# Cambodia

**Temples of Angkor**
p129

**Siem Reap**
p93

**Northwestern Cambodia**
p228

**Eastern Cambodia**
p270

**Phnom Penh**
p36

**South Coast**
p172

## WITHDRAWN

THIS EDITION WRITTEN AND RESEARCHED BY
Nick Ray, Jessica Lee

PSAR THMEI P79,
PHNOM PENH

CHRISTOPHER GROENHOUT / GETTY IMAGES ©

MAN IN TRADITIONAL
COSTUME, BAYON P149

TIM HUGHES / GETTY IMAGES ©

# Contents

# Welcome to Cambodia

*Ascend to the realm of the gods, Angkor Wat. Descend into hell at Tuol Sleng Prison. With a history both inspiring and depressing, Cambodia delivers an intoxicating present.*

## An Empire of Temples

Contemporary Cambodia is the successor state to the mighty Khmer empire, which, during the Angkorian period, ruled much of what is now Laos, Thailand and Vietnam. The remains of this empire can be seen at the fabled temples of Angkor, monuments unrivalled in scale and grandeur in Southeast Asia. The traveller's first glimpse of Angkor Wat, the ultimate expression of Khmer genius, is sublime and is matched by only a few select spots on earth, such as Machu Picchu or Petra.

## The Urban Scene

Just as Angkor is more than its wat, so too is Cambodia more than its temples, and its urban areas can surprise with their sophistication. Chaotic yet charismatic capital Phnom Penh is a revitalised city earning plaudits for its gorgeous riverside location, cultural renaissance and world-class wining-and-dining scene. Second city Siem Reap, with its cosmopolitan cafes and a diverse nightlife, is as much a destination as the nearby iconic Angkor temples. And up-and-coming Battambang, reminiscent of Siem Reap before the advent of mass tourism, charms with graceful French architecture and a thriving contemporary art scene.

## Upcountry Adventures

Siem Reap and Phnom Penh may be the heavyweights, but to some extent they are a world away from the Cambodia of the countryside. This is the place to experience the rhythm of rural life and timeless landscapes of dazzling rice paddies and swaying sugar palms. The South Coast is fringed by tropical islands, with just a handful of beach huts in sight. Inland lie the Cardamom Mountains, part of a vast tropical wilderness and the gateway to emerging ecotourism adventures. The mighty Mekong River cuts through the country and is home to some of the region's last remaining freshwater dolphins, while the northeast is a world of wild and mountainous landscapes and home to Cambodia's ethnic minorities.

## The Cambodian Spirit

Despite having the eighth wonder of the world in its backyard, Cambodia's real treasure is its people. The Khmers have been to hell and back, struggling through years of bloodshed, poverty and political instability. Thanks to an unbreakable spirit and infectious optimism, they have prevailed with their smiles intact. No visitor comes away without a measure of admiration and affection for the inhabitants of this enigmatic kingdom.

## Why I Love Cambodia

By Nick Ray, Writer

Where to start? I first came through Cambodia as a young backpacker in 1995 and the turbulent history captured my attention. However, the people were the most memorable part of that first trip, their smiles infectious. Angkor is spectacular and special, and continues to reward no matter how many times you visit. The coastline is beautiful and blissfully undeveloped compared with some of the region. And it remains a frontier for motorbike rides from the Cardamoms in the southwest to Mondulkiri and Ratanakiri in the northeast. Even as it develops, Cambodia remains an authentic adventure.

**For more about our writers, see page 384**

Above: Monks at Ta Prohm (p158)

# Cambodia

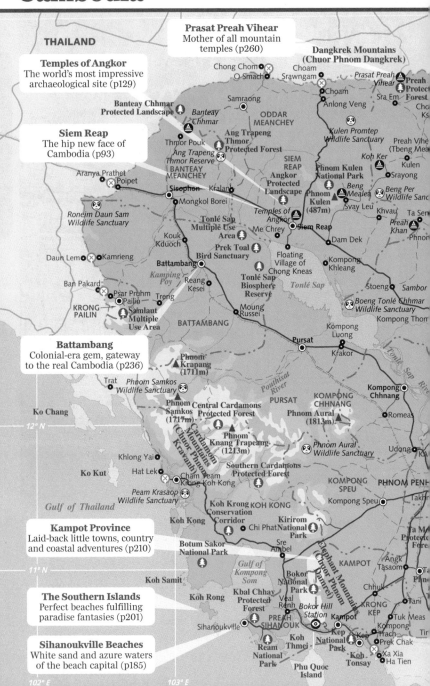

**THAILAND**

**Prasat Preah Vihear**
Mother of all mountain
temples (p260)

**Dangkrek Mountains
(Chuor Phnom Dangkrek)**

Chong Chom ⊗  Choam
O Smach  Srawngam ⊗  Choam  Prasat Preah  Preah
Vihear  Protec
Samraong  Choam  Sra Em  Forest  Cho
Anlong Veng  Ks

**Temples of Angkor**
The world's most impressive
archaeological site (p129)

**Banteay Chhmar
Protected Landscape** ▲ *Banteay
Chhmar*  **ODDAR
MEANCHEY**  Kulen Promtep
Wildlife Sanctuary  Preah Vihe
(Tbeng Mea

**Siem Reap**
The hip new face of
Cambodia (p93)

Thmor Pouk  Ang Trapeng
Thmor  Koh Ker ▲  Kulen
*Ang Trapeng
Thmor Reserve*  **Thmor
Protected Forest**  **SIEM
REAP**  Srayong

Aranya Prathet  Poipet ⊗  **BANTEAY
MEANCHEY**  **Angkor
Protected
Landscape**  **Phnom Kulen
National Park**  *Beng
Mealea* ▲  Beng Per
Wildlife Sanc

Sisophon  Kralanh  *Phnom
Kulen
(487m)* ▲  Svay Leu  Khvau  Ta Se

Mongkol Borei  *Temples of
Angkor*  **Siem Reap**  *Preah
Khan* ▲  Phnor

*Roneim Daun Sam
Wildlife Sanctuary*  **Tonlé Sap
Multiple Use
Area** ▲  Me Chrey  Dam Dek

Kouk
Kduoch  **Prek Toal
Bird Sanctuary** ▲  Floating
Village of
Chong Kneas  Kompong
Khleang

Daun Lem ⊗ Kamrieng  **Battambang**  Reang
Kesei  **Tonlé Sap
Biosphere
Reserve**  *Tonlé Sap*  Stoeng  Sambor

Ban Pakard  *Kamping
Poy*  *Boeng Tonlé Chhmar
Wildlife Sanctuary*

Psar Pruhm  Treng  Kompong Thom

Pailin ⊗  Moung
Russei

**KRONG
PAILIN**  **Samlaut
Multiple
Use
Area** ▲  **BATTAMBANG**  Kompong
Luong

**Battambang**
Colonial-era gem, gateway
to the real Cambodia (p236)

Trat  *Phnom Samkos
Wildlife Sanctuary*  *Phnom
Krapang
(1711m)* ▲  **Pursat**  Krakor

Ko Chang  *Phnom
Samkos
(1717m)* ▲  **Central Cardamons
Protected Forest** ▲  *Pouthisat
River*  **KOMPONG
CHHNANG**  Kompong
Chhnang

— 12° N —  *Cardamom
Mountains
(Chuor Phnom
Kravanh)*  **PURSAT**  *Phnom Aural
(1813m)* ▲  Romeas

*Phnom
Knang Trapeang
(1213m)* ▲  *Phnom Aural
Wildlife Sanctuary*  Udong

Khlong Yai  **Southern Cardamons
Protected Forest** ▲  **KOMPONG
SPEU**  **PHNOM PENH**

Ko Kut  Hat Lek ⊗  Cham Yeam
Krong Koh Kong  Kompong Speu

*Peam Krasaop
Wildlife Sanctuary*  **Koh Krong KOH KONG
Conservation
Corridor** ▲  *Kirirom
National
Park* ▲  Ta M
Protec
For

*Gulf of Thailand*  Koh Kong  Chi Phat

**Kampot Province**
Laid-back little towns, country
and coastal adventures (p210)

**Botum Sakor
National Park** ▲  Sre
Ambel  **KAMPOT**  Angk
Tasaom  Ta
Phn

— 11° N —  Koh Samit  *Gulf of
Kompong
Som*  **Bokor
National
Park** ▲  Chhuk

**The Southern Islands**
Perfect beaches fulfilling
paradise fantasies (p201)

Koh Rong  **Kbal Chhay
Protected
Forest** ▲  Veal
Renh  *Bokor Hill
Station* ◎  **KRONG
KEP**  Tani  Tuk Meas

Kep  Kompong
Trach

Sihanoukville ⊗  **PREAH
SIHANOUK**  Koh
Thmei  **Kep
National Park** ▲  Prek Chak

**Sihanoukville Beaches**
White sand and azure waters
of the beach capital (p185)

**Ream
National
Park** ▲  *Koh
Tonsay*  Xa Xia ⊗  Ha Tien

*Phu Quoc
Island*

102° E  103° E

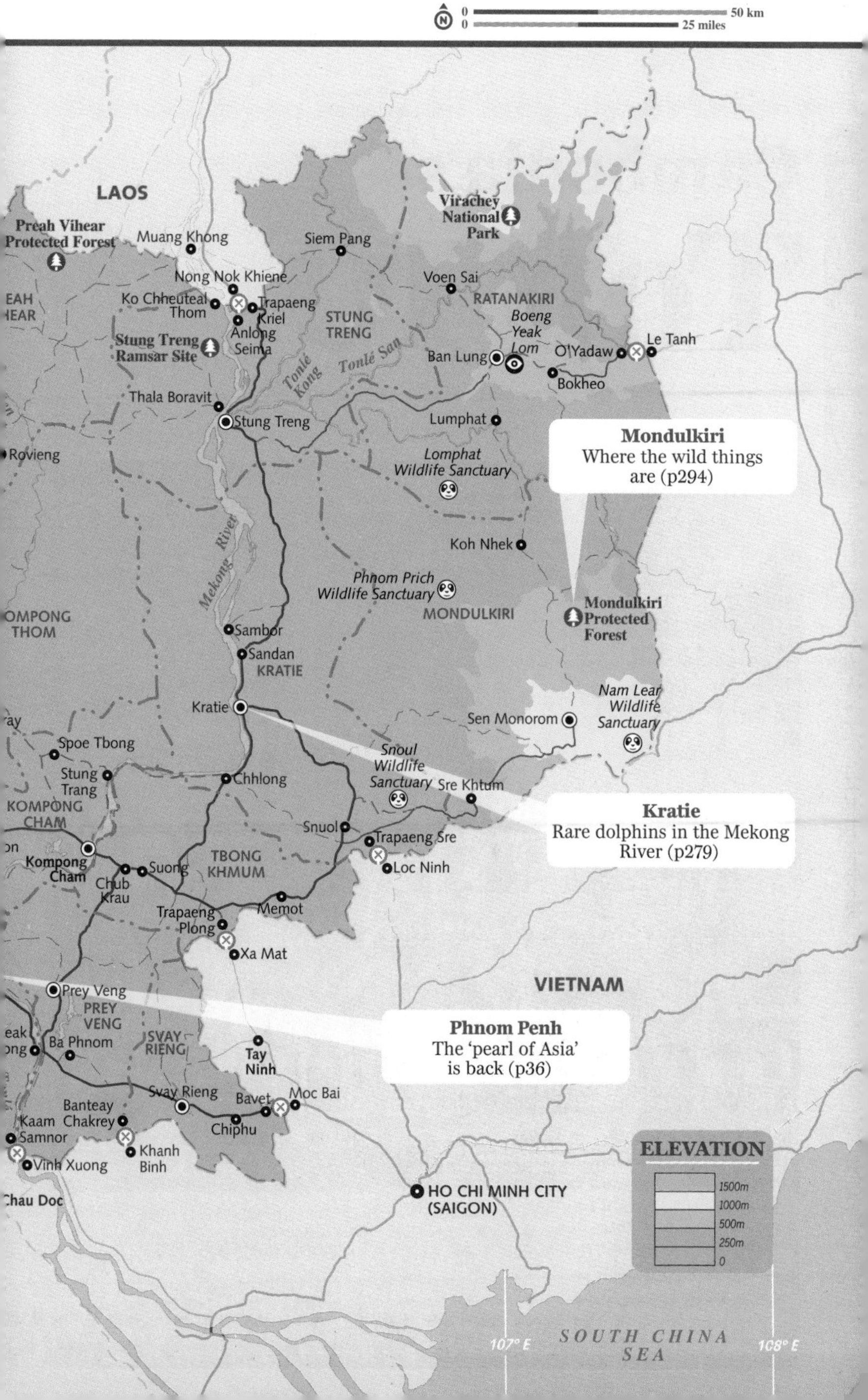

**0** ────────────────── **50 km**
**0** ────────────────── **25 miles**

LAOS

Preah Vihear
Protected Forest

Muang Khong

Siem Pang

Virachey
National
Park

Voen Sai

RATANAKIRI

Nong Nok Khiene

Ko Chheuteal
Thom

Trapaeng
Kriel

Anlong
Seima

EAH
HEAR

STUNG
TRENG

*Boeng
Yeak
Lom*

O'Yadaw

Le Tanh

Stung Treng
Ramsar Site

Ban Lung

Bokheo

Thala Boravit

Stung Treng

Lumphat

Rovieng

*Lomphat
Wildlife Sanctuary*

**Mondulkiri**
Where the wild things
are (p294)

Koh Nhek

OMPONG
THOM

*Phnom Prich
Wildlife Sanctuary*

MONDULKIRI

Sambor

**Mondulkiri
Protected
Forest**

Sandan
KRATIE

Kratie

Sen Monorom

*Nam Lear
Wildlife
Sanctuary*

ay

Spoe Tbong

Chhlong

*Snoul
Wildlife
Sanctuary*

Sre Khtum

**Kratie**
Rare dolphins in the Mekong
River (p279)

Stung
Trang

KOMPONG
CHAM

Snuol

Trapaeng Sre

on

Kompong
Cham

Suong

Loc Ninh

Chub
Krau

TBONG
KHMUM

Trapaeng
Plong

Memot

Xa Mat

**VIETNAM**

Prey Veng

PREY
VENG

eak
ong

Ba Phnom

SVAY
RIENG

Tay
Ninh

**Phnom Penh**
The 'pearl of Asia'
is back (p36)

Banteay
Kaam Chakrey

Svay Rieng

Bavet

Moc Bai

Samnor

Chiphu

Vinh Xuong

Khanh
Binh

hau Doc

**HO CHI MINH CITY
(SAIGON)**

**ELEVATION**

| | |
|---|---|
| | 1500m |
| | 1000m |
| | 500m |
| | 250m |
| | 0 |

107° E

*SOUTH CHINA
SEA*

108° E

# Cambodia's
# Top 10

# Siem Reap & the Temples of Angkor

**1** One of the world's most magnificent sights, the temples of Angkor (p129) are so much better than the superlatives. Choose from Angkor Wat (pictured below left; p144), the world's largest religious building; Bayon, one of the world's weirdest, with its immense stone faces; or Ta Prohm, where nature runs amok. Buzzing Siem Reap, with a superb selection of restaurants and bars, is the base for temple exploration. Beyond lie floating villages on the Tonlé Sap, adrenaline-fuelled activities such as quad biking and ziplining, and such cultured pursuits as cooking classes and birdwatching.

# Phnom Penh

**2** The Cambodian capital is a chaotic yet charming city that has stepped out of the shadows of the past to embrace a brighter future. Boasting one of the most beguiling riverfronts in the region, Phnom Penh (p36) is surprisingly sophisticated thanks to its hip hotels, epicurean eateries and boho bars ready to welcome urban explorers. Experience emotional extremes at the inspiring National Museum (pictured below; p42) and the depressing Tuol Sleng prison, showcasing the best and worst of Cambodian history. Once known as the 'pearl of Asia', Phnom Penh is glistening once more.

WAJ / SHUTTERSTOCK ©

MARCEL TOUNG / SHUTTERSTOCK ©

## Sihanoukville Beaches

**3** Despite a reputation for hedonism Sihanoukville's real appeal lies in its bustling beaches (p185). It's only a short hop from Sihanoukville's gritty centre to popular Otres Beach, a still mellow and sublime stretch of sand despite the looming threat of development. More central, and the town's prettiest beach, is Sokha Beach, its tiny eastern end rarely crowded. The original traveller magnet is Serendipity Beach, which blends right into Occheuteal Beach (pictured top; p185), popular with locals by day and 24-hour party people by night.

## Battambang

**4** This is the real Cambodia. Unfurling along the banks of the Sangker River, Battambang (pictured above; p236) is one of the country's best-preserved colonial-era towns. Streets of French shophouses host everything from fair-trade cafes to art galleries. Beyond the town is the Cambodian countryside and a cluster of ancient temples, which, although not exactly Angkor Wat, do, mercifully, lack the crowds. Then there's the 'bamboo train', a unique form of handmade local transport only found here. Battambang in a word? Charming.

## Kampot Province

**5** Kampot Province (p210) offers atmospheric towns and attractions including national parks, cave pagodas and beaches. In laid-back Kampot town, choose from hostels, riverside resorts or boutique hotels to take in the French architectural legacy or explore the pretty river by paddle-board or kayak. Sleepier Kep has its famous Crab Market, hiking in Kep National Park and nearby Koh Tonsay (Rabbit Island; pictured top; p219). Countryside romps include the ascent to Bokor Hill Station or exploring Kampot's famous working pepper farms.

## Mondulkiri

**6** Eventually the endless rice fields and sugar palms that characterise the Cambodian landscape give way to rolling hills and the wild east of Mondulkiri (p294), home to the hardy Bunong people (pictured above), who still practise animism and ancestor worship. Wildlife is a big draw here with the opportunity to walk with elephants or spot doucs or gibbons on a trek through the Seima Protected Forest. Add thunderous waterfalls, a jungle zipline and quad biking to the mix and you have the perfect ingredients for an authentic adventure.

ALEKSANDAR TODOROVIC / SHUTTERSTOCK ©

### The Southern Islands

**7** Cambodia's up-and-coming southern islands (p201) are reminiscent of 1980s Thailand. Koh Rong (pictured above left; p202) and Koh Rong Sanloem, off the Sihanoukville coast, fulfil those Asian paradise fantasies. Koh Rong is party central, with its hippy travel hub of Koh Tuch village, while mellow, family-friendly Koh Rong Sanloem has some tropical hideaway resorts and gentle, shallow bays. There are more islands strung along the coast, including the Koh Sdach archipelago and large, almost undeveloped Koh Kong.

### Kratie

**8** Gateway to the rare freshwater Irrawaddy dolphins of the Mekong, Kratie (p277) is a busy crossroads on the overland route between Phnom Penh and northeastern Cambodia or southern Laos. The town has a certain decaying colonial grandeur and boasts some of the country's best Mekong sunsets. Nearby Koh Trong island is a relaxing place to experience a homestay or explore on two wheels. North of Kratie lies the Mekong Discovery Trail, with adventures and experiences themed around the mother river, including community-based homestays, bicycle rides and boat trips.

### Prasat Preah Vihear

**9** The mother of all mountain temples, Prasat Preah Vihear (p262) stands majestically atop the Dangkrek Mountains, forming a controversial border post between Cambodia and Thailand. Its foundation stones stretch to the edge of the cliff, and the views across northern Cambodia are incredible. The 300-year chronology of its construction also offers an insight into the metamorphosis of carving and sculpture during the Angkorian period. It's all about location, though, and it doesn't get better than this.

## Khmer Cuisine

**10** Khmer cuisine (p339) is an unexpected epicurean adventure that remains under the culinary radar. *Amok* (baked fish with lemongrass, chilli and coconut; pictured right) is the national dish, but sumptuous seafood and fresh-fish dishes are plentiful, including Kep crab infused with Kampot pepper. It wouldn't be Asia without street snacks, and Cambodia delivers everything from noodles *(mee)* and congee *(bobor*; rice porridge) to deep-fried tarantulas and roasted crickets, some of which can be sampled on a foodie tour in Siem Reap.

GUENTER FISCHER / GETTY IMAGES ©

# Need to Know

**For more information, see Survival Guide (p347)**

### Currency
Riel (r); US dollars (US$) universally accepted

### Language
Khmer; English and Chinese widely spoken, plus some French

### Visas
A one-month tourist visa costs US$30 on arrival and requires one passport-sized photo. Easily extendable business visas are available for US$35.

### Money
ATMs widely available, including in all major tourist centres and provincial capitals. Credit cards accepted by many hotels and restaurants in larger cities.

### Mobile Phones
Roaming is possible but is expensive. Local SIM cards and unlocked mobile phones readily available.

### Time
Indochina Time Zone (GMT/UTC plus seven hours)

## When to Go

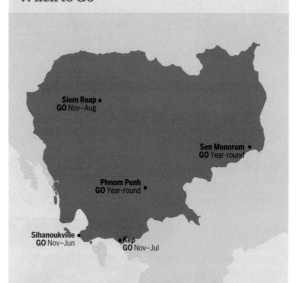

Siem Reap •
**GO** Nov–Aug

Sen Monorom •
**GO** Year-round

Phnom Penh
**GO** Year-round •

Sihanoukville •
**GO** Nov–Jun

• Kep
**GO** Nov–Jul

Tropical climate, wet & dry seasons

### High Season
(Nov–Mar)

➡ Cool and windy, with almost Mediterranean temperatures; the best all-round time to be here.

➡ Book accommodation in advance during the peak Christmas and New Year period.

### Shoulder
(Jul & Aug)

➡ Wet in most parts of Cambodia, with high humidity, but the landscapes are emerald green.

➡ The South Coast can be busy as Western visitors escape for summer holidays while school is out.

### Low Season
(Apr–Jun & Sep & Oct)

➡ April and May spells hot season, when the mercury hits 40°C and visitors melt.

➡ September and October can be wet, but awesome storms and cloud formations accompany the deluge.

**PLAN YOUR TRIP** NEED TO KNOW

## Useful Websites

**Lonely Planet** (www.lonely planet.com) The online authority on travel in the Mekong region.

**Phnom Penh Post** (www. phnompenhpost.com) Cambodia's newspaper of record.

**Travelfish** (www.travelfish. org) Opinionated articles and reviews.

**Move to Cambodia** (www. movetocambodia.com) Insightful blog on living and working in Cambodia.

**Cambodia Tribunal Monitor** (www.cambodiatribunal.org) Detailed coverage of the Khmer Rouge trials.

## Important Numbers

Drop the 0 from a regional (city) code when calling Cambodia from another country.

| Cambodia code | 855 |
| --- | --- |
| International access code | 001 |
| Police | 117 |
| Fire | 118 |
| Ambulance | 119 |

## Exchange Rates

| Australia | A$1 | 3031r |
| --- | --- | --- |
| Canada | C$1 | 3048r |
| Euro zone | €1 | 4480r |
| Japan | ¥100 | 3549r |
| New Zealand | NZ$1 | 3700r |
| Thailand | 1B | 115r |
| UK | UK£1 | 5688r |
| USA | US$1 | 3994r |

For current exchange rates see www.xe.com.

## Daily Costs

**Budget: less than US$50**

➡ Cheap guesthouse room: US$5–10

➡ Local meals and street eats: US$1–3

➡ Local buses: US$2–3 per 100km

**Midrange: US$50–200**

➡ Air-con hotel room: US$15–50

➡ Decent local restaurant meal: US$5–10

➡ Local tour guide per day: US$25

**Top End: more than US$200**

➡ Boutique hotel or resort: US$50–500

➡ Gastronomic meal with drinks: US$25–50

➡ 4WD rental per day: US$60–120

## Opening Hours

Opening hours can vary throughout the year. These are high-season opening hours and may decrease in the low season.

**Banks** 8am–3.30pm Monday to Friday, Saturday mornings

**Bars** 5pm–late

**Government offices** 7.30–11.30am and 2–5pm Monday to Friday

**Restaurants** 7am–9pm or meal times

**Shops** 8am–6pm daily

## Arriving in Cambodia

**Phnom Penh International Airport** (p358) The airport is 7km west of central Phnom Penh. Official taxis/*remork-motos (tuk tuks)* to anywhere in the city cost a flat US$12/9 (30 minutes to one hour).

**Siem Reap International Airport** (p358) The airport is 7km from the town centre; taxis cost US$9 (15 minutes). A trip to the town centre on the back of a *moto* (motorcycle taxi) is about US$3. Many city hotels and guesthouses offer a free airport pick-up service with advance bookings.

**Land borders** Shared with Laos, Thailand and Vietnam; Cambodian visas are available on arrival. Most borders are open during the core hours of 7am to 5pm. Overcharging for the Cambodian visa is very common at the borders with Thailand. Poipet and Cham Yeam (Koh Kong) are particularly notorious, so some travellers like the convenience of arranging an e-visa in advance.

## Getting Around

**Bus** The most popular form of transport for most travellers, connecting all major towns and cities.

**Car** Private car or 4WD is an affordable option for those who value time above money.

**Motorbike** An amazing way to travel for experienced riders.

**Air** Domestic flights link Phnom Penh and Siem Reap.

**Boat** Less common than in the old days of bad roads, but Siem Reap to either Battambang or Phnom Penh remain popular routes.

For much more on **getting around**, see p361

# If You Like...

## Temples

**Angkor Wat** The one and only – the mother temple that puts all others in the shade, with epic bas-reliefs and iconic *apsaras* (nymphs; p144).

**Ta Prohm** Nature has run riot here, where iconic tree roots are locked in a muscular embrace with ancient stones. It's the stuff of Indiana Jones fantasies. (p158)

**Prasat Preah Vihear** The most mountainous of all the Khmer mountain temples, it is perched imperiously on the cliff-face of the Dangkrek Mountains. (p260)

**Sambor Prei Kuk** The pre-Angkorian capital of Isanapura was the first temple city in the Mekong region and is a chronological staging post on the road to Angkor. (p267)

## Islands & Beaches

**Sihanoukville** King of the Cambodian beach resorts, with a headland ringed by squeaky white sands and azure waters. (p184)

**Koh Rong & Koh Rong Sanloem** Up-and-coming islands near Sihanoukville with long and lonely white-sand beaches, backpacker and flashpacker resorts, plus diving. (p202)

**Koh Kong** There's no shortage of dreamy beaches on practically uninhabited Koh Kong Island and the cluster of islands just off Botum Sakor National Park. (p178)

**Kep** Cambodia's original beach resort, Kep was devastated by war but is back from the brink with boutique resorts, seafood specialities and the backpacker beach of Koh Tonsay (Rabbit Island; p219).

## Epicurean Experiences

**Phnom Penh** Dine to make a difference at one of Phnom Penh's many training restaurants to help the disadvantaged. (p62)

**Siem Reap** Try one of the new specialist foodie tours or browse the lively restaurants of the Old Market area, choosing from exotic barbecues, mod Khmer cuisine and stop-and-dip market stalls. (p107)

**Sihanoukville** Sample succulent seafood at Cambodia's leading beach resort, including fresh crab, prawns and squid, cooked up with Kampot pepper. (p194)

**Battambang** Discover the delights of Cambodian cooking with a cheap and cheerful cooking class in this relaxed riverside town. (p242)

## Water Features

**Mekong Discovery Trail** See rare freshwater dolphins, cycle around remote Mekong islands or experience a local family homestay. (p283)

**Tonlé Sap** Discover floating villages, bamboo skyscrapers, flooded forests and rare birdlife with a boat trip on Cambodia's Great Lake. (p127)

**Boeng Yeak Lom** Small but perfectly formed, this jungle-clad crater lake is Cambodia's most inviting natural swimming pool, located in the heart of Ratanakiri Province. (p286)

**Bou Sraa Waterfall** One of Cambodia's biggest set of falls, this roars out of the jungle in remote Mondulkiri Province and now includes the breathtaking Mayura Zipline. (p300)

## Markets & Shopping

**Russian Market** & **Psar Thmei** Phnom Penh is home to the most markets in the country, including the iconic Psar Thmei and the shopping magnet that is the Russian Market. Throw in good-cause shops, designer silk boutiques and some bustling malls, and you can shop till you drop. (p79)

**Psar Chaa** Temple town (aka Siem Reap) is a major shopping destination, especially popular for its Psar Chaa (Old Market; p119). The town is also dotted with creative-clothing boutiques and shops supporting community projects. (p118)

**Battambang's Galleries** There's an emerging art scene in up-and-coming Battambang, with several galleries selling local artists' work. It's also home to Psar Nath, a landmark market from the French days. (p237)

**Otres Market** It's more a beach town than a shopping hub, but Sihanoukville's Otres Village plays host to the weekly Otres Market, more Camden than Cambodia, and lots of fun on a Saturday evening. (p197)

## Nightlife

**Phnom Penh** This is where Cambodia rocks. Warm up with a riverfront happy hour, bar crawl around the Bassac Lane area and end up in a nightclub. (p74)

**Siem Reap** There are so many bars around the Old Market that one strip has earned itself the accolade of Pub St. Nearby lanes hide more mellow bars. Stay late for the alternative Angkor sunrise. (p115)

**Sihanoukville** Home to a hedonistic crowd, the beachfront strips of Serendipity and Occheuteal have long been party central on the coast, but Otres Beach is no slouch either. (p196)

**Top**: Atmospheric Ta Prohm (p158), temples of Angkor
**Bottom**: Buzzing Pub St (p115), Siem Reap

# Month by Month

## January

This is peak tourist season in Cambodia with Phnom Penh, Siem Reap and the South Coast heaving. Chinese and Vietnamese New Years sometimes fall in this month too.

### ⭐ Chaul Chnam Chen (Chinese New Year)

The Chinese inhabitants of Cambodia celebrate their New Year somewhere between late January and mid-February – for the Vietnamese, this is Tet. As many of Phnom Penh's businesses are run by Chinese-Khmers, commerce grinds to a halt around this time and there are lion dances all over town. Many Vietnamese living in Cambodia return to their homeland for a week or more.

## February

Still one of the busiest times of year for tourist arrivals, February is also often the month for Chinese and Vietnamese New Years.

### ⭐ Giant Puppet Parade

This colourful annual fundraising event (www.giantpuppetproject.com) takes place in Siem Reap. Local organisations, orphanages and businesses come together to create giant puppets in the shape of animals, deities and contemporary characters, and the whole ensemble winds its way along the Siem Reap River like a scene from the Mardi Gras.

## April

This is the most important month in the calendar for Khmers, as the New Year comes in the middle of April. For tourists it's a possible month to avoid, as the mercury regularly hits 40°C.

### ⭐ Chaul Chnam Khmer (Khmer New Year)

This is a three-day celebration of the Khmer New Year, and it's like Christmas, New Year and a birthday all rolled into one. Cambodians make offerings at wats, clean out their homes and exchange gifts. It is a lively time to visit the country as the Khmers go wild with water in the countryside. Throngs of Khmers flock to Angkor for the Sangkranta Festival, and it's absolute madness at most temples, so avoid the celebration if you want a quiet, reflective Angkor experience. That said, it is nowhere near as excessive as in Thailand or Laos, so it might seem tame by comparison.

## May

This is the beginning of the low season for visitors as the monsoon arrives (and lasts till October), but there may be a last blast of hot weather to welcome mango season and some delicious ripe fruits.

### ⭐ Chat Preah Nengkal (Royal Ploughing Ceremony)

Led by the royal family, the Royal Ploughing Ceremony is a ritual agricultural festival marking the traditional beginning of the rice-growing season. It takes place in early May in front of the National Museum, near the Royal Palace in Phnom Penh, and the royal oxen are said to have a nose for whether it will be a good harvest or a bad one.

### ✨ Visakha Puja (Buddha Day)

A celebration of Buddha's birth, enlightenment and *parinibbana* (passing). Activities are centred on wats. The festival falls on the eighth day of the fourth moon (May or June) and is best observed at Angkor Wat, where you can see candle-lit processions of monks.

## September

Traditionally the wettest month in Cambodia, September is usually a time of sporadic flooding along the Mekong. The calendar's second most important festival, P'chum Ben, usually falls in this month.

### ✨ P'chum Ben (Festival of the Dead)

This festival is a kind of All Souls' Day, when respects are paid to the dead through offerings made at wats. Offerings include paper money, candles, flowers and incense, as well as food and drink, all passed through the medium of the monks. P'chum Ben lasts for several days and devout Buddhists are expected to visit seven wats during the festival. Head to the village of Vihear Sour in Kandal Province, about 35km northeast of Phnom Penh, to witness authentic bareback buffalo racing and traditional Khmer wrestling.

## October

The rains often linger long into October and this has led to some major flooding in Siem Reap in recent years. However, the countryside is extraordinarily green at this time.

### ✨ Bon Om Tuk (Water Festival)

Celebrating the epic victory of Jayavarman VII over the Chams, who occupied Angkor in 1177, this festival also marks the extraordinary natural phenomenon of the reversal of the current of Tonlé Sap River. It's one of the most important festivals in the Khmer calendar and is a wonderful, chaotic time to be in Phnom Penh or Siem Reap. Boat races are held on the Tonlé Sap and Siem Reap Rivers, with each boat colourfully decorated and holding 40 rowers. As many as two million people flood the capital for the fun and frolics; book ahead for accommodation. Sadly, this event was marred by tragedy in 2010 when 350 people died in a stampede on a bridge connecting the city with nearby Koh Pich (Diamond Island). The event was cancelled for three years in a row, but was reinstated in 2014.

## November

November brings the dry, windy season and signals the start of the best period to be in the country (which extends through until January or February). Bon Om Tuk often comes around in November.

### ✨ Angkor Photo Festival

In Siem Reap, resident and regional photographers descend on the temples and team up with local youths to teach them the tricks of the trade (www.angkorphoto.com). Photography exhibitions are staged all over town.

### ✨ Kampot Writers & Readers Festival

Launched in 2015, this festival (www.kampot writersfestival.com) brings four days of literary discussions, poetry readings, art exhibitions, concerts and creative workshops to Kampot.

## December

Christmas and New Year are the peak of the peak season at Angkor and leading beach resorts; book a long way ahead. Sign up for a half marathon or bike ride if you fancy doing something for charity.

### 🏃 Angkor Wat International Half Marathon

This half marathon (www.angkormarathon.org) has been a fixture in the Angkor calendar for more than 15 years. Choose from a 21km half marathon, a 10km fun run or various bicycle races and rides. It's hard to imagine a better backdrop to a road race than the incredible temples of Angkor. Launched in 2014, there is now also a full Angkor Empire Marathon (www.angkor empiremarathon.org) held in August.

# Plan Your Trip
# Itineraries

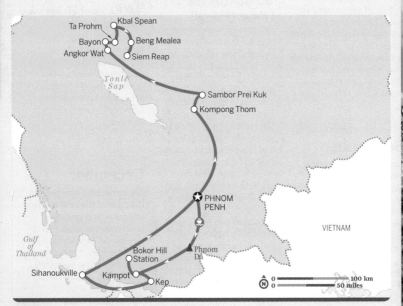

## Cambodia Snapshot

This is the ultimate journey, via temples, beaches and the capital. It can be run in any direction, but it is best followed to the letter, starting in the capital, exploring the coastline and winding up at the world's most impressive collection of temples, Angkor.

Hit **Phnom Penh** for its impressive National Museum and stunning Silver Pagoda. It's home to the most eclectic dining scene in Cambodia, with fine-dining Khmer restaurants, an international array of eateries and some safe street food eating. There's also superb shopping at the Psar Tuol Tom Pong, and a night shift that never sleeps.

Take a fast boat to the hilltop temple of **Phnom Da**, dating from the pre-Angkorian time, and then continue south to the colonial-era town of **Kampot**, which makes a good base for this area. From here, visit the seaside town of **Kep** (and Rabbit Island, just off the coast) and nearby cave pagodas. It is also possible to make a side trip to **Bokor Hill Station** or visit a pepper plantation.

Bayon (p149), Angkor Thom

Go west to **Sihanoukville**, Cambodia's beach capital, to sample the seafood, dive or snorkel the nearby waters or just soak up the sun. Choose from party-central Serendipity Beach, chilled-out Otres Beach or the up-and-coming islands of Koh Rong or Koh Rong Sanloem. Backtrack via Phnom Penh to **Kompong Thom** and visit the pre-Angkorian brick temples of **Sambor Prei Kuk**.

Finish at Angkor, a mind-blowing experience that few other sights can compare with. See **Angkor Wat**, perfection in stone; **Bayon**, weirdness in stone; and **Ta Prohm**, nature triumphing over stone –

before venturing further afield to **Kbal Spean** or jungle-clad **Beng Mealea**.

Save some time for soaking up **Siem Reap**, one of the most diverse destinations in Cambodia, with a host of activities on tap. Everything from cooking classes to Vespa tours is on offer, and some of these activities are a great way to punctuate the temple tours.

This trip can take two weeks at a steady pace or three weeks at a slow pace. Public transport serves most of this route, although some of the side trips will require chartered transport or a motorbike trip.

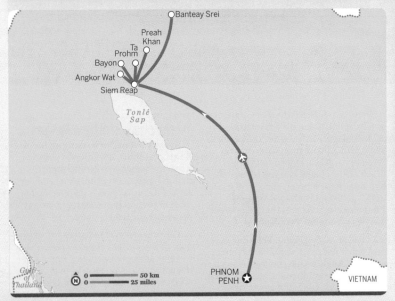

# 1 WEEK A Tale of Two Cities

If time is tight, focus on the big hitters of Phnom Penh and Siem Reap, gateway to the temples of Angkor. With two nights in the capital and three or four nights in Siem Reap, discover the best of modern and ancient Cambodia.

Start out in **Phnom Penh** with a look at Cambodia's contrasting history. Relive the glories of the past at the National Museum, home to the world's finest collection of Angkorian sculpture, and the Royal Palace, housing a glittering array of priceless artefacts. Discover a darker past with a visit to the Tuol Sleng Museum and the Killing Fields of Choeung Ek, both profoundly depressing places but essential to understanding the modern political landscape of Cambodia.

History aside, Phnom Penh is cool Cambodia, a dynamic if disorienting city of chic boutique hotels, funky fashion, contemporary cafes, fusion restaurants and hip bars, so spend at least two nights here to relish the scene.

From the capital, take the 30-minute flight northwest to **Siem Reap**, or take a day-long road trip if you want to see more of the Cambodian countryside. The first order of business is to spend a couple of days touring the nearby temples of Angkor, including the headline names like **Angkor Wat**, **Bayon** and **Ta Prohm**. Make sure you also allow some time to catch some of the support acts, like beautiful **Banteay Srei** and enormous **Preah Khan**. Add some activities to the mix with a zipline adventure at Flight of the Gibbon Angkor or a quad-bike ride through the rice fields.

Or you could simply relax and enjoy fine dining and the lively bars in the town of Siem Reap. From authentic Khmer countryside cooking to fine French cuisine, the gastronomic scene in Siem Reap is something to be savoured. Extend your nights out here by exploring the lanes and alleys around Pub St. Visit one of the sumptuous spas in town to round out your stay.

If you decide to travel overland between these two cities, the months from July to December are best for this – during this time the landscape is lush and green.

Top: Banteay Srei (p165), emples of Angkor;
Bottom: Independence Monument (p45), Phnom Penh

# The Big One

**4 WEEKS**

Cambodia is a small country and even though the roads are sometimes bad and travel can be slow, most of the highlights can be visited in a month.

Setting out from the hip capital that is **Phnom Penh**, pass through the bustling Mekong town of **Kompong Cham** before heading on to **Kratie** for an encounter with the elusive Irrawaddy river dolphins. Then it is time to make a tricky choice to experience the beauty of the northeast. To ensure maximum time elsewhere, choose between **Ratanakiri Province** and the volcanic crater lake of Boeng Yeak Lom, or **Mondulkiri Province** and the original Elephant Valley Project. Both offer primate experiences for those who fancy a bit of monkey business along the way. If you have a bit of extra time up your sleeve, you could combine the two in a grand loop, now that the road between Sen Monorom and Ban Lung is in good shape.

Next up, head to the south coast. Take your time and consider a few nights in **Kep** or on one of the nearby islands, and a boat trip from **Sihanoukville** to explore the up-and-coming islands off the coast. Turning back inland, check out **Kirirom National Park**, home to pine trees, black bears and some spectacular views of the Cardamom Mountains.

Then it's time to go northwest to charming **Battambang**, one of Cambodia's best-preserved colonial-era towns and a base from which to discover rural life. Take the proverbial slow boat to **Siem Reap**, passing through stunning scenery along the snaking Sangker River, and turn your attention to the **temples of Angkor**.

Visit all the greatest hits in and around Angkor, but set aside some extra time to venture further to the rival capital of **Koh Ker**, which is cloaked in thick jungle, or **Prasat Preah Vihear**, a mountain temple perched precariously atop a cliff on the Thai border.

Overlanders can run this route in reverse, setting out from Siem Reap and exiting Cambodia by river into Vietnam or Laos. Entering from Laos, divert east to Ratanakiri before heading south. Getting around is generally easy as there are buses on the big roads, taxis on the small roads and buzzing boats on the many rivers.

Top: Floating village (p229) near Battambang;
Bottom: Elephant Valley Project (p298).
Mondulkiri Province

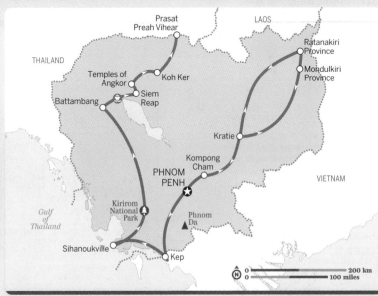

# Off the Beaten Track: Cambodia

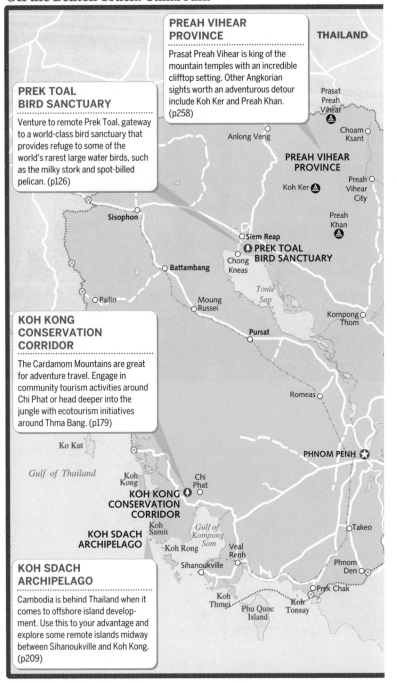

**PREAH VIHEAR PROVINCE**

Prasat Preah Vihear is king of the mountain temples with an incredible clifftop setting. Other Angkorian sights worth an adventurous detour include Koh Ker and Preah Khan. (p258)

THAILAND

**PREK TOAL BIRD SANCTUARY**

Venture to remote Prek Toal, gateway to a world-class bird sanctuary that provides refuge to some of the world's rarest large water birds, such as the milky stork and spot-billed pelican. (p126)

**KOH KONG CONSERVATION CORRIDOR**

The Cardamom Mountains are great for adventure travel. Engage in community tourism activities around Chi Phat or head deeper into the jungle with ecotourism initiatives around Thma Bang. (p179)

**KOH SDACH ARCHIPELAGO**

Cambodia is behind Thailand when it comes to offshore island development. Use this to your advantage and explore some remote islands midway between Sihanoukville and Koh Kong. (p209)

Prasat Preah Vihear

Choam Ksant

Anlong Veng

PREAH VIHEAR PROVINCE

Koh Ker

Preah Vihear City

Preah Khan

Sisophon

Siem Reap

PREK TOAL BIRD SANCTUARY

Chong Kneas

Battambang

*Tonlé Sap*

Pailin

Moung Russei

Kompong Thom

Pursat

Romeas

PHNOM PENH

Ko Kut

*Gulf of Thailand*

Koh Kong

Chi Phat

KOH KONG CONSERVATION CORRIDOR

Koh Samit

*Gulf of Kompong Som*

KOH SDACH ARCHIPELAGO

Koh Rong

Veal Renh

Takeo

Sihanoukville

Phnom Den

Koh Thmei

Phu Quoc Island

Koh Tonsay

Prek Chak

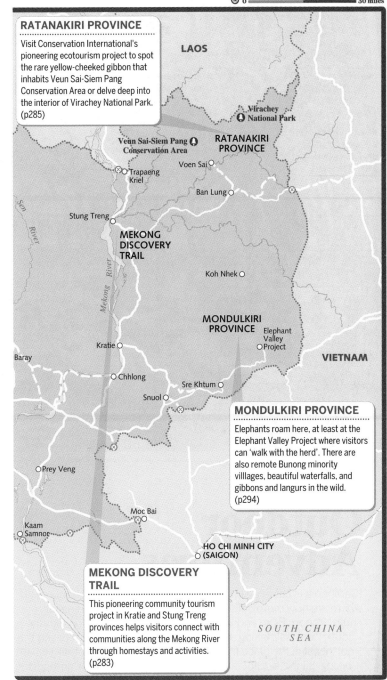

0 ___ 50 km
0 ___ 30 miles

**RATANAKIRI PROVINCE**

Visit Conservation International's pioneering ecotourism project to spot the rare yellow-cheeked gibbon that inhabits Veun Sai-Siem Pang Conservation Area or delve deep into the interior of Virachey National Park. (p285)

LAOS

Virachey National Park

Veun Sai-Siem Pang Conservation Area

**RATANAKIRI PROVINCE**

Voen Sai

Trapaeng Kriel

Ban Lung

Stung Treng

**MEKONG DISCOVERY TRAIL**

Sen River

Mekong River

Koh Nhek

**MONDULKIRI PROVINCE**

Elephant Valley Project

Kratie

Baray

VIETNAM

Chhlong

Sre Khtum

Snuol

**MONDULKIRI PROVINCE**

Elephants roam here, at least at the Elephant Valley Project where visitors can 'walk with the herd'. There are also remote Bunong minority villlages, beautiful waterfalls, and gibbons and langurs in the wild. (p294)

Prey Veng

Moc Bai

Kaam Samnor

**HO CHI MINH CITY (SAIGON)**

**MEKONG DISCOVERY TRAIL**

This pioneering community tourism project in Kratie and Stung Treng provinces helps visitors connect with communities along the Mekong River through homestays and activities. (p283)

SOUTH CHINA SEA

Kompong Pluk (p126), a stilt village on the banks of the Tonlé Sap

# Outdoor Adventures

Cambodia is catching up with its more developed neighbours and there are now more activities than ever to get that adrenaline buzz. Phnom Penh and Siem Reap have plenty of action, but the South Coast is making a name for itself with water sports and the northeast is the place for a walk on the wild side. Whether you are hiking, biking, ascending peaks or plumbing depths, Cambodia can deliver the action.

# When to Go

## November to February

This is the cooler dry season and the best time for strenuous activities like trekking and cycling. Higher altitude places like Mondulkiri and Ratanakiri are worth considering any time of year because they're always cooler, although they can get chilly at night.

## March to May

The mercury regularly hits 40°C during the hot season, so this is the perfect time to cool off with some water sports such as scuba diving, stand-up paddle-boarding or sailing, all down on the South Coast.

## June to October

The wet season is not ideal for hiking or biking due to torrential downpours and the presence of leeches in many jungle areas. However, it's a great time for boat trips and kayaking on Cambodia's extensive network of rivers.

# Boat Trips

With so much water around the country, it's hardly surprising that boat trips are popular with visitors. Some of these are functional, such as travelling up the Tonlé Sap River from Phnom Penh to Siem Reap, or along the Sangker River from Siem Reap to Battambang. There is a lot of water in Cambodia, particularly in the wet season when the Mekong is in full flow and the Tonlé Sap at its maximum extent, so when in Cambodia, do as the locals do and travel by boat.

# Where to Go

**Chi Phat** Explore the untamed rivers of the Cardamoms from this jungle base (p181), which includes the possibility of spotting rare Siamese crocs.

**Kampot** The riverside town of Kampot (p210) offers boat trips up river to mangroves and down river to isolated beaches and the open sea.

**Mekong River** The mother river flows through the heart of Cambodia and offers some rewarding opportunities for discovering tranquil islands and quiet homestays along the Mekong Discovery Trail (p283).

**Tonlé Sap** Explore floating villages (p127), flooded forests (p128) and bird sanctuaries (p126) with a boat trip on the Great Lake.

# Cycling

Cambodia is a great country for adventurous cyclists to explore. Given the country's legendary potholes, a mountain bike is the best bet. Many roads remain in poor condition, but there is usually a flat unpaved trail along the side. Travelling at such a gentle speed allows for much more interaction with the locals. Bicycles can be transported around the country in the back of pick-ups or on the roof of minibuses.

Cycling around Angkor is a rewarding experience as it really helps to get a measure of the size and scale of the temple complex. Mountain biking is likely to take off in Mondulkiri and Ratanakiri Provinces in coming years, as there are some great trails. Guesthouses and hotels throughout Cambodia rent out bicycles for around US$2 per day, or US$7 to US$15 for an imported brand.

# Where to Go

**Battambang** The beautiful countryside around Battambang (p236) is perfect for two-wheeled exploring.

**Chi Phat** This ecotourism hub (p181) in the Cardamom Mountains offers mountain biking on jungle trails to remote waterfalls.

**Mondulkiri Province** The meeting of the hills is an appropriate name for this mountainous province and there are some great biking trails to Bunong villages (p301) and jungle waterfalls (p300).

**Temples of Angkor** The temples (p129) can get very busy in peak season, so leave the crowds

PLAN YOUR TRIP OUTDOOR ADVENTURES

HUGO / GETTY IMAGES ©

## QUAD BIKING

Quad bikes or ATVs are growing in popularity in Cambodia thanks to the prevalence of dirt roads across the country. Siem Reap has three operators (p101) offering countryside tours around temple town. Phnom Penh has one quad bike outfit (p56), which offers a very different experience to city life. Up in Mondulkiri, a new operator (p297) gives you the chance to explore the hilltops and viewpoints around Sen Monorom. Prices for quad biking range from US$25 per hour to more than US$100 for a full-day adventure.

behind and follow local jungle trails (p102). Organised tours are available.

# Dirt Biking

For experienced riders, Cambodia is one of the most rewarding off-road biking destinations in the world. The roads are generally considered some of the worst in Asia (or best in Asia for die-hard biking enthusiasts). There are incredible rides all over the country, particularly in the provinces of Preah Vihear, Mondulkiri, Ratanakiri and the Cardamom Mountains, but it is best to stay away from the main highways as traffic and dust make them a choking experience. The advantage of motorcycle travel is that it allows for complete freedom of movement and you can stop in small villages that Westerners rarely visit. It is possible to take motorcycles upcountry for tours, but only experienced off-road bikers should take to these roads with a dirt bike.

Motorcycles are available for hire in Phnom Penh and some other popular tourist destinations. In Siem Reap, motorcycle rental is forbidden, so anyone planning rides in the northwest will need to arrange a bike elsewhere. Costs are US$5 to US$10 per day for a 100cc motorcycle and around US$10 to US$25 for a 250cc dirt bike.

## Where to Go

**Cardamom Mountains** Not for the faint-hearted, the Cardamom Mountains offer some tough jungle trails north to Pailin or Pursat. Seek an experienced operator (p363).

**Kampot** The landscapes around Kampot (p210) include rice fields, salt pans, pepper farms, karst peaks and Bokor Hill Station (p218).

**Mondulkiri Province** The rolling hills of Mondulkiri are perfect for dirt biking, and include the stunning road that follows the Seima Protected Forest (p301) to Sen Monorom (p295).

**Preah Vihear Province** Get your kicks on Cambodia's Route 66 (NH66), which runs from Beng Mealea (p168) to the remote temple of Preah Khan (p264). Or ascend to the realm of the gods at Prasat Preah Vihear (p262).

# Trekking & Walking

Trekking is not the first activity most people would associate with Cambodia, due to the ongoing presence of land mines, but there are plenty of safe areas in the country – including the nascent national parks – where walking can be enjoyed. The northeastern provinces of Mondulkiri and Ratanakiri, with their wild, natural scenery, abundant waterfalls and ethnic-minority populations, are emerging as the country's leading trekking destinations.

Cambodia is steadily establishing a network of national parks with visitor facilities; Bokor National Park, Kirirom National Park and Ream National Park all promise trekking potential, while Virachey National Park in Ratanakiri has multiday treks. Chi Phat and the Cardamom Mountains also offer the possibility of a walk on the wild side.

Angkor is emerging as a good place for gentle walks between the temples; as visitor numbers skyrocket, this is one way to experience peace and solitude.

## Where to Go

**Koh Kong Province** Coastal gateway to the Cardamoms, Koh Kong has several trekking companies offering jungle treks around Tatai (p179).

**Mondulkiri Province** One of the most rewarding trekking destinations in Cambodia thanks to cooler climes, Bunong minority encounters (p295) and thundering waterfalls, not to mention tracking elephants (p298) or gibbons (p301).

**Ratanakiri Province** Choose from gentle treks to ethnic minority villages or hard-core treks into the heart of Virachey National Park (p293).

Top: Northern gate of Angkor Thom (p148)

Bottom: Prek Toal Bird Sanctuary (p126)

ROCBJAS / GETTY IMAGES ©

**Temples of Angkor** From a base in Siem Reap, explore Angkor Thom (p148) on foot or ascend to the River of a Thousand Lingas at Kbal Spean (p166).

# Water Sports

Snorkelling and diving are available off the coast of Sihanoukville, and while the scenery may not be as spectacular as in Indonesia or the Philippines, there is still plenty out there in the deep blue yonder. It's best to venture to the more remote dive sites, such as Koh Tang and Koh Prins, by staying overnight on a boat. There are many unexplored areas off the coast between Koh Kong and Sihanoukville that could one day put Cambodia on the dive map of Asia.

As the Cambodian coast takes off, there are more water sports available, including boating, windsurfing and kitesurfing off the beaches of Sihanoukville. In Kampot, stand-up paddle-boarding has taken off in a big way and it's a great way to appreciate the river scenery.

## Where to Go

**Kep** Hit the waterfront Sailing Club (p220) to rent a hobie cat sailing boat or windsurfer to explore the calm waters off the coast.

**Kampot** Explore the river and mangroves on a stand-up paddle-board (p211), or laze around in an inner tube if that sounds like too much hard work.

**Sihanoukville** Water sports capital of Cambodia (p187); choose from diving, snorkelling, windsurfing, wake-boarding, jet skiing and more.

### ZIPLINING IN CAMBODIA

Ziplining has recently taken off in Cambodia. Flight of the Gibbon Angkor (p98) offers the longest zipline course in the country with 10 lines and the chance to spot some gibbons in the wild. Mayura Zipline (p300) is a new adrenaline-fuelled adventure above the Bou Sraa Waterfall in Mondulkiri Province. There is also a zipline on Koh Rong Island (p204) if you need more than a beach buzz. Ziplining doesn't come cheap though – Flight of the Gibbon Angkor charges around US$109 per person and the Mayura Zipline around US$69 per person.

### ROCK CLIMBING

Rock climbing is very much in its infancy compared with neighbouring Laos, Thailand and Vietnam, but there is a climbing outfit down in Kampot Province where the landscape is peppered with karst outcrops. Climbodia (p211) offers cabled routes up Phnom Kbal Romeas, about 5km south of Kampot town, from US$35 for a half day.

**Southern Islands** Koh Rong and Koh Rong Sanloem (p202) provide an up-and-coming base for serious divers wanting some big-fish action.

# Wildlife Spotting

Cambodia is home to rich and varied wildlife that has somehow survived the dramatic events that engulfed the country in the past decades. Big cats, small cats, elephants, primates and some curious critters all call the Cambodian jungle their home, and it's possible to see them across the country. Birdwatching is a big draw, as Cambodia is home to some of the region's rarest large waterbirds, including adjutants, storks and pelicans.

## Where to Go

**Kratie Province** Extremely rare freshwater river dolphins inhabit stretches of the Mekong River between Kratie (p279) and the Laos border.

**Mondulkiri Province** Walk with the herd at Elephant Valley Project (p294) or spot gibbons and doucs in the Seima Protected Forest (p301).

**Phnom Tamao Wildlife Rescue Centre** So much more than a zoo, this wildlife sanctuary (p90) offers behind-the-scenes tours to meet the animals.

**Prek Toal Bird Sanctuary** Cambodia's world-class bird sanctuary (p126); see rare waterbirds like the spot-billed pelican, black headed ibis and painted stork.

**Ratanakiri Province** This remote jungle province is home to a pioneering gibbon spotting project.

**Siem Reap** Try the Flight of the Gibbon zipline (p98) or visit the Angkor Centre for Conservation of Biodiversity (p166), where rare animals, including the giant ibis, pangolin, silvery langur and leopard cat, can be seen.

# Regions at a Glance

Phnom Penh, Cambodia's resurgent capital, is the place to check the pulse of contemporary life. Siem Reap, gateway to the majestic temples of Angkor, is starting to give the capital a run for its money with sophisticated restaurants, funky bars and chic boutiques. World Heritage Site Angkor houses some of the most spectacular temples on earth.

Down on the South Coast are several up-and-coming beach resorts and a smattering of tropical islands that are just beginning to take off, unlike those of neighbouring countries. Northwestern Cambodia is home to Battambang, a slice of more traditional life, and several remote jungle temples. The country's wild east is where elephants roam, waterfalls thunder and freshwater dolphins can be found.

## Phnom Penh

Dining
Bars
Shopping

### Creative Cuisine

French bistros abound, and outstanding fusion restaurants blend the best of Cambodian and European flavours. Ubiquitous Cambodian barbecues offer a local experience, or try gourmet Khmer cuisine in a designer restaurant.

### Happy Hour

Get started early in a breezy establishment overlooking the Mekong, move on to a live-music bar, and dance till dawn in a club. Phnom Penh is 24/7, one of the liveliest capitals in Asia.

### Chic Boutiques

Choose from colourful local markets where bargains abound or check out the impressive collections of local designers. There are plenty of good-cause shops where your spending assists Cambodia.

**p36**

## Siem Reap

Temples
Dining
Activities

### Divine Inspiration

It's not just all about Angkor Wat. True, it's one of the world's most iconic buildings, but down the road are the enigmatic faces of the Bayon and the jungle temple of Ta Prohm.

### Eclectic Epicurean Experiences

Contemporary Khmer cuisine, spiced-up street food, fine French dining and more: Siem Reap is a dining destination in itself. Continue the night along Pub St and the gentrified lanes beyond.

### Adventures Beyond Angkor

Take to the skies by helicopter to see Angkor from a different angle. Zipline through the jungle or quad bike through rice fields. Experience a cooking class or unwind with a massage.

**p93**

PLAN YOUR TRIP REGIONS AT A GLANCE

# South Coast

**Beaches**
**Activities**
**Dining**

### Tropical Bliss

Claim a strip of sand all to yourself or relax in a beach-front bar. Choose life in the fast lane in Sihanoukville, the slow lane in Kep or forget the roads altogether and escape to the islands.

### Land or Sea

National parks and protected areas dot the region, offering trekking, mountain biking, kayaking, rock climbing and kitesurfing. Water sports abound or venture underwater to experience snorkelling or scuba diving.

### Seafood Specialities

Each coastal town has its speciality. In Kep it's delectable crab. In Takeo it's lobster. In Kampot it's anything cooked with the region's famous pepper. Sihanoukville offers a seafood extravaganza.

p172

# North-western Cambodia

**Temples**
**Towns**
**Boat Trips**

### Beyond the Crowds

Heard enough about Angkor Wat? Don't forget the pre-Angkorian capital of Sambor Prei Kuk, the jungle temples of Preah Vihear Province and atmospheric Banteay Chhmar.

### The Real Cambodia

Riverside Battambang has some of the country's best-preserved French architecture, while Kompongs Chhnang and Thom are off the tourist trail and offer a slice of real Cambodia.

### Floating Villages

One of the best boat rides in Cambodia links Battambang to Siem Reap following the Sangker River. Explore the largest floating village on the Tonlé Sap lake, Kompong Luong.

p228

# Eastern Cambodia

**Wildlife**
**Culture**
**River Life**

### The Wild Things

View rare freshwater river dolphins around Kratie, walk with a herd of elephants in Mondulkiri or spot primates in community-based forest treks around Mondulkiri or Ratanakiri.

### A World Apart

Northeast Cambodia is home to a mosaic of ethnic minorities. Encounter the Bunong people of Mondulkiri or venture up jungle rivers to visit the remote tribal cemeteries in Ratanakiri.

### The Mighty Mekong

The Mekong cuts through the region's heart and includes the Mekong Discovery Trail, a community tourism initiative. Beyond the Mekong is the Tonlé Srepok tributary, as depicted in *Apocalypse Now*.

p270

# On the Road

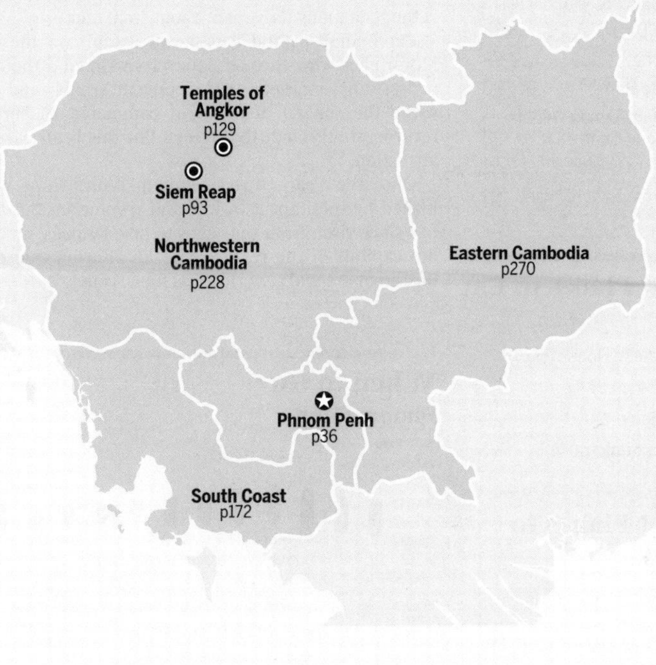

**Temples of Angkor**
p129

**Siem Reap**
p93

**Northwestern Cambodia**
p228

**Eastern Cambodia**
p270

**Phnom Penh**
p36

**South Coast**
p172

# Phnom Penh

023 / POP 2 MILLION / AREA 290 SQ KM

## Best Places to Eat

➡ Boat Noodle (p70)
➡ Chinese House (p63)
➡ Deco (p72)
➡ Malis (p70)
➡ Romdeng (p64)

## Best Places to Stay

➡ Eighty8 Backpackers (p57)
➡ Foreign Correspondents' Club (p57)
➡ Pavilion (p60)
➡ Raffles Hotel Le Royal (p59)
➡ Rambutan Resort (p61)

## Why Go?

Phnom Penh (ភ្នំពេញ): the name can't help but conjure up an image of the exotic. The glimmering spires of the Royal Palace, the fluttering saffron of the monks' robes and the luscious location on the banks of the mighty Mekong – this is the Asia many daydream about from afar.

Cambodia's capital can be an assault on the senses. Motorbikes whiz through laneways without a thought for pedestrians; markets exude pungent scents; and all the while the sounds of life – of commerce, of survival – reverberate through the streets. But this is all part of the attraction.

Once the 'Pearl of Asia', Phnom Penh's shine was tarnished by the impact of war and revolution. But the city has since risen from the ashes to take its place among the hip capitals of the region, with an alluring cafe culture, bustling bars and a world-class food scene.

## When to Go
### Phnom Penh

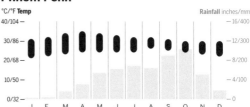

**Jan & Feb** The holiday crush is over and pleasant northeasterly breezes massage the riverfront.

**Sep & Oct** Heavy rains provide welcome relief from searing sun; many hotels offer steep discounts.

**Oct & Nov** The water festival Bon Om Tuk is one giant street party on the banks of the river.

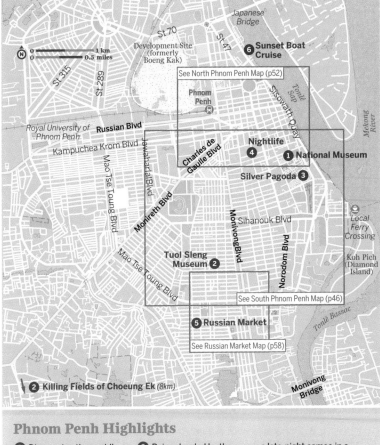

N
0                    1 km
0              0.5 miles

St 70
St 47
Japanese Bridge
St 315
St 289
Development Site (formerly Boeng Kak)
Phnom Penh
**6** Sunset Boat Cruise
See North Phnom Penh Map (p52)
Tonlé Sap
Stsowath Quay
Mekong River
Royal University of Phnom Penh
Russian Blvd
Kampuchea Krom Blvd
Jawaharlal Blvd
Charles de Gaulle Blvd
Nightlife **4**
**1** National Museum
Silver Pagoda **3**
Mao Tse Toung Blvd
Monireth Blvd
Sihanouk Blvd
Monivong Blvd
Norodom Blvd
Local Ferry Crossing
Tuol Sleng Museum **2**
Koh Pich (Diamond Island)
Mao Tse Toung Blvd
See South Phnom Penh Map (p46)
Tonlé Bassac
**5** Russian Market
See Russian Market Map (p58)
**2** Killing Fields of Choeung Ek (8km)
Monivong Bridge

## Phnom Penh Highlights

**1** Discovering the world's finest collection of Khmer sculpture at the stunning **National Museum** (p42).

**2** Delving into the dark side of Cambodian history with visits to the **Tuol Sleng Museum** (p43) and the **Killing Fields** (p44).

**3** Being dazzled by the 5000 silver floor tiles of the **Silver Pagoda** (p40), part of the Royal Palace.

**4** Diving into Phnom Penh's frenzied **nightlife** (p73) with a happy-hour cocktail, a bar crawl and

a late-night cameo in a legendary disco.

**5** Shopping till you drop (of heat exhaustion) at bounteous **Russian Market** (p79).

**6** Cruising the mighty Mekong, cocktail in hand, on a sunset **boat cruise** (p50).

## History

Legend has it that the city of Phnom Penh was founded when an old woman named Penh found four Buddha images that had come to rest on the banks of the Mekong River. She housed them on a nearby hill, and the town that grew up here came to be known as Phnom Penh (Hill of Penh).

In the 1430s, Angkor was abandoned and Phnom Penh chosen as the site of the new Cambodian capital. Angkor was poorly situated for trade and subject to attacks from the Siamese (Thai) kingdom of Ayuthaya. Phnom Penh commanded a more central position in the Khmer territories and was perfectly located for riverine trade with Laos and China via the Mekong Delta.

# Greater Phnom Penh

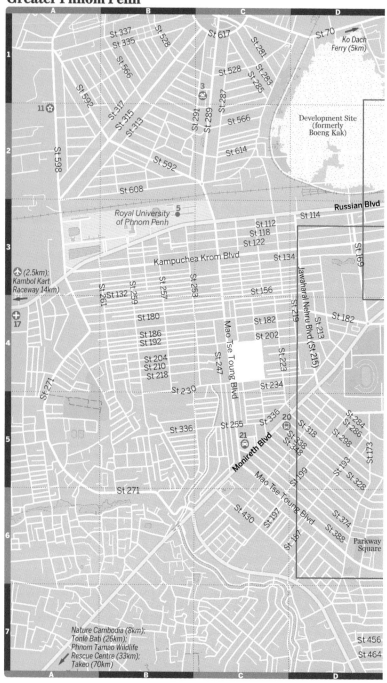

St 337
St 335
St 528
St 617
St 70
Ko Dach
Ferry (5km)
St 281
St 528
St 283
St 566
3
St 285
St 287
St 291
St 289
St 317
St 315
St 313
St 566
Development Site
(formerly
Boeng Kak)
11
St 592
St 598
St 592
St 614
St 608
Russian Blvd
Royal University
of Phnom Penh
5
St 114
St 112
St 118
St 122
St 134
Kampuchea Krom Blvd
St 169
(2.5km);
Kambol Kart
Raceway 14km)
St 132
St 259
St 257
St 253
St 156
St 182
17
St 180
St 261
Jawaharal Nehru Blvd (St 215)
St 213
St 182
St 186
St 192
St 182
St 202
St 219
St 204
St 210
St 218
St 247
St 223
St 230
St 234
St 271
St 284
St 286
St 336
St 255
St 336
20
St 318
St 298
St 173
St 336
21
St 338
St 348
Monireth Blvd
St 199
St 193
St 328
St 271
Mao Tse Toung Blvd
St 430
St 197
St 374
St 388
St 187
Parkway
Square
Mao Tse Toung Blvd
Nature Cambodia (8km);
Tonlé Bati (26km);
Phnom Tamao Wildlife
Rescue Centre (33km);
Takeo (70km)
St 456
St 464

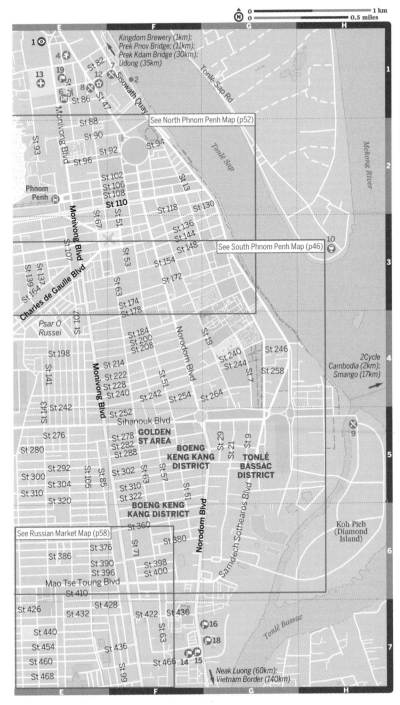

# Greater Phnom Penh

By the mid-16th century, trade had turned Phnom Penh into a regional power. Indonesian and Chinese traders were drawn to the city in large numbers. A century later, however, the landlocked and increasingly isolated kingdom had become little more than a buffer between the ascendant Thais and Vietnamese, until the French took over in 1863.

The French protectorate in Cambodia gave Phnom Penh the layout we know today. They divided the city into districts or *quartiers* – the French and European traders inhabited the area north of Wat Phnom between Monivong Blvd and Tonlé Sap River. By the time the French departed in 1953, they had left many important landmarks, including the Royal Palace, the National Museum, Psar Thmei (Central Market) and many impressive government ministries.

The city grew quickly in the post-independence peacetime years of Norodom

Sihanouk's rule: by the time he was overthrown in 1970, the population of Phnom Penh was approximately 500,000. As the Vietnam War spread into Cambodian territory, the city's population swelled with refugees and reached nearly three million in early 1975. The Khmer Rouge took the city on 17 April 1975, and as part of its radical revolution immediately forced the entire population into the countryside. Whole families were split up on those first fateful days of 'liberation'.

During the time of Democratic Kampuchea, many tens of thousands of former Phnom Penhois – including the vast majority of the capital's educated residents – were killed. The population of Phnom Penh during the Khmer Rouge regime was never more than about 50,000, a figure made up of senior party members, factory workers and trusted military leaders.

Repopulation of the city began when the Vietnamese arrived in 1979, although at first it was strictly controlled by the new government. During much of the 1980s, cows were more common than cars on the streets of the capital. The 1990s were boom years for some: along with the arrival of the UN Transitional Authority in Cambodia (Untac) came US$2 billion (much of it in salaries for expats).

Phnom Penh has really begun to change in the last 15 years, with roads being repaired, sewage pipes laid, parks inaugurated and riverbanks reclaimed. Business is booming in many parts of the city, with skyscrapers under development, investors rubbing their hands with the sort of glee once reserved for Bangkok or Hanoi, and swanky new restaurants opening. Phnom Penh is back, and bigger changes are set to come.

## ⊙ Sights

Phnom Penh, a relatively small city, is easy to navigate as it is laid out in a numbered grid. The most important cultural sights can be visited on foot and are located near the riverfront in the most beautiful part of the city. Most other sights are also fairly central, just a short *remork-moto (tuk tuk)* ride from the riverfront.

★**Royal Palace**                    PALACE
(ព្រះបរមរាជវាំង; Map p42; Sothearos Blvd; admission incl camera 25,000r, guide per hr US$10; ⊙ 7.30-11am & 2-5pm) With its classic Khmer roofs and ornate gilding, the Royal Palace dominates the diminutive skyline of Phnom Penh. It's a striking structure near the river-

PHNOM PENH SIGHTS

front, bearing a remarkable likeness to its counterpart in Bangkok.

Being the official residence of King Sihamoni, parts of the massive palace compound are closed to the public. Visitors are allowed to visit only the throne hall and a clutch of buildings surrounding it. Adjacent to the palace, the Silver Pagoda complex is also open to the public.

Visitors need to wear shorts that reach to the knee, and T-shirts or blouses that reach to the elbow; otherwise they will have to hire an appropriate covering. The palace gets very busy on Sundays, when countryside Khmers come to pay their respects, but being amid the thronging locals can be a fun way to experience the place.

➡ Palace Compound

All visitors enter into the eastern portion of the palace compound near the Chan Chaya Pavilion. Performances of classical Cambodian dance were once staged in this pavilion, which is sometimes lit up at night to commemorate festivals or anniversaries.

The main attraction in the palace compound is the Throne Hall. Topped by a 59m-high tower inspired by the Bayon at Angkor, it was inaugurated in 1919 by King Sisowath.

The Throne Hall is used for coronations and ceremonies such as the presentation of credentials by diplomats. Many of the items once displayed here were destroyed by the Khmer Rouge.

South of the Throne Hall, check out the curious iron Napoleon III Pavilion. Given to King Norodom by Napoleon III of France, it was hardly designed with the Cambodian climate in mind.

➡ Silver Pagoda Complex

From the palace compound you enter the Silver Pagoda complex through its north gate. The Silver Pagoda (Map p42; Samdech Sothearos Blvd; incl in admission to Royal Palace; ⊙7.30-11am & 2-5pm) was so named in honour of the floor, which is covered with more than 5000 silver tiles weighing 1kg each, adding up to five tonnes of gleaming silver. You can sneak a peek at some near the entrance – most are covered for their protection. It is also known as Wat Preah Keo (Pagoda of the Emerald Buddha).

It was originally constructed of wood in 1892 during the rule of King Norodom, who was apparently inspired by Bangkok's Wat Phra Keo, and was rebuilt in 1962. The Silver Pagoda was preserved by the Khmer Rouge to demonstrate its concern for the conservation of Cambodia's cultural riches to the outside world. Although more than half of the pagoda's contents were lost, stolen or destroyed in the turmoil that followed the Vietnamese invasion, what remains is spectacular. This is one of the few places in Cambodia where bejewelled objects embodying some of the brilliance and richness of Khmer civilisation can still be seen.

The staircase leading to the Silver Pagoda is made of Italian marble. Inside, the Emerald Buddha, believed to be made of Baccarat crystal, sits on a gilded pedestal high atop the dais. In front of the dais stands a life-sized gold Buddha decorated with 2086 diamonds, the largest of which, set in the crown, is a whopping 25 carats. Created in the palace workshops around 1907, the gold Buddha weighs in at 90kg.

Along the walls of the pagoda are examples of extraordinary Khmer artisanship,

## PHNOM PENH IN...

### Two Days

Start early to observe the aerobics sessions on the riverfront, then grab breakfast before venturing into the Royal Palace (p40). Next is the National Museum (p42) and the world's most wondrous collection of Khmer sculpture. After lunch at Friends (p64) restaurant, check out the funky architecture of Psar Thmei (p79), but save the heavy shopping for Russian Market (p79). Celebrate your shopping coups with a riverside happy-hour drink at Foreign Correspondents' Club (p74), and then a night out on the town.

Start day two with a walking tour of the centre, or just wander around Wat Phnom (p44), where Khmers pray for luck. Have lunch on the riverside, then visit the sobering Tuol Sleng Museum (p43) before continuing on to the Killing Fields of Choeung Ek (p44). It is a grim afternoon, but essential for understanding just how far Cambodia has come in the intervening years. Wind up your weekend with a sunset cruise on the Mekong River, offering a beautiful view over the Royal Palace.

# Royal Palace & Silver Pagoda

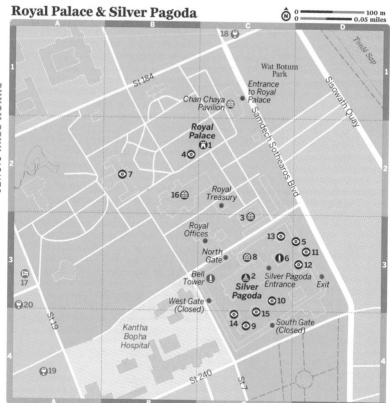

PHNOM PENH SIGHTS

including intricate masks used in classical dance and dozens of gold Buddhas. The many precious gifts given to Cambodia's monarchs by foreign heads of state appear rather spiritless when displayed next to such exuberant Khmer art. (Note that photography is not permitted inside the Silver Pagoda.)

The Silver Pagoda complex is enclosed by walls plastered with an extensive **mural** depicting the classic Indian epic of the *Ramayana* (known as the *Reamker* in Cambodia). The story begins just south of the east gate and includes vivid images of the battle of Lanka. The mural was created around 1900 and is definitely showing its age in parts.

Other structures to be found in the complex (listed clockwise from the north gate) include the **mondap** (library), which once housed richly decorated sacred texts written on palm leaves (now moved to the safety of air-conditioned storage); the **shrine** of

King Norodom (r 1860–1904); an **equestrian statue** of King Norodom; the **shrine** of King Ang Duong (r 1845–59); a pavilion housing a huge footprint of the Buddha; **Phnom Mondap**, an artificial hill with a structure containing a bronze footprint of the Buddha from Sri Lanka; a **shrine** dedicated to Kantha Bopha, one of Prince Sihanouk's daughters; a **pavilion** for celebrations held by the royal family; the **shrine** of King Norodom Sihanouk's father, King Norodom Suramarit (r 1955–60); and a **bell tower**, whose bell is rung to order the gates to be opened or closed.

## ★ National Museum of Cambodia

MUSEUM

(សារមន្ទីរជាតិ; Map p52; www.cambodiamuseum.info; cnr St 13 & St 178; admission US$5; ⊙8am–5pm) Located just north of the Royal Palace, the National Museum of Cambodia is housed in a graceful terracotta structure of traditional design (built from 1917 to 1920), with

# Royal Palace & Silver Pagoda

an inviting courtyard garden. The museum is home to the world's finest collection of Khmer sculpture – a millennium's worth and more of masterful Khmer design. The museum comprises four pavilions, facing a pretty garden. Most visitors start left and continue in a clockwise, chronological direction.

The first significant sculpture to greet visitors is a large fragment – including the relatively intact head, shoulders and arms – of an immense bronze reclining Vishnu statue that was recovered from the Western Mebon temple near Angkor Wat in 1936. Continue into the left pavilion, where the pre-Angkorian collection begins, illustrating the journey from the human form of Indian sculpture to the more divine form of Khmer sculpture from the 5th to 8th centuries. Highlights include an imposing, eight-armed Vishnu statue from the 6th century found at Phnom Da, and a staring Harihara, combining the attributes of Shiva and Vishnu, from Prasat Andet in Kompong Thom province. The Angkor collection includes several striking statues of Shiva from the 9th, 10th and 11th centuries; a giant pair of wrestling monkeys (Ko Ker, 10th century); a beautiful 12th-century stele (stone) from Oddar Meanchey Province inscribed with scenes from the life of Shiva; and the

sublime statue of a seated Jayavarman VII (r 1181–1219), his head bowed slightly in a meditative pose (Angkor Thom, late 12th century).

The museum also contains displays of pottery and bronzes dating from the pre-Angkorian periods of Funan and Chenla (4th to 9th centuries), the Indravarman period (9th and 10th centuries) and the classical Angkorian period (10th to 14th centuries), as well as more recent works, such as a beautiful wooden royal barge.

Visitors are not allowed to photograph the collection, only the central courtyard. English-, French- and Japanese-speaking guides are available for tours (US$6). The comprehensive *The New Guide to the National Museum* (US$10) is available at the front desk, while the smaller *Khmer Art in Stone* (US$2) covers some signature pieces.

★Tuol Sleng Museum
of Genocidal Crimes          MUSEUM
(សារមន្ទីរប្រល័យពូជសាសន៍; Map p46; cnr St 113 & St 350; admission US$2, guide US$6; ⊙7am-5.30pm) In 1975, Tuol Svay Prey High School was taken over by Pol Pot's security forces and turned into a prison known as Security Prison 21 (S-21); it soon became the largest centre of detention and torture in the country. Between 1975 and 1978 more than 17,000 people held at S-21 were taken to the killing fields of Choeung Ek (p44). S-21 has been turned into the Tuol Sleng Museum, which serves as a testament to the crimes of the Khmer Rouge.

Like the Nazis, the Khmer Rouge leaders were meticulous in keeping records of their barbarism. Each prisoner who passed through S-21 was photographed, sometimes before and after torture. The museum displays include room after room of harrowing B&W photographs; virtually all of the men, women and children pictured were later killed. You can tell which year a picture was taken by the style of number-board that appears on the prisoner's chest. Several foreigners from Australia, New Zealand and the USA were also held at S-21 before being murdered. It's worth hiring a guide, as they can tell you the stories behind some of the people in the photographs.

As the Khmer Rouge 'revolution' reached ever greater heights of insanity, it began devouring its own. Generations of torturers and executioners who worked here were in turn killed by those who took their places. During early 1977, when the party purges of

PHNOM PENH SIGHTS

Eastern Zone cadres were getting under way, S-21 claimed an average of 100 victims a day.

When the Vietnamese army liberated Phnom Penh in early 1979, there were only seven prisoners alive at S-21, all of whom had used their skills, such as painting or photography, to stay alive. Fourteen others had been tortured to death as Vietnamese forces were closing in on the city. Photographs of their gruesome deaths are on display in the rooms where their decomposing corpses were found. Their graves are nearby in the courtyard.

A visit to Tuol Sleng is a profoundly depressing experience. The sheer ordinariness of the place makes it even more horrific: the suburban setting, the plain school buildings, the grassy playing area where children kick around balls juxtaposed with rusted beds, instruments of torture and wall after wall of disturbing portraits. It demonstrates the darkest side of the human spirit that lurks within us all. Tuol Sleng is not for the squeamish.

Behind many of the displays at Tuol Sleng is the Documentation Center of Cambodia. DC-Cam was established in 1995 through Yale University's Cambodian Genocide Program to research and document the crimes of the Khmer Rouge. It became an independent organisation in 1997 and researchers have spent years translating confessions and paperwork from Tuol Sleng, mapping mass graves and preserving evidence of Khmer Rouge crimes.

French-Cambodian director Rithy Panh's 1996 film *Bophana* tells the true story of Hout Bophana, a young woman, and Ly Sitha, a regional Khmer Rouge leader, who fall in love but are made to pay for this 'crime' with imprisonment and execution at S-21 prison. It is well worth investing an hour to watch this powerful documentary, which is screened here at 10am and 3pm daily. Rithy Panh also directed *The Khmer Rouge Killing Machine,* which includes interviews with former prison guards. A DC-

Cam slide presentation takes place Monday and Friday at 2pm and Wednesday at 9am.

**Killing Fields of Choeung Ek**  MUSEUM
( វាលពិឃាតជើងឯក; admission incl audio tour US$6; ☺7.30am-5.30pm) Between 1975 and 1978 about 17,000 men, women and children who had been detained and tortured at S-21 were transported to the extermination camp of Choeung Ek. They were often bludgeoned to death to avoid wasting precious bullets.

The remains of 8985 people, many of whom were bound and blindfolded, were exhumed in 1980 from mass graves in this onetime longan orchard; 43 of the 129 communal graves here have been left untouched. Fragments of human bone and bits of cloth are scattered around the disinterred pits. More than 8000 skulls, arranged by sex and age, are visible behind the clear glass panels of the Memorial Stupa, which was erected in 1988. It is a peaceful place today, masking the horrors that unfolded here several decades ago.

Admission to the Killing Fields includes an excellent audio tour, available in several languages. The site is well signposted in English about 7.5km south of the city limits. Figure on about US$10 for a *remork* (drivers may ask for more).

The audio tour includes stories by those who survived the Khmer Rouge, plus a chilling account by Him Huy, a Choeung Ek guard and executioner, about some of the techniques they used to kill innocent and defenceless prisoners, including women and children. There's also a museum here with some interesting information on the Khmer Rouge leadership and the ongoing trial. A memorial ceremony is held annually at Choeung Ek on 9 May.

A shuttle bus tour is available with **Phnom Penh Hop On Hop Off** (☎016 745880; www.phnompenhhoponhopoff.com; 1/2 passengers, excl entry fees US$15/25), which includes hotel pick-up from 8am in the morning or 1.30pm in the afternoon.

**Wat Phnom**  BUDDHIST TEMPLE
(វត្តភ្នំ; Map p52; Norodom Blvd at St 94; temple admission US$1, museum admission US$2; ☺7am-6.30pm, museum 7am-6pm) Set on top of a 27m-high tree-covered knoll, Wat Phnom is on the only 'hill' in town. According to legend, the first pagoda on this site was erected in 1373 to house four statues of Buddha deposited here by the waters of the Mekong River and discovered by Penh. The main entrance to Wat Phnom is via the

---

**GIVE BLOOD!**

Cambodia has a critical shortage of blood as there's a local stigma against donating blood and a high rate of thalassaemia. If you want to help, donate at the **National Blood Transfusion Centre** (Map p52; Preah Ang Doung Hospital, cnr Norodom Blvd & St 114; ☺8am-5pm). It's perfectly safe and you get a T-shirt.

grand eastern staircase, which is guarded by lions and *naga* (mythical serpent) balustrades.

Today, many people come here to pray for good luck and success in school exams or business affairs. When a wish is granted, the faithful return to deliver on the offering promised, such as a garland of jasmine flowers or a bunch of bananas (of which the spirits are said to be especially fond).

The *vihara* (temple sanctuary) was rebuilt in 1434, 1806, 1894 and 1926. West of the *vihara* is a huge stupa containing the ashes of King Ponhea Yat (r 1405–67). In a pavilion on the southern side of the passage between the *vihara* and the stupa is a statue of a smiling and rather plump Penh.

A bit to the north of and below the *vihara* is an eclectic shrine dedicated to the genie Preah Chau, who is especially revered by the Vietnamese. On either side of the entrance to the central altar are guardian spirits bearing iron bats. In the chamber to the right of the statue are drawings of Confucius, as well as two Chinese-style figures of the sages Thang Cheng (right) and Thang Thay (left).

Down the hill from the *vihara*, in the northwest corner of the complex, is a museum with some old statues and historical artefacts, which you can probably skip if you've been to the National Museum.

Be aware that Wat Phnom can be a bit of a circus, with beggars, street urchins and drink- and caged-bird sellers. You pay to set the bird free, but they are trained to return to their cage afterwards.

### Wat Ounalom                    BUDDHIST TEMPLE

(វត្តឧណ្ណាលោម; Map p52; Sothearos Blvd; ⊗ 6am-6pm) FREE This wat is the headquarters of Cambodian Buddhism. It was founded in 1443 and comprises 44 structures. It received a battering during the Pol Pot era, but today the wat has come back to life – the head of the country's Buddhist brotherhood lives here, with a large number of monks.

On the 2nd floor of the main building, to the left of the dais, is a statue of Huot Tat, fourth patriarch of Cambodian Buddhism, who was killed by Pol Pot. The statue, made in 1971 when the patriarch was 80 years old, was thrown in the Mekong by the Khmer Rouge to show that Buddhism was no longer the driving force in Cambodia. It was retrieved after 1979. To the right of the dais is a statue of a former patriarch of the Thummayuth sect (to which the royal family belongs).

Seek out the stairway to the left behind the dais. It leads up to the 3rd floor, where a glass case houses a small marble Buddha of Burmese origin that was broken into pieces by the Khmer Rouge and later reassembled. There are some nice views of the Mekong from up here.

Behind the main building is a stupa containing an eyebrow hair of Buddha with an inscription in Pali (an ancient Indian language) over the entrance.

### Olympic Stadium                    LANDMARK

(ពហុកីឡុដ្ឋានជាតិអូឡាំពិក; Map p46; near cnr Sihanouk & Monireth Blvds; ⊗ 6am-10pm) FREE Known collectively as the National Sports Complex, the Olympic Stadium is a striking example of 1960s 'New Khmer' architecture and includes a sports arena and facilities for boxing, gymnastics, volleyball and other sports. Turn up after 5pm to see countless football matches, *pétanque* duels or badminton games. It's also a popular spot for sunrise or sunset mass musical aerobics.

### Wat Moha Montrei                    BUDDHIST TEMPLE

(វត្តមហាមន្ត្រី; Map p46; Sihanouk Blvd at St 161) Situated close to the Olympic Stadium, Wat Moha Montrei was named in honour of one of King Monivong's ministers, Chakrue Ponn, who initiated the founding of the pagod a (*moha montrei* means 'the great minister'). The cement *vihara,* topped with a 35m-high tower, was completed in 1970. Between 1975 and 1979, it was used by the Khmer Rouge to store rice and corn.

Check out the assorted Cambodian touches incorporated into the wall murals of the *vihara*, which tell the story of Buddha. The angels accompanying Buddha to heaven are dressed as classical Khmer dancers, while the assembled officials wear the white military uniforms of the Sihanouk period.

### Independence Monument                    MONUMENT

(វិមានឯករាជ្យ; Map p46; cnr Norodom & Sihanouk Blvds) Modelled on the central tower of Angkor Wat, Independence Monument was built in 1958 to commemorate the country's independence from France in 1953. It also serves as a memorial to Cambodia's war dead. Wreaths are laid here on national holidays. In the park just east of here is an impressive statue (Map p46; Sihanouk Blvd) of the legendary former king/prime minister/statesman King Father Norodom Sihanouk, who died a national hero in 2012.

Near by, in Wat Botum Park (ឧទ្យានវត្តបុទុម) opposite photogenic Wat

# South Phnom Penh

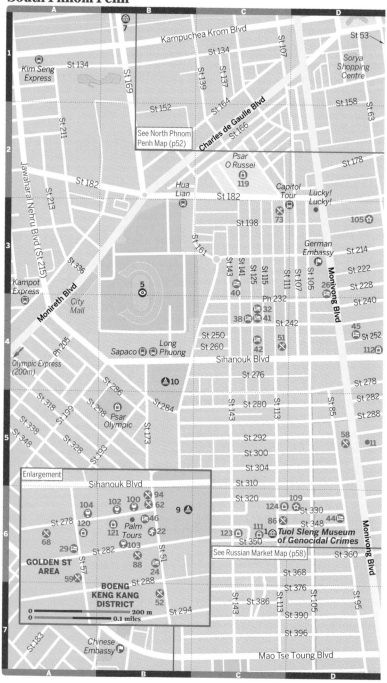

See North Phnom Penh Map (p52)

Kampuchea Krom Blvd

St 53

St 134

St 107

Sorya Shopping Centre

Kim Seng Express

St 134

St 158

St 63

St 211

St 169

St 139

St 137

St 152

St 164

Charles de Gaulle Blvd

St 166

Psar O Russei
119

St 178

Jawaharal Nehru Blvd (St 215)

St 182

St 213

Hua Lian

St 182

Capitol Tour

Lucky! Lucky!

St 198

73

105

St 161

St 143

St 141

St 125

St 115

St 107

St 111

St 105

German Embassy

St 214

St 222

St 228

St 240

Kampot Express

St 336

Monireth Blvd

City Mall

5

40

Ph 232

32

38

41

St 242

St 250

St 260

42

St 252

112

45

51

Sihanouk Blvd

Long Phuong

Sapaco

10

St 276

St 278

St 282

St 288

Olympic Express (200m)

Ph 205

St 286

St 284

St 143

St 280

St 113

St 85

St 318

St 199

St 298

Psar Olympic

St 173

St 292

St 300

58

11

St 338

St 328

St 193

St 304

St 310

St 348

St 320

## Enlargement

Sihanouk Blvd

102

100

94

62

St 330

124

109

104

120

46

9

St 278

Palm Tours

22

86

St 348

44

68

121

103

123

111

1

Tuol Sleng Museum of Genocidal Crimes

29

St 282

88

St 350

See Russian Market Map (p58)

St 360

24

51

**GOLDEN ST AREA**

St 57

59

**BOENG KENG KANG DISTRICT**

St 288

52

St 368

St 376

St 386

St 390

St 105

St 95

St 294

St 143

St 113

0 ——— 200 m
0 ——— 0.1 miles

St 183

St 396

Chinese Embassy

Mao Tse Toung Blvd

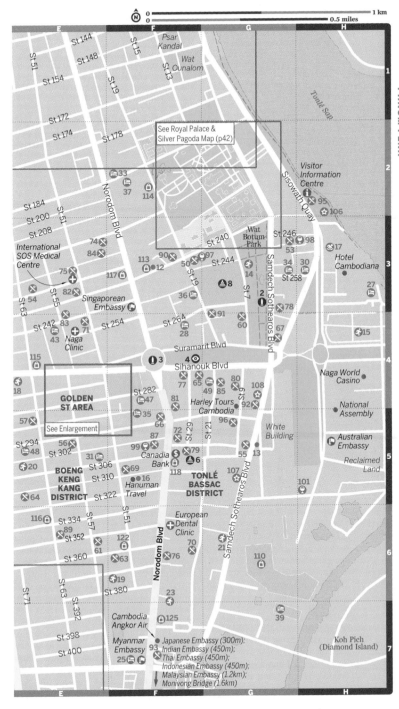

# South Phnom Penh

Botum (Map p46; btwn St 7 & St 19), is opti- mistically named **Cambodia-Vietnam Friendship Monument** (Map p46), built to a Vietnamese (and rather communist) design in 1979. Concerts are often held in the park, which springs to life with aerobics, football and *takraw* (foot juggling with a rattan ball) enthusiasts after 5pm.

**Vann Nath Gallery**                        ART GALLERY
(Map p46; Kith Eng Restaurant; 33B St 169) FREE
The late Cambodian artist Vann Nath is world famous for his depictions of Khmer Rouge torture scenes at Phnom Penh's noto- rious S-21 Security Prison, where he was one of only seven survivors. Many of Vann Nath's

later works can be viewed here at his family's Kith Eng Restaurant. There are no set hours, so just drop by; his wife or his son-in-law (who speaks English) will usually let you in.

Vann Nath continued to paint vivid can- vases of S-21 right up until his death in 2011; some of his most famous images are on display at the Tuol Sleng Museum. The Vietnamese brought him back to S-21 from 1980 to 1982 specifically to paint these. 'We must think of the souls of those who died there,' Vann Nath told us in an interview not long before he passed away. 'These souls died without hope, without light, without a future. They had no life. So I paint my scenes to tell the world the stories of those who did not survive.' In the wake of Vann Nath's death, fellow prisoners Chum Mey and Bou Meng are the last remaining survivors of S-21.

**French Embassy** LANDMARK
(Map p38; 1 Monivong Blvd) Located at the northern end of Monivong Blvd, the French embassy played a significant role in the dramas that unfolded after the fall of Phnom Penh on 17 April 1975. About 800 foreigners and 600 Cambodians took refuge in the embassy. Within 48 hours, the Khmer Rouge informed the French vice-consul that they did not recognise diplomatic privileges – and if the Cambodians

in the compound were not handed over, the lives of the foreigners inside would also be forfeited.

Cambodian women married to foreigners could stay; Cambodian men married to foreign women could not. Foreigners wept as servants, colleagues, friends, lovers and husbands were escorted out of the embassy gates. At the end of the month the foreigners were expelled from Cambodia by truck. Many of the Cambodians were never seen again. Today a high, whitewashed wall surrounds the massive complex, and the French have returned to Cambodia in a big way, promoting French language and culture in their former colony.

### National Library
LANDMARK

(បណ្ណាល័យជាតិ; Bibliothèque Nationale; Map p52; St 92; ⊘8-11am & 2-5pm Mon-Fri) The National Library is in a graceful building constructed in 1924, near Wat Phnom. During its rule, the Khmer Rouge turned the building into a stable and destroyed most of the books. Many were thrown out into the streets, where they were picked up by people, some of whom donated them back to the library after 1979; others used them as food wrappings. Today it houses, among other things, a time-worn collection of English and French titles (including some ancient Lonely Planet books).

### Prayuvong Buddha Factories
BUDDHIST

(សិប្បកម្មសាងព្រះពុទ្ធរូប ព្រះយួវង្ស; Map p46; btwn St 308 & St 310) ✐ In order to replace the countless Buddhas and ritual objects smashed by the Khmer Rouge, a whole neighbourhood of private workshops making cement Buddhas, *naga* and small stupas has grown up on the grounds of Wat Prayuvong. While the graceless cement figures painted in gaudy colours are hardly works of art, they are an effort by the Cambodian people to restore Buddhism to a place of honour in their culture. The factories are 300m south of Independence Monument.

## 🏃 Activities

### Aerobics
Every morning at the crack of dawn, and again at dusk, Cambodians gather in several pockets throughout the city to participate in quirky and colourful aerobics sessions. This quintessential Cambodian phenomenon sees a ringleader, equipped with boom box and microphone, whip protégés into shape with a mix of 1980s, Soviet-style calisthenics and *Thriller*-inspired line-dancing moves. It's favoured by middle-aged Khmer women, but you'll see both sexes and all ages participating, and tourists are more than welcome.

There are many places to join in the fun or just observe. Olympic Stadium (p45) is probably the best spot for the sheer volume of participants; several instructors compete for clients and the upper level of the grandstand becomes a cacophony of competing boom boxes.

The riverfront usually sees some action: the space opposite Blue Pumpkin (p62) at the terminus of St 144 is a good bet. Another popular place that usually sees several groups in action is Wat Botum Park (p45), along Sothearos Blvd.

### Boat Cruises
Boat trips on the Tonlé Sap and Mekong Rivers are very popular with visitors. Sunset cruises are ideal, the burning sun sinking slowly behind the glistening spires of the Royal Palace. A slew of cruising boats (Map p38) are available for hire on the riverfront about 500m north of the tourist boat dock. Just rock up and arrange one on the spot for around US$20 an hour, depending on negotiations and numbers. You can bring your own drinks or buy beer and soft drinks on the boat. Public river cruises are another option. They leave every 30 minutes from 5pm to 7.30pm from the tourist boat dock (p84) and last about 45 minutes (US$5 per head).

### Kanika Boat Tour
BOAT TOUR

(Map p52; ☑089 848959; www.kanika-boat.com; US$7 sunset/dinner cruise US$7/20) The *Kanika* is a striking white catamaran that sails the waters of the Tonlé Sap and Mekong nightly (except Mondays). Choose from a sunset cruise (US$15 with free-flow draught beer or tasting platters) at 5pm, or a longer dinner cruise from 7pm.

### Cycling
You can hire a bike and go it alone. Koh Dach (p88) is a doable DIY trip, or venture across the Mekong River on a local ferry (1000r including bike) behind Imperial Garden Hotel (p50) and pick up bucolic back roads on the other side. Or opt for something more organised (with or without a guide) through one of the companies below; Vicious Cycle runs daily group tours to Udong (p88) or Koh Dach, departing before 8am.

### Bike Shop
CYCLING

(Map p46; ☑089 834704; www.bicycletours cambodia.com; 31 St 302) Has premium mountain and road bikes for rent (US$10 to US$30) and specialises in multiday cycling tours that criss-cross the country (from US$80 per person per day for a couple).

### Vicious Cycle
CYCLING

(Map p52; ☑012 430622; www.grasshopper adventures.com; 23 St 144; road/mountain bike per day US$4/8) Plenty of excellent mountain and other bikes available here. Kiddie seats can be attached to your mountain bike for US$3. Vicious represents well-respected Grasshopper Adventures in Phnom Penh.

### Fitness Centres & Swimming
The fanciest hotels listed in this chapter will let you use their gyms and pools for a fee,

while **Sofitel** (Map p46; ☑023-999200; www.
sofitel.com; 26 Sothearos Blvd) and **Imperial
Garden** (Map p46; ☑023-219991; www.imperial
garden-hotel.com; 315 Sisowath Quay) include
access to tennis courts.

A few of the hotels will let you swim if
you buy a few bucks' worth of food or cocktails: try Teahouse (p60) or the **252** (Map
p46; ☑023-998252; www.the-252.com; 19 St 152).

Keep in mind that the pools at these places are pretty small, more for dipping and
cooling off than for doing laps. Most other
midrange boutiques charge US$5 for pool
rights.

**Himawari Hotel**                                    SWIMMING
(Map p46; ☑023-214555; 313 Sisowath Quay;
admission weekday/weekend US$7/8) Has a
larger pool fit for laps.

**Long Beach Plaza Hotel**                    SWIMMING
(Map p38; ☑023-998007; 3 St 289; admission
US$1) A bargain for a lap-sized pool but far
from the centre.

**Muscle Fitness**                                        GYM
(Map p58; cnr St 95 & St 386; per session US$3.50;
☺6am-8pm) A pretty good deal considering
the range of equipment, albeit with dysfunctional air-con.

**The Place**                                                  GYM
(Map p46; ☑023-999799; 11 St 51; walk-in US$15;
☺6am-10pm) This is absolutely state of the
art, with myriad machines, a big pool and a
range of cardio classes.

### Go-Carting

**Kambol Kart Raceway**                        GO CARTS
(☑012 232332; per 10min US$12) Kambol Kart
Raceway is a professional circuit in a rural
setting just outside of Phnom Penh. Prices

## PHNOM PENH FOR CHILDREN

With chaotic traffic, a lack of green spaces and sights that are predominantly morbid,
Phnom Penh would not seem like the most child-friendly city. Think again. There are
plenty of little gems to help you pass the time with your children in the capital. (Plus, most
children love a remork ride.)

Kids also love Buddhist temples – especially colourful temples such as Wat Langka
(p55) or Wat Ounalom (p45), and hill temples such as Wat Phnom (p44) or, outside of
town, Udong (p88). Shimmering gold Buddhas, shiny stupas, animal statues and the
occasional monkey give children plenty of visual stimulation (hide little ones' eyes
from potentially scary demons). The Royal Palace (p40) is similarly rich in Buddhist
iconography.

Alternatively consider renting bicycles and crossing the Mekong by ferry from the dock
behind Imperial Garden Hotel (p50). On the other side, smooth roads and trails lead 15km
or so north to **Smango** (☑016 994555; www.smangohouse.com; pool admission US$5), a
guesthouse with decent food and a refreshing swimming pool. Best check its website for
exact directions.

Phnom Penh has decent public play spaces, including a **playground** (Map p46; Samdech Sotharos Blvd) northwest of the Cambodia-Vietnam Friendship Memorial in Wat
Botum Park, and another **playground** (Map p52) just south of Wat Phnom. Swimming
pools are another popular option in a hot, hot city: many hotels with pools allow outside
guests to swim for a fee or a minimum spend. **Kingdom Resort** (☑023-721514; www.
thekingdomresort.net; off NH1; adult/child US$5/3) is a great option for those willing to make
a short excursion (6km) out of town; it has a huge pool and some slides.

Great for escaping the heat (or the rain), **Kids City** (Map p46; www.kidscityasia.com;
Sihanouk Blvd; 1hr from US$5; ☺8am-9.30pm) is a vast indoor play palace, with a first-rate
climbing gym, an elaborate jungle gym, a science gallery and an ice rink. Other indoor
playgrounds (bring socks) with elaborate slides, bouncy castles and the like can be found
at amusement park **Dream Land** (Map p46; www.dreamland.com.kh; 8 Sisowath Quay; admission US$6, playground 2000r; ☺9am-9pm), which also has a Ferris wheel and other rides;
and, for younger children, **Monkey Business** (Map p46; St 370 at St 57; child US$2-4, adult
free; ☺9am-7pm), which has wi-fi and a cafe for adults. Many of the restaurants and cafes
are child-friendly.

The most interesting attraction is beyond the city limits and makes a good day trip:
Phnom Tamao Wildlife Sanctuary (p90), a rescue centre for Cambodia's incredible wildlife.

# North Phnom Penh

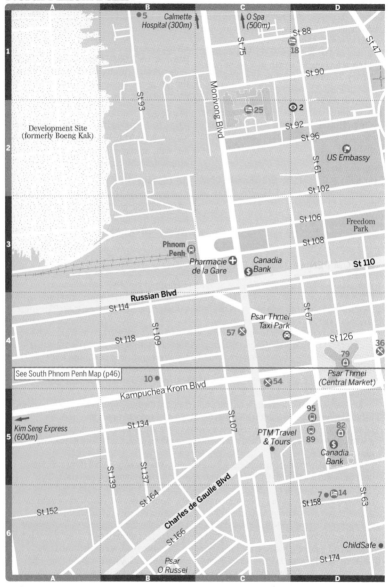

include helmets and racing suits. It's about 2km off the road to Sihanoukville. Look for a hard-to-spot sign on the right, 8km beyond the airport; if you hit the toll booth, you've gone too far.

## Golf

If you can't survive without a swing, Phnom Penh has several 18-hole courses, but most of them lie about 30km or more out of town.

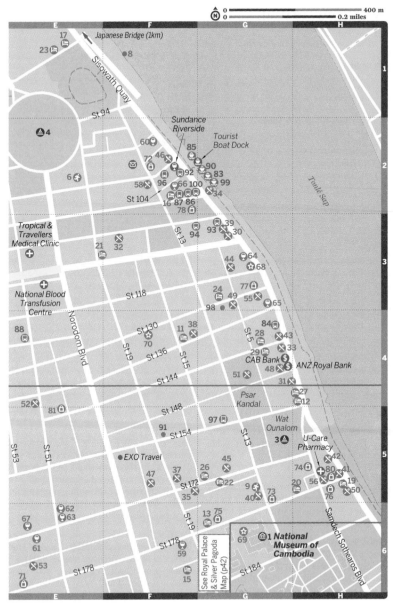

See Royal Palace & Silver Pagoda Map (p42)

**Grand Phnom Penh Golf Club** GOLF
(☏ 023-690 0888; www.grandphnompenhgolf.com; Hanoi Rd; weekdays/weekends US$85/129, plus caddy & cart US$40) The most convenient of the 18-hole golf courses around the capital, this was designed by none other than Jack Nicklaus. Turn north off the Airport Rd and follow Hanoi Rd for 5km until you spot the imposing entrance on the right.

## Massage & Spas

There are plenty of massage parlours in Phnom Penh, though some offer 'naughty' massages. However, there are also scores

# North Phnom Penh

of legitimate massage centres and some superb spas for that pampering palace experience.

**Spa Bliss**  SPA
(Map p46; ☎ 023-215754; www.blissspacambodia. com; 29 St 240; massages from US$22) One of the most established spas in town, set in a lovely old French house on popular St 240.

**Bodia Spa**  SPA
(Map p52; ☎ 023-226199; www.bodia-spa.com; cnr Sotheuros Blvd & St 178; massages from US$26; ⊙ 10am-11pm) Just about the best rubdowns in town, in a Zen-like setting just off the riverfront.

**O Spa**  SPA
(Map p38; ☎ 023-992405; www.ospacambodia. com; 4B St 75; massages from US$20; ⊙ 11am-10pm) An oasis of calm, with rejuvenating hot-stone massage, plus Balinese and Thai treatments.

**Daughters**  SPA
(Map p52; ☎ 077 657678; www.daughtersof cambodia.org; 65 St 178; 1hr foot spa US$10; ⊙ 9am-5.30pm Mon-Sat) Hand and foot massages are administered by participants in this NGO's vocational training program for at-risk women. Shorter (15- to 30-minute) treatments also available.

**Nail Bar**  MASSAGE
(Map p52; www.mithsamlanh.org; Friends n' Stuff store, 215 St 13; 30/60min massages US$4/7; ⊙ 11am-9pm) Cheap manicures, pedicures, foot massages, hand massages and nail painting, all to help Mith Samlanh train street children in a new vocation.

**Seeing Hand**
**Massage Chan Tharith**  MASSAGE
(Map p46; ☎ 092 260910; www.seeinghand massage.com; 77 Sotheuros Blvd; massages US$5-7.50; ⊙ 7am-10pm) This place helps you ease those aches and pains and helps blind mas-

seurs stay self-sufficient. One of the best-value massages in the capital.

### Meditation & Yoga

Free one-hour Vipassana meditation sessions take place in the central *vihara* of **Wat Langka** (Map p46; cnr St 51 & Sihanouk Blvd) at 6pm on Mondays, Thursdays and Saturdays, and on Sunday morning at 8am. If you've never done it before, an hour will seem like an eternity – it's OK to just do 20 or 30 minutes.

Yoga studios around town hold regular classes – check their websites for schedules. Some offer discounts for multiple classes.

**NaṭaRāj Yoga**                    YOGA
(Map p46; ☏ 090 311341; www.yogacambodia. com; 52 St 302; classes from US$9) Popular yoga studio with a range of classes.

**Yoga Phnom Penh**                 YOGA
(Map p46; ☏ 012 739419; www.yogaphnom penh.com; 172 Norodom Blvd; classes from US$8)

### Running

**Hash House Harriers**             RUNNING
(www.p2h3.com) A good opportunity to meet local expatriates is via the Hash House Harriers, usually referred to simply as 'the Hash'. A run/walk takes place every Sunday. Participants meet in front of Phnom Penh train station (p86) at 2pm. The US$5 fee includes refreshments – mainly beer – at the end.

## 🍴 Courses

**Cambodia Cooking Class**     COOKING COURSE
(Map p46; ☏ 012 524801; www.cambodia-cooking-class.com; booking office 67 St 240; half/full day US$15/23) Learn the art of Khmer cuisine through Frizz Restaurant. Classes are held near the Russian embassy. Reserve ahead.

## ☞ Tours

There are some interesting niche tours in and around Phnom Penh. For an organised

## CAMBODIAN FIGHT CLUB

The whole world knows about *muay Thai* (Thai boxing) and kickboxing, but what is not so well known is that this contact sport probably originated in Cambodia. *Pradal serey* (literally 'free fighting') is Cambodia's very own version of kickboxing; you can see some fights in Phnom Penh. Popular Cambodian TV channel CTN hosts live bouts at 2pm on Friday, Saturday and Sunday out at its main studio on National Hwy 5, about 4km north of the Japanese Bridge. Entry is free and there is usually a rowdy local crowd surreptitiously betting on the fights. Most bouts are ended by a violent elbow move and there's a lot more ducking and diving than with other kickboxing genres.

An even older martial art is *bokator*, or *labokatao*, which some say dates back to the time of Angkor. It translates as 'pounding a lion' and was originally conceived for battle-field confrontations. Weapons include bamboo staffs and short sticks, as well as the *krama* (scarf) in certain situations. The **Pras Khan Chey Bokator School** (Map p52; ☑ 095 455555; www.bokatorcambodia.com; 10 St 109; ⊙ 8-10am & 6-8pm) in Phnom Penh offers lessons (US$5 per hour) or full brown-belt courses (US$1500). Call ahead to ensure you get an English-speaking instructor.

city tour, most of the leading guesthouses and travel agencies can arrange one for about US$6 per person, not including entrance fees.

### Khmer
#### Architecture Tours                       CULTURAL TOUR
(www.ka-tours.org; tours US$10-55, depending on numbers) Those interested in the new-wave Khmer architecture from the Sangkum era (1953–70) should look no further. These two- to three-hour introductory tours take in some of the most prominent buildings in the city and take place on foot or by *cyclo* (pedicab), starting at 8.30am two or three Sundays per month. The website also includes a DIY map of the most popular walking tour.

For more on this landmark architecture, pick up a copy of *Cultures of Independence* (2001) or *Building Cambodia: New Khmer Architecture 1953–70* (2006).

#### Cambodian Living Arts          CULTURAL TOUR
(CLA; Map p46; ☑ 017 998570; www.cambodian livingarts.org; 128 Sothearos Blvd) Cambodian Living Arts supports elder Cambodian musicians to train young and at-risk Cambodians in traditional music, dance and other forms. You can visit many of these classes through CLA's 'Living Arts Tours'. Among the most interesting is the **Pinpeat ensemble class** (⊙ 10.45am-12.15pm Mon-Fri) in the decrepit modernist 'White Building', where students learn to play melodies that were used in the royal courts of Angkor to accompany ceremonies, dances and masked plays.

There are many more tours, both in Phnom Penh and in Siem Reap, Takeo and other provinces; see the website for details.

#### Cyclo Centre                              TOUR
(Map p52; ☑ 097 700 9762; www.cyclo.org.kh; 95 St 158; per hour/day from US$3/12) Dedicated to supporting *cyclo* drivers in Phnom Penh, these tours are a great way to see the sights. Themed trips such as pub crawls or cultural tours are also available.

#### Kingdom Brewery                           TOUR
(☑ 023-430180; 1748 NH5; tours US$6; ⊙ 1-5pm Mon-Fri) It costs just US$6 to tour the facilities of Kingdom Brewery. Tours include two drinks and you don't even have to book ahead – just show up. It's exactly 1km north of the Japanese Bridge on NH5.

#### Nature Cambodia                     BICYCLE TOUR
(☑ 012 676381; www.nature-cambodia.com; tours per 90min/half-day/full-day US$25/55/110) Offers quad biking in the countryside around Phnom Penh. The quads are automatic, and so are easy to handle for beginners (maximum two passengers per bike). Full-day tours take in Tonlé Bati and Phnom Tamao; despite its proximity to the capital, this is rural Cambodia and very beautiful. Longer trips and jeep tours are also available.

Follow signs to the Killing Fields of Choeung Ek (p44); it's about 300m before the entrance. Call ahead as numbers are limited.

## 🛏 Sleeping

Accommodation in Phnom Penh, as in the rest of the country, is great value no matter your budget, with quite literally hundreds of guesthouses and hotels to choose from.

## North Central (Riverfront)

While the idea of resting up on the riverfront has obvious appeal, you'll find better value elsewhere. Also keep in mind that hotels along the river tend to be noisy, and most budget rooms are windowless or face away from the river. A few superb options exist in the top end options, but worthwhile pickings are much slimmer in the budget and midrange categories.

### ★Foreign

**Correspondents' Club**   BOUTIQUE HOTEL **$$**
(FCC; Map p52; ☑ 023-210142; www.fcc cambodia.com; 363 Sisowath Quay; standard/ deluxe incl breakfast from US$59/79; ❄ 🛜) This landmark location is a fine place to recapture the heady days of the war correspondents. The rooms are exquisitely finished in polished wood and include fine art, top-of-the-line furniture and vintage *Phnom Penh Post* covers on the wall. The deluxe rooms have breezy balconies with prime river views.

**Bougainvillier Hotel**   HOTEL **$$**
(Map p52; ☑ 023-220528; www.bougainvillier hotel.com; 277G Sisowath Quay; r without/with river views incl breakfast from US$55/90; ❄ 🛜) These tastefully decorated rooms include amply proportioned river-view suites with a private balcony. You can also ascend to the rooftop bar (p74) for serious views (but be aware there's no lift).

**Amanjaya Pancam Hotel**   BOUTIQUE HOTEL **$$$**
(Map p52; ☑ 023-214747; www.amanjaya-suites-phnom-penh.com; 1 St 154; r incl breakfast US$135-175; ❄ @ 🛜) Amanjaya boasts a superb riverfront location and spacious rooms finished with luxuriant dark-wood floors, elegant Khmer drapes and tropical furnishings. Luscious Le Moon (p74) bar is on the roof, trendy **K West** cafe at ground level.

**The Quay**   BOUTIQUE HOTEL **$$$**
(Map p52; ☑ 023-224894; www.thequayhotel. com; 277 Sisowath Quay; r/ste incl breakfast from US$50/90; ❄ @ 🛜) The Quay is the home of contemporary style right on the riverfront. The river-view panoramic suites, with big balconies, are the beds of choice, as they are far more spacious than the also-stylish-but-dark rooms at the rear. Ascend to the rooftop Chow (p74) bar to catch views and breezes.

## North Central (Off-River)

If you want to be near the riverfront but not pay riverfront prices, this area is a happy hunting ground. Be aware, though, that the blocks running west off the river from St 104 to about St 144 are gritty and have sleazy areas; a handful of delectable new boutique hotels point to the slow gentrification of this prime real estate. Meanwhile, St 172 between St 19 and St 13 has become Phnom Penh's most popular backpacker area.

★**Eighty8 Backpackers**   HOSTEL **$**
(Map p52; ☑ 023-500 2440; www.88backpackers. com; 98 St 88; dm US$5.25-7.75, r US$18-26; ❄ @ 🛜 🏊) A hostel with a swimming pool means party time – this place hosts a big one on the first Friday of every month. The pool and the extensive villa are home to a variety of dorms and private rooms. The courtyard has a central bar, with a pool table and plenty of spots to lounge around the pool.

The dorms come in air-con and fan varieties, plus a female dorm.

**DoDo Guesthouse**   GUESTHOUSE **$**
(Map p52; ☑ 023-999912; http://dodoguest house.wordpress.com; 2B St 90; r US$15-25; ❄ 🛜) An impressive little guesthouse north of Wat Phnom, the rooms here are clean, spacious and top value, including bathrooms that are as big as some of the cell-like rooms in other places. Downstairs is a funky little cafe-bar.

**Me Mate's Place**   GUESTHOUSE **$**
(Map p52; ☑ 023-500 2497; www.memates place.com; 5 St 90; dm US$6-7, s/d from US$18/20; ❄ @ 🛜 🏊) This is a smart little guesthouse-bar on a quiet strip north of Wat Phnom. The six-bed dorms include sturdy double bunk beds and crisp air-con. The spartan private rooms, some windowless, are less memorable. Guests here get to swim at Eighty8 Backpackers' (p57) swimming pool. **New Me Mate's Villa** (Map p46; ☑ 012 795961; 21A St 184; dm US$6-10, r US$20-25; ❄ 🛜) on St 184 is a flashpacker alternative.

**Mama Veary's Guesthouse**   GUESTHOUSE **$**
(Map p52; ☑ 023-989696; www.mamaveary guesthouse.com; 26 St 172; dm/s/d US$4/15/20; ❄ @ 🛜) Standard hotel rooms at guesthouse prices make Mama Veary's a great little place on the popular St 172 backpacker strip. The dorms are clean and air-conditioned and among the cheapest beds in town.

## Russian Market

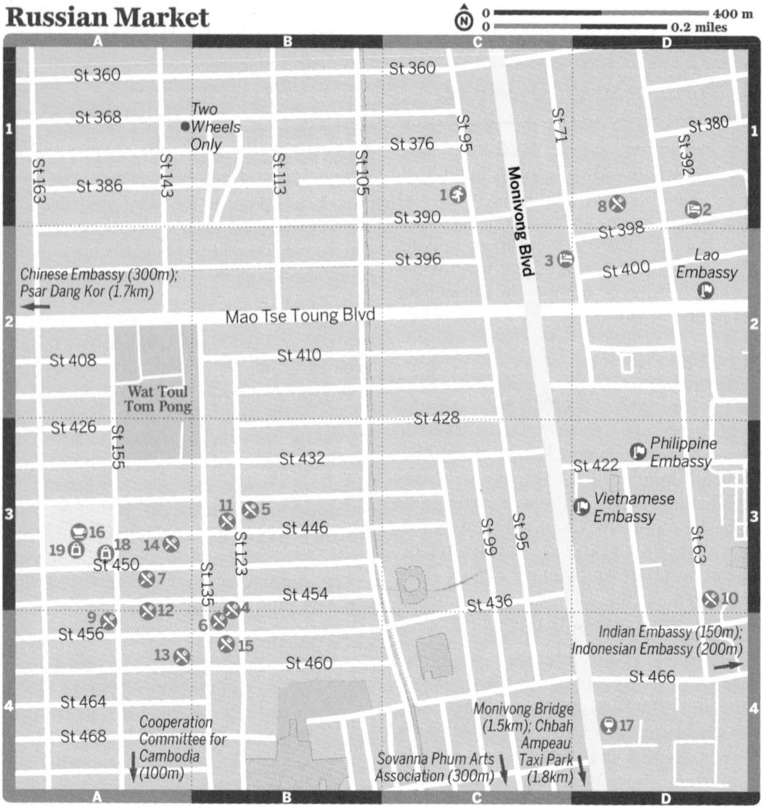


**Velkommen Backpackers** GUESTHOUSE **$**
(Map p52; ☎077 757701; www.velkommenbackpackers.com; 17 St 144; dm US$5, r US$8-30; ❄📶) The popular Velkommen has been looking after travellers for the better part of a decade now. Dorms are air-conditioned and rooms come in a pick 'n' mix of shapes and sizes. There is a bar-restaurant downstairs and lots of useful travel info. Directly across the road is the **Velkommen Guesthouse** (Map p52; ☎077 757701; www.velkommenguesthouse.com; 18 St 144; r US$18-45; ❄📶), with smarter rooms.

**11 Happy Backpacker** HOSTEL **$**
(Map p52; ☎088 777 7421; happy11gt@hotmail.com; 87-89 St 136; dm US$5, r US$8-15; ❄@📶) At one of the original backpacker pads in Phnom Penh, the sprawling rooftop bar-restaurant offers chairs for chilling out and a pool table; it's mellow by day, fun by night. The white-tiled rooms are clean and functional. The **Flicks 2 cinema** is conveniently located downstairs.

★**Blue Lime** BOUTIQUE HOTEL **$$**
(Map p52; ☎023-222260; www.bluelime.asia; 42 St 19z; r incl breakfast US$50-85; ❄@📶≋) The Blue Lime offers smart, minimalist rooms and a leafy pool area that invites relaxation. The pricier rooms have private plunge pools, four-poster beds and concrete love seats. The cheaper rooms upstairs in the main building are similarly appealing. No children.

**Monsoon Boutique Hotel** BOUTIQUE HOTEL **$$**
(Map p52; ☎023-989856; www.monsoonhotel.com; 53-55 St 130; r incl breakfast US$30-45; ❄@📶) Blink and you'll miss this little oasis on chaotic St 130. Hidden inside are attractive rooms with polished concrete walls and pleasing murals. It's a real deal considering the sophistication of the design and a location close to the river.

**De Art Hotel** BOUTIQUE HOTEL **$$**
(Map p52; ☎023-622 2298; www.dearthotel.com; 9-12 St 106; r US$30-70; ❄@📶) A new

# Russian Market

boutique hotel that adds to a legion of chic sleeps in the city, De Art has some incredible specials on their rooms, making them a real steal. Four-star comfort at two-star prices, rooms are ultra-modern with some contemporary art adorning the walls. (Though it can be noisy as it's near bus company offices.)

**Billabong**     BOUTIQUE HOTEL $$
(Map p52; ✆023-223703; www.thebillabong hotel.com; 5 St 158; s/d/tr incl breakfast from US$36/60/75; ❇@🛜🏊) Near Psar Thmei but an oasis of calm by comparison, Billabong has 41 stylish rooms surrounding an open courtyard with a large swimming pool. Aim for the ground-level pool-view rooms, which have private verandahs and more space compared with rooms at the back.

**Sundance Inn & Saloon**     GUESTHOUSE $$
(Map p52; ✆016 802090; www.sundance cambodia.com; 61 St 172; r US$23-38; ❇@🛜🏊) Sundance is a step above the guesthouse pack on St 172 with oversize beds, designer bathrooms, kitchenettes and computers that hook up to flat-screens in every room. With open-mic Mondays, frequent live music, all-day US$1 cocktails and a pool out back, it is

quite the party pad. Free airport pick-up with 24 hours' notice.

**Artist Guesthouse**     GUESTHOUSE $$
(Map p52; ✆023-213930; www.the-artist-guest house.com; 69 St 178; US$28-58; ❇🛜) Small but perfectly formed, this is a B&B-style guesthouse overlooking the National Museum. Rooms at the front come with balconies and are worth the extra investment. Downstairs is newcomer restaurant **Jay's Diner**.

**Sangkum**     BOUTIQUE HOTEL $$
(Map p38; ✆023-987775; www.thesangkum.com; 35A St 75; r US$55-85; ❇@🛜🏊) Set in a '60s villa to the north of Wat Phnom, the name pays homage to Cambodia's so-called Golden Years, under the rule of Sihanouk and his Sangkum political party. Rooms are decorated with a contemporary flourish and there's a small swimming pool for cooling off after exploring the city.

⭐**Raffles Hotel Le Royal**     HOTEL $$$
(Map p52; ✆023-981888; www.raffles.com/phnom penh; cnr Monivong Blvd & St 92; r from US$250; ❇@🛜🏊) From the golden age of travel, this is one of Asia's grand old dames, in the illustrious company of the Oriental in Bangkok and Raffles in Singapore. This classic colonial-era property is Phnom Penh's leading address, with a heritage to match its service and style. Indulgent diversions include two swimming pools, a gym, spa and lavish bars and restaurants. Between 1970 and 1975 many famous journalists working in Phnom Penh stayed here. More recent celebrated guests have included Barack Obama and Angelina Jolie.

⭐**La Maison D'Ambre**     BOUTIQUE HOTEL $$$
(Map p52; ✆023-222780; www.lamaisondambre. com; 123 St 110; ste incl breakfast US$100-190; ❇@🛜) A designer hotel linked to leading house of couture Ambre, this place is fit for a fashion shoot. The ample themed suites feature stunning contemporary art, space-age lamps and designer kitchens. The psychedelic rooftop bar, **The Fifth Element**, has prime views of Wat Phnom and funky furniture, making it a great place for breakfast or a sundowner.

**Frangipani Royal Palace Hotel**     BOUTIQUE HOTEL $$$
(Map p52; ✆023-223320; www.frangipani palacehotel.com; 27 St 178; US$80-135; ❇@🛜🏊) Frangipani is a homegrown chain of boutique hotels in Phnom Penh and Siem Reap; this is their flagship property overlooking the

Royal Palace. Aim to live the high life and ask for a room on the upper floors. There's a rooftop swimming pool with a palace view and happy hours at the **skybar** from 5pm to 7.30pm.

## St 240 & Around

The hotels in this zone are ideally positioned – on or within walking distance of the river and close to the Royal Palace. Cosy boutique hotels set around a pool are in abundance here. Walk-in backpackers can target St 258, which has a clutch of cheap guesthouses.

### Number 9 Guesthouse                    FLASHPACKER $
(Map p46; ☑ 023-984999; www.number9hotel. com; 7C St 258; r from US$15; ❄ 🛜 🏊) The first of Phnom Penh's old school backpacker pads to undergo a transformation into a flash-packer hotel, it is still going strong thanks to great rates, a rooftop pool and a lively bar-restaurant. Worth a splash for backpackers who have been exploring rural Cambodia.

### Aura Thematic Hostel                         HOSTEL $
(Map p42; ☑ 023-986211; www.aurahostel.com; 205A St 19; dm US$8-12; ❄ @ 🛜) A funky new hostel behind the Royal Palace, the rooms here are themed along the lines of 'Desert', 'Jungle' and 'Sea'. In reality this is more about a large image on the wall, but the rooms are spotless and include boutique bathrooms. Head to the rooftop to wind down at the stylish Eluvium Lounge.

### Lazy Gecko Guesthouse               GUESTHOUSE $
(Map p46; ☑ 078 786025; lazygeckocafe@gmail. com; 1D St 258; r with fan US$6-10, with air-con US$14-20; ❄ 🛜) Best known as a cafe, Lazy Gecko's rooms are hit and miss. The air-con doubles are plain, but do have flat-screen TVs and plenty of space, while the fan rooms are on the small side. But it's a great location amid the backpacker haunts of St 258.

### ★ Pavilion                         BOUTIQUE HOTEL $$
(Map p46; ☑ 023-222280; www.thepavilion.asia; 227 St 19; r incl breakfast US$50-100, apt US$110-120; ❄ @ 🛜 🏊) Housed in an elegant French villa, this immensely popular and atmospheric place kick-started Phnom Penh's boutique hotel obsession. All rooms have inviting four-poster beds, stunning furniture, personal computers and iPod docks. Some of the newer rooms include a private plunge pool. Guests can use bamboo bikes for free. No children allowed.

### Teahouse                           BOUTIQUE HOTEL $$
(Map p46; ☑ 023-212789; www.theteahouse.asia; 32 St 242; r incl breakfast US$33-89; ❄ @ 🛜 🏊) A smaller, cheaper version of sister hotel Plantation, the rooms are exceptional value given the chic look. The open-air reception area under a Chinese-style pavilion has relaxing seating and free internet.

### Kabiki                             BOUTIQUE HOTEL $$
(Map p46; ☑ 023-222290; www.thekabiki.com; 22 St 264; r incl breakfast US$50-80; ❄ @ 🛜 🏊) The most family-friendly place in town, the Kabiki offers a large, lush garden and an inviting swimming pool with a kiddie pool. Family rooms include bunks and most rooms have a private garden terrace.

### Plantation                       BOUTIQUE HOTEL $$$
(Map p46; ☑ 023-215151; www.theplantation.asia; 28 St 184; r incl breakfast US$85-298; ❄ @ 🛜 🏊) This is the largest and most ambitious hotel among the Pavilion properties. It ticks all the boxes with high ceilings, stylish fixtures and fittings, open-plan bathrooms and bal-conies. There are two swimming pools here and a beautiful courtyard reception that hosts regular art exhibitions.

## Boeng Keng Kang & Tonlé Bassac

Popular among NGO workers and expats, the Boeng Keng Kang (BKK) and Tonlé Bassac districts, south of Independence Monument, comprise the flashpacker zone, with an expanding selection of fine midrange hotels to go with a wealth of trendy bars and restaurants (plus a few good hostels). Many of the hotels are centred on St 278, dubbed 'Golden St' because of the preponderance of hotels that feature 'Golden' in their name.

### ★ Mad Monkey                            HOSTEL $
(Map p46; ☑ 023-987091; www.phnompenh hostels.com; 26 St 302; dm US$4-7, r from US$14-30; ❄ @ 🛜) This colourful and vibrant hostel is justifiably popular. The spacious dorms have air-con and sleep six to 20; the smaller ones have double-width bunk beds that can sleep two. The private rooms are swish for the price but lack TVs and, often, windows. The **rooftop bar** above quiet St 302 serves free beer on Mondays from 6pm to 8pm.

### Top Banana Guesthouse                    HOSTEL $
(Map p46; ☑ 012 885572; www.topbanana.biz; 9 St 278; dm US$5, r US$8-18; ❄ @ 🛜) Fifteen years on, a facelift has greatly improved the rooms

and there are some dorms available, including a four-bed female dorm. The main draw is the strategic location overlooking Wat Langka and Golden St, plus the open-air chill-out area. Book way ahead. **One Up Banana Hotel** (Map p46; ☑023-211344; www.1uphotelcambodia.com; Z9-132 St 51; s/d from US$33/39; ❋@⬀) is its nearby flashpacker upgrade.

**White Rabbit** HOSTEL $
(Map p46; ☑023-223170; www.whiterabbitguesthouse.com; 40A St 294; dm with fan/air-con from US$3/5, r US$6-15; ❋⬀) This convivial hostel is a hidden gem, with an attractive ground-level bar and hang-out area with a thousand movies or Sony PS3 games on a big screen. The private rooms are good value, but most opt for the comfortable dorms with clean bathrooms and wide bunk beds.

**Blue Dog Guesthouse** HOSTEL $
(Map p46; ☑012 658075; bluedogguesthouse@gmail.com; 13 St 51; dm US$5-6, r US$9-22; @⬀) The location and price are right, plus there's a cosy common area and a popular bar downstairs, so you won't end up spending too much time in the clean but basic rooms. Mains at the bar-restaurant include a free drink.

★**Rambutan Resort** BOUTIQUE HOTEL $$
(Map p58; ☑017 992240; www.rambutanresort.com; 29 St 71; r incl breakfast US$55-150; ❋⬀⬆) Sixties-groovy, gay-friendly and very well run, this striking villa once belonged to the American Embassy. The soaring original structure and a newer wing shade a boot-shaped swimming pool. Concrete floors set an industrial tone in the 19 smart rooms, which are outfitted with top-quality furnishings.

★**Villa Langka** BOUTIQUE HOTEL $$
(Map p46; ☑023-726771; www.villalangka.com; 14 St 282; r incl breakfast US$50-120; ❋❋⬀⬆) One of the first players in the poolside-boutique game, it's long been a Phnom Penh favourite, even as the competition heats up. The 48 rooms ooze postmodern panache, although there are big differences in size and style.

**Palm Tree Boutique Hotel** BOUTIQUE HOTEL $$
(Map p58; ☑023-229933; www.palmtreeboutiquehotel.com; 7 St 398; US$42-96; ❋⬀⬆) This brand new boutique hotel is set in a spacious villa in BKK. Rooms are finished with polished-wood floors and saffron silk furnishings. Best of all, the minibar is included in the rates, with some beers and soft drinks. Bicycles are also available for free.

**Khmer Surin Boutique Guesthouse** BOUTIQUE HOTEL $$
(Map p46; ☑012 731909; www.khmersurin.com.kh; 11A St 57; r incl breakfast US$40-65; ❋⬀) This guesthouse is attached to the long-running restaurant of the same name, set in a sumptuous villa. The 19 rooms come with flat-screen TVs, leafy balconies and antique furnishings, not to mention bathrooms that would put most four-star properties to shame.

**Willow** BOUTIQUE HOTEL $$
(Map p46; ☑023-996256; www.thewillowpp.com; 1 St 21; r incl breakfast US$40-70; ❋⬀⬆) Another hip little boutique hotel, the Willow has 12 spacious rooms in a splendid 1960s villa that now includes a small pool. Four-poster beds, modern art, wood furniture, rain showers and flat-screen TVs set an enticing mood. Also known for its sandwiches and its Wednesday night pub quizzes.

**Governor's House** BOUTIQUE HOTEL $$$
(Map p46; ☑023-987025; www.governorshouse.net; 3 Mao Tse Tung Blvd; r incl breakfast from US$75-185; ❋⬀⬆) There's a definite 'wow' factor at Governor's House – predictable when you furnish sumptuous rooms with centuries-old European furniture (part of the collection of the antique-dealing Belgian owner). The building itself, a restored colonial number, also impresses. The suites (US$185) are fit for Belgian royalty.

## Psar O Russei & Tuol Sleng

With the downfall of the Boeng Kak area, the zone south of Psar O Russei has emerged as a popular alternative for budget travellers. It's a mix of high-rise hotels and backpacker-oriented guesthouses.

**Narin Guesthouse** GUESTHOUSE $
(Map p46; ☑099 881133; www.naringuesthouse.com; 50 St 125; r with fan/air-con US$12/17; ❋@⬀) One of the stalwarts of the Phnom Penh guesthouse scene (we first stayed here back in 1995); rooms are smart, bathrooms smarter still and the price is right. There is a super-relaxed, open-air restaurant-terrace where you can take some time out.

**Smiley's Hotel** HOTEL $
(Map p46; ☑012 365959; smileyhotel.pp@gmail.com; 37 St 125; s with fan US$6, d US$15-20; ❋@⬀) A migrant from Siem Reap, Smiley's is a huge seven-storey hotel with 40 spacious rooms that border on chic. The US$20 rooms have big flat-screen TVs. Includes a lift.

### Sunday Guesthouse
GUESTHOUSE $

(Map p46; ☎ 023-211623; gech_sundayguest house@hotmail.com; 97 St 141; d/tr from US$7/11; ❋ @ ☎) It's a *real* guesthouse: a three-storey, walk-up affair run by an amiable family who can cook you meals and help with travel arrangements.

### Tat Guesthouse
GUESTHOUSE $

(Map p46; ☎ 012 921211; tatcambodia@yahoo.com; 52 St 125; s without bathroom US$4, r US$7-15; ❋ @ ☎) A super-friendly spot with a breezy rooftop hang-out perfect for chilling. The rooms aren't going to wow you but they are functional. For US$12 you get air-con. They also own nearby **Tattoo Guesthouse** (Map p46; ☎ 011 801000; 62A St 125; r US$5-10; ❋ ☎), which has a great name and smarter rooms.

### Terrace on 95
BOUTIQUE HOTEL $$

(Map p46; ☎ 023-996143; www.theterraceon95. com; 43 St 95; r US$35-45; ❋ ☎) This hotel has the intimate feel of a B&B. The six attractively furnished rooms share an impeccably restored traditional house, with vegan-friendly K'nyay (p72) restaurant upstairs. Downstairs rooms share an outdoor patio.

### H 22
CAPSULE HOTEL $$

(Map p46; ☎ 023-964020; www.d22h22.com; 22nd Floor, Phnom Penh Hotel, 445 Monivong Blvd; capsule r from US$29, r US$60-110; ❋ ☎) The capsule rooms are almost as minimalist as the hotel name, squeezing a bunk, a desk and a tidy trim into a very small space. Normal rooms are a lot more expensive, but offer expansive views across the developing city.

---

### THE FATE OF BOENG KAK 'LAKE'

Boeng Kak Lake was backpacker central – a lakeside version of Bangkok's Khao San Rd – until Boeng Kak ('the lake') was completely filled in with sand in 2011 as part of a massive development project for apartments. The area has an abandoned feel these days, as most guesthouses moved south to St 172 or St 258. Some residents are still holding out for compensation from the government, and there are still a handful of guesthouses here, but the main reason to venture north is the street art scene, with lots of Banksy-style art on the remaining walls.

##  Eating

For foodies, Phnom Penh is a real delight, boasting a superb selection of restaurants that showcase the best in Khmer cooking, as well as the greatest hits from world cuisines such as Chinese, Vietnamese, Thai, Indian, French, Italian, Spanish, Mexican and more. Visitors to Phnom Penh are quite literally spoilt for choice these days.

### North Central (Riverfront)

#### Blue Pumpkin
CAFE $

(Map p52; 245 Sisowath Quay; mains US$3-7; ⊙ 6am-11pm; ☎) Healthy breakfasts, pasta, sandwiches and some of the capital's best ice cream lead the menu, and you can watch the nightly aerobics spectacle on the riverfront as you eat. There are plenty of branches around town, including one at Kids City (p51) and another at Monument Books (p81).

#### Anjali/Karma Cafe
CAFE $

(Map p52; 273 Sisowath Quay; mains US$3-6; ⊙ 7am-late) Twin-sister restaurants practically under one roof. The prices are more than reasonable for this part of town. Anjali has some Indian offerings, but otherwise they share an identical menu – pub grub and some Asian highlights.

#### Kandal House
INTERNATIONAL $

(Map p52; ☎ 012 525612; 239B Sisowath Quay; mains US$4-6; ☎) So small that it's easy to miss, this riverfront restaurant turns out delicious *amok* and other Cambodian faves, plus homemade pasta, salads and soups. Anchor draught is available in pints.

#### ¡Viva!
MEXICAN $

(Map p52; 139 Sisowath Quay; dishes US$4-6; ⊙ 10am-11pm; ☎) It doesn't look like much, but this riverfront place has raised the bar for Mexican food in Phnom Penh. A bucket of margaritas costs US$5. It's on the same strip as a potpourri of international restaurants if you'd rather window shop.

#### ★ Yi Sang
CHINESE $$

(Map p46; Sisowath Quay; US$6-20; ⊙ 6am-11pm; ☎) The riverfront location is one of the only places in the city where you can dine right on the riverside – perfect for a relaxing sunset cocktail. The menu here includes a mix of well-presented Cambodian street flavours including *nam ben choc* (rice noodles with curry), plus plenty of dim sum and some international flavours.

### Pop Café
ITALIAN **$$**

(Map p52; ☑ 012 562892; 371 Sisowath Quay; pasta dishes US$6-9; ⊙ 11am-2pm & 6-10pm) Owner Giorgio welcomes diners as if you are coming to his own home for dinner, making this a popular spot for authentic Italian cooking. Thin-crust pizza, homemade pasta and tasty gnocchi – it could be Roma.

### Grand River
INTERNATIONAL **$$**

(Map p52; ☑ 023-220244; 357 Sisowath Quay; US$3-12; ⊙ 7am-midnight) One of the newer riverfront restaurants, this is a great spot for watching the world go by. The menu includes moderately priced Cambodian and international dishes, plus a quaffable drinks selection.

### La Croisette
INTERNATIONAL **$$**

(Map p52; ☑ 023-220554; 241 Sisowath Quay; mains US$5-18; ⊙ 7am-1am; 🐾) The stylish La Croisette is a popular riverfront spot with homemade pasta and gnocchi, plus hearty steaks, lamb chops and even some Cambodian offerings.

### Limoncello
ITALIAN **$$**

(Map p52; 81 Sisowath Quay; pizzas US$5.50-8; ⊙ 11.30am-2pm & 5.30-10pm; 🐾) The pizza here is simply outstanding – arguably the best in town – and it's got a plum riverfront setting to boot. Great desserts, too. Wash them all down with an eponymous *limoncello* shot.

### Fish
SEAFOOD **$$**

(Map p52; ☑ 023-222685; cnr St 108 & Sisowath Quay; mains US$6-17; ⊙ 7am-11pm; 🐾) No prizes for guessing its speciality. Sophisticated tapas and mains, including a superb bouillabaisse, dot the menu. The Pacific dory fish and chips is among the best in town.

### Happy Herb Pizza
PIZZA **$$**

(Map p52; ☑ 012 921915; 345 Sisowath Quay; medium pizzas US$6-8.50; ⊙ 8am-11pm; 🐾) Happy doesn't mean it comes with free toppings – it means pizza à la ganja. The non-marijuana pizzas are also pretty good, but don't involve the free trip. It's a good place to sip a cheap beer and watch the riverfront action unfold.

### Bopha Phnom Penh Restaurant
CAMBODIAN **$$**

(Map p52; Sisowath Quay; mains US$5-10; ⊙ 6am-11pm; 🐾) Also known as Titanic, it's right on the river and designed to impress, with Angkorian-style carvings and elegant wicker furniture. The menu is punctuated with exotic flavours, especially water buffalo, but there's a European menu for the less adventurous.

### ★ Chinese House
FUSION **$$$**

(Map p38; ☑ 023-991514; 45 Sisowath Quay, cnr St 84; mains US$12-20; ⊙ 5-10.30pm Mon-Sat) Housed in one of the city's true colonial-era masterpieces, Chinese House is worth a visit for the ambience alone. The relaunched menu promises contemporary Asian flavours. A three-course lunch is available for US$12.50. Doubles as a chic cocktail bar downstairs, with regular music events.

### Metro
FUSION **$$$**

(Map p52; ☑ 023-222275; 271 Sisowath Quay; small plates US$4-8, large plates US$8-24; ⊙ 9.30am-1am; 🐾) Metro is the trendiest spot on the riverfront strip thanks to a striking design and an adventurous menu. Small plates are for sampling and include beef with red ants and tequila black-pepper prawns; large plates include steaks and honey-soy roasted chicken. They also do a mean eggs Benedict. The new **Mara Metro** (Map p46; ☑ 092 776552; www.mara restaurant.com; 16 St 214; mains US$4.80-13.70; ⊙ 10am-1am Mon-Fri, 5pm-1am Sat & Sun) lounge bar is a glitzy alternative on St 214.

## North Central (Off-river)

### Feel Good Cafe
CAFE **$**

(Map p52; 79 St 136; mains US$2-5) One of the only cafes in town to roast and grind its own coffee, with blends that are a fusion of Cambodian, Lao and Thai coffee beans. The menu is international with influences from the Med to Mexico, including wraps and burgers.

### Noodle House
ASIAN **$**

(Map p52; ☑ 077 919110; 32A St 130; mains US$3.50-5.50; ⊙ 6am-10pm) Set in a lovingly restored French-era gem, this place looks more expensive than it actually is. The menu is a regional tour of noodle soups with stops everywhere from Cambodian *kyteow* to Malaysian *laksa*.

### Sorya Food Court
ASIAN **$**

(Map p52; 11 St 63; 5000-10,000r; ⊙ 9am-9pm) The top-floor food court is a more sanitised way to experience a variety of local fare, with stalls serving a wide range of affordable Cambodian, Chinese, Vietnamese, Malaysian and Korean dishes. It works on a coupon system.

### Special Pho
VIETNAMESE **$**

(Map p52; 11 St 178; mains US$2.50-4.50; ⊙ 8am-9pm) Boasting a great location near the riverfront for good *pho* – the noodle soup

## GOOD-CAUSE DINING

There are several restaurants around town that are run by aid organisations to help fund their social programs in Cambodia. The proceeds of a hearty meal go towards helping Cambodia's recovery and allow restaurant staff to gain valuable work experience.

### North Central

Veiyo Tonlé (Map p52; 237 Sisowath Quay; mains US$3.50-6.50; ⊘7am-11pm; 🕿) A little restaurant on the riverfront, the menu here features mainly Khmer and Italian cuisine, including tasty pizzas. Not-for-profit, with proceeds going towards helping a local orphanage.

Romdeng (Map p52; 🗗092 219565; 74 St 174; mains US$5-8; ⊘11am-9pm; 🕿) Set in a gorgeous colonial villa with a small pool, Romdeng specialises in Cambodian country fare, including a famous fish *amok*, two-toned pomelo salad and tiger-prawn curry. Sample deep-fried tarantulas or stir-fried tree ants with beef and holy basil if you dare. Part of the Friends' extended family, it is staffed by former street youth and their teachers.

Friends (Map p52; 🗗012 802072; www.friends-restaurant.org; 215 St 13; tapas US$4-7, mains from US$6-10; ⊘11am-10.30pm; 🕿) One of Phnom Penh's best-loved restaurants, this place is a must, with tasty tapas bites, heavenly smoothies and creative cocktails. It offers former street children a head start in the hospitality industry.

Sugar 'n Spice Cafe (Map p52; www.daughtersofcambodia.org; 65 St 178; sandwiches US$3.50-7; ⊘9am-6pm Mon-Sat; 🕿) This fantastic cafe on the top floor of the Daughters visitors centre features soups, smoothies, original coffee drinks, cupcakes and fusion-y mains served by former victims of trafficking, who are being trained by Daughters to reintegrate into society.

### South Central

Café Yejj (Map p58; www.cafeyejj.com; 170 St 450; mains US$3.50-6; ⊘8am-9pm; 🕿🗗) An air-con escape from Russian Market (walk upstairs), this bistro-style cafe uses organic ingredients to prepare pasta, salads and wraps, as well as a few more ambitious dishes like Moroccan lamb stew and chilli con carne. Promotes fair trade and responsible employment.

Jars of Clay (Map p58; 39B St 155; cakes US$1.50, mains US$3-5.50; ⊘7.30am-9pm Mon-Sat; 🕿) Much more than just a bakery, with authentic Khmer mains like their patented *lok lak* (a traditional Cambodian beef dish), plus thirst-quenching drinks and welcome air-conditioning on a hot day. Ten per cent of profits go to those in need, including women rescued from trafficking.

Hagar (Map p46; 44 St 310; lunch/dinner buffet US$6.50/11; ⊘7am-2pm & 6-9pm Thu-Sat, 7am-2pm Sun-Wed; 🕿) Proceeds from the all-you-can-eat buffets here go towards assisting destitute or abused women. The spread is usually Asian fusion or barbecue, except for Wednesday lunches and Thursday dinners, when Hagar lays out its legendary Italian buffet.

Le Lotus Blanc (Map p46; 152 St 51; mains US$4-8.50; ⊘7am-10pm Mon-Sat; 🕿) This upmarket diner acts as a training centre for youths who previously scoured the city dump. Run by French NGO Pour un Sourire d'Enfant (For the Smile of a Child), it serves classy French and Khmer cuisine, including set lunches.

Restore One Cafe (Map p58; 🗗016 302727; http://restoreone.org; 23 St 123; burgers US$5.75-6.50; ⊘11am-9pm; 🕿) Set in a handsome wooden house near the Russian Market, this is not your typical burger joint. Choose from themed burgers like American Oink or Rugged Cowboy, plus fish and chicken options, all with sauces and a side of fries. The restorative power of burgers support training and villages in extreme poverty.

Craft Peace Cafe (Map p58; https://www.facebook.com/craftpeacecafe; 14 St 392; US$2.50-4.50; ⊘8am-7.30pm; 🕿) This Jesuit-run cafe produces smoothies, fresh juices, fair-trade coffee, salads and delicious pocket sandwiches, plus textiles crafted by their disabled staff. Cosy, attractive and well air-conditioned.

that keeps Vietnam driving forward – plus dirt-cheap fried rice and fried noodles.

### Laughing Fatman
CAMBODIAN **$**

(Map p52; 63 St 172; mains US$2.50-6.50; ☺7am-midnight) A welcoming backpacker cafe with cheap food and big breakfasts, formerly called Oh My Buddha – 'New name, same body', joked the corpulent owner on our visit.

### Restaurant Soksan
CAMBODIAN **$**

(Map p52; 30 St 136; mains 4000-10,000r; ☺5.30am-9pm) This local curbside eatery, just a hop, skip or jump away from Psar Thmei, is popular for *lok lak,* spicy fried chicken and noodle soups.

### ★Sam Doo Restaurant
CHINESE **$$**

(Map p52; 56-58 Kampuchea Krom Blvd; mains US$2.50-15; ☺7am-2am; ❄) Many Chinese Khmers swear that this upstairs eatery near Central Market has the best Middle Kingdom food in town. Choose from their signature Sam Doo fried rice, *trey chamhoy* (steamed fish with soy sauce and ginger), fresh seafood, hot pots and dim sum.

### Boston
CAMBODIAN **$$**

(Map p52; 54 St 172; mains US$3-10; ☺7.30am-11pm; ☎) This is a sophisticated backpacker cafe, popular with expats and serving a range of Cambodian and international dishes. With enjoyable music, a wine list and some care given to presentation, it's a step above most dining options on the busy St 172 strip. Try the signature beef Wellington.

### Exchange
INTERNATIONAL **$$**

(Map p38; ☏023-992865; 28 St 47; US$5-15; ☺10am-midnight) One of the grandest old French houses in the city is home to this stylish bistro and bar. The menu takes diners on a global tour and includes some excellent sharing platters with Mediterranean and ocean themes, plus some top imported steaks.

### La Patate
BELGIAN **$$**

(Map p52; 14 St 5; mains US$4-15; ☺7am-2am; ☎) Head here for hearty Belgian fare where meat dishes arrive swimming in one of several rich sauces. If you're really hungry, try the footlong 'bazooka burger', served on a king-sized bed of Phnom Penh's best Belgian *frites*.

### Dim Sum Emperors
CHINESE **$$**

(Map p52; ☏023-650 7452; 48 St 130; dim sum US$2-3, mains US$5-15; ☺7am-9pm; ☎) Wildly popular for both its dim sum and its power-

ful air-con, which comes as welcome relief after a shopping session at nearby Psar Thmei.

### Lemongrass
THAI **$$**

(Map p52; ☏012 996707; 14 St 130; mains US$4.50-9; ☺9am-11pm; ☎) A higher-class Thai restaurant with a fair selection of Khmer classics. The prices are pretty reasonable given the look of the place. Splurge for the *choo chee goong* (ocean tiger prawns in red curry).

### Sher-e-Punjab
INDIAN **$$**

(Map p52; ☏023-216360; 16 St 130; mains US$3-7; ☺11am-11pm; ✎) The top spot for a curry fix according to many members of Phnom Penh's Indian community – the tandoori dishes here are particularly good. Even the prawn dishes cost just US$6.

### Lone Star
TEX-MEX **$$**

(Map p52; 30 St 23; US$4.50-7; ☺7am-11pm; ☎) Missing the US of A? You won't after a morning in here watching American football via satellite and digging into the calorific mains, like meatloaf and Baja fish tacos. The smoked pork ribs and the wings are both among the best in town.

### ★Van's Restaurant
FRENCH **$$$**

(Map p52; ☏023-722067; www.vans-restaurant.com; 5 St 13; mains US$16-43; ☺11.30am-2.30pm & 5-10.30pm) Located in one of the city's grandest buildings, the former Banque Indochine, you can still see the old vault doors en route to the refined dining room upstairs. Dishes are presented with decorative flourish; menu highlights include langoustine ravioli, tender veal and boneless quail. Business lunches (US$15) include a glass of wine and a coffee.

### Armand's
FRENCH **$$$**

(Map p52; ☏015 548966; 33 St 108; meals US$12-25; ☺from 6pm Tue-Sun) The best steak in town is served flambé style by the eponymous owner of this French bistro. The meat is simply superb, but every item on the chalkboard menu shines. Space is tight, so book ahead.

### Dine in the Dark
INTERNATIONAL **$$$**

(DID; Map p52; ☏077 589458; www.didexperience.com; 126 St 19; set menu US$18; ☺6-11pm) It's the Tea Garden by day (from 8am), with a verdant hidden courtyard and speciality loose-leaf teas, but by night the lights go out and the upstairs is transformed into Dine in the Dark. Choose from a set menu of Khmer, Western or vegetarian dishes and eat them in darkness with the help of your sight-impaired guide. A meaningful experience.

## Self-Catering

**Thai Huot**                          SUPERMARKET **$**
(Map p52; 103 Monivong Blvd; ☉ 7.30am-8.30pm)
This is the place for French travellers who
are missing home, as it stocks many French
products, including Bonne Maman jam and
the city's best cheese selection. Additional
location in BKK (Map p46; cnr St 63 & St 352;
☉ 7.30am-8.30pm).

## South Central

**The Vegetarian**           CAMBODIAN, VEGETARIAN **$**
(Map p46; 158 St 19; mains US$1.75-2.50;
☉ 10.30am-8.30pm Mon-Sat; ☑) This is one
of the best-value spots in Phnom Penh. All
dishes are US$2.50 or under – and it doesn't
skimp on portions either. Noodles and fried
rice are the specialties. The leafy setting in a
quiet nook off central Sihanouk Blvd is yet
another plus.

★ **The Shop**                              CAFE **$**
(Map p46; ☎ 023-986964; 39 St 240; mains
US$3.50-6; ☉ 7am-7pm, to 3pm Sun; ☑) If you
are craving the local deli back home, make
for this haven, which has a changing selection of sandwiches and salads with healthy
and creative ingredients including wild
lentils, forest mushrooms and lamb. The
pastries, cakes and chocolates are delectable – and worth the indulgence.

**Mercy House**
**Coffee Restaurant**          ASIAN, VEGETARIAN **$**
(Map p46; 157 St 51; mains 7500-15,000r; ☉ 7am-
6pm; ☑) This outdoor vegetarian eatery serves
Japanese dishes with a Cambodian twist. Go
for the teppan-yaki hot plates – sizzling fake
meat topped with an egg and served over
rice – or the sweet-and-sour 'pork ribs'.

**ARTillery**                              CAFE **$$**
(Map p46; St 240½; mains US$4-6; ☉ 7.30am-
9pm Tue-Sun, to 5pm Mon; ☎☑) Healthy
salads, sandwiches, shakes and snacks such
as hummus and felafel are served in this
creative space on an artsy alley off St 240.
The menu is mostly vegetarian, and pizza
is among the offerings on its small raw-food
menu. The daily specials are worth a sample.

**Public House**             FUSION, PUB FOOD **$$**
(Map p46; ☎ 017 770754; St 240½; mains US$5-8;
☉ 11.30am-11pm Tue-Sun; ☎) The first gastro
pub on trendy St 240½, Kiwi-owned Public
House attracts hip expats with its long bar
and linear design. The food is the real highlight, however: a mix of fusion fare (eg roast
duck breast on couscous) and gentrified
pub grub (fish and chips). High tea is from
3pm to 5.30pm; reserve ahead.

**Backyard Cafe**                          VEGAN **$$**
(Map p46; ☎ 078 751715; www.backyardeats.com;
11b St 246; mains US$4-7; ☉ 7.30am-4.30pm;
☎☑) A cool and contemporary superfoods
cafe, this is the place to check the pulse(s)
of the vegetarian dining scene in the capital.
Raw foods include stuffed avocado and a ve-
gan abundance bowl. The mouthwatering
desserts are also vegan.

**Sleuk Chark**                          CAMBODIAN **$$**
(Map p46; ☎ 012 979199; 165 St 51; mains US$3-
10; ☉ 10.30am-3pm & 5-10pm; ☎) This place
doesn't look like much from the street, but
venture inside for a dining experience that
includes a zesty frogs legs and quails eggs in
a sugar-palm and black-pepper clay pot, or
a fish egg soup. Or test your taste buds with
fried spiders or beef with red ants.

**Magnolia**                              ASIAN **$$**
(Map p46; ☎ 012 529977; 55 St 51; mains US$3-8;
☉ 6am-10pm; ☎) Set in a gracefully restored
old house, this place offers an affordable
lunchtime buffet, wafer-thin *ban xeo* (Viet-
namese savoury pancakes) and an array of
classics from Hanoi to Saigon.

**Sonoma Oyster Bar**                      SEAFOOD **$$**
(Map p46; ☎ 077 723911; 159 St 222; 6-oyster
platters US$7.50-9; ☉ 5-11pm; ☎) The owner
here sells premium imported oysters wholesale to top-end hotels – or sells them here
to drop-in diners at bargain prices. A must
for raw oyster lovers. Scallops and steaks are
among other tempting options.

**Kravanh**                              CAMBODIAN **$$**
(Map p46; ☎ 012 792088; 112 Sothearos Blvd;
mains US$3-8; ☉ 11.30am-10pm; ☎) A stylish
Khmer restaurant under the stewardship
of a Franco-Khmer, the linen and decor set
this place apart from its neighbours. The
menu includes traditional salads, scented
soups and regional specialities.

**Black Bambu**                          FUSION **$$$**
(Map p46; ☎ 023-966895; www.black-bambu.com;
29 St 228; US$3.50-21.50; ☉ 8.30am-11pm Tue-
Sun) This contemporary space is home to the
stylish Black Bambu, which works with the
Cambodia Children's Fund to help train former dump children in the art of hospitality.
The menu includes delicious sharing plates,
like homemade lamb-and-lemongrass sausages and black-pepper caramel pork belly.

LOCAL KNOWLEDGE

# GOING LOCAL

## Khmer Barbecues & Soup Restaurants

After dark, Khmer eateries scattered across town illuminate their neon signs, hailing locals in for fine fare and generous jugs of draught beer. Don't be shy – the food is great and the atmosphere lively.

The speciality at most of these places is grilled strips of meat or seafood, but they also serve fried noodles and rice, curries and other pan-fried faves, along with some vegie options.

Many of these places also offer *phnom pleung* (hill of fire), which amounts to cook-your-own meat over a personal barbecue. Another speciality is *soup chhnang dei* (cook-your-own soup in a clay pot), which is great fun if you go in a group. Other diners will often help with protocol, as it is important to cook things in the right order so as not to overcook half the ingredients and eat the rest raw.

Khmer barbecues are literally all over the place, so it won't be hard to find one.

**Koh Pich** (Diamond Island; Map p38; US$2-6), east of hulking Naga World casino, has a cluster of well-reputed barbecues.

**Red Cow** (Map p46; 126 Norodom Blvd; mains US$2.50-7; ☺4-11pm) Grills up everything imaginable – eel, eggplant, frog, pig intestine, quail – along with curries and other traditional Khmer dishes.

**Sovanna** (Map p46; 2C St 21; mains US$2-8; ☺6-11am & 3-11pm) Always jumping with locals and a smattering of expats who have made this their barbecue of choice thanks to the huge menu. It's as good a place as any to sample the national breakfast, *bei sait chrouk* (pork and rice).

**Psar Kabco Restaurant** (Map p46; ☑012 702708; 5 St 9; mains US$1.50-4; ☺6am-9pm) Located opposite the very local Psar Kabco (Kabco Market), this is great Cambodian-Chinese restaurant serving a panoply of street flavours, including noodle soups, point-and-eat curries and stews, and Khmer desserts.

**Sonivid** (Map p46; 39 St 242; meals US$5-10; ☺3pm-midnight) Steamed or fried crab, squid, fish and shellfish are the specialities at this wildly popular corner eatery. It's not a barbecue, it just looks like one.

**Master Suki** (Map p52; 7th fl, Sorya Shopping Centre; soup from US$5; ☺9am-10pm) It may be a Japanese concept, but it has a very Khmer touch and is a great way to try *chhnang dei* soup (cook-your-own hotpot), with photos to help choose the ingredients. Great views as well. Additional outlets all over the city.

## Street Fare & Markets

Street fare is not quite as familiar or user-friendly here as in, say, Bangkok. But if you're a little adventurous and want to save boatloads of money, look no further. Breakfast is when the street-side eateries really get hopping, as most Cambodian men eat out for breakfast. Look for filled seats and you can't go wrong.

Phnom Penh's many markets all have large central eating areas, where stalls serve up local faves like noodle soup and fried noodles. Most dishes cost a reasonable 4000r to 6000r. The best market for eating is Russian Market (p79), with an interior food zone that's easy to find and has a nice variety of Cambodian specialties; the large car park on the west side converts to seafood barbecues and more from around 4pm. Psar Thmei (p79) and Psar O Russei (p79) are other great choices. **Psar Kandal** (Map p52; btwn St 144 & St 154), just off the riverfront, gets going a little later and is an early-evening option where Cambodians come for takeaways.

If the markets are just too hot or claustrophobic for your taste, look out for the mobile street sellers carrying their wares on their shoulders or wheeling them around in small carts. Another popular all-day option is a row of **curry noodle stalls** (Map p46) opposite Wat Botum Park.

# Phnom Penh

Cambodia's capital casts its spell over all who enter. It might be the gleaming spires of the Royal Palace, or the graceful French architecture, a waft of lemongrass from a street stall, or the infectious buzz of the cafe-lined riverfront. Somehow, some way, Phnom Penh will grab you.

2

TOM COCKREM / GETTY IMAGES ©

3

BEN PIPE / ROBERTHARDING / GETTY IMAGES ©

### 1. Royal Palace (p40)
Buddhist monks walk the grounds of the king's official residence.

### 2. Phnom Penh streets
A family rides the capital's busy streets.

### 3. Food markets (p67)
Phnom Penh is packed with busy markets selling fresh food.

### 4. Throne Hall (p41)
Used for coronations and important ceremonies, it features classic Khmer roofs and ornate gilding.

4

STUART DEE / GETTY IMAGES ©

**Origami**                                    JAPANESE **$$$**
(Map p46; ☑012 968095; 88 Sothearos Blvd; sushi sets from US$25; ⏱11.30am-2pm & 6-10pm; 📶) This outstanding Japanese eatery takes the art of Japanese food to another level. It's expensive, but real sushi connoisseurs wouldn't settle for anything less. Set menus include beautifully presented sushi, sashimi and tempura boxes.

## Boeng Keng Kang & Tonlé Bassac

⭐ **Boat Noodle Restaurant**              THAI **$**
(Map p46; ☑012 774287; 57 Sothearos Blvd; mains US$3-7; ⏱7am-9pm; 📶) Relocated to Sothearos Blvd, this long-running Thai-Khmer restaurant has some of the best-value regional dishes in town. Choose from the contemporary but traditionally decorated space at the front or a traditional wooden house behind. Delicious noodle soups and lots of local specialities.

**Aeon Mall Food Court**                    ASIAN **$**
(Map p46; 132 Sothearos Blvd; US$1-6; ⏱9am-10pm; 📶) It may be surprising to venture into the country's swankiest mall to find cheap eats, but there are two food courts here covering the best of Asia and beyond. Downstairs is the more local option with noodles soups, fried rice and fresh sushi. Upstairs on Level 2 is the World Dining Food Court, with fancier furnishings and live music.

**Brown Coffee**                             CAFE **$**
(Map p46; cnr St 294 & St 57; mains US$2-5; ⏱7am-9pm; 📶) The flagship outlet of a homegrown coffee chain has outgrown all the expensive imports to produce some of the most refined spaces and best coffee in town. There are lots of branches around town, as they've set their sights on cracking Cambodia.

**My Burger Lab**                            BURGERS **$**
(Map p46; ☑099-666424; www.myburgerlab.com.kh; 160B Norodom Blvd; burgers from US$1.50; ⏱10.30am-9pm; 📶) This new burger joint takes an experimental approach to burgers, creating fusion flavours with creative names – choose from 'Say Cheese' to 'Kick in the Face'. Our personal fave was 'The A+', with cheddar, caramelised onions and shiitake mushrooms, but the charcoal buns do have a tendency to disintegrate.

**JoMa Bakery Cafe**                         CAFE **$**
(Map p46; www.joma.biz; cnr Norodom Blvd & St 294; mains US$2-6; ⏱8am-10pm; 📶) A recent arrival from Laos, JoMa Bakery Cafe has used a winning formula to expand rapidly in the Cambodian capital. Salads, soups and sandwiches in various combinations make up the menu, but the coffee, cakes and shakes are not to be missed.

**Jidaiya**                                  JAPANESE **$**
(Map p58; ☑097 230 6301; 79A St 63; mains US$1-7; ⏱5pm-midnight; 📶) Set in the heart of 'Little Tokyo' at the southern end of St 63, this feels like a little piece of Japan transported to Cambodia when the staff shout *irasshaimase* (welcome) as you walk in. Barbecued skewers are cheap and plentiful and a mix of soba and ramen dishes is available. Sapporo beer is just US$2 a bottle.

**Dosa Corner**                              INDIAN **$**
(Map p46; 5E St 51; mains US$1.50-5; ⏱8.30am-2pm & 5-10pm) Fans of Indian dosas will be pleased to discover this place does just what it says on the label – namely, a generous variety of savoury pancakes from the south. Vegetarian thalis are US$4.

**Mama Wong's**                   CHINESE, FUSION **$$**
(Map p46; ☑097 850 8383; 41 St 308; mains US$3-8; ⏱10am-10pm; 📶) This brings a contemporary touch to the Chinese dining scene in the city, serving up traditional noodle soups, steamed buns and congee, but with mini burgers, sliders and more that mix Asian and European flavours. Good value, good fun.

⭐ **Malis**                               CAMBODIAN **$$**
(Map p46; ☑023-221022; www.malis-restaurant.com; 136 Norodom Blvd; mains US$6-12; ⏱7am-11pm; 📶) The leading Khmer restaurant in the Cambodian capital, Malis is a chic place to dine alfresco. The original menu includes beef in bamboo, goby with Kampot peppercorns, and traditional soups and salads. It's popular for a boutique breakfast: the breakfast sets are a good deal at US$3 to US$4. Book ahead for dinner.

**Java Café**                                CAFE **$$**
(Map p46; www.javaarts.org; 56 Sihanouk Blvd; mains US$4-8; ⏱7am-10pm; 📶) Consistently popular thanks to a breezy balcony and a creative menu that includes crisp salads, delicious homemade sandwiches, burgers and excellent coffee from several continents. The upstairs doubles as an art gallery, the downstairs as a bakery.

**Piccola Italia Da Luigi**                  PIZZA **$$**
(Map p46; ☑017 323273; 36 St 308; pizzas US$4.50-9; ⏱11am-2pm & 6-10pm; 📶) This is

the place that kickstarted the St 308 scene. A bustling curbside eatery just like in Italy, Luigi's certainly has a claim to making some of the best pizza in Phnom Penh. Also has a small deli attached if you're in the mood for some zingy antipasti. After dark, reservations recommended.

### Lost Room
INTERNATIONAL $$

(Map p46; ☑ 078 700001; www.thelostroom.asia; 43 St 21; mains US$4-12; ☺ 5pm-late Mon-Sat; 🛜) Located in the back streets of Bassac, look out for the symbolic key and you have found a hidden gem. The menu is all about small plates and sharing, so bring along some friends. Try the signature seared kangaroo steak or sea bass with goat-cheese tartare.

### Chicky
BARBECUE $$

(Map p46; ☑ 023-430606; 165 St 63; mains US$3-10; ☺ 11.30am-10pm) A French-style rotisserie, the menu here is all about chicken. It's a simple concept: just pick from a quarter chicken to a whole chicken and choose some sides such as new potatoes or salad. Tasty.

### Ngon
HAWKER $$

(Map p46; ☑ 023-987151; www.ngonpnh.com; 60 Sihanouk Blvd; mains US$3-9; ☺ 6.30am-10pm; 🛜) A Cambodian outpost of the popular Quan An Ngon in Saigon, this place brings street food to a sophisticated setting. The concept is simple: just wander around the hawkers with their wares and choose the tastiest looking dishes – although it's also fine to order straight from the menu.

### From Farm to Table
CAFE $$

(Map p46; ☑ 078 899722; 16 St 360; mains US$3.50-7; ☺ 8am-10pm; 🛜) Formerly Le Jardin, it's no longer an out-and-out family place, but still has a lush garden laden with jackfruit trees and an old tractor for kids to clamber around on. Owned by the team behind ARTillery (p66), it aims to promote organic farming methods in Cambodia and has a healthy menu of all-day breakfasts, salads, sandwiches and shakes. Live music from 6pm on Fridays.

### Comme à la Maison
FRENCH $$

(Map p46; ☑ 023-360801; www.commeala maison-delicatessen.com; 13 St 57; mains US$5-9; ☺ 6am-10.30pm; 🛜) This attractive open-air restaurant under a thatched Balinese-style roof has an extensive menu of provincial French fare, plus pizza and pasta and enticing weekly specials. An on-site bakery makes this a good spot for delicious pastries.

### Zino Wine Bar
INTERNATIONAL $$

(Map p46; ☑ 023-998519; 12 St 294; mains US$5-15; ☺ 10.30am-midnight; 🛜) A popular wine bar and bistro, the menu here is eclectic. It's popular for its weekend brunch for US$7.50; there's also a lengthy happy hour (from 4pm to 7pm) daily. Set lunches of starter plus main and coffee are US$9, and the wine selection is impressively extensive.

### Aussie XL
INTERNATIONAL $$

(Map p46; www.aussiexl.com; 205A St 51; mains US$7-14; ☺ 9am-11pm) The name says it all: this is a place for serious stuffing. Super-sized fish, lamb, chicken, steak and about every type of burger imaginable is available. Weekends sometimes see pigs roasted on spits. Also the place for Aussie sports on the telly.

### Sushi Bar
JAPANESE $$

(Map p46; ☑ 023-215041; www.sushibar-kh.com; 2D St 302; sushi sets from US$6; ☺ 11am-10pm; 🛜) Purists will scoff at the low sushi prices, but it's always packed for a reason. Definitely the best place in town for quick-and-easy raw fish. Sit downstairs at the bar, outside on the patio or in private rooms upstairs.

### La Plaza
SPANISH $$

(Map p46; 22B St 278; tapas US$2.50-10; ☺ 11am-2pm & 5-10pm; 🛜) An authentic Spanish tapas bar in a snug shophouse on Golden St, La Plaza's wide-ranging menu covers the basics (garlic shrimp, Spanish meatballs) and adds Cambodia-inspired creations like *boquerones del Mekong* (small Mekong fish in vinegar).

### Vego Salad Bar
CAFE $$

(Map p46; ☑ 011 457711; 3 St 51; mains US$4-7; ☺ 7.30am-9pm; 🛜✏) Vego attracts health nuts with its design-your-own salads and wraps. Choose your leaves, vegies, meat or dairy and condiments and you have a bespoke salad. Set combos available with health drinks.

### Taste Budz
INDIAN $$

(Map p46; ☑ 092 961554; 13E St 282; mains US$3-6; ☺ 10am-2.30pm & 5-10pm) This pint-sized outfit with the curious moniker is one of the best of Phnom Penh's many Indian restaurants. The speciality is Kerala (South Indian) cuisine, including spicy *kedai* dishes, which are divine. Order *porotta* (flat bread) on the side and dig in with your hands.

### ★ Deco
EUROPEAN $$$

(Map p46; ☑ 017 577327; www.decophnompenh. com; cnr St 352 & St 57; mains US$7-15; ☺ noon-2pm & 5-10pm; 🛜) With an enviable setting in an impeccably restored '60s modernist house and a rotating menu of progressive European cuisine, Deco is one of Phnom Penh's most sophisticated restaurants. The menu might include duck breast or Kampot crab cakes at any given time, and the creative cocktails are legendary. Also serves craft beer.

**Topaz** FRENCH $$$
(Map p46; ☎ 023-221622; www.topaz-restaurant. com; 182 Norodom Blvd; dishes US$5-25; ☺ 11am-2pm & 6-11pm; 🐦) One of Phnom Penh's original restaurants, Topaz is housed in a elegant villa with reflective pools and a walk-in wine cellar. The menu is classic Paris, including delicate Bourgogne snails drizzled in garlic, and steak tartare for those with rare tastes.

**Tiger's Eye** FUSION $$$
(Map p46; ☎ 023-212917; http://thetigerseye.asia; 49 Sothearos Blvd; mains US$12-23, degustation menu US$55; ☺ 7.30am-10.30pm; 🐦) Formerly The Common Tiger, now The Tiger's Eye, the fusion flavours here are some of the most innovative in town. The South African chef personally presents his creations to diners on super-sized plates. The regularly rotating menu usually includes just a handful of main courses. Cocktails and craft beers round things off.

## Psar O Russei & Tuol Sleng

**Asian Spice** ASIAN $
(Map p46; 79 St 111; mains US$2-3.50; ☺ 6am-9pm; 🐦) The house speciality is the zesty Singapore laksa, but you'll also find a host of appropriately spicy Indonesian and Malaysian specialties on the menu, along with some European fare. One of Phnom Penh's best bargains.

**Mama Restaurant** CAMBODIAN $
(Map p46; 10C St 111; mains US$1.50-4; ☺ 7.30am-8.30pm) This long-running backpacker cafe in the heart of Psar O Russei serves tasty, French-influenced Khmer food, such as beef stew and *hachi parmentier* (Shepherd's pie).

**Spider Restaurant** CAMBODIAN $
(Map p46; 50 St 113; mains US$2.50-6; ☺ 8am-5pm; 🐦) A relaxing little fan-cooled cafe opposite Tuol Sleng, with good curries, coffee, a jazz soundtrack and a charming chequered floor.

**Chinese Noodle/ China Restaurant** CHINESE $
(Map p46; 553 Monivong Blvd; mains US$1.50-3; ☺ 6am-2am) Twin bargain eateries popular with locals and expats. Chinese Noodle is all about – what else – noodles, with anything from duck to pig stomach. China Restaurant is famous for its dumpling-like pork buns.

★ **K'nyay** CAMBODIAN, VEGAN $$
(Map p46; ☎ 011 454282; 43 St 95; mains US$4-7; ☺ noon-10pm Tue-Fri, 8am-10pm Sat-Sun; 🐦 🍴) A handsome restaurant upstairs at the Terrace on 95 (p62) boutique hotel, K'nyay complements meat-infused traditional Cambodian fare with a vegan menu and prepares vegan lunch boxes for daytrippers. Try the tasty banana or pumpkin curry or drop by for an original health shake after visiting sweltering Tuol Sleng nearby.

## Russian Market Area

There is nothing better than an iced coffee or fresh fruit shake after surviving the scrum that is the Russian Market (p79). In the market's central food stall area, look out for the charismatic **Mr Bounnareth** (Map p58; Shop 547, Russian Market), whose patented 'best iced coffee in Phnom Penh' has been living up to its name for some 35 years. Other stalls sell fried noodles and *banh cheav* (meat or seafood and vegies wrapped inside a thin egg pancake and lettuce leaf) for US$1 to US$2.

The streets emanating east and south from Russian Market are home to several stand-out lunch spots, some so successful that they are now open for dinner.

**Sesame Noodle Bar** NOODLES $
(Map p58; www.sesamenoodlebar.com; 9 St 460; mains US$3.75-4.50; ☺ 11.30am-2.30pm & 5-9.30pm; 🐦) A Japanese-American duo is behind Russian Market's trendiest lunch spot. Cold noodles arrive in vegetarian or egg varieties and come heaped with an egg and carmelised pork or grilled tofu. Simply delicious.

**Alma Cucina Mexicana** MEXICAN $
(Map p58; 43A St 454; meals US$3-5; ☺ 7am-2pm; 🐦) How real, home-cooked Mexican cuisine made its way here we'll never know, but we're glad it did. The scrumptious rotating menu might include chorizo quesadillas one day, *bistec encebollado* (steak and onions) the next. The huevos rancheros breakfasts are legendary. Note the limited opening hours.

## FLOWER DISEMPOWER

Anyone who spends a night or two on the town in Phnom Penh will soon be familiar with young girls and boys hovering around popular bars and restaurants to sell decorative flowers. The kids are incredibly sweet and most people succumb to their charms and buy a flower or two. All these late nights for young children might not be so bad if they were benefiting from their hard-earned cash, but usually they're not. Look down the road and there will be a *moto* driver with an ice bucket full of these flowers waiting to ferry the children to another popular spot. Yet again, the charms of children are exploited for the benefit of adults who should know better. Think twice before buying from them, as the child is unlikely to reap the reward.

**Buffalo Sister**                        SANDWICHES **$$**
(Map p58; ☑017 879403; 55D Street 456; sandwiches from US$4.25; ☺11am-7.30pm; ☎) The extensive sandwich list is written on a chalkboard on the walls of this self-described carvery. Dig into a roast pork with applesauce sandwich or go healthy with a roast vegie or felafel wrap. Famous for its Sunday roast.

**Sumatra**                        INDONESIAN **$**
(Map p58; 35 St 456; mains US$1.50-3.50; ☺11am-8pm; ☎🖉) The vegetarian dishes, which average around US$2, are fantastic value, although hearty eaters may want to order two. The spicy *balado* (tomato and chilli sauce) dishes are good. Seating is on a leafy garden patio under a tin roof.

**Sisters**                        BAKERY **$**
(Map p58; 26B St 446; sandwiches US$2.50-3.50; ☺7am-6pm; ☎) A tiny little place that punches above its weight with light bites, all-day breakfasts, a few Cambodian mains and excellent homemade cakes, including cheap cupcakes.

★**Brooklyn Bistro**            INTERNATIONAL **$$**
(Map p58; ☑089 925926; 20 St 123; mains US$3-17; ☺11am-10pm; ☎) A stylish American diner that points where the Russian Market area is heading, this is incredibly popular with Phnom Penh expats in the know. The 16in pizzas are the largest in town, plus there's a dedicated menu of wings – as well as great deli sandwiches and the best New York cheesecake we've tasted in this part of the world.

**Roots & Burgers/Tipico**    FUSION, TAPAS **$$**
(Map p58; 80 St 454; ☺10am-10pm; ☎) This new concept restaurant offers the perfect two-for-one deal. Downstairs is **Roots & Burgers**, offering fusion flavours served in a *bao* bun. Upstairs is a stylish little Spanish tapas cafe called **Tipico**, one of the only bars in this part of town and open a little later.

### Self-Catering

**Super Duper**                        SUPERMARKET
(www.super-duper.biz; 21 St 488; ☺24hr) Phnom Penh's only 24hr supermarket, this could be very handy if the midnight munchies strike. It has one of the best product ranges in town, as the owners bring in their own containers from the US and Australia.

 **Drinking & Nightlife**

Phnom Penh has some great bars and clubs – it's definitely worth planning at least one big night on the town. There are some good pub-crawl strips around town, with lots of late-night spots clustered around the intersection of St 51 and St 172, where seemingly everybody ends up for a late night. 'Golden St' (St 278) is also popular, and the riverfront also has its share of bars. Another up-and-coming area is St 308 and the adjacent Bassac Lane. Further north off the riverfront, the bar strips take on a sleazier complexion, while many of the drinking spots clustered on St 104 and St 136 are hostess bars (aka 'girlie bars'), where female staff are employed mainly to flirt with and entertain customers.

 Bars

Happy hours are a big thing in Phnom Penh, so it pays to get started early, when even such luminaries as the Foreign Correspondents' Club and the Raffles offer two-for-one specials. Wednesday is 'Ladies' Night' at some of the smarter bars around town, with two-for-one deals all night or even free drinks. Most bars are open until at least midnight, which is about the time that Phnom Penh's bangin' nightclubs swing into action.

#### North Central (Riverfront)

★**FCC**                        BAR
(Foreign Correspondents' Club; Map p52; 363 Sisowath Quay; ☺6am-midnight; ☎) A Phnom

Penh institution, the 'F' is housed in a colonial gem with great views and cool breezes. One of those must-see places in Cambodia, almost everyone swings by for a drink – happy hours are 5pm to 7pm and 10pm to midnight. If the main bar is too crowded, head up to the rooftop, which often sees live music at weekends.It also offers an excellent menu both day and night.

**Blue Dragon**                                    BAR
(Map p42; 391 St 184; ⊘5.30pm-1pm) The location doesn't get better than this, with a front-row view of the royal palace and the chance for some river breezes on a balmy evening. Beers, wines and spirits flow.

**Oskar Bistro**                                   BAR
(Map p52; www.oskar-bistro.com; 159 Sisowath Quay; 🔊) This new gastro-pub blends the bar and restaurant to perfection. Choose from creative cocktails and a huge wine list of 55 tipples, set to subtle DJ beats. A top spot for a late-night feed: the kitchen stays open until 11pm.

**Paddy Rice**                                  IRISH PUB
(Map p52; 213 Sisowath Quay; ⊘24hr; 🔊) A real jack of all trades – good pub grub, big screens for sports viewing, and occasional live music, plus Thursday is open-mic night. All this in a perfect riverside location.

**Pickled Parrot**                            SPORTS BAR
(Map p52; 4 St 104; ⊘24hr; 🔊) One of the few bars in town where you can wash up any time of the day and find a fellow drinker sipping a beer, this is a friendly spot with air-con, big screens, a pool table and cheap drinks. (And not a hostess bar, unlike many others in this strip.)

**Chez Rina**                              COCKTAIL BAR
(Map p52; 6 St 98; ⊘5pm-midnight; 🔊) A blink-and-you'll-miss-it cocktail bar tucked away between the riverfront and the post office, set in a small section of a French-era building that has been renovated to perfection. The martinis are renowned.

### North Central (Off-river)
⭐**Dusk Till Dawn**                              BAR
(Map p52; 46 St 172) Also known as Reggae Bar because of the clientele and the music, the rooftop setting makes it a great spot for a sundowner, but the party lasts well into the night. The bar is split over two levels, so continue upstairs if the first level is quiet. Ride the lift to the top floor in the tall building opposite Pontoon.

**Elephant Bar**                                  BAR
(Map p52; Raffles Hotel Le Royal, St 92; ⊘happy hour 4-9pm; 🔊) Few places are more atmospheric than this sophisticated bar at the Raffles. It has been drawing journalists, politicos, and the rich and famous for more than 80 years. Singapore slings and many more drinks are half-price during the generous happy hour.

## BARS WITH A VIEW

As Phnom Penh grows up and the skyline starts to head higher, there is an increasing number of rooftop bars with a view. Here are some of the best in town:

**Chow** (Map p52; 277 Sisowath Quay; ⊘7am-11pm) The Quay hotel's swanky rooftop has river views, cooling breezes and half-price happy hours from 4pm to 8.30pm. The cocktail list includes zesty infusions such as ginger and lemongrass, plus a passionfruit caipirinha.

**Eclipse** (Map p46; Phnom Penh Tower, 445 Monivong Blvd; ⊘5pm-2am) Located on the 24th floor, this open-air venue is the dry-season venue of choice for big breezes and bigger views. When the wet season kicks in, venture two floors down to **D-22** (⊘7am-midnight), a stylish, enclosed bar-restaurant offering the same views without the elements.

**Ibiza Lounge** (Map p52; 277 Sisowath Quay; ⊘5pm-midnight) Spacious riverfront bar above the Bougainvillier Hotel. You have to earn your happy-hour (5pm to 7pm) reward here, as there is no lift to the 5th floor.

**Le Moon** (Map p52; 1 St 154; ⊘5pm-1am) Another hotel bar, the Amanjaya's rooftop number scores points for atmosphere and views over the river, though service is spotty. Bring patience.

**Tonle Sab Sky Bar** (Map p38; Sokha Phnom Penh Hotel) See Phnom Penh from another perspective with a drink at this bar located atop the huge Sokha Hotel, on the other side of the Tonlé Sap River.

### Howie Bar
BAR

(Map p52; 32 St 51; ☺7pm-6am) Friendly, fun and unpredictable, the way-cool Howie is the perfect spillover when neighbouring places are packed. It draws a convivial crowd of expats, travellers and locals into the wee hours.

### Zeppelin Bar
BAR

(Map p46; St 278; ☺5pm-late) Who says vinyl is dead? It lives on here thanks to the owner of this old-school rock bar spinning the turntables every night. The mainstay on the menu is '70s big rock. There is also a pool table. Zeppelin recently relocated to popular Golden St.

### Dodo Rhum House
BAR

(Map p52; 42C St 178; ☺5pm-late) This French favourite specialises in homemade, flavoured rums infused with tropical fruits and spices. Also serves an excellent fish fillet and other tasty treats.

### Blue Chili
GAY

(Map p52; 36 St 178; ☺6pm-late; ☎) The owner of this long-running, gay-friendly bar stages his own drag show every Friday and Saturday at 10.30pm.

## South Central

### Bar Sito
BAR

(Map p46; St 240½; ☺5pm-midnight; ☎) The bar that kick-started 240½ – it feels like private club as you seek out the hidden entrance, but once inside it reveals itself as a hip hideaway with impressive cocktails, wine by the glass and bottled beers.

### Strangefruit Bar
BAR

(Map p42; 213 St 19½; ☺5pm-11pm; ☎) Small, but perfectly formed, Strangefruit is a new, gay-friendly bar tucked away down a small alley behind the royal palace. It's an artistic little bolt hole for classy cocktails, wine by the glass and sharp collection of photographs and art.

### Bouchon
WINE BAR

(Map p46; 3 St 246; ☺4pm-midnight) Bouchon has a great selection of French wines, plus pâtés and other French nibbles, in a contemporary space on a quiet side street. A glass of house red is US$3.50.

## Boeng Keng Kang & Tonlé Bassac

### Che Culo
BAR

(Map p46; www.checulocambodia.com; 6b St 302; ☺11am-late Mon-Sat; ☎) A funky new spot in popular BKK district, this bar is all retro tiles and seated alcoves, making for an intimate atmosphere. Great cocktails are even greater during happy hours from 5pm to 7pm. A tapas-style menu is available day and night.

### Duplex
BAR

(Map p46; www.duplex.com.kh; 3 St 278; ☺10am-2am; ☎) A self-styled Belgian *taverne* with an extensive beer selection, it's also an uber-cool contemporary space that hosts regular salsa and Latin evenings. Great cocktails and a good range of light meals are available.

### Score
BAR

(Map p46; ☎023-221357; www.scorekh.com; 5 St 282; ☺8am-late; ☎) With its cinema-sized screen and television banks on every wall, this cavernous bar is the best place to watch a big game. It's not just the usual footie and rugby – almost all sports are catered for here. Several pool tables tempt those who would rather play than watch.

### Liquid
BAR

(Map p46; 3b St 278; ☺11am-midnight; ☎) A long-running bar on this popular street, with cheap drinks, an even cheaper happy hour and a popular pool table. There are some great tunes lurking if you can work out how to operate the music player.

### Red Bar
BAR

(Map p46; cnr St 308 & St 29; ☺5pm-1am; ☎) A friendly little local bar in the popular 308 St. The drinks here are so cheap that drinkers find themselves lingering long into the night...or maybe that's just us?

## Nightclubs

For the low-down on club nights, check out Phnom Penh Underground (www.phnom-penh-underground.com), an online guide to the club scene in Cambodia's capital.

### ★Heart of Darkness
CLUB

(Map p52; www.heartofdarknessclub.com.kh; 26 St 51; ☺8pm-late) This Phnom Penh institution with an alluring Angkor theme has evolved more into a nightclub than a bar over the years. It goes off every night of the week, attracting all – and we mean *all* – sorts. Everybody should stop in at least once just to bask in the aura and atmosphere of the place.

### ★Pontoon
CLUB

(Map p52; www.pontoonclub.com; 80 St 172; admission weekends US$3-5, weekdays free; ☺9.30pm-

PHNOM PENH DRINKING & NIGHTLIFE

## BASSAC LANE BARS

Bassac Lane is the moniker given to an alley that leads south off St 308. The brainchild of Kiwi brothers the Norbert-Munns, who have a flair for drinks and design, there are half a dozen or more hole-in-the-wall boozers open from 5pm to 1am in this eclectic spot (Map p46). Choose from fusion wraps and burgers at the original Meat & Drink, tiny and intimate Seibur, the refined Library, newcomer Harry's Bar or custom-bike tribute bar, Hangar 44. There's even a gin palace, the tiny Cicada Bar, plus Indian and Mexican eateries planned, and the chic Paperdolls (p80) dress shop. From out of nowhere, Bassac Lane has become the new Bohemian district of Phnom Penh and is well worth a visit.

late) After floating around from pier to pier for a few years (hence the name), the city's premier nightclub has finally found a permanent home on terra firma. It draws top local DJs and occasional big foreign acts. Thursday is gay-friendly night, with a 1am lady-boy show. Adjacent Pontoon Pulse is more of a lounge-club, with electronica and ambient music.

**Vito**                                               CLUB
(Map p42; 8 St 214; ⊙9pm-3am) A popular new retro club spinning some older dance tunes, from the '90s to noughties, and even back to the '80s. Popular with a slightly older crowd who want to have a conversation as well as a dance.

**Epic**                                               CLUB
(Map p46; ☑010 600608; www.epic.com.kh; 122b Tonlé Bassac; ⊙9pm-5am) The super-club comes to Phnom Penh with the opening of Epic. This is a huge warehouse space but the decor and design is anything but 'warehouse' – this is aimed at Cambodia's rich young things.

**Rock**                                               CLUB
(Map p58; 468 Monivong Blvd; admission varies; ⊙until late) If you want a more authentic local experience, Rock is your best bet – replete with karaoke rooms and all. It looks like a gigantic Home Depot, but Khmers go crazy for the place.

## ☆ Entertainment

For news on what's happening in town, *AsiaLife* is a free monthly with entertainment features and some listings. Online, try www.ladypenh.com or www.khmer440.com.

### Cinemas

**★ Meta House**                                       CINEMA
(Map p46; www.meta-house.com; 37 Sotharos Blvd; ⊙4pm-midnight Tue-Sun; ☎) This German-run cinema screens art-house films, documentaries and shorts from Cambodia and around the world most evenings at 4pm (admission free) and 7pm (admission varies). Films are sometimes followed by Q&As with those involved. Order German sausages, pizza-like 'flamecakes' and beer to supplement your viewing experience.

**Major Cineplex**                                     CINEMA
(Map p46; ☑023-901111; www.majorcineplex.com.kh; Aeon Mall, 132 Sotharos Blvd; tickets US$3-15; ⊙9am-midnight) The smartest cinema in town, with seven screens, including a business-class-like VIP screen and a 4DX screen for interactive viewing (complete with moving seats and surprise effects).

**Flicks**                                             CINEMA
(Map p46; www.theflicks-cambodia.com; 39B St 95; tickets US$3.50; ☎) It shows at least two movies a day in an uber-comfortable air-conditioned screening room. You can watch both films on one ticket.

**Bophana Centre**                                 FILM CENTRE
(Map p46; ☑023-992174; www.bophana.org; 64 St 200; admission free; ⊙8am-noon & 2-6pm Mon-Fri, 2-6pm Sat) Established by Cambodian-French filmmaker Rithy Panh, this is an audiovisual resource for filmmakers and researchers. Visitors can explore its archive of old photographs and films and attend free film screenings on Saturdays at 4pm.

**Mekong River Restaurant**                            CINEMA
(Map p52; cnr St 118 & Sisowath Quay; tickets US$3) Screens two original films in English or French, one covering the Khmer Rouge and the other on the subject of land mines. Showings are hourly from 11am to 9pm.

### Classical Dance & Arts

**★ Plae Pakaa**                             PERFORMING ARTS
(Fruitful; Map p52; ☑023-986032; www.cambodianlivingarts.org; National Museum, St 178; adult/child US$15/6; ⊙7pm Mon-Sat Oct-Mar, Fri & Sat May-Sep, closed Apr) Plae Pakaa is a series of must-see performances put on by

**LOCAL KNOWLEDGE**

## ARN CHORN-POND, MUSICIAN

Arn Chorn-Pond is the founder of Cambodian Living Arts (CLA; p56), an organisation dedicated to reviving traditional music, dance and other Cambodian art forms that were nearly lost during the Khmer Rouge years. Arn himself almost didn't survive that dark time. His parents ran a respected traditional opera company in Battambang, which made them immediate targets of the Khmer Rouge – who murdered almost all of the performing artists and 25 members of Arn's immediate family, including five of his eight siblings.

But the Khmer Rouge needed to keep some musicians around to play their revolutionary songs. Arn was among several children in Battambang recruited to dance and play the flute and the *khim* (a traditional Cambodian string instrument) at a local killing temple. 'They killed three kids who were slow to learn,' Arn says. 'I was a fast learner because I had music in my blood. If there was no music at that time, I probably would have been killed. Music saved my life.'

At the killing temple, Arn witnessed all sorts of atrocities. The Khmer Rouge made him play music to drown out the sounds of the screams. In the late 1970s, at the age of 12, Arn was forced to trade in his *khim* for a gun when he was recruited into the beleaguered Khmer Rouge army. He eventually managed to escape over the border to a refugee camp in Thailand, where he was ultimately adopted, along with several other refugees, by an American family from New Hampshire. When Arn returned to Cambodia several years later, people in Battambang still recognised him as 'that little boy who played the *khim*'. He founded CLA in 1998.

Arn shared with us his top five places for cultural connections in Phnom Penh:

➡ **Amrita Performing Arts** (www.amritaperformingarts.org) They create new stories with traditional Apsara dancers, and worked closely with CLA to organise the 2013 'Season of Cambodia' in New York.

➡ **Apsara Arts Association** (p78) A great, family-run organisation that's working with a new generation to preserve forms like Apsara and traditional folk dance.

➡ **Plae Pakaa** (p78) CLA puts on these performances almost every evening in front of the National Museum.

➡ **CLA's Yike Class** (Map p46; 65 Sothearos Blvd) These daily traditional-opera classes for at-risk youth are run by master theatre performer Ieng Sithul, and are open to tourists. Many of the kids here would be prostitutes if not for this class.

➡ **Sovanna Phum Arts Association** (p78) They do a great job creating new stories and new dances out of old Cambodian traditional forms.

Cambodian Living Arts (p56). There are three rotating shows, each lasting about an hour. *Children of Bassac* showcases traditional dance styles. *Passage of Life* depicts the various celebrations and rituals that Khmers go through in their lifetimes (weddings, funerals etc). *Mak Therng* is a traditional *yike* opera.

**Apsara Arts Association**      DANCE
(Map p38; ☑ 012 979335; www.apsara-art.org; 71 St 598; tickets US$6-7) ✆ Alternate performances of classical dance and folk dance are held most Saturdays at 7pm (call to confirm). Visitors are also welcome from 7.30am to 10.30am and from 2pm to 5pm Monday to Saturday to watch the students in training (suggested donation: US$3).

Please remember that this is a training school – noise and flash photography should be kept to a minimum. It's in Tuol Kork district, in the far north of the city.

**Sovanna Phum
Arts Association**      PERFORMING ARTS
(☑ 023-987564; www.shadow-puppets.org; 166 St 99, btwn St 484 & St 498; adult/child US$5/3) ✆ Regular traditional shadow-puppet performances and occasional classical dance and traditional drum shows are held here at 7.30pm every Friday and Saturday night. Audience members are invited to try their hand at the shadow puppets after the 50-minute performance. Classes are available here in the art of shadow puppetry, puppet making, classical and folk dance, and traditional Khmer musical instruments.

### Chatomuk Theatre
THEATRE

(Map p46; Sisowath Quay) Check the flyer out front for information on performances at the Chatomuk Theatre, located at the heart of Phnom Penh's popular riverfront. Officially, it has been turned into a government conference centre, but it regularly plays host to cultural performances.

### Live Music

Phnom Penh boasts a surprisingly active music scene, with several talented expat and mixed Khmer-expat bands. Check out Leng Pleng (www.lengpleng.com) for weekly live music listings in Phnom Penh.

#### Showbox
BAR

(Map p46; 11 St 330; ⊙11am-1am; ☎) This grungy music bar supports regular live acts and open-mic nights, as well as doubling up as a popular clubbing venue and occasional comedy club. Look out for cheap deals, including a rather generous free beer from 6.30pm to 7pm daily. Stick around afterwards for a rockin' night.

#### Sharky's
LIVE MUSIC

(Map p52; www.sharkybarblog.com; 126 St 130; ⊙5pm-late; ☎) An old-school Phnom Penh hang-out long famous for billiards and babes, Sharky's has done a good job of redirecting its focus towards quality live music. Claims to be Indochina's longest-running rock and roll bar.

### Doors
LIVE MUSIC

(Map p38; 18 St 84; ⊙7am-midnight; ☎) Self-described as a 'music and tapas' bar, the Doors is a sophisticated place with a long bar, mouth-watering Spanish bites, expensive drinks, live jazz and more.

 Shopping

There is some great shopping to be had in Phnom Penh, but don't forget to bargain in the markets or you'll have your 'head shaved' – local-speak for being ripped off.

### Markets & Malls

As well as the markets, there are now some shopping malls in Phnom Penh. While they are not quite as glamorous as the likes of the Siam Paragon in Bangkok, they are good places to browse (especially thanks to the air-conditioning).

#### Russian Market
MARKET

(Psar Tuol Tom Pong; Map p58; St 155; ⊙6am-5pm) This sweltering bazaar is the one market all visitors should come to at least once during a trip to Phnom Penh. It is *the* place to shop for souvenirs and discounted name-brand clothing. We can't vouch for the authenticity of everything, but along with plenty of knock-offs you'll find genuine articles stitched in local factories. You'll pay as little as 20% of the price back home for brands like Banana Republic, Billabong, Calvin Klein, Colombia, Gap and Next.

---

### SHOPPING TO HELP CAMBODIA

There are a host of tasteful shops selling handicrafts and textiles to raise money for projects to assist disadvantaged Cambodians. These are a good place to spend some dollars, as it helps to put a little bit back into the country.

**Cambodian Handicraft Association** (CHA; Map p46; 1 St 350; ⊙8am-7pm) This well-stocked showroom and workshop sells fine, handmade silk clothing, scarves, toys and bags produced by victims of land mines and polio.

**Daughters** (Map p52; www.daughtersofcambodia.org; 65 St 178; ⊙9am-6pm Mon-Sat) Daughters is an NGO that runs a range of programs to train and assist former prostitutes and victims of sex trafficking. The fashionable clothes, bags and accessories here are made with eco-friendly cotton and natural dyes by program participants.

**Mekong Blue** (Map p52; www.bluesilk.org; 9 St 130; ⊙8am-6pm) This is the Phnom Penh boutique for Stung Treng's best-known silk cooperative to empower women. Produces beautiful scarves and shawls, as well as jewellery.

**Rajana** (Map p58; www.rajanacrafts.org; 170 St 450; ⊙7am-6pm Mon-Sat, 10.30am-5pm Sun) One of the best all-round handicraft stores, Rajana aims to promote fair wages and training. It has a beautiful selection of cards, some quirky metalware products, jewellery, bamboo crafts, lovely shirts, gorgeous wall hangings, candles – you name it. Also has a **shop** (Map p58; ⊙10am-6pm) at the Russian Market.

Russian Market, so-called by foreigners because the predominantly Russian expat population shopped here in the 1980s, also has a large range of handicrafts and antiquities (many fake), including miniature Buddhas, woodcarvings, betel-nut boxes, silks, silver jewellery, musical instruments and so on. Bargain hard, as hundreds of tourists pass through here every day.

**Psar Thmei**  MARKET
(ផ្សារធំ, Central Market; Map p52; St 130; ⊙ 6.30am-5.30pm) A landmark building in the capital, the art-deco Psar Thmei is often called the Central Market, a reference to its location and size. The huge domed hall resembles a Babylonian ziggurat – some claim it ranks as one of the 10 largest domes in the world. The design allows for maximum ventilation, and even on a sweltering day the central hall is cool and airy. The market was recently renovated with French government assistance and is looking good.

The market has four wings filled with stalls selling gold and silver jewellery, antique coins, dodgy watches, clothing and other such items. For photographers, the fresh-food section affords many opportunities. For a local lunch, there are a host of food stalls located on the western side, which faces Monivong Blvd.

Psar Thmei is undoubtedly the best market for browsing. However, it has a reputation among Cambodians for overcharging on most products.

**Night Market**  MARKET
(Psar Reatrey; Map p52; cnr St 108 & Sisowath Quay; ⊙ 5-11pm Fri-Sun) A cooler, alfresco version of Russian Market, this night market takes place every Friday, Saturday and Sunday evening if it's not raining. Bargain vigorously, as prices can be on the high side. Interestingly, it's probably more popular with Khmers than foreigners.

**Psar O Russei**  MARKET
(Map p46; St 182; ⊙ 6.30am-5.30pm) Much bigger than other noted markets in town, Psar O Russei sells foodstuffs, costume jewellery, imported toiletries, secondhand clothes and everything else you can imagine from hundreds of stalls. The market is housed in a huge labyrinth of a building that looks like a shopping mall from the outside.

**Aeon Mall**  MALL
(Map p46; www.aeonmallphnompenh.com; 132 Sothearos Blvd) The swankiest mall in Phnom Penh, this Japanese-run establishment has international boutiques, several food courts and extensive dining outlets, plus a seven-screen multiplex cinema, ice skating and a bowling alley.

**Sorya Shopping Centre**  MALL
(Map p52; cnr St 63 & St 154; ⊙ 9am-9pm) Still a popular mall, this long-running place has a good range of shops, a food court, a cinema, a central location and superb views over the more traditional Psar Thmei.

**Rehab Craft** (Map p46; 1 St 278; ⊙ 9am-9pm) Sells carvings, weavings, wallets, jewellery and bags produced in the workshop by disabled artisans, and often using recycled materials.

**Sobbhana** (Map p52; www.sobbhana.org; 23 St 144; ⊙ 8am-noon & 1-6pm) Established by Princess Marie, the Sobbhana Foundation is a not-for-profit organisation training women in traditional weaving. Beautiful silks in a stylish boutique.

**Tabitha** (Map p46; 239 St 360; ⊙ 7am-6pm Mon-Sat) A leading NGO shop with a good collection of silk bags, tableware, bedroom decorations and children's toys. Proceeds go towards rural community development, such as well-drilling.

**Villageworks** (Map p46; www.villageworks.biz; 118 St 113; ⊙ 8am-5pm Mon-Sat) Opposite Tuol Sleng Museum, this shop has the inevitable silk and bags, as well as coconut-shell utensils made by poor and disadvantaged artisans in Kompong Thom province.

**Watthan Artisans** (Map p46; www.wac.khmerproducts.com; 180 Norodom Blvd; ⊙ 8am-6.30pm) Located at the entrance to Wat Than, it sells silk and other products, including wonderful contemporary handbags, made by a project-supported cooperative of land mine and polio victims. You can visit the on-site woodworking and weaving workshops.

**Women for Women** (WFW; Map p52; www.womanforwoman.net; 9 St 178; ⊙ 7am-10pm) Pillows, throws, bags, scarves, jewellery, silver and more, hand-fashioned by women with disabilities.

## Clothing, Silks & Accessories

While the markets are best-known for knock-off clothing, a few stores surrounding Russian Market sell authentic brand-name gear, made locally and in neighbouring Vietnam. There are also several boutiques around town specialising in silk furnishings and stylish original clothing, as well as glam accessories. Many are conveniently located on St 240, Cambodia's answer to London's King's Rd.

**Ambre** CLOTHING
(Map p52; ☑ 023-217935; 37 St 178; ⊗10am-6pm) Leading Cambodian fashion designer Romyda Keth has turned this striking French-era mansion into the perfect showcase for her stunning silk collection.

**Bliss Boutique** CLOTHING, BEAUTY
(Map p46; 29 St 240; ⊗9am-9pm) Casual dresses, blouses and men's shirts made of wonderfully airy materials, plus pillows and scented creams and oils.

**Couleurs d'Asie** ACCESSORIES
(Map p46; www.couleursdasie.net; 33 St 240; ⊗8am-7pm) Great place for gift shopping, with lots of kids' clothes, silks, chunky jewellery, beautiful bags, knick-knacks and fragrant soaps, lotions, incense and oils.

**DAH Export** CLOTHING, CHILDREN
(Map p46; 87 Sihanouk Blvd; ⊗9am-9pm) This is the biggest and best of the factory outlets, with an impressive winter collection (North Face Gore-Tex ski jackets for US$99, anyone?), plenty of kiddie clothing and a prominent location.

**Lost 'N' Found Vintage Shop** CLOTHING
(Map p46; http://lostnfoundvintagestore.weebly.com; 321 St 63; ⊗9am-8pm) A vintage clothing store that hand-picks the funkiest pieces from the retro market collections around town. Predominantly women's clothing and accessories.

**Paperdolls** CLOTHING
(Map p46; Bassac Lane; ⊗10am-6pm Tue-Sun) Great stuff for women, including sundresses, shoes, movie-star shades, handbags, jewellery – you name it.

**Spicy Green Mango** CLOTHING, CHILDREN
(Map p46; www.spicygreenmango.com; 4A St 278; ⊗9am-9pm) *The* place to shop for original and creative kids' clothes, plus quality T-shirts and a hippie-esque adult female line.

**Smateria** ACCESSORIES, CHILDREN
(Map p52; 7 St 178; ⊗9am-9.30pm) They do some clothing but the speciality is bags, including a line of quirky kids' backpacks, made from fishing net and other recycled materials. There's another branch in BKK (Map p46; 8 St 57; ⊗8am-9pm).

**Subtyl** CLOTHING, CHILDREN
(Map p46; www.subtyl.com; 43 St 240; ⊗9am-7pm) French-run boutique offering stylish accessories and clothes for women, plus the Chilli Kids line for hip youngsters.

**Tuol Sleng Shoes** SHOES
(Map p46; 136 St 143; ⊗7.30am-5pm) Scary name, but there's nothing scary about the price of these custom-fit, handmade shoes. Neighbouring Beautiful Shoes is another good option.

**Waterlily** ACCESSORIES
(Map p46; 37 St 240; ⊗10am-7pm Mon-Fri, 9am-5pm Sat) Strikingly original bags, jewellery, art and dolls, all made from recycled materials.

## Art & Books

Plenty of shops sell locally produced paintings along St 178, opposite the Royal University of Fine Arts between streets 13 and 19. With a new generation of artists coming up, the selection is much stronger than it once was. Lots of reproduction busts of famous Angkorian sculptures are available along this stretch, great for the mantelpiece back home. Be sure to bargain.

**Artisans Angkor** CRAFTS
(Map p52; 12 St 13; ⊗9am-6pm) Classy Phnom Penh branch of the venerable Siem Reap sculpture and silk specialist.

**Asasax Art Gallery** ARTS
(Map p52; 192 St 178; ⊗8am-7.30pm) High-end gallery featuring the striking work of artist Asasax.

**Bohr's Books** BOOKS
(Map p52; 5 Sothearos Blvd; ⊗8am-8pm) Secondhand bookshop near the riverfront with a great selection of novels and nonfiction.

**D's Books** BOOKS
(Map p52; 7 St 178; ⊗9am-9pm) The largest chain of secondhand bookshops in the capital, with a good range of titles. There's a second branch (Map p46; 79 St 240; ⊗9am-9pm) just east of Norodom Blvd.

### Estampe
VINTAGE

(Map p46; 197A St 19; ⊙10am-7pm Mon-Sat)
Reproduction images, posters, journals
and more, plus original collectibles from
old Indochine, including books, maps and
postcards.

### International
### Book Center
BOOKS, ACCESSORIES

(IBC; Map p46; 59 Sihanouk Blvd; ⊙8am-8pm)
Lost something on the road? Chances are
you can replace it here. High-quality head-
phones, flashlights, swimming goggles,
notebooks, pens and more.

### Monument Books
BOOKS

(Map p46; 111 Norodom Blvd; ⊙7am-8.30pm) The
best-stocked bookshop in town, with almost
every Cambodia-related book available,
a superb maps and travel section – plus a
wi-fi-enabled branch of Blue Pumpkin (p62)
cafe.

### Open Book
BOOKS, CHILDREN

(Map p46; 41 St 240; ⊙10am-5pm) Run by an
NGO, this is essentially a library where you
can drop in to read a variety of books in
French or English. Also has a fair selection
of Cambodia-themed children's books for
sale.

### Theam's House
CRAFTS

(Map p52; www.theamshouse.com; 47 St 178;
⊙8am-6pm) Renowned Siem Reap–based
lacquerware designer Theam has opened a
flagship gallery in the old Reyum premises.
Both contemporary and classic.

## ❶ Information

### DANGERS & ANNOYANCES
➡ Phnom Penh is not as dangerous as people
imagine, but it is important to take care. Armed
robberies do sometimes occur, but statistically
you would be very unlucky to be a victim. However, bag- and smartphone-snatching is a huge

problem, and victims are often hurt when they
are dragged off their bicycles or motorbikes.
Should you become the victim of a robbery, do
not panic and do not, under any circumstances,
struggle. Calmly raise your hands and let your
attacker take what they want. *Do not* reach for
your pockets, as the assailant may think you
are reaching for a gun. Do not carry a bag at
night, because it is more likely to make you a
target.

➡ If you ride your own motorbike during the
day, some police may try to fine you for the
most trivial of offences, such as turning left
in violation of a no-left-turn sign. At their
most audacious, they may try to get you for
riding with your headlights on during the day
although, worryingly, it does not seem to be
illegal for Cambodians to travel without their
headlights on at night. The police will most
likely demand US$5 from you and threaten to
take you to the police station for an official
US$20 fine if you do not pay. If you are patient
with them and smile, you can usually get away
with handing over US$1. The trick is not to stop
in the first place by not catching their eye.

➡ The riverfront area of Phnom Penh, particularly places with outdoor seating, attracts many
beggars, as do Psar Thmei and Russian Market.
Generally, however, there is little in the way of
push and shove.

➡ Flooding is a major problem in the wet season
(June to October), and heavy downpours see
some streets turn into canals for a few hours.

### EMERGENCIES
In the event of a medical emergency it may be
necessary to be evacuated to Bangkok.
**Ambulance** (☑119, ☑in English 023-724891)
**Fire** (☑in Khmer 118)
**Police** (☑in Khmer 117)

### INTERNET ACCESS
Phnom Penh is now well and truly wired, and
pretty much all hotels, guesthouses, cafes
and restaurants offer free wi-fi connections.
Internet cafes are less common since the wi-fi
explosion, but the main backpacker strips –

---

### ❶ WARNING: BAG-SNATCHING

Bag-snatching has become a real problem in Phnom Penh, with foreigners often targeted. Hot spots include the riverfront and busy areas around popular markets, but there is
no real pattern; the speeding motorbike thieves, usually operating in pairs, can strike any
time, any place. Countless expats and tourists have been injured falling off their bikes in
the process of being robbed, and in 2007 a French woman was killed after being dragged
from a speeding *moto* (motorcycle taxi) into the path of a vehicle. Wear close-fitting bags
(such as backpacks) that don't dangle from the body temptingly. Don't hang expensive
cameras around the neck and keep things close to the body and out of sight, particularly
when walking along the road, crossing the road or travelling by *remork-moto (tuk tuk)* or
especially by *moto*. These people are real pros and only need one chance.

St 258, St 278 and St 172 – have a few places. Most internet cafes are set up for Skype or similar services, and offer cheap VOIP (Voice-Over-Internet Protocol) calls as well.

### MEDIA

The *Cambodia Daily* and the *Phnom Penh Post* are widely available. They mix original local-news content with international stories pulled from wire services. *AsiaLife* is a monthly listings mag full of features targeted at Phnom Penh's expat community. Pick up *Drinking & Dining* and *Out & About*, both produced by **Cambodia Pocket Guide** (www.cambodiapocketguide.com). The *Phnom Penh Visitors Guide* (www.canby publications.com) is brimming with useful information on the capital and beyond, plus detailed maps of the entire city.

### MEDICAL SERVICES

It is important to be aware of the difference between a clinic and a hospital in Phnom Penh.

Clinics are good for most situations, but in a genuine emergency, it is best to go to a hospital.

**Calmette Hospital** (Map p38; ☑ 023-426948; 3 Monivong Blvd; ⊙ 24hr) The best of the local hospitals, with the most comprehensive services and an intensive care unit.

**Royal Phnom Penh Hospital** (Map p38; ☑ 023-991000; www.royalphnompenh hospital.com; 888 Russian Blvd; ⊙ 24hr) International hospital affiliated with Bangkok Hospital. Boasts top facilities. Expensive.

**International SOS Medical Centre** (Map p46; ☑ 023-216911, 012 816911; www.internationalsos.com; 161 St 51; ⊙ 8am-5.30pm Mon-Fri, to noon Sat, emergency 24hr) Top clinic with a host of international doctors (and prices to match).

**Tropical & Travellers Medical Clinic** (Map p52; ☑ 023-306802; www.travellers medicalclinic.com; 88 St 108; ⊙ 9.30-11.30am & 2.30-5pm Mon-Fri, 9.30-11.30am Sat) Well-regarded clinic run by a British general practitioner for more than a decade.

## CHILD PROSTITUTION

The sexual abuse of children by foreign paedophiles is a serious problem in Cambodia. Paedophilia is a crime in Cambodia and several foreigners have served or are serving jail sentences. There is no such thing as an isolation unit for sex offenders in Cambodia. Countries such as Australia, France, Germany, the UK and the USA have also introduced much-needed legislation that sees nationals prosecuted in their home country for having under-age sex abroad.

This child abuse is slowly but surely being combated, although in a country as poor as Cambodia, money can tempt people into selling babies for adoption and children for sex. The trafficking of innocent children has many shapes and forms, and the sex trade is just the thin end of the wedge. Poor parents have been known to rent out their children as beggars, labourers or sellers; many child prostitutes in Cambodia are Vietnamese and have been sold into the business by family back in Vietnam. Once in the trade, it is difficult to escape a life of violence and abuse. Drugs are also being used to keep children dependent on their pimps, with bosses giving out *yama* (a dirty methamphetamine) or heroin to dull their senses.

Paedophilia is not unique to Western societies and it is a big problem with Asian tourists as well. The problem is that some of the home governments don't treat it as seriously as some of their Western counterparts. Even more problematic is the domestic industry of virgin-buying in Cambodia, founded on the superstition that taking a virgin will enhance one's power. Even if NGOs succeed in putting off Western paedophiles, confronting local traditions may be a greater challenge.

Visitors can do their bit by keeping an eye out for any suspicious behaviour. Don't ignore it – pass on any relevant information such as the name and nationality of the individual to the embassy concerned. To report abuse there is a Cambodian hotline (☑ 023-997919) and ChildSafe (details opposite) maintains confidential hotlines in Phnom Penh (☑ 012 311112), Siem Reap (☑ 017 358758) and Sihanoukville (☑ 012 478100). When booking into a hotel or jumping on transport, look out for the ChildSafe logo, as each establishment or driver who earns this logo is trained to identify and respond to child abuse. End Child Prostitution and Trafficking (ECPAT; www.ecpat.net) is a global network aimed at stopping child prostitution, child pornography and the trafficking of children for sexual purposes, and has affiliates in most Western countries.

**Naga Clinic** (Map p46; ☐ 023-211300; www. nagaclinic.com; 11 St 254; ⊙ 24hr) A reliable, French-run clinic.

**European Dental Clinic** (Map p46; ☐ 023-211363; 160A Norodom Blvd; ⊙ 8am-noon & 2-7pm Mon-Fri, 8am-noon Sat, closed Sun) Has international-standard dental services and a good reputation.

**Pharmacie de la Gare** (Map p52; 81 Monivong Blvd; ⊙ 7am-9pm) A pharmacy with English- and French-speaking consultants.

**U-Care Pharmacy** (Map p52; 26 Sothearos Blvd; ⊙ 8am-10pm) International-style pharmacy with a convenient location near the river.

### MONEY

There's little need to turn US dollars into riel, as greenbacks are universally accepted in the capital. You can change a wide variety of other currencies into dollars or riel in the jewellery stalls around Psar Thmei and Russian Market. Many upmarket hotels offer 24-hour money-changing services, although this is usually reserved for their guests. Banks with ATMs and money-changing facilities are ubiquitous. Malls and supermarkets are good bets, and there are dozens of ATMs along the riverfront.

**ANZ Royal Bank** (Map p52; 265 Sisowath Quay; ⊙ 8.30am-4pm Mon-Fri, to noon Sat) ANZ has ATMs galore all over town, including at supermarkets and petrol stations, but there is a US$5 charge per transaction.

**CAB Bank** (Map p52; 263 Sisowath Quay; ⊙ 8am-9pm) Convenient hours and location; cashes travellers cheques in a range of currencies (3% commission). There's also a Western Union office here (one of several in the city).

**Canadia Bank** (Map p52; cnr St 110 & Monivong Blvd; ⊙ 8am-3.30pm Mon-Fri, to 11.30am Sat) Has ATMs around town, with a US$4 charge. At their flagship branch you can also change travellers cheques of several currencies for a 2% commission, plus get free cash advances on MasterCard and Visa. Also represents MoneyGram.

### POST

**Central Post Office** (Map p52; St 13 at St 100; ⊙ 8am-6pm) A landmark, it's in a French colonial classic just east of Wat Phnom.

### TOURIST INFORMATION

**Visitor Information Centre** (Map p46; Sisowath Quay; ⊙ 8am-5pm Mon-Sat; 🐾) Located on the riverfront near the Chatomuk Theatre. While it doesn't carry a whole lot of information, it does offer free internet access, free wi-fi, air-con and clean public toilets.

**ChildSafe** (Map p52; ☐ 023-986601, hotline 012 311112; www.childsafe-cambodia.org; 71 St 174; ⊙ 8am-5pm Mon-Fri) There's a centre here for tourists to learn about best behaviour relat-ing to child begging, the dangers of orphanage tours, exploitation and other risks to children (see www.thinkchildsafe.org for tips). You can also look out for the ChildSafe logo on *remorks* and hotels: this network of people are trained to protect children in Cambodia.

### TRAVEL AGENCIES

There are plenty of travel agents around town. The following are good bets for air tickets and all manner of domestic excursions, and can also arrange local transport and tour guides in multi-ple languages.

**EXO Travel** (Map p52; ☐ 023-218948; www. exotravel.com; 66 Norodom Blvd) Runs tours all over Cambodia and the Mekong region.

**Hanuman Travel** (Map p46; ☐ 023-218396; www.hanuman.travel; 12 St 310) Guides in several languages, tours and more, all over the country.

**Palm Tours** (Map p46; ☐ 023-726291; www. palmtours.biz; 1B St 278; ⊙ 8am-9pm) Efficient Volak and her team are a great option for bus tickets (no commission) and the like.

**PTM Travel & Tours** (Map p52; ☐ 023-219268; www.ptmcambodia.com; 200 Monivong Blvd; ⊙ 8am-5.30pm Mon-Sat) Good place for out-going air tickets.

## 🛈 Getting There & Away

### AIR

Many international air services run to/from Phnom Penh. Domestically, there are now three airlines connecting Phnom Penh and Siem Reap. **Cambodia Angkor Air** (Map p46; ☐ 023-666 6786; www.cambodiaangkorair.com; 206A Norodom Blvd) flies four to six times daily to Siem Reap (from US$60 one way, 30 minutes), while newcomers **Bassaka Air** (☐ 023-217613; www. bassakaair.com) and **Cambodia Bayon Airlines** (☐ 023-231555; www.bayonairlines.com) have at least one flight a day, from US$40 one way.

### BOAT

Fast boats up the Tonlé Sap to Siem Reap and down the Mekong to Chau Doc in Vietnam op-erate from the **tourist boat dock** (Map p52; 93 Sisowath Quay) at the eastern end of St 104. Public boats up the Mekong to Kompong Cham and Kratie stopped running years ago.

The fast boats to Siem Reap (US$35, five to six hours) aren't as popular as they used to be. When it costs from as little as US$6 for an air-conditioned bus or US$35 to be bundled on the roof of a boat, it's not hard to see why. It is better to save your boat experience for elsewhere in Cambodia. Several companies have daily ser-vices departing at 7am and usually take it in turns to make the run. The first stretch of the journey along the river is scenic, but once the boat hits the lake, the fun is over: it's a vast inland sea with

## GETTING TO VIETNAM: PHNOM PENH TO HO CHI MINH CITY

**Getting to the border** The original Bavet/Moc Bai land crossing between Vietnam and Cambodia has seen steady traffic for two decades. The easiest way to get to Ho Chi Minh City (Saigon) is to catch an international bus (US$8 to US$13, seven hours) from Phnom Penh. We recommend taking a Vietnamese company, such as Sapaco (p84), as it will speed entry into Vietnam in the event of long lines at the border. There are several companies making this trip.

**At the border** Long lines entering either country are not uncommon, but it's straightforward provided you purchase a Vietnamese visa in advance (should you require one).

**Moving on** If you are not on the international bus, it's not hard to find onward transport to HCMC or elsewhere.

not a village in sight. The boats to Siem Reap run from roughly August through March (water levels are too low at other times).

### LAND
#### Bus

All major towns in Cambodia are accessible by air-conditioned bus from Phnom Penh. Most buses leave from company offices, which are generally clustered around Psar Thmei or located near the corner of St 106 and Sisowath Quay. Buying tickets in advance is a good idea for peace of mind, although it's not always necessary.

Not all buses are created equal, or priced the same. Buses run by Capitol Tour and Phnom Penh Sorya are usually among the cheapest, while Giant Ibis, Mekong Express and Orient Express 1907 buses are smarter and pricier.

Most of the long-distance buses drop off and pick up in major towns along the way, such as Kompong Thom en route to Siem Reap, Pursat on the way to Battambang, or Kompong Cham en route to Kratie. However, full fare is usually charged anyway.

Another popular bus route is to Ho Chi Minh City.

**Capitol Tour** (Map p46; ☑ 023-724104; 14 St 182) Offers trips all the way through to Chau Doc using a combination of bus and boat. Capitol Tour services depart at 8am; the trip is about six to seven hours.

**Giant Ibis** (Map p52; ☑ 023-999333; www.giantibis.com; 3 St 106; ☎) 'VIP' bus and express-van specialist. Big bus to Siem Reap has plenty of legroom and dysfunctional wi-fi. A portion of profits go toward giant ibis conservation.

**Gold VIP** (Map p52; ☑ 070 988888; 3 St 106)

**GST** (Map p52; ☑ 023-218114; 13 St 142)

**Long Phuong** (Map p46; ☑ 097 311 0999; 274 Sihanouk Blvd)

**Mekong Express** (☑ 023-427518; http://catmekongexpress.com; 2020 NH5) Has a riverside booking office (Map p52; Sisowath Quay).

**Olympic Express** (Map p38; ☑ 092 868782; 70 Monireth Blvd)

**Orient Express 1907** (Map p52; ☑ 090 896666; 18 St 108)

**Phnom Penh Sorya** (Map p52; ☑ 023-210359; cnr St 217 & St 67, Psar Thmei area)

**Rith Mony** (Map p52; ☑ 017 525388; 24 St 102) Double-decker buses to Battambang, Kampot, Krong Koh Kong, Kompong Cham, Kratie, Pailin, Pakse, Poipet, Siem Reap and Sihanoukville.

**Sapaco** (Map p46; ☑ 023-210300; www.sapacotourist.com; 309 Sihanouk Blvd)

**Virak Buntham** (Kampuchea Angkor Express; Map p52; ☑ 016 786270; 1 St 106) Night-bus specialist with services to Siem Reap, Sihanoukville and Koh Kong.

#### Express Van

Speedy express vans (minibuses) with 12 to 14 seats serve popular destinations like Siem Reap and Sihanoukville. These cut travel times significantly, but they tend to be cramped and often travel at very high speeds – not for the faint of heart. Several of the big bus companies also run vans, most famously Mekong Express. It's a good idea to book express vans in advance.

**CTT Net** (Map p52; ☑ 023-217217; 223 Sisowath Quay)

**Golden Bayon Express** (Map p52; ☑ 023-966968; 3 St 126)

**Kampot Express** (Map p46; ☑ 077 555123; 2 St 215)

**Kim Seng Express** (Map p46; ☑ 012 786000; 506 Kampuchea Krom Blvd) To Sen Monorom in Mondulkiri.

**Mey Hong Transport** (☑ 023-637 2722) Call for pick-up.

**Neak Krorhorm** (Map p52; ☑ 092 966669; 4 St 108)

**Seila Angkor** (Map p52; ☑ 077 888080; 43 St 154)

## Local Transport (Share Taxi, Minibus & Pick-up)

Share taxis and local minibuses leave Phnom Penh for destinations all over the country. Taxis to Kampot, Kep and Takeo leave from **Psar Dang Kor** (Map p38; Mao Tse Toung Blvd), while packed local minibuses and taxis for most other places leave from the northwest corner of **Psar Thmei** (Map p52). Vehicles for the Vietnam border leave from **Chbah Ampeau** taxi park, on the eastern side of Monivong Bridge in the south of town. You may have to wait awhile (possibly until the next day if you arrive in the afternoon) before your vehicle fills up, or pay for the vacant seats yourself.

Local minibuses aren't much fun and are best avoided when there are larger air-con buses or faster share taxis available, which is pretty much everywhere. However, they will save you a buck or two if you're pinching pennies.

### Train

There are currently no passenger services operating on the Cambodian rail network – but this should be seen as a blessing in disguise, given that the trains are extremely slow, travelling at

## BUSES FROM PHNOM PENH

| DESTINATION | DURATION (HR) | PRICE | COMPANIES | FREQUENCY |
|---|---|---|---|---|
| Ban Lung | 11 | US$12 | PP Sorya, Rith Mony | morning only |
| Bangkok, Thailand | 12 | US$18-23 | Mekong Express, PP Sorya, Virak Buntham | once daily |
| Battambang (day) | 5-6 | US$5-6 | GST, Phnom Penh Sorya, Rith Mony | several daily |
| Battambang (night) | 6 | US$8-10 | Virak Buntham | 4 per night |
| Ho Chi Minh City, Vietnam | 7 | US$8-13 | Capitol Tour, Long Phuong, Mekong Express, PP Sorya, Sapaco, Virak Buntham (night bus) | several daily until about 3pm |
| Kampot (direct) | 3 | US$5-6 | Capitol Tour, Rith Mony | 2 daily |
| Kampot (via Kep) | 4 | US$6 | PP Sorya | 7.30am, 9.30am, 2.45pm |
| Kep | 3 | US$5 | PP Sorya | 7.30am, 9.30am, 2.45pm |
| Koh Kong | 5½ | US$7 | Olympic Express, PP Sorya, Virak Buntham | 2-3 daily (before noon) |
| Kompong Cham | 3 | US$5 | PP Sorya, Rith Mony | hourly until 4pm |
| Kratie | 6-8 | US$8 | PP Sorya, Rith Mony | 6.45am, 7.15am, 7.30am, 9.30am, 10.30am |
| Pakse via Don Det, Laos | 12-14 | US$28 | PP Sorya | 6.45am |
| Poipet (day) | 8 | US$9-11 | Capitol Tour, Gold VIP, PP Sorya, Rith Mony | frequent until noon |
| Poipet (night) | 7 | US$10-11 | Gold VIP, Rith Mony, Virak Buntham, | at least once daily |
| Preah Vihear City | 7 | US$10 | GST, PP Sorya | morning only |
| Sen Monorom | 8 | 35,000r | PP Sorya | 7.30am |
| Siem Reap (day) | 6 | US$6-8 | most companies | frequent |
| Siem Reap (VIP) | 6 | US$13-15 | Giant Ibis, Mekong Express, Orient Express 1907 | 7.45am, 8.45am, 12.30pm |
| Siem Reap (night) | 6hr | US$10 | Gold VIP, Virak Buntham | 6pm, 8pm, 11pm, 12.30am |
| Sihanoukville | 5½ | US$5-6 | Capitol Tour, GST, Mekong Express, PP Sorya, Rith Mony, Virak Buntham | frequent |
| Stung Treng | 9 | US$10 | PP Sorya, Rith Mony | 6.45am, 7.30am |

## GETTING TO VIETNAM: PHNOM PENH TO CHAU DOC

The most scenic way to end your travels in Cambodia is to sail the Mekong to Kaam Samnor (about 100km south-southeast of Phnom Penh), cross the border to Vinh Xuong in Vietnam, and proceed to Chau Doc on the Tonlé Bassac River via a small channel or overland. Chau Doc has onward land and river connections to points in the Mekong Delta and elsewhere in Vietnam. Various companies do trips all the way through to Chau Doc using a single boat or some combination of bus and boat; prices vary according to speed and level of service. **Delta Adventure** (Map p52; ☑ 012 733191; www.saigonmekong.info; US$19) and Capitol Tour (p84) depart Phnom Penh at 8am and involve a bus transfer; the trip is about six to seven hours. **Hang Chau** (Map p52; ☑ 088 878 7871; US$25) departs at noon and the entire journey is by boat; the more upmarket and slightly faster **Blue Cruiser** (Map p52; ☑ 023-633 3666; www.bluecruiser.com; US$35) departs at 1.30pm; **Victoria Hotels** (Map p52; www.victoriahotels.asia; US$95) also has a boat making several runs a week between Phnom Penh and its Victoria Chau Doc Hotel. These companies take about four hours, including a slow border check, and use a single boat to Chau Doc. Backpacker guesthouses and tour companies offer cheaper bus/boat combo trips. All boats depart from Phnom Penh's **tourist boat dock** (Map p52; 93 Sisowath Quay).

about 20km/h. (Yes, for a few minutes at least, you could outrun the train.)

Just for reference, Phnom Penh's train station is located at the western end of St 106 and St 108, in a grand old colonial-era building that is a shambles inside. The railway is being overhauled and has been reopened to cargo services, so there may be the option of passenger services at some point in the future.

# ❶ Getting Around

Being such a small city, Phnom Penh is quite easy to get around, although traffic is getting worse by the year and traffic jams are common around the morning and evening rush hour, particularly around the two main north–south boulevards, Monivong and Norodom.

### TO/FROM THE AIRPORT

Phnom Penh International Airport (p358) is 7km west of central Phnom Penh, via Russian Blvd.

An official booth outside the airport arrivals area arranges taxis to the centre for US$12; a *remork* costs a flat US$9. You can get a *remork* for US$5 and a *moto* for about US$3 if you walk one minute out to the street. Heading to the airport from central Phnom Penh, a taxi/*remork*/ *moto* will cost about US$10/5/3. The journey usually takes between 30 minutes and one hour depending on the traffic.

### BICYCLE

It's possible to hire bicycles at some of the guesthouses around town for about US$1 to US$2 a day, but take a look at the chaotic traffic conditions before venturing forth. Once you get used to the anarchy, it can be a fun way to get around.

There are also shops (p50) that rent out road bicycles and mountain bikes.

### CAR & MOTORCYCLE

Car hire is available through travel agencies, guesthouses and hotels in Phnom Penh. Everything from cars (from US$25) to 4WDs (from US$60) are available for travelling around the city, but prices rise fast once you venture beyond.

Exploring Phnom Penh and the surrounding areas on a motorbike is a very liberating experience if you are used to chaotic traffic conditions.

There are numerous motorbike hire places around town. A 100cc Honda costs US$4 to US$7 per day and 250cc dirt bikes run from US$12 to US$30 per day. You'll have to leave your passport – a driver's licence or other form of ID isn't enough. Remember you usually get what you pay for when choosing a bike.

A Cambodia licence isn't a bad idea if you'll be doing extensive riding. Motorbike rental shops get you one for about US$40. Otherwise you technically need an international licence to drive in Cambodia (although a small bribe gets you out of most infractions if you don't have one). If you want to purchase insurance (available at motorbike rental shops for about US$22 per month), you'll need an international or Cambodian licence. Remember to lock your bike, as motorbike theft is common.

**Harley Tours Cambodia** (Map p46; ☑ 012 948529; www.harleycambodia.com) For those looking for a little more muscle on the road, Harley Tours organise Harley rides around Phnom Penh, including overnighters to places like Kompong Cham or Kep. Day rental is available, but prices are similar to luxury-car rental back home.

## EXPRESS VANS FROM PHNOM PENH

| DESTINATION | DURATION (HR) | PRICE (US$) | COMPANIES | FREQUENCY |
|---|---|---|---|---|
| Battambang | 4½ | 10-12 | Golden Bayon, Mekong Express | several daily |
| Kampot | 2 | 8-9 | Giant Ibis, Kampot Express, Olympic Express | 3 daily |
| Kep | 2½ | 8 | Olympic Express | 7.15am, 1.30pm |
| Sen Monorom | 5½ | 11 | Kim Seng Express | 7am, 7.30am, 11am, 1.30pm |
| Siem Reap | 5 | 10-12 | Golden Bayon, Mekong Express, Mey Hong, Neak Krohorm, Olympic Express, Seila Angkor | 3-5 daily |
| Sihanoukville | 4 | 10-12 | CTT Net, Giant Ibis, Golden Bayon, Mekong Express, Mey Hong | 2-4 daily |

**Little Bikes** (Map p52; ☑ 017 329338; 97 St 154) High-quality trail bikes from US$18, and 125cc bikes for US$7/30 per day/week.

**Lucky! Lucky!** (Map p46; ☑ 023-212788; 413 Monivong Blvd) Motorbikes are US$4 to US$7 per day, less for multiple days. Trail bikes from US$12.

**Two Wheels Only** (Map p58; ☑ 012 200513; www.twocambodia.com; 34L St 368) Has well-maintained bikes available to rent (motorbike/trail bike US$25/5 per day).

**Vannak Bikes Rental** (Map p52; ☑ 012 220970; 46 St 130) Has high-performance trail bikes up to 600cc for US$15 to US$30 per day, and smaller motorbikes for US$5 to US$7.

### CYCLO

Travelling by *cyclo* (pedicab) is a more relaxing way to see the sights in the centre of town, although they don't work well for long distances. For a day of sightseeing, expect to pay around US$10 – find one on your own or negotiate a tour through the Cyclo Centre (p56). For short, one-way jaunts costs are similar to *moto* fares. You won't see many *cyclos* on the road late at night.

### MOTO

In areas frequented by foreigners, *moto* drivers generally speak English and sometimes a little French. Elsewhere around town it can be difficult to find anyone who understands where you want to go. Most short trips are about 2000r, although if you want to get from one end of the city to the other, you have to pay US$1 or more.

Cambodians never negotiate when taking rides (they just pay what they think is fair), but foreigners should always work out the price in advance, especially with *motodups* who hang out in touristy areas like the riverside or outside luxury hotels. Likewise, night owls taking a *moto* home from popular drinking holes should definitely negotiate to avoid an expensive surprise.

Many of the *moto* drivers who wait outside the popular guesthouses and hotels have good

English and are able to act as guides for a daily rate of about US$10 and up, depending on the destinations.

### REMORK-MOTO

Better known as *tuk tuks, remorks* are motorbikes with carriages and are the main way of getting around Phnom Penh for tourists. Average fares are about double those of *moto*: US$2 for short rides around the centre, US$3 and up for longer trips. *Remork* drivers will try to charge more for multiple passengers but don't let them; pay per ride not per person (although groups of four or should pay an extra US$1 or so).

### TAXI

At 3000r per kilometre, taxis are cheap, but don't expect to flag one down on the street. Call **Global Meter Taxi** (☑ 011 311888), **Choice Taxi** (☑ 023-888023, 010 888010) or **Taxi Vantha** (☑ 012 855000) for a pick-up.

## SHARE TAXIS FROM PHNOM PENH

| DESTINATION | PRICE (US$) | DURATION (HR) |
|---|---|---|
| Battambang | 55 | 4½ |
| Kampot | 35 | 3 |
| Kep | 40 | 3 |
| Koh Kong | 65 | 4½ |
| Kompong Cham | 35 | 2½ |
| Kompong Thom | 45 | 3 |
| Kratie | 50 | 5 |
| Pursat | 45 | 3 |
| Siem Reap | 70 | 5 |
| Sihanoukville | 50 | 4 |
| Takeo | 25 | 2 |
| Vietnam border | 50 | 3 |

# AROUND PHNOM PENH

There are several attractions around Phnom Penh that make good day trips. Koh Dach is the easiest trip and is best done by mountain bike, *moto* or *remork*. The other sights listed here are at least an hour by car and longer still by *moto* or *remork*.

The Angkorian temple of Tonlé Bati, Phnom Tamao Wildlife Rescue Centre and the hilltop pagoda of Phnom Chisor are near each other off NH2. You can easily combine two of these into one trip (all three might be a stretch). These can also be built into a journey south to either Takeo or Kep/Kampot.

Udong, once the capital of Cambodia, is a separate half-day trip and can be combined with a visit to Kompong Chhnang, known for being a 'genuine' Cambodian town. Kirirom National Park lies further afield, about halfway to Sihanoukville off NH4.

## Koh Dach                    កោះដាច់

Known as 'Silk Island' by foreigners, this is actually a pair of islands lying in the Mekong River about 5km northeast of the Japanese Friendship Bridge. They make for an easy, half-day DIY excursion for those who want to experience the 'real Cambodia'. The hustle and bustle of Phnom Penh feels light years away here.

The name derives from the preponderance of silk weavers who inhabit the islands. When you arrive by ferry, you'll undoubtedly be approached by one or more smiling women who speak a bit of English and will invite you to their house to observe weavers in action and – they hope – buy some *kramas*, sarongs or other silk items. If you are in the market for silk, you might follow them and have a look. Otherwise, feel free to smile back and politely decline their offer. You'll see plenty of weavers as you journey around the islands.

Other attractions include a few colourful modern temple complexes and rural scenery.

### ❶ Getting There & Around

*Remork* drivers offer half-day tours to Koh Dach; US$20 should cover it (less if you just want to be dropped off at the ferry), but they have been known to charge as much as US$40. The daily **boat tours** (per person US$10), departing at 8.30am, 9.30am and 1pm from the tourist boat dock in Phnom Penh (p84), are another option

(minimum four people). **Cambocruise** (☑ 092 290077; www.cambocruise.com; without/with lunch US$14/22) offers a daily trip to Koh Dach at 12.30pm with optional lunch, plus a free pick-up in town.

Otherwise, hire a mountain bike or motorbike and go it alone. Ferries cross the Mekong in three places and cost 500r per person, plus 500r per bike. The southernmost ferry crossing is the most convenient; it takes you to the larger, closer island. Cross the Japanese Bridge and follow NH6 for 4km, then turn right just before the Medical Supply Pharmaceutical Enterprise. You immediately hit a small dirt road that parallels the Mekong. Turn left and follow it north for about 500m until you see the ferry crossing.

Over on the larger island, you are just a short cycle ride to a bridge that links the two islands. The smaller island (technically named Koh Okhna Tey, or Mekong Island) has better infrastructure, including a paved main road; the larger island is more rustic and remote feeling, especially as you venture north.

## Udong                    ឧដុង្គ

Udong (literally, 'victorious') served as the capital of Cambodia under several sovereigns between 1618 and 1866, during which time 'victorious' was an optimistic epithet, as Cambodia was in near-terminal decline. A number of kings, including King Norodom, were crowned here. The main attractions today are the twin humps of **Phnom Udong** (ភ្នំឧដុង្គ), which have several stupas on them. Both ends of the ridge have good views of the Cambodian countryside, dotted with innumerable sugar palm trees.

The larger main ridge – the one you'll hit first if approaching from NH5 – is known as **Phnom Preah Reach Throap** (ភ្នំព្រះរាជទ្រព្យ; Hill of the Royal Fortune). It is so named because a 16th-century Khmer king is said to have hidden the national treasury here during a war with the Thais.

Ascending the main, monkey-lined north stairway from the parking area, the first structure you come to at the top of the ridge is a modern temple containing a relic of the Buddha, believed to be an eyebrow hair and fragments of teeth and bones. The relics were brazenly stolen in 2013 (though later recovered). Follow the path behind this stupa along the ridge and you'll come to a line of three large stupas. The first (northwesternmost) is **Damrei Sam Poan**, built by King Chey Chetha II (r 1618–26) to hold the ashes of his predecessor, King Soriyopor. The second stupa, **Ang Doung**, is decorated with coloured tiles; it was built in 1891 by King Norodom to house the ashes of his father, King Ang Duong (r 1845–59), but some say King Ang Duong was in fact buried next to the Silver Pagoda in Phnom Penh. The last stupa is **Mak Proum**, the final resting place of King Monivong (r 1927–41). Decorated with *garudas* (mythical half-man, half-bird creatures), floral designs and elephants, it has four faces on top.

Continuing along the path beyond Mak Proum, you'll pass a stone *vihara* with a cement roof and a seated Buddha inside (looking resplendent in a sailor's cap when we dropped in), then arrive at a clearing dotted by a gaggle of structures, including three small *vihara* and a stupa. The first *vihara* you come to is **Vihear Prak Neak**, its cracked walls topped with a tin roof. Inside this *vihara* is a seated Buddha who is guarded by a *naga* (*prak neak* means 'protected by a *naga*'). The second structure also has a seated Buddha inside. The third structure is **Vihear Preah Keo**, a cement-roofed structure that contains a statue of Preah Ko, the sacred bull; the original statue was carried away by the Thais long ago. Beyond this, near the stupa, red and black mountain lions guard the entrance to a modern brick-walled *vihara*.

Continue southeast along a lotus-flower-lined concrete path to the most impressive structure on Phnom Preah Reach Throap, **Vihear Preah Ath Roes**. The *vihara* and an enormous seated Buddha, dedicated in 1911 by King Sisowath, were blown up by the Khmer Rouge in 1977. The *vihara*, supported by eight enormous columns and topped by a soaring tin roof, was recently rebuilt, as was the 20m-high Buddha.

At the base of the main (northern) staircase leading up to Phnom Preah Reach Throap, near the restaurants, is a **memorial** to the victims of Pol Pot. It contains the bones of some of the people who were buried in approximately a hundred mass graves, each containing about a dozen bodies. Instruments of torture were unearthed along with the bones when a number of the pits were disinterred in 1981 and 1982. Just north of the memorial is a pavilion decorated with graphic murals depicting Khmer Rouge atrocities.

Southeast of Phnom Preah Reach Throap, the smaller ridge has two structures and several stupas on top. **Ta San Mosque** faces westward towards Mecca. Across the plains to the south of the mosque you can see **Phnom Vihear Leu**, a small hill on which a *vihara* (temple sanctuary) stands between two white poles. To the right of the *vihara* is a building used as a prison under Pol Pot's rule. To the left of the *vihara* and below it is a pagoda known as **Arey Ka Sap** (អារ៉ែយកៈស្រុប).

Phnom Udong really fills up with locals at weekends but is quiet during the week. Admission is free but myriad beggars and vendors will do their best to get money out of you.

## 🛏 Sleeping & Eating

The sprawling and impressive **Cambodia Vipassana Dhura Buddhist Meditation Centre** (✆ contact Mr Um Sovann 016 883090; www.cambodiavipassanacenter.com) is near the base of the western staircase up Phnom Preah Reach Throap. Foreigners are welcome to practise meditation here with experienced monks or nuns for one or several days. Meditation sessions are daily from 7am to 9pm and from 2pm to 5pm. In between you can hang out in the library, which contains scores of books on Buddhism (not to mention an impressive collection of pirated Lonely Planet books). The en suite guest rooms are fairly comfortable by monastic standards, albeit sans mattresses (wicker mats are as good as it gets). You'll be fed breakfast and lunch, but no dinner. There is no fixed price for a meditative retreat here, so donate according to your means; US$25 per day would be considered about average. Meditation sessions are free.

There are scores of food stalls around the bustling main parking area at the base of the northern staircase.

## ❶ Getting There & Away

Udong is 37km from the capital. Take a Phnom Penh Sorya bus bound for Kompong Chhnang (10,000r, one hour to Udong). It will drop you off at the access road to Phnom Udong, and from there it's 3km (4000r by *moto*). Other bus companies (p84) also make the trip to Udong. To return to Phnom Penh flag down a bus on NH5.

If going it alone, head north out of Phnom Penh on NH5 and turn left (south) at a prominent archway between the 36km and 37km markers.

A taxi for the day trip from Phnom Penh will cost around US$40. *Moto* drivers also run people to Udong for about US$15 or so for the day, but compared with the bus this isn't the most pleasant way to go, as the road is pretty busy and very dusty.

# Tonlé Bati ទន្លេបាទី

Tonlé Bati (admission US$3) is the collective name for a pair of old Angkorian-era temples and a popular lakeside picnic area. It's worth a detour if you are on the way to Phnom Tamao and Phnom Chisor. You can eat at one of many picnic restaurants here and rent an inner tube to float around the lake for 2000r. Just avoid Tonlé Bati at weekends, when it's mobbed by locals.

## ◉ Sights

### Ta Prohm HINDU TEMPLE

(តាព្រហ្ម) The laterite temple of Ta Prohm was built by King Jayavarman VII (r 1181–1219) on the site of a 6th-century Khmer shrine. The main sanctuary consists of five chambers, each containing a modern Buddha. The facades of the chambers contain intricate and well-preserved bas-reliefs. In the central chamber is a *linga* (phallic symbol) that shows signs of the destruction wrought by the Khmer Rouge.

### Yeay Peau HINDU TEMPLE

(យាយពៅ) Yeay Peau temple, named after King Prohm's mother, is 150m north of Ta Prohm in the grounds of a modern pagoda. Legend has it that Peau gave birth to a son, Prohm. When Prohm discovered his father was King Preah Ket Mealea, he set off to live with the king. After a few years, he returned to his mother but did not recognise her; taken by her beauty, asked her to become his wife. He refused to believe Peau's protests that she was his mother. To put off his advances, she suggested a contest to avoid the impending marriage. For the outcome of the contest, see p275.

## ❶ Getting There & Away

The access road heading to Tonlé Bati is signposted on the right on NH2, 33km south of Independence Monument in Phnom Penh. The entrance to the complex is 1.8km from the highway.

Most people hire private transport to get here. Figure on US$12/25 return for a *moto/remork* from Phnom Penh. Add US$5 to combine with

Phnom Tamao, and more still to throw Phnom Chisor into the mix.

Another option is to take a Takeo-bound Phnom Penh Sorya bus (four daily – aim for the 7am or the 10.30am) and jump off at the access road. Returning to Phnom Penh can be problematic, however. The best advice is to buy a ticket in advance on the Takeo–Phnom Penh bus. Otherwise, hire a *moto*.

# Phnom Tamao Wildlife Rescue Centre ភ្នំតាម៉ៅ (សួនសត្វ)

This wonderful wildlife sanctuary (adult/child US$5/2; ☉ 8am-5pm) for rescued animals is home to gibbons, sun bears, elephants, tigers, lions, deer, enormous pythons and a massive bird enclosure. They were all taken from poachers or abusive owners and receive care and shelter here as part of a sustainable breeding program. Wherever possible animals are released back into the wild once they have recovered. The centre operates breeding programs for a number of globally threatened species.

The sanctuary occupies a vast site south of the capital and its animals are kept in excellent conditions by Southeast Asian standards, with plenty of room to roam in enclosures that have been improved and expanded over the years with help from international wildlife NGOs. Spread out as it is, it feels like a zoo crossed with a safari park.

The centre is home to the world's largest captive collections of pileated gibbons and Malayan sun bears, as well as other rarities such as Siamese crocodiles and greater adjutant storks. Other popular enclosures include huge areas for the large tiger population, and there are elephants that sometimes take part in activities such as painting. You'll also find a walk-through area with macaques and deer, and a huge aviary.

Cambodia's wildlife is usually very difficult to spot, as larger mammals inhabit remote areas of the country, so Phnom Tamao is the perfect place to discover more about the incredible variety of animals in Cambodia. If you don't like zoos, you might not like this wildlife sanctuary, but remember that these animals have been rescued from traffickers and poachers and need a home. Visitors who come here will be doing their own small bit to help in the protection and survival of Cambodia's varied and wonderful wildlife.

##  Tours

**Free the Bears** TOUR
(Map p46; www.freethebears.org; per person US$70, groups of five or more each US$50) Free the Bears operates a 'Bear Keeper for a Day' program to allow students and adults with a genuine interest in wildlife a better understanding of the Asian black bear and Malayan sun bear. Participants have no contact with the bears, but spend the day behind the scenes of the Phnom Tamao sanctuary learning the ins and outs of caring for the 130-plus bears being looked after here. One- to 12-week volunteer positions are also available.

**Wildlife Tours** TOUR
(☑ 095 970175; www.wildlifealliance.org; minimum donation US$150) Wildlife Alliance has created an exciting, full-day interactive tour to raise funds for Phnom Tamao. Donors get to interact with a variety of rescued animals, including elephants, macaques and gibbons, and get up close with tigers, crocodiles and what is possibly the world's only captive hairy-nosed otter. All proceeds go towards the rescue and care of wildlife at Phnom Tamao.

Tours include walks with elephants in the forest and you get to feed various baby animals in the sanctuary's nursery, which is normally off-limits to the public.

**Betelnut Jeep Tours** TOUR
(Map p52; ☑ 012 619924; www.betelnuttours. com; per person US$40) Betelnut Jeep Tours offers guided open-top jeep trips to Phnom Tamao from Tuesday to Saturday, departing at 9.45am from the Lazy Gecko Guesthouse (p60) in Phnom Penh. The price includes admission, lunch and a *krama* to protect against the elements.

### ❶ Getting There & Away

The access road to Phnom Tamao is clearly signposted on the right, 6.5km south of the turnoff to Tonlé Bati on NH2. The sanctuary is 5km from the highway on an incredibly dusty road lined with elderly beggars. If coming by bus ask to be let off at the turnoff, where *motos* await to whisk you to the sanctuary.

## Phnom Chisor ភ្នំជីសូរ

A **temple** (admission US$2) from the Angkorian era, Phnom Chisor is set upon a solitary hill in Takeo Province, offering superb views of the countryside. Try to get to Phnom Chisor early in the morning or late in the afternoon, as it is an uncomfortable climb in the heat of the midday sun.

The main temple stands on the eastern side of the hilltop. Constructed of laterite and brick with carved sandstone lintels, the complex is surrounded by the partially ruined walls of a 2.5m-wide gallery with windows. Inscriptions found here date from the 11th century, when this site was known as Suryagiri.

On the plain to the west of Phnom Chisor are the sanctuaries of **Sen Thmol** (just below Phnom Chisor), **Sen Ravang** and the former sacred pond of **Tonlé Om**. All three of these features form a straight line from Phnom Chisor in the direction of Angkor. During rituals held here 900 years ago, the king, his Brahmans and their entourage would climb a monumental 400 steps to Suryagiri from this direction.

If you haven't got the stamina for an overland adventure to Preah Vihear or Phnom Bayong (near Takeo), this is the next best thing for a temple with a view. Near the main temple is a modern Buddhist *vihara* that is used by resident monks.

### ❶ Getting There & Away

Phnom Chisor lies about 55km south of Phnom Penh. The eastward-bound access road to Phnom Chisor is signposted (in Khmer) on the left, 12km south of the Phnom Tamao turnoff on NH2. The temple is 4.5km from the highway and *motos* wait at the turnoff. To get here follow the directions for Tonlé Bati and Phnom Tamao, adding a few dollars more if you are hiring private transport.

## Kirirom National Park
ឧទ្យានជាតិគិរីរម្យ

You can really get away from it all at this lush, elevated **park** (admission US$5) a two-hour drive southwest of Phnom Penh. Winding trails lead through pine forests to cascading wet-season waterfalls and cliffs with amazing views of the Cardamom Mountains, and there's some great mountain-biking to be done if you're feeling adventurous.

From the NH4 highway it's 10km on a sealed road to a small village near the park entrance. From the village you have two choices: the left fork takes you 50m to the park entrance and then 17km up a fairly steep sealed road to the unmanned Kirirom Information Centre inside the park proper; the right fork takes you 10km along the perimeter of the park on a dirt road to Chambok commune, the site of an excellent community based eco-tourism (CBET; ☑ 012 698529; mlup@online.com.kh; adult/child US$3/1) program. These are two vastly different experiences, and they are nowhere near each other, so it's recommended to devote a day to each.

## Protected Area

Up in the actual national park, you'll find myriad walking trails and dirt roads that lead to small wet-season waterfalls, lakes, wats and abandoned buildings, but you'll need a map or a guide to navigate them. There's a great map of the park trails and roads made by a Phnom Penh–based mountain bike enthusiast if you can track down a copy.

Mr Mik (☑ 015 810271) is a park ranger and guide who can usually be found at the barbecue shacks near the busy main parking area, about 500m northeast of the information centre. For US$10 he can take you on a two-hour hike up to Phnom Dat Chivit (End of Life Mountain), where an abrupt cliff face offers an unbroken view of the Elephant Mountains and Cardamom Mountains to the west.

## Chambok Commune

The main attraction at the Chambok CBET site is a 4km hike to a series of three waterfalls (no guide required). The second waterfall has a swimming hole; the third one is an impressive 40m high. Bikes are available for US$1.50 but won't get you very far as the trail deteriorates fairly quickly. Other attractions include traditional ox-cart rides, a bat cave and guided nature walks (guides cost US$15 per day).

## 🛏 Sleeping & Eating

**Chambok Homestays** HOMESTAY $
(☑ 012 938920; per person US$3, home-cooked meals each US$3) Multiple homestays are available in Chambok commune proper as part of the CBET program.

**Romantic Waterfall & Cafe** GUESTHOUSE $
(☑ 012 733694; www.romantic-cafe.org; r US$8) About 1km south of Chambok commune, Romantic has a few basic rooms and a Khmer restaurant, but be sure to pre-order.

⭐ **vKirirom Pine Resort** RESORT $$
(☑ 078 777384; www.vkirirom.com; camping US$20, r US$50-230; 🌐@🛜) A smart, Japanese-run resort that has a dizzying array of rooms, including slightly surreal circular-pipe rooms, some impressively simple, open-plan Khmer cottages made of rattan, and luxurious bungalows with all the trimmings. There's an attractive open-plan restaurant here, which is the best lunch stop for day-trippers to the park.

**Kirirom Mountain Lodge** GUESTHOUSE $$
(☑ 092 490216; www.kirirom.asia; r weekday/weekend US$40/65; 🌐🛜) This long-running guesthouse has been given a makeover by the hotel group behind the Plantation in Phnom Penh. Rooms are simple but stylish and there's a good restaurant serving a mix of French, Moroccan and Asian flavours. With only six rooms you can rent the whole place for US$200 if you want to party amid the pines.

**Kirirom Hillside Resort** RESORT $$
(☑ 016 303888; www.kiriromresort.com; room/bungalow from US$50/65; 🌐🛜🏊) Located beneath the park, this place has attractive Scandinavian-style bungalows, some with glorious balconies overlooking a small lake, dotting the sprawling grounds. There's a nice pool, a hit-or-miss restaurant, a zoo and even a plastic dinosaur park. Beware: advertised services like horse riding, wi-fi and mountain-bike rental are rarely available.

## ⓘ Getting There & Away

Kirirom National Park is accessed from the village of Treng Trayern, which straddles the NH4 87km southwest of Phnom Penh and 139km northeast of Sihanoukville. A taxi from either city is about US$60; or have a bus drop you off at the turnoff in Treng Trayern, where *motos* demand a stiff US$5 per person to get you to the entrance (a bit more to Chambok commune, and still more to ascend into the park proper). Travelling under your own steam is highly recommended.

# Siem Reap

🎵 063 / POP 175,000 (TOWN) / AREA 10,299 SQ KM (PROVINCE)

### Best Places to Eat

➜ Cuisine Wat Damnak (p115)

➜ Flow (p114)

➜ Haven (p108)

➜ Marum (p108)

➜ Mie Cafe (p114)

### Best Places to Stay

➜ Ivy Guesthouse 2 (p104)

➜ La Résidence d'Angkor (p105)

➜ Sala Lodges (p107)

➜ Soria Moria Hotel (p106)

➜ Viroth's Hotel (p106)

## Why Go?

The life-support system for the temples of Angkor, Siem Reap (*see*-em ree-*ep*; សៀមរាប) was always destined for great things. It has reinvented itself as the epicentre of chic Cambodia, with everything from backpacker party pads to hip hotels, world-class wining and dining, and sumptuous spas.

This is good news for the long-suffering Khmers riding the wave, but it can make the town a little bling in places. While it's not exactly authentic, just a short distance away lies Siem Reap Province and the real Cambodia of rural beauty. Explore floating villages and rare-bird sanctuaries or just cycle (or quad bike or pony trek) through the paddies as an antidote to the bustle of town.

Angkor is a place to be savoured, not rushed, and this is the base from which to plan your adventures. Still think three days at the temples is enough? Think again, with Siem Reap on the doorstep.

## When to Go
### Siem Reap

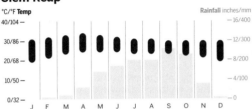

**Nov–Mar** To dodge crowds, avoid peak season. There's a Giant Puppet Parade in February.

**Apr & May** Shockingly hot, making exploring hard work and the countryside barren.

**Jun–Oct** Wet season. The town centre may be under water for several days in October.

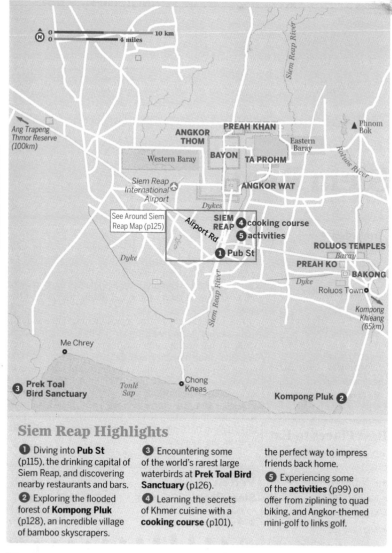

## Siem Reap Highlights

**1** Diving into **Pub St** (p115), the drinking capital of Siem Reap, and discovering nearby restaurants and bars.

**2** Exploring the flooded forest of **Kompong Pluk** (p128), an incredible village of bamboo skyscrapers.

**3** Encountering some of the world's rarest large waterbirds at **Prek Toal Bird Sanctuary** (p126).

**4** Learning the secrets of Khmer cuisine with a **cooking course** (p101),

the perfect way to impress friends back home.

**5** Experiencing some of the **activities** (p99) on offer from ziplining to quad biking, and Angkor-themed mini-golf to links golf.

## History

Siem Reap was little more than a village when French explorers discovered Angkor in the 19th century. With the return of Angkor to Cambodian – or should that be French – control in 1907, Siem Reap began to grow, absorbing the first wave of tourists. The Grand Hotel d'Angkor opened its doors in 1932 and the temples of Angkor remained one of Asia's leading draws until the late 1960s, luring luminaries such as Charlie Chaplin and Jackie Kennedy. With the

advent of war and the Khmer Rouge, Siem Reap entered a long slumber from which it only began to awaken in the mid-1990s.

Tourism is the lifeblood of Siem Reap and, without careful management, it could become Siem Reapolinos, the not-so-Costa-del-Culture of Southeast Asia. However, there are promising signs that developers are learning from the mistakes that have blighted other regional hot spots, with restrictions on hotel height and bus size. Either way, Angkor is centre stage on the world travel map right now, and there's no going back for its supply line, Siem Reap.

## ◉ Sights

Visitors come to Siem Reap to see the temples of Angkor. The sights in and around the town pale in comparison, but they are a good diversion for those who find themselves templed out after a few days. That said, some of the best sights are...yet more temples. The modern pagodas around Siem Reap offer an interesting contrast to the ancient sandstone structures of Angkor.

You'll find even more attractions just outside town in Siem Reap Province, including up and coming Banteay Srei District (p124) and the floating villages (p127) of the Tonlé Sap Lake. And don't forget to include a visit to the Angkor Centre for Conservation of Biodiversity (p166) out near Kbal Spean, one of the more remote Angkorian sites.

★ **Angkor National Museum**　　MUSEUM
(សារមន្ទីរអង្គរ; Map p96; ☏ 063-966601; www.angkornationalmuseum.com; 968 Charles de Gaulle Blvd; adult/child under 1.2m US$12/6; ⊙ 8.30am-6pm, to 6.30pm 1 Oct-30 Apr) Looming large on the road to Angkor is the Angkor National Museum, a state-of-the-art showpiece on the Khmer civilisation and the majesty of Angkor. Displays are themed by era, religion and royalty as visitors move through the impressive galleries. After a short presentation, visitors enter the Zen-like 'Gallery of a Thousand Buddhas', which has a fine collection of images. Other exhibits include the pre-Angkorian periods of Funan and Chenla; the great Khmer kings; Angkor Wat; Angkor Thom; and the inscriptions.

Exhibits include touch-screen video, epic commentary and the chance to experience a panoramic sunrise at Angkor Wat, though there seems to be less sculpture on display here than in the National Museum (p42) in Phnom Penh. The US$12 admission fee is a little high, given that US$20 buys admission to all the temples at Angkor. That said, it remains a very useful experience for first-time visitors, putting the story of Angkor and the Khmer empire in context before exploring the temples. An audio tour is available for US$3.

**Artisans Angkor –**
**Les Chantiers Écoles**　　ARTS CENTRE
(អា ទីសង់អង្គរ; Map p96; www.artisansdangkor.com; ⊙ 7.30am-6.30pm) 🏷 FREE Siem Reap is the epicentre of the drive to revitalise Cambodian traditional culture, which was dealt a harsh blow by the Khmer Rouge and the years of instability that followed its rule. Les Chantiers Écoles teaches wood- and stone-carving techniques, traditional silk painting, lacquerware and other artisan skills to impoverished young Cambodians. Free guided tours explaining traditional techniques are available daily from 7.30am to 6.30pm. Tucked down a side road, the school is well signposted from Sivatha St.

On the premises the school runs a beautiful shop called Artisans Angkor (p118), which sells everything from stone and wood reproductions of Angkorian-era statues to household furnishings. There's also a second shop opposite Angkor Wat in the Angkor Cafe building, and outlets at Phnom Penh and Siem Reap international airports. All the profits go back into funding the school and bringing more young Cambodians into the training program, which is 20% owned by the artisans themselves.

Les Chantiers Écoles also maintains a silk farm (⊙ 7.30am-5.30pm), which produces some of the best work in the country, including clothing, interior-design products and accessories. All stages of the production

SIEM REAP SIGHTS

---

### SIEM REAP FOR CHILDREN

Siem Reap is a great city for children thanks to the range of activities on offer beyond the temples. A temple visit may appeal to older children, particularly the Indiana Jones atmosphere found at Ta Prohm and Beng Mealea, the sheer size and scale of Angkor Wat, and the weird faces at the Bayon.

Other activities include boat trips on the Tonlé Sap to visit other-worldly villages (p127), swimming (p99) at a hotel or resort, ziplining (p98) in the jungle, exploring the countryside on horseback or quad bike (p101), goofing around at the Cambodian Cultural Village (p98), playing mini-golf at the Angkor Wat Putt (p99), exploring the Banteay Srei Butterfly Centre (p124) or just enjoying the cafes and restaurants of Siem Reap at a leisurely pace. Ice-cream shops will be popular, if a little naughty, while the local barbecue restaurants are always enjoyably interactive for older children.

# Siem Reap

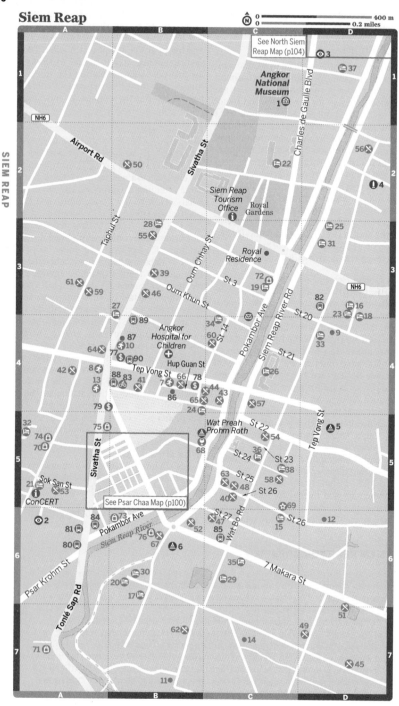

See North Siem Reap Map (p104)

0 — 400 m
0 — 0.2 miles

NH6

Airport Rd

Sivatha St

Charles de Gaulle Blvd

Angkor National Museum

Taphul St

Siem Reap Tourism Office

Royal Gardens

Oum Chhay St

Royal Residence

St 3

Oum Khun St

NH6

St 20

Pokambor Ave

Siem Reap River Rd

Angkor Hospital for Children

St 14

St 21

Hup Guan St

Tep Vong St

Wat Preah Prohm Roth

St 22

Tep Vong St

St 24

St 23

See Psar Chaa Map (p100)

Sivatha St

St 25

St 26

Sok San St

ConCERT

Pokambor Ave

Wat Bo Rd

St 27

St 26

Siem Reap River

7 Makara St

Psar Krohm St

Tonlé Sap Rd

# Siem Reap

## ◎ Top Sights
1 Angkor National Museum.......................C1

## ◎ Sights
2 Artisans Angkor – Les Chantiers
   Écoles .........................................A6
3 Khmer Ceramics Centre..................D1
4 Miniature Replicas of Angkor's
   Temples ....................................D2
5 Wat Bo................................................D5
6 Wat Dam Nak ...................................B6

## ✦ Activities, Courses & Tours
7 Frangipani Spa .......................................B4
   Grasshopper Adventures ........... (see 48)
8 Helistar.............................................A4
9 KKO (Khmer for Khmer
   Organisation) Bike Tours.................D4
   KKO Countryside Moto Tour.........(see 9)
10 Lemongrass Garden Spa......................B4
11 Quad Adventure Cambodia..................B7
12 Sam Veasna Center...............................D6
13 Seeing Hands Massage 4 .....................A4
14 Siem Reap Quad Bike Adventure .........C7

## 🛏 Sleeping
15 Angkor Village ........................................C6
16 Babel Guesthouse ................................D3
17 Downtown Siem Reap Hostel................B6
18 European Guesthouse ...........................D3
19 FCC Angkor ...........................................C3
20 Golden Banana B&B...............................B6
21 Golden Temple Villa...............................A5
22 Grand Hotel d'Angkor ...........................C2
23 Happy Guesthouse.................................D3
24 Ivy Guesthouse 2 ..................................B4
25 La Noria Guesthouse.............................D3
26 La Résidence d'Angkor ..........................C4
27 Mad Monkey ..........................................B3
28 Memoire d'Angkor Boutique Hotel.......B3
29 Petit Villa Boutique ...............................C6
30 Rambutan Resort ..................................B6
31 Rosy Guesthouse...................................D3
32 Secrets Pavilion .....................................A5
33 Seven Candles Guesthouse ..................D4
34 Shinta Mani............................................C4
35 Siem Reap Hostel ..................................C6
36 Soria Moria Hotel...................................C5
37 Velkommen Guesthouse .......................D1
38 Viroth's Hotel.........................................C5

## 🍴 Eating
39 Angkor Market .......................................B3
   Armand's........................................(see 78)
40 Banllé Vegetarian Restaurant...............C5
41 Blossom Cafe .........................................B4
42 Bugs Cafe...............................................A4
43 Chanrey Tree..........................................C4
44 Common Grounds..................................C4
45 Cuisine Wat Damnak..............................D7
46 Curry Walla ............................................B3
47 Embassy..................................................C6

FCC Angkor .....................................(see 19)
48 Flow........................................................C5
49 Haven.....................................................D7
50 Japanese Restaurant Genkiya...............B2
   Jungle Burger..................................(see 48)
51 Kanell......................................................D7
52 King's Road ............................................B6
53 Kuriosity Kafe ........................................A5
54 Le Café ...................................................C5
55 Lucky Market ..........................................B3
56 Marum.....................................................D2
57 Moloppor Cafe .......................................C4
58 Pages Cafe .............................................C5
59 Sala Bai Hotel & Restaurant School .....A3
60 Siem Reap Brewpub ..............................C4
61 Sugar Palm .............................................A3
62 Tangram Garden .....................................B7
63 Temple Coffee & Bakery ........................C5
64 The Glasshouse .....................................A4
65 The Hive Siem Reap................................B4
66 The Little Red Fox Espresso ..................B4
67 Wat Damnak BBQs.................................B6

## 🍷 Drinking & Nightlife
68 Barcode..................................................B5
   Nest................................................(see 27)

## ✪ Entertainment
69 Apsara Theatre.......................................C5
   La Noria Restaurant.......................(see 25)
   Plae Pakaa......................................(see 2)

## 🛍 Shopping
70 Angkor Night Market .............................A5
   Artisans Angkor..............................(see 2)
71 IKTT........................................................A7
72 McDermott Gallery.................................C3
73 Monument Books....................................B6
74 Nyemo.....................................................A5
75 Rajana.....................................................A5
   Samatoa ..........................................(see 48)
76 Siem Reap Art Center............................B6

## ℹ Information
77 ABA Bank................................................B4
78 ANZ Royal Bank......................................B4
79 Canadia Bank.........................................A4

## ℹ Transport
80 Giant Ibis...............................................A6
81 Gold VIP.................................................A6
82 Golden Bayon Express...........................D3
83 Green e-bikes.........................................B4
84 GST.........................................................A6
85 Hang Tep................................................C6
86 Helicopters Cambodia...........................B4
87 Helistar...................................................B4
88 Mekong Express ....................................B4
89 Nattakan.................................................B4
90 Orient Express 1907..............................B4
   Sapaco Transport .........................(see 81)
   Virak Buntham...............................(see 84)

## FLIGHT OF THE GIBBON ANGKOR

Angkor provides the ultimate backdrop for a zipline experience, although you won't actually see the temples while navigating the course. **Flight of the Gibbon Angkor** (Map p130; ☑096 999 9101; www.treetopasia.com; near Ta Nei Temple, Angkor; per person US$109; ☺7am-5pm) is located inside the Angkor protected area and the course includes 10 ziplines, 21 treetop platforms, four skybridges and an abseil finish. There is a panoramic refreshment stop at the halfway stage and highlights include a tandem line for couples.

Safety is a priority and high-flyers are permanently clipped to lines via karabiners, with clear English instruction throughout. There is also a conservation element to the project, with a pair of gibbons released in the surrounding forest and a plan for more introductions in the future. The price includes transfer to any Siem Reap hotel, plus lunch before or after the trip near Sra Srang. Located near Ta Nei temple, it's a great addition to the activities on offer around Siem Reap and Angkor. Watch a Lonely Planet YouTube video of the experience at www.youtube.com/watch?v=UJzEtKoITrg.

process can be seen here, from the cultivation of mulberry trees to the nurturing of silk worms to the dyeing and weaving of silk. Free tours are available daily and there is a free shuttle bus departing from Les Chantiers Écoles in Siem Reap at 9.30am and 1.30pm. The farm is about 16km west of Siem Reap, just off the road to Sisophon in the village of Puok.

**Cambolac** ARTS CENTRE
(ខេមបូឡាក់; Map p125; ☑097 843 1790; www.cambolac.com; ☺8-11.30am & 1-5pm Mon-Sat) **FREE** Cambodia has a long tradition of producing beautiful lacquerware, although the years of upheaval resulted in some of the skills being forgotten. Cambolac is a social enterprise helping restore Cambodia's lacquer tradition and create a new contemporary scene. You can tour the workshop to learn more about the perfectionist approach required to produce a piece of lacquerware. Most of the guides are hearing-impaired and a tour allows some great interaction and the opportunity to learn some basic sign commands.

It's a worthy cause with some beautiful handmade souvenirs for sale. Shops around town are open from 9.30am to 10.30pm.

**Khmer Ceramics Centre** ARTS CENTRE
(មជ្ឈមណ្ឌលស្មាតខ្មែរ; Map p96; ☑017 843014; www.khmerceramics.com; Charles de Gaulle Blvd; ☺8am-7.30pm) ∅ Located on the road to the temples, this ceramics centre is dedicated to reviving the Khmer tradition of pottery, which was an intricate art during the time of Angkor. It's possible to visit and try your hand at the potter's wheel, and courses in traditional techniques are available for US$20, including pottery and ceramic painting.

Free tours are available, including information on Angkorian techniques and a new kiln museum. There is also a walk-in shop in Alley West.

**House of Peace Association** GALLERY
(សមាគមនិផ្ទះសន្តិភាព; Map p125; Airport Road; ☺9am-6pm) The creation of leather *sbei tuoi* (shadow puppets) is a traditional Khmer art form, and the figures make a memorable souvenir. Characters include gods and demons from the *Reamker*, as well as exquisite elephants with intricate armour. The House of Peace Association, about 4km down NH6 on the way to the airport, makes and sells these puppets; small pieces start at US$15, while larger ones can be as much as US$150.

**Miniature Replicas of Angkor's Temples** SCULPTURE GARDEN
(គំរូចម្លងប្រាសាទអង្គរវត្ត; Map p96; 16 Slokram District; admission US$2; ☺9am-5pm) One of the more quirky places in town is the garden of local master sculptor Dy Proeung, which houses miniature replicas of Angkor Wat, the Bayon, Banteay Srei and other temples. It is the bluffer's way to get an aerial shot of Angkor without chartering a helicopter, although the astute might question the presence of oversized insects in the shot. There is also a display of scale miniatures at Preah Ko Temple.

**Cambodian Cultural Village** CULTURAL CENTRE
(ភូមិវប្បធម៌កម្ពុជា; Map p125; ☑063-963836; www.cambodianculturalvillage.com; Airport Rd; adult/child under 1.1m US$9/free; ☺8am-7pm) It may be kitsch, it may be kooky, but it's very popular with Cambodians and provides a diversion for families travelling with children. This is the Cambodian Cul-

tural Village, which tries to represent all of Cambodia in a whirlwind tour of re-created houses and villages. The visit begins with a wax museum and includes homes of the Cham, Chinese, Kreung and Khmer people, as well as miniature replicas of landmark buildings in Cambodia.

There are dance shows and performances throughout the day, but it still doesn't add up to much for most foreign visitors, unless they have the kids in tow. It's located about midway between Siem Reap and the airport.

**War Museum** MUSEUM
(សារមន្ទីរប្រវត្តិសាស្ត្រសង្គ្រាម; Map p125; ☑ 097 457 8666; www.warmuseumcambodia.com; Kaksekam Village; incl guide US$5) The unique selling point here is that the museum encourages visitors to handle the old weapons, from an AK-47 right through to a rocket launcher. We are not sure what health and safety think about it, but it makes for a good photo op. Other war junk includes Soviet-era T-54 tanks and MiG-19 fighters.

**Wat Bo** BUDDHIST TEMPLE
(វត្តបូ; Map p96; Tep Vong St; ⏱ 6am-6pm) This is one of the town's oldest temples and has a collection of well-preserved wall paintings from the late 19th century depicting the *Reamker,* Cambodia's interpretation of the *Ramayana.*

**Wat Preah Inkosei** BUDDHIST TEMPLE
(វត្តព្រះឥន្ទកោសិយ៍; Map p104; ⏱ 6am-6pm) This wat, north of town, is built on the site of an early Angkorian brick temple, which still stands today at the rear of the compound.

**Wat Athvea** BUDDHIST TEMPLE
(វត្តអធ្វា; Map p130; ⏱ 6am-6pm) South of the city centre, Wat Athvea is an attractive pagoda on the site of an ancient temple. The old temple is still in very good condition and sees far fewer visitors than the main temples in the Angkor area, making it a peaceful spot in the late afternoon.

**Wat Thmei** BUDDHIST TEMPLE
(វត្តថ្មី; Map p125; ⏱ 6am-6pm) Wat Thmei has a small memorial stupa containing the skulls and bones of victims of the Khmer Rouge. It also has plenty of young monks eager to practise their English.

**Wat Dam Nak** BUDDHIST TEMPLE
(វត្ត ដំណាក់; Map p96; ⏱ 6am-6pm) Formerly a royal palace during the reign of King Sisowath, hence the name *dam nak* (palace),

today Wat Dam Nak is home to the Centre for Khmer Studies (www.khmerstudies. org), an independent institution promoting a greater understanding of Khmer culture with a drop-in research library on site.

## 🏃 Activities

There is an incredible array of activities on offer in Siem Reap, ranging from predictable swimming pools, spa centres and golf courses right through to less predictable ziplining, horse riding, quad biking and an Angkor-themed mini-golf course.

It's hot work clambering about the temples and there's no better way to wind down than with a dip in a swimming pool. You can pay by the day for use of the pool and/ or gym at most hotels; prices range from just US$5 at some of the midrange hotels to US$20 at the five-star palaces. More and more of the cheaper hotels and resorts are putting in pools and this can be a worthwhile splash for weary travellers. Locals like to swim in the waters of the Western Baray at the weekend.

**The Great Escape** CHALLENGE
(Map p125; ☑ 063-506 9777; www.greatescape cambodia.com; C-39 Angkor Shopping Arcade, Airport Rd; per person US$18-25) Escape the room in 60 minutes using only your wits. That's the premise of The Great Escape, Siem Reap's answer to the Crystal Maze. Try the Warehouse of Jack Travis, an Angkor-themed mystery.

### Golf

**Angkor Golf Resort** GOLF
(Map p125; ☑ 063-761139; www.angkor-golf.com; green fees US$115) This world-class course was designed by British golfer Nick Faldo. Fees rise to US$175 with clubs, caddies, carts and all.

**Angkor Wat Putt** GOLF
(☑ 012 302330; www.angkorwatputt.com; adult/ child US$5/4; ⏱ 7.30am-10pm) Crazy golf to the Brits among us, this home-grown mini-golf course contrasts with the big golf courses out of town. Navigate mini temples and creative obstacles for 14 holes. Win a beer for a hole-in-one.

**Phokheetra Country Club** GOLF
(☑ 063-964600; www.sofitel.com; green fees US$100) This club hosts a tournament on the Asian tour annually and includes an ancient Angkor bridge amid its manicured fairways and greens.

# Psar Chaa

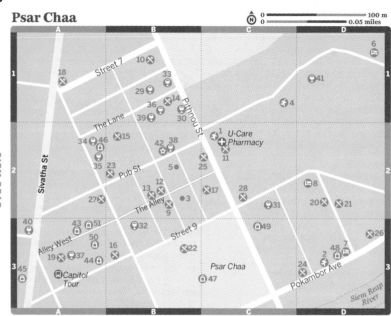

# Psar Chaa

SIEM REAP

## Horse Riding

**Happy Ranch** HORSE RIDING
(Map p125; ☑ 012 920002; www.thehappyranch.
com; 1hr/half-day US$28/59) Forget the Wild
West – try your hand at horse riding in the
Wild East. Happy Ranch offers the chance
to explore Siem Reap on horseback, taking
in surrounding villages and secluded temples. This is a calm way to experience the
countryside, far from the traffic and crowds.
Popular rides take in Wat Athvea (p99), a
modern pagoda with an ancient temple on
its grounds, and Wat Chedi, a temple set on
a flood plain near the Tonlé Sap lake. Riding
lessons are available for children and begin-
ners. Book direct for the best prices.

## Massage & Spas

Foot massages are a big hit in Siem Reap –
not surprising given all those steep stair-
ways at the temples. There are half a dozen
or more places offering a massage for about
US$6 to US$8 an hour on the strip running
northwest of Psar Chaa. Some are more authentic than others, so dip your toe in first
before selling your sole.

For an alternative foot massage, brave the
waters of Dr Fish: you dip your feet into a
paddling pool full of cleaner-fish, who nibble
away at your dead skin. It's heaven for some,
tickly for others. The original is housed in
the Angkor Night Market, but copycats have
sprung up all over town, including a dozen
or so tanks around Pub St and Psar Chaa.

**Bodia Spa** SPA
(Map p100; ☑ 063-761593; www.bodia-spa.com;
Pithnou St; ☺10am-midnight) Sophisticated
spa near Psar Chaa offering a full range of
scrubs, rubs and natural remedies, including
its own line of herbal products.

**Bodytune** SPA
(Map p100; ☑ 063-764141; www.bodytune.co.th;
293 Pokambor Ave; ☺10am-10pm) A lavish outpost of a popular Thai spa, this is a fine place
to relax and unwind on the riverfront.

**Frangipani Spa** SPA
(Map p96; ☑ 063-964391; www.frangipanisiem
reap.com; 615 Hup Guan St; ☺10am-10pm) This
delightful hideaway offers massages and a
whole range of spa treatments.

**Krousar Thmey** MASSAGE
(Map p104; www.krousar-thmey.org; Charles de
Gaulle Blvd; massage US$7) 🖉 Massages here are
performed by blind masseurs. In the same location is the free Tonlé Sap Exhibition, which

includes a 'Seeing in the Dark' interactive exhibition exploring what it is like to be blind,
guided by a sight-impaired student.

**Lemongrass Garden Spa** SPA
(Map p96; ☑ 012 387385; www.lemongrass
garden.com; 105B Sivatha St; ☺11am-11pm)
Smart spa in a central location, offering a
range of affordable treatments.

**Seeing Hands Massage 4** MASSAGE
(Map p96; ☑ 012 836487; 324 Sivatha St; fan/
air-con per hr US$5/7) 🖉 Seeing Hands trains
blind people in the art of massage. Watch
out for copycats, as some of these are just
exploiting the blind for profit.

## Quad Biking

**Cambodia Quad Bike** ADVENTURE TOUR
(Map p125; ☑ 012 893447; www.cambodiaquadbike.
com; 1hr/half day US$30/100) Quad-bike tours
around the Siem Reap countryside, including sunrise and sunset options.

**Quad Adventure Cambodia** ADVENTURE TOUR
(Map p96; ☑ 092-787216; www.quad-adventure-
cambodia.com; sunset ride US$30, full day US$170)
The original quad-bike operator in town.
Rides around Siem Reap involve rice fields
at sunset, pretty temples, and back roads
through traditional villages.

**Siem Reap Quad
Bike Adventure** ADVENTURE TOUR
(Map p96; ☑ 012 324009; www.srquadbiking
adventure.com; 1hr US$30, with 1 child US$40)
A locally owned ATV company with fully
automatic quad bikes.

## Yoga & Meditation

**Peace Cafe Yoga** YOGA
(Map p104; ☑ 063-965210; www.peacecafeangkor.
org; Siem Reap River Rd; per session US$6) This
popular community centre-cum-cafe has
daily yoga sessions at 8.30am and 6.30pm,
including ashtanga and hatha sessions.

## ✎ Courses

Cooking classes have really taken off in Siem
Reap with a number of restaurants and
hotels, including many of the top-end places,
now offering an introduction to the secrets
of Cambodian cooking.

**Cambodian Cooking Cottage** COOKING COURSE
(Map p100; ☑ 077 566455; www.restaurant-siem
reap.com; Champey Restaurant, The Alley; per person US$25) This sophisticated cooking class
includes tips on decorative presentation, rec-
ipe book, a DVD and some take-away spices.

### Cooks in Tuk Tuks
COOKING COURSE

(Map p104; ☑ 063-963400; www.therivergarden.
info; River Rd West; per person US$25) Starts at
10am daily with a visit to Psar Leu market,
then returns to the River Garden for a professional class.

### Le Tigre de Papier
COOKING COURSE

(Map p100; ☑ 012 265811; www.angkor-cooking-
class-cambodia.com; Pub St; per person US$14)
✎ Daily classes are held at 10am and 1pm
in English, and at 5pm in French. Classes
include a visit to the market.

### Vegetarian Cooking Class
COOKING COURSE

(Map p104; ☑ 092 177127; peacecafeangkor.org;
Siem Reap River Rd; per person US$20) A vege-
tarian cooking class with tofu amok, papaya
salad and vegie spring rolls.

## ☞ Tours

Most visitors are in Siem Reap to tour the
temples of Angkor, but not all operators are
created equal. Be sure to ask around before
booking. Non-temple tours include two-
wheeled adventures on bicycles or motorbikes, as well as some foodie tours.

### Tours To & Around Angkor

#### Beyond
TOUR

(www.beyonduniqueescapes.com) ✎ Responsible operator offering tours to Beng Mealea
and Kompong Pluk plus cycling trips and
cooking classes.

#### Buffalo Trails
TOUR

(☑ 012 297506; www.buffalotrails-cambodia.
com) ✎ Ecotours and lifestyle adventures
around Siem Reap.

#### Indochine Exploration
TOUR

(www.indochineex.com) ✎ Me Chrey kayaking
and remote temple tours.

#### Terre Cambodge
TOUR

(☑ 077 448255; www.terrecambodge.com) Tours
to remote sites around Angkor, bicycle tours,
and boat trips on the Tonlé Sap lake.

### Cycling Tours

The beautiful countryside around Siem
Reap is perfect for two-wheeled adventures.

#### Camouflage
BICYCLE TOUR

(Map p100; ☑ 012 884909; www.camouflage
cambodia.com; 37 New St A; tours US$25-85) This
specialist cycling operator has a range of 10
tours taking in temples, remote sites and the
beautiful countryside. Choose from gentle

family rides to challenging Phnom Kulen
and Beng Mealea adventures.

#### Grasshopper Adventures
BICYCLE TOUR

(Map p96; ☑ 012 462165; www.grasshopper
adventures.com; 586 St 26; per person from US$39)
Rides around the Siem Reap countryside,
plus a dedicated temple tour on two wheels
and a long-distance trip to Beng Mealea.

#### KKO (Khmer for Khmer Organisation) Bike Tours
BICYCLE TOUR

(Map p96; ☑ 093 903024; www.kko-cambodia.
org; cnr St 20 & Wat Bo Rd; tours US$35-50) ✎
Good-cause cycling tours around the paths
of Angkor or into the countryside beyond
the Western Baray. Proceeds go towards the
Khmer for Khmer Organisation, which supports education and vocational training.

#### PURE! Countryside Cycling Tour
BICYCLE TOUR

(http://www.puredreamcentre.nl/en/community/
4509-pure-bicycle-tour.html; per person US$25)
✎ Long half-day tour that takes in local life
around Siem Reap, including lunch with a
local family. All proceeds go towards supporting Pure's educational and vocational-
training projects.

### Foodie Tours

Cambodian food is now on the map and
there are some cracking culinary tours to
give you an insight into the food scene in
Siem Reap. The Cambodia Vespa Adventures' After Dark Foodie Tour (opposite) is a
good option for those who want to combine
a Vespa ride with a culinary experience.

**Siem Reap Food Tours**  FOOD TOUR
(☎ 012 505542; www.siemreapfoodtours.com; per person US$75) Operated by an experienced Scottish chef with a penchant for stand-up comedy and an American food writer, these tours are a recipe for engaging food encounters. Choose from a morning tour that takes in local markets and the *naom banchok* noodle stalls of Preah Dak or an evening tour that takes in street stalls and local barbecue restaurants.

### Motorbike Tours

Most Cambodians still use motorbikes to get around the countryside. 'When in Rome' also applies to 'When in Siem Reap', so consider taking a motorbike adventure deep into the Cambodian countryside. You can also customise a motorbike tour with any of the English-speaking *moto* drivers in Siem Rea, which will work out a lot cheaper than taking an organised tour.

**Cambodia Vespa Adventures**  TOUR
(Map p125; ☎ 012 861610; www.cambodiavespa adventures.com; tours per person US$60-99) The modern Vespa is a cut above the average *moto* and is a comfortable way to explore the temples, learn about local life in the countryside or check out some street food after dark, all in the company of excellent and knowledgeable local guides.

**Khmer Ways**  TOUR
(Map p125; ☎ 088 606 3374; www.khmerways.com; tours US$60-95) Live the dream with Khmer Ways...or at least ride the Honda Dream. Choose from a countryside tour, a longer ride to Beng Mealea or an adventure on the jungle roads of Phnom Kulen.

---

### SUPPORTING RESPONSIBLE TOURISM IN SIEM REAP

Many travellers passing through Siem Reap are interested in contributing something to the communities they visit as they explore the temples and surrounding areas. ConCERT (Map p96; ☎ 063-963511; www.concertcambodia.org; 560 Phum Stoueng Thmey; ⊙ 9am-5pm Mon-Fri) is a Siem Reap–based organisation that is working to build bridges between tourists and good-cause projects in the Siem Reap–Angkor area. It offers information on anything from ecotourism initiatives to volunteering opportunities.

---

**KKO Countryside Moto Tour**  TOUR
(Map p96; ☎ 093 903024; www.kko-cambodia.org; St 20; donation US$30-60) Take a good-cause ride through the history of Siem Reap taking in remote Angkorian temples off the tourist trail and the real countryside. All proceeds goes towards supporting education and vocational training.

## 🛏 Sleeping

Siem Reap has the best range of accommodation in Cambodia. A vast number of family-run guesthouses charging US$5 to US$20 a room cater for budget travellers, while those looking for midrange accommodation can choose from upmarket guesthouses or small hotels from US$20 per room.

Touts for budget guesthouses wait at the taxi park and at the airport. Even if you've not yet decided where to stay in Siem Reap, don't be surprised to see a noticeboard displaying your name, as most guesthouses in Phnom Penh either have partners up here or sell your name on to another guesthouse. This system usually involves a free ride into town. There's no obligation to stay at the guesthouse if you don't like the look of it, but the 'free lift' might suddenly cost US$2 or more.

There has been an explosion in backpacker hostels and even flashpacker pads, but bear in mind that a dorm bed in some of these places costs as much (or more) than a private room in a Cambodian-run guesthouse.

There are plenty of great midrange deals available in quality boutique accommodation. Most rates include a free transfer from the airport or boat dock.

Many top-end hotels levy an additional 10% government tax, 2% tourist tax and sometimes an extra 10% for service, but breakfast is included. It's essential to book ahead at most places from November to March, particularly for the glamorous spots.

During the low season (April to September), there are lots of offers available ranging from stay three/pay two to big discounts in the range of 30% to 50%. Top-end hotels usually publish high- and low-season rates.

There are many good places around town, with the total number of guesthouses and hotels now hovering around the 600 or more mark. Commission scams abound in Siem Reap, so keep your antennae up.

---

### 🏠 Psar Chaa Area

Psar Chaa is the liveliest part of town, brimming with restaurants, bars and boutiques.

SIEM REAP SLEEPING

# North Siem Reap

0 — 100 m
0 — 0.05 miles

## North Siem Reap

### ◎ Sights
1 Wat Preah Inkosei.................................B2

### ◉ Activities, Courses & Tours
2 Cooks in Tuk Tuks ...............................A3
3 Krousar Thmey ....................................A1
Peace Cafe Yoga.........................(see 10)
Vegetarian Cooking Class .........(see 10)

### ⊜ Sleeping
4 HanumanAlaya.......................................A2
5 River Garden........................................A3

### ⊗ Eating
6 Angkor Palm..........................................A1
7 L'Oasi Italiana.......................................B2
8 Mahob ..................................................A2
9 Mie Cafe ...............................................A2
10 Peace Cafe...........................................A3
11 Touich...................................................B2

### ⊛ Entertainment
12 Beatocello............................................A1

### ⋒ Shopping
13 AHA Local Handicraft Market.............A1

---

Staying here can be a lot of fun, but it's not the quietest area.

**★ Ivy Guesthouse 2** GUESTHOUSE $
(Map p96; ☑012 800860; www.ivy-guesthouse. com; Psar Kandal St; r US$6-15; ❋@🖥) An inviting guesthouse with a chill-out area and bar, the Ivy is a lively place to stay. The restaurant is as good as it gets among the guesthouses in town, with a huge vegetarian selection and US$1 'Tapas Fridays'.

**Downtown Siem Reap Hostel** HOSTEL $
(Map p96; ☑012 675881; www.downtownsiem reaphostel.hostel.com; Wat Dam Nak area; dm US$6-8, r US$12-18; ❋🖥⛱) The rates here are particularly inviting when you factor in the small pool in the garden. Chill out with air-con in the more expensive dorms or rooms. Outside visitors can use the pool with a US$6 spend on food and drink.

**Prohm Roth Guesthouse** GUESTHOUSE $
(Map p100; ☑012 466495; www.prohmroth-guest house.com; near Wat Preah Prohm Roth; r US$12-33; ❋@🖥) Central, yet tucked away down a side street that runs parallel to Wat Preah Prohm Roth, this is a friendly place with a wide range of rooms, including triples and quads. Free pick-up from airport, port or bus station.

**Shadow of Angkor Guesthouse** GUESTHOUSE $$
(Map p100; ☑063-964774; www.shadowofangkor. com; 353 Pokambor Ave; r US$15-25; ❋@🖥⛱) In a grand old French-era building overlooking the river, this friendly place offers affordable air-conditioned rooms in a superb setting. A recent major renovation propelled it into the lower midrange category, like its annexe across the river, which has a swimming pool.

**Steung Siem Reap Hotel** HOTEL $$
(Map p100; ☑063-965167; www.steungsiem reaphotel.com; near Psar Chaa; r from US$65; ❋@🖥⛱) In keeping with the French colonial–era legacy around Psar Chaa, this hotel has high ceilings, louvre shutters and wrought-iron balconies. Three-star rooms feature smart wooden trim. The location is hard to beat.

**Golden Banana B&B** GUESTHOUSE $$
(Map p96; ☑063-761259; www.golden-banana.com; Wat Dam Nak area; s/d US$30/34; ❋@🖥⛱) The original Golden Banana, this B&B is set in attractive temple-like pavilions with Sino-Khmer furnishings. Breakfast is included in the rates and nearby annexes are available for spillovers.

### Rambutan Resort

RESORT $$

(Map p96; ☑063-766655; http://rambutans.info; Wat Dam Nak area; r US$49-89; ❋@☎☀) Long a part of the iconic Golden Banana B&B empire, the (Golden) Banana Republic has now split and the outcome is this atmospheric, gay-friendly resort. Rambutan has spacious and stylish rooms overlooking an inviting courtyard swimming pool.

## Sivatha St Area

The area to the west of Sivatha St includes a good selection of budget guesthouses and midrange boutique hotels.

### Mad Monkey

HOSTEL $

(Map p96; www.madmonkeyhostels.com; Sivatha St; dm US$7-9, r US$16-26; ❋@☎) The Siem Reap outpost of an expanding Monkey business, this is a classic backpacker crash pad with several dorms, good-value rooms for those wanting privacy and the obligatory rooftop bar, only this one's a beach bar!

### Funky Flashpacker

HOSTEL $

(Map p125; ☑070 221524; www.funkyflashpacker.com; Funky Lane; dm US$7, r US$16-35; ❋@☎☀) This upmarket backpackers has a funky vibe – the entire downstairs courtyard is taken up with a swimming pool where water polo regularly take place. A great hostel, but not ideal for recovering partyholics as there's always a buzz about the place.

### Garden Village

GUESTHOUSE $

(Map p125; ☑012 217373; www.gardenvillage guesthouse.com; 434 Sok San St; dm US$4, r US$8-25; ❋@☎) This traditional backpacker hangout offers some of the cheapest beds in town and is a good place to meet other travellers. Options among its 70 rooms are eight-bed dorms at a reasonable US$4 per bed. The rooftop bar is a draw around sunset.

### Golden Temple Villa

HOTEL $$

(Map p96; ☑012 943459; www.goldentemple villa.com; r US$15-40; ❋@☎) A long-running, popular place that's recently relocated, Golden Temple Villa has a bar-restaurant downstairs, plus all sorts of generous freebies ranging from a one-hour massage to a dance show at Temple Club (p118). The associated Golden Temple Residence is pretty spectacular too, offering the four-star high life.

### Secrets Pavilion

BOUTIQUE HOTEL $$

(Map p96; www.secretspavilion.com; 120 Angkor Night Market St; US$25-75; ❋@☎☀) A cool, contemporary hotel offering great value for money, the rooms here include impressive motifs from the bas-reliefs of Angkor Wat and sumptuous silk decorations. Billing itself as an 'urban boutique hotel', they are on to something good here.

### Memoire d'Angkor Boutique Hotel

BOUTIQUE HOTEL $$

(Map p96; ☑063-766999; www.memoiredangkor. com; Sivatha St; US$65-150; ❋@☎☀) Centrally located on the popular Sivatha St strip, this hotel pays homage to its Angkor heritage with some incredible pieces of local lacquer art on display. Rooms are spacious, colourful and contemporary, and there is an inviting swimming pool in which to wind down after visiting the temples.

## Riverfront & Royal Gardens

The smart end of town, this is where the royal residence is to be found, along with many of the luxury hotels and boutique resorts.

### Rosy Guesthouse

GUESTHOUSE $

(Map p96; ☑063-965059; www.rosyguest house.com; Siem Reap River Rd; r US$9-35; ❋☎) 🌿 A Brit-run establishment whose 13 rooms come with TV and DVD. The lively pub downstairs has great grub and hosts regular events to support community causes, including a popular quiz night.

### La Noria Guesthouse

GUESTHOUSE $$

(Map p96; ☑063-964242; www.lanoriaangkor. com; Siem Reap River Rd; r US$49-69; ❋@☎☀) Long-running and lovely La Noria is set in a lush tropical garden with a pretty swimming pool. Rooms have a traditional trim and include a verandah but no TV or fridge. Sister hotel Borann is almost identical. Rates vary seasonally.

### ★ La Résidence d'Angkor

RESORT $$$

(Map p96; ☑063-963390; www.residence dangkor.com; Siem Reap River Rd; r from US$220; ❋@☎☀) The 54 wood-appointed rooms, among the most tasteful and inviting in town, come with verandahs and huge Jacuzzi-sized tubs. The gorgeous swimming pool is perfect for laps. The newer wing is ultra-contemporary, as is the sumptuous Kong Kea Spa.

### Shinta Mani

RESORT $$$

(Map p96; ☑063-761998; www.shintamani.com; Oum Khun St; r US$140-305; ❋@☎☀) 🌿 With a contemporary chic design by renowned architect Bill Bensley, Shinta Mani Resort features an inviting central pool, while Shinta

Mani Club offers more exclusive rooms. Shinta Mani has won international awards for responsible tourism practices and hosts a regular 'Well Made in Cambodia' market.

### Grand Hotel d'Angkor    HOTEL $$$
(Map p96; ☑ 063-963888; www.raffles.com; 1 Charles de Gaulle Blvd; r from US$220; �snowflake@🖥⌨) This historic hotel has been welcoming guests such as Charlie Chaplin, Charles de Gaulle, Jackie Kennedy and Bill Clinton since 1932. Ensconced in opulent surroundings, you can imagine what it was like to be a tourist in colonial days. Rooms include classic touches and a dizzying array of bathroom gifts.

### FCC Angkor    BOUTIQUE HOTEL $$$
(Map p96; ☑ 063-760280; www.fcccambodia.com; Pokambor Ave; r/ste from US$95/150; ✸@🖥⌨) This funky property wouldn't look out of place in any chic European capital. Rooms feature large baths, Cambodian silks and wi-fi throughout. The black-tiled swimming pool and Visaya Spa complete the picture. Breakfast is available free in the room from 4.30am for those sunrise starts.

## 🏠 Wat Bo Rd Area

This up-and-coming area features socially responsible guesthouses as well as some hip boutique hotels. There is a great guesthouse ghetto in a backstreet running parallel to the north end of Wat Bo Rd, which is a good option for browsers without a booking.

### Babel Guesthouse    GUESTHOUSE $
(Map p96; ☑ 063-965474; www.babel-siemreap. com; 738 Wat Bo Village; r incl breakfast US$18-33; ✸@🖥) 🌿 A Norwegian-run guesthouse set in a relaxing tropical garden, the service and presentation here are a cut above the nearby budget places and rates include breakfast. The Babel owners are keen supporters of responsible tourism.

### European Guesthouse    GUESTHOUSE $
(Map p96; ☑ 012 582237; www.european-guesthouse.com; 566 Wat Bo Village; dm US$7, r US$22; ✸@🖥⌨) 🌿 Rooms are well presented at this friendly place, which now boasts a swimming pool to go with the relaxing garden. The European is a member of local NGO networks Childsafe and ConCERT, and supports projects such as the White Bicycles.

### Happy Guesthouse    GUESTHOUSE $
(Map p96; ☑ 063-963815; www.happyangkor guesthouse.com; 134 Wat Bo Village; r US$7-14; ✸@🖥) This place will really make you

happy thanks to welcoming owners who speak English well *et un peu de Français*. Great-value rooms start at the price of dorms elsewhere and there's free internet.

### Siem Reap Hostel    HOSTEL $
(Map p96; ☑ 063-964660; www.thesiemreap hostel.com; 10 Makara St; dm US$8-10, r incl breakfast US$34-45; ✸@🖥⌨) Angkor's original backpacker hostel is pretty slick. The dorms are well tended, while the rooms are definitely flashpacker and include breakfast. There is a lively bar-restaurant and a covered pool, plus a well-organised travel desk.

### ★ Soria Moria Hotel    BOUTIQUE HOTEL $$
(Map p96; ☑ 063-964768; www.thesoriamoria. com; Wat Bo Rd; r US$39-63; ✸@🖥⌨) 🌿 A hotel with a heart, promoting local causes to help the community, this boutique place has attractive rooms with smart bathroom fittings. There's a fusion restaurant downstairs, sky hot tub upstairs and a new swimming pool. Half the hotel was transferred to staff ownership in 2011, a visionary move.

### ★ Viroth's Hotel    BOUTIQUE HOTEL $$
(Map p96; ☑ 063-766107; www.viroth-hotel.com; St 24; r from US$86; ✸@🖥⌨) The new Viroth's is an ultra-stylish, retro-chic property with 30 rooms fitted out with classy contemporary furnishings. Behind the impressive facade lies a 30m swimming pool, a gym and a spa. The original seven-bedroom hotel is still operating as Viroth's Villa.

### Seven Candles Guesthouse    GUESTHOUSE $$
(Map p96; ☑ 063-963380; www.seven candlesguesthouse.com; 307 Wat Bo Rd; r US$20-38; ✸@🖥) 🌿 A good-cause guesthouse, the profits from Seven Candles help a local foundation that seeks to promote education to rural communities. Rooms include hot water, TV and fridge, plus some decorative flourishes.

### Petit Villa Boutique    BOUTIQUE HOTEL $$
(Map p96; ☑ 063-764234; www.petitvilla.com; Wat Dam Nak area; US$40-80; ✸@🖥⌨) A blissful little boutique hideaway in the suburbs of Wat Dam Nak, there is a mellow retreat vibe to this place. Rooms are spacious and include a balcony looking out over the central swimming pool and lush gardens. Cooking classes are available and there's a small spa.

### Angkor Village    BOUTIQUE HOTEL $$$
(Map p96; ☑ 063-963561; www.angkorvillage. com; St 26; US$75-350; ✸@🖥⌨) The original boutique hotel in Siem Reap (when boutique

was still an upmarket shopping experience to most), Angkor Village remains one of the most atmospheric places in temple town. Rooms are set in beautiful wooden bungalows around a stunning pond with a central restaurant. Sister hotel, Angkor Village Resort, is even more opulent.

## Further Afield

Don't shy away from venturing further afield, as some of the most memorable boutique hotels lie hidden beyond.

### Velkommen Guesthouse GUESTHOUSE $
(Map p96; 012 477270; www.velkommen guesthouse.com; off Charles de Gaulle Blvd; dm US$5, r from US$22) The Siem Reap outpost of a popular Phnom Penh pad, the Velkommen is set in a large Khmer villa with a mix of cheap dorms and comfortable rooms. Handy travel information is available, plus there is a pool table.

### HanumanAlaya BOUTIQUE HOTEL $$
(Map p104; 063-760582; www.hanumanalaya. com; 5 Krom 2, Phoum Treang, just off Charles de Gaulle Blvd; r US$60-100; ❄@🛜🏊) The most traditionally Cambodian of the boutique hotels in town, HanumanAlaya is set around a lush garden and pretty swimming pool. Rooms are decorated with antiques and handicrafts but include modern touches such as flatscreen TV, minibar and safe.

### Pavillon Indochine BOUTIQUE HOTEL $$
(Map p125; 012 849681; www.pavillon-indochine.com; r US$55-70, ste US$75-95; ❄@🛜🏊) The Pavillon offers charming colonial-chic rooms set around a small swimming pool. Trims includes Asian antiques, billowing mosquito nets and a safe. Also included in the rates is a *remork* driver for the day to tour the temples, making it good value.

### River Garden BOUTIQUE HOTEL $$
(Map p104; 063-963400; www.theriver garden.info; Siem Reap River Rd West; r US$40-115; ❄@🛜🏊) Invitingly set amid a verdant garden, this wooden resort has a small selection of atmospheric rooms, some with large balconies. Renowned for its 'cooks in *tuk tuks*' culinary class and street-food tour.

### ★ Sala Lodges BOUTIQUE HOTEL $$$
(063-766699; www.salalodges.com; 498 Salakom-roeuk; r US$230-510; ❄🛜🏊) An original concept, Sala Lodges offers 11 traditional Khmer houses that have been retro-fitted inside to bring them up to the standard of a rustic boutique hotel. Enter the resort and you'll think you have stumbled on an idyllic Cambodian village, but the pool and restaurant will soon confirm you have stumbled on a gem.

### Navutu Dreams BOUTIQUE HOTEL $$$
(063-688 0607; www.navutudreams.com; US$80-230; ❄🛜🏊) Set in the semi-rural suburbs of Siem Reap, Navutu Dreams offers a selection of open-plan villas set around lush gardens and three swimming pools. A recent expansion has added a yoga and wellness centre.

### Heritage Suites BOUTIQUE HOTEL $$$
(Map p125; 063-969100; www.relaischateaux. com/heritage; Wat Polanka; r US$120-380; ❄@🛜🏊) Designed in a colonial style, the open-plan suites are spectacular, and many include a small garden and free-standing bath. Lanterns Restaurant is highly regarded, plus there's Thursday night jazz.

## Eating

The dining scene in Siem Reap is something to savour, offering a superb selection of street food, Asian eateries and sumptuous restaurants. The range encompasses something from every continent, with new temptations regularly opening up. Sample the subtleties of Khmer cuisine in town, or indulge in home comforts or gastronomic delights prior to, or after, hitting the remote provinces. Some of the very best restaurants (p108) also put something back into community projects or offer vocational training.

Tourist numbers mean many top restaurants are heaving during the high season. But with so many places to choose from, keep walking and you'll find somewhere more tranquil. Quite a lot of restaurants work with tour groups to some degree. If you prefer to avoid places with tour groups, stick to the Psar Chaa area and explore on foot.

Some of the budget guesthouses have good menus offering a selection of local dishes and Western meals; while it's easy to order in-house food, it hardly counts as the full Siem Reap experience. Several of the midrange hotels and all of the top-end places have restaurants, some of them excellent. Several hotels and restaurants around town feature dinner and a performance of classical dance.

The Alley is wall-to-wall with good Cambodian restaurants, many of which are family owned. Most have 'Khmer' in the name and offer cheap beers and meal deals. Take a stroll and see what takes your fancy.

## DINING FOR A CAUSE

There are some good restaurants in Siem Reap that support worthy causes or assist in the training of Cambodia's future hospitality staff with a subsidised ticket into the tourism industry. When you dine at the training places, it provides the trainees with a good opportunity to hone their skills with real customers.

**Marum** (Map p96; www.marum-restaurant.org; Wat Polanka area; mains US$3.25-6.75; ⊙11am-10pm Mon-Sat; 🕾🖉) Set in a delightful wooden house with a spacious garden, Marum serves up lots of vegetarian and seafood dishes, plus some mouth-watering desserts. Menu highlights include red-tree-ant fritters and ginger basil meatballs. Marum is part of the Tree Alliance group of training restaurants; the experience is a must.

**Haven** (Map p96; 🖉078-342404; www.haven-cambodia.com; Chocolate Rd; mains US$3-7; ⊙11.30am-2.30pm & 5.30-9.30pm Mon-Sat; 🕾) A culinary haven indeed – dine here for the best of east meets west; the fish fillet with green mango is particularly zesty. Proceeds go towards helping young adult orphans make the step from institution to employment. It recently relocated to the Wat Dam Nak area, just near Angkor High School.

**Blossom Cafe** (Map p96; www.blossomcakes.org; St 6; cupcakes US$1.50; ⊙10am-5pm Mon-Sat; 🕾) Cupcakes are elevated to an art form at this elegant cafe, with beautifully presented creations available in a rotating array of 48 flavours. Creative coffees, teas and juices are also on offer and profits assist Cambodian women in vocational training.

**Common Grounds** (Map p96; 719 St 14; light meals US$3-5; ⊙7am-10pm; 🕾) This sophisticated international cafe, akin to Starbucks, has great coffee, homemade cakes, light bites, and free wi-fi and internet terminals. Offers free computer classes and English classes for Cambodians, and supports good causes.

**Joe-to-Go** (Map p100; near Psar Chaa; mains US$2-5; ⊙7am-9.30pm) If you need coffee coursing through your veins to tackle the temples, then head here. Gourmet coffees, shakes and light bites, with proceeds supporting street children. Upstairs is a small boutique supporting the associated NGO, The Global Child.

**New Leaf Book Cafe** (Map p100; near Psar Chaa; mains US$3-6; ⊙7am-10pm) The profits from this new cafe and secondhand bookshop go towards supporting NGOs working in Siem Reap province. The menu includes some home favourites, an Italian twist and some local Cambodian specials.

**Peace Cafe** (Map p104; www.peacecafeangkor.org; River Rd; mains US$2.50-4.50; ⊙7am-9pm; 🖉) This popular garden cafe serves affordable vegetarian meals, while healthy drinks include a tempting selection of vegetable juices. A focal point for community activities, daily yoga sessions and Khmer classes are held every weekend at 4pm.

**Sister Srey Cafe** (Map p100; 200 Pokambor Ave; mains US$3-6; ⊙7am-7pm Tue-Sun) Sister Srey, a funky and fun cafe on the riverfront near Psar Chaa, offers an ambitious breakfast menu, including eggs bene-delicious, that is perfect after a sunrise at the temples. Lunch is Western food with a creative twist, including burgers, wraps and salads.

**Les Jardins des Delices** (Map p125; 🖉063-963673; Paul Dubrule Hotel & Tourism School, NH6; set lunch US$15; ⊙noon-2pm Mon-Fri) Enjoy Sofitel standards at an affordable price with a three-course meal of Asian and Western food prepared by students training in the culinary arts. It also runs a 'Khmer Food Lovers' cooking class.

**Sala Bai Hotel & Restaurant School** (Map p96; www.salabai.com; Taphul St; set lunch US$10-12; ⊙7-9am & noon-2pm Mon-Fri) This school trains young Khmers in the art of hospitality and serves an affordable menu of Western and Cambodian cuisine. The training program includes an upstairs guesthouse with four rooms available.

The markets are well stocked with fruit and fresh bread. For more substantial treats, such as cheese and chocolate, try the local supermarkets. Eating locally usually works out cheaper than self-catering, but some folks like to make up a picnic for longer days on the road.

## Pub St & Around

Pub St may not seem to be the most relaxing dining area, particularly at night, but the criss-crossing alleys and lanes reveal some atmospheric places.

### Khmer Kitchen Restaurant    CAMBODIAN $
(Map p100; www.khmerkitchens.com; The Alley; mains US$2-5; ⊙11am-10pm) Can't get no (culinary) satisfaction? Then follow in the footsteps of Sir Mick Jagger and try this popular place, which offers an affordable selection of Khmer and Thai favourites, including zesty curries.

### Red Piano    ASIAN, INTERNATIONAL $$
(Map p100; www.redpianocambodia.com; Pub St; mains US$3-10; 🛜) Strikingly set in a restored colonial gem, Red Piano has a big balcony for watching the action unfold below. The menu has a reliable selection of Asian and international food, all at decent prices. Former celebrity guest Angelina Jolie has a cocktail named in her honour.

### The Sun    INTERNATIONAL $$
(Map p100; 📱092 844362; St 11; mains US$2.25-12.75; ⊙7am-midnight) A cafe, bistro and tapas bar all rolled into one, The Sun occupies a handsome building on the corner of Pub St. The tapas is east meets west, and there are some authentic pizzas as well as some Cambodian dishes. The coffee is highly regarded thanks to the La Marzocco coffee machine. Happy hour runs from 5.30pm to 6.30pm.

### Le Tigre de Papier    INTERNATIONAL $$
(Map p100; www.letigredepapier.com; Pub St; mains US$2-9; ⊙24hr; 🛜📱) One of the best all-rounders in Siem Reap, the popular Tigre serves up authentic Khmer food, great Italian dishes and a selection of favourites from most other corners of the globe. It conveniently offers frontage on both Pub St and the Alley; the latter is generally a lot quieter.

### Chamkar    VEGETARIAN $$
(Map p100; www.chamkar-vegetarian.com; The Alley; mains US$4-8; ⊙11am-11pm, closed lunch Sun; 🛜📱) The name translates as 'farm' and the ingredients must be coming from a pretty impressive organic vegetable supplier given the creative dishes on the menu here. Asian flavours dominate and include dishes such as stuffed pumpkin and vegetable kebabs in black pepper sauce.

### Cambodian BBQ    BARBECUE $$
(Map p100; www.restaurant-siemreap.com/html/cambodianbbq.php; The Alley; mains US$5-9; ⊙11am-11pm; 🛜) Crocodile, snake, ostrich and kangaroo meat add an exotic twist to the traditional *phnom pleung* (hill of fire) grills. Cambodian BBQ has spawned half a dozen or more copycats in the surrounding streets, many of which offer discount specials.

### Amok    CAMBODIAN $$
(Map p100; www.angkorw.com; The Alley; mains US$4-9; ⊙10am-11pm; 🛜) The name pays homage to Cambodia's national dish, *amok* (baked fish), and this is indeed a fine place to try baked fish curry in banana leaf or, better still, an *amok* tasting platter with four varieties. It is in the heart of the Alley.

### Il Forno    ITALIAN $$
(Map p100; http://ilforno.restaurant; The Lane; mains US$5-15; ⊙11am-11pm; 🛜) Aficionados of fine Italian cuisine will be delighted to know that there is, as the name suggests, a full-blown brick oven in this cosy little *trattoria*. The menu includes fresh antipasti, authentic pizzas and some home-cooked Italian dishes.

### Soup Dragon    ASIAN, INTERNATIONAL $$
(Map p100; Pub St; mains US$2-10; ⊙6am-11pm; 🛜) This three-level restaurant has a split personality: the ground floor serves up cheap, classic Asian breakfasts, while upstairs there's a diverse menu featuring Asian and international dishes, including Italian and Moroccan flavours.

### Little Italy    ITALIAN $$
(Map p100; Alley West; mains US$4-12; ⊙11am-11pm) This elegant Italian restaurant is much more affordable than its sophisticated exterior might suggest. As well as wood-fired pizzas, the menu includes a wide range of homemade pasta and imported Italian cuts.

### Dakshin's    INDIAN $$
(Map p100; 📱012 808011; The Lane; US$2-8; ⊙11am-11.30pm) Such is their confidence in their subcontinental selection that they have an open-plan kitchen. Arguably the best of Siem Reap's numerous Indian restaurants, Dakshin's serves up a delicious butter chicken alongside the highlights of northern and southern cuisine.

### Belmiro's Pizzas & Subs    INTERNATIONAL $$
(Map p100; 📱095 331875; St 7; pizza US$3-12; ⊙noon-midnight) No prizes for guessing what is served here, but they do rightly claim to serve the biggest pizzas in town, conveniently

# Siem Reap

Siem Reap is known as gateway to the temples of Angkor; however, there is much going on in and around town to warrant a visit on its own merit. Floating villages on the nearby Tonlé Sap, a superb selection of restaurants and bars, first-class shopping, first-rate cooking classes and a host of other activities as diverse as birdwatching and Vespa tours are all on offer.

MAROZNC / GETTY IMAGES ©

PETER STUCKINGS / GETTY IMAGES ©

### 1. Psar Chaa (p119)

The produce section at the Old Market is an atmospheric place to visit.

### 2. Kompong Pluk (p128)

Houses on stilts make up the floating village of Kompong Pluk.

### 3. Street food (p107)

Get your fried-noodle fix at Psar Chaa, where the food is cheap, tasty and filling.

### 4. Banteay Srei Butterfly Centre (p124)

The largest enclosed butterfly centre in Southeast Asia provides a sustainable living for locals.

LEONID SEREBRENNIKOV / ALAMY STOCK PHOTO ©

sold by the slice if you can't cope with a whole pie. Regular specials include anything from an original French dip sandwich to big burritos.

## Psar Chaa Area

### Blue Pumpkin CAFE $

(Map p100; http://tbpumpkin.com; Pithnou St; mains US$3-7; ⊘6am-10pm) The original branch of an expanding local chain, venture upstairs for a world of white minimalism, with beds to lounge on and free wi-fi. The menu includes light bites, great sandwiches, filling specials and divine shakes. The homemade ice-cream comes in some exotic flavours.

### Psar Chaa CAMBODIAN $

(Map p100; mains US$1.50-4; ⊘7am-9pm) When it comes to cheap Khmer eats, Psar Chaa itself has plenty of food stalls on the north-west side, all with signs and menus in English. These are atmospheric places for a local meal at local-ish prices. Some dishes are on display, others are freshly wok-fried to order, but most are wholesome and filling.

### Olive FRENCH $$

(Map p100; ☑063-769899; near Angkor Trade Center; US$5-15; ⊘11am-11pm) A fine French restaurant hidden away down a side street near the Old Market, the air-conditioning and crisp white linens beckon diners in. The menu includes a good range of Gallic classics, including a lamb shank and a pork tenderloin. Save space for the desserts or a cheese platter.

### Viva MEXICAN $$

(Map p100; www.ivivasiemreap.com; Pithnou St; mains US$2.50-12.50; ⊘7am-late) Spice up your life with Mexican food and margaritas at this long-running place, which includes a guesthouse located above. In a strategic set-ting opposite Psar Chaa.

## Sivatha St Area

### The Little Red Fox Espresso CAFE $

(Map p96; www.thelittleredfoxrespresso.com; Hup Guan St; dishes US$2-8; ⊘6.30am-6.30pm, closed Wed) This foxy little cafe is incredibly popular with long-term residents in Siem Reap who swear that the regionally sourced Feel Good coffee is the best in town. Add to that designer breakfasts, creative juices and lunch specials and it's easy to while away some time here. Upstairs is one of Siem Reap's leading hair salons.

### Curry Walla INDIAN $

(Map p96; Sivatha St; mains US$2-5; ⊘10.30am-11pm) For good-value Indian food, this place is hard to beat. The *thalis* (set meals) are a bargain and the owner, long-time resident Ranjit, knows his share of spicy specials from the subcontinent.

### The Hive Siem Reap CAFE $

(Map p96; Psar Kandal St; dishes US$2-6; ⊘7am-6pm) This place has generated a buzz among foreign residents in Siem Reap thanks to its creative coffees, jam-jar juices and healthy open sandwiches on rye, such as smashed avocado or smoked salmon. Try an espresso martini if you like your coffee with a kick.

### Bugs Cafe INSECTS $

(Map p96; ☑017-764560; www.bugs-cafe.com; Steung Thmei St; mains US$2-8; ⊘5pm-midnight; ☎) Cambodians were on to insects long be-fore the food scientists started bugging us about the merits of critters. Choose from a veritable feast of crickets, water bugs, silk worms and spiders. Bee cream soup, feta and tarantula samosas, and pan fried scorpions – you won't forget this menu in a hurry.

### ★Sugar Palm CAMBODIAN $$

(Map p96; www.sugarpalmrestaurant.com; Taphul St; mains US$5-9; ⊘11.30am-3pm & 5.30-10pm Mon-Sat; ☎) Set in a beautiful wooden house; the Sugar Palm is the place to sample traditional flavours infused with herbs and spices, including delicious *char kreung* (curried lemongrass) dishes. Owner Ketha-na showed celebrity chef Gordon Ramsay how to prepare *amok*.

### Kuriosity Kafe INTERNATIONAL $$

(Map p96; ☑063-963240; Sok San Rd; mains US$4-12; ⊘10am-midnight) Impressively set over three floors, this place has a quirky and kitsch look that stands out from the pack in up-and-coming Sok San Rd. The menu blends home comfort food such as sand-wiches and wraps with authentic Khmer food, including an aromatic chicken curry. The barbecued pork ribs are divine.

### Le Malraux FRENCH-ASIAN $$

(Map p100; www.le-malraux-siem-reap.com; Siva-tha St; mains US$5-15; ⊘7am-midnight) A good spot for gastronomes, this classy art-deco restaurant offers fine French food. Try the combination beef or salmon tartar and car-paccio to start. The Cognac and Armagnac selection is to die for. Asian dishes also available.

## CRAVING ICE CREAM?

After a hot day exploring the temples, there's nothing quite like an ice-cream fix and Siem Reap delivers some superb surprises:

**Blue Pumpkin** (p112) Homemade ice cream in original tropical flavours from ginger to passionfruit.

**The Glasshouse** (Map p96; Park Hyatt, Sivatha St; cones US$2; ☺6am-10pm) Velvety ice creams including white chocolate and tangy sorbets.

**Swenson's Ice Cream** (Map p100; Pokambor Ave; cones US$1.25; ☺9am-9pm) One of America's favourites has become one of Siem Reap's favourites. Located in the Angkor Trade Centre.

**Japanese Restaurant Genkiya**　JAPANESE $$
(Map p96; ☑063-967978; www.genkiya-restaurant.com; Airport Rd; US$6-18; ☺11.30am-2pm & 6-10pm) There are lots of Japanese restaurants in Siem Reap these days, but Genkiya is noteworthy for its bargain set lunches (US$7). Choose from a variety of sets, including grilled mackerel, sashimi, shrimp and salmon, fried chicken or tempura.

**Armand's**　FRENCH $$$
(Map p96; ☑092 305401; 586 Tep Vong St; mains US$5-25; ☺5pm-late Mon-Sat) The new Siem Reap outpost of Phnom Penh's most flamboyant French restaurant, Armand's lives up to its reputation. It's a sophisticated space turning out the best steaks in town, including the signature tenderloin *rossini*. Doubles as one of the longest bars in town with quaffable wines by the glass and premium whisky.

### Self-Catering

**Angkor Market**　SUPERMARKET $
(Map p96; Sivatha St) The best all-round supermarket in town, this place has a steady supply of international treats.

**Lucky Market**　SUPERMARKET $
(Map p96; Sivatha St) Part of a big shopping mall on Sivatha St, this is the biggest supermarket in town.

## Riverfront & Royal Gardens

**Chanrey Tree**　CAMBODIAN $$
(Map p96; www.chanreytree.com; Pokambor Ave; mains US$5-12; ☺11am-10pm) Cool and contemporary, Chantrey Tree is the new face of Khmer cuisine, combining a stylish setting with expressive presentation, while retaining the essentials of traditional Cambodian cooking. Try the eggplant with pork ribs or grilled stuffed frog.

**FCC Angkor**　INTERNATIONAL $$
(Map p96; ☑063-760280; Pokambor Ave; mains US$5-15; ☺7am-midnight; ☎) This landmark building draws people in from the riverside thanks to a reflective pool, torchlit dining and a garden bar. Inside, the colonial chic atmosphere continues with lounge chairs and an open kitchen turning out a range of Asian and international food.

**Siem Reap Brewpub**　INTERNATIONAL $$
(Map p96; ☑080 888555; www.siemreapbrewpub.asia; St 5; US$4-15; ☺11am-11pm) Designer dining meets designer brewing. Set in an open-plan villa, the menu is international fusion, including everything from light bites and tapas to gourmet meals. The beer comes in four flavours, including Blonde, Golden, Amber and Dark, and a US$3 sampling platter is available.

## Wat Bo Rd Area

**Pages Cafe**　CAFE $
(Map p96; ☑092 966812; www.pages-siemreap.com; St 24; dishes US$2-6; ☺6am-10pm; ☎) This hip hideaway is no longer so hidden, with the new Viroth's Hotel opposite. Exposed brickwork and designer decor make it a good place to linger over an excellent breakfast or light tapas bites. On Saturdays it offers an outdoor grill with wine and pool access. Rooms also available.

**Le Café**　CAFE $
(Map p96; French Cultural Centre; snacks US$2-4; ☺7.30am-9pm; ☎) ✒ Run in partnership with the Paul Dubrule Hotel & Tourism School, this cafe brings five-star sandwiches, salads and shakes to the French Cultural Centre.

**Banllé Vegetarian Restaurant**　VEGETARIAN $
(Map p96; ☑085 330160; www.banlle-vegetarian.com; St 26; mains US$2-4; ☺9am-9.30pm, closed Tue; ☎✒) Set in a traditional wooden house with its own organic vegetable garden, this is a great place for a healthy bite. The menu offers a blend of international and Cambodian dishes, including a vegetable *amok*, and zesty fruit and vegetable shakes.

**Moloppor Cafe**　JAPANESE, INTERNATIONAL $
(Map p96; Siem Reap River Rd; mains US$1-4; ☺10am-11pm; ☎) One of the cheapest deals

in Siem Reap, Moloppor Cafe serves up Japanese, Asian and Italian dishes at almost give-away prices for what is a real restaurant. Nice location offering river views.

### Wat Damnak BBQs
BARBECUE $

(Map p96; Wat Dam Nak St; mains US$2-5; ☺11am-11pm) Located opposite the venerable Wat Dam Nak, these local barbecue restaurants are popular for barbecued beef, other local meats and lake fish. They also double as beer emporiums and turn out some of the cheapest draught in town.

### ★Flow
FUSION $$

(Map p96; ☑012 655285; St 26; mains US$5-12; ☺5-11pm) This chic, contemporary space is earning a resident following for its creative cuisine that mixes the best of east and west. Starters include octopus carpaccio, mains include a tender beef cheek and the chocolate lava is divine. The wine list is extensive so go with the Flow!

### Jungle Burger
INTERNATIONAL $$

(Map p96; ☑098 293400; St 26; mains US$2.50-10; ☺11am-10pm) There are more than 10 types of burger on offer here, including the huge Burg Kalifa burger, plus pizzas, footlong subs and Kiwi comfort food such as home-made pies. It doubles as a small sports bar with a popular pool table.

### Temple Coffee & Bakery
INTERNATIONAL $$

(Map p96; Siem Reap River Rd; dishes US$3-12; ☺7am-11pm) The latest, greatest offering from the Temple group, this huge place is a mash-up of a bakery, restaurant and cocktail lounge. Downstairs there are vintage motobikes and inviting cakes or continue up to the rooftop bar with a pool and bean bags, a popular romantic retreat for young Cambodians.

### Tangram Garden
INTERNATIONAL $$

(Map p96; www.tangramgarden.com; mains US$4.75-9.50; ☺11am-2pm & 5-10pm; ☏☑♨) An alfresco garden restaurant with a children's garden, in a quiet suburb near Wat Dam Nak, Tangram Garden specialises in barbecue grills, creative vegetarian dishes and Khmer staples. It is atmospheric at night.

### Embassy
CAMBODIAN $$$

(Map p96; ☑063-963840; www.restaurant-siemreap.com; King's Rd; set menus from US$27; ☺11am-11pm) Part of the King's Rd village, Embassy is all about Khmer gastronomy, offering an evolving menu that changes with the seasons. Under the supervision of the Kimsan twins, who studied with Michelin-starred chef Regis Marcon, this is Khmer cuisine at its most creative.

## ✵ Further Afield

### ★Mie Cafe
CAMBODIAN, INTERNATIONAL $$

(Map p104; ☑069 999096; www.miecafe-siemreap.com; near Angkor Conservation; mains US$4-8; ☺11am-2pm & 5.30-10pm, closed Tue) An impressive Cambodian eatery offering a fusion take on traditional flavours. It is set in a wooden house just off the road to Angkor and offers a gourmet set menu for US$24. Dishes include everything from succulent marinated pork ribs to squid-ink ravioli.

### Mahob
CAMBODIAN $$

(Map p104; ☑063-966986; www.mahobkhmer.com; near Angkor Conservation; mains US$3.50-15; ☺11am-11pm) The Cambodian word for food, the *mahob* at this restaurant is delicious. Set in a traditional wooden house with a contemporary twist, they take the same approach to cuisine as they do to decor, serving up dishes such as caramelised pork shank with ginger and black pepper, or wok-fried local beef with red tree ants. Hot stone barbecue available.

### Touich
CAMBODIAN $$

(Map p104; http://the-touich-restaurant-bar.blogspot.com; mains US$2.50-8; ☺5.30-10.30pm) Hidden away but worth the search, this traditional Khmer restaurant is set in the backstreet suburbs of Wat Preah Inkosei. The menu includes regional specialities and seafood such as Mekong prawns and Koh Kong red snapper. Check the blog to avoid getting lost.

### Por Cuisine

CAMBODIAN **$$**

(Map p125; ☑063-967797; www.porcuisine.com; mains US$3.50-18; ⊙10.30am-10.30pm) A stylish contemporary restaurant, Por Cuisine offers a wide selection of Asian and international dishes, including the best of Cambodian flavours. The nightly classical dance show is one of the more sophisticated on offer and is an affordable way to get a cultural fix in Siem Reap.

### L'Oasi Italiana

ITALIAN **$$**

(Map p104; www.oasiitaliana.com; mains US$5-17, pizzas US$5-9; ⊙6-10pm Mon, 11am-2pm & 6-10pm Tue-Sun; 🛜) L'Oasi Italiana really is something of an oasis, hidden away in a forest near Wat Preah Inkosei. Expats swear by the gnocchi and homemade pasta, including ravioli with porcini mushrooms, plus wood-fired pizzas.

### Madame Butterfly

ASIAN **$$**

(Map p125; www.madamebutterflyrestaurant.com; Airport Rd; mains US$4-10; ⊙10am-11pm; 🛜) This traditional wooden house has been sumptuously decorated with fine silks and billowing drapes. Lovely atmosphere, but sometimes dampened by the sheer number of tour groups who come to sample the Asian and Khmer cuisine.

### Angkor Palm

CAMBODIAN **$$**

(Map p104; www.angkorpalm.com; Charles de Gaulle Blvd; mains US$3-9; ⊙10am-10pm) Relocated on the road to Angkor, this popular restaurant offers the authentic taste of Cambodia. Even Khmers rave about the legendary *amok* here, and it offers a great-value sampling platter. Cooking classes available.

### Kanell

INTERNATIONAL **$$**

(Map p96; www.kanellrestaurant.com; 7 Makara St; mains US$4-13; ⊙10am-10pm; 🛜) Set in a handsome Khmer villa on the edge of town, Kanell offers extensive gardens and a swimming pool (free with US$5 spend) for those seeking to dine and unwind. The menu includes French-accented dishes, plus some Cambodian favourites.

### ★Cuisine Wat Damnak

CAMBODIAN **$$$**

(Map p96; www.cuisinewatdamnak.com; Wat Dam Nak village; 5-/6-course menu US$24/28; ⊙6.30-10.30pm Tue-Sat, last orders 9.30pm) Set in a traditional wooden house is this highly regarded restaurant from Siem Reap celeb chef Johannes Rivieres. The menu delivers the ultimate contemporary Khmer dining experience. Seasonal set menus focus on market-fresh ingredients and change week-

ly; vegetarian options are available with advance notice.

### Abacus

FRENCH **$$$**

(Map p125; www.cafeabacus.com; mains US$10-22; ⊙11am-late; 🛜) This place has the finest French dining in town with steaks in black-truffle sauce, succulent lamb and superb seafood, including tuna *maguro*. Dine in the garden or cool interior. The menu includes some beautifully presented Khmer dishes.

 ## Drinking & Nightlife

The transformation from sleepy overgrown village to an international destination for the jet set has been dramatic and Siem Reap is now firmly on the nightlife map of Southeast Asia. By night it feels more like a beach town than a cultural capital. The Psar Chaa area is a good hunting ground, with one street even earning the moniker 'Pub St', where you can dive in and crawl out. Pub St is closed to traffic every evening.

Great spots running parallel to Pub St include the Alley, to the south, where the volume control is just a little lower, plus a series of smaller lanes to the north. There are plenty more places around town, so make sure you plan at least one big night out. Late night, the crowd wanders on to Wat Prohm Roth St, X Bar and, eventually, to Sok San St, where there are a number of 'late-night' bars – although 'early morning' might be more apt as they stay open until daybreak. Most of the bars here have happy hours, as do some of the fancier hotels, which is a good way to sample the high life even if you're not staying at there, although the atmosphere can be a little austere.

A number of restaurants double as bars by night, including atmospheric Abacus, classic FCC Angkor, the popular Red Piano and rooftop Soup Dragon, which donates 7% of the take to the Angkor Children's Hospital, so you're helping someone else's liver, if not your own.

### ★Charlie's

BAR

(Map p100; www.charliessiemreap.com; 98 Pithnou St; ⊙10am-1am; 🛜) A cracking retro Americana bar with cheap drinks and a convivial crowd. This is the missing link between the more sophisticated bars around the alleyways and the madness unfolding nightly on Pub St. Food optional, shots obligatory.

### Laundry Bar

BAR

(Map p100; St 9; ⊙4pm-late; 🛜) One of the most chilled bars in town thanks to low lighting

## THE CAMBODIAN BEER GARDEN EXPERIENCE

There are dozens of beer gardens around Siem Reap that cater to young Cambodians working in the tourism industry. These can be great places to get some cheap beer and local snacks, as well as getting to know some Cambodians beyond your driver or guide. All serve up ice-cold beer, some in 3L beer towers complete with chiller. They can be a bit laddish by Cambodian standards, so solo female travellers might want to hook up with a traveller crowd before venturing forth.

The best strip is just north of Airport Rd from the first set of traffic lights after Sivatha St, known locally as 'Cambodian Pub St'. **Samut Siem Reap** (Map p125; Cambodian Pub St; ☉ 5pm-late) is one of the best of the bunch, with a huge central bar, regular football on big screens and mighty beer towers. Wander around this area to see where the locals are hanging out.

and discerning decor, this is the place to come for electronica and ambient sounds. It heaves on weekends or when guest DJs crank up the volume. Happy hour until 9pm.

**Asana** BAR
(Map p100; www.asana-cambodia.com; The Lane; ☉ 11am-late; ☎) Also known as the wooden house, this is a traditional Cambodian countryside home dropped into the backstreets of Siem Reap, which makes for an atmospheric place to drink. Lounge on kapok-filled rice sacks over a classic cocktail made with infused rice wine. Khmer cocktail classes with Sombai spirits available at US$15 per person.

**Miss Wong** BAR
(Map p100; www.misswong.net; The Lane; ☉ 5pm-late; ☎) Miss Wong carries you back to chic 1920s Shanghai. The cocktails are a draw here, making it a cool place to while away an evening, with a new menu offering dim sum. Gay-friendly and extremely popular with the well-heeled expat crowd.

**The Yellow Sub** BAR
(Map p100; www.theyellow-sub.com; The Lane; ☉ 11am-11pm; ☎) No prizes for guessing the theme here, but as Beatles tribute bars go, this has to be one of the best. Memorabilia plasters the walls, including signed album covers and artworks. Venture upstairs and there are multiple levels, including a pool table and a 4th-floor whisky bar with single malts. Great food as well, including Beatle-themed burgers.

**Picasso** BAR
(Map p100; Alley West; ☉ 5pm-late; ☎) This tiny tapas bar in the Alley West area is a convivial spot for a bit of over-the-counter banter. With only a dozen or so stools, expect spill-over into the street, especially once the cheap sangria, worldly wines and cheap Tiger bottles start flowing.

**Angkor What?** BAR
(Map p100; Pub St; ☉ 5pm-late; ☎) Siem Reap's original bar claims to have been promoting irresponsible drinking since 1998. The happy hour (to 9pm) lightens the mood for later when everyone's bouncing along to indie anthems, sometimes on the tables, sometimes under them.

**YOLO Bar** BAR
(Map p100; Wat Prohm Roth St; ☉ 5pm-late; ☎) A popular backpacker bar down a side street, YOLO specialises in cheap cocktails by the bucketload (quite literally) and DIY tunes played through their open table laptop. Give it a try...after all, you only live once.

**Barcode** BAR
(Map p96; http://barcodesiemreap.com; Wat Prohm Roth St; ☉ 5pm-late; ☎) A super-stylin' gay bar that is metrosexual friendly, the cocktails here are worth the stop, as is the regular drag show at 9.30pm. There is a happy hour from 5pm to 7pm daily.

**Mezze Bar** BAR
(Map p100; www.mezzesiemreap.com; St 11; ☉ 6pm-late; ☎) One of the hippest bars in Siem Reap, Mezze is located above the circus that surrounds Pub St. Ascend the stairs to a contemporary lounge bar complete with original art and regular DJs.

**Malone's** BAR
(Map p100; St 11; ☉ 8am-midnight; ☎) This upstairs bar brings the sparkle of the Emerald Isle to homesick Irish and a whole host of honorary Dubliners. Serves up Powers whiskey, Guinness and excellent pub grub.

**Long's Bar** BAR
(Map p100; The Lane; ☉ 5pm-late; ☎) A great little bolt hole hidden away among the Lanes, Long's has some creative cocktails such as

pomelo and basil infusion or ginger and lemongrass mojito. Cheap beers for a proper bar, blissfully air-conditioned and no smoking inside.

### Linga Bar
COCKTAIL LOUNGE

(Map p100; The Alley; ⊙4pm-late; 🛜) This chic gay bar attracts all comers thanks to a relaxed atmosphere, a cracking cocktail list and some ambient sounds. Relocated across the Alley, it's still popular.

### Temple Club
BAR

(Map p100; Pub St; ⊙10am-late; 🛜) The only worshipping going on at this temple is 'all hail the ale'. This place starts moving early and doesn't stop, but it's not for the hard of hearing as the music is permanently cranked up to 11. Dangerous happy hours from 10am to 10pm.

### X Bar
BAR

(Map p100; Sivatha St; ⊙4pm-sunrise; 🛜) One of *the* late-night spots in town, X Bar draws revellers for the witching hour when other places are closing up. Early-evening movies on the big screen, pool tables and even a skateboard pipe...take a breath test first!

### Nest
BAR-RESTAURANT

(Map p96; http://nestangkor.com; Sivatha St; ⊙11am-late; 🛜) A memorable bar thanks to its sweeping sail-like shelters and stylish seating, this place has one of the most creative cocktail lists in town. Curl up in a sleigh bed and relax for the night. Also has an impressive menu of fusion and international cuisine should the munchies strike.

### Sombai
DISTILLERY

(Map p125; ☑095 810890; www.sombai.com; Sombai Rd) Is it drinking or is it shopping? A bit of both actually, as this rice-wine distillery produces infused spirits sold in beautiful hand-painted bottles. Choose from eight flavours including ginger and chilli or anise coffee. Free tastings available by appointment. It's also on sale in bars around Siem Reap.

## ★ Entertainment

Several restaurants and hotels offer cultural performances during the evening, and for many visitors such shows offer the only opportunity to see Cambodian classical dance. While they may be aimed at tourists and are nowhere near as sophisticated as a performance of the Royal Ballet in Phnom Penh, to the untrained eye they are nonetheless graceful and alluring. Prices usually include a buffet meal.

### Apsara Theatre
DANCE

(Map p96; ☑063-963561; www.angkorvillage.com/theatre.php; St 26; admission US$25) The setting is a striking wooden pavilion finished in the style of a wat. There are two Cambodian classical dance shows per night, including dinner, and it's packed to the rafters with tour groups.

### Plae Pakaa
PERFORMING ARTS

(Map p96; ☑099 516580; www.cambodianliving arts.org; Artisans Angkor – Les Chantiers Écoles; adult/child US$15/6; ⊙7pm Mon-Sat) 🍴 Plae Pakaa is a series of traditional dance performances hosted by the talented dancers of Cambodian Living Arts. Originating in

SIEM REAP ENTERTAINMENT

---

### ROLL UP, ROLL UP, THE CIRCUS HAS COME TO TOWN

Cambodia's answer to Cirque du Soleil, **Phare the Cambodian Circus** (Map p125; ☑015 499480; www.pharecambodiancircus.org; west end of Sok San Rd; adult/child US$18/10, premium seats US$35/18; ⊙8pm) is so much more than a conventional circus, with an emphasis on performance art and a subtle yet striking social message behind each production. Cambodia's leading circus, theatre and performing arts organisation, Phare Ponleu Selpak opened its big top for nightly shows in 2013 and the result is a unique form of entertainment that should be considered unmissable when staying in Siem Reap. Several generations of performers have graduated through Phare's original Battambang campus and have gone on to perform in international venues around the world. Many of the performers have deeply moving personal stories of abuse and hardship, making their talents a triumph against the odds. An inspiring night out for adults and children alike, all proceeds are reinvested into Phare Ponleu Selpak activities. Animal lovers will be pleased to note there are no animals used in any performance. Return visitors should note that the circus has recently moved location to the western outskirts of town and is no longer behind the Angkor National Museum.

Phnom Penh, the show now runs at Artisans Angkor during high season from November to the end of March, but there may also be a reduced schedule during the low season.

**Beatocello**                                    CLASSICAL MUSIC
(Map p104; www.beatocello.com; Charles de Gaulle Blvd; ⊗ 7.15pm Thu & Sat) ◢ Better known as Dr Beat Richner, Beatocello performs cello compositions at Jayavarman VII Children's Hospital. Entry is free, but donations are welcome as they assist the hospital in offering free medical treatment to the children of Cambodia.

**La Noria Restaurant**                          PERFORMING ARTS
(Map p96; ☑ 063-964242; Siem Reap River Rd; show US$6, mains US$4-8) ◢ For something a bit different, try the Wednesday-evening shadow-puppet show with classical dance at La Noria (p105). Part of the fee is donated to a charity supporting local children.

**Rosana Broadway**                                      CABARET
(Map p125; ☑ 063-769991; www.rosanabroadway. com; NH6; show US$25-45; ⊗ 7.30pm) Bringing a bit of Bangkok-style Broadway to Siem Reap, this show includes cultural dances from the region and a not-so-cultural ladyboy cabaret; ticket prices are on the high side.

**Temple Club**                                            DANCE
(Map p100; Pub St; ☎) Temple Club stages a free traditional dance show from 7.30pm,

providing punters order some food and drink from the very reasonably priced menu.

# 🛍 Shopping

Much of what you see on sale in the markets of Siem Reap can also be purchased from children and vendors throughout the temple area. Some visitors get fed up with the endless sales pitches as they navigate the ancient wonders, while others enjoy the banter and a chance to interact with Cambodian people. It's often children out selling, and some visitors will argue that they should be at school instead. However, most do attend school at least half of the time, joining for morning or afternoon classes, alternating with siblings.

Items touted at the temples include postcards, T-shirts, temple bas-relief rubbings, curious musical instruments, ornamental knives and crossbows – the latter may raise a few eyebrows when customs should you try to take one home! Be sure to bargain, as overcharging is pretty common.

Cheap books on Angkor and Cambodia are hawked by kids around the temples, and by amputees trying to make a new start in Siem Reap. Be aware that many are illegal photocopies and the print quality is poor.

Shinta Mani Resort (p105) holds its 'Well Made in Cambodia' community market

---

## SHOPPING FOR A CAUSE

Several shops support Cambodia's disabled and disenfranchised through their production process or their profits.

**AHA Local Handicraft Market** (Map p104; ☑ 078 341454; www.aha-kh.com; Rd 60, Trang Village) For locally produced souvenirs (unlike much of the imported stuff that turns up in Psar Chaa) drop in on this handicraft market. It's a little out of the way, but there are more than 20 stalls selling a wide range of traditional items.

**Artisans Angkor** (Map p96; www.artisansdangkor.com; ⊗ 7.30am-6.30pm) On the premises of Les Chantiers Écoles (p95) is this shop that sells everything from stone and wood reproductions of Angkorian-era statues to household furnishings. There's a second shop opposite Angkor Wat in the Angkor Cafe building, and outlets at Phnom Penh and Siem Reap international airports. All profits from sales go back into funding the school and bringing more young Cambodians into the training program, which is 20% owned by the artisans themselves.

**IKTT** (Map p96; Tonlé Sap Rd; ⊗ 9am-5pm) This traditional wooden house is home to the Institute for Khmer Traditional Textiles. Fine *krama*, scarves, throws and more.

**Mekong Quilts** (Map p100; www.mekong-quilts.org; 5 Sivatha St; ⊗ 8am-10pm) Handmade bed covers, quilts, home accessories and more in cotton, linen and silk. Supports women from poor rural areas and helps them earn money within their community.

**Nyemo** (Map p96; www.nyemo.com; Angkor Night Market; ⊗ 4pm-midnight) Silk products such as cushions, hangings and throws, plus children's toys. Proceeds are used to help HIV/AIDS sufferers and vulnerable women.

from 4pm to 9pm on Saturdays, Sundays and Tuesdays, bringing together many of the best local craftsfolk and creators in Siem Reap.

### Psar Chaa                                    MARKET

(Old Market; Map p100) When it comes to shopping in town, Psar Chaa is well stocked with anything you may want to buy, and lots that you don't. Silverware, silk, wood carvings, stone carvings, Buddhas, paintings, rubbings, notes and coins, T-shirts, table mats... the list goes on. There are bargains to be had if you haggle patiently and humorously. Avoid buying old stone carvings that vendors claim are from Angkor. Whether or not they are real, buying these artefacts serves only to encourage their plunder and they will usually be confiscated by customs.

### Angkor Night Market                          MARKET

(Map p96; www.angkornightmarket.com; ☺4pm-midnight) Near Sivatha St, this is a popular place on the Siem Reap shopping scene. It's packed with stalls selling a variety of handicrafts, souvenirs and silks and is well worth a browse to take advantage of cooler temperatures. It's also possible to chill out in the Island Bar, indulge in a Dr Fish massage or watch a 3D event movie (US$3) about the Khmer Rouge or the scourge of land mines. There are now half a dozen copycats in the near vicinity.

### Siem Reap Art Center                         MARKET

(Map p96; www.siemreapartcenter.com; south bank of Siem Reap River; ☺4-11pm) One of the newer night markets in town, the Siem Reap Art Center has a range of handicrafts and souvenirs, and is connected to the Psar Chaa area via a traditional wooden bridge across the Siem Reap River.

### Bambou Indochine                           CLOTHING

(Map p100; Alley West; ☺10am-10pm) Original clothing designs inspired by Indochina. A cut above the average souvenir T-shirts.

### Blue Apsara                                  BOOKS

(Map p100; St 9; ☺9am-9pm) The longest-running secondhand bookstore in town has a good selection of English, French and German titles.

### Diwo Gallery                                  ARTS

(www.tdiwo.com; Wat Svay district; ☺9am-6pm) Sells French photographer and writer Thierry Diwo's collection of art photography from around Angkor, as well as high-quality replica bronze, stone and wood sculptures.

### Eric Raisina Workshop                      FASHION

(Map p125; ☎063-965207; www.ericraisina.com; Wat Thmei area; ☺by appointment) Renowned designer Eric Raisina brings a unique cocktail of influences to his couture. Born in Madagascar, raised in France and resident in Cambodia, he offers a striking collection

**SIEM REAP** SHOPPING

**Rajana** (Map p96; ☎063-964744; www.rajanacrafts.org; Sivatha St; ☺9am-9pm Mon-Sat) Sells quirky wooden and metalwork objects, well-designed silver jewellery and handmade cards. Rajana promotes fair-trade employment opportunities for Cambodians.

**Rehab Craft** (Map p100; Pokambar Ave; ☺8am-5.30pm) Small shop selling traditional scarves, silk items, carvings, paintings and postcards, all to assist the disabled community in Cambodia.

**Samatoa** (Map p96; ☎063-965310; www.samatoa.com; St 26; ☺8am-11pm) If you find yourself in need of a party frock, this designer dress shop offers original threads in silk, with the option of a tailored fit in 48 hours. Samatoa employs fair-trade practices.

**Senteurs d'Angkor** (Map p100; ☎063-964860; Pithnou St; ☺8.30am-9.30pm) Opposite Psar Chaa, this shop has an eclectic collection of silk and carvings, as well as a superb range of traditional beauty products and spices, all made locally. It targets rural poor and disadvantaged Cambodians for jobs and training, and sources local products from farmers. Visit its

**Botanic Garden** (Map p125; Airport Rd; ☺7.30am-5.30pm) on Airport Rd, a sort of Willy Wonka's for the senses, where you can sample infused teas and speciality coffees.

**Smateria** (Map p100; www.smateria.com; Alley West; ☺10am-10pm) Recycling rocks here with funky bags made from construction nets, plastic bags, motorbike seat covers and more. Fair-trade enterprise employing some disabled Cambodians.

of clothing and accessories with several locations around town.

### Jayav Art
ARTS

(Map p125; ☑ 89 787345; A25 Charles de Gaulle Blvd; ☺ 9am-6pm) Inspired by all the beautiful Angkorian sculpture around the temples, but lacking the excess baggage limit to carry replica statues all the way home? Talk to Jayav Art, which specialises in exquisite papier mâché replica sculptures in various sizes.

### McDermott Gallery
ARTS

(Map p96; www.mcdermottgallery.com; FCC Angkor, Pokambor Ave; ☺ 10am-10pm) These are the famous sepia images you have seen of Angkor. Calendars, cards and striking images of the temples, plus regular exhibitions.

### Monument Books
BOOKS

(Map p96; Pokambor Ave; ☺ 9am-9pm) Well-stocked new bookstore near Psar Chaa, with an additional branch at the airport.

### Mooglee
CLOTHING

(Map p100; www.mooglee.com; The Lane; ☺ 10am-10pm) Fun T-shirt shop with some original designs including elephants at Angkor, tigers at the temples and old Angkor travel posters.

### Rogue
MUSIC

(Map p125; Sok San St; ☺ 10am-10pm) Dedicated to selling iPods, downloads, accessories and T-shirts.

### Spicy Green Mango
FASHION

(Map p100; www.spicygreenmango.com; Alley West; ☺ 8am-10pm) Small designer boutique with fun and funky fashion and accessories, in an old house that looks like it's straight out of Provence.

### Theam's House
ARTS

(Map p125; www.theamshouse.com; 25 Veal, Kokchak district; ☺ 8am-7pm) Cambodian artist and designer Theam spent years helping Artisans Angkor (p95) revitalise Khmer handicrafts and now operates his own studio of lacquer creations and artwork. Highly original, just make sure you find a driver who knows where it is.

## ⓘ Orientation

Siem Reap is still a small town at heart and is easy enough to navigate. The centre is around Psar Chaa (Old Market) and accommodation is spread throughout town. National Hwy 6 (NH6) cuts across the northern part of town, passing Psar Leu (Main Market) in the east of town and the Royal Residence and the Grand Hotel

d'Angkor in the centre, and then heads to the airport and beyond to the Thai border. The Siem Reap River (Stung Siem Reap) flows north–south through the centre of town, and has enough bridges that you won't have to worry too much about being on the wrong side. Street numbering is haphazard to say the least, so take care when hunting down specific addresses.

Angkor Wat and Angkor Thom are only 6km and 8km north of town respectively.

Buses and share taxis usually drop passengers off at the bus station/taxi park about 3km east of the town centre, from where it's a short *moto* or *remork-moto (tuk tuk)* ride to nearby guesthouses and hotels. Fast boats from Phnom Penh and Battambang arrive at Phnom Krom, about 11km south of town, and most places to stay include a free transfer by *moto* or minibus. Siem Reap International Airport is 7km west of town and there are plenty of taxis and *motos* available for transfers to the town centre.

## ⓘ Information

### DANGERS & ANNOYANCES

Siem Reap is a pretty safe city, even at night. However, if you rent a bike, don't keep your bag in the basket as it will be easy pickings for a drive-by snatch. Likewise, lone females should try to walk home with travelling companions when leaving late-night spots, particularly if heading through poorly lit areas.

There are a lot of commission scams in Siem Reap that involve certain guesthouses and small hotels paying *moto* and taxi drivers to deliver guests. Ways to avoid these scams include booking ahead via the internet and arranging a pick-up, or sticking with a partner guesthouse if you are coming from Phnom Penh. Alternatively, just go with the flow and negotiate with the hotel or guesthouse on arrival.

There are a lot of beggars around town and some visitors quickly develop beggar fatigue. However, try to remember that with no social-security network and no government support, life is pretty tough for the poorest of the poor in Cambodia. In the case of children, it is often better not to encourage begging, but if you are compelled to help, then offer food, as money usually ends up being passed on to someone else. These days the problem is less serious, as many former beggars have been retrained to sell books or postcards to tourists instead of simply begging.

Watch out for the baby milk powder scam taking place in Siem Reap. A woman and baby approach asking for help to buy milk for the baby. Visitor agrees and gets asked to buy the most expensive brand in the nearby minimart. Transaction over, woman and baby then take the formula back to the shop and split the profit.

Out at the remote temple sites beyond Angkor, stick to clearly marked trails. There are still land mines at locations such as Phnom Kulen and Koh Ker.

### EMERGENCY

**Tourist Police** (Map p125; ☑ 012 402424) Located at the main ticket checkpoint (Map p125) for the Angkor area, this is the place to lodge a complaint if you encounter any serious problems while in Siem Reap.

### INTERNET ACCESS

Internet shops are fast disappearing as most restaurants and bars offer reliable free wi-fi. A few remain and prices are around US$0.50 per hour and cheap internet-based telephone calls are also offered. Almost all guesthouses and hotels also offer free internet access for guests, either via a free terminal, free wi-fi or both.

### MEDICAL SERVICES

Siem Reap now has an international-standard hospital for emergencies. However, any serious complications will still require relocation to Bangkok.

**Angkor Hospital for Children** (AHC; Map p96; ☑ 063-963409; angkorhospital.org; cnr Oum Chhay St & Tep Vong St; ☺24hr) This international-standard paediatric hospital is the place to take your children if they fall sick. They will also assist adults in an emergency for up to 24 hours. Donations accepted.

**Royal Angkor International Hospital** (Map p125; ☑ 063-761888; www.royalangkor hospital.com; Airport Rd) This international facility affiliated with the Bangkok Hospital is on the expensive side as it's used to dealing with insurance companies.

**U-Care Pharmacy** (Map p100; ☑ 063-965396; Pithnou St; ☺8am-10pm) Smart pharmacy and shop similar to Boots in Thailand (and the UK). English spoken.

### MONEY

For cash exchanges, markets (usually at jewellery stalls or dedicated money-changing stalls) are faster and less bureaucratic than the banks.

**ABA Bank** (Map p96; Tep Vong St ) Withdrawals are limited to US$100 per transaction and there is a US$4 transaction fee per withdrawl.

**ANZ Royal Bank** (Map p96; Achar Mean St) Credit-card advances and can change travellers cheques in most major currencies. Several branches and many ATMs (US$5 per withdrawal) around town.

**Canadia Bank** (Map p96; Sivatha St) Offers credit-card cash advances (US$4) and changes travellers cheques in most major currencies at a 2% commission.

### POST

**Main Post Office** (Map p96; Pokambor Ave; ☺7am-5.30pm) Services are more reliable these days, but it doesn't hurt to see your stamps franked. Includes a branch of EMS express mail.

### TELEPHONE & FAX

Making international calls is all about Facetime, Skype or Viber these days. Download the apps before you travel and consider purchasing a local SIM card if you have an unlocked phone and will be in the country for a while. Or even a local mobile and SIM, which won't break the bank. Hotels impose hefty surcharges on calls, so check the rates before you dial.

### TOURIST INFORMATION

There is an official tourist office in Siem Reap, but it offers little more than take-away leaflets. Guesthouses and hotels are often a more reliable source of information, as are fellow travellers who have been in town for a few days.

Check out *Drinking and Dining* for the low-down on bars and restaurants, or *Out and About* for shops and services, both produced by Cambodia Pocket Guide (www.cambodiapocketguide.com) and widely available. Pick up a copy of the *Siem Reap Angkor Visitors Guide* (www.canby publications.com), which is packed with listings and comes out quarterly.

**Siem Reap Tourism Office** (Map p96; ☑ 063-959600; http://siemreaptourism.gov.kh; Royal Gardens) Conveniently located in the Royal Gardens but not much local intel available here.

---

### INTERNATIONAL BUS TO BANGKOK

Many guesthouses and travel companies offer 'international' bus tickets to Bangkok (around US$15) with a change of bus at the border. There are even some 'night' buses advertised, but these are pretty pointless given the Poipet border does not open until 7am!

**Nattakan** (Map p96; ☑ 078 795333; Sivatha St) offers a 'direct' bus to Bangkok (US$25) daily at 8am departing from its Sivatha St office, including fast-track immigration at the border. It may not be so advantageous departing Cambodia but might prove very useful for travellers entering Cambodia this way. However, visa-overcharging is a risk; arranging a Cambodian e-visa (US$25) in advance of travel is one way to avoid this. From Bangkok to Siem Reap, the bus departs Mo Chit Bus Terminal at 9am and tickets cost 750B.

SIEM REAP INFORMATION

## TRANSPORT OPTIONS FROM SIEM REAP

| DESTINATION | CAR & MOTORBIKE | BUS | BOAT | AIR |
| --- | --- | --- | --- | --- |
| Bangkok, Thailand | 8hr | US$15-28, 10hr, frequent | N/A | from US$90, 1hr, 8 daily |
| Battambang | 3hr | US$5-8, 4hr, regular | US$20, 6-8hr, 7am | N/A |
| Kompong Thom | 2hr | US$5, 3hr, frequent | N/A | N/A |
| Phnom Penh | 6hr | US$6-15, 7hr, frequent | US$35, 5hr, 7am | from US$40, 30min, 9 daily |
| Poipet | 3hr | US$5-8, 3hr, regular | N/A | N/A |

# ❶ Getting There & Away

### AIR

There are direct international flights from Siem Reap to Bangkok in Thailand; Vientiane, Luang Prabang and Pakse in Laos; Ho Chi Minh City (Saigon), Hanoi and Danang in Vietnam; Kuala Lumpur in Malaysia; Beijing, Guangzhou, Hong Kong, Kunming and Shanghai in China; Busan and Seoul in South Korea; Singapore; Taipei in Taiwan; Manila in the Philippines; and Yangon in Myanmar.

Domestic links are currently limited to Phnom Penh (from US$40 one way) and Sihanoukville (from US$50 one way). Airlines operating domestic flights include Bassaka Air, Cambodia Angkor Air and Cambodia Bayon Airlines. Demand for seats is high during peak season, so book as far in advance as possible. Some of the discount fares are reserved for Cambodian nationals.

### BOAT

There are daily express boat services between Siem Reap and Phnom Penh (US$35, five to six hours) or Battambang (US$20, four to eight hours or more, depending on the season). The boat to Phnom Penh is rather overpriced these days, given it is just as fast by road and so much cheaper. The Battambang trip is seriously scenic, but breakdowns are *very* common.

Boats from Siem Reap leave from the floating village of Chong Kneas near Phnom Krom, about 11km south of Siem Reap. The boats dock in different places at different times of the year; when the lake recedes in the dry season, both the port and floating village move with it. An all-weather road has improved access around the lake area, but the main road out to the lake takes a pummelling in the annual monsoon.

Most of the guesthouses in town sell boat tickets. Buying the ticket from a guesthouse usually includes a *moto* or minibus ride to the port. Otherwise, a *moto* out there costs about US$3, a *remork-moto* about US$7 and a taxi about US$15.

### BUS

The road linking Siem Reap to Phnom Penh varies in condition from year to year. Currently the section from Phnom Penh to Skuon is excellent with

two-lanes in either direction. However, the section between Skuon and Kompong Thom is still under repair. The road west to Sisophon, Thailand and Battambang is generally in pretty good condition.

All buses depart from the **bus station/taxi park** (Map p125), which is 3km east of town and nearly 1km south of NH6. Tickets are available at guesthouses, hotels, bus offices, travel agencies and ticket kiosks. Some bus companies send a minibus around to pick up passengers at their place of lodging. Departures to Phnom Penh run throughout the day, and night buses are available. Buses to other destinations generally leave early in the morning. Upon arrival in Siem Reap, be prepared for a rugby scrum of eager *moto* drivers when getting off the bus. Express minibus services to Phnom Penh (from US$10) are gaining in popularity as they can save considerable time on the poor sections of road.

Be aware that several long-distance services require a change of bus, particularly where an international border is involved, such as services to Bangkok, Ho Chi Minh City, or Pakse in Southern Laos. Also services to some South Coast destinations such as Kampot and Kep require a lengthy detour via Sihanoukville, so ask about the routing and timing when making a booking. In some cases, it may be better to take a bus to Phnom Penh and change there.

Night buses are now a popular option between Siem Reap and Phnom Penh and on longer routes from temple town to Sihanoukville and points beyond. Most night buses go via Sihanoukville, meaning a diversion to Kampot or Koh Kong, but this can help towards a more reasonable hour of arrival. Check the schedules!

**Capitol Tour** (Map p100; ☎ 063-963883; www.capitoltourscambodia.com)

**Giant Ibis** (Map p96; ☎ 023-999333; www.giantibis.com) Smartest operator with daily service to Phnom Penh (US$15) and free wi-fi.

**GST** (Map p96; ☎ 092 905016)

**Gold VIP** (Map p96; ☎ 063-632 7600) Express minibuses to Phnom Penh and Sihanoukville.

**Golden Bayon Express** (Map p96; ☎ 063-966968; goldenbayonexpress.com)

**Hang Tep** (Map p96; ☎ 012 645264)

**Larryta Express** (Map p125; ☏ 066 202020) Smart new Ford Transit minibuses hourly to Phnom Penh through the day.

**Mekong Express** (Map p96; ☏ 063-963662; catmekongexpress.com/) Upmarket bus company with hostesses and drinks.

**Mey Hong** (Map p125; ☏ 063-965979) Express minivans to Phnom Penh.

**Orient Express 1907** (Map p96; ☏ 069 881907; www.orientexpress1907.com) One of the smarter operators to the capital.

**Phnom Penh Sorya** (Map p125; ☏ 012 235618; www.ppsoryatransport.com)

**Sapaco Transport** (Map p96; ☏ 063-761434; www.sapacotourist.vn) Buses to Ho Chi Minh City with a change in Phnom Penh.

**Virak Buntham** (Map p96; ☏ 017 790440) The night-bus specialist to Phnom Penh, Sihanoukville and Koh Kong.

### SHARE TAXI, MINIBUS & PICK-UP

Share taxis and other vehicles operate along some of the main routes and these can be a little quicker than buses. Destinations include Phnom Penh (US$10, five hours), Kompong Thom (US$5, two hours), Sisophon (US$5, two hours) and Poipet (US$7, three hours). To get to the

temple of Banteay Chhmar, head to Sisophon and arrange onward transport there.

## ⊕ Getting Around

Common forms of transport used for getting around Siem Reap include *motos* (motorcycle taxis) and *remork-motos* (tuk tuks). Travellers looking to stretch their legs can hire a bicycle for the day, and many guesthouses and hotels can organise car hire for trips further afield.

### TO/FROM THE AIRPORT

Siem Reap International Airport is 7km from the town centre. Many hotels and guesthouses in Siem Reap offer a free airport pick-up service with advance bookings. Official taxis are available next to the terminal for US$9. A trip to the city centre on the back of a *moto* is US$3 or US$7 by *remork-moto*.

### BICYCLE

Some of the guesthouses around town hire out bicycles, as do a few shops around Psar Chaa, usually for US$1 to US$2 a day. The **White Bicycles** (www.thewhitebicycles.org) project rents bikes through over 50 guesthouses and hotels in Siem Reap, with all proceeds going towards supporting local development projects around Siem

SIEM REAP GETTING AROUND

## BUSES FROM SIEM REAP

| DESTINATION | DURATION (HR) | PRICE (US$) | COMPANIES | FREQUENCY |
|---|---|---|---|---|
| Anlong Veng | 3 | 5 | GST | 1 daily at 7.15am |
| Bangkok, Thailand | 10 | 15-28 | Capitol Tour, Hang Tep, Nattakan, Virak Buntham | Frequent until 4pm |
| Battambang | 4 | 5-8 | Capitol Tour, Phnom Penh Sorya | Regular in the morning |
| Ho Chi Minh City, Vietnam | 12 | 22-27 | Mekong Express, Sapaco Transport | 2 per day at 7.30am |
| Kampot | 13 | 13 | Virak Buntham | 1 daily at 7pm |
| Koh Kong | 13-14 | 17-22 | Virak Buntham | 2 daily at 7pm & 11pm |
| Kompong Cham | 5-6 | 5 | Capitol Tour, GST | Frequent in the morning |
| Kratie | 7-8 | 8-13 | GST | 2 daily at 6am & 7.15am |
| Phnom Penh | 6-7 | 6-15 | Capitol Tour, Giant Ibis, Gold VIP, Golden Bayon Express, GST, Larryta Express, Mekong Express, Mey Hong, Orient Express 1907, Phnom Penh Sorya, Virak Buntham | Frequent both day and night until midnight |
| Poipet | 3 | 5-8 | Capitol Tour, Hang Tep | Frequent in the morning |
| Preah Vihear City | 3-4 | 8-12 | AVT, GST | 2 in the morning |
| Sihanoukville | 10-11 | 13-25 | Capitol Tour, Mekong Express, Virak Buntham | 3 in the morning, 5 between 7pm and midnight |
| Stung Treng | 7 | 20 | AVT | 1 daily at 8.15am |

Reap. Imported mountain bikes are available from cycling tour operators for around US$8 to US$10. Another option is **Green e-bikes** (Map p96; ☑ 095 700130; www.greene-bike.com; Central Market; per 24hr US$10; ⊙ 7.30am-7pm daily), an environmentally sound compromise between the bicycle and the motorbike.

### CAR & MOTORCYCLE

Most hotels and guesthouses can organise car hire for the day, with a going rate of US$30 and up. Upmarket hotels may charge more. Foreigners are forbidden to rent motorcycles in and around Siem Reap. If you want to get around on your own motorcycle, you need to hire one in Phnom Penh and ride it to Siem Reap.

### MOTO

A *moto* (motorcycle taxi) with a driver will cost from US$10 per day depending on the destination. Far-flung temples will involve a higher fee. The average cost for a short trip within town is 2000r or so, and around US$1 or more to places strung out along the roads to Angkor or the airport. It is probably best to negotiate in advance as a lot of drivers have got into the habit of overcharging.

### REMORK-MOTO

*Remork-motos* are sweet little motorcycles with carriages (commonly called *tuk tuks* around town), and are a nice way for couples to get about Siem Reap, although drivers like to inflate the prices. Trips around town start from US$2, but you'll need to pay more to the edge of town at night. Prices rise when you add more people.

# AROUND SIEM REAP

## Banteay Srei District
ស្រុក បន្ទាយស្រី

Famous for its petite pink-coloured temple (p165), there is more to Banteay Srei than its headline Angkor sites, such as the 'River of a Thousand Lingas' at Kbal Spean (p166) and the 12th-century temple of Banteay Samré (p163). New destinations and experiences, including homestays, lifestyle experiences and handicraft workshops, are under development to encourage visitors to stay longer in the district and explore further.

### ◉ Sights & Activities

While the temples (p165) of the Banteay Srei district are the main attraction, make sure you also check out the Angkor Centre for Conservation of Biodiversity (p166) when visiting the River of a Thousand Lingas at

Kbal Spean. Other activities include walks in the Kbal Teuk Community Forest, home to rare carnivorous pitcher plants.

★ **Cambodia Landmine Museum**   MUSEUM
(សារមន្ទីរគ្រាប់មីនកម្ពុជា និងមូលនិធិសង្គ្រោះ; ☑ 012 598951; www.cambodialandminemuseum.org; donation US$3; ⊙ 7.30am-5pm) Established by DIY de-miner Aki Ra, this museum has eye-opening displays on the curse of land mines in Cambodia. The collection includes mines, mortars, guns and weaponry, and there's a mock minefield where visitors can attempt to locate the deactivated mines. Proceeds from the museum are ploughed into mine-awareness campaigns. It's about 25km from Siem Reap, near Banteay Srei.

**Banteay Srei
Butterfly Centre**   WILDLIFE RESERVE
(សួនមេអំបៅបន្ទាយស្រី; ☑ 097 852 7852; www.angkorbutterfly.com; adult/child US$4/2; ⊙ 9am-5pm) 🦋 The centre is the largest fully enclosed butterfly centre in southeast Asia, with more than 30 species of Cambodian butterflies fluttering about. It is a good experience for children, as they can see the whole life cycle from egg to caterpillar to cocoon to butterfly. The centre aims to provide a sustainable living for the rural poor and most of the butterflies are farmed around Phnom Kulen. It's about 7km before Banteay Srei temple on the left side of the road.

**Tani Museum of Ceramics**   MUSEUM
(សារមន្ទីរកុលាល ភា ជន៍ ភូមិតានី; Tani Village; admission US$1) This tiny museum is located in Tani commune and showcases a collection of Angkorian pottery from the days of the Khmer empire. Only pottery enthusiasts are likely to get fired up by the limited displays, but go with a good guide and they can show you some Angkor-era kilns in the area.

### 🛏 Sleeping & Eating

There are several homestay options in the Banteay Srei district ranging from the rural and rustic to the boutique.

**Bayon Smile Homestay**   HOMESTAY $
(☑ 086 595402; sarouensean@gmail.com; Banteay Srei Village; s/d US$10/15 ) Run by the enthusiastic Mr Sarouen is this group of six spacious and attractive village homes set just north of the Banteay Srei temple. Lots of activities are promoted here, including wood-carving, village tours, cycling and some more adventurous treks to remote sites such as Phnom Cheur and Phnom Hop. Recommended.

# Around Siem Reap

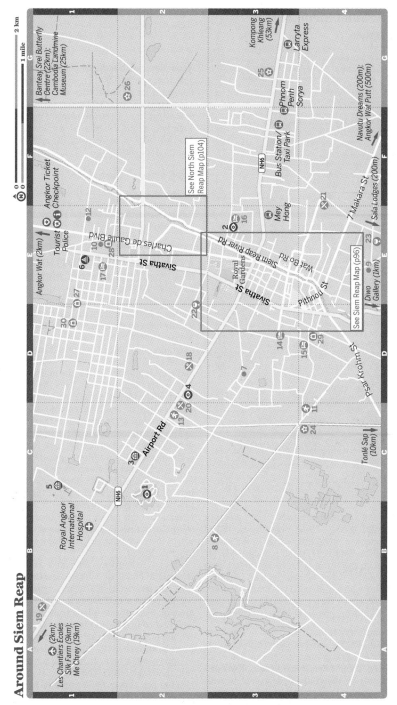

0   1 mile
0   2 km

Banteay Srei Butterfly
Centre (22km);
Cambodia Landmine
Museum (25km)

Kompong
Khleang
(53km)

Larryta
Express

Angkor Ticket
Checkpoint

Angkor Wat (2km)

Tourist
Police

Phnom
Penh
Sorya

Navutu Dreams (200m);
Angkor Wat Putt (500m)

Charles de Gaulle Blvd

Bus Station/
Taxi Park

7 Makara St

Sala Lodges (200m)

Sivatha St

Mey
Hong

Siem Reap River Rd

Wat Bo Rd

Royal
Gardens

Sivatha St

Pithnou St

Psar Krohm St

Diwo
Gallery (1km)

See North Siem
Reap Map (p104)

See Siem Reap Map (p96)

NH6

Airport Rd

NH6

Royal Angkor
International
Hospital

Tonlé Sap
(10km)

Les Chantiers Ecoles
Silk Farm (9km);
Me Chrey (19km)

(2km)

# Around Siem Reap

## ◎ Sights
1  Cambodian Cultural Village................C2
2  Cambolac......................................E3
3  House of Peace Association................C2
4  Senteurs d'Angkor Botanic Garden ...D2
5  War Museum ................................C1
6  Wat Thmei....................................E1

## ◎ Activities, Courses & Tours
7  Angkor Fight Club ..........................D3
8  Angkor Golf Resort ........................B3
9  Cambodia Quad Bike........................E4
10  Cambodia Vespa Adventures ............E1
11  Happy Ranch ................................C4
12  Khmer Ways .................................E1
13  The Great Escape ..........................C2

## ◎ Sleeping
14  Funky Flashpacker...........................D3
15  Garden Village ...............................D4
16  Heritage Suites ..............................E3
17  Pavillon Indochine..........................E1

## ◎ Eating
18  Abacus .........................................D2
19  Les Jardins des Delices.....................A1
20  Madame Butterfly............................C2
21  Por Cuisine ...................................F4

## ◎ Drinking & Nightlife
22  Samut Siem Reap............................D2
23  Sombai ........................................E4

## ◎ Entertainment
24  Phare the Cambodian Circus............C4
25  Rosana Broadway............................G3
26  Smile of Angkor.............................G2

## ◎ Shopping
27  Eric Raisina Workshop .....................E1
28  Jayav Art .....................................E1
29  Rogue .........................................D4
30  Theam's House ..............................D1

### Tbeng Village Homestays          HOMESTAY $
(☏ 092 966047; Tbeng Village; house US$15)
Tbeng is a pretty little village in the east of
Banteay Srei where local schoolteacher Mr
Khuon has set up a homestay project with
around a dozen houses. Try and opt for a
house with a tiled roof if you have the option,
as it's cooler than corrugated metal. Village
activities on offer and local interaction.

### Bong Thom Home Stay          HOMESTAY $$
(☏ 012 520092; www.thebongthomhomestay.com;
r US$60-80) Very much a boutique homestay,
Bong Thom offers some beautiful wooden
houses in the countryside complete with
four-poster beds and tasteful decor. Lots of

activities are available including cooking
classes, cycling, ox-cart rides and more. The
restaurant here is well regarded and open
to non-guests with an advance booking.

### Naom Banchok Noodle Stalls          NOODLES $
(Preah Dak; noodles 4000r) Preah Dak village is
renowned for its *naom banchok* (thick rice
noodles) stalls, which hug the main road
to Banteay Srei. These homemade noodles
come with a mild fish broth or a mild chick-
en curry, plus an assortment of vegetables
and condiments.

### ❶ Getting There & Away
Banteay Srei is about 32km northeast of Siem
Reap on good roads. It should take about 45
minutes to reach by car or one hour by *remork*;
agree to a price before setting off.

# Prek Toal Bird Sanctuary

Prek Toal (ជម្រកសត្វស្លាបទឹកព្រែកទាល់;
admission US$25-50) is one of three bio-
spheres on the Tonlé Sap lake, and this
stunning bird sanctuary makes it the most
worthwhile and straightforward of the three
to visit. It is an ornithologist's fantasy, with
a significant number of rare breeds gathered
in one small area, including the huge lesser
and greater adjutant storks, the milky stork
and the spot-billed pelican. Even the uninitiated will be impressed, as these birds have
a huge wingspan and build enormous nests.

Visitors during the dry season (December
to April) will find the concentration of birds
like something out of a Hitchcock film. It
is also possible to visit from September, but
the numbers may be lower. As water starts
to dry up elsewhere, the birds congregate
here. Serious twitchers know that the best
time to see birds is early morning or late afternoon and this means an early start or an
overnight at Prek Toal's environment office,
where there are basic single beds for US$15
(doubles US$20).

Several ecotourism companies arrange
trips out to Prek Toal. **Sam Veasna Center**
(SVC; Map p96; ☏ 063-963710; www.samveasna.
org; per person from US$100), in the Wat Bo
area of Siem Reap, offers trips to Prek
Toal that contribute to the conservation of
the area. Sam Veasna uses ecotourism to
provide an income for local communities
in return for a ban on hunting and cutting down the forest. The trips cost about
US$100 per person for a group of five or

more, with additional charges for smaller groups. Osmose (☎ 012 832812; www.osmose tonlesap.net; per person US$95) also runs organised day trips to Prek Toal with a minimum group of four.

Tours include transport, entrance fees, guides, breakfast, lunch and water. Binoculars are available on request, plus the Sam Veasna Center has spotting scopes. Both outfits can arrange overnight trips for serious enthusiasts. Some proceeds from the tours go towards educating children and villagers about the importance of the birds and the unique flooded-forest environment, and the trip includes a visit to one of the local communities. Day trips include a hotel pick-up around 6am and a return by nightfall.

Getting to the sanctuary under your own steam requires you to take a 20-minute *moto* (US$3 or so) or taxi (US$15 one way) ride to the floating village of Chong Kneas (depending on the time of day additional fees may have to be paid at the new port), and then a boat to the environment office (around US$55 return, one hour each way). From here, a small boat (US$30 including a guide) will take you into the sanctuary, which is about one hour beyond.

Sunscreen and head protection are essential, as it can get very hot in the dry season. The guides are equipped with booklets with the bird names in English, but they speak little English themselves, hence the advantage of travelling with the Sam Veasna Center or Osmose (both of which provide English-speaking guides).

## Ang Trapeng Thmor Reserve

This **bird sanctuary** (អាងត្រពាំងថ្ម; admission US$10) is just across the border in the Phnom Srok region of Banteay Meanchey Province, about 100km from Siem Reap. It's one of only a handful of places in the world where it's possible to see the extremely rare sarus crane, as depicted on bas-reliefs at Bayon. These grey-feathered birds have immensely long legs and striking red heads. The reserve is based around a reservoir created by forced labour during the Khmer Rouge regime and facilities are very basic, but it is an incredibly beautiful place. Bring your own binoculars as none are available.

To reach here, follow the road to Sisophon for about 72km before turning north at Prey Mon. It's 22km to the site, passing

### A GOLDEN SILK REVIVAL

**Golden Silk** (☎ 012 596811; www.golden silk.org; Phum Thmey) is a working silk farm located in Banteay Srei district, about 30km from Siem Reap. Golden silk also happens to be the name of a refined thread of silk produced by the yellow silkworm. Once common in Cambodia, its production has been in decline in recent years due to the fragile constitution of the silkworm and the weaving methods involved in producing silk items. It's an intensive process involving 100kg of cocoons and 1500kg of mulberry leaves just to produce 10kg of silk. Visitors are welcome to visit the weaving centre and learn more about the weaving process. A donation of US$10 is requested to assist the work of the NGO, which employs former orphans and disadvantaged women from the Banteay Srei area.

through some famous silk-weaving villages. The Sam Veasna Center (opposite) arranges birdwatching trips (US$100 per person with a group of four) out here, which is probably the easiest way to undertake the trip.

## Floating Village of Chong Kneas ភូមិអណ្ដែតទឹកចុងឃ្នាស

This famous floating village is now extremely popular with visitors wanting a break from the temples, and is an easy excursion to arrange yourself. If you want something a bit more peaceful, try venturing to one of the other Tonlé Sap villages further afield. Visitors arriving by boat from Phnom Penh or Battambang get a sneak preview, as the floating village is near Phnom Krom, where the boat docks. It is very scenic in the warm light of early morning or late afternoon and can be combined with a view of the sunset from the hilltop temple of Phnom Krom. The downside is that tour groups tend to take over, and boats end up chugging up and down the channels in convoy. Avoid the crowds by asking your boat driver to take you down some back channels.

Visitors should stop at the **Gecko Centre** (www.tsbr-ed.org; ⊙ 8.30am-5.30pm), an informative exhibition that is located in the floating village and helps to unlock the secrets of the Tonlé Sap. It has displays on flora and fauna of the area, as well as information on communities living around the lake.

The village moves depending on the season and you will need to rent a boat to get around it properly. However, Sou Ching, the company that runs the tours here, has fixed boat prices at a stiff US$15 per person for independent travellers. This makes it very poor value by comparison with the temples of Angkor. Tour operators can generally get a much cheaper rate if you can join a budget tour.

One of the best ways to visit Chong Kneas is to hook up with the Tara Boat (☑092 957765; www.taraboat.com; per person incl lunch/dinner US$29/36), which offers all-inclusive trips with a meal aboard its converted cargo boat. Prices include transfers, entry fees, local boats, a tour guide and a two-course meal, starting from US$29 for a lunch to US$36 for a sunset buffet and all-you-can-drink tour.

Getting to the floating village from Siem Reap costs US$3 by *moto* each way (more if the driver waits), or US$15 or so by taxi. The trip takes 20 minutes. Alternatively rent a bicycle in town and just pedal out here, as it is a leisurely 11km through pretty villages and rice fields.

## Kompong Pluk ព្រៃលិចទឹកកំពង់ភ្លុក

Kompong Pluk (per person US$20) is an otherworldly place that looks straight out of a film set. The village itself is a friendly place, where most of the houses are built on stilts of about 6m high. Nearby is a flooded forest, inundated every year when the lake rises to take the Mekong's overflow. As the lake drops, the petrified trees are revealed. Exploring this area by wooden dugout in the wet season is very atmospheric.

Prices to visit have been fixed too high at US$20 per person for a boat and, when you add up all the separate costs, it may work out cheaper to sign up to a budget tour out of Siem Reap.

There are two ways to get to Kompong Pluk: one is to come via the floating village of Chong Kneas, where a boat (1¼ hours) can be arranged from US$55 return; the other is to come via the small town of Roluos by a combination of road (about US$7 by *moto* or US$20 by taxi) and then the boat. All said, the road-and-boat route will take up to two hours, but it depends on the sea-

son – sometimes it's more by road, sometimes more by boat. The new road brings the dry season access time to around one hour. Tara Boat (opposite) offers day trips here for US$60 per person.

## Kompong Khleang កំពង់ឃ្លាំង

One of the largest communities on the Tonlé Sap, Kompong Khleang is more of a town than the other villages, and comes complete with several ornate pagodas. Most of the houses here are built on towering stilts to allow for a dramatic change in water level. Fewer tourists visit here compared with the floating villages closer to Siem Reap, so that might be a reason to visit in itself. There is only a small floating community on the lake, but the stilted town is an interesting place to browse for an hour or two. A boat trip around the town and out to the lake is about US$20 per person for a couple of hours, but they may ask for US$30.

Kompong Khleang is not difficult to reach from Siem Reap thanks to an all-weather road via the junction town of Dam Dek, but the trip will cost about US$40 return by taxi.

## Me Chrey មេជ្រៃ

One of the more recently 'discovered' floating villages, Me Chrey (admission US$1) lies midway between Siem Reap and Prek Toal. It is one of the smaller villages in the area and sees far fewer tourists than busy Chong Kneas. Me Chrey moves with the water level and is prettier during the wet season, when houses are anchored around an island pagoda. It is located to the south of Puok district, about 25km from Siem Reap on a pretty dirt road through lush rice fields. Arrange transport by road for about US$8 for a *moto* or US$25 for a taxi before switching to a boat (a steep $20 per person) to explore the area.

Unique Kayak Cambodia (☑097 456 2000; http://uniquekayakcambodia.com; half day US$70-115, full day US$100-150) offers kayaking trips to explore the flooded forest near Me Chrey and paddle around the village. A half day is probably enough unless you are an Olympic rower. The flooded forest is really beautiful and it's possible to spot some waterbirds. Tours include all car and boat transfers so are quite reasonable if you have a group. They also include a stop at the Artisans Angkor Silk Farm in Pouk District.

# Temples of Angkor

## Best Temples for Sunrise or Sunset

➡ Angkor Wat (p144)

➡ Phnom Bakheng (p156)

➡ Pre Rup (p162)

➡ Sra Srang (p159)

## Best Temples for Film Buffs

➡ Angkor Wat (p144)

➡ Bayon (p149)

➡ Beng Mealea (p168)

➡ East Gate of Angkor Thom (p149)

➡ Ta Prohm (p158)

## Why Go?

Welcome to heaven on earth. Angkor (ប្រាសាទអង្គរ) is the earthly representation of Mt Meru, the Mt Olympus of the Hindu faith and the abode of ancient gods. The temples are the perfect fusion of creative ambition and spiritual devotion. The Cambodian 'god-kings' of old each strove to better their ancestors in size, scale and symmetry, culminating in the world's largest religious building, Angkor Wat.

The temples of Angkor are a source of inspiration and national pride to all Khmers as they struggle to rebuild their lives after the years of terror and trauma. Today, the temples are a point of pilgrimage for all Cambodians, and no traveller to the region will want to miss their extravagant beauty. Angkor is one of the world's foremost ancient sites, with the epic proportions of the Great Wall of China, the detail and intricacy of the Taj Mahal, and the symbolism and symmetry of the pyramids, all rolled into one.

## Don't Miss

➡ Seeing the sun rise over the holiest of holies, Angkor Wat (p144), the world's largest religious building.

➡ Contemplating the serenity and splendour of Bayon (p149), its 216 enigmatic faces staring out into the jungle.

➡ Witnessing nature reclaiming the stones at the mysterious ruin of Ta Prohm (p158), the *Tomb Raider* temple.

➡ Staring in wonder at the delicate carvings adorning Banteay Srei (p165), the finest seen at Angkor.

➡ Trekking deep into the jungle to discover the River of a Thousand Lingas at Kbal Spean (p166).

➡ Exploring the tangled vines, crumbling corridors and jumbled sandstone blocks of Beng Mealea (p168).

# Temples of Angkor

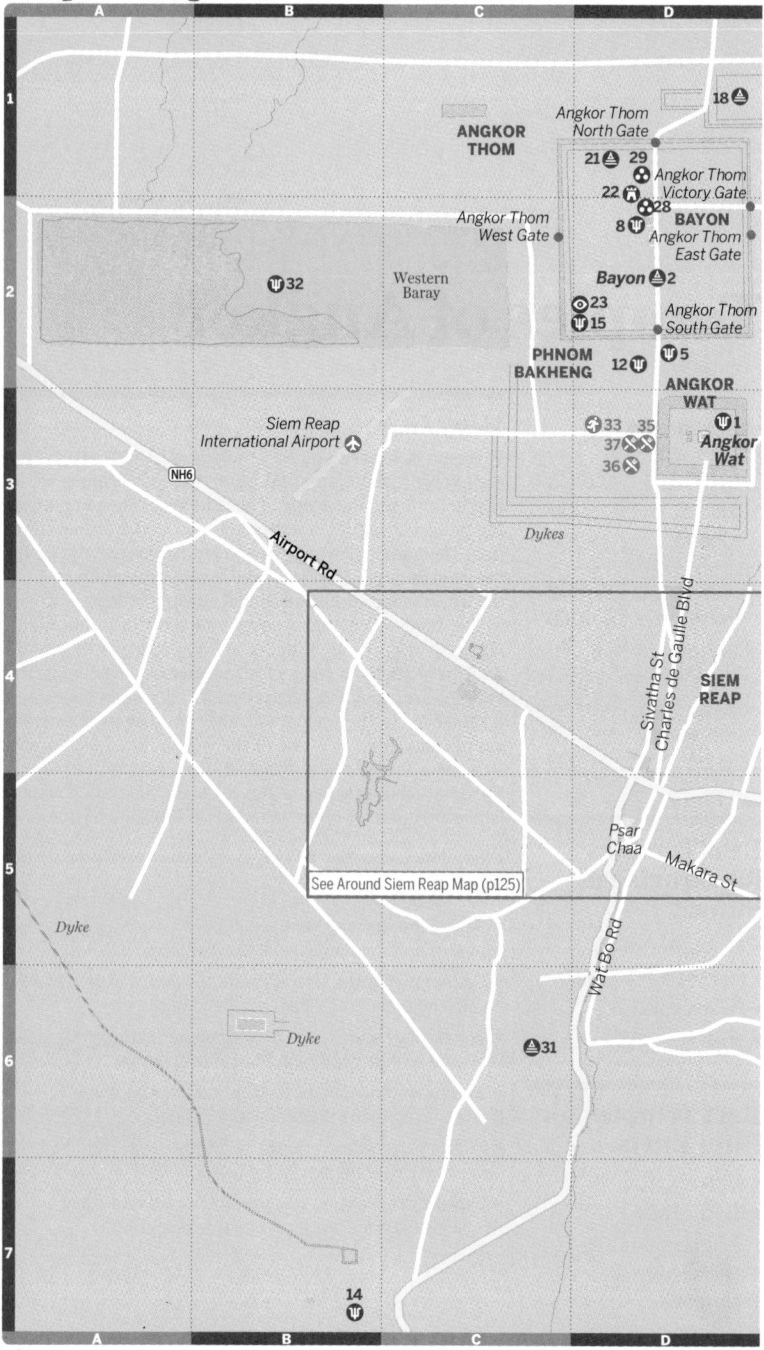

18 ▲

ANGKOR
THOM

*Angkor Thom
North Gate*

21 ▲  29 ✪

22 🏛  *Angkor Thom
Victory Gate*

28 ✪

*Angkor Thom
West Gate*

8 🛕  **BAYON**
*Angkor Thom
East Gate*

🛕 32

Western
Baray

*Bayon* 🏛 2

◉ 23

🛕 15  *Angkor Thom
South Gate*

**PHNOM
BAKHENG**

12 🛕  🛕 5

**ANGKOR
WAT**

🛕 1

*Siem Reap
International Airport* ✈

33 ✈  35

37 ✪

36 ✪

*Angkor
Wat*

NH6

*Airport Rd*

*Dykes*

See Around Siem Reap Map (p125)

Sivatha St
Charles de Gaulle Blvd

**SIEM
REAP**

*Psar
Chaa*

*Makara St*

Wat Bo Rd

*Dyke*

*Dyke*

▲ 31

14
🛕

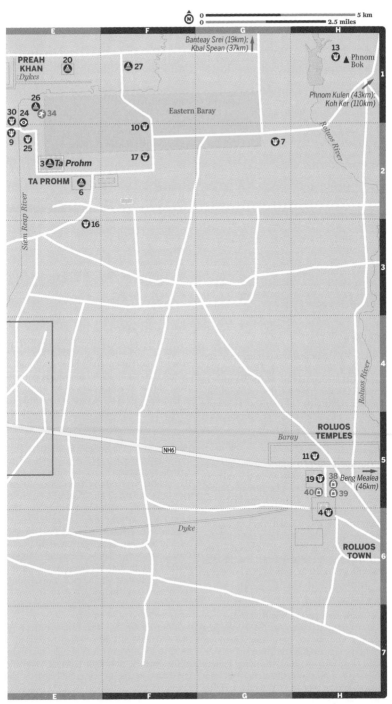

# Temples of Angkor

## History

The Angkorian period spans more than 600 years from AD 802 to 1432. This incredible age saw the construction of the temples of Angkor and the consolidation of the Khmer empire's position as one of the great powers in Southeast Asia. This era encompassed periods of decline and revival, and wars with rival powers in Vietnam, Thailand and Myanmar.

The hundreds of temples surviving today are but the sacred skeleton of the vast political, religious and social centre of Cambodia's ancient Khmer empire, a city that, at its zenith, boasted a population of one million when London was a small town of 50,000. The houses, public buildings and palaces of Angkor were constructed of wood – now long decayed – because the right to dwell in structures of brick or stone was reserved for the gods.

### An Empire is Born

The Angkorian period began with the rule of Jayavarman II (r 802–50). He was the first to unify Cambodia's competing kingdoms before the birth of Angkor. His court was situated at various locations, including Phnom Kulen, 40km northeast of Angkor Wat, and Roluos (known then as Hariharalaya), 13km east of Siem Reap.

Jayavarman II proclaimed himself a *devaraja* (god-king), the earthly representative of the Hindu god Shiva, and built a 'temple-mountain' at Phnom Kulen, symbolising Shiva's dwelling place of Mt Meru, the holy mountain at the centre of the universe. This set a precedent that became a dominant feature of the Angkorian period and accounts for the staggering architectural productivity of the Khmers at this time.

Indravarman I (r 877–89) is believed to have been a usurper, and probably inherited the mantle of *devaraja* through conquest. He built a 6.5-sq-km *baray* (reservoir) at Roluos and established Preah Ko. The *baray* was the first stage of an irrigation system that created a hydraulic city, the ancient Khmers mastering the cycle of nature to water their lands. Form and function worked together in harmony, as the *baray* also had religious significance, representing the oceans surrounding Mt Meru. Indravarman's final work was Bakong, a pyramidal representation of Mt Meru.

Indravarman I's son Yasovarman I (r 889–910) looked further afield to celebrate his divinity and glory in a temple-mountain of his own. He first built Lolei on an artificial island in the *baray* established by his father, before beginning work on the Bakheng. Today this hill is known as Phnom Bakheng, and is a favoured spot for viewing the sunset over Angkor Wat. A raised highway was constructed to connect Phnom Bakheng with Roluos, 16km to the southeast, and a large *baray* was constructed to the east of Phnom Bakheng. Today it is known as the Eastern Baray but has entirely silted up. Yasovarman I also established the temple-mountains of Phnom Krom and Phnom Bok.

After the death of Yasovarman I, power briefly shifted from the Angkor region to Koh Ker, around 80km to the northeast, under another usurper king, Jayavarman IV (r 924–42). In AD 944 power returned again to Angkor under the leadership of Rajendravarman II (r 944–68), who built the Eastern Mebon and Pre Rup. The reign of his son Jayavarman V (r 968–1001) produced the temples Ta Keo and Banteay Srei, the latter built by a Brahman rather than the king.

### The Golden Age of Angkor

The temples that are now the highlight of a visit to Angkor – Angkor Wat and those in and around the walled city of Angkor Thom – were built during the golden age or classical period. While this period is marked by fits of remarkable productivity, it was also a time of turmoil, conquests and setbacks. The great city of Angkor Thom owes its existence to the fact that the old city of Angkor, which stood on the same site, was destroyed during the Cham invasion of 1177.

Suryavarman I (r 1002–49) was a usurper to the throne who won the day through strategic alliances and military conquests. Although he adopted the Hindu cult of the god-king, he is thought to have come from a Mahayana Buddhist tradition and may even have sponsored the growth of Buddhism in Cambodia. Buddhist sculpture certainly became more commonplace in the Angkor region during his time.

Little physical evidence of Suryavarman I's reign remains at Angkor, but his military exploits brought much of central Thailand and southern-central Laos under the control of Angkor. His son Udayadityavarman II (r 1049–65) embarked on further military expeditions, extending the empire once more, and building Baphuon and the Western Mebon. Many major cities in the Mekong region were important Khmer settlements in the 11th and 12th centuries, including the Lao capital of Vientiane and the Thai city of Lopburi.

From 1066 until the end of the century, Angkor was again divided as rival factions contested the throne. The first important monarch of this new era was Suryavarman II (r 1112–52), who unified Cambodia and extended Khmer influence to Malaya and Burma (Myanmar). He also set himself apart religiously from earlier kings through his devotion to the Hindu deity Vishnu, to whom he consecrated the largest and arguably most magnificent of all the Angkorian temples, Angkor Wat.

The reign of Suryavarman II and the construction of Angkor Wat signifies one of the high-water marks of Khmer civilisation. However, there were signs that decline was lurking. It is thought that the hydraulic system of reservoirs and canals that supported the agriculture of Angkor had by this time been pushed beyond its limits, and was slowly starting to silt up due to overpopulation and deforestation. The construction of Angkor Wat was a major strain on resources, and, on top of this, Suryavarman II led a disastrous campaign against the Dai Viet (Vietnamese) late in his reign, during the course of which he was killed in battle.

### Enter Jayavarman VII

In 1177 the Chams of southern Vietnam, then the Kingdom of Champa and long annexed by the Khmer empire, rose up and sacked Angkor. This attack caught the Khmers completely unawares, as it came via sea, river and lake rather than the traditional land routes. The Chams burnt the wooden city

> ### ❶ TEMPLE ETIQUETTE
>
> While the temples of Angkor are not a million miles away from the beaches of Sihanoukville, it is important to remember that the temples of Angkor represent a sacred religious site to the Khmer people. Inappropriate dress is not appreciated, despite that the friendly Cambodians may say nothing. Sleeveless tops for men and women, hot pants, short skirts – none of these should be worn when exploring Angkor. Certain temples even stipulate a dress code and it is not possible to visit the highest level of Angkor Wat without upper arms covered and shorts to the knees. Local authorities have recently released visitor 'code of conduct' guidelines and a video to encourage dressing appropriately, as well as reminding tourists not to touch or sit on the ancient structures, to pay attention to restricted areas, and to be respectful of monks.

# Temples of Angkor

## THREE-DAY EXPLORATION

The temple complex at Angkor is simply enormous and the superlatives don't do it justice. This is the site of the world's largest religious building, a multitude of temples and a vast, long-abandoned walled city that was arguably Southeast Asia's first metropolis, long before Bangkok and Singapore got in on the action.

Starting at the Roluos group of temples, one of the earliest capitals of Angkor, move on to the big circuit, which includes the Buddhist-Hindu fusion temple of **1 Preah Khan** and the ornate water temple of **2 Preah Neak Poan**.

On the second day downsize to the small circuit, starting with an early visit to **3 Ta Prohm**, before continuing to the temple pyramid of Ta Keo, the Buddhist monastery of Banteay Kdei and the immense royal bathing pond of **4 Sra Srang**.

Next venture further afield to Banteay Srei temple, the jewel in the crown of Angkorian art, and Beng Mealea, a remote jungle temple.

Saving the biggest and best until last, experience sunrise at **5 Angkor Wat** and stick around for breakfast in the temple to discover its amazing architecture without the crowds. In the afternoon, explore **6 Angkor Thom**, an immense complex that is home to the enigmatic **7 Bayon**.

Three days around Angkor? That's just for starters.

### TOP TIPS

» **Dodging the Crowds** To avoid the hordes, try dawn at Sra Srang, post sunrise at Angkor Wat, and lunchtime at Banteay Srei.

» **Extended Explorations** Three-day passes can be used on non-consecutive days over the period of a week but be sure to request this.

**Bayon**
The surreal state temple of legendary king Jayavarman VII where 216 faces bear down on pilgrims, asserting religious and regal authority.

Terrace of the Leper King

Preah Palilay

Phimeanakas Temple

Tep Pran

West Gate Angkor Thom

Baphuon Temple

Terrace of the Elephan

**7**

South Gate Angkor Thom

Phnom Bakheng

Baksei Chamrong

**5**

**Angkor Wat**
The world's largest religious building. Experience sunrise at the holiest of holies, then explore the beautiful bas-reliefs – devotion etched in stone.

## Angkor Thom
The last great capital of the Khmer empire conceals a wealth of temples and its epic proportions would have inspired and terrified in equal measure.

### Preah Khan
A fusion temple dedicated to Buddha, Brahma, Shiva and Vishnu; the immense corridors are like an unending hall of mirrors.

### Preah Neak Poan
If Vegas ever adopts the Angkor theme, this will be the swimming pool; a petite tower set in a lake, surrounded by four smaller ponds.

**North Gate, Angkor Thom**

**Preah Pithu**

**Thommanon Temple**

❻

**Prasat Suor Prat**

**Victory Gate Angkor Thom**

**East Gate Angkor Thom**

**Chau Say Tevoda**

**Ta Keo Temple**

**Ta Nei Temple**

**Banteay Srei** →

❸

**Banteay Kdei Temple**

**Roluos, Beng Mealea** ↓

❹

**Prasat Kravan**

**Bat Chum Temple**

## Ta Prohm
Nicknamed the *Tomb Raider* temple; *Indiana Jones* would be equally apt. Nature has run riot, leaving iconic tree roots strangling the surviving stones.

### Sra Srang
Once the royal bathing pond, this is the ablutions pool to beat all ablutions pools and makes a good stop for sunrise or sunset.

and plundered its wealth. Four years later Jayavarman VII (r 1181–1219) struck back, emphatically driving the Chams out of Cambodia and reclaiming Angkor.

Jayavarman VII's reign has given scholars much to debate. It represents a radical departure from the reigns of his predecessors. For centuries the fount of royal divinity had reposed in the Hindu deity Shiva (and, occasionally, Vishnu). Jayavarman VII adopted Mahayana Buddhism and looked to Avalokiteshvara, the Bodhisattva of Compassion, for patronage during his reign. In doing so he may well have been converting to a religion that already enjoyed wide popular support among his subjects. It may also be that the destruction of Angkor was such a blow to royal divinity that a new religious foundation was thought to be needed.

During his reign, Jayavarman VII embarked on a dizzying array of temple projects that centred on Baphuon, which was the site of the capital city destroyed by the Chams. Angkor Thom, Jayavarman VII's new city, was surrounded by walls and a moat, which became another component of Angkor's complex irrigation system. The centrepiece of Angkor Thom was Bayon, the temple-mountain studded with faces that, along with Angkor Wat, is the most famous of Cambodia's temples. Other temples built during his reign include Ta Prohm, Banteay Kdei and Preah Khan. Further away, he rebuilt vast temple complexes, such as Banteay Chhmar and Preah Khan in Preah Vihear Province, making him by far the most prolific builder of Angkor's many kings.

Jayavarman VII also embarked on a major public-works program, building roads, schools and hospitals across the empire. Remains of many of these roads and their magnificent bridges can be seen across Cambodia. Spean Praptos at Kompong Kdei, 65km southeast of Siem Reap on National Hwy 6 (NH6), is the most famous, but there are many more lost in the forest on the old Angkorian road to the great Preah Khan, including the now accessible Spean Ta Ong, about 28km east of Beng Mealea near the village of Khvau.

After the death of Jayavarman VII around 1219, the Khmer empire went into decline. The state religion reverted to Hinduism for a century or more and outbreaks of iconoclasm saw Buddhist sculpture adorning the Hindu temples vandalised or altered. The Thais sacked Angkor in 1351, and again with devastating efficiency in 1431. The glorious Siamese capital of Ayuthaya, which enjoyed a golden age from the 14th to the 18th centuries, was in many ways a re-creation of the glories of Angkor from which the Thai conquerors drew inspiration. The Khmer court moved to Phnom Penh, only to return fleetingly to Angkor in the 16th century; in the meantime, it was abandoned to pilgrims, holy men and the elements.

## TOP 10 KINGS OF ANGKOR

A mind-numbing array of kings ruled the Khmer empire from the 9th to the 14th centuries AD. All of their names include the word 'varman', which means 'armour' or 'protector'. Forget the small fry and focus on the big fish in our Top 10:

**Jayavarman II** (r 802–50) Founded the Khmer empire in AD 802.

**Indravarman I** (r 877–89) Built the first *baray* (reservoir), Preah Ko and Bakong.

**Yasovarman I** (r 889–910) Moved the capital to Angkor and built Lolei and Phnom Bakheng.

**Jayavarman IV** (r 924–42) Usurper king who moved the capital to Koh Ker.

**Rajendravarman II** (r 944–68) Built Eastern Mebon, Pre Rup and Phimeanakas.

**Jayavarman V** (r 968–1001) Oversaw construction of Ta Keo and Banteay Srei.

**Suryavarman I** (r 1002–49) Expanded the empire into much of Laos and Thailand.

**Udayadityavarman II** (r 1049–65) Built the pyramidal Baphuon and the Western Mebon.

**Suryavarman II** (r 1112–52) Legendary builder of Angkor Wat and Beng Mealea.

**Jayavarman VII** (r 1181–1219) The king of the god-kings, who built Angkor Thom, Preah Khan and Ta Prohm.

## Angkor Rediscovered

The French 'discovery' of Angkor in the 1860s made an international splash and created a great deal of outside interest in Cambodia. But 'discovery', with all the romance it implied, was something of a misnomer. When French explorer Henri Mouhot first stumbled across Angkor Wat on his Royal Geographic Society expedition, it included a wealthy, working monastery with monks and slaves. Moreover, Portuguese travellers in the 16th century encountered Angkor, referring to it as the Walled City. Diego do Couto produced an accurate description of Angkor in 1614, but it was not published until 1958. A 17th-century Japanese pilgrim drew a detailed plan of Angkor Wat, though he mistakenly recalled that he had seen it in India.

Still, it was the publication of *Voyage à Siam et dans le Cambodge* by Mouhot, posthumously released in 1868, that first brought Angkor to the public eye. Although the explorer himself made no such claims, by the 1870s he was being celebrated as the discoverer of the lost temple-city of Cambodia. In fact, a French missionary known as Charles-Emile Bouillevaux had visited Angkor 10 years before Mouhot and had published an account of his own findings. However, the Bouillevaux account was roundly ignored and it was Mouhot's account, with its rich descriptions and tantalising pen-and-ink colour sketches of the temples, that turned the ruins into an international obsession.

Soon after Mouhot, other adventurers and explorers began to arrive. Scottish photographer John Thomson took the first photographs of the temples in 1866. He was the first Westerner to posit the idea that they were symbolic representations of the mythical Mt Meru. French architect Lucien Fournereau travelled to Angkor in 1887 and produced plans and meticulously executed cross-sections that were to stand as the best available until the 1960s.

From this time Angkor became the target of French-financed expeditions and, in 1901, the École Française d'Extrême-Orient (www.efeo.fr) began a long association with Angkor by funding an expedition to Bayon. In 1907 Angkor was returned to Cambodia, having been under Thai control for more than a century, and the EFEO took responsibility for clearing and restoring the whole site. In the same year, the first foreign tourists arrived in Angkor – an unprecedented 200 of them in three months. Angkor had

### TEMPLE ADDICTS

The god-kings of Angkor were dedicated builders. Each king was expected to dedicate a temple to his patron god, most commonly Shiva or Vishnu, during the time of Angkor. Then there were the ancestors, including mother, father and grandparents (both maternal and paternal), which meant another half dozen temples or more. Finally there was the mausoleum or king's temple, intended to deify the monarch and project his power, and each of these had to be bigger and better than one's predecessor. This accounts for the staggering architectural productivity of the Khmers at this time and the epic evolution of temple architecture.

been 'rescued' from the jungle and was assuming its place in the modern world.

## Archaeology of Angkor

With the exception of Angkor Wat, which was restored for use as a Buddhist shrine in the 16th century by the Khmer royalty, the temples of Angkor were left to the jungle for many centuries. The majority of temples are made of sandstone, which tends to dissolve when in prolonged contact with dampness. Bat droppings took their toll, as did sporadic pilfering of sculptures and cut stones. At some monuments, such as Ta Prohm, the jungle had stealthily waged an all-out invasion, and plant life could only be removed at great risk to the structures it now supported in its web of roots.

Initial attempts to clear Angkor under the aegis of the École Française d'Extrême-Orient were fraught with technical difficulties and theoretical disputes. On a technical front, the jungle tended to grow back as soon as it was cleared; on a theoretical front, scholars debated the extent to which temples should be restored and whether later additions, such as Buddha images in Hindu temples, should be removed.

It was not until the 1920s that a solution was found, known as anastylosis. This was the method the Dutch had used to restore Borobudur in Java. Put simply, it was a way of reconstructing monuments using the original materials and in keeping with the original form of the structure. New materials were permitted only where the originals

## MOTIFS, SYMBOLS & CHARACTERS AROUND ANGKOR

The temples of Angkor are intricately carved with myths and legends, symbols and signs, and a cast of characters in the thousands. Deciphering them can be quite a challenge, so we've highlighted some of the most commonly seen around the majestic temples. For more help understanding the carvings of Angkor, pick up a copy of *Images of the Gods* by Vittorio Roveda.

**Apsaras** Heavenly nymphs or goddesses, also known as *devadas;* these beautiful female forms decorate the walls of many temples.

**Asuras** These devils feature extensively in representations of the Churning of the Ocean of Milk, such as at Angkor Wat.

**Devas** The 'good gods' in the creation myth of the Churning of the Ocean of Milk.

**Flame** The flame motif is found flanking steps and doorways and is intended to purify pilgrims as they enter the temple.

**Garuda** Vehicle of Vishnu; this half-man, half-bird features in some temples and was combined with his old enemy the *nagas* to promote religious unity under Jayavarman VII.

**Kala** The temple guardian appointed by Shiva; he had such an appetite that he devoured his own body and appears only as a giant head above doorways. Also known as Rehu.

**Linga** A phallic symbol of fertility, *lingas* would have originally been located within the towers of most Hindu temples.

**Lotus** A symbol of purity, the lotus features extensively in the shape of towers, the shape of steps to entrances and in decoration.

**Makara** A giant sea serpent with a reticulated jaw; features on the corner of pediments, spewing forth a *naga* or some other creature.

**Naga** The multiheaded serpent, half-brother and enemy of *garudas*. Controls the rains and, therefore, the prosperity of the kingdom; seen on causeways, doorways and roofs. The seven-headed *naga,* a feature at many temples, represents the rainbow, which acts as a bridge between heaven and earth.

**Nandi** The mount of Shiva; there are several statues of Nandi dotted about the temples, although many have been damaged or stolen by looters.

**Rishi** A Hindu wise man or ascetic, also known as *essai;* these bearded characters are often seen sitting cross-legged at the base of pillars or flanking walls.

**Vine** Another symbol of purity, the vine graces doorways and lintels and is meant to help cleanse the visitor on their journey to this heaven on earth, the abode of the gods.

**Yama** God of death who presides over the underworld and passes judgement on whether people continue to heaven or hell.

**Yoni** Female fertility symbol that is combined with the *linga* to produce holy water infused with the essence of life.

could not be found, and were to be used discreetly. An example of this method can be seen on the causeway leading to the entrance of Angkor Wat, as the right-hand side was originally restored by the French.

The first major restoration job was carried out on Banteay Srei in 1930. It was deemed such a success that many more extensive restoration projects were undertaken elsewhere around Angkor, culminating in the massive Angkor Wat restoration in the 1960s. Large cranes and earth-moving machines were brought in, and the operation was backed by a veritable army of surveying equipment.

The Khmer Rouge victory and Cambodia's subsequent slide into an intractable civil war resulted in far less damage to Angkor than many had assumed, as EFEO and Ministry of Culture teams had removed many of the statues from the temple sites for protection. Nevertheless, turmoil in Cambodia resulted in a long interruption of restoration work, allowing the jungle to resume its assault on the monuments. The illegal trade of *objets d'art* on the world art market has also been a major threat to Angkor, although it is the more remote sites that have been targeted recently. Angkor has been under the jurisdiction of Unesco since 1992 as a World Heritage Site, and international and local efforts continue to preserve and reconstruct the monuments. In a sign of real progress, Angkor was removed from Unesco's endangered list in 2003.

Many of Angkor's secrets remain to be discovered, as most of the work at the temples has concentrated on restoration efforts above ground rather than archaeological digs and surveys below. Underground is where the real story of Angkor and its people lies – the inscriptions on the temples give us only a partial picture of the gods to whom each structure was dedicated, and the kings who built them.

To learn more about Unesco's activities at Angkor, visit http://whc.unesco.org, or take a virtual tour of Angkor in 360 degrees at www.world-heritage-tour.org. For a great online photographic resource on the temples of Angkor, look no further than www.angkor-ruins.com, a Japanese website with an English translation.

## Architectural Styles

From the time of the earliest Angkorian monuments at Roluos, Khmer architecture was continually evolving, often from the rule of one king to the next. Archaeologists therefore divide the monuments of Angkor into nine periods, named after the foremost example of each period's architectural style.

The evolution of Khmer architecture was based on a central theme of the temple-mountain, preferably set on a real hill (but an artificial hill was allowed if there weren't any mountains to hand). The earlier a temple was constructed, the more closely it adheres to this fundamental idea. Essentially, the mountain was represented by a tower mounted on a tiered base. At the summit was the central sanctuary, usually with an open door to the east, and three false doors at the remaining cardinal points of the compass. For Indian Hindus, the Himalayas represent Mt Meru, the home of the gods, while the Khmer kings of old adopted Phnom Kulen as their symbolic Mt Meru.

By the time of the Bakheng period, this layout was being embellished. The summit of the central tower was crowned with five 'peaks' – four at the points of the compass and one in the centre. Even Angkor Wat features this layout, though on a grandiose scale. Other features that came to be favoured include an entry tower and a causeway lined with *naga* (mythical serpent) balustrades leading up to the temple.

As the temples grew in ambition, the central tower became a less prominent feature, although it remained the focus of the temple. Later temples saw the central tower flanked by courtyards and richly decorated galleries. Smaller towers were placed on gates and on the corners of walls, their overall number often of religious or astrological significance.

These refinements and additions eventually culminated in Angkor Wat, which effectively showcases the evolution of Angkorian architecture. The architecture of the Bayon period breaks with tradition in temples such as Ta Prohm and Preah Khan. In these temples, the horizontal layout of the galleries, corridors and courtyards seems to completely eclipse the central tower.

The curious narrowness of the corridors and doorways in these structures can be explained by the fact that Angkorian architects never mastered the flying buttress to build a full arch. They engineered arches by laying blocks on top of each other, until they met at a central point; known as false arches, they can only support very short spans.

### ON LOCATION WITH TOMB RAIDER

Several sequences for the film *Tomb Raider*, starring Angelina Jolie as Lara Croft, were shot around the temples of Angkor. The Cambodia shoot opened at Phnom Bakheng, with Lara looking through binoculars for the mysterious temple. The baddies were already trying to break in through the east gate of Angkor Thom by pulling down a giant polystyrene *apsara*. Reunited with her custom Land Rover, Lara made a few laps around Bayon before discovering a back way into the temple from Ta Prohm. After battling a living statue and dodging Daniel Craig (aka 007) by diving off the waterfall at Phnom Kulen, she emerged in a floating market in front of Angkor Wat, as you do. She came ashore here before borrowing a mobile phone from a local monk and venturing into the Gallery of a Thousand Buddhas, where she was healed by the abbot.

> **ℹ WHERE TO STAY AROUND ANGKOR**
>
> The nearby town of Siem Reap is the base for exploring the temples of Angkor, with an incredible array of accommodation (p103) on offer from budget hostels to opulent hotels. There is no accommodation around Angkor as such, although there are some homestays in Banteay Srei district (p124) for those seeking a local experience.

Most of the major sandstone blocks around Angkor include small circular holes. These originally held wooden stakes that were used to lift and position the stones during construction before being sawn off.

## When to Go

Avoid the sweltering temperatures of March to May. November to February is the best time of year to travel, but this is no secret, so it coincides with peak season. And peak season really is mountainous in this day and age, with more than two million visitors a year descending on Angkor. The summer months of July and August can be a surprisingly rewarding time, as the landscape is emerald green, the moats overflowing with water, and the moss and lichen in bright contrast to the grey sandstone. The Angkor Wat International Half Marathon takes place annually in December, including the option of bicycle rides for those not into running.

## Itineraries

Back in the early days of tourism, the decision of what to see and in what order came down to a choice between two basic temple itineraries: the Small (Petit) Circuit and the Big (Grand) Circuit. It's difficult to imagine anyone following these to the letter any more, but in their time they were an essential component of the Angkor experience and were often undertaken on the back of an elephant.

Today most budget and midrange travellers prefer to take in the temples at their own pace, and tend to use a combination of transport options, such as car, *remork*, bicycle or minivan. Plan a dawn-to-dusk itinerary with a long, leisurely lunch to avoid the heat of the midday sun. Alternatively, explore the temples through lunch, when it can be considerably quieter than during the peak morning and afternoon visit times.

However, it will be hot as hell and the light is not conducive to photography.

### Small Circuit

The 17km Small Circuit begins at Angkor Wat and heads north to Phnom Bakheng, Baksei Chamkrong and Angkor Thom, including the city wall and gates, the Bayon, the Baphuon, the Royal Enclosure, Phimeanakas, Preah Palilay, the Terrace of the Leper King, the Terrace of Elephants, the Kleangs and Prasat Suor Prat. It exits from Angkor Thom via the Victory Gate in the eastern wall, and continues to Chau Say Tevoda, Thommanon, Spean Thmor and Ta Keo. It then heads northeast of the road to Ta Nei, turns south to Ta Prohm, continues east to Banteay Kdei and Sra Srang, and finally returns to Angkor Wat via Prasat Kravan.

### Big Circuit

The 26km Big Circuit is an extension of the Small Circuit: instead of exiting the walled city of Angkor Thom at the east gate, the Grand Circuit exits at the north gate and continues to Preah Khan and Preah Neak Poan, east to Ta Som, then south via the Eastern Mebon to Pre Rup. From there it heads west and then southwest on its return to Angkor Wat.

### One Day

If you have only one day to visit Angkor, arrive at Angkor Wat in time for sunrise and stick around to explore the mighty temple while it's quieter. From there continue to the tree roots of Ta Prohm before breaking for lunch. In the afternoon, explore the temples within the walled city of Angkor Thom and the beauty of the Bayon in the late-afternoon light.

### Two Days

A two-day itinerary allows you to include some of the big hitters around Angkor. Spend the first morning visiting petite Banteay Srei, with its fabulous carvings; stop at Banteay Samré on the return leg. In the afternoon, visit immense Preah Khan, delicate Preah Neak Poan and the tree roots of Ta Som, before taking in a sunset at Pre Rup. Get up early the second morning to arrive at Angkor Wat for sunrise, then spend a few hours enjoying the relative quiet before heading to Ta Prohm. Devote the afternoon to explorations of Angkor Thom.

### Three to Five Days

If you have three to five days to explore Angkor, it's possible to see most of the important sites. One approach is to see as much as possible on the first day or two and then spend the final days combining visits to other sites such as the Roluos temples and Banteay Kdei. Better still is a gradual build-up to the most important monuments. After all, if you see Angkor Wat on the first day, then a temple like Ta Keo just won't cut it. Another option is a chronological approach, starting with the earliest Angkorian temples and working steadily forwards in time to Angkor Thom, taking stock of the evolution of Khmer architecture and artistry.

It is well worth making the trip to the River of a Thousand Lingas at Kbal Spean for the chance to stretch your legs amid natural and human-made splendour, or the remote, vast and overgrown temple of Beng Mealea. Both can be combined with Banteay Srei in one long day.

### One Week

Those with the time to spend a week at Angkor will be richly rewarded. Not only is it possible to visit all the temples of the region, but a longer stay also allows for non-temple activities, such as relaxing by a pool, indulging in a spa treatment or shopping around Siem Reap. You may also want to throw in some of the more remote sites such as Koh Ker, Prasat Preah Vihear or Banteay Chhmar.

### ☞ Tours

Visitors who have only a day or two at this incredible site may prefer something organised locally. It is possible to link up with an official tour guide in Siem Reap (p102), where a number of operators run tours ranging from simple day trips to cycling tours to excursions to more remote temple sites. The **Khmer Angkor Tour Guides Association** (☑ 063-964347; www.khmerangkortourguide.com) represents some of Angkor's authorised guides. English- or French-speaking guides can be booked from US$20 to US$40 a day; guides speaking other languages, such as Italian, German, Spanish, Japanese and Chinese, are available at a higher rate as there are fewer of them.

### ℹ Orientation

Heading north from Siem Reap, Angkor Wat is the first major temple, followed by the walled city of Angkor Thom. To the east and west of this city are two vast former reservoirs (the eastern reservoir now completely dried up), which once helped to sustain the huge population. Further east are temples including Ta Prohm, Banteay Kdei and Pre Rup. North of Angkor Thom is Preah Khan

and way beyond in the northeast, Banteay Srei, Kbal Spean, Phnom Kulen and Beng Mealea. To the southeast of Siem Reap is the early Angkorian Roluos Group of Temples.

### ℹ Information

#### ADMISSION FEES

While the cost of entry to Angkor is relatively expensive by Cambodian standards, the fees represent excellent value on an international scale. Visitors have the choice of a one-day pass (US$20), a three-day pass (US$40) or a one-week pass (US$60). The three-day passes can be used over three non-consecutive days in a one-week period, while one-week passes can be used on seven days over a month. Purchase the entry pass from the large official entrance booth on the road to Angkor Wat. The Angkor ticket checkpoint is due to move in the very near future and will reopen on a parallel newer road to Angkor. Passes include a digital photo snapped at the entrance booth, so queues can be slow at peak times. Visitors entering after 5pm get a free sunset, as the ticket starts from the following day. The fee includes access to all the monuments in the Siem Reap area but not the sacred mountain of Phnom Kulen (US$20) or the remote complexes of Beng Mealea (US$5) and Koh Ker (US$10).

Most of the major temples now have uniformed staff to check the tickets, which has reduced the opportunity for scams. A pass is not required for excursions to villages around or beyond Angkor, but you still have to stop at the checkpoint to explain your movements to the staff.

#### MAPS

There are several free maps covering Angkor, including the *Siem Reap Angkor 3D Map*, which is available at certain hotels, guesthouses and restaurants in town. River Books of Thailand publishes a fold-out *Angkor Map*, which is one of the more detailed offerings available.

#### USEFUL WEBSITES

**Angkor – Unesco World Heritage Site** (http://whc.unesco.org/en/list/668) Information, images and videos on the world's top temples.

**National Geographic** (http://ngm.nationalgeographic.com/2009/07/angkor/angkor-animation) Animated illustrations of life in the Khmer Empire.

**Heritage Watch** (www.heritagewatch international.org) Sustainable tourism initiatives involving the local community.

---

### TEMPLE-PASS WARNING!

Visitors found inside any of the main temples without a ticket will be fined a whopping US$100.

## DODGING THE CROWDS

Angkor is on the tourist trail and is only getting busier, with over two million visitors annually, but with a little planning it is still possible to escape the crowds. One important thing to remember, particularly when it comes to sunrise and sunset, is that places are popular for a reason, and it is worth going with the flow at least once.

It is received wisdom that as Angkor Wat faces west, one should be there for late afternoon, and in the case of the Bayon, which faces east, in the morning. Ta Prohm, most people seem to agree, can be visited in the middle of the day because of its umbrella of foliage. This is all well and good, but if you reverse the order, the temples will still look good – and you can avoid some of the crowds.

Only four temples are open at 5am for sunrise: Angkor Wat, Phnom Bakheng, Sra Rang and Pre Rup. The most popular place is Angkor Wat. Most tour groups head back to town for breakfast, so stick around and explore the temple while it's cool and quiet between 7am and 9am. Sra Srang is usually pretty quiet, and sunrise here can be spectacular thanks to reflections in the extensive waters. Phnom Bakheng could be an attractive option, because the sun comes up behind Angkor Wat and you are far from the madding crowd that gathers here at sunset, but there are now strict limitations on visitor numbers each day.

The hilltop temple of Phnom Bakheng is the definitive sunset spot. This was getting well out of control, with as many as 1000 tourists clambering around the small structure. However, new restrictions limit visitors to no more than 300 at any one time. It is generally better to check it out for sunrise or early morning and miss the crowds. Staying within the confines of Angkor Wat for sunset is a rewarding option, as it can be pretty peaceful when most tourists head off to Phnom Bakheng around 4.30pm or so. Pre Rup is popular with some for an authentic rural sunset over the countryside, but this is starting to get very busy. Better is the hilltop temple of Phnom Krom, which offers commanding views across Tonlé Sap lake, but involves a long drive back to town in the dark. The Western Baray takes in the sunset from the eastern end, across its vast waters, or from Western Mebon island, and is generally a quiet option.

When it comes to the most popular temples, the middle of the day is generally the quietest time. This is because the majority of the large tour groups head back to Siem Reap for lunch. It is also the hottest part of the day, which makes it tough going around relatively open temples such as Banteay Srei and the Bayon, but fine at well-covered temples such as Ta Prohm, Preah Khan and Beng Mealea, or even the bas-reliefs at Angkor Wat. The busiest times at Angkor Wat are from 6am to 7am and 3pm to 5pm; at the Bayon, from 8am to 10am; and at Banteay Srei, mid-morning and mid-afternoon. However, at other popular temples, such as Ta Prohm and Preah Khan, the crowds are harder to predict, and at most other temples in the Angkor region it's just a case of pot luck. If you pull up outside and see a car park full of tour buses, you may want to move on to somewhere quieter. The wonderful thing about Angkor is that there is always another temple to explore.

**Lonely Planet** (www.lonelyplanet.com/cambodia/temples-of-angkor) Destination information, bookings and more.

## ℹ Getting There & Around

Visitors heading to the temples of Angkor – in other words, pretty much everybody coming to Cambodia – need to consider the most suitable way to travel between the temples. Many of the best-known temples are no more than a few kilometres from the walled city of Angkor Thom, which is just 8km from Siem Reap, and can be visited using anything from a car or motorcycle to a sturdy pair of walking boots. For the independent traveller, there is a daunting range of alternatives to consider.

For the ultimate Angkor experience, try a pick-and-mix approach, with a *moto, remork-moto* or car for one day to cover the remote sites, a bicycle to experience the central temples, and an exploration on foot for a spot of peace and serenity. Transport will be more expensive for remote temples such as Banteay Srei or Beng Mealea, due to extra fuel costs.

### BICYCLE

A great way to get around the temples, bicycles are environmentally friendly and are used by most locals. There are few hills and the roads are good, so there's no need for much cycling experience. Moving about at a slower speed, you soon find that you take in more than from out of a car window or on the back of a speeding *moto*.

**White Bicycles** (www.thewhitebicycles.org; per day US$2) is supported by some guesthouses around Siem Reap, with proceeds from the hire fee going towards community projects. Many guesthouses and hotels in town rent bikes for around US$1 to US$2 per day.

Some rental places offer better mountain bikes, such as Trek or Giant, for US$7 to US$10 per day. Try Grasshopper Adventures (p102), which offers international mountain bikes and helmets for US$8 per day.

### CAR & MOTORCYCLE

Cars are a popular choice for getting about the temples. The obvious advantage is protection from the elements, be it heavy downpours or the punishing sun. Shared between several travellers, they can also be an economical way to explore. The downside is that visitors are a little more isolated from the sights, sounds and smells as they travel between temples. A car for the day around the central temples is US$25 to US$35 and can be arranged through hotels, guesthouses and agencies in Siem Reap.

Motorcycle rental in Siem Reap is currently prohibited, but some travellers bring a motorcycle from Phnom Penh. If you manage to get a bike up here, leave it at a guarded parking area or with a stallholder outside each temple; otherwise it could get stolen.

### ELEPHANT

Travelling by elephant was the traditional way to see the temples way back in the early days of tourism at Angkor, at the start of the 20th century. While you will see tourists taking an elephant ride between the south gate of Angkor Thom and the Bayon in the morning, or up to the summit of Phnom Bakheng for sunset, several elephant welfare organisations suggest it is not in the best interests of these majestic creatures (p276).

### HELICOPTER & HOT-AIR BALLOON

For those with plenty of spending money, there are tourist flights around Angkor Wat (US$90) and the temples outside Angkor Thom (US$150). There are two companies operating out of Siem Reap Airport and both also offer charters to remote temples such as Prasat Preah Vihear and Preah Khan: **Helicopters Cambodia** (☏ 012 814500; www.helicopterscambodia.com; 658 Hup Quan St, Siem Reap) or **Helistar** (Map p96; ☏ 063-966072; www.helistarcambodia.com; 24 Sivatha St, Siem Reap).

**Angkor Balloon** (Map p130; ☏ 012 759698; per person US$15) offers a bird's-eye view of Angkor Wat. The balloon carries up to 30 people, is on a fixed line and rises 200m above the landscape. It doesn't drift across the temples like Balloons over Bagan, so don't get the wrong idea.

### MINIBUS

Minibuses are available from various hotels and travel agents around town. A 12-seat minibus costs from US$50 per day, while a 25- or 30-seat coaster bus is around US$80 to US$100 per day.

### MOTO

Many independent travellers end up visiting the temples by *moto* (motorcycle taxi). *Moto* drivers accost visitors from the moment they set foot in Siem Reap, but they often end up being knowledgeable and friendly, and good companions for a tour around the temples, starting at around US$10 per day. They can drop you off and pick you up at allotted times and places, and even tell you a bit of background about the temples as you zip around. Many of the better drivers go on to become official tour guides.

### REMORK-MOTO

*Remork-motos*, motorcycles with twee little hooded carriages towed behind, are also known around town as *tuk tuks*. They are a popular way to get around Angkor as fellow travellers can still talk to each other as they explore (unlike on the back of a *moto*). They also offer some protection from the rain. Some *remork* drivers are very good companions for a tour of the temples. Prices run from US$15 to US$25 for the day, depending on the destination and number of passengers.

### WALKING

Why not simply explore on foot? There are obvious limitations to what can be seen, as some temples are just too far from Siem Reap. However, it is easy enough to walk to Angkor Wat and the temples of Angkor Thom, and this is a great way to meet up with villagers in the area. Those who want to get away from the roads should try the peaceful walk along the walls of Angkor Thom. It is about 13km in total, and offers access to several small, remote temples and some bird life. Another rewarding walk is from Ta Nei to Ta Keo through the forest.

> ### LINGAS LOW-DOWN
>
> Fertility symbols are prominent around the temples of Angkor. The *linga* is a phallic symbol and would have originally been located within the towers of most Hindu temples. It sits inside a *yoni*, the female fertility symbol, combining to produce holy water, charged with the sexual energy of creation. Brahmans poured the water over the *linga* and it drained through the *yoni* and out of the temples through elaborate gutters to anoint the pilgrims outside.

# ANGKOR WAT

The traveller's first glimpse of **Angkor Wat** (អង្គរវត្ត; Map p130; ⊙5am-5.30pm), the ultimate expression of Khmer genius, is matched by only a few select spots on earth. Built by Suryavarman II (r 1112–52) and surrounded by a vast moat, Angkor Wat is one of the most inspired monuments ever conceived by the human mind. Stretching around the central temple complex is an 800m-long series of bas-reliefs, and rising 55m above the ground is the central tower, which gives the whole ensemble its sublime unity.

Angkor Wat is, literally, heaven on earth. Angkor is the earthly representation of Mt Meru, the Mt Olympus of the Hindu faith and the abode of ancient gods. The 'temple that is a city', Angkor Wat is the perfect fusion of creative ambition and spiritual devotion. The Cambodian god-kings of old each strove to better their ancestors' structures in size, scale and symmetry, culminating in what is believed to be the world's largest religious building, the mother of all temples, Angkor Wat.

The temple is the heart and soul of Cambodia. It is the national symbol, the epicentre of Khmer civilisation and a source of fierce national pride. Soaring skyward and surrounded by a moat that would make its European castle counterparts blush, Angkor Wat was never abandoned to the elements and has been in virtually continuous use since it was built.

Simply unique, it is a stunning blend of spirituality and symmetry, an enduring example of humanity's devotion to its gods. Relish the very first approach, as that spine-tingling moment when you emerge on the inner causeway will rarely be felt again. It's the best-preserved temple at Angkor. Repeat visits are rewarded with previously unnoticed details.

There is much about Angkor Wat that is unique among the temples of Angkor. The most significant fact is that the temple is oriented towards the west. Symbolically, west is the direction of death, which once led a large number of scholars to conclude that Angkor Wat must have existed primarily as a tomb. This idea was supported by the fact that the magnificent bas-reliefs of the temple were designed to be viewed in an anticlockwise direction, a practice that has precedents in ancient Hindu funerary rites. Vishnu, however, is also frequently associated with west, and it is now commonly accepted that Angkor Wat most likely served both as a temple and as a mausoleum for Suryavarman II.

Angkor Wat is famous for its beguiling *apsaras* (heavenly nymphs). More than 3000 *apsaras* are carved into the walls of Angkor Wat, each of them unique, and there are 37 different hairstyles for budding styl-

## Angkor Wat

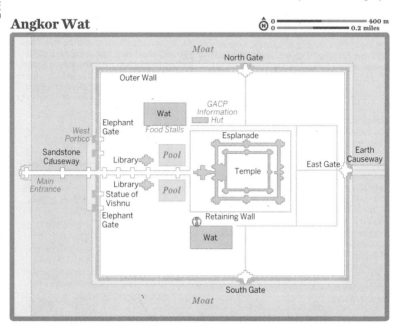

# Angkor Wat – Central Structure

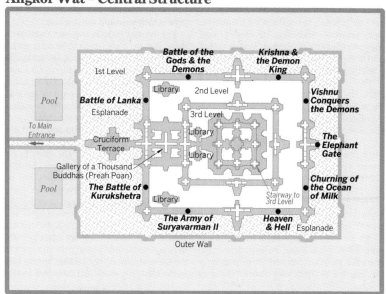

Battle of the Gods & the Demons

Krishna & the Demon King

1st Level

Library

2nd Level

Battle of Lanka

Esplanade

Vishnu Conquers the Demons

To Main Entrance

3rd Level

Cruciform Terrace

Library

The Elephant Gate

Gallery of a Thousand Buddhas (Preah Poan)

Library

Pool

Churning of the Ocean of Milk

The Battle of Kurukshetra

Library

Stairway to 3rd Level

Pool

The Army of Suryavarman II

Heaven & Hell

Esplanade

Outer Wall

ists to check out. Many of these exquisite *apsaras* have been damaged by centuries of bat droppings and urine, but they are now being restored by the German Apsara Conservation Project (GACP; www.gacp-angkor.de). The organisation operates a small information booth in the northwest corner of Angkor Wat, near the modern wat, where beautiful black-and-white postcards and images of Angkor are available.

Allow at least two hours for a visit to Angkor Wat and plan a half day if you want to decipher the bas-reliefs with a tour guide and ascend to Bakan, the upper level, which is open to visitors on a timed ticketing system.

## Symbolism

Visitors to Angkor Wat are struck by its imposing grandeur and, at close quarters, its fascinating decorative flourishes and extensive bas-reliefs. Holy men at the time of Angkor must have revelled in its multilayered levels of meaning in much the same way a contemporary literary scholar might delight in James Joyce's *Ulysses*.

Eleanor Mannikka explains in her book *Angkor Wat: Time, Space and Kingship* that the spatial dimensions of Angkor Wat parallel the lengths of the four ages (Yuga) of classical Hindu thought. Thus the visitor to Angkor Wat who walks the causeway to the main entrance and through the courtyards to the final main tower, which once contained a statue of Vishnu, is metaphorically travelling back to the first age of the creation of the universe.

Like the other temple-mountains of Angkor, Angkor Wat also replicates the spatial universe in miniature. The central tower is Mt Meru, with its surrounding smaller peaks, bounded in turn by continents (the lower courtyards) and the oceans (the moat). The seven-headed *naga* becomes a symbolic rainbow bridge for humanity to reach the abode of the gods.

While Suryavarman II may have planned Angkor Wat as his funerary temple or mausoleum, he was never buried there as he died in battle during a failed expedition to subdue the Dai Viet (Vietnamese).

## Architectural Layout

Angkor Wat is surrounded by a 190m-wide moat, which forms a giant rectangle measuring 1.5km by 1.3km. From the west, a sandstone causeway crosses the moat. The sandstone blocks from which Angkor Wat was built were quarried more than 50km away (from the holy mountain of Phnom Kulen) and floated down the Siem Reap River on rafts. The logistics of such an operation are mind-blowing, consuming the labour of thousands – an unbelievable feat given the lack of cranes and trucks that we take for granted in contemporary construction projects. According to inscriptions, the construction of Angkor Wat involved 300,000 workers and 6000 elephants, yet it was still not fully completed.

The rectangular outer wall, measuring 1025m by 800m, has a gate on each side, but the main entrance, a 235m-wide porch richly decorated with carvings and sculptures, is on the western side. There is a statue of Vishnu, 3.25m in height and hewn from a single block of sandstone, located in the right-hand tower. Vishnu's eight arms hold a mace, a spear, a disc, a conch and other items. You may also see locks of hair lying about. These are offerings both from young people preparing to get married and from pilgrims giving thanks for their good fortune.

An avenue, 475m long and 9.5m wide and lined with *naga* balustrades, leads from the main entrance to the central temple, passing between two graceful libraries

(restored by a Japanese team) and then two pools, the northern one a popular spot from which to watch the sun rise.

The central temple complex consists of three storeys, each made of laterite, which enclose a square surrounded by intricately interlinked galleries. The Gallery of a Thousand Buddhas (Preah Poan) used to house hundreds of Buddha images before the war, but many of these were removed or stolen, leaving just the handful we see today.

The corners of the second and third storeys are marked by towers, each topped with symbolic lotus-bud towers. The stairs to the upper level are immensely steep, because reaching the kingdom of the gods was no easy task. Also known as Bakan, the upper level of Angkor Wat was closed to visitors for several years, but it is once again open to a limited number per day with a timed queuing system. This means it is once again possible to complete the pilgrimage with an ascent to the summit: savour the cooling breeze, take in the extensive views and then find a quiet

## TREKKING AROUND THE TEMPLES

Spread over a vast area of the steamy tropical lowlands of Cambodia, the temples of Angkor aren't the ideal candidates to tackle on foot. However, the area is blanketed in mature forest, offering plenty of shade, and following back roads into temples is the perfect way to leave the crowds behind.

Angkor Thom is the top trekking spot thanks to its manageable size and plenty of rewarding temples within its walls. Starting out at the spectacular south gate of Angkor Thom, admire the immense representation of the Churning of the Ocean of Milk before bidding farewell to the masses and their motorised transport. Ascend the wall of this ancient city and then head west, enjoying views of the vast moat to the left and the thick jungle to the right. It is often possible to see forest birds along this route, as it is very peaceful. Reaching the southwest corner, admire Prasat Chrung, one of four identical temples marking the corners of the city. Head down below to see the water outlet of Run Ta Dev, as this once powerful city was criss-crossed by canals in its heyday.

Back on the gargantuan wall, continue to the west gate, looking out for a view to the immense Western Baray on your left. Descend at the west gate and admire the artistry of the central tower. Wander east along the path into the heart of Angkor Thom, but don't be diverted by the beauty of Bayon, as this is best saved until last. If you are with a tour guide you will have to travel this first and follow the designated running order, but independent travellers can plot their own course.

Veer north into Baphuon and wander to the back of what some have called the 'world's largest jigsaw puzzle'. Pass through the small temple of Phimeanakas and the former royal palace compound, an area of towering trees, tumbling walls and atmospheric foliage. Continue further north to petite but pretty Preah Palilay.

It's time to make for the mainstream with a walk through the Terrace of the Leper King and along the front of the royal viewing gallery, the Terrace of Elephants. If there is time, you may want to zigzag east to visit the laterite towers of Prasat Suor Prat and the atmospheric Buddhist temple of Preah Pithu. Otherwise, continue to the top billing of Bayon: weird yet wonderful, this is one of the most enigmatic of the temples at Angkor. Take your time to decipher the bas-reliefs before venturing up to the legendary faces of the upper level.

corner in which to contemplate the symmetry and symbolism of this Everest of temples.

## Bas-Reliefs

Stretching around the outside of the central temple complex is an 800m-long series of intricate and astonishing bas-reliefs. The following is a brief description of the epic events depicted on the panels. They are described in the order in which you'll come to them if you begin on the western side and keep the bas-reliefs to your left. The majority were completed in the 12th century, but in the 16th century several new reliefs were added to unfinished panels. The bas-reliefs at Angkor Wat were once sheltered by the cloister's wooden roof, which long ago rotted away except for one original beam in the western half of the north gallery. The other roofed sections are reconstructions.

### The Battle of Kurukshetra    BAS-RELIEF
The southern portion of the west gallery depicts a battle scene from the Hindu *Mahabharata* epic, in which the Kauravas (coming from the north) and the Pandavas (coming from the south) advance upon each other, meeting in furious battle. Infantry are shown on the lowest tier, with officers on elephants, and chiefs on the second and third tiers. Some of the more interesting details (from left to right): a dead chief lying on a pile of arrows, surrounded by his grieving parents and troops; a warrior on an elephant who, by putting down his weapon, has accepted defeat; and a mortally wounded officer, falling from his carriage into the arms of his soldiers. Over the centuries, some sections have been polished (by the millions of hands that fall upon them) to look like black marble. The portico at the southwestern corner is decorated with sculptures representing characters from the *Ramayana*.

### The Army of Suryavarman II    BAS-RELIEF
The remarkable western section of the south gallery depicts a triumphal battle march of Suryavarman II's army. In the southwestern corner about 2m from the floor is Suryavarman II on an elephant, wearing the royal tiara and armed with a battleaxe; he is shaded by 15 parasols and fanned by legions of servants. Compare this image of the king and with the image of Rama in the northern gallery and you'll notice an uncanny likeness that helped reinforce the aura of the god-king.

Further on is a procession of well-armed soldiers and officers on horseback; among them are bold and warlike chiefs on elephants. Just before the end of this panel is the rather disorderly Siamese mercenary army, with their long headdresses and ragged marching, at that time allied with the Khmers in their conflict with the Chams. The Khmer troops have square breastplates and are armed with spears; the Thais wear skirts and carry tridents.

The rectangular holes seen in the Army of Suryavarman II relief were created when, so the story goes, Thai soldiers removed pieces of the scene containing inscriptions that reportedly gave clues to the location of the golden treasures of Suryavarman II, later buried during the reign of Jayavarman VII.

### Heaven & Hell    BAS-RELIEF
The eastern half of the south gallery depicts the punishments and rewards of the 37 heavens and 32 hells. On the left, the upper and middle tiers show fine gentlemen and ladies proceeding towards 18-armed Yama (the judge of the dead) seated on a bull; below him are his assistants, Dharma and Sitragupta. On the lower tier, devils drag the wicked along the road to hell. To Yama's right, the tableau is divided into two parts by a horizontal line of *garudas*: above, the elect dwell in beautiful mansions, served by women and attendants; below, the condemned suffer horrible tortures that might have inspired the Khmer Rouge. The ceiling in this section was restored by the French in the 1930s.

### Churning of the Ocean of Milk    BAS-RELIEF
The southern section of the east gallery is decorated by the most famous of the bas-relief scenes at Angkor Wat, the Churning of the Ocean of Milk. This brilliantly executed carving depicts 88 *asuras* on the left, and 92 *devas*, with crested helmets, churning up the sea to extract from it the elixir of immortality. The demons hold the head of the serpent Vasuki and the gods hold its tail. At the centre of the sea, Vasuki is coiled around Mt Mandala, which turns and churns up the water in the tug of war between the demons and the gods. Vishnu, incarnated as a huge turtle, lends his shell to serve as the base and pivot of Mt Mandala. Brahma, Shiva, Hanuman (the monkey god) and Lakshmi (the goddess of wealth and prosperity) all make appearances, while overhead a host of heavenly female spirits sing and dance in encouragement. Luckily for us, the gods won through, as the *apsaras* above were too much for the hot-blooded devils to take. Restoration work on this incredible panel by the

## PROFESSOR ANG CHOULEAN, ARCHAEOLOGY EXPERT

**What is the most important Khmer temple?** Angkor Thom is the most striking and challenging for archaeologists, since it was a living city, humans and gods co-habiting there.

**What is the most important archaeological site in Cambodia?** Sambor Prei Kuk is among the most important for its homogeneity given the period and its artistic style.

**Who is the most important king in Cambodian history?** Suryavarman I, who had a real political vision which can be measured by the monuments he built, such as Preah Vihear and Wat Phu.

**What is your position on the debate between romance and restoration at Ta Prohm?** It is a matter of balance. The trees are most impressive, but maintaining the monument is our duty.

**Which other civilisation interests you greatly?** Japanese civilisation, as it is so different from Khmer civilisation, allowing me to better understand mine.

*Professor Ang Choulean is one of Cambodia's leading experts on anthropology and archaeology and is a renowned scholar on Cambodian history. He was awarded the 2011 Grand Fukuoka Prize for his outstanding contribution to Asian culture.*

World Monuments Fund (WMF; www.wmf. org) was completed in 2012.

### The Elephant Gate
BAS-RELIEF

This gate, which has no stairway, was used by the king and others for mounting and dismounting elephants directly from the gallery. North of the gate is a Khmer inscription recording the erection of a nearby stupa in the 18th century.

### Vishnu Conquers the Demons
BAS-RELIEF

The northern section of the east gallery shows a furious and desperate encounter between Vishnu, riding on a *garuda,* and innumerable devils. Needless to say, he slays all comers. This gallery was most likely completed in the 16th century, and the later carving is notably inferior to the original work from the 12th century.

### Krishna & the Demon King
BAS-RELIEF

The eastern section of the north gallery shows Vishnu incarnated as Krishna riding a *garuda.* He confronts a burning walled city, the residence of Bana, the demon king. The *garuda* puts out the fire and Bana is captured. In the final scene Krishna kneels before Shiva and asks that Bana's life be spared.

### Battle of the Gods & the Demons
BAS-RELIEF

The western section of the north gallery depicts the battle between the 21 gods of the Brahmanic pantheon and various demons. The gods are featured with their traditional attributes and mounts. Vishnu has four arms and is seated on a *garuda,* while Shiva rides a sacred goose.

### Battle of Lanka
BAS-RELIEF

The northern half of the west gallery shows scenes from the *Ramayana.* In the Battle of Lanka, Rama (on the shoulders of Hanuman), along with his army of monkeys, battles 10-headed, 20-armed Ravana, captor of Rama's beautiful wife Sita. Ravana rides a chariot drawn by monsters and commands an army of giants.

# ANGKOR THOM

It is hard to imagine any building bigger or more beautiful than Angkor Wat, but in Angkor Thom the sum of the parts add up to a greater whole. Aptly named, the fortified city of Angkor Thom (អង្គរធំ) is indeed a 'Great City' on an epic scale. The last great capital of the Khmer empire, and set over 10 sq km, Angkor Thom took monumental to a whole new level.

It was built in part as a reaction to the surprise sacking of Angkor by the Chams, after Jayavarman VII (r 1181–1219) decided that his empire would never again be vulnerable at home. At the city's height, it may have supported a population of one million people in the surrounding region. Centred on Bayon, the surreal state temple of Jayavarman VII, Angkor Thom is enclosed by a formidable *jayagiri* (square wall) 8m high and 12km in length and encircled by a

100m-wide *jayasindhu* (moat) that would have stopped all but the hardiest invaders in their tracks. This architectural layout is an expression of Mt Meru surrounded by the oceans.

It is the gates that grab you first, flanked by a vast representation of the Churning of the Ocean of Milk, 54 demons and 54 gods engaged in an epic tug of war on the causeway. Each gate towers above the visitor, the magnanimous faces of the Bodhisattva Avalokiteshvara staring out over the kingdom. Imagine being a peasant in the 13th century approaching the forbidding capital for the first time. It would have been an awe-inspiring yet unsettling experience to enter such a gateway and come face to face with the divine power of the god-kings.

The **south gate** (Map p130) is most popular with visitors, as it has been fully restored and many of the heads (mostly copies) remain in place. The gate is on the main road into Angkor Thom from Angkor Wat, and it gets very busy. More peaceful are the east

and west gates, found at the end of dirt trails. The **east gate** (Map p130) was used as a location in *Tomb Raider,* where the bad guys broke into the 'tomb' by pulling down a giant (polystyrene!) *apsara.* The causeway at the **west gate** (Map p130) of Angkor Thom has completely collapsed, leaving a jumble of ancient stones sticking out of the soil, like victims of a terrible historical pile-up.

In the centre of the walled enclosure are the city's most important monuments, including Bayon, Baphuon, the Royal Enclosure, Phimeanakas and the Terrace of Elephants. With all these temples and sites to discover, visitors should set aside a half day to explore Angkor Thom in depth.

## Bayon                                    បាយ័ន

At the heart of Angkor Thom is the 12th-century **Bayon** (បាយ័ន; Map p130; ☉7.30am-5.30pm), the mesmerising, if slightly mind-bending, state temple of

## Central Area of Angkor Thom

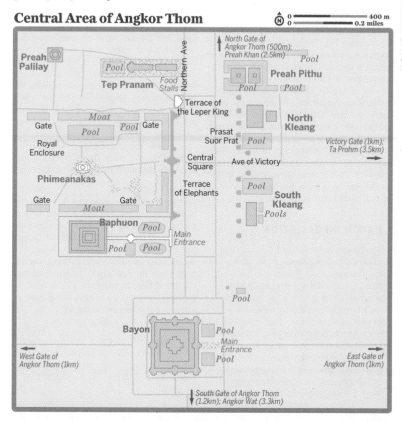

Jayavarman VII. It epitomises the creative genius and inflated ego of Cambodia's most celebrated king. Its 54 Gothic towers are famously decorated with 216 gargantuan smiling faces of Avalokiteshvara that bear more than a passing resemblance to the great king himself. The Bayon is decorated with 1.2km of extraordinary bas-reliefs incorporating more than 11,000 figures, depicting everyday life in 12th-century Cambodia.

Unique even among its cherished contemporaries, the architectural audacity was a definitive political statement about the change from Hinduism to Mahayana Buddhism. Known as the 'face temple' thanks to its iconic visages, these huge heads glare down from every angle, exuding power and control with a hint of humanity. This was precisely the blend required to hold sway over such a vast empire, ensuring the disparate and far-flung population yielded to his magnanimous will. As you walk around, a dozen or more of the heads are visible at any one time: full face or in profile, sometimes level with your eyes, sometimes staring down from on high.

Bayon is now known to have been built by Jayavarman VII, though for many years its origins were unknown. Shrouded by dense jungle, it also took researchers some time to realise that it stands in the exact centre of the city of Angkor Thom. There is still much mystery associated with Bayon – such as its exact function and symbolism – and this seems only appropriate for a monument whose signature is an enigmatic smiling face.

The eastward orientation of Bayon leads most people to visit early in the morning. However, Bayon looks equally good in the late afternoon. A Japanese team is restoring several outer areas of the temple.

---

### BAYON INFORMATION

The **Bayon Information Center** (Map p104; ☑ 092-165083; www.angkor-jsa.org/bic; admission US$2; ☺ 8am-4pm Tue, Wed & Fri-Sun) is a well-presented and informative exhibition on the history of the Khmer empire and the restoration projects around Angkor, that includes some short documentary films. Set in the beautiful compound of the Japanese government team for Safeguarding Angkor (JSA) on the outskirts of Siem Reap, it's a big saving on the Angkor National Museum.

---

## Architectural Layout

Unlike Angkor Wat, which looks impressive from all angles, Bayon looks rather like a glorified pile of rubble from a distance. It's only when you enter the temple and make your way up to the third level that its magic becomes apparent.

The basic structure of Bayon comprises a simple three levels, which correspond more or less to three distinct phases of building. This is because Jayavarman VII began construction of this temple at an advanced age, so he was never confident it would be completed. Each time one phase was completed, he moved on to the next. The first two levels are square and adorned with bas-reliefs. They lead up to a third, circular level, with the towers and their faces.

Some say that the Khmer empire was divided into 54 provinces at the time of Bayon's construction, hence the all-seeing eyes of Avalokiteshvara (or Jayavarman VII) keeping watch on the kingdom's outlying subjects.

## Bas-Reliefs

Angkor Wat's bas-reliefs may grab the headlines, but Bayon's are even more extensive, decorated with 1.2km of extraordinary carvings depicting more than 11,000 figures. The famous carvings on the outer wall of the first level show vivid scenes of everyday life in 12th-century Cambodia. The bas-reliefs on the second level do not have the epic proportions of those on the first level and tend to be fragmented. The reliefs described are those on the first level. The sequence assumes that you enter Bayon from the east and view the reliefs in a clockwise direction.

### Chams on the Run                    BAS-RELIEF

Just south of the east gate is a three-level panorama. On the first tier, Khmer soldiers march off to battle – check out the elephants and the ox-carts, which are almost exactly like those still used in Cambodia today. The second tier depicts coffins being carried back from the battlefield. In the centre of the third tier, Jayavarman VII, shaded by parasols, is shown on horseback followed by legions of concubines (to the left).

### Linga Worship                       BAS-RELIEF

The first panel north of the southeastern corner shows Hindus praying to a *linga* (phallic symbol). This image was probably originally a Buddha, later modified by a Hindu king.

# Bayon

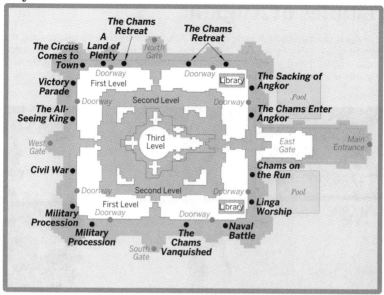

### Naval Battle          BAS-RELIEF
The Naval Battle panel has some of the best-carved reliefs. The scenes depict a naval battle between the Khmers and the Chams (the latter with head coverings), and everyday life around Tonlé Sap lake where the battle was fought. Look for images of people picking lice from each other's hair, of hunters and, towards the western end of the panel, of a woman giving birth.

### The Chams Vanquished          BAS-RELIEF
In the Chams Vanquished, scenes from daily life are featured while the battle between the Khmers and the Chams takes place on the shore of Tonlé Sap lake, where the Chams are soundly thrashed. Scenes include two people playing chess, a cockfight and women selling fish in the market. The scenes of meals being prepared and served are in celebration of the Khmer victory.

### Military Procession          BAS-RELIEF
The most western relief of the south gallery, depicting a military procession, is unfinished, as is the panel showing elephants being led down from the mountains. Brahmans have been chased up two trees by tigers.

### Civil War          BAS-RELIEF
This panel depicts scenes that some scholars maintain is a civil war. Groups of people, some armed, confront each other, and the violence escalates until elephants and warriors join the melee.

### The All-Seeing King          BAS-RELIEF
The fighting depicted in the Civil War panel, just south of this panel, continues on a smaller scale. An antelope is being swallowed by a gargantuan fish; among the smaller fish is a prawn, under which an inscription proclaims that the king will seek out those in hiding.

### Victory Parade          BAS-RELIEF
This panel depicts a procession that includes the king (carrying a bow). Presumably it is a celebration of his victory.

### The Circus Comes to Town          BAS-RELIEF
At the western corner of the northern wall is a Khmer circus. A strongman holds three dwarfs, and a man on his back is spinning a wheel with his feet; above is a group of tightrope walkers. To the right of the circus, the royal court watches from a terrace, below which is a procession of animals. Some of the reliefs in this section remain unfinished.

### A Land of Plenty          BAS-RELIEF
The two rivers, one next to the doorpost and the other a few metres to the right, are teeming with fish.

# Temples of Angkor

Cambodia is the undisputed temple capital of Asia, and we're not just talking about the holiest of holies – the one and only Angkor Wat. Angkor is heaven on earth, but there are also temples dotted all over Siem Reap, the epicentre of the empire, that attest to the glories of Khmer civilisation.

### 1. Ta Prohm (p158)
Jungle trees are entwined with temples at Angkor's most atmospheric ruin.

### 2. Sra Srang (p159)
Only the stone base remains of the temple that once stood in this peaceful basin.

### 3. Bayon (p149)
There are more than 210 faces of Cambodia's most celebrated king, Avalokiteshvara, carved here.

### 4. Banteay Srei (p165)
A Hindu temple with stunning stone carvings, known as the art gallery of Angkor.

### The Chams Retreat                    BAS-RELIEF

On the lowest level of this unfinished three-tiered scene, the Cham armies are being defeated and expelled from the Khmer kingdom. The next panel depicts the Cham armies advancing, and the badly deteriorated panel shows the Chams (on the left) chasing the Khmers.

### The Sacking of Angkor               BAS-RELIEF

This panel shows the war of 1177, when the Khmers were defeated by the Chams, and Angkor was pillaged. The wounded Khmer king is being lowered from the back of an elephant and a wounded Khmer general is being carried on a hammock suspended from a pole. Directly above, despairing Khmers are getting drunk. The Chams (on the right) are in hot pursuit of their vanquished enemy.

### The Chams Enter Angkor             BAS-RELIEF

This panel depicts a meeting of the Khmer and Cham armies. Notice the flag bearers among the Cham troops (on the right). The Chams were defeated in the war, which ended in 1181, as depicted on the first panel in the sequence.

## Baphuon                              បាពួន

Some have called Baphuon (Map p130; ☺7.30am-5.30pm) the 'world's largest jigsaw puzzle'. Before the civil war the Baphuon was painstakingly taken apart piece-by-piece by a team of archaeologists, but their meticulous records were destroyed during the Khmer Rouge regime, leaving experts with 300,000 stones to put back into place. After years of excruciating research, this temple has been partially restored. On the western

---

### THE RECLINING BUDDHA OF BAPHUON

On the western side of Baphuon is a reclining Buddha about 60m in length. The unfinished figure is difficult to make out, but the head is on the northern side of the wall and the gate is where the hips should be; to the left of the gate protrudes an arm. When it comes to the legs and feet – the latter are entirely gone – imagination must suffice. This huge project, undertaken by the Buddhist faithful 500 years ago, reinforces the notion that Angkor was never entirely abandoned.

---

side, the retaining wall of the second level was fashioned, in the 16th century, into a reclining Buddha (p154) 60m in length.

Baphuon is approached by a 200m elevated walkway made of sandstone, and the central structure is 43m high. Clamber under the elevated causeway leading to Baphuon for an incredible view of the hundreds of pillars supporting it.

In its heyday, Baphuon would have been one of the most spectacular of Angkor's temples. Located 200m northwest of Bayon, it's a pyramidal representation of mythical Mt Meru. Construction probably began under Suryavarman I and was later completed by Udayadityavarman II. It marked the centre of the capital that existed before the construction of Angkor Thom.

## Royal Enclosure & Phimeanakas        ភិមានអាកាស

Phimeanakas (Map p130) stands close to the centre of a walled area that once housed the royal palace. There's very little left of the palace today except for two sandstone pools near the northern wall. Once the site of royal ablutions, these are now used as swimming holes by local children. Phimeanakas means 'Celestial Palace', and some scholars say that it was once topped by a golden spire.

Today, Phimeanakas only hints at its former splendour and looks a little worse for wear. The temple is another pyramidal representation of Mt Meru, with three levels. Most of the decorative features are broken or have disappeared. Still, it is worth clambering up to the second and third levels for good views of Baphuon.

Construction of the palace began under Rajendravarman II, although it was used by Jayavarman V and Udayadityavarman I. It was later added to and embellished by Jayavarman VII and his successors. The royal enclosure is fronted to the east by the Terrace of Elephants. The northwestern wall of the Royal Enclosure is very atmospheric, with immense trees and jungle vines cloaking the outer side, easily visible on a forest walk from Preah Palilay to Phimeanakas.

## Preah Palilay                        ព្រះបាលិឡៃ

Preah Palilay (Map p130; ☺7.30am-5.30pm) is about 200m north of the Royal Enclosure's northern wall. It was erected during the rule of Jayavarman VII and originally housed a Buddha, which has long since vanished. Sadly, the immense trees that used to loom large over the temple have been cut down, removing some of the romance of the place in the process, although the large trunks are already showing some signs of regrowth.

## Tep Pranam        ទេពប្រណម្យ

**Tep Pranam** (⊘7.30am-5.30pm), an 82m by 34m cruciform Buddhist terrace 150m east of Preah Palilay, was once the base of a pagoda of lightweight construction. Nearby is a 4.5m-high Buddha, but it's a reconstruction of the original. A group of Buddhist nuns lives in a wooden structure close by.

## Preah Pithu        ព្រះពិធូរ

**Preah Pithu** (⊘7.30am-5.30pm), located across Northern Ave from Tep Pranam, is a group of 12th-century Hindu and Buddhist temples enclosed by a wall. It includes some beautifully decorated terraces and guardian animals in the form of elephants and lions. It sees few tourists so is a good place to explore at a leisurely pace, taking in the impressive jungle backdrop.

## Terrace of the Leper King        ទីលានព្រះគម្ងង់

The **Terrace of the Leper King** (Map p130) is just north of the Terrace of Elephants. Dating from the late 12th century, it is a 7m-high platform, on top of which stands a nude, though sexless, statue. The front retaining walls of the terrace are decorated with at least five tiers of meticulously executed carvings. On the southern side of the Terrace of the Leper King, there is access to a hidden terrace with exquisitely preserved carvings.

The aforementioned statue is yet another of Angkor's mysteries. The original of the statue is held at Phnom Penh's National Museum, and various theories have been advanced to explain its meaning. Legend has it that at least two of the Angkor kings had leprosy, and the statue may represent one of them. Another theory – a more likely explanation – is that the statue is of Yama, the god of death, and that the Terrace of the Leper King housed the royal crematorium.

The carved walls include seated *apsaras*, kings wearing pointed diadems, armed with short double-edged swords and accompa-

nied by the court and princesses, the latter adorned with beautiful rows of pearls.

On the southern side of the Terrace of the Leper King (facing the Terrace of Elephants), there is access to the front wall of a hidden terrace that was covered up when the outer structure was built – a terrace within a terrace. The four tiers of *apsaras* and other figures, including *nagas*, look as fresh as if they had been carved yesterday, thanks to being covered up for centuries. Some of the figures carry fearsome expressions. As you follow the inner wall of the Terrace of the Leper King, notice the increasingly rough chisel marks on the figures, an indication that this wall was never completed, like many of the temples at Angkor.

## Terrace of Elephants        ទីលានដល់ដំរី

The 350m-long **Terrace of Elephants** (Map p130) was used as a giant viewing stand for public ceremonies and served as a base for the king's grand audience hall. Try to imagine the pomp and grandeur of the Khmer empire at its height, with infantry, cavalry, horse-drawn chariots and elephants parading across Central Square in a colourful procession, pennants and standards aloft. Looking on is the god-king, shaded by multitiered parasols and attended by mandarins and handmaidens bearing gold and silver utensils.

The Terrace of Elephants has five piers extending towards the Central Square – three in the centre and one at each end. The middle section of the retaining wall is decorated with life-size *garudas* and lions; towards either end are the two parts of the famous parade of elephants, complete with their Khmer mahouts.

## Kleangs & Prasat Suor Prat        ប្រាសាទឃ្លាំង និងប្រាសាទស្វ័យ្រ្រ័ត

Along the east side of Central Square are two groups of buildings called **Kleangs**. The North Kleang and South Kleang may at one time have been palaces. The North Kleang has been dated from the period of Jayavarman V. Along Central Square in front of the two Kleangs are 12 laterite towers – 10 in a row and two more at right angles facing the Ave of Victory – known as the Prasat Suor Prat, meaning 'Temple of the Tightrope Dancers'.

Archaeologists believe the towers, which form an honour guard along Central Square, were constructed by Jayavarman VII. It is likely that each one originally contained either a *linga* or a statue. It is said artists performed for the king on tightropes or rope bridges strung between these towers, hence the name. According to 13th-century Chinese emissary Chou Ta-Kuan, the towers of **Prasat Suor Prat** were also used for public trials of sorts. During a dispute the two parties would be made to sit inside two towers, one party eventually succumbing to illness and proven guilty.

# AROUND ANGKOR THOM

## Baksei Chamkrong បក្សីចាំក្រុង

Located southwest of the south gate of Angkor Thom, **Baksei Chamkrong** (Map p130; ⊙7.30am-5.30pm) is one of the few brick edifices in the immediate vicinity of Angkor. A well-proportioned though petite temple, it was once decorated with a covering of lime mortar. Like virtually all of the structures of Angkor, it opens to the east. In the early 10th century, Harshavarman I erected five statues in this temple: two of Shiva, one of Vishnu and two of Devi.

## Phnom Bakheng ភ្នំបាខែង

Located around 400m south of Angkor Thom, the main attraction at **Phnom Bak-** heng (Map p130; ⊙5am-7pm) is the sunset view over Angkor Wat. For many years, the whole affair turned into a circus, with crowds of tourists ascending the slopes of the hill and jockeying for space. Numbers are restricted to just 300 visitors at any one time, so get here early (4pm) to guarantee a sunset spot. The temple, built by Yasovarman I (r 889–910), has five tiers, with seven levels.

Phnom Bakheng also lays claim to being home to the first of the temple-mountains built in the vicinity of Angkor. Yasovarman I chose Phnom Bakheng over the Roluos area, where the earlier capital (and temple-mountains) had been located.

The temple-mountain has five tiers, with seven levels (including the base and the summit). At the base are – or were – 44 towers. Each of the five tiers had 12 towers. The summit of the temple has four towers at the cardinal points of the compass as well as a central sanctuary. All of these numbers are of symbolic significance. The seven levels, for example, represent the seven Hindu heavens, while the total number of towers, excluding the central sanctuary, is 108, a particularly auspicious number and one that correlates to the lunar calendar.

Some prefer to visit in the early morning, when it's cool (and crowds are light), to climb the hill. That said, the sunset over the Western Baray is very impressive from here. Allow about two hours for the sunset experience.

To get a good picture of Angkor Wat in the glow of the late-afternoon sun from the summit of Phnom Bakheng, you will need at least a 300mm lens, as the temple is 1.3km away.

## Phnom Bakheng

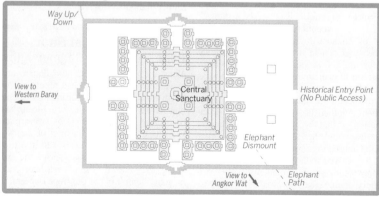

## ANGKORIN' FOR LUNCH

Many of the tour groups buzzing around Angkor head back to Siem Reap for lunch. This is as good a reason as any to stick around the temples, taking advantage of the lack of crowds to explore some popular sites and enjoy a local lunch at one of the many stalls. Almost all of the major temples have some sort of nourishment available beyond the walls. Anyone travelling with a *moto* or *remork-moto (tuk tuk)* should ask the driver for tips on cheap eats, as these guys eat around the temples every day. They know the best spots, at the best price, and should be able to sort you out (assuming you are getting along well).

The most extensive selection of restaurants is lined up opposite the entrance to Angkor Wat and includes several choices such as **Khmer Angkor Restaurant** (Map p130; mains US$3-6; ☺6am-6pm) and **Angkor Reach Restaurant** (Map p130; mains US$3-6; ☺6am-6pm). There is also a handy branch of **Blue Pumpkin** (Map p130; Angkor Cafe; dishes US$2-8; ☺7am-7pm) turning out sandwiches, salads and ice creams, as well as divine fruit shakes, all to take away if required. **Chez Sophea** (Map p130; ☎012 858003; meals US$10-20; ☺11am-10pm) offers barbecued meats and fish, accompanied by a cracking homemade salad, but prices are at the high end.

There are dozens of local noodle stalls just north of Angkor Thom's Terrace of the Leper King, which are a good spot for a quick bite to eat. Other central temples with food available include Ta Prohm, Preah Khan and Ta Keo. There is also a cluster of excellent Khmer restaurants located along the northern shore of Sra Srang.

Further afield, Banteay Srei has several small restaurants, complete with ornate wood furnishings cut from Cambodia's forests. Further north at Kbal Spean, food stalls at the bottom of the hill can cook up fried rice or a noodle soup. The excellent **Borey Sovann Restaurant** (meals US$3-6; ☺11am-6pm), located near the entrance to Kbal Spean, is a great place to wind down before or after an ascent to the River of a Thousand Lingas. There are also stop-and-dip stalls (dishes US$2 to US$4) near the entrance to Beng Mealea temple.

Water and soft drinks are available throughout the temple area, and many sellers lurk outside the temples, ready to pounce with offers of cold drinks. Sometimes they ask at just the right moment; on other occasions it is the 27th time in an hour that you've been approached and you are ready to scream. Try not to – you'll scare your fellow travellers and lose face with the locals.

## Chau Say Tevoda ចៅសាយទេវតា

Just east of Angkor Thom's Victory Gate is **Chau Say Tevoda** (Map p130; ☺7.30am-5.30pm). It was probably built during the second quarter of the 12th century, under the reign of Suryavarman II, and dedicated to Shiva and Vishnu. It has been renovated by the Chinese to bring it up to the condition of its twin temple, Thommanon.

## Thommanon ប្រាសាទធម្មនន្ទ

Just north of Chau Say Tevoda is **Thommanon** (Map p130; ☺7.30am-5.30pm). Although unique, the temple complements its neighbour, as it was built to a similar design around the same time and was dedicated to Shiva and Vishnu. Thommanon is in good

condition thanks to extensive work undertaken by the EFEO in the 1960s.

## Spean Thmor ស្ពានថ្ម

**Spean Thmor** (Stone Bridge; Map p130), of which an arch and several piers remain, is 200m east of Thommanon. Jayavarman VII constructed many roads with these immense stone bridges spanning watercourses. This is the only large bridge remaining in the immediate vicinity of Angkor. It vividly highlights how the water level has changed course over the centuries and may offer another clue to the collapse of Angkor's extensive irrigation system. Just north of Spean Thmor is a large water wheel.

There are more-spectacular examples of these ancient bridges elsewhere in Siem Reap Province, such as Spean Praptos, with 19 arches, in Kompong Kdei on NH6 from

Phnom Penh; and Spean Ta Ong, a 77m bridge with a beautiful *naga*, forgotten in the forest about 28km east of Beng Mealea.

# Ta Keo តាកែវ

**Ta Keo** (Map p130; ⊘ 7.30am-5.30pm) is a stark, undecorated temple that undoubtedly would have been one of the finest of Angkor's structures, had it been finished. Built by Jayavarman V, it was dedicated to Shiva and was the first Angkorian monument built entirely of sandstone. The summit of the central tower, which is surrounded by four lower towers, is almost 50m high. The four towers at the corners of a square and a fifth tower in the centre is typical of many Angkorian temple-mountains.

No one is certain why work was never completed, but a likely cause may have been the death of Jayavarman V. Others contend that the hard sandstone was impossible to carve and that explains the lack of decoration. According to inscriptions, Ta Keo was struck by lightning during construction, which may have been a bad omen and led to its abandonment. Allow about 30 minutes to visit Ta Keo.

# Ta Nei តានី

**Ta Nei** (Map p130; ⊘ 7.30am-5.30pm), 800m north of Ta Keo, was built by Jayavarman VII (r 1181–1219). There is something of the spirit of Ta Prohm here, albeit on a lesser scale, with moss and tentacle-like roots covering many outer areas of this small temple. However, the number of visitors are also on a lesser scale, making it very atmospheric.

It can be accessed by walking across a French-built dam or via a short trek from Ta Nei to Ta Keo through the forest, a guaranteed way to leave the crowds behind. Including the access walk, allow about two hours to visit Ta Nei. Close by is the new Flight of the Gibbon Angkor zipline experience.

# Ta Prohm តាព្រហ្ម

The ultimate Indiana Jones fantasy; **Ta Prohm** (Map p130; ⊘ 7.30am-5.30pm) is cloaked in dappled shadow, its crumbling towers and walls locked in the slow muscular embrace of vast root systems. Undoubtedly the most atmospheric ruin at Angkor, Ta Prohm should be high on the hit list of every visitor. Its appeal lies in the fact that, unlike the other monuments of Angkor, it has been swallowed by the jungle, and looks very much the way most of the monuments of Angkor appeared when European explorers first stumbled upon them.

Well, that's the theory, but in fact the jungle is pegged back and only the largest trees are left in place, making it manicured rather than raw like Beng Mealea. Still, a visit to Ta Prohm is a unique, other-worldly experience. There is a poetic cycle to this venerable ruin, with humanity first conquering nature to rapidly create, and nature once again conquering humanity to slowly destroy. If Angkor Wat is testimony to the genius of the ancient Khmers, Ta Prohm reminds us equally of the awesome fecundity and power of the jungle.

Built from 1186 and originally known as Rajavihara (Monastery of the King), Ta Prohm was a Buddhist temple dedicated to the mother of Jayavarman VII. It is one of the few temples in the Angkor region where an inscription provides information about the temple's dependents and inhabitants. Almost 80,000 people were required to maintain or attend at the temple, among them more than 2700 officials and 615 dancers.

Ta Prohm is a temple of towers, closed courtyards and narrow corridors. Many of the corridors are impassable, clogged with jumbled piles of delicately carved stone blocks dislodged by the roots of long-decayed trees. Bas-reliefs on bulging walls are carpeted with lichen, moss and creeping plants, and shrubs sprout from the roofs of monumental porches. Trees, hundreds of years old, tower overhead, their leaves filtering the sunlight and casting a greenish pall over the whole scene.

The most popular of the many strangulating root formations is that on the inside of the easternmost gopura (entrance pavilion) of the central enclosure, nicknamed the Crocodile Tree. One of the most famous spots in Ta Prohm is the so-called 'Tomb Raider tree', where Angelina Jolie's Lara Croft picked a jasmine flower before falling through the earth into...Pinewood Studios.

It used to be possible to climb onto the damaged galleries, but this is now prohibited, to protect both temple and visitor. Many of these precariously balanced stones weigh a tonne or more and would do some serious damage if they came down. Ta Prohm is currently under stabilisation and restoration by an Indian team of archaeologists working with their Cambodian counterparts.

# Ta Prohm

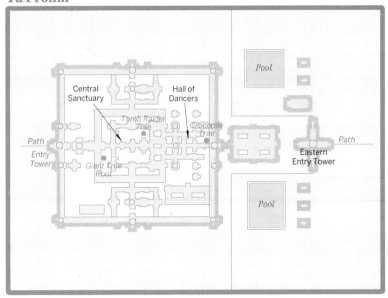

Central Sanctuary

Hall of Dancers

Tomb Raider Tree

Crocodile Tree

Path

Entry Tower

Giant Tree Root

Path

Eastern Entry Tower

Pool

Pool

Ta Prohm is at its most impressive early in the day. Allow as much as two hours to visit, especially if you want to explore the maze-like corridors and iconic tree roots.

## Banteay Kdei & Sra Srang   បន្ទាយក្តីនិងស្រះស្រង់

**Banteay Kdei** (Map p130; ☺ 7.30am-5.30pm), a massive Buddhist monastery from the latter part of the 12th century, is surrounded by four concentric walls. Each of its four entrances is decorated with *garudas*, which hold aloft one of Jayavarman VII's favourite themes: the four faces of Avalokiteshvara. East of Banteay Kdei is an earlier basin, Sra Srang, measuring 800m by 400m, reserved for the king and his consorts.

The outer wall of Banteay Kdei measures 500m by 700m. The inside of the central tower was never finished and much of the temple is in a ruinous state due to hasty construction. It is considerably less busy than nearby Ta Prohm and this alone can justify a visit.

A tiny island in the middle of Sra Srang once bore a wooden temple, of which only the stone base remains. This is a beautiful body of water from which to take in a quiet sunrise.

Allow about one hour to visit Banteay Kdei and take in the view over nearby Sra Srang.

## Prasat Kravan   ប្រាសាទក្រវ៉ាន់

Uninspiring from the outside, the interior brick carvings concealed within its towers are the hidden treasure of **Prasat Kravan** (Map p130; ☺ 7.30am-5.30pm). The five brick towers, arranged in a north–south line and oriented to the east, were built for Hindu worship in AD 921. The structure is unusual in that it was not constructed by royalty; this accounts for its slightly distant location, away from the centre of the capital. Prasat

### THE LONG STRIDER

One of Vishnu's best-loved incarnations was when he appeared as the dwarf Vamana, and proceeded to reclaim the world from the evil demon king Bali. The dwarf politely asked the demon king for a comfortable patch of ground upon which to meditate, saying that the patch need only be big enough so that he could easily walk across it in three paces. The demon agreed, only to see the dwarf swell into a mighty giant who strode across the universe in three enormous steps. From this legend, depicted at Prasat Kravan, Vishnu is sometimes known as the 'long strider'.

Kravan is just south of the road between Angkor Wat and Banteay Kdei.

Prasat Kravan was partially restored in 1968, returning the brick carvings to their former glory. The images of Vishnu in the largest central tower show the eight-armed deity on the back wall, taking the three gigantic steps with which he reclaimed the world (p159) on the left wall; and riding a *garuda* on the right wall. The northernmost tower displays bas-reliefs of Vishnu's consort, Lakshmi.

# Preah Khan ព្រះខ័ន្ធ

The temple of **Preah Khan** (Sacred Sword; Map p130; ☉ 7.30am-5.30pm) is one of the largest complexes at Angkor, a maze of vaulted corridors, fine carvings and lichen-clad stonework. It is a good counterpoint to Ta Prohm and generally sees slightly fewer visitors. Like Ta Prohm it is a place of towered enclosures and shoulder-hugging corridors. Unlike Ta Prohm, however, the temple of Preah Khan is in a reasonable state of preservation thanks to the ongoing restoration efforts of the World Monuments Fund (WMF; www.wmf.org).

Preah Khan was built by Jayavarman VII and probably served as his temporary residence while Angkor Thom was being built.

The central sanctuary of the temple was dedicated in AD 1191.

A large stone stela tells us much about Preah Khan's role as a centre for worship and learning. Originally located within the first eastern enclosure, this stela is now housed safely at Angkor Conservation. The temple was dedicated to 515 divinities and during the course of a year 18 major festivals took place here, requiring a team of thousands just to maintain the place.

Preah Khan covers a very large area, but the temple itself is within a rectangular enclosing wall of around 700m by 800m. Four processional walkways approach the gates of the temple, and these are bordered by another stunning depiction of the Churning of the Ocean of Milk, as in the approach to Angkor Thom, although most of the heads have disappeared. From the central sanctuary, four long, vaulted galleries extend in the cardinal directions. Many of the interior walls of Preah Khan were once coated with plaster that was held in place by holes in the stone. Today, many delicate reliefs remain, including *rishi* and *apsara* carvings.

The main entrance to Preah Khan is in the east, but most tourists enter at the west gate near the main road, walk the length of the temple to the east gate before doubling back to the central sanctuary, and exit at the

## Preah Khan

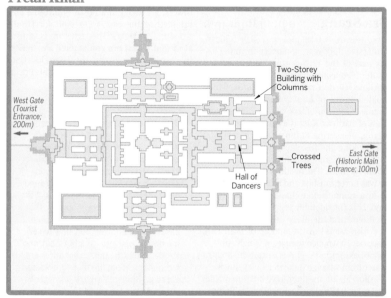

West Gate (Tourist Entrance; 200m)

Two-Storey Building with Columns

East Gate (Historic Main Entrance; 100m)

Crossed Trees

Hall of Dancers

north gate. Approaching from the west, there is little clue to nature's genius, but on the outer retaining wall of the east gate is a pair of trees with monstrous roots embracing, one still reaching for the sky. There is also a curious, Grecian-style, two-storey structure in the temple grounds, the purpose of which is unknown, but it looks like an exile from Athens. Another option is to enter from the north and exit from the east. Given its vast size, it is sensible to set aside at least 90 minutes to explore this temple, even two hours.

Preah Khan is a genuine fusion temple, the eastern entrance dedicated to Mahayana Buddhism with equal-sized doors, and the other cardinal directions dedicated to Shiva, Vishnu and Brahma with successively smaller doors, emphasising the unequal nature of Hinduism.

## Preah Neak Poan  ព្រះនាគព័ន្ធ

The Buddhist temple of **Preah Neak Poan** (Temple of the Intertwined Nagas; Map p130; ⊙7.30am-5.30pm) is a petite yet perfect temple constructed by Jayavarman VII in the late 12th century. It has a large square pool surrounded by four smaller square pools. In the middle of the central pool is a circular 'island' encircled by the two *nagas* whose intertwined tails give the temple its name.

It's a safe bet that if an 'Encore Angkor' casino is eventually developed in Las Vegas or Macau, Preah Neak Poan will provide the blueprint for the swimming complex.

In the pool around the central island there were once four statues, but only one remains, reconstructed from the debris by the French archaeologists who cleared the site. The curious figure has the body of a horse supported by a tangle of human legs. It relates to a legend that Avalokiteshvara once saved a group of shipwrecked followers from an island of ghouls by transforming into a flying horse. A beautiful replica of this statue decorates the main roundabout at Siem Reap International Airport.

Water once flowed from the central pool into the four peripheral pools via ornamental spouts, which can still be seen in the pavilions at each axis of the pool. The spouts are in the form of an elephant's head, a horse's head, a lion's head and a human head. The pool was used for ritual purification rites.

Preah Neak Poan was once in the centre of a huge 3km-by-900m *baray* serving Preah Khan, known as Jayatataka, which is once again partially filled with water due to a new opening in the dyke road. Access is currently restricted to the edge of the complex via a wooden causeway, so a visit takes only 30 minutes.

## Preah Neak Poan

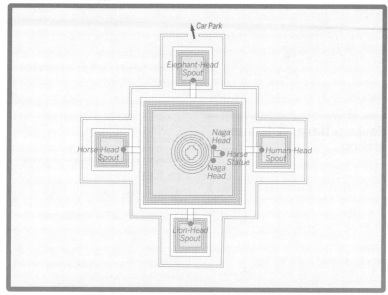

## GUIDE TO THE GUIDES

Countless books on Angkor have been written over the years, with more and more new titles coming out, reflecting Angkor's rebirth as the world's top cultural hot spot. Here are just a few of the best:

**A Guide to the Angkor Monuments** (Maurice Glaize) The definitive 1944 guide, downloadable for free at www.theangkorguide.com.

**A Passage Through Angkor** (Mark Standen) One of the best photographic records of the temples.

**A Pilgrimage to Angkor** (Pierre Loti) One of the most beautifully written books on Angkor, based on the author's 1910 journey.

**Ancient Angkor** (Claude Jacques) Written by one of the foremost scholars on Angkor, this is a very readable guide to the temples, with photos by Michael Freeman.

**Angkor: An Introduction to the Temples** (Dawn Rooney) Probably the most popular contemporary guide.

**Angkor – Heart of an Asian Empire** (Bruno Dagens) The story of the 'discovery' of Angkor, complete with lavish illustrations.

**Angkor: Millennium of Glory** (various authors) A fascinating introduction to the history, culture, sculpture and religion of the Angkorian period.

**Khmer Heritage in the Old Siamese Provinces of Cambodia** (Etienne Aymonier) Aymonier journeyed through Cambodia in 1901 and visited many of the major temples.

**The Angkor Guide** (Andrew Booth) Excellent guide to the temples of Angkor with input from leading academics, beautiful overlay illustrations and profits helping to fund education in Siem Reap (see www.angkorguidebook.com).

**The Customs of Cambodia** (Chou Ta-Kuan) The only eyewitness account of Angkor, by a Chinese emissary who spent a year at the Khmer capital in the late 13th century.

## Ta Som តាសោម

Ta Som (Map p130; ⊙ 7.30am-5.30pm), which stands to the east of Preah Neak Poan, is one of the late-12th-century Buddhist temples of prolific builder Jayavarman VII. The most impressive feature at Ta Som is the huge tree completely overwhelming the eastern *gopura*, providing one of the most popular photo opportunities in the Angkor area.

## Eastern Baray & Eastern Mebon បារាយណ៍ខាងកើត និងមេបុណ្យខាងកើត

The enormous one-time reservoir known as the **Eastern Baray** was excavated by Yasovarman I, who marked its four corners with stelae. This basin, now entirely dried up, was the most important of the public works of Yasodharapura, Yasovarman I's capital, and was 7km by 1.8km. It was originally fed by the Siem Reap River.

The Hindu temple, **Eastern Mebon** (Map p130; ⊙ 7.30am-5.30pm), erected by Rajendra-varman II, would once have been situated on an islet in the centre of the Eastern Baray reservoir, but is now very much on dry land. Its temple-mountain form is topped off by a quintet of towers. The elaborate brick shrines are dotted with neatly arranged holes, which attached the original plaster-work. The base of the temple is guarded at its corners by perfectly carved stone figures of elephants.

The Eastern Mebon is flanked by earthen ramps, a clue that this temple was never finished and a good visual guide to how the temples were constructed.

## Pre Rup ប្រែរូប

Built by Rajendravarman II, **Pre Rup** (Map p130; ⊙ 5am-7pm) is about 1km south of the Eastern Mebon and is a popular spot for sunset. The temple consists of a pyramid-shaped temple-mountain with the uppermost of the three tiers carrying five lotus towers. Pre Rup means 'Turning the Body' and refers to a traditional method of cremation in which a corpse's outline is traced in the cinders: this

suggests that the temple may have served as an early royal crematorium.

The brick sanctuaries here were once decorated with a plaster coating, fragments of which remain on the southwestern tower; there are some amazingly detailed lintel carvings here. Several of the outermost eastern towers are perilously close to collapse and are propped up by an army of wooden supports.

Pre Rup is one of the most popular sunset spots around Angkor as the view over the surrounding rice fields of the Eastern Baray is beautiful, although some trees have rather obscured it these days. It gets pretty crowded.

## Banteay Samré បន្ទាយសំរែ

Banteay Samré (Map p130; ⏱7.30am-5.30pm) dates from the same period as Angkor Wat and was built by Suryavarman II. The temple is in a fairly healthy state of preservation due to some extensive renovation work, although its isolation has resulted in some looting during the past few decades. The area consists of a central temple with four wings, preceded by a hall and also accompanied by two libraries, the southern one remarkably well preserved.

The whole ensemble is enclosed by two large concentric walls around what would have been the unique feature of an inner moat, now dry.

Banteay Samré is 400m east of the Eastern Baray. A visit here can be combined with a trip to Banteay Srei or Phnom Bok.

## Western Baray & Western Mebon បារាយណ៍ខាងលិច និងមេបុណ្យខាងលិច

The Western Baray, measuring an incredible 8km by 2.3km, was excavated by hand to provide water for the intensive cultivation of lands around Angkor. These enormous *barays* weren't dug out, but were huge dykes built up around the edges.

The Western Baray is the main local swimming pool around Siem Reap. There is a small beach of sorts at the western extreme, complete with picnic huts and inner tubes for hire, which attracts plenty of Khmers at weekends. In the centre of the Western Baray is the ruin of the Western Mebon (Map p130; ⏱7.30am-5.30pm) temple, where the giant bronze statue of Vishnu, now in the National Museum (p42) in Phnom Penh, was found. The Western Mebon is accessible by boat.

## ROLUOS TEMPLES

The monuments of Roluos (រលួស), which served as Indravarman I's capital, Hariharalaya, are among the earliest large, permanent temples built by the Khmers and mark the dawn of Khmer classical art. Before the construction of Roluos, generally only lighter (and less durable) construction materials such as brick were employed.

The temples can be found 13km east of Siem Reap along NH6 near the modern-day town of Roluos. Plan a half-day visit together with the stilted village of Kompong Pluk or allow two to three hours to explore the three temples.

### Preah Ko HINDU TEMPLE
(ប្រះគោ; Map p130; ⏱7.30am-5.30pm) Preah Ko was erected by Indravarman I in the late 9th century, and was dedicated to Shiva. Preah Ko was also dedicated to his deified ancestors in AD 880. The front towers relate to male ancestors or gods, the rear towers to female ancestors or goddesses. Lions guard the steps up to the temple. The towers of Preah Ko (Sacred Ox) feature three *nandis* (sacred oxen), all of whom look like a few

### GOOD-CAUSE PROJECTS AROUND ROLUOS

Several good-cause initiatives have sprung up around the Roluos area. Look out for Prolung Khmer (Map p130; www.prolungkhmer.blogspot.com) on the road between Preah Ko and Bakong. It's a weaving centre producing stylish cotton *kramas* (scarves), set up as a training collaboration between Cambodia and Japan. Also here is the Lo-Yuyu (Map p130) ceramics workshop, producing traditional Angkorian-style pottery.

Right opposite Preah Ko is the Khmer Group Art of Weaving (Map p130), turning out silk and cotton scarves on traditional looms. Also here is Dy Proeung Master Sculptor (Map p130; donations accepted), who has created scale replicas of Preah Ko, Bakong and Lolei, plus Angkor Wat, Preah Vihear and Banteay Srei for good measure.

## HIDDEN RICHES, POLITICAL HITCHES

Angkor Conservation is a Ministry of Culture compound on the banks of the Siem Reap River, about 400m east of the Sofitel Phokheetra Royal Angkor Hotel. The compound houses more than 5000 statues, lingas (phallic symbols) and inscribed stelae, stored here to protect them from the wanton looting that has blighted hundreds of sites around Angkor. The finest statuary is hidden away inside Angkor Conservation's warehouses, meticulously numbered and catalogued. Unfortunately, without the right contacts, trying to get a peek at the statues is a lost cause. Some of the statuary is on public display in the Angkor National Museum (p95) in Siem Reap, but it is only a fraction of the collection.

Formerly housed at Angkor Conservation, but now going it alone in an impressive head-quarters is **Apsara Authority** (Authority for Protection & Management of Angkor & the Region of Siem Reap; www.autoriteapsara.org). This organisation is responsible for the research, protection and conservation of cultural heritage around Angkor, as well as urban planning in Siem Reap and tourism development in the region. Quite a mandate, quite a challenge, especially now that the government is taking such a keen interest in its work. Angkor is a money-spinner; it remains to be seen whether Apsara will put preservation before profits. It is a powerful authority that some have nicknamed the Ministry of Angkor.

steaks have been sliced off over the years. The six *prasats* (stone halls), aligned in two rows and decorated with carved sandstone and plaster reliefs, face east; the central tower of the front row is a great deal larger than the other towers. Preah Ko has some of the best surviving examples of plaster-work seen at Angkor and is currently under restoration by a German team. There are elaborate inscriptions in the ancient Hindu language of Sanskrit on the doorposts of each tower.

### Bakong
HINDU TEMPLE

( បាគង; Map p130; ☉ 7.30am-5.30pm) Bakong is the largest and most interesting of the Roluos Group. Built and dedicated to Shiva by Indravarman I, it's a representation of Mt Meru, and it served as the city's central temple. The east-facing complex consists of a five-tier central pyramid of sandstone, 60m square at the base, flanked by eight towers of brick and sandstone, and by other minor sanctuaries. A number of the lower towers are still partly covered by their original plaster-work. The complex is enclosed by three concentric walls and a moat. There are well-preserved statues of stone elephants on each corner of the first three levels of the central temple. There are 12 stupas – three to each side – on the third tier. The sanctuary on the fifth level of Bakong temple was a later addition during the reign of Suryavarman II, in the style of Angkor Wat's central tower. There is an active Buddhist monastery here, dating back a century or more, which has recently been restored.

### Lolei
HINDU TEMPLE

(លលៃ; Map p130; ☉ 7.30am-5.30pm) The four brick towers of Lolei, an almost exact replica of the towers of Preah Ko (although in much worse shape), were built on an islet in the centre of a large reservoir (now rice fields) by Yasovarman I, the founder of the first city at Angkor. The sandstone carvings in the niches of the temples are worth a look and there are Sanskrit inscriptions on the doorposts. According to one of the inscriptions, the four towers were dedicated by Yasovarman I to his mother, his father and his maternal grandparents on 12 July 893.

## AROUND ANGKOR

## Phnom Krom
ភ្នំក្រោម

The Hindu temple of **Phnom Krom** (Map p130; ☉ 7.30am-5.30pm), 12km south of Siem Reap on a hill overlooking Tonlé Sap, dates from the reign of Yasovarman I in the late 9th or early 10th century. The name means 'Lower Hill' and is a reference to its geographic location in relation to its sister temples of Phnom Bakheng and Phnom Bok. Phnom Krom remains one of the more tranquil spots from which to view the sunset, complete with an active wat.

The three towers, dedicated (from north to south) to Vishnu, Shiva and Brahma, are in a ruined state. It is necessary to have an Angkor pass to visit the temple at the summit of Phnom Krom, so don't come all the way out here without one, as the guards won't allow you access to the summit of the hill. If coming here by *moto* or car, try to get the driver to take you to the summit, as it is a long, hot climb otherwise. Plan on a half-day visit in tandem with exploring the floating village of Chong Kneas (p127).

# Phnom Bok ភ្នំបូក

One of three temple-mountains built by Yasovarman I in the late 9th or early 10th century, **Phnom Bok** (Map p130; ◷ 7.30am-5.30pm) is in a peaceful but remote location and sees few visitors. The small temple is in reasonable shape, but it is the views of Phnom Kulen to the north and the plains of Angkor to the south from this 212m hill that make it worth the trip. The remains of a 5m *linga* are also visible at the opposite end of the hill and it's believed there were similar *linga* at Phnom Bakheng and Phnom Krom. Phnom Bok is about 25km from Siem Reap.

There is a long, winding trail snaking up the hill at Phnom Bok, which takes about 20 minutes to climb, plus a faster cement staircase, but the latter is fairly exposed. Avoid the heat in the middle of the day and carry plenty of water, which can be purchased locally.

Phnom Bok is clearly visible from the road to Banteay Srei. It is accessed by continuing east on the road to Banteay Samré for another 6km. It is possible to loop back to Siem Reap via the temples of Roluos by heading south instead of west on the return journey, and gain some rewarding glimpses of the countryside. Unfortunately, it is not a sensible place for sunrise or sunset, as it would require a long journey in the dark.

# Chau Srei Vibol ចៅស្រីវិបុល

A petite hilltop temple, **Chau Srei Vibol** (◷ 7.30am-5.30pm) used to see few visitors as it was difficult to access, but new roads have put it on the temple map at last. The central sanctuary is in a ruined state but is nicely complemented by the construction of a modern wat nearby.

Surrounding the base of the hill are laterite walls, each with a small entrance hall in reasonable condition. To get here, turn east off the Roluos to Anlong Veng highway at a point about 8km north of NH6, or 5km south of Phnom Bok. There is a small sign (easy to miss) that marks the turn. Locals are friendly and helpful should you find yourself lost.

# Banteay Srei បន្ទាយស្រី

Considered by many to be the jewel in the crown of Angkorian art, **Banteay Srei** (◷ 7.30am-5.30pm) is cut from stone of a pinkish hue and includes some of the finest stone carving anywhere on earth. Begun in AD 967, it is one of the smallest sites at Angkor, but what it lacks in size it makes up for in stature. The art gallery of Angkor, Banteay Srei, a Hindu temple dedicated to Shiva, is wonderfully well preserved and many of its carvings are three-dimensional.

Banteay Srei means 'Citadel of the Women' and it is said that it must have been built by a woman, as the elaborate carvings are supposedly too fine for the hand of a man.

Banteay Srei is one of the few temples around Angkor to be commissioned not by a king but by a Brahman, who may have been a tutor to Jayavarman V. The temple is square and has entrances at the east and west, with the east approached by a causeway. Of interest are the lavishly decorated libraries and the three central towers, which are decorated with male and female divinities and beautiful filigree relief work.

Classic carvings at Banteay Srei include delicate women with lotus flowers in hand and traditional skirts clearly visible, as well as breathtaking re-creations of scenes from the epic *Ramayana* adorning the library pediments (carved inlays above a lintel).

**TEMPLES OF ANGKOR PHNOM BOK**

## WHEN NATURE CALLS

Angkor is now blessed with some of the finest public toilets in Asia. Designed in wooden chalets and complete with amenities such as electronic flush, they wouldn't be out of place in a fancy hotel. The trouble is that the guardians often choose not to run the generators that power the toilets, meaning it is pretty dark inside the cubicles (but, thankfully, you can flush manually, too!). Entrance is free if you show your Angkor pass; and the toilets are found near most of the major temples.

Remember, in remote areas don't stray off the path; being seen in a compromising position is infinitely better than stepping on a land mine.

---

**DON'T MISS**

## ANGKOR CENTRE FOR CONSERVATION OF BIODIVERSITY

Conveniently located near the base of the trail to Kbal Spean is the **Angkor Centre for Conservation of Biodiversity** (មជ្ឈមណ្ឌលអង្គរសម្រាប់ការអភិរក្សជីវចម្រុះ; ACCB; www.accb-cambodia.org; donation US$3; ⊙ tours 9am & 1pm Mon-Sat), committed to rescuing, rehabilitating and reintroducing threatened wildlife to the Cambodian forests. Tours of the centre are available daily at 9am and 1pm, taking about 90 minutes. The 9am tour is the better option as animals are fed at this time and are more lively than during the heat of the day in the afternoon. Species currently under protection here include pangolin, pileated gibbon, silvered langur, slow loris, civet cat and leopard cat. There are also several large water birds, including the impressive sarus crane and the extremely rare giant ibis, the national bird of Cambodia, the only known one in captivity.

Private tours of the centre are available outside core hours but must be booked in advance and will cost US$25 per person or US$10 for a group of five or more. Note that you don't need an Angkor pass to visit ACCB, only to visit Kbal Spean.

---

However, the sum of the parts is no greater than the whole – almost every inch of these interior buildings is covered in decoration. Standing watch over such perfect creations are the mythical guardians, all of which are copies of originals stored in the National Museum.

Banteay Srei was the first major temple restoration undertaken by the EFEO in 1930 using the anastylosis method. The project, as evidenced today, was a major success and soon led to other larger projects such as the restoration of Bayon. Banteay Srei is also the first to have been given a full makeover in terms of facilities, with a large car park, a designated dining and shopping area, clear visitor information and a state-of-the-art exhibition on the history of the temple and its restoration. There is also a small *baray* (reservoir) behind the temple where local boat trips (US$7 per boat) are possible through the lotus pond.

When Banteay Srei was first rediscovered, it was assumed to be from the 13th or 14th centuries, as it was thought that the refined carving must have come at the end of the Angkor period. It was later dated to AD 967, from inscriptions found at the site.

In 1923 Frenchman André Malraux was arrested in Phnom Penh for attempting to steal several of Banteay Srei's major statues and pieces of sculpture. Ironically, Malraux was later appointed Minister of Culture under Charles de Gaulle.

Banteay Srei is about 32km northeast of Siem Reap and 21km northeast of Bayon. Banteay Srei is well signposted and the road is surfaced all the way, so a trip from Siem Reap should take about 45 minutes by car or one hour by *remork-moto. Moto* and *remork-moto* drivers will want a bit of extra cash to come out here, so agree on a sum first.

There's plenty to do in Banteay Srei district as well as several homestays (p124) should you wish to stay and explore the area. It is possible to combine a visit to Banteay Srei as part of a long day trip to the River of a Thousand Lingas at Kbal Spean and Beng Mealea. A half-day itinerary might include Banteay Srei, the Cambodia Landmine Museum and Banteay Samre. It takes 45 minutes to explore Banteay Srei temple, but allow 90 minutes to visit the information centre and explore the area.

## Kbal Spean ក្បាលស្ពាន

A spectacularly carved riverbed, **Kbal Spean** (⊙ 7.30am-5.30pm) is set deep in the jungle to the northeast of Angkor. More commonly referred to in English as the 'River of a Thousand Lingas', the name actually means 'bridgehead', a reference to the natural rock bridge at the site. *Lingas* have been elaborately carved into the riverbed, and images of Hindu deities are dotted about the area. Kbal Spean was 'discovered' in 1969, when ethnologist Jean Boulbet was shown the area by a hermit.

It is a 2km uphill walk to the carvings, along a pretty path that winds its way up into the jungle, passing by some interesting boulder formations along the way. Carry plenty of water up the hill, as there is none available beyond the parking area. The path eventually splits to the waterfall or the river carvings. There is an impressive carving of Vishnu on the upper section of the river, followed by a series of carvings at the bridgehead itself, some of which were hacked off in the past few years, but have since been replaced by excellent replicas. This area is now roped off to protect the carvings from further damage.

Following the river down, there are several more impressive carvings of Vishnu, and Shiva with his consort Uma, and further downstream hundreds of *lingas* appear on the riverbed. At the top of the waterfall are many animal images, including a cow and a frog, and a path winds around the boulders to a wooden staircase leading down to the base of the falls. Visitors between January and June will be disappointed to see very little water here. The best time to visit is between July and December. When exploring Kbal Spean it is best to start with the river carvings and work back down to the waterfall to cool off. From the car park, the visit takes about two hours including the walk and nearer to three hours with a natural shower or a picnic. It's the best part of a day trip if you include Angkor Centre for Conservation of Biodiversity (opposite), Banteay Srei temple (p165) and the Cambodia Landmine Museum (p124).

Kbal Spean is about 50km northeast of Siem Reap or about 18km beyond the temple of Banteay Srei. The road is now excellent, as it forms part of the new road north to Anlong Veng and the Thai border, so it takes just one hour or so from town.

*Moto* drivers will no doubt want a bit of extra money to take you here, such as US$15 or so for the day, including a trip to Banteay Srei. Likewise, *remork-moto* drivers will probably up the price to US$25 or so. A surcharge is also levied to come out here by car. Admission to Kbal Spean is included in the general Angkor pass; the last entry to the site is at 3.30pm.

# Phnom Kulen ភ្នំគូលែន

Considered by Khmers to be the most sacred mountain in Cambodia, **Phnom Kulen** (admission US$20) is a popular place of pilgrimage on weekends and during festivals. It played a significant role in the history of the Khmer empire, as it was from here in AD 802 that Jayavarman II proclaimed himself a *devaraja* (god-king), giving birth to the Cambodian kingdom. Attractions include a giant reclining Buddha, hundreds of *lingas* carved in the riverbed, an impressive waterfall and some remote temples.

In 1999 a private businessman bulldozed a road up here and now charges a US$20 toll per foreign visitor, an ambitious fee compared with what you get for your money at Angkor, especially as very little of the toll goes towards preserving the site. The road winds its way through some spectacular jungle scenery, emerging on the plateau after a 20km ascent. The road eventually splits: the left fork leads to the picnic spot, waterfalls and ruins of a 9th-century temple; the right fork continues over a bridge and some riverbed carvings to the reclining Buddha. Wat Preah Ang Thom sits at the summit of the mountain and houses the large reclining Buddha carved into the sandstone boulder upon which it is built. This is the focal point of a pilgrimage for Khmer people, so it is important to take off your shoes and any head covering before climbing the stairs to the sanctuary. The views from the 487m peak are tremendous, as you can see right across the forested plateau.

The waterfall is an attractive spot and was featured in *Lara Croft: Tomb Raider*. However, it could be much more beautiful were it not for all the litter left here by families picnicking at the weekend. Near the top of the waterfall is a jungle-clad temple known as Prasat Krau Romeas, dating from the 9th century.

## THE LOST CITY OF MAHENDRAPRAVARTA

Phnom Kulen hit the headlines in 2013 thanks to the 'discovery' of a lost city known as Mahendrapravarta in Angkorian times. Using jungle-piercing LIDAR radar technology, the structures of a more extensive archaeological site have been unveiled beneath the jungle canopy. However, it wasn't quite as dramatic a discovery as initially reported, as Phnom Kulen had long been known as an important archaeological site. The LIDAR research confirmed the size and scale of the ancient city, complete with canals and *barays*, in the same way NASA satellite imagery had helped identify the size and scale of the greater Angkor hydraulic water system more than a decade ago. Some new temples and features were identified beneath the jungle, but remain remote and inaccessible due to terrain and the possibility of land mines. An additional LIDAR survey of the entire Kulen plateau was conducted in 2015.

## LAND MINE ALERT!

At no point during a visit to Kbal Spean or Phnom Kulen should you leave well-trodden paths, as there may be land mines in the area.

There are plenty of other Angkorian sites on Phnom Kulen, including as many as 20 minor temples around the plateau, the most important of which is Prasat Rong Chen, the first pyramid or temple-mountain to be constructed in the Angkor area. Most impressive of all are the giant stone animals or guardians of the mountain, known as Sra Damrei (Elephant Pond). These are quite difficult to reach, particularly during the wet season. The few people who make it, however, are rewarded with a life-size replica of a stone elephant – a full 4m long and 3m tall – and smaller statues of lions, a frog and a cow. These were constructed on the southern face of the mountain and from here there are spectacular views across the plains below. Getting to Sra Damrei requires taking a *moto* from Wat Preah Ang Thom for about 12km on very rough trails. From here it is a 1km walk to the animals through the forest. Don't try to find it on your own; expect to pay the *moto* driver about US$10 for a half day exploring this area and carry plenty of water. Other impressive sites that could be included in an adventurous day trip around Phnom Kulen include the ancient rock carvings of **Poeng Tbal**, an atmospheric site of enormous boulders, and the partially restored temple of **Damrei Krap**.

Phnom Kulen is a huge plateau around 50km from Siem Reap and about 15km from Banteay Srei. To get here on the toll road, take the well-signposted right fork just before Banteay Srei village and go straight ahead at the crossroads. Just before the road starts to climb the mountain, there is a barrier and it is here that the US$20 charge is levied. It is possible to buy a cheaper entrance ticket to Phnom Kulen for US$12 from the **City Angkor Hotel** (☎ 063-760336; www.cityangkorhotel.com; Airport Rd) in Siem Reap. It is only possible to go up Phnom Kulen before 11am and only possible to come down after midday, to avoid vehicles meeting on the narrow road. There are plenty of small restaurants and food stalls located near the waterfall or in the small village near Wat Preah Ang Thom.

*Moto* drivers are likely to want about US$20 or more to bring you out here, and rented cars will hit passengers with a surcharge, more than double the going rate for Angkor; forget coming by *remork-moto* as the hill climb is just too tough. With the long journey here, it is best to plan on spending the best part of a day exploring, although it can be combined with either Banteay Srei or Beng Mealea.

# Beng Mealea    បឹងមាលា

A spectacular sight to behold, **Beng Mealea** (admission US$5; ⏰ 7.30am-5.30pm), located about 68km northeast of Siem Reap, is one of the most mysterious temples at Angkor, as nature has well and truly run riot. Built to the same floorplan as Angkor Wat, exploring this titanic of temples is Angkor's ultimate Indiana Jones experience. Built in the 12th century under Suryavarman II, Beng Mealea is enclosed by a massive moat measuring 1.2km by 900m.

This Buddhist temple used to be utterly consumed by jungle, but some of the dense foliage has been cut back and cleaned up in recent years. Entering from the south, visitors wend their way over piles of finely chiselled sandstone blocks, through long, dark chambers and between hanging vines. The central tower has completely collapsed, but hidden away among the rubble and foliage are several impressive carvings, as well as a well-preserved library in the northeastern quadrant. The temple is a special place and it is worth taking the time to explore it thoroughly – Apsara caretakers can show you where rock-hopping and climbing is permitted. The large wooden walkway to and around the centre was originally constructed for the filming of Jean-Jacques Annaud's *Two Brothers* (2004), set in 1920s French Indochina and starring two tiger cubs. The filming included 20 tigers of all ages for continuity throughout the story.

There are several very basic, unmarked family homestays a few hundred metres behind the restaurants opposite the temple entrance. The best restaurant is **Romduol Angkor II** (mains US$5; ⏰ 7am-7pm), a sister restaurant to the Romduol Angkor near Sra Srang. Wholesome Cambodian food is on offer, plus ice-cold drinks.

It costs US$5 to visit Beng Mealea and there are additional small charges for transport, so

# Beng Mealea

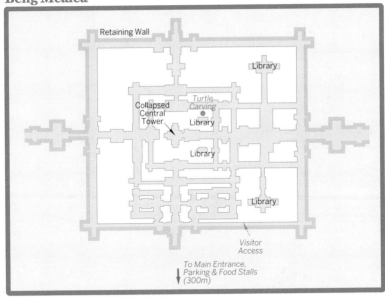

Retaining Wall

Library

Collapsed
Central
Tower

Turtle
Carving

Library

Library

Library

Visitor
Access

To Main Entrance,
Parking & Food Stalls
(300m)

make sure you work out in advance with the driver or guide who is paying for these.

Beng Mealea is about 40km east of Bayon (as the crow flies) and 6.5km southeast of Phnom Kulen. By road it is about 68km (one hour by car, longer by *moto* or *remork-moto*) from Siem Reap. The shortest route is via the junction town of Dam Dek, located on NH6 about 37km from Siem Reap in the direction of Phnom Penh. Turn north immediately after the market and continue on this road for 31km. The entrance to the temple lies just beyond the left-hand turn to Koh Ker. Allow a half day to visit, including the journey time from Siem Reap or combine it with Koh Ker in a long day trip best undertaken by car or 4WD.

Beng Mealea is at the centre of an ancient Angkorian road connecting Angkor Thom and Preah Khan in Preah Vihear Province, now evocatively numbered route 66. A small Angkorian bridge just west of Chau Srei Vibol temple is the only remaining trace of the old Angkorian road between Beng Mealea and Angkor Thom; between Preah Khan and Beng Mealea there are at least 10 bridges abandoned in the forest. This is a way for extreme adventurers to get to Preah Khan temple, but do not undertake this journey lightly.

# REMOTE ANGKORIAN SITES

## Koh Ker                         ភ្នំភ្លើង

Abandoned to the forests of the north, **Koh Ker** (admission US$10; ⊙ 7.30am-5.30pm), capital of the Angkorian empire from AD 928 to AD 944, is now within day-trip distance of Siem Reap. Most visitors start at Prasat Krahom where impressive stone carvings grace lintels, doorposts and slender window columns. The principal monument is Mayan-looking Prasat Thom, a 55m-wide, 40m-high sandstone-faced pyramid whose seven tiers offer spectacular views across the forest. Koh Ker is 127km northeast of Siem Reap.

Long one of Cambodia's most remote and inaccessible temple complexes, the opening of a toll road from Dam Dek (via Beng Mealea) has placed Koh Ker (pronounced ko-kaye) within striking distance of Siem Reap. To really appreciate the temples – the ensemble has 42 major structures in an area that measures 9km by 4km – it's necessary to spend at least one night.

**Prasat Krahom** (Red Temple), the second-largest structure at Koh Ker, is so named

## Koh Ker

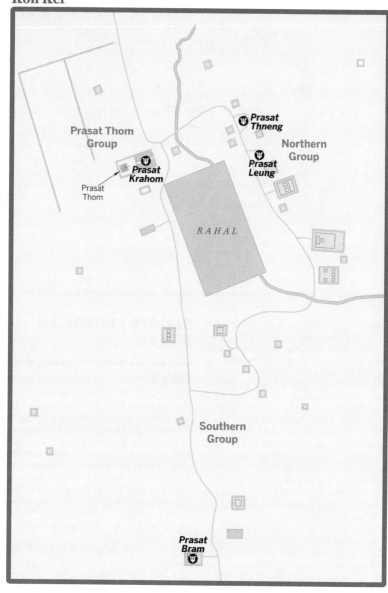

Prasat Thom Group

Prasat Thneng

Northern Group

Prasat Leung

Prasat Krahom

Prasat Thom

*R A H A L*

Southern Group

Prasat Bram

for the red bricks from which it is constructed. Sadly, none of the carved lions for which this temple was once known remain, though there's still plenty to see, with stone archways and galleries leaning hither and thither. A *naga*-flanked causeway and a series of sanctuaries, libraries and gates lead past trees and vegetation-covered ponds. Just west of Prasat Krahom, at the far western end of a half-fallen colonnade, are the remains (most of the head) of a statue of Nandin.

The principal monument at Koh Ker is **Prasat Thom** (also known as Prasat Kompeng). The staircase to the top is open to a limited number of visitors and the views are spectacular if you can stomach the heights. Some 40 inscriptions, dating from AD 932 to AD 1010, have been found here.

South of this central group is a 1185m-by-548m *baray* known as the Rahal. It is fed by the Sen River, which supplied water to irrigate the land in this arid area.

Some of the largest Shiva *linga* in Cambodia can still be seen in four temples about 1km northeast of Prasat Thom. The largest is found in **Prasat Thneng**, while **Prasat Leung** is similarly well endowed.

Among the many other temples that are found around Koh Ker, **Prasat Bram** is a real highlight. It consists of a collection of brick towers, at least two of which have been completely smothered by voracious strangler figs; the probing roots cut through the brickwork like liquid mercury.

Koh Ker is one of the least-studied temple areas from the Angkorian period. Louis Delaporte visited in 1880 during his extensive investigations into Angkorian temples. It was surveyed in 1921 by the great Henri Parmentier for an article in the *Bulletin de l'École d'Extrême Orient*, but no restoration work was ever undertaken here. Archaeological surveys were carried out by Cambodian teams in the 1950s and 1960s. But all records

vanished during the destruction of the 1970s, helping to preserve this complex as something of an enigma.

Several of the most impressive pieces in the National Museum (p42) in Phnom Penh come from Koh Ker, including the huge *garuda* (mythical half-man, half-bird creature) that greets visitors in the entrance hall and a unique carving depicting a pair of wrestling monkey-kings.

## 🛏 Sleeping & Eating

Near the main temple of Prasat Thom there are a few small eateries (open during daylight hours) run by the wives of the heritage police stationed here. The nearby village of Srayong (10km) also has a few eateries.

**Mom Morokod**
**Koh Ker Guesthouse** GUESTHOUSE $
(☑ 011 935114; r from US$10) About 200m south of the Koh Ker toll plaza, 8km south of Prasat Krahom, this quiet guesthouse has 11 clean, spacious rooms with elaborately carved wooden doors and bathrooms.

**Ponloeu Preah**
**Chan Guesthouse** GUESTHOUSE $
(☑ 012 489058; r US$5) Located in the village of Srayong, this friendly, family-run guesthouse has 14 rooms with bare walls, mosquito nets and barely enough space for a double bed. Toilets and showers are out the back.

## ❶ Getting There & Away

Koh Ker is 127km northeast of Siem Reap (2½ hours by car) and 72km west of Tbeng Meanchey (1½ hours). The toll road from Dam Dek, paved only as far as the Preah Vihear Province line, passes by Beng Mealea, 61km southwest of Koh Ker; one-day excursions from Siem Reap often visit both temple complexes. Admission fees are collected at the toll barrier near Beng Mealea if travelling from Siem Reap.

From Siem Reap, hiring a private car for a day trip to Koh Ker costs about US$80. There's no public transport to Koh Ker, although a few pick-ups (10,000r) link Srayong, 10km south of Prasat Krahom, with Siem Reap. It might also be possible to take one of the share taxis that link Siem Reap with Tbeng Meanchey and get off at Srayong.

**TEMPLES OF ANGKOR KOH KER**

---

### LAND MINE ALERT!

Many of the Koh Ker temples were mined during the war, but by 2008 most had been cleared: de-mining teams reported removing from the area a total of 1382 mines and 1,447,212 pieces of exploded and unexploded ordnance. However, considering what's at stake, it's best to err on the side of caution. Do not stray from previously trodden paths or wander off into the forest, as there may be land mines within a few hundred metres of the temples.

# South Coast

AREA 27,817 SQ KM / POP 2 MILLION

## Best Nature & Adventure

➡ CBET Treks (p182)

➡ Climbodia (p211)

➡ Ream National Park (p200)

➡ Kep National Park (p219)

➡ SUP Asia (p211)

## Best Places to Stay

➡ Rikitikitavi (p213)

➡ Rainbow Lodge (p179)

➡ Mushroom Point (p192)

➡ Green House (p214)

➡ Cita Resort (p208)

## Why Go?

Cambodia's South Coast (ផ្លូវខាងត្បូង) provides the antidote to temple-hopping tick lists. The beaches draw most folk here, but stick around and you'll see this region is more than its sandy bits.

The Koh Kong Conservation Corridor's emerald-green vistas offer trekking potential that is only now being tapped into, providing both day-hikers and intrepid types with a host of nature-filled adventures. Down south travellers can dig into history, admiring Kampot's preserved architecture, then dig into plates piled with crab in Kep, before exploring the surrounding countryside, patch-worked with rice fields and studded with caves.

Here to answer the call of the beach? The South Coast doesn't disappoint. While brash Sihanoukville isn't everyone's cup of tea, the islands offshore have something for everyone from die-hard partiers to those seeking solitude. Pick your beach, sprawl on the sand, make friends with your hammock. There's a reason many visitors decide to never leave.

## When to Go
### Sihanoukville

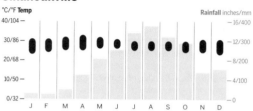

**Nov–Jan** Prime hiking time. Hit the Cardamoms while comfortable temperatures reign.

**Feb** Peak season finishes on the islands. The crowds fizzle out but the weather's still glorious.

**Jun–Oct** Hotel prices nosedive across the coast with bargains ahoy, but pack an umbrella.

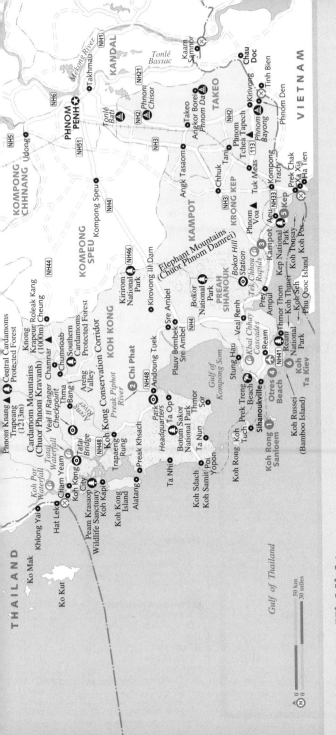

## South Coast Highlights

**1** De-stressing upon the photogenic white sands of Saracen Bay on **Koh Rong Sanloem** (p202).

**2** Exploring the forest with local guides and bedding down for the night in a friendly homestay at Cambodia's most successful ecotourism project in **Chi Phat** (p181).

**3** Ambling the alleys of Cambodia's best-preserved old town in **Kampot** (p210), then heading out for river and cave adventures in the surrounding countryside.

**4** Topping-up your tan by day and downing cocktails by night on the meandering sands of Sihanoukville's mellow **Otres Beach** (p186).

**5** Feasting on the famous Kampot pepper crab of **Kep** (p223), then working off the calories in Kep National Park.

**6** Tuning out on **Koh Ta Kiev** (p201) where hammock-time is a way of life.

# KOH KONG PROVINCE

Cambodia's vast and sparsely populated far southwestern province of Koh Kong (ខេត្ត កោះកុង) shelters some of the country's most remarkable and important natural sites.

Until relatively recently the entire province was effectively cut off from the rest of the country due to dreadful roads. The provincial capital of Koh Kong (Krong Koh Kong) was easier to visit from Thailand, the Thai baht was king and the vast majority of foreigners in town were the wrong type of tourists on visa runs from Pattaya. That has all changed as National Hwy 48 (NH48) is now paved and bus connections to Phnom Penh and Sihanoukville are frequent.

The best base for exploring the province's untamed jungle and coastline, spread out along the Koh Kong Conservation Corridor, is the riverine town of Koh Kong, 8km from the Thai border. From here, motorboats can whisk you to rushing waterfalls, secluded islands, sandy coves and Venice-like fishing villages on stilts.

## Koh Kong City   ក្រុងកោះកុង

📞 035 / POP 36,053

Sleepy Koh Kong was once Cambodia's Wild West with its isolated frontier economy dominated by smuggling, prostitution and gambling. Although remnants of its less salubrious past still cling on, today this low-slung town is striding towards respectability as ecotourists, aiming to explore the Cardamoms, shoo away the sleaze. The dusty sprawl of streets sits on the banks of the Koh Poi River which spills into the Gulf of Thailand a few kilometres south of the centre.

### ⊙ Sights & Activities

Koh Kong's main appeal is as a launching pad for adventures in and around the Cardamom Mountains and the Koh Kong Conservation Corridor, but there are a few diversions around town as well. If you want a dip, the pool at Oasis Bungalow Resort (p176) is open to non-guests (children/adults US$2/4). Sun-worshippers will discover additional beaches further north on the Gulf of Thailand near the Thai border.

**Koh Yor Beach**                               BEACH
(ឆ្នេរកោះយ៉ នៅបាក់ខ្លង) This long, wind-swept beach is on the far (western) side of the peninsula that forms the west bank of the Koh Poi River opposite Koh Kong. Although it's not the world's prettiest beach, it offers good shell-collecting and you're nearly guaranteed to have it to yourself. To

## Koh Kong City

**❸ Activities, Courses & Tours**

get there, cross the toll bridge that spans the river north of the town centre and look for a left turn about 1.5km beyond the tollbooth. The beach is about 6km from the turnoff.

### Wat Neang Kok
BUDDHIST TEMPLE

(វត្តនាងកុក) A rocky promontory on the right (western) bank of the Koh Poi River is decorated with life-size statues demonstrating the violent punishments that await sinners in the Buddhist hell. This graphic tableau belongs to Wat Neang Kok, a Buddhist temple. To get there, cross the bridge, turn right 600m past the tollbooth (*motos* cost 1400r), and proceed 150m beyond the temple to the statues.

## ☞ Tours

Boat tours are an excellent way to view Koh Kong's many coastal attractions. English-speaking **Teur** (☎ 016 278668) hangs around the **boat dock** (cnr St 1 & St 9) and can help you hire six-passenger (40-horsepower) and three-passenger (15-horsepower) outboards (speedboats). Destinations include Koh Kong Island western beaches (big/small boats US$80/50), around Koh Kong Island (big/small boats US$120/90) and Peam Krasaop Wildlife Sanctuary (big/small boats US$40/30).

The most popular tour is to **Koh Kong Island** (full day per person incl lunch & snorkelling equipment US$25, overnight US$55). Trips take in some of the mangroves of **Peam Krasaop Wildlife Sanctuary**, where there's a good chance of spotting Irrawaddy dolphins early in the morning. Overnight trips involve beach camping or a homestay on the island. Note that tours don't take place in the rainy season (July to October) because of strong onshore (southwesterly) breezes. However, private boat trips to Peam Krasaop are possible year-round.

As tours become more popular, garbage is beginning to pile up on some of the island's western beaches, which is mainly the fault of irresponsible boatmen and tour operators. Choose a reputable tour company. Most operators offer overland trips in the Cardamom Mountains as well as boat tours.

### Ritthy's Koh Kong Eco Adventure Tours
ADVENTURE TOUR

(☎ 012 707719; www.kohkongecoadventure.com; St 1; ⊙ 8am-9pm) A one-stop shop for all your tour needs in Koh Kong, this is the longest-running ecotourism operator in town. Ritthy's excursions include excellent Koh Kong Island boat tours, birdwatching,

and jungle treks in the Koh Kong Conservation Corridor. Their overnight jungle trekking and camping excursions (one/two nights per person US$35/70) get great reviews from travellers.

### Neptune Adventure
ECOTOUR

(☎ 088 777 0576; neptuneadventure-cambodia. com; Tatai River) 🌿 This well-established ecotourism operator is based at Neptune River Bungalows (p179) on the Tatai River and offers highly recommended jungle treks as well as multi-activity adventures combining trekking, kayaking and boating. Day tours range from US$10 to US$25 per person.

### Jungle Cross
ADVENTURE TOUR

(☎ 015 601633; www.junglecross.com; dirt-bike rental per day US$25; ⊙ 9am-6pm) Specialises in dirt-bike and 4WD safaris deep into the Cardamoms, with riverside camping in hammocks. Also runs trekking tours to more remote bits of the Cardamoms, with transport by 4WD to the launch point. Based out of Koh Kong Safari World near the Thai border.

## 🛏 Sleeping

Koh Kong is a popular holiday destination for Khmer families; hotels fill up and raise their rates during Cambodian holidays. If staying in town doesn't appeal, check out the Tatai River (18km east), with its handful of fabulous eco-accommodation options.

### ★ Koh Kong City Hotel
HOTEL $

(☎ 035-936777; http://kkcthotel.netkhmer.com; St 1; r US$15-20; ❄@🛜) Ludicrous value for what you get; squeaky-clean rooms include a huge bathroom, two double beds, 50 TV channels, a full complement of toiletries, free water and – in the US$20 rooms – glorious river views. Friendly staff top off the experience.

### Asian Hotel
HOTEL $

(☎ 035-936667; www.asiankohkong.com; St 1; r US$15-20; ❄@) While it may lack the river views of rival hotels across the road, the Asian makes up for it with spacious, clean and comfortable rooms with a touch of old-time class. Bag a front (roadside) room for a balcony.

### 99 Guesthouse
HOTEL $

(☎ 035-936799; 99guesthouse@gmail.com; St 6; s/d with fan US$8/10, with air-con US$13/15; ❄🛜) Managed by friendly Piseth, 99 is a solid budget choice with a range of bright and neat as a pin, decent-sized rooms in a central, yet quiet, location.

### PS Guesthouse
GUESTHOUSE $

(☑ 097 729 1600; St 1; r with fan/air-con US$7/12; ❄ �🛜) The ultra simple rooms at this riverfront place are spick and span, and decked out in a rainbow of colours.

### ★ Oasis Bungalow Resort
BUNGALOW $$

(☑ 092 228342; http://oasisresort.netkhmer.com; d/tr US$30/35; ❄ 🛜 ≋) Surrounded by lush forest, 2km north of Koh Kong centre, Oasis really lives up to its name. Five large, airy bungalows set around a gorgeous infinity pool with views of the Cardamoms provide a tranquil base in which to chill out and reset your travel batteries. To get here, follow the blue signs from Acleda Bank. During the December to January high season bungalows are US$5 extra. The no-sex-tourist policy here is a refreshing approach for Koh Kong.

### Koh Kong Bay Hotel
BOUTIQUE HOTEL $$

(☑ 035-936367; www.kohkongbay.com; St 1; r incl breakfast US$32-45, ste from US$60; ❄ 🛜 ≋) Koh Kong's first attempt at a boutique hotel has wood-floored rooms designed in minimalist European style with balconies and rain showers in the bathrooms, but at this price we'd have expected someone to vacuum the hallways. If there was a tad more attention to detail it could be a winner.

### Thmorda Garden Riverside Resort
RESORT $$

(☑ 035-690 0324; www.thmordagarden.com; Neang Kok; standard/deluxe r US$35/60; ❄ 🛜) The standard rooms may be only slightly bigger than a postage stamp but you can't beat the location. Smack on the peninsula overlooking the Koh Poi River (just across the toll bridge from Koh Kong), this small resort is a peaceful choice for travellers looking to fully unwind. Kayaks are free and bikes can be hired.

## ✖ Eating & Drinking

The best cheap food stalls are in the southeast corner of **Psar Leu** (Market; St 3; ⊙ 8am-11pm); fruit stalls can be found near the southwest corner. Riverfront food carts sell noodles and cans of beer for a few thousand riel, doubling up as sunset drinking spots.

### Baan Peakmai
ASIAN $

(St 1; mains 7000-15,000r; ⊙ 11am-2pm & 5-10pm; 🍴) Sure, you'd find more ambience in a paper bag but don't be put off by the plain-Jane decor. Baan Peakmai does a fine line in pan-Asian dishes with large portions and on-the-ball service. The menu romps through Thai, Chinese and Khmer favourites and there are plenty of vegetarian options.

### Crab Shack
SEAFOOD $

(Koh Yor Beach; mains US$4-8; ⊙ 11am-9pm) A family-run place over the bridge on Koh Yor, it's known for perfect sunsets and heaping portions of fried crab with pepper (on request).

### ★ Café Laurent
INTERNATIONAL $$

(St 1; mains US$4-15; ⊙ 10.30am-11pm Wed-Mon; 🛜) This chic waterfront cafe and restaurant offers atmospheric dining in over-water pavilions where you can sit back and watch the sunset while feasting on refined Western and Khmer cuisine. As well as French-accented steaks and a decent pasta menu, there's a huge range of fresh seafood and Asian classics, all served with fine-dining panache.

### Thmorda Crab House
SEAFOOD $$

(☑ 035-690 1252; Neang Kok; mains US$4-20; ⊙ 7am-10pm) For dining with a different perspective, head across the bridge to this attractive restaurant set on stilts over the river. Part of the Thmorda Garden Riverside Resort, the restaurant includes some private pavilions. Crab is a speciality, plus there's a good range of Thai dishes available.

### Seta Ice Cream
INTERNATIONAL $$

(St 1; mains US$4-10; ⊙ 7am-10pm) Seta covers most bases offering everything from pizza to curry and baguettes to noodles, with breakfast options (US$1.50 to $4.50) thrown in for good measure. Its road-front terrace also doubles up as a popular drinking spot in the evening.

### Fat Sam's
BAR

(off St 3; ⊙ 9am-10pm Mon-Sat, 4-10pm Sun; 🛜) This informal, Welsh-run bar-restaurant has a decent selection of beers, spirits and wines and an impressive food menu that runs the full gamut from fish-and-chips and chilli con carne to authentic Khmer and Thai favourites. Useful travel information is dished out for free, plus there are motorbikes available for rent.

### Paddy's Bamboo Pub
BAR

(St 7; mains US$2-4) Paddy's angles for the backpacker market with US$1 beers, a pool table and affordable Khmer food, plus some home-grown comfort flavours. If you're down to your last dollars, they also have extremely basic rooms out the back (singles/doubles US$4.50/5.50). Paddy is also a good source of travel info and can arrange boat tours and other excursions.

# ❶ Information

## MEDICAL SERVICES

In a medical emergency, evacuation to Thailand via the Cham Yeam-Hat Lek border crossing is possible 24 hours a day. In Thailand there's a hospital in Trat, 92km from the border.

**Sen Sok Clinic** (☑ 012 555060; kkpao@camintel.com; St 3; ⊘24hr) Has doctors who speak English and French.

## MONEY

Thai baht are widely used so there's no urgent need to change baht into dollars or riel. To do so, use one of the many mobile-phone shops around Psar Leu.

**Acleda Bank** (St 3; ⊘8am-3.30pm Mon-Fri, to 11.30am Sat, ATM 24hr)

**Canadia Bank** (St 1; ⊘8am-3.30pm Mon-Fri, to 11.30am Sat, ATM 24hr)

## TOURIST INFORMATION

Ritthy's Koh Kong Eco Adventure Tours (p175) and guesthouses are the best places to get the local low-down. You can also look for the free *Koh Kong Visitors Guide* (www.koh-kong.com), which is mostly advertisements.

# ❶ Getting There & Away

Koh Kong is on NH48, 220km northwest of Sihanoukville and 290km west of Phnom Penh. It's linked to the Thai border by a paved toll road that begins on the other side of the 1.9km bridge over the Koh Poi River.

## BUS

Most buses drop passengers at Koh Kong's unpaved **bus station** (St 12), on the northeast edge of town, where *motos* (motorbike taxis) and *remork-motos (tuk tuks)* await, eager to overcharge tourists. Don't pay more than US$1/2

for the three-minute *moto/remork* ride into the centre. Pick-ups are at the company offices in town. Bus companies usually offer free transfer by *remork* from your guesthouse to their respective offices.

➡ To Phnom Penh (US$7, six hours), **Virak Buntham** (☑ 089 998760; St 3) and **Phnom Penh Sorya** (☑ 077 563447; St 3) each have a 7.45am departure; **Olympic Transport** (☑ 011 363678; St 3) buses leave at 7.45am and 11.45am; and **Rith Mony** (☑ 012 640344; St 3) has services at 7.30am and 11.30am.

➡ For Sihanoukville (five hours), Virak Buntham (US$8, 8am), Olympic Transport (US$10, 11.45am) and Rith Mony (US$8, 2pm) all have one bus daily.

➡ Note that Virak Buntham and Rith Mony claim to offer night buses from Siem Reap to Koh Kong, but these arrive in Sihanoukville early morning and require a second five-hour bus to Koh Kong, leaving many a backpacker justifiably annoyed.

➡ The same two companies offer midday trips to Bangkok with a bus change at the border (US$20, eight hours). There are also trips to Koh Chang in Thailand (US$14 including ferry) with a change of bus at the border, plus a local ferry to the island.

## TAXI

From the **taxi lot** (St 12) next to the bus station, shared taxis head to Phnom Penh (US$11, five hours) and occasionally to Sihanoukville (US$10, four hours) and Andoung Tuek (US$5, two hours). As with anywhere, the best chance for a ride is in the morning. Guesthouses can set you up with a private taxi to Phnom Penh (US$55) or Sihanoukville (US$50).

Hiring a taxi to or from the Thai border costs about US$10 (plus 6000r for the toll), while a *moto/remork* will cost about US$3/8.

---

## GETTING TO THAILAND: KOH KONG CITY TO TRAT

**Getting to the border** The Cham Yeam–Hat Lek **border crossing** (⊘8am-10pm), between Cambodia's Koh Kong and Trat in Thailand, links the beaches of Cambodia and Thailand. Leaving Cambodia, take a taxi (US$10 plus toll), *remork* (US$8) or *moto* (US$3) from Koh Kong across the toll bridge to the border. Once in Thailand, catch a minibus to Trat, from where there are regular buses to Bangkok.

**At the border** Departing Cambodia via the Hat Lek border is pretty straightforward. Coming in the other direction and arriving in Cambodia, be aware that the Cham Yeam border is notorious for visa overcharging; although these days you'll usually pay 1300B, which is basically the same price as buying an e-visa in advance.

**Moving on** From the Hat Lek border, take a minibus straight to Trat (120B). From here there are regular buses to Bangkok (254B, six hours) heading to the Thai capital's Eastern or North and Northeastern bus stations. Buses depart hourly from 6am until 11.30pm. Anyone heading to the nearby island of Koh Chang can arrange onward transport in Trat.

Coming into Cambodia, note that you'll get a better deal on all transport from the border to Koh Kong if you pay in dollars not baht.

## ⓘ Getting Around

### BICYCLE

Ritthy's Koh Kong Eco Adventure Tours (p175) rents out bicycles for half (US$1) and full days (US$2).

### CAR, MOTO & MOTORBIKE

Short *moto* rides within the centre are 2000r; *remorks* are double that, but overcharging is common.

Motorbike hire is available from most guesthouses, Ritthy's Koh Kong Eco Adventure Tours (p175) and Jungle Cross (p175).

# Around Koh Kong City

## Koh Kong Island កោះកុង

Cambodia's largest island towers over seas so crystal clear you can make out individual grains of sand in a couple of metres of water. The island has seven beaches, all of them along the Western coast. Unfortunately they're becoming increasingly polluted as irresponsible tour operators fail to properly dispose of waste. Hopefully the situation can be reversed, as the island is a real gem.

Several of the beaches – lined with coconut palms and lush vegetation, just as you'd expect in a tropical paradise – are at the mouths of little streams. At the sixth beach from the north, a narrow channel leads to a hidden lagoon.

On Koh Kong Island's eastern side, half a dozen forested hills – the highest towering 407m above the sea – drop steeply to the mangrove-lined coast. The Venice-like fishing village of Alatang, with its stilted houses and colourful fishing boats, is on the southeast coast facing the northwest corner of Botum Sakor National Park.

It's forbidden to explore the thickly forested interior, but there are now two bungalow resorts on the island. Overnight camping is available with a guide.

## 🛏 Sleeping

**Koh Kong Island Resort** RESORT $$
(☑ 035-936371; www.kohkongisland.net; Koh Kong Island; bungalows d US$25-50, f US$70) The first accommodation to open on Koh Kong Island, the rustic wooden bungalows here have solar-powered electricity, fans and dinky porches out front, perfect for a spot of lazing. Standard bungalows are pretty poky so it's worth splashing out on the deluxe option (US$50).

## ⓘ Getting There & Away

Koh Kong Island lies about 25km south of Koh Kong City. The most practical way to get there is on a boat tour from Koh Kong City.

Koh Kong Island Resort offers daily transport on its boat for US$15 per person, departing Koh Kong at 8.30am and returning to Koh Kong from Koh Kong Island at 3pm. This must be booked beforehand.

## Peam Krasaop Mangrove Sanctuary
ជម្រកសត្វព្រៃបឹងក្រឃាំក នៅពាមក្រសោប

Anchored to alluvial islands – some no larger than a house – the magnificent mangroves of the 260-sq-km **Peam Krasaop Mangrove Sanctuary** (admission 5000r; ⊙ 6.30am-6pm) protect the coast from erosion, serve as a vital breeding and feeding ground for fish, shrimp and shellfish, and are home to myriad birds.

To get a feel for the delicate mangrove ecosystem, explore the 600m-long concrete mangrove walk, which wends its way above the briny waters to a 15m observation tower. The entrance is 5.5km southeast of Koh Kong. A *moto/remork* costs US$5/10 return.

Although the main raised walkway is made from concrete blocks, there are various wooden paths that shoot off from the main trail. Travellers with little ones in tow should keep a vigilant eye on children as the walkway (particularly on the wooden sections) is not maintained well. If you're lucky, you'll come across cavorting monkeys with a fondness for fizzy drinks.

Unfortunately, a new resort has built 30 stilted bungalows amid the mangroves near the sanctuary entrance. The resort is a shrine to wood-crete that falls well short of blending with the beauty of the surroundings.

You can avoid confronting this eyesore by hiring a motorboat to take you through the sanctuary. Wooden boats are available for hire from the dock at the sanctuary entrance (short/long tours US$5/10), but a better plan is to head into the park's interior on a boat tour out of Koh Kong.

On a boat tour you'll have a chance to visit **fishing hamlets** where residents use spindly traps to catch fish, which they keep alive till market time in partly submerged nets attached to floating wooden frames. Further out, on some of the more remote mangrove islands, you pass isolated little beaches where you can land and lounge alongside fearless hermit crabs.

Much of Peam Krasaop is on the prestigious Ramsar List of Wetlands of International Importance (www.ramsar.org). The area, which is part of the Koh Kong Conservation Corridor, is all the more valuable from an ecological standpoint because similar forests in Thailand have been trashed by short-sighted development. Today Peam Krasaop's habitats and fisheries are threatened by the large-scale dredging of sand for Singapore.

# Koh Kong Conservation Corridor

របៀងអភិរក្សខេត្តកោះកុង

Stretching along both sides of NH48 from Koh Kong to the Gulf of Kompong Som (the bay northwest of Sihanoukville), the Koh Kong Conservation Corridor encompasses many of Cambodia's most outstanding natural sites, including the southern reaches of the fabled Cardamom Mountains, an area of breathtaking beauty and astonishing biodiversity.

The Cardamoms cover 20,000 sq km of southwestern Cambodia. The remote peaks – up to 1800m high – and 18 major waterways are home to at least 59 globally threatened animal species including tigers, Asian elephants, bears, Siamese crocodiles, pangolins and eight species of tortoise and turtle.

The second-largest virgin rainforest on mainland Southeast Asia, the Cardamoms are one of only two sites in the region where unbroken forests still connect mountain summits with the sea (the other is in Myanmar). Some highland areas receive up to 5m of rain a year. Conservationists hope the Cardamoms will someday be declared a Unesco World Heritage Forest.

While forests and coastlines elsewhere in Southeast Asia were being ravaged by developers and well-connected logging companies, the Cardamom Mountains and the adjacent mangrove forests were protected from the worst ecological outrages by their sheer remoteness and, at least in part, by Cambodia's long civil war. As a result, much of the area is still in pretty good shape, ecologically speaking, so the potential for ecotourism is huge – akin, some say, to that of Kenya's game reserves or Costa Rica's national parks.

The next few years will be critical in determining the future of the Cardamom Mountains. NGOs such as Conservation International (www.conservation.org), Fauna & Flora International (www.fauna-flora.org) and Wildlife Alliance (www.wildlifealliance.

org), along with teams of armed enforcement rangers, are working to help protect the area's 16 distinct ecosystems from loggers and poachers. Ecotourism, too, can play a role in providing local people with sustainable alternatives to logging and poaching.

## Tatai River & Waterfall
ស្ទឹងតាតៃ និងទឹកធ្លាក់តាតៃ

The Phun Daung (Tatai) Bridge, about 18km east of Koh Kong on the NH48, is your gateway to jungle living. The main sight here is the **Tatai Waterfall**, a thundering set of rapids during the wet season, plunging over a 4m rock shelf. Water levels drop in the dry season, but you can swim year-round in refreshing pools around the waterfall.

However, the real attraction of the Tatai River is its isolated setting with dense forest plunging down to the riverbank. Spending a few days here, either exploring the lush and tranquil natural environment or swinging in a hammock while contemplating river-life, is a pure get-away-from-it-all experience that offers extra kudos for sustainability.

### 🛏 Sleeping

Most places have their own restaurants and offer a range of trekking, boating and kayaking adventures on and around the river.

⭐ **Rainbow Lodge**     ECOLODGE **$$**
(☑012 160 2585; www.rainbowlodgecambodia.com; Tatai River; s/d/f incl all meals US$75/100/140; 📶) 🦋 A slice of jungle-chic, Rainbow Lodge proves being sustainable doesn't mean you have to sacrifice creature comforts. Powered by solar panels and bio-fuel, the bungalows here are set back from the river. They are reached by elevated walkways hugged by foliage and centred around a sleek open-air lounge with an impressive bar. Access is by boat; free transfers to/from Tatai Bridge.

Activities include kayaking, day treks, river cruises, local village visits and overnight camping, while a riverfront spa pavilion provides pampering massages.

**Neptune River Bungalows**    ECOLODGE **$$**
(☑0887770576; http://neptuneadventure-cambodia.com; Tatai River; bungalow incl breakfast US$35-50) 🦋 Want to play Robinson Crusoe? You're in the right place. Thomas – ecotour operator of long-running Neptune Adventure (p175) – has created a jungle getaway with bags of rustic charm. The four stilted bungalows, made of all natural materials, are set amid

SOUTH COAST KOH KONG CONSERVATION CORRIDOR

fruit trees. Meals (US$3 to $7), using produce from their gardens, are usually eaten communally, which adds to the homely vibe. Excellent jungle trekking and boat trips are easily arranged and there's free use of kayaks. Transfers to/from Tatai Bridge are included.

**Four Rivers Floating Lodge** RESORT **$$$**
(☑ 097 758 9676; www.ecolodges.asia; Tatai River; d incl breakfast US$259; 🛜) The 12 canvas tent-villas here float on a pontoon situated on a branch of the Tatai River estuary 6km downriver from Tatai Bridge. Inside, the lavish use of wicker and richly dark wood provides a colonial-cool ambience, topped off by the most sumptuous bathrooms you'll see under canvas anywhere. Boat transfers to/from Tatai Bridge are included.

## ❶ Getting There & Away

Access to Tatai Waterfall is by car or motorbike. The clearly marked turnoff is on the NH48 about 15km southeast of Koh Kong, or 2.8km northwest of the Tatai Bridge. From the highway it's about 2km to the falls along a rough access road. There's a stream crossing about halfway – at the height of the wet season you may have to cross it on foot and walk the last kilometre.

From Koh Kong, a half-day *moto* excursion to Tatai Waterfall costs US$10 return (*remork-moto* US$15), or less to go one way to the bridge. If travelling by public transport from Phnom Penh to one of the resorts, ask the driver to let you off at the bridge.

## Central Cardamoms Protected Forest ឧទ្យានជាតិជួរភ្នំក្រវាញ

The Central Cardamoms Protected Forest (CCPF; 4013 sq km) encompasses three of Southeast Asia's most threatened ecosystems: lowland evergreen forests, riparian forests and wetlands.

The rangers and military police who protect this vast area from illegal hunting and logging, with the help of Conservation International, are based at six strategically sited ranger stations, including one in **Thma Bang**. Here you'll find two basic **guesthouses** (per person US$5) (one run by the rangers, the other by the local community) both with a couple of rooms and a dorm, and with electricity from 6pm to 9pm. Meals can be prepared for US$2. Bring warm clothes, as the temperature can drop as low as 10°C.

Mostly covered with dense rainforest, Thma Bang is perfect for birdwatching or hiking to a waterfall with a local guide (rangers can help you find one). A new **community-based ecotourism (CBET) project** (☑ 097 752 9960; ccheb@conservation.org) was also set to launch here. The nearby **Areng Valley**, some of whose inhabitants belong to the Khmer Daeum minority community, is home to Asian elephants and the dragonfish (Asian arowana), which is almost extinct in the wild. It also has the world's second-largest population of critically endangered wild Siamese crocodiles, toothy critters up to 3.5m long, which don't eat people, preferring fish, snakes, frogs and small mammals.

The valley and its fauna are under threat from a proposed huge Chinese-built hydroelectric dam that, if constructed, will displace 1500 people, flood 90 to 120 sq km of land and inundate an important elephant-migration route. Government proponents of the dam counter that this and several additional Chinese-funded dams being built in Cambodia will provide much needed electricity to a power-starved country.

From December to May the truly intrepid can take an eight-day trek from Thma Bang north to Kravanh, or from Chamnar (linked to Thma Bang by road) over the mountains to Kravanh, a five- or six-day affair.

An easier, year-round option is the three- or four-day hike from Chumnoab, east of Thma Bang, eastwards to Roleak Kang Cheung, linked to Kompong Speu by road. Between the two is Knong Krapeur (1000m), set amid high-elevation grassland and pines. Inhabited five centuries ago, the area is known for its giant ceramic funeral jars, still filled with human bones.

There's no reservation system in Thma Bang; just show up and arrange trekking and accommodation on the spot.

## ❶ Getting There & Away

The southern reaches of the Central Cardamoms Protected Forest are easiest to reach from the south. The road to Thma Bang from NH48 has been widened and it now takes only about an hour to drive from Koh Kong. Turn off NH48 about 10km east of the Tatai River bridge at the Veal II (Veal Pii) ranger checkpoint.

Thma Bang is linked to Chi Phat by a difficult trail that can be handled by motorbike, but just barely and only in the dry season. We don't recommend it. Only attempt it in a large group of experienced bikers to help navigate bikes over the more difficult river crossings and dried out waterfall beds.

An improved road (though still much easier to navigate in the dry season), goes north from Koh Kong through the Cardamoms to Pursat, Pailin and Battambang, passing by remote mountain towns such as Veal Veng, Ou Som (where there's a fledgling ecotourism project) and Promouy (the main town in the Phnom Samkos Wildlife Sanctuary). Near Koh Kong, the turnoff is on the old road to Phnom Penh past the airport, a few hundred metres beyond the army base.

Going south, share taxis link Pursat with Promouy, Ou Som and Koh Kong during the dry season. In the wet season, it may still be possible to hire a *moto* for the long trip from Promouy to Koh Kong, depending on local road conditions and seasonal rainfall. Heading north from Koh Kong, share taxis are rare on this route. The CCPF's northern sections are accessible from Pursat (p232).

## Botum Sakor National Park
រមណីយដ្ឋានឧទ្យានជាតិបុទុមសាគរ

Occupying almost the entirety of the 35km-wide peninsula northwest across the Gulf of Kompong Som from Sihanoukville, this 1834-sq-km national park, encircled by mangroves and beaches, is home to a profusion of wildlife, including elephants, deer, leopards and sun bears.

Alas, Botum Sakor appears to be a national park in name only. A US$3.5 billion Chinese-run tourism project is developing the western third of the park into seven resort-cities. Launched in 2010, the project will take 25 years to complete, but hundreds of local families have already been evicted from the area, a four-lane highway has been laid through the heart of the park, and a golf course is already up and running.The new highway, which begins 6km west of Andoung Tuek, also provides access to the Koh Sdach Archipelago (p209).

Meanwhile, Cambodian businessman Ly Yong Phat has been granted a concession to develop a large central swath of the park.

That leaves the eastern third of the peninsula as the only viable area to visit. Boats can be hired in Andoung Tuek to take you up into four mangrove-lined streams that are rich with wildlife, including the pileated gibbon, long-tailed macaque and black-shanked douc langur. The streams are Ta Op, the largest, on the east coast; Ta Nun in the middle of the south coast; and Ta Nhi and Preak Khsach on the east coast.

At the **park headquarters** (☑ 099 374797, 081 414988; NH48), 3.5km west of Andoung Tuek, you can arrange a hike with a ranger (US$5 a day) or a boat excursion out of Andoung Tuek.

Trail bikers and intrepid *moto* riders can bypass the newer highway and take the rugged road around the park's east coast via the scenic fishing village of Thmor Sor, which is largely built on stilts over the alluvial bay, stretching almost 1km out to sea.

---

## Chi Phat សហគមន៍ទេសចរណ៍ជីជាត់

In an effort to protect the southern Cardamom Mountains from poaching, logging and land grabbing, Wildlife Alliance (www.wildlifealliance.org) launched a multiphase project to transform the rainforest into a source of jobs and income for local people. The **Southern Cardamoms Protected Forest** (1443 sq km), whose southern boundary is NH48 between Koh Kong and Andoung Tuek, is becoming a world-class ecotourism destination.

Once notorious for its loggers and poachers, the river village of Chi Phat (population 630 families) is now home to Wildlife Alliance's pioneering community-based eco-tourism project (CBET). Chi Phat offers travellers a rare opportunity to stay in a rural community where tourism is controlled by the local villagers themselves; and to explore the Cardamoms ecosystems while contributing to their conservation and providing an alternative livelihood to the former poachers who act as its protectors and guides.

### 🎣 Activities & Tours

All activities in Chi Phat are controlled through the exceptionally organised **CBET Community Visitor Centre** (☑ 092 720925, 035-675 6444; www.chi-phat.org; Chi Phat; ⏱ 7am-7pm; 🛜), a two-minute walk from the river pier. The visitor centre has free wi-fi, solar-powered electricity and a good restaurant serving both meat and vegetarian Khmer food.

Prices for all tours are extremely reasonable, ranging from US$15 to US$25 per person including lunch, transport and equipment. All-inclusive multiday trips cost a bit more per day. Prices include a contribution to the community conservation fund. All tours require guides, most of whom once worked as poachers and loggers.

On arrival in Chi Phat, head to the visitor centre to organise activities, which must be booked by 5pm the day before. At the centre you can meet the guides and other guests returning from treks. This is the time to get information about activities and the condition of the trails, and learn how the local community is now a force to protect the forests it once plundered.

As well as the many trekking, boating and mountain-biking activities on offer, it is also possible to visit Wildlife Alliance's million-tree nursery, where it nurtures saplings for its impressive reforestation program. This is an educational experience and involves the chance to make a lasting mark with a plant-a-tree initiative. You can also hire kayaks to explore the river by yourself. When we last called through town they were busy setting up new Khmer cooking classes.

### Treks

CBET treks (US$15 to US$25 per person per day) range from one to seven days with shorter trips exploring the bat caves, waterfalls, mountain communities and mysterious burial jar sites in the surroundings. The more adventurous can also get a glimpse into the work involved in protecting the forest from illegal logging and poaching on three- to five-day patrol with forest ranger treks.

On overnight trips you either sleep in hammocks or at one of five campsites set up by Wildlife Alliance, equipped with eco-toilets, field kitchens and comfortable hammocks with mosquito-proof nets. Wildlife spotting isn't guaranteed but there are usually plenty of opportunities to shoot (with a camera) monkeys and hornbills. Although the guides wear flip-flops, it's recommended to bring walking shoes for the treks.

### Boat Tours

CBET's sunrise birdwatching boat trips and sunset star-gazing cruises (US$12 to US$35 per person) are a great way to experience the languid beauty of the Preak Piphot River. The former involves a 1½ hour longtail boat ride before jumping in a traditional stand-up rowing boat (with rower) and silently paddling along the placid Stung Proat, an unlogged tributary of the river.

Silver langurs, long-tailed macaques, greater hornbills and other rainforest creatures can often be seen along the banks of Stung Proat. Gibbons are hard to spot, but can often be heard calling to each other through the forest canopy.

### Mountain-Biking Tours

CBET's one- to two-day mountain-biking tours (US$20 to US$25 per person per day) follow trails to waterholes, burial jar sites,

## CHI PHAT: AN ECOTOURISM CASE STUDY

The Chi Phat community has long supplemented its meagre agricultural income with products from the nearby forests. Gathering nontimber forest products (known in development lingo as NTFPs) and small quantities of firewood can be ecologically sustainable, but around Chi Phat the wholesale forest destruction carried out during 'the logging time' – the anarchic 1990s – left the whole ecosystem, and the villagers' livelihoods, way out of kilter. For many, poaching endangered animals became a way of life.

When Wildlife Alliance (www.wildlifealliance.org) came on the scene in 2002 in a last-ditch effort to save the southern Cardamoms, local villagers and outsiders were encroaching on protected land, destroying the forest by illegal logging, and hunting endangered animals for local consumption and sale on the black market. The only way to prevent ecological catastrophe – and, among other things, to save macaques from being trapped, sold for US$60 and shipped to Vietnam to be eaten – was to send in teams of enforcement rangers to crack down on 'forestry and wildlife crimes'.

But enforcing the law impinged on local people's ability to earn income, generating a great deal of resentment. Wildlife Alliance realised that in order to save the Cardamoms, it needed the cooperation of locals, which would be forthcoming only if income-generating alternatives to poaching and logging were available.

Thus Wildlife Alliance launched what's known in NGO parlance as a community-based ecotourism (CBET) project. The first step was empowering the local community. A committee of 14 elected representatives was established to assess positive and negative impacts, set goals and manage the project. Many of those who joined as 'stakeholders' were former loggers and wildlife traders.

Today the Chi Phat CBET project is flourishing. The initially sceptical locals have warmed to the idea, and the income generated from ecotourism – income that goes into both the villagers' pockets and a community development fund – is starting to make a real difference. Chi Phat is seen as a model for other CBET projects, and delegations from around Cambodia now come here to see how it's done.

waterfalls and rural communities in the surrounding forest. Overnight trips use hammocks (with mosquito nets) for sleeping. If you want to explore the countryside around Chi Phat village solo, you can also hire mountain bikes at the CBET visitor centre.

### Release Station Tours

**Wildlife Alliance Release Station Tours** TOUR
(☑010 690864; www.wildlifealliance.org/page/view/507/wildlife-release-station-tours; adult/child 1 night US$120/50, 2 nights US$200/75) Wildlife Alliance operate tours to their release station (about 30 minutes from Chi Phat), where animals such as sun bears and binturongs are released into the wild after being rescued from illegal trafficking. Accommodation, food and activities – jungle trekking, wildlife tracking, and helping set up camera traps – are included. Transport (by motorbike) is provided from either Andoung Tuek =or Chi Phat. Advance bookings essential.

## 🛏 Sleeping

Chi Phat's CBET project has a selection of places to stay. Some are in town, others are out in the countryside, surrounded by orchards. There's not a huge difference in accommodation standards, particularly between the guesthouses and the homestays. All rooms – inspected monthly by the CBET committee – are clean and commodious and come with fans, mosquito nets, cotton sheets, foam mattresses, towel, free bottled water and a laminated sheet on local customs. The village only has electricity in the morning between 5am and 9am, and in the evening from 6pm to 9pm (bring a torch/flashlight).

You can either book your room in advance or simply call in at the visitor centre when you arrive and choose your accommodation then. The guesthouse owner will come and meet you.

**CBET Homestays** HOMESTAY $
(www.chi-phat.org; r US$4) 🌿 Many of Chi Phat's 13 homestays are in wooden, stilted Khmer houses that offer a glimpse into rural life. Rooms are cosy and simple, and bathrooms are shared with the family. Some homestays have squat toilets and traditional shower facilities (a rainwater cistern with a plastic bucket). Dinner (US$2.50) can be provided.

Visitors can let CBET staff know if they need Western-style bathroom facilities when choosing where to stay. Some

homestays also have 12V fans powered overnight by rechargeable car batteries.

**CBET Guesthouses** GUESTHOUSE $
(www.chi-phat.org; r US$5, with bathroom US$6) 🌿 Chi Phat's CBET project has 18 family-run guesthouses that provide small, clean rooms. While some only have shared bathrooms, others come with en suite facilities. You can specify your preference when booking at the CBET visitor centre. All guesthouses are connected to the village's electricity grid, which operates mornings and evenings only.

**CBET Bungalows** BUNGALOW $
(www.chi-phat.org; bungalow US$10-15) 🌿 Chi Phat has two bungalow options providing a greater degree of privacy than the village's guesthouse and homestay accommodation. Both sets of bungalows are built from natural materials and come with en suite bathrooms and dinky balconies. They have electricity in the mornings and evenings.

**Butterfly Island** BUNGALOW $$
(www.chi-phat.org; bungalow US$30-35) 🌿 Chi Phat's most upmarket and peaceful place to stay is Butterfly Island, a set of simple but sturdy bungalows, surrounded by lush forest, on a small island in the middle of a river reached by a swing bridge. It has been closed recently, but reopening was on the cards. Check on the CBET website before arriving.

## 🍴 Eating & Drinking

Several food stalls on the main strip between the river pier and the visitor centre sell simple local food for about US$2 a dish. Soft drinks and beer are available in local stores. The visitor centre boasts the only real bar in town, which (when it's open) offers some of the best cocktails this side of Phnom Penh.

**Visitor Centre Restaurant** RESTAURANT $
(breakfast US$2.50, lunch & dinner US$3.50; 🍴) The only restaurant in town is located at the visitor centre. Everybody enjoys the same selection of three dishes for lunch, and three dishes for dinner, and the menu changes daily. Vegetarians are catered for and packed lunches are available. All of the food is sourced locally, and much is locally grown or reared.

## ℹ Information

Chi Phat has no bank or ATM; bring all the cash you need with you. For information on all activities, tours, accommodation and getting to Chi Phat check out www.chi-phat.org.

Very occasionally, at the boat dock in Andoung Tuek and in nearby coffee shops, scammers accost travellers, purveying misinformation, offering bogus tourist services and demanding spurious payments.

### ❶ Getting There & Away

Chi Phat is on the scenic Preak Piphot River, 21km upriver from Andoung Tuek. Andoung Tuek is on NH48, 98km from Koh Kong. All buses travelling between Koh Kong and Phnom Penh or Sihanoukville pass through here.

Arriving in Andoung Tuek, buses usually stop outside Kim Chhoun Guesthouse (the restaurant with blue pillars), where the management work in conjunction with CBET to help organise onward transport to Chi Phat. This is the place to organise a *moto* or ask about the CBET boat if you haven't already booked through the CBET website (www.chi-phat.org).

CBET's longtail boat (US$10), which makes the two-hour trip from Andoung Tuek every day, is the most atmospheric way to get to Chi Phat. It's best to book at least 48 hours in advance through the CBET website to be sure of a place on the boat. The boat leaves Andoung Tuek at 1pm (or whenever the Virak Buntham bus from Phnom Penh arrives). The CBET community works only with local boatmen who have been trained in safety standards and whose boats have been remodelled to offer tourists a degree of comfort. The CBET-sanctioned boats have life-vests and carry a spare engine.

You can also book a *moto* (US$7, 45 minutes) in advance to travel the 17km unsealed road to Chi Phat, although this is also easily organised upon arrival in Andoung Tuek. *Moto* drivers drop passengers off across the river from Chi Phat and a tiny raft-ferry (1000r) takes passengers to the village itself.

Travelling from Chi Phat, boats and *motos* can be booked the night before to return to Andoung Tuek in the morning, in time to catch onward buses. The CBET office can also book bus tickets.

If you have your own transport, the road to Chi Phat is unsealed but in pretty good shape. Follow the telephone lines and use the car ferry to cross the river. Motorbikers can use the smaller raft-ferry, located 100m to the left of the main ferry.

## PREAH SIHANOUK PROVINCE

Sandwiched between Kampot and Koh Kong Provinces, diminutive Preah Sihanouk Province (ខេត្តព្រះសីហនុ; also known as Kompong Som Province) is dominated by its main city, the dynamic port of Sihanoukville.

Besides the surrounding islands, natural sites include Ream National Park, 18km east of Sihanoukville, and the Kbal Chhay Cascades.

## Sihanoukville ក្រុងព្រះសីហនុ

♪ 034 / POP 91,000

Sure, Sihanoukville would never win first prize in a beauty competition, but thanks to a surrounding coastline of white-sand beaches this is Cambodia's most happening sun-sloth destination. Named in honour of the then head-of-state, Sihanoukville (Kong Preah Sihanouk; also known as Kompong Som) was hacked out of the jungle in the late 1950s to create Cambodia's first and only deep-water port, strategically vital because it meant that the country's international trade no longer had to pass through Vietnam's Mekong Delta.

Today it is a bustling and ever expanding city, but its sandy bits are one step removed from the hubbub. The Serendipity Beach area is a sort of decompression chamber for backpackers, who flock here to rest up between travels and party through the night.

Even further away from the hustle, in the far south of town, is relaxed Otres Beach, where cheap bungalow joints and bohemian-flavoured guesthouses are now neighbours with rather swish boutique resorts. The mellow scene here ticks all the boxes if you're looking for lazy days of sunbathing rather than night-time bar-hopping.

Although none of Sihanoukville's beaches qualify as Southeast Asia's finest, the sandy strips rimmed by casuarina trees and coconut palms have plenty of tropical charm and it's easy to find stretches of sand to yourself, especially if you venture outside the centre. If they're not picture-postcard-perfect enough for you, Sihanoukville is also the jumping-off point to Cambodia's southern islands, where castaway-cool beckons.

## ⊙ Sights

On most days in the late afternoon, three troupes of tame monkeys gather on 2 Thnou St – behind and on the chain-link fence enclosing the grounds of the Independence Hotel (p192) – hoping to score peanuts and bananas from passing humans. Locals often stop by with their kids, generating a great deal of mirth and mutual inter-primate admiration.

### Wat Leu BUDDHIST TEMPLE

(វត្តលើ, Wat Chhnothean; Map p185; Wat Leu Rd) Spectacular views of almost the entire city and gorgeous sunset panoramas await at Wat Leu, situated on a peaceful, forested hilltop 1.5km northwest of the city centre. From the city centre, a *moto* ride due north up the hill costs 6000r, but drivers will likely want US$2. *Remorks* have to take the long way around and ask US$5.

## 🏖 Beaches

Sihanoukville's beaches all have wildly different characters, offering something for just about everyone. For a more isolated sandy strip, the beaches of Ream National Park (p200) are only a short ride away.

### Occheuteal Beach BEACH

(ឆ្នេរអូរឈើទាល; Map p190) This 4km-long beach is by far Sihanoukville's most popular. The rocky strip at the northwestern end is known as **Serendipity Beach** (Map

## Sihanoukville

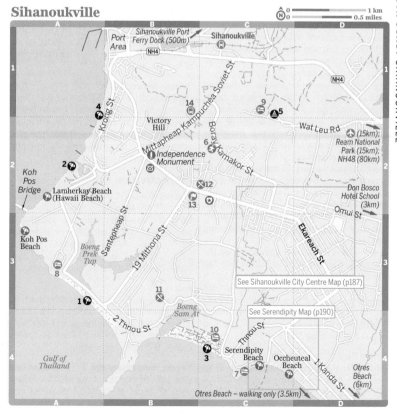

p190), which has a few resort bar-restaurants where waves lap a few metres from the tables, providing a romantic backdrop. Turning left from the pier, a string of beach-bars rim the white sand. During the day this area is busy with vendors, beggars and nuisances such as jet skis. Escape the mayhem by walking to the southern section of the beach.

Occheuteal can get packed, especially at weekends when local families arrive for some beach time. It's also far from clean, particularly along the beach-bar section; note the rivulets of waste water that flow from the shacks into the surf. The southern section of the beach is ultimately slated to become another exclusive Sokha resort, but is for now pretty empty.

### ★ Otres Beach                             BEACH

(ឆ្នេរអូរត្រេះ; Map p194) Past the southern end of Occheuteal Beach, beyond the **Phnom Som Nak Sdach** (Hill of the King's Palace) headland, lies stunning Otres Beach; a seemingly infinite strip of casuarinas that gives southern Thailand a run for its money.

Although no longer the empty stretch of beach it once was, Otres has cleaner water and is more relaxed than anything in Sihanoukville proper, and is lengthy enough that finding your own patch of sand is not a challenge…just walk south.

Long eyed-up by large-scale developers, Otres has so far managed to shun major construction work and DIY development is blossoming with more than 30 small-scale independent resorts and beach bungalow places in the area, including a handful of upmarket boutique hotels. Otres is split into three distinct sections: **Otres 1** (Map p194) is the first and busiest stretch, while about 2km south is quieter **Otres 2** (Map p194), separated by a slated resort development currently known as 'Long Beach'. Inland lies laid-back **Otres Village**, an up-and-coming estuary area.

Otres Beach is about 5km south of the Serendipity area. It's a US$2 *moto* ride (*remork* US$5) to get here (more at night). If going it alone, follow the road southeast along the beach and skirt the hill by heading inland on the inviting tarmac. From the city centre, you can take Omui St from Psar Leu east out of town for 5km.

### Sokha Beach                              BEACH

(ឆ្នេរ សុខា; Map p185) Midway between Independence and Serendipity beaches lies Sihanoukville's prettiest beach, 1.5km-long Sokha Beach. Its fine, silicon-like sand squeaks loudly underfoot. The tiny eastern end of Sokha Beach is open to the public and is rarely crowded. The rest is part of the exclusive **Sokha Beach Resort** (Map p185; ☎034-935999; www.sokhahotels.com; Thnou St; r/ste from US$171/210; ❄@🛜🏊). Tourists are welcome to enjoy the sand near Sokha but are expected to buy something to drink or eat. You might even duck into the resort to use the pool (US$5).

### Victory Beach                            BEACH

(ឆ្នេរជ័យជំនះ; Map p185) Though it's not the best beach in town due to the looming backdrop of Sihanoukville Port, it is hassle-free and family-friendly, with plenty of midrange beach eateries.

### Lamherkay Beach                          BEACH

(ឆ្នេរលម្ហែរកាយ; Map p185) About 1.5km southwest of Victory Beach is Lamherkay Beach, also known as Hawaii Seaview Beach. It's hugely popular with car-owning Khmers on weekends and holidays but quiet on weekdays. **Koh Pos** (Snake Island), the island 800m offshore, has been leased by Russians with big resort plans, which explains the flashy new bridge linking it with the mainland. It's currently a bridge to nowhere, as work on the actual resort appears to have stalled.

### Independence Beach                       BEACH

(ឆ្នេរ ឯ ក រាជ្យ; Map p185) Northwest of Sokha Beach Independence Beach (7-Chann Beach) has mostly been taken over by a gargantuan new property development. The only open section is beneath the classic hotel for which the beach is named.

## 🏃 Activities

### Starfish Bakery & Café                   MASSAGE

(Map p187; off 7 Makara St; per hr US$6-10; ⊙7am-6pm) 🌀 Masseuses who are visually or physically disabled and have been trained by Western massage therapists perform Khmer, Thai, oil, foot and Indian head massages. Profits go towards social projects.

### Relax                                     SPA

(Map p190; ☎085 352213; Serendipity Beach Rd; per hr from US$10; ⊙10am-9.30pm) This place's Khmer, lavender, jasmine-oil and foot massages get great reviews. They also offer facials, pedicures and waxing.

### Seeing Hands Massage 3                   MASSAGE

(Map p187; 95 Ekareach St; per hr US$6; ⊙8am-9pm) 🌀 Some of the blind masseurs who work their magic here speak English.

# Sihanoukville City Centre

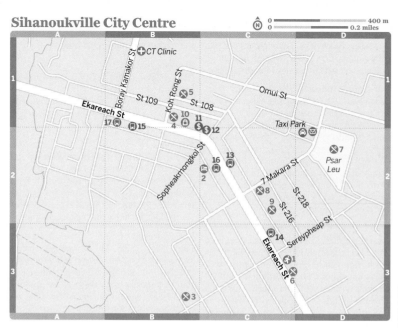

## Sihanoukville City Centre

### 🔵 Activities, Courses & Tours
1 Seeing Hands Massage 3 ..................... C3
Starfish Bakery & Café..................(see 9)

### 🔵 Sleeping
2 Small Hotel .............................................. C2

### 🔵 Eating
3 Cabbage Farm Restaurant.................... B3
4 Espresso Kampuchea ...........................B1
5 Gelato Italiano ....................................... B1
6 Holy Cow................................................ C3
7 Psar Leu ................................................. D2
8 Samudera Supermarket....................... C2
9 Starfish Bakery & Café.......................... C2

### 🔵 Shopping
10 Mr Heinz ................................................. B1
Starfish .............................................(see 9)

### 🔵 Information
11 ANZ Royal Bank...................................... B1
12 Canadia Bank.........................................C2

### 🔵 Transport
13 Capitol Tour ...........................................C2
14 GST..........................................................C3
15 Phnom Penh Sorya ................................ B1
16 Rith Mony ...............................................C2
17 Virak Buntham....................................... B1

**Fitness Resort**                                    GYM

(Map p185; ☑015 620534; www.fitness-sihanoukville.com; Boray Kamakor St; day pass/class US$5/6; ☺6am-8pm Mon-Sat, to noon Sun) A French-run complex with a huge open-air gym, free weights, aerobics, and Khmer and Thai boxing classes.

### Diving & Water Sports

**Scuba Nation**                                   DIVING

(Map p190; ☑012 604680; www.divecambodia.com; Serendipity Beach Rd; 2-dive package US$85, PADI Open Water US$445; ☺8am-6.30pm) The longest-running dive operator in Sihanoukville, Scuba Nation is a PADI five-star centre with a comfortable boat for day and liveaboard trips.

**Dive Shop**                                       DIVING

(Map p190; ☑034-933664; www.diveshopcambodia.com; Serendipity Beach Rd; PADI Discover Scuba US$95, 1-/2-dive package US$65/80; ☺9am-7pm) PADI five-star dive centre offering the full gamut of PADI courses, as well as fun dives and liveaboards. Also has a dive shop on Koh Rong Sanloem.

### EcoSea Dive
DIVING

(Map p190; ☑034-934631; www.ecoseadive.com; Serendipity Beach Rd; 3-dive package US$90; ☺9am-7pm) Offers both PADI and SSI courses and has competitively priced fun-dive rates.

### Hurricane Windsurfing
WATER SPORTS

(Map p194; ☑017 471604; sydney.victor@yahoo.fr; Queenco Palm Beach Resort, Otres 1; ☺9am-6.30pm) Rents paddleboards (US$8 per hour), windsurfers (basic US$10 per hour, high-performance US$20), sea kayaks (single US$4 per hour, tandem US$6) and skimboards (try bungee skimboarding). Otres Beach sometimes gets surf from May to October; you can rent surfboards and bodyboards here too.

### Blue Lagoon Kitesurf Centre
WATER SPORTS

(Map p194; ☑085 511145; Papa Pippo, Otres 1; 1hr lesson incl equipment US$50; ☺9am-7pm) This kitesurfing centre rents equipment as well as running kitesurfing lessons and multiday courses. Located on Otres Beach, near Papa Pippo restaurant, they also run boat tours to four islands (US$15 per person including breakfast, lunch and snorkelling).

##  Courses

### Don Bosco Hotel Khmer Cooking Course
COOKING COURSE

(☑034-934478; www.donboscohotelschool.com/cooking; Don Bosco Hotel School, Ou Phram St; per person US$30) ✐ The cooking classes here provide a great opportunity to support the worthy Don Bosco Hotel School plus learn some Khmer culinary skills. They include a trip to the market and a slap-up three-course lunch (which you've helped create), as well as a tour of the hotel school. Classes usually run from 10am to 12.30pm on Tuesdays, Thursdays and Saturdays.

## Tours

Popular day tours go to some of the closer islands and to Ream National Park (US$20 per person). You can also hire a boat and make your own way to the islands: most travel agencies and guesthouses can arrange a boat. Budget US$50 for a boat to Koh Ta Kiev from Occheuteal, and a bit less for Koh Russei. You'll save money going from Otres Beach.

Booze cruises offer backpackers the chance to spend the day onboard getting sloshed under the sun. Be aware that accidents have occurred (including one boat sinking due to overloading passengers) and there are rarely enough life jackets onboard.

Check out the boat operator thoroughly before signing up. Drowning kind of takes the fun out of a day on the water.

### Eco-Trek Tours
ADVENTURE TOUR

(Map p190; ☑012 987073; www.ecotourscambodia.com; ☺8am-10pm) This travel agency runs highly recommended boat tours and trekking trips to Ream National Park as well as boat trips around the islands.

### Suntours
BOAT TOUR

(☑016 396201; www.suntours-cambodia.com; per person US$30) Suntours offers upmarket island cruises. Their day cruises to Koh Rong Sanloam, which get rave reviews, include snacks, buffet lunch, coffee and tea, as well as snorkelling, kayaking and fishing equipment.

### Liberty Ranch
HORSE RIDING

(Map p194; ☑016 339774; www.libertyranch-sihanoukville.com; Otres Village; 1/2/3hr trail ride US$25/45/60; ☺7-11am & 3-6pm) A horseback tour is a great way to discover the tranquil countryside around Sihanoukville. Total beginners can opt for trails along Otres Beach and explore the small villages nearby, while more advanced riders can venture on longer tours that head further out towards the hills.

### Party Boat
BOAT TOUR

(Map p190; www.thepartyboat.asia; Serendipity Beach Pier; per person US$25) The daily trip (9.30am to 5pm) to Koh Rong Sanloem includes snacks, lunch, snorkelling and a free drink. They also run return transport to Koh Rong Island's full moon parties leaving Sihanoukville at 5pm and returning around 8am.

### Stray Dogs of Asia
ADVENTURE TOUR

(Map p190; ☑017 810125; www.straydogasia.com; Mithona St; tours US$100; ☺9am-6pm) Runs all-day countryside dirt-bike tours that take in some of the natural attractions around Sihanoukville.

## Sleeping

Location, location, location; each Sihanoukville district has its own distinct character and attracts a different type of clientele. We quote prices for the high season (November to March). Rates drop between June and October, especially on Serendipity and Otres Beaches, but can skyrocket on Khmer holidays at some establishments.

### Serendipity & Occheuteal

The main backpacker hang-out is Serendipity Beach Rd, which runs up the hill from

Serendipity Beach, connecting to Ekareach St at the **Golden Lions Roundabout** (Map p190; Ekareach St). A string of wallet-friendly crash pads and guesthouses meander all the way up the street. Decent midrange options can be found on the roads running south-east from here.

Late-night noise from the nearby clubs affects most of the accommodation here. The din lessens substantially in the hotels slightly further east but light sleepers may want to bunk elsewhere.

⭐**Chochi Garden**  GUESTHOUSE $
(Map p190; ☑070 865640; www.chochigarden. com; Serendipity Beach Rd; r with fan/air-con US$15/25; ⊜❄�widehat{}) Finally! Serendipity gets its first boutique backpacker pad. Italian-Japanese couple Francesca and Taka have created the nearest Serendipity gets to a tranquil oasis right in the heart of the action. Out the front is a cool bar/restaurant while simple rooms, some with palm-thatch roofs and pretty painted window-grills, are in a plant-filled garden strewn with comfy seating areas.

**The Gypsies**  GUESTHOUSE $
(Map p190; ☑088 788 2100; www.the-gypsies. com; Serendipity Beach Rd; dm/r US$7/25; ❄�widehat{}) Right beside Serendipity's pier Gypsies is a cute-as-a-button yellow building. Upstairs are four breezy rooms with bags of bohemian flair that share a wide balcony overlooking the mayhem below. The cafe downstairs serves up some decent grub and there's a (poky) dorm too.

**One Stop Hostel**  HOSTEL $
(Map p190; ☑096 339 0005; onestophostelshv@ gmail.com; Golden Lions Roundabout; dm US$7; ❄�widehat{}) Dorm beds just got a makeover. The eight-bed dorms here, decked out in lashings of white-on-white, boast beds with individual reading lamps and luggage lock-boxes. Rooms are set around a wall-to-ceiling glassed courtyard with a small pool, proving slick styling doesn't have to cost the earth.

**Monkey Republic**  HOSTEL $
(Map p190; ☑012 490290; http://monkey republic.info; Serendipity Beach Rd; dm US$6, r with fan US$15-22, r with air-con US$18-30; ❄@�widehat{}) Self-proclaimed 'backpacker central', Monkey Republic rose from the ashes in 2013 following a dramatic fire (no casualties). It offers decent dorms and plain, affordable rooms in a building fronted by a yellow French colonial facade. The bar-restaurant constantly heaves with young travellers.

**Big Easy**  HOSTEL $
(Map p190; ☑081 943930; Serendipity Beach Rd; dm US$3, r US$6-10; �widehat{}) This classic backpacker joint is accommodation, comfort food and a lively rock bar all rolled into one. Rooms are basic but you'll most likely spend your time in the bar, which has a great vibe with occasional live music and live EPL games.

⭐**Ropanha Boutique Hotel**  BOUTIQUE HOTEL $$
(Map p190; ☑012 556654; www.ropanha-boutique hotel.com; 23 Tola St; r incl breakfast US$45-55; ❄�widehat{}❆) The pick of the pack when it comes to affordable atmosphere in the Serendipity area. Set around a lush courtyard garden and pool, Ropanha's rooms include flat-screen TVs and accompanying DVD players, plus rain showers in the bathroom. Deluxe rooms have pool views but all have lashings of white and are exceptionally well cared for.

**OC Hotel**  HOTEL $$
(Map p190; ☑034-933658; www.ochotel.asia; 23 Tola St; r incl breakfast US$49-86; ❄�widehat{}❆) There are two OC hotels in one location: choose either the slick deluxe rooms in the new annexe, with swags of contemporary style and pool views; or the less expensive options in the old building, which have great amenities but a lot less pizzazz. Guests get free transfers to Otres Beach.

**Coolabah Resort**  HOTEL $$
(Map p190; ☑017 678218; www.coolabah-hotel. com; 14 Mithona St; r US$42-65; ❄@�widehat{}❆) This popular Aussie-run hotel gets kudos for having the most on-the-ball staff in the Serendipity area. Rooms are classically styled in soothing neutrals with smart art and contemporary bathrooms, and come in a variety of sizes including family options.The bar here is one of Serendipity's more relaxed places to sit down with a beer.

**Reef Resort**  HOTEL $$
(Map p190; ☑034-934281; www.reefresort.com. kh; Serendipity Beach Rd; incl breakfast d US$30-40, f US$55-60; ❄�widehat{}❆) Reef's enthusiastic new owners were giving the property a modern-Mediterranean makeover when we last pulled through town. This was the first upmarket property to open in the Serendipity area and the generously proportioned rooms, well-kitted-out family suites and 12.5m pool still make it a smart choice.

**Cloud 9**  BUNGALOW $$
(Map p185; ☑098 215166; www.cloud9bungalows. com; Serendipity Beach; bungalow US$40-100;

# Serendipity

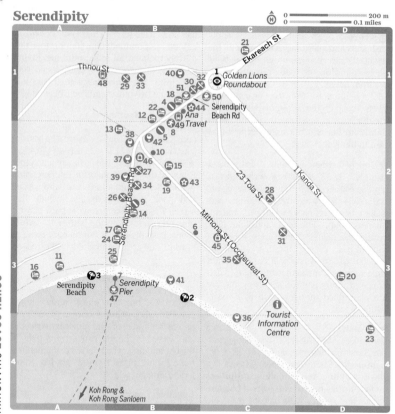

🗺) The last place on Serendipity Beach is a fine choice, and not just because it's furthest removed from the club noise. It has a cosy tropical bar and we really like their range of rustic, Khmer-style wooden bungalows with fans and ocean-view balconies.

### Cove
BUNGALOW **$$**

(Map p190; ☑034-638 0296; www.thecovebeach. com; Serendipity Beach; r with air-con from US$29, bungalow from US$40; ❄🗺) This clutch of bungalows nestles into the hillside. Most directly face the sea and come with balconies and hammocks. Be aware that bungalows here are close together so there's not much privacy. There's also a row of rooms in a concrete block higher up the hill.

### Blue Sea Boutique Hotel
HOTEL **$$**

(Map p190; ☑034-933999; www.bluesea-boutique.com; Serendipity Beach Rd; r incl breakfast US$60-80; ❄🗺🏊) These bungalows are set amid a lush garden with pool. Rooms, with

Asian decorative touches, come with great amenities (including kettles and decent bathroom toiletries) and the larger ones are great for travelling families.

### Nice Beach Hotel
HOTEL **$$**

(Map p190; ☑034-659 4999; www.nicebeach-hotel.com; 14 Mithona St; r incl breakfast US$25-35; ❄🗺) This Cambodian villa-style hotel offers enticing value for money with powerful air-con, fridge and cable TV (that actually works) in all rooms. Bag a front-facing room for a swish bathroom and balcony.

### Diamond Ocean Resort
HOTEL **$$**

(Map p190; ☑034-683 3999; www.diamond oceanresort.com; Serendipity Beach Rd; r incl breakfast US$55-75; ♿❄🗺🏊) The facade is business-bland but this new hotel provides the bells and whistles necessary for those who can't live without their mod-cons. Large rooms have subtle touches of Khmer artistry and come with contemporary bathrooms.

# Serendipity

**SOUTH COAST** SIHANOUKVILLE

**Serendipity Beach Resort**     HOTEL **$$**
(Map p190; ☑034-938888; www.serendipity
beachresort.com; Serendipity Beach Rd; r US$45-75;
❄@🌐☎) Ignore the ugly ducking exterior,
for inside a Serendipity swan awaits. Prices
here remain good value given the impressive
size and style of the rooms. The huge pool is
often partially shaded.

**Above Us Only Sky**     BUNGALOW **$$$**
(Map p190; ☑089 822318; www.aboveusonlysky.
net; Serendipity Beach; bungalow $80-100;
❄☎) The bungalows here are attractive-
ly minimalist inside with tiled floors and
glass-fronted doors to make the most of the
sea panoramas. Chances are you'll spend
most of your time parked on the cosy balcony in a comfy cane chair, taking in the view.
The bar-restaurant, perched over the rocks
by the seashore, is a real gem.

## 🛏 City Centre & Around

The shabby city centre, spread out along
and north of Ekareach St, is preferred by

some long-termers because it's cheap and
it's removed from the traveller scene. Most
banks and businesses are here too, as is Sihanoukville's main market.

Victory Hill (Weather Station Hill, also
known as 'The Hill'), once a backpacker
haven, is up the hill from Victory Beach.
The main drag is pretty sleazy and far removed from its original hippy-trippy vibe,
but one of the longest-running guesthouses
here remains a good locally owned option.
Independence Beach and Sokha Beach both
have high-end resorts occupying the prime
beach real estate.

**Small Hotel**     HOTEL **$**
(Map p187; ☑034-630 6161; www.thesmallhotel.
info; s/d US$17/25; ⊜❄@☎) Run by a clued-
up Swedish-Khmer couple, this guesthouse
is as cosy as sitting in front of a fireplace on
a snowy Scandinavian night. The 11 rooms
lack the immense character of the lobby
but are spotless and have hot water, fridge
and TV.

### Don Bosco Hotel School
HOTEL $$

(☏034-934478; www.donboscohotelschool.com; Ou Phram St; s US$35, d US$40-65; 🅿❄🛜🏊) 🏊 This excellent training hotel offers disadvantaged youngsters a helping hand into hospitality. Rooms are great value with a three-star trim throughout. Facilities include a pool, a gym and an Italian restaurant. The location isn't great but the experience more than compensates. It's signposted from Omui St when travelling out of the city centre on the road to Otres Beach.

### Pagoda Rocks
BOUTIQUE HOTEL $$

(Map p185; ☏077 524275; www.pagodarocks.com; Wat Leu Area; d/f US$65/105; ❄🛜🏊) If you're going to stay far away from the beach you might as well stay somewhere memorable. Pagoda Rocks has a swanky restaurant, a blissful infinity pool with prime views of the port area, and chic cottages. Unfortunately, getting here is a hassle if you don't have your own wheels; *remork* drivers demand US$5 one way. Ask for 'Wat Leu'.

### Independence Hotel
HOTEL $$$

(Map p185; ☏034-934300; www.independence hotel.net; 2 Thnou St; d/ste from US$130/155; ❄@🛜🏊) Opened in 1963, this striking seven-storey hotel still has the jet-set feel of Sihanoukville's movie-star heyday. After years of neglect it was reopened in 2007. It features fresh contemporary rooms with sea panoramas or views of the landscaped gardens, and a few bungalows overlooking the water. Ride the elevator to the private beach.

## 🛏 Otres Beach

Groovy little Otres is Sihanoukville's laid-back beach colony with a cluster of bungalows, guesthouses and stylish boutique resorts running along the sand. The beach is split into two sections, separated by a 2.5km section of empty beach. Otres 1 has most of the accommodation while quieter Otres 2, further south, is home to the boutique resorts. Just inland is Otres Village with a scattering of relaxed places nestled on a river estuary.

### ★Wish You Were Here
HOSTEL $

(Map p194; ☏097 241 5884; http://wishotres. com; Otres 1; dm US$6, r US$14-16, bungalows US$18; 🅿🛜) This rickety wooden building is one of the hippest hang-outs in Otres. Rooms are simple but the balcony upstairs encourages serious sloth-time and the bar-restaurant downstairs has a great vibe thanks to chilled-out tunes and friendly staff.

Even if you're not staying, stop in for a drink or to sample their Aussie meat pies ($4.50 to $7) or quesadillas ($3 to $4.50).

### Otres Orchid
BUNGALOW $

(Map p194; ☏034-633 8484; www.otresorchid. com; Otres 1; bungalow with fan/air-con US$20/35; ❄🛜) Cracking value, the Orchid offers simple bungalows at sensible prices in a garden setting a hop-skip-jump to the beach. The fan-only bungalows have more character than the air-con options and come with hammock-strung balconies.

### SeaGarden
BUNGALOW $

(Map p194; ☏096 253 8131; www.seagarden otres.com; Otres 1; dm US$5, r US$15-20; 🛜) Look no further for a cheap bungalow right on the sand. SeaGarden offers basic beach huts, and rooms in a stilted building, both on the beach. The new owner keeps everything neat as a pin and was building a spacious dorm when we last pulled into town.

### Castaways
BUNGALOW $

(Map p194; ☏012 998492; Otres 2; bungalow US$15-25) Castaways has just five wood-floored bungalows, brightened by wall murals, on the sand. More expensive options come with en suite. This place's quiet location suits those looking for serious downtime.

### Hacienda
HOSTEL $

(Map p194; ☏070 814643; Otres Village; dm US$4, r US$8-15; 🛜) Hacienda is a laid-back backpacker zone on Otres' estuary with cheap dorm beds and basic bungalows. There's also a popular bar-restaurant that often breaks into a party.

### ★Mushroom Point
BUNGALOW $$

(Map p194; ☏078 509079; www.mushroompoint. com; Otres 1; dm US$8, bungalow US$25-30; 🛜) The open-air dorm in the shape of a mushroom wins the award for most creative in Cambodia. Even those averse to communal living will be content in their mosquito-net-draped pods, good for two. Quirky 'shroom-shaped bungalows are beautifully conceived with hammocks outside for lounging. Their beach annex has more bungalows and a bar.

### Elephant Garden
RESORT $$

(Map p194; ☏034-659 0222; www.elephant-garden.com; Otres 2; bungalow US$35-50, f US$60; ❄🛜) This intimate resort is on a quiet stretch of sand and has shaded terraces strewn with cushions. Bed down in either stilted Khmer houses or opt for the tidy palm-thatched bungalows. The split-level family suite is perfect for travellers with little ones in tow.

### Otres Lodge
BUNGALOW $$

(Map p194; ☑070 857391; www.otreslodge.com; Otres 1; bungalow with fan/air-con US$45/55; ✳🛜🏊) Otres Lodge has roomy thatch-roofed, wooden bungalows amid a flower-filled garden. Out the front the small pool is on hand if you're too lazy to make it across the road to the beach. The restaurant is renowned for its burgers.

### Papa Pippo
BUNGALOW $$

(Map p194; ☑010 359725; www.papapippo.com; Otres 1; bungalow US$30-35) Sandy-toed bliss is at hand with these cosy, and rather classy, beachfront bungalows. Glass doors make the most of the sea views while the interiors, with painted-wood walls and tiled floors, add a touch of individual style.

### Mama Clare's
BUNGALOW $$

(Map p194; ☑097 690 2914; www.mamaclares.com; Otres Village; bungalow US$30-35; 🛜) Peaceful downtime is on the cards at this homely place on Otres' riverbank. The wood-and-thatch stilted bungalows are a rustic retreat from the world and vegetarian dinners (US$4 to $5) are eaten communally.

### Ren
RESORT $$$

(Map p194; ☑078 539999; www.ren-resort.com; Otres 2; r incl breakfast US$95-107; ➿✳🛜🏊) Ren has gone for super-slick minimalism with a nod to mid-century modern in its 24 stylish rooms set around an inviting pool and surrounded by lush foliage. Three rooms have rather sumptuous outdoor bathrooms, while others have balconies that flow right into the pool – great for those who fancy a swim as soon as they wake up.

### Secret Garden
RESORT $$$

(Map p194; ☑097 649 5131; www.secretgarden otres.com; Otres 2; bungalow incl breakfast from US$119; ✳🛜🏊) Otres' first upmarket boutique resort is still one of its best. Cute bungalows, set amid a manicured garden with swimming pool, have bright and breezy decor, while sun-lounging heaven is available at the beachside bar-restaurant across the road.

### Tamu
BOUTIQUE HOTEL $$$

(Map p194; ☑088 901 7451; www.tamucambodia.com; Otres 2; r incl breakfast US$110-170; ✳🛜🏊) This ultra-contemporary boutique hotel offers a range of simple yet chic rooms set around a courtyard pool. Bag a pool-front room for a Balinese-style alfresco bathroom. There's also a hip beachside restaurant open to all.

## THE LAST BATTLE OF THE VIETNAM WAR

The final bloody confrontation of the Vietnam or Indochina War took place off the coast of Sihanoukville.

On 12 May 1975, two weeks after the fall of Saigon, Khmer Rouge forces used captured US-made Swift boats to seize an American merchant ship, the SS *Mayagüez* (named after a city in Puerto Rico), while it was on a routine voyage from Hong Kong to Thailand. The vessel was anchored 50km southwest of Sihanoukville off Koh Tang – now a popular scuba-diving destination – while the 39 crew members were taken to Sihanoukville.

Determined to show resolve in the face of this 'act of piracy', President Gerald Ford ordered that the ship and its crew be freed. Naval planes from the US aircraft carrier *Coral Sea* bombed Sihanoukville's oil refinery and the Ream airbase, and Marines prepared for their first hostile boarding of a ship at sea since 1826.

On 15 May, Marines stormed aboard the *Mayagüez* like swashbuckling pirates but found it deserted. In parallel, airborne Marine units landed on Koh Tang. Thought to be lightly defended, the island turned out to have been fortified in anticipation of a Vietnamese attack (Vietnam also claimed the island). In the course of the assault, most of the US helicopters were destroyed or damaged and 14 Americans were killed.

Unbeknown to the Americans, early on 15 May the Khmer Rouge had placed the crew of the *Mayagüez* aboard a Thai fishing boat and set it adrift – but the men weren't discovered by US ships until after the assault on Koh Tang had begun. In the chaotic withdrawal from the island, three Marines were accidentally left behind and, it is believed, later executed by the Khmer Rouge.

The Vietnam War Memorial in Washington DC lists American war dead chronologically, which is why the names of the Marines who perished in the '*Mayagüez* Incident' appear at the bottom of the very last panel.

SOUTH COAST SIHANOUKVILLE

# Otres Beach

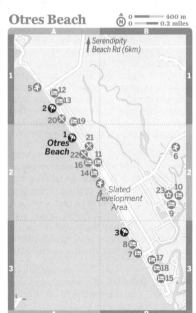

## Eating

If you've had your fill of noodles for a while, Sihanoukville's globetrotting mash-up menus of quesadillas, burgers, kebabs, and plenty of pizza and pasta should hit the right spot. The Serendipity area has the most dining choice, but the gritty commercial centre also holds a few culinary surprises. Otres is your best bet for atmospheric meals on the beach.

### Serendipity & Occheuteal

For ambience, check out the over-the-water resort restaurants at Serendipity Beach. Two blocks inland, Tola St is developing into a restaurant zone, with a plethora of barbecue places in the evening.

★**Nyam**                                CAMBODIAN $
(Map p190; www.nyamsihanoukville.com; 23 Tola St; mains US$2-4.25; ⊙ 5-10pm; 🛜) Translating as 'Eat' in Khmer, this is a great spot for a contemporary Cambodian dinner experience. All the favourites are here such as *amok* (baked fish), but there are also some healthy seafood offerings reflecting its coastal location.

**Cafe Mango**                              ITALIAN $
(Map p190; Serendipity St; mains US$3-6; ⊙ 7am-10pm; 🛜) A cracking little Italian cafe turning out wood-fired pizzas, homemade pasta and delicate gnocchi. Dine at lunchtime or before 6.30pm for a main course accompanied by garlic bread or bruschetta and a drink for just US$5.

**Leisure Cafe**                              CAFE $
(Map p190; 23 Tola St; mains US$1.50-3.50; ⊙ 7am-9pm; 🛜) This contemporary cafe is located in the grounds of the Golden Sands Hotel. With turbo air-con, this is a great place to hide from the heat and sample its coffee creations and the New Zealand Natural ice cream.

★**Sandan**                              CAMBODIAN $$
(Map p190; 2 Thnou St; mains US$4-10; ⊙ 7am-9pm Mon-Sat; 🛜♿) 🌱 Loosely modelled on the beloved Phnom Penh restaurant Romdeng (p64), this superb restaurant is an extension of the vocational-training programs for at-risk Cambodians run by local NGO

M'lop Tapang. The menu features creative Cambodian cuisine targeted at a slightly upmarket clientele. There's a kids' play area and occasional cultural shows.

### Invito
ASIAN $$

(Map p190; Serendipity Beach Rd; mains US$4.50-10.50; ☺10am-10pm; 🐾) The Thai and Khmer dishes coming out of the kitchen here are among Serendipity Beach Rd's best. Splash out on the *nium tre* salmon (salmon in a mango sauce) or tuck into their Panang curry or fish *amok*. There's also a range of pasta and meaty options such as rib-eye steak if you're not after Asian flavours.

### So
INTERNATIONAL $$

(Map p190; Serendipity Beach Rd; mains US$4-10; ☺8am-10pm; 🐾) So is renowned for serving up some of Serendipity's tastiest cuisine. Come for dinner when the candles come out, the menu changes and the top chef is in action. Specialities include wasabi prawns and baked scallops in wine sauce. Early diners benefit from two courses for US$5 between 5pm and 6.30pm.

### Marco Polo
ITALIAN $$

(Map p190; Thnou St; mains US$3-8; ☺11am-10pm; 🐾) Some of the best Italian food around is created by the Italian owner and chef of Marco Polo. The pasta dishes are perfectly *al dente* and the thin-crust pizzas emerging from the wood-fired oven are divine.

### Taj Mahal
INDIAN $$

(Map p190; 23 Mithana St; curries US$3-10; ☺7am-9pm; 🐾) Curry-craving British expats rave about the food here. Selecting bespoke dishes can add up to an expensive spread, making the *thalis* (set meals, US$4 to $7) a particularly good deal.

### Olive & Olive
MEDITERRANEAN $$

(Map p190; 🖉086 283151; Serendipity Beach Rd; mains US$7-13; ☺7am-10pm) A pinch of Greek cuisine, a touch of Turkish influence and swags of Italian favourites are on the menu here. There's plenty of pasta, seafood and steaks, but most people order the wood-fired pizzas, which are ridiculously huge.

### Mick & Craig's
INTERNATIONAL $$

(Map p190; www.mickandcraigs.com; Serendipity Beach Rd; mains US$4-7; ☺7am-10pm; 🐾) This long-running guesthouse and restaurant serves up classic comfort food from around the globe. Indian meals are just US$6, while Thursday and Friday barbecue nights include a rack of ribs.

## 🍽 City Centre & Around

For Sihanoukville's cheapest dining, head to the food stalls in and around **Psar Leu** (Map p187; 7 Makara St; ☺7am-9pm). The vendors across the street, next to the Kampot taxis, are open 24 hours.

### Dao of Life
VEGAN $

(Map p185; Ekareach St; mains US$3.50-6; ☺noon-9pm Tue-Sun; 🐾🖉) 🍃 This rooftop cafe, full of hammocks and recycled furniture, dishes up creative and tasty vegan meals. Its vegie burger (made from sweet potato and black beans) is particularly good, or tuck into healthy options such as spiralised zucchini linguine. It has movie nights every Wednesday and regularly host social projects with local community involvement.

### Starfish Bakery & Café
CAFE $

(Map p187; www.starfishcambodia.org; off 7 Makara St; sandwiches US$2.50-4.50; ☺7am-6pm; 🐾🖉) 🍃 This relaxing, NGO-run garden cafe specialises in filling Western breakfasts, cakes and tarts, and healthy, innovative sandwiches heavy on Mexican and Middle Eastern flavours. Sitting down for coffee here on the shady terrace is a peaceful reprieve from Sihanoukville's hustle. Income goes to sustainable development projects.

### Espresso Kampuchea
CAFE $

(Map p187; Boray Kamakor St; mains US$2-4; ☺8am-5pm) Espresso Kampuchea is hidden away on a nondescript side street in Sihanoukville centre but serious caffeine aficionados should definitely make the trip here. Owner Sophal personally sources her coffee from Laos and serves up excellent double-shot cappuccinos and espresso. There's a small menu of baguettes and fried noodles.

### Cabbage Farm Restaurant
CAMBODIAN $

(Map p187; small/large mains 8000r/15,000r; ☺11am-10pm) Known to locals as Chom Ka Spey, this restaurant gets rave reviews for its seafood and spicy seasonings. An authentic Khmer dining experience. A sign in English on Sereypheap St points the way.

### Gelato Italiano
ICE CREAM $

(Map p187; St 108; gelato per scoop US$1; ☺8am-9pm; 🐾) Run by students from Don Bosco Hotel School (p192), this cafe specialises in *gelatos* (Italian ices) in a dizzying array of flavours, and also serves various coffee drinks and light meals in a bright, airy space.

**Samudera Supermarket**     SUPERMARKET **$**
(Map p187; 64 7 Makara St; ⊙6am-10pm) Good selection of fruit, vegies and imported food brands, including European cheeses and wine.

★**Chez Claude**     FRENCH **$$**
(Map p185; www.claudecambodge.com; above 2 Thnou St; mains US$5-15; ⊙7am-11pm; 🕾) Dou Dou and Claude are your hosts at this all-wood lookout perched high above Sokha Beach with panoramic views and outstanding French, Vietnamese and Cambodian cuisine, especially seafood. Time your visit for sunset to see Sihanoukville's twinkling lights turn on. Access is via an innovative tractor-pulled cable car.

**Holy Cow**     INTERNATIONAL **$$**
(Map p187; 83 Ekareach St; mains US$2.50-7; ⊙8.30am-11pm; 🕾🍴) As well as solid comfort food such as pasta, burgers and shepherd's pie, this funky cafe-restaurant dishes up bagels with cream cheese, sandwiches on homemade bread and a good selection of vegie options. The menu includes two vegan desserts, both involving chocolate.

## 🍴 Otres Beach

**Mom's Kitchen**     CAMBODIAN **$**
(Map p194; Otres 1; mains US$1.50-2.50; ⊙8am-7pm) Plonk yourself down on a streetside seat here and dig into cheap and cheerful rice and noodle dishes cooked by the ladies in the little store behind. Nothing fancy – just fresh and tasty Khmer home cooking.

★**Chez Paou**     INTERNATIONAL **$$**
(Map p194; Otres 1; mains US$5-8, khmer specials US$15-22; ⊙7am-10pm; 🕾) This is fine dining Otres style – right on the beach. The menu contains a good selection of steaks, pasta and burgers, but it's the Khmer specials (order in advance) of sting ray cooked on embers with fresh Kampot pepper, prawns flambéed in pastis, and crabs in two different ways that makes this place really stand out.

**Mushroom Point**     INTERNATIONAL **$$**
(Map p194; Otres 1; mains $3.50-12; ⊙8am-10pm) Mushroom Point's breakfasts are a winner featuring homemade baguettes with mango jam and homemade muesli. Later in the day their pizzas (with original topping combinations) and barbecued seafood plates get plaudits from travellers. There's an excellent wine list to boot.

**Papa Pippo**     ITALIAN **$$**
(Map p194; www.papapippo.com; Otres 1; mains US$5-7; ⊙9am-9.30pm; 🕾) Located on the beachfront Papa Pippo brings Italian flair to Otres. Their homemade pasta is some of the best on the coast and there are plenty of regional specialities from Emelia-Romagna (where the owners hail from) on the menu.

**Shin**     JAPANESE **$$**
(Map p194; Otres 1; mains US$6-9; ⊙9am-4am) On the beachfront, Shin is all about sand-between-your-toes dining while sipping a cocktail and munching on freshly prepared sushi. Later in the evening a bar atmosphere takes over – if you're up for a late-night drink in Otres, this is the place to be.

## 🍷 Drinking & Nightlife

There's no shortage of venues in which to quaff locally brewed Angkor Beer, available on draught for as little as US$0.50. Many of the hostels on Serendipity Beach Rd have lively bars, including Monkey Republic (p189) (happy hour 6pm to 9pm), Big Easy (p189) (sport and live music) and Utopia (Map p190; cnr Serendipity Beach Rd & Mithona St; ⊙24hr), with regular US$0.25 beer promotions: yes, that does equal 20 beers for US$5.

Occheuteal Beach is lined with beach-shack bars but the scene here seems to attract a fair number of sex-tourists sofemale travellers may find this area too sleazy. Hit the bar-restaurant of Above Us Only Sky (p191) and the other Serendipity Beach resorts for a more laid-back scene. Off the beach, the bars at Coolabah Resort (p189) and Chochi Garden (p189) both have a friendly vibe.

The bar courts of Golden Lions Plaza, at the top of Serendipity Beach Rd, are mostly heavy on hostesses and light on atmosphere. A few long-standing regular bars remain amid the hostess bars of Victory Hill, but the overall impression is Sinville rather than the beach vibe of Serendipity. For relaxed sunset drinks with plenty of sand-between-the-toes appeal, Otres Beach can't be beaten.

**La Rhumerie**     BAR
(Map p190; Serendipity Beach Rd; ⊙6pm-2am) Pull up a bar stool at La Rhumerie for salsa music and yummy rum infused with ingredients such as Kampot pepper and ginger. We're not big fans of their weird blue back-lighting, but we're more than a tad partial to the coffee-infused rum. Not a rum fan? They whip up mean cocktails as well.

**Maybe Later** BAR

(Map p190; Serendipity Beach Rd; ⏰5pm-2am) This popular little Mexican taqueria that doubles as a late-night bar serves top margheritas and some refined tequilas for those who prefer sips to shots. It's a civilised escape from the beachside party scene.

**Led Zephyr** BAR

(Map p190; Serendipity Beach Rd; ⏰7am-midnight) Sihanoukville's premier live-music venue, the house band (and friends from time to time) are rockin' here most nights. Covers include many of the big anthems from the '60s to '80s, with a bit of Chili Peppers thrown in for good measure.

**Sessions** BAR

(Map p190; Occheuteal Beach; ⏰5pm-1am) The music selection makes Sessions the top sundowner bar on Occheuteal Beach. The crowd of expats and backpackers assembled usually lingers well into the evening before the hard-core partiers move on to the late-night venues.

**JJ's Playground** BAR

(Map p190; Occheuteal Beach; ⏰6pm-6am) For a while now JJ's has been the go-to spot for those seeking late-night debauchery. The scene here is pretty much summed up by their tag line 'let's get wasted'. Expect shots, loud techno, a fire show or two, and a lot of chaos. And don't say we didn't warn you about the toilets.

**Reggae Bar** BAR

(Map p190; Thnou St; ⏰5pm-1am) It has more Marley on the walls than we've seen in quite some time (owner Dell is an avid collector) and the clientele diligently pay homage in the most appropriate way available.

## ☆ Entertainment

**Otres Market** LIVE MUSIC

(Map p194; www.otresmarket.com; Otres Village; ⏰noon-9pm Sat Nov-Apr) Located on Otres Village's estuary, this wooden shack, known as 'the barn', is a live-music venue every Saturday during high season. Vendors have food and craft stalls while DJ's and bands take to the stage from around 4pm. Look out for their special events – in the past they've hosted top local bands such as Cambodian Space Project.

**Top Cat Cinema** CINEMA

(Map p190; ☎012 790630; Serendipity Beach Rd; tickets US$3.50; ⏰11am-3am) Shows films on an 8m high-definition screen (for groups of

at least six) or on large flat-screen TVs (for smaller groups). Has cosy satellite chairs and powerful air-con.

**Galaxy Cinema** CINEMA

(Map p190; ☎017 721677; Mithona St; tickets US$3; ⏰11am-1pm) Regular screenings at 7pm or you can rent it out for private viewings.

## 🛍 Shopping

Funky restaurant Holy Cow (opposite) sells some fashionable clothing upstairs.

**Tapang** HANDICRAFTS

(Map p190; www.mloptapang.org; Serendipity Beach Rd; ⏰10am-8pm) 🖉 Run by a local NGO that works with at-risk children, this shop sells good-quality bags, scarves and T-shirts made by street kids (and their families) so that they can attend school instead of peddling on the beach.

**Starfish** HANDICRAFTS

(Map p187; www.starfishcambodia.org; off 7 Makara St; ⏰7am-6pm) 🖉 On the premises of the bakery of the same name, the silks and other gifts sold here support a sustainable livelihood for poor local families.

**Q&A** BOOKS

(Map p190; Mithona St; ⏰7.30am-7.30pm) An inviting secondhand bookshop behind Occheuteal Beach with 8000 titles in more than 20 languages, plus a small cafe.

**Mr Heinz** BOOKS

(Map p187; 219 Ekareach St; ⏰9am-6pm) Stocks thousands of books in 57 varieties... well not quite, but at least 10 languages.

## ℹ Information

Most guesthouses and hotels offer free wi-fi, as do the majority of cafes, restaurants and bars. There are also a few shops on Serendipity Beach Rd and on Ekareach St that have public internet terminals.

Sihanoukville's banks – all with ATMs – are in the city centre along Ekareach St. There are plentiful standalone ATMs along Serendipity Beach Rd and a couple on Otres 1 at Otres Beach.

**Ana Travel** (Map p190; ☎034-933929; Serendipity Beach Rd; ⏰8am-10pm) Handles Cambodia visa extensions and arranges Vietnam visas the same day.

**ANZ Royal Bank** (Map p187; 215 Ekareach St; ⏰8am-3.30pm Mon-Fri, to 11.30am Sat, ATM 24hr)

**Canadia Bank** (Map p187; 197 Ekareach St; ⏰8am-3.30pm Mon-Fri, to 11.30am Sat, ATM 24hr)

**CT Clinic** (Map p187; ☎ 081 886666, 034-936666; 47 Boray Kamakor St; ☺ emergencies 24hr) The best medical clinic in town. Can administer rabies shots, and antivenin in the event of a snake bite.

**Post Office** (Map p187; 19 7 Makara St; ☺ 7am-5pm)

**Tourist Information Centre** (Map p190; 14 Mithona St; ☺ 9am-11.30am & 2-5pm Mon-Sat) Don't expect much out of Sihanoukville's tourist information centres. The best is this one just off Occheuteal Beach. It has brochures and can help you with hotel reservations.

### DANGERS & ANNOYANCES

Theft is a problem on the beaches (especially Occheuteal Beach) so leave valuables in your room. It's often children who do the deed, sometimes in conjunction with adults. Arriving in a team, one or more will distract you while another lifts whatever valuables are lying on your towel. Or they'll strike when you're out swimming.

You'll probably tire of the steady stream of beggars, many of them children or amputees, on Occheuteal Beach. NGO M'lop Tapang, which exists to improve the welfare of street kids, advises you never give money or food to children begging.

As in Phnom Penh, drive-by bag snatchings occasionally happen and are especially dangerous when you're riding a *moto*. Hold your shoulder bags tightly in front of you, especially at night. The road between Otres and Sihanoukville is considered especially risky after dark, so arrange a *remork* or *moto* via your guesthouse if staying in this area, and not just a random stranger in town.

At night, travellers (especially women) should avoid walking alone along dark, isolated beaches and roads.

The currents off Occheuteal can be deceptively strong, especially during the wet season.

## ❶ Getting There & Away

National Highway 4 (NH4), which links Sihanoukville to Phnom Penh (230km), is in excellent condition, but because of heavy truck traffic and the prevalence of high-speed overtaking on blind corners, this is one of Cambodia's most dangerous highways; it's doubly dicey around dusk and at night.

NH3 to Kampot (105km) and NH48 to Koh Kong (220km) and the Thailand border (230km) are also in good shape.

### AIR

Sihanoukville International Airport has one daily direct flight to Phnom Penh and another to Siem Reap from US$115 one way. Both routes are operated by **Cambodia Angkor Airlines** (☎ 023 6660330; www.cambodiaangkorair.com).

The airport is 15km east of town, just off the NH4. A taxi to/from the airport costs about US$20. Figure on US$5 one way for a *moto*; US$10 for a *remork*.

### BOAT

Sihanoukville is the gateway to Cambodia's southern islands. Only Koh Rong and Koh Rong Sanloem have scheduled public ferry services. Transport to other islands is by day-trip boats or on private boats owned by the resorts.

## BUS SERVICES FROM SIHANOUKVILLE

| DESTINATION | DURATION (HR) | PRICE (US$) | COMPANIES | FREQUENCY |
| --- | --- | --- | --- | --- |
| Bangkok | 14 | 28 | Rith Mony, Virak Buntham (night) | 8.15am, 9.15am, 7pm |
| Battambang | 12 | 17 | Capitol Tour, Rith Mony, Virak Buntham (night) | 7 services 7am-2.15pm, 7pm |
| Kampot (minivan) | 2 | 5-6 | Champa Mekong Travel (book through Ana Travel), Kampot Tours & Travel | 7.30am, 11.30am, 1.30pm, 3.30pm |
| Kep (minivan) | 2¼ | 7-8 | Champa Mekong Travel (book through Ana Travel), Kampot Tours & Travel | 7.30am, 11.30am, 1.30pm, 3.30pm |
| Koh Kong | 4½ | 8 | Rith Mony, Virak Buntham | 6 services 7.45am-2.45pm |
| Phnom Penh | 4½ | 5-11 | Capitol Tour, Giant Ibis, GST, Phnom Penh Sorya, Rith Mony | regular 7am-2.30pm |
| Phnom Penh (minivan) | 4 | 10 | Virak Buntham | 6 services 7.45am-2.45pm |
| Siem Reap | 12 | 13-17 | GST, Rith Mony, Virak Buntham (night) | 6 services 7am-12.30pm, 8pm |

## ℹ SINS OF COMMISSION, SINS OF OMISSION

At Sihanoukville's bus station, only members of the official 'motodup association' are allowed to pick up arriving passengers (independent drivers sent to fetch someone must show their charge's name). As a result, you may be quoted inflated prices for onward local transport. Bargaining is usually futile – if you don't agree to the set price (usually 8000r to the beaches) no one else will take you. You can try walking out to the street, but there's not a whole lot of traffic in this part of town. You may also have trouble shaking the persistent driver the cartel has assigned you according to a rotation system. Confrontations between independents and cartel drivers sometimes develop. The situation with remorks – ideal for travel with a big pack – is similar. The set price for remorks to the Serendipity area is US$6.

Many guesthouses pay US$2 to moto drivers who bring them customers, but some places pay drivers far higher sums – US$4 or even US$5 – to send custom their way, so if you've just arrived, getting your moto guy to take you where you want may turn into a battle of wills. If your chosen hostelry is one that won't pay up, don't be surprised to hear that it's closed, has contaminated water or is 'full of prostitutes'.

Ferry companies tend to come and go. The two main companies (at the moment) servicing Koh Rong and Koh Rong Sanloem are **Speed Ferry Cambodia** (Map p190; www.speedferry cambodia.com; Koh Rong Dive Centre, Serendipity Beach Rd; return ticket US$26) and **TBC Speed Boat** (Map p190; ☑ 088 781 1711; www.tbckohrongspeedboat.com; Serendipity Beach Rd; return ticket US$20).

Speed Ferry Cambodia has sailings to Koh Rong Sanloem and Koh Rong at 8am and 3pm, and another departure only to Koh Rong at 11am. TBC Speed Boat leaves for Koh Rong Sanloem and Koh Rong at 10am, 1pm and 3.30pm.

Of the two companies, Speed Ferry Cambodia tends to be the more reliable but sailing schedules of both tend to change regularly. Ticket prices drop substantially from June to October.

Both services leave from Serendipity Beach Rd pier, although in adverse sea conditions departure is moved to the ferry dock at Sihanoukville Port (7km north of the Serendipity Beach area).

A cheaper option is the cargo 'slow boat' ferry that usually chugs from the ferry dock at Sihanoukville Port to Koh Rong Sanloem and Koh Rong twice daily (8am and 2pm, return US$10, three hours). Note that safety isn't a top priority – to put it mildly – on this boat. Slow boat tickets can be purchased from most travel agencies around Serendipity Beach Rd.

### BUS

All of the major bus companies have frequent connections to Phnom Penh from early morning until at least 2pm. Capital Tour and Rith Mony are the cheapest. Giant Ibis runs a 'luxury' service, complete with hostess and wi-fi, at 7.30am, 9.30am and 1.30pm.

Bookings made through hotels and travel agencies incur a commission. Most travel agents only work with two or three bus companies, so ask around if you need to leave at a different time than what's being offered.

Minivans to Kampot and Kep can be booked through Ana Travel (p197).

Most bus departures leave from the company terminals on Ekareach St and stop at the **bus station** (Map p185; Mittapheap Kampuchea Soviet St) on the way out of town. Most bus companies will include free pick up from the Serendipity and central Sihanoukville area.

**Capitol Tour** (Map p187; ☑ 034-934042; 169 Ekareach St)

**Giant Ibis** (Map p190; ☑ 089 999818; www.giantibis.com; Thnou St)

**GST** (Map p187; ☑ 015 995950; Ekareach St)

**Phnom Penh Sorya** (Map p187; ☑ 034-933888; 236 Ekareach St)

**Rith Mony** (Map p187; ☑ 093 465858; Ekareach St)

**Virak Buntham** (Map p187; ☑ 016 754358; Ekareach St)

#### SHARE TAXI

Cramped share taxis (US$6 per person or US$45 per car) and minibuses (15,000r) to Phnom Penh depart from the bus station until about 8pm. Avoid the minibuses if you value things like comfort and your life. Hotels can arrange taxis to Phnom Penh for US$50 to US$60 (about four hours). Share taxis to Kampot (US$5, 1½ hours) leave mornings only from a **taxi park** (Map p187; 7 Makara St ) opposite Psar Leu. This taxi park and the bus station are good places to look for share taxis to Koh Kong or the Thai border. If nobody's sharing, expect to pay US$45 to US$60 to the Thai border.

## ℹ Getting Around

### TO/FROM THE BUS STATION

Arriving in Sihanoukville, buses stop at the bus station then some, if you're lucky, continue to their central terminals. Prices to the Serendipity Beach area from the station are fixed at a pricey

US$2 for a *moto* and US$6 for a *remork*, so continue to the centre if possible and get a cheaper, shorter *remork* ride from there.

### BICYCLE

Bicycles can be hired from many guesthouses for about US$2 a day.

### MOTO & REMORK

Sihanoukville's *moto* drivers are notorious for aggressively hassling passers-by and, more than anywhere else in Cambodia, shamelessly trying to overcharge, so haggle hard (with a smile) over the price before setting out.

A *moto* should cost about US$1 from the centre to Serendipity, Occheuteal and Victory Beaches, and Victory Hill; *remorks* around US$2. *Remorks* from Serendipity to Victory Hill/Beach should cost US$3, but drivers ask US$5 for this trip.

Motorbikes can be rented from many guesthouses for US$5 to US$7 a day. The police sometimes 'crack down' on foreign drivers. Common violations: no driver's licence, no helmet, no wing mirrors and, everybody's favourite, driving with the lights on during the day. Hiring a *moto* (including the driver) for the day costs US$10 plus petrol; a *remork* is about US$20 a day.

# Ream National Park

Just 15km east of Sihanoukville, Ream National Park (ឧទ្យានជាតិរាម) offers trekking opportunities in primary forest, invigorating boat trips through coastal mangroves and long stretches of unspoilt beach. This is an easy escape for those looking to flee the crowds of Sihanoukville. The park is home to breeding populations of several regionally and globally endangered birds of prey, including the Brahminy kite, grey-headed fish eagle and white-bellied sea eagle: look for them soaring over Prek Toeuk Sap Estuary. Endangered birds that feed on the mudflats include the lesser adjutant, milky stork and painted stork.

Despite its protected status, Ream is endangered by planned tourism development, especially along its coastline. By visiting, you can demonstrate that the park, in its natural state, is not only priceless to humanity but also a valuable economic resource. Major roads have been bulldozed through the heart of the park to access the beaches and a main road will eventually connect NH4 with Otres Beach directly via this route.

## ☉ Sights & Activities

Hiking and boating trips through Ream National Park can either be booked beforehand with a tour operator in Sihanoukville

or arranged at the Ream National Park Headquarters (☏016 767686, 012 875096; NH4; ⏰7am-5pm) itself, opposite Sihanoukville Airport entrance. When booking directly with the park HQ, it's best (but not obligatory) to phone ahead. The income generated goes to help protect the park.

To get to some deserted beaches on your own, drive south from the park HQ and the airport for about 9km along a sealed road until you get to Ream Naval Base. Jog left around the base and follow the dirt roads to a series of long white beaches lined with casuarina trees. Road access to Koh Sampoach Beach is possible by taking an immediate left-hand turn off the Ream National Park road when leaving NH4. If you pass the airport entrance, you've gone too far. Follow this major road for about 12km and you will eventually arrive at a small beachside restaurant on Koh Sampoach.

Ream National Park's territory includes two islands with some fine snorkelling, Koh Thmei (p202) and – just off Vietnam's Phu Quoc Island – Koh Seh, which is best accessed from Koh Thmei.

### Boat Trips

Popular ranger-led boat trips head through the mangrove channels of the Prek Toeuk Sap Estuary. These leave from the Prek Toeuk Sap ranger station, which is located about 3km east of Ream National Park Headquarters next to a major bridge on NH4 – the rangers at HQ will help you get there and arrange for a boat to be waiting.

From the Prek Toeuk Sap ranger station it's a one-hour boat ride (US$35 return for one to three persons) to the fishing village of Ta Ben. Full-day trips (US$50 per group) continue another hour east to the village of Andoung Toeuk. From here a path leads 25 minutes through the jungle to the park's finest beach, Koh Sampoach Beach, which is also nicknamed the Chinese beach as Chinese developers have the concession for this area.

### Jungle Walks

Jungle walks led by rangers are easy to arrange, but hiking unaccompanied is not allowed. Two-hour walks in the forest behind the Ream National Park Headquarters cost US$6 per person. Four- to six-hour treks going further into the park's mountainous interior cost US$10 per person.

## ❶ Getting There & Around

Sihanoukville travel agencies offer day trips to Ream National Park for about US$20, including a boat ride, a jungle walk and lunch.

Ream National Park is a breeze to get to – just follow NH4 east from Sihanoukville to the airport turnoff, which is 15km from the Cambrew brewery at the junction of NH4 and Wat Leu Rd. Go right and drive 500m to the park headquarters.

A return trip from Sihanoukville by *moto* should cost US$7 to US$15; a *remork* US$15 to US$20. The price depends on how well the driver speaks English and how long you stay.

## Kbal Chhay Cascades

Thanks to their appearance in *Pos Keng Kong* (*The Giant Snake*; 2000), one of the most successful Cambodian films of the post-civil war era, these cascades (ទឹកធ្លាក់ក្បាលឆាយ; admission US$1, picnicking platforms per day 5000r) on the Prek Toeuk Sap River draw huge numbers of domestic tourists.

From the parking area, a rough log tollbridge (locals 300r, tourists 500r) leads to several miniature sandy coves and some perilous rapids. The best spot for a safe, refreshing dip (for children as well as adults) is across another bridge, on the far bank of a cool, crystal-clear tributary of the brown-tinted main river. Not much water flows here in the dry season.

To get here from Sihanoukville, head east along NH4 for 5.5km from the Cambrew junction then, at the sign, head north along a wide dirt road for 8km. By *moto/remork* a return trip should cost US$7/15.

## THE SOUTHERN ISLANDS

For many a traveller Cambodia's southern islands are the tropical Shangri-La they've been seeking – as yet untouched by the mega-resorts that have sprouted like mushrooms across Thailand's cachet of islands. Many of the islands have been tagged for major development by well-connected foreign investors but, thanks to the global recession, the big boys have been slow to press go, paving the way for DIY development to move in with rustic bungalow resorts targeting independent travellers.

That's not to say that all small-scale development is fine. Koh Rong, in particular, has changed dramatically in the past couple of years due to unchecked construction in the Koh Tuch area. But for the most part, Cambodia's islands are still paradise the way you imagined it: endless crescents of powdered, sugary-soft sand, hammocks swaying in the breeze, photogenic fishing villages on stilts,

technicolour sunsets and the patter of raindrops on thatch as you slumber. It seems too good to last, so enjoy it while it does.

### ℹ️ Getting There & Away

The logical jumping-off point for any of the main habitable islands between the Koh Kong Conservation Corridor and Ream National Park is Sihanoukville.

Scheduled boat services link Sihanoukville with Koh Rong and Koh Rong Sanloem while other islands, such as Koh Ta Kiev, can be reached by private boats, usually owned by the resort you're visiting.

The Koh Sdach Archipelago is most easily accessed from the four-lane highway that cuts through Botum Sakor National Park.

Koh Kong is the base for visiting Cambodia's largest island, Koh Kong Island.

## Koh Ta Kiev    កោះតាកៀវ

If your beach break perfection is about logging off and slothing out, this little island off Ream National Park ticks all the right boxes. Despite the fact that the island has been leased to French and Chinese property companies – and a proper road has recently been sliced through the jungle interior signalling major development may not be far off – for the moment Koh Ta Kiev has a handful of budget-friendly, basic digs with serious chill-out factor.

Most of the beach bungalow accommodation is along Long Beach, a white-sand beach on the west side. Various tracks branch off from here through the forest for those who want to explore, including one to an even more secluded beach on the south coast. Unfortunately rubbish regularly washes up on the island, so don't expect pristine swaths of sand.

Koh Ta Kiev, along with Koh Russei and smaller uninhabited islands in the area, appears on most island-hopping itineraries out of Sihanoukville. Day trips run from US$12 to US$15 depending on whether you launch from Otres Beach or Serendipity Beach.

## 🛏 Sleeping

There's no wi-fi at any of Koh Ta Kiev's accommodation, electricity is limited (bring a torch/flashlight) and most places only have rudimentary shared bathrooms (bucket showers and squat toilets).

**Ten103 Treehouse Bay**  BUNGALOW $

(☑097 943 7587; www.ten103cambodia.com; Koh Ta Kiev; hammock/dm US$5/7, hut without bathroom US$20-25) Unplug, unwind, de-stress – Ten103 is a beachfront backpacker bolt hole that dishes up simple beach living the way it used to be. Stilted open-air 'treehouse' huts have sea views, while the open-air dorm and palm-thatch hammock shelters provide even more basic back-to-nature options. Book transport on their boat (US$13 return) from Otres one day in advance.

**The Last Point**  BUNGALOW $

(☑088 502 6930; www.lastpointisland.com; Koh Ta Kiev; dm/tent US$4/6, bungalows US$15-20) The Last Point sits in splendid isolation on a sandy stretch of Koh Ta Kiev's south coast, a 40-minute walk from the island's other accommodation options. There's a variety of small, sweet palm-thatch bungalows to play out Robinson Crusoe dreams, as well as a breezy open-air dorm just steps from the sand.

# Koh Russei  កោះឫស្សី

Less than an hour by boat from Sihanoukville, tiny Koh Russei (Bamboo Island) was cleared of most resorts in preparation for a high-end development – a five-star Alila Hotels (www.alilahotels.com) resort – that is still in the construction phase.

Most boat day trips from Sihanoukville call in at Koh Russei as part of their itinerary.

# Koh Thmei  កោះថ្មី

The large island of Koh Thmei is part of Ream National Park. There's only one resort on the island, German-managed **Koh Thmei**

**Resort** (☑097 737 0400; www.koh-thmei-resort. com; bungalows US$35, f US$60) 🍃. It's a real gem with super-simple bungalows, which use solar-panels and biofuel for electricity, that are just right for the setting. The resort sits on a great beach, and you can easily walk to several more, plus go sea-kayaking or snorkelling (visibility varies). Khmer meals are tasty and cost US$6.

Getting here requires private transport to the mainland fishing village of Koh Kchhang; turn off the NH4 in the town of Bat Kokir, about 12km east of Sihanoukville airport. From Koh Kchhang the resort is a 1¼ hour boat ride (six-passenger boat US$15). Koh Thmei Resort can organise pick-ups from Sihanoukville, as well as the boat ride.

# Koh Rong  កោះរ៉ុង

If you're here to party, you're in the right place. A few years back, Koh Rong was little more than a jungle-clad wilderness rimmed by swaths of sugary-white sand, with a few beach-hut resorts speckling the shore around tiny Koh Tuch village. Today the Koh Tuch village street-strip that leads out from the pier is a bottleneck of back-to-back backpacker crash pads, restaurants, and hole-in-the-wall bars blasting competing music. Look, you'll either love it or hate it, but for young travellers who descend off the ferry in droves, Koh Rong (particularly Koh Tuch beach) is a vital stop on any Southeast Asia party itinerary.

It's still possible to escape the mayhem though. The further you walk away from the village, the more sedate it gets. The evening frog chorus overpowers the drifting bass from the late-night raves, phosphorescence shimmers in the sea and the island's natural charms of head-turning beaches, backed by lush forest interior, are clear to see.

Koh Rong's full-tilt surge into tourism is not without problems that threaten the pristine environment that attracted travellers here in the first place. Many hastily knocked-up hostels and bars don't have proper septic systems, with waste running directly into the sea, and the sand nearest the village can become strewn with rubbish. The threat of even bigger development also hangs over the island with a ring-road cutting through the interior and the initial planning stages of a big resort on beautiful Long Beach now materialising.

If you want to hang out with fellow travellers, hit an all-night rave (or three) and crash out on the sand during the day, Koh Rong's the spot. Those looking for a more relaxed vibe would be wise to pick a bungalow-resort well away from Koh Tuch village or to look at Koh Rong Sanloem instead.

## 🏖 Beaches

### Koh Tuch Beach                                    BEACH
The wide sweep of Koh Tuch Beach extends for about 1km northeast from Koh Tuch village pier and gets lovelier the further out you go. Walk towards the headland (near Treehouse Bungalows) for white sand and a more mellow scene.

### Long Beach                                       BEACH
On the back (west) side of the island is Koh Rong's finest beach, a 7km stretch of drop-dead gorgeous white sand, dubbed Long Beach (also called Sok San Beach after the fishing village at its northern end). Longtail boats head here from Koh Tuch pier, depositing sun-seekers on the sand for a day of

sunbathing and swimming. There are simple resorts at the north and south end of this beach, with virtually nothing in between.

During our last visit, one of the basic resorts on the southern end was being knocked down to make way for a new hotel construction, so expect part of this sandy sweep to see more development in the future.

### 4km Beach                                        BEACH
Past the Koh Tuch Beach headland (near Treehouse Bungalows) is 4km Beach, where you can walk at least another hour along the sand and encounter little more than hermit crabs. A clutch of small bungalow resorts are moving in but it's still very peaceful. Further on, 4km Beach runs into Nature Beach; another worthy white-sand stretch.

## 🏃 Activities

Longtail **boat day trips** to Long Beach (with snorkelling, fishing and swimming

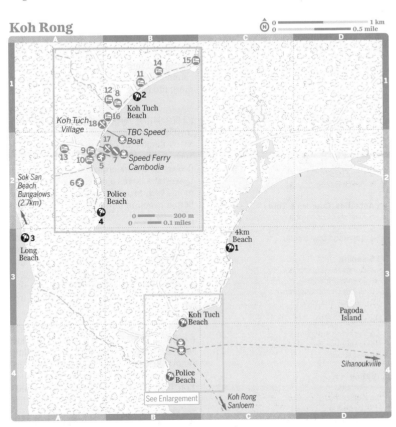

Koh Rong

SOUTH COAST KOH RONG

thrown in) are the main Koh Rong activity. Pretty much every place in Koh Tuch village organises them for about US$10 per person.

For an adventurous day out packed full of scenery, it's possible to organise a boat to Sangker village on the island's east coast, then hire a *moto* driver to whiz you around the island. Vagabonds can help organise this (about US$25 per person).

It's also viable to walk 1½ hours from the main beach to Long Beach via a rigorous jungle track, but be aware that it involves scrambling and is definitely not flip-flops territory.

There's good snorkelling around the island and resorts rent out gear for about US$5 per day. Several places hire sea kayaks for about US$5 per hour for a single kayak (US$8 for a tandem). From Koh Tuch Beach, it's a 30-minute paddle out to Pagoda Island, an idyllic islet topped by a wat, just offshore.

**High Point**

**Rope Adventure** ADVENTURE SPORTS
(☑ 016 839993; www.high-point.asia; Koh Tuch village; per person US$35; ☺ 9am-6pm) A collection of ziplines, swing bridges and walking cables take thrill-seekers on an adrenaline-packed, 400m-long journey through the forest canopy, not far from Koh Tuch. Your ticket gets you unlimited access to the course for the entire day. From April to October, tickets are US$10 cheaper.

**Koh Rong Dive Center** DIVING
(☑ 034-934744; http://kohrong-divecenter.com; Koh Rong Pier) Koh Rong's main dive centre organises trips in the waters around both Koh Rong and Koh Rong Sanloem.

**Friends of Koh Rong** VOLUNTEERING
(☑ 096 552 0416; www.friendsofkohrong.org; Local Pier, Koh Tuch village) 🖋 This grassroots NGO takes on qualified teachers (minimum two-month commitment) to volunteer with its education programs. They also have volunteer opportunities in community development and local health projects. They run regular beach clean-ups that travellers can get involved in.

## 🛏 Sleeping

During high season (particularly December and January) Koh Rong's accommodation fills up fast. This is compounded by the fact that some backpacker crash pads don't accept advance bookings. If you're nervous about turning up on the island without a bed, it's worthwhile to book a place for the first night and, once here, check out the rest of the hostel scene. Travellers with no bed for the night during busy periods usually end up renting a hammock. Nearly all accommodation has 24-hour electricity, wi-fi, mosquito nets and fans. Air-con is a rarity.

**Natural Lounge** GUESTHOUSE $
(☑ 069 541177; hengseksa@gmail.com; Koh Tuch; dm US$8, r with/without bathroom from US$30/20; ☎) A family-run calm oasis amid the Koh Tuch hubbub with small, spotless, wood-floored rooms set around a leafy courtyard. Downstairs there's a couple of bijou en suite rooms with two double beds that you could fit four people in if you don't mind a squeeze.

**Bongs** HOSTEL $
(☑ 093 924856; www.bongsguesthouse.com; Koh Tuch; r US$20; ☎) Bongs' well looked-after wooden rooms (above the bar of the same name) are a great deal if you want to stay in the centre of the action. All come with tiny but adequate bathrooms and guests get free water refills, tea and coffee.

**Green Ocean Guesthouse** HOSTEL $
(☑ 096 916 9267; mengly007@gmail.com; Koh Tuch; dm US$8-10, d US$25; ☎) The recently renovated rooms with tiled floors here are some of the nicest, and most spacious, in Koh Tuch village. There's a great communal balcony out front and the 12-bed dorm has sea views.

### Vagabonds HOSTEL $

(www.vagabondskohrong.com; Koh Tuch; dm US$5; r with shared bathroom US$10) Firstly, you don't come here for the facilities. Bare-bones rooms and four-bed dorms (with lockers) are made cheery by colourful murals. Vagabonds' following is instead due to friendly staff and the fun vibe of the cafe downstairs, which dishes up huge portions of comfort food (US$3 to $5). Walk-ins only.

### Dreamcatch Inn GUESTHOUSE $

(kohrongdreamcatch@gmail.com; Koh Tuch; r with shared bathroom US$15; 🐦) A more mellow alternative to most of the Koh Tuch village offerings, Dreamcatch Inn has super-basic rooms leading onto a colourful terrace strung with hammocks and swing chairs. Shared bathrooms have squat toilets. Walk-ins only.

### Nam Nam GUESTHOUSE $

(Koh Tuch; r US$25; 🐦) Fronted by a communal terrace, the three rooms at this Khmer-managed place are among the most spacious in town and come with decent bathrooms. It's in a back alley off the beach strip but you'll find the manager at their restaurant next to Bong's Bar. Walk-ins only.

### ★Treehouse Bungalows BUNGALOWS $$

(📞 034-934744; www.treehouse-bungalows.com; Koh Tuch Beach; bungalows US$45-55, treehouses US$45-60; 🐦) Nestled on a secluded cove about a 15-minute beach walk from Koh Tuch pier, Treehouse has more than a touch of the fairy tale about it. Bungalow balconies are strung with seashells (nab B3 for great sea views), high-raised bungalow 'treehouses' have prime vistas, and the restaurant is set beside a natural reservoir with an organic garden out back. Even if you're not staying here, drop by to sample their delicious wood-fired pizza and Khmer seafood menu.

### Paradise Bungalows BUNGALOWS $$

(📞 092 548883; www.paradise-bungalows.com; Koh Tuch Beach; bungalows US$35-100; 🐦) Delightfully rustic, bungalows here (in all shapes and sizes) climb up the hill amid rambling jungle foliage. US$35 rooms are way up on the hill while more expensive options are practically lapped by waves at high tide. The loungey restaurant, with soaring palm-leaf panel roof and shoreline panorama, is a real highlight.

### Monkey Island BUNGALOW $$

(📞 081 830992; www.monkeyisland-kohrong.com; Koh Tuch Beach; bungalows with bathroom US$35-40, without bathroom US$30; 🐦) Linked to the popular Monkey Republic in Sihanoukville, Monkey Island's action revolves around its bamboo-and-thatch bar, which is always jam-packed with backpackers. Some of the basic bungalows can fit up to five people at a squeeze and come with hammocks on the porches.

### Sok San Beach Bungalows BUNGALOW $$

(📞 034-5000127; Soksan village, Long Beach; bungalows US$20-25) You're paying for the Long Beach setting here. Bungalows are decidedly rickety, electricity is limited and, it's fair to say, amenities are few. But you're far from the hoopla of Koh Tuch and travellers looking for a slice of old-school Koh Rong beach life will revel in the spartan solitude.

## ✗ Eating & Drinking

Both Bongs and Vagabonds are great places to relax with a beer and are often home to a lively crowd. Bongs regularly has live music in the evening.

During high season there are frequent all-night parties on **Police Beach**, just south of Koh Tuch village. Check out flyers around town for information. Police Beach is also the main location for full moon parties.

### Loops Bar INTERNATIONAL $

(Koh Tuch; mains US$2.50-5.50; ⊙8am-11pm; 🐦) Downstairs from Dreamcatch Inn is this cafe-bar decorated with recycled water bottles, strung from the ceiling as pot plants. Breakfast options are stellar and include fruity French toast with a tropical twist and coconut muesli. Lunch and dinner feature decent Khmer options along with comfort food classics such as bangers and mash. Manager Te puts on a fire-poi show every Saturday night.

### Koh Lanta INTERNATIONAL $

(Koh Tuch; US$3-6; ⊙7am-10pm) Named after the famous French *Survivor* show, which is filmed on Koh Rong, this place offers the best wood-fired pizzas on the island.

### Buffalo INTERNATIONAL $$

(Cambodia Speed Ferry Pier, Koh Tuch; mains US$7-10; ⊙8am-late; 🐦) With a breezy pier position, Buffalo tries to please everyone with a menu featuring everything from fajitas to pizza to *gözleme* (Turkish pancakes). Happy hour (3pm to 5pm) heralds US$0.75 draught beer.

## ❶ Information

Bring all the cash you think you'll need with you. If you do run out of money, Vagabonds has a useful money-lending service (10% fee).

## DANGERS & ANNOYANCES

Theft is becoming a problem on Koh Rong. Use lock-boxes if supplied in dorms, or leave valuables in your accommodation's safe.

In 2013 an American woman was murdered while hiking the jungle trail to Long Beach, and in 2015 there was an attempted attack on a Japanese tourist. Travellers – both male and female – should buddy up when walking in more isolated areas of the island, and on the beach late at night.

## ⓘ Getting There & Away

From Koh Tuch **Speed Ferry Cambodia** (www.speedferrycambodia.com; one way/return US$13/26) departs for Sihanoukville at 10am, noon and 4pm daily; and the **TBC Speed Boat** (☑ 088 7811711; www.tbckohrongspeedboat.com; one way/return US$12.50/$20) to Sihanoukville leaves at 10.30am, 1.30am and 4pm. Both journeys take between 45 minutes to one hour. If you don't have a return ticket, you can buy one-way tickets at the ferry offices on the Koh Tuch piers. If you have a return ticket, go to the relevant ferry office the day before you want to travel to make sure of a seat. Ticket prices drop from June to October.

During high season extra ferry times are usually added. When sea conditions are bad (particularly from June to October) ferries can be cancelled at short notice.

If you're travelling to a resort not on the island's eastern side, book transport through the resort itself.

## Koh Rong Sanloem កោះរ៉ុងសន្លឹម

This horseshoe-shaped, 10km-long island is many people's ideal vision of island bliss. Koh Rong Sanloem's most popular destination is Saracen Bay – a crescent-shaped sweep of white sand on the island's east coast, lined by a row of small beach-bungalow resorts backed by lush jungle. If that's not isolated enough though, the southwestern side of the island (reached by walking trail or private boat) is home to just a couple of secluded

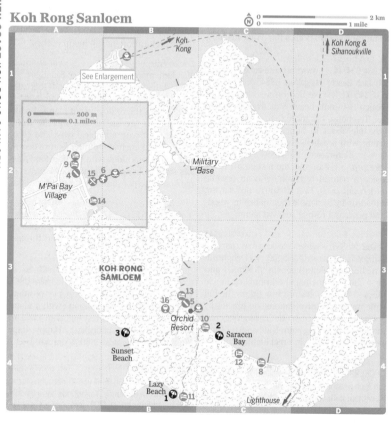

### Koh Rong Sanloem

resorts, where the cares of the world seem a million miles away.

Those looking for an alternative island experience can head to the village of M'Pai Bay at the island's northern tip. There's no romantically photogenic white sands here (the beach is a grainy-yellow hue), but the clutch of budget guesthouses that have set up shop provide serious chill factor with a proper local vibe that will suit the more intrepid.

## ◉ Sights & Activities

From **Saracen Bay** it's an easy 25-minute walk to **Lazy Beach** (non-guests will need to buy a drink or meal at the resort restaurant to stay and admire the beach), and a 45-minute hike (sneakers necessary) to **Sunset Beach**. There's also a harder trail, taking about 1½ hours to the lighthouse on a hill overlooking the ocean at the island's extreme southern tip, which is also a prime nesting spot for sea eagles. Be aware that there are soldiers stationed at the lighthouse and they may ask you for a tip (US$1 is usually fine).

If you want to explore the island interior further, talk to **Gil** (☑ 088 379 6528), usually based at Paradise Villas on Saracen Bay from around November to March. He can guide treks for between US$12 to $15 per person.

The Beach Resort's (p208) activity centre rents kayaks (US$10) and can organise guided kayaking trips and snorkelling ex-

cursions. Tom at Coral Garden Dive Resort is one of the best people to talk to about organising fishing trips (US$30).

**Cambodian Diving Group**  DIVING

(☑ 088 685 6986; www.cambodiandiving.com; M'Pai Bay; 2-dive package US$65, PADI Discover Scuba US$75, 3-day PADI Open Water US$345) ✐ Based in M'Pai Bay, these guys have expert knowledge of the surrounding underwater world that only comes from years of experience diving here. As well as excellent one-day dive packages and a range of PADI courses, they run longer three-day exploration dive trips for experienced divers and are involved in local marine conservation efforts.

**Coral Garden Dive Resort**  DIVING

(☑ 088 611 5770; www.coraldivers.org; Saracen Bay; 2-dive package US$80, Discover Scuba 2-dive package US$95, 3-day PADI Open Water US$385) Master scuba-diver trainer Tom Mellon knows the dive sites around Koh Rong Sanloem and Koh Rong like few others and guides highly recommended, professional dive excursions for both absolute beginners and advanced divers on a 12m catamaran. Two-dive packages stop at M'Pai Bay for a local lunch. Snorkellers (US$25 for two locations) are also welcome.

**Save Cambodian Marine Life**  VOLUNTEERING

(☑ 096 807 3236; www.savecambodianmarinelife. com; M'Pai Bay; 1-week volunteer package US$250) ✐ This NGO works to protect the local reefs surrounding Koh Rong Sanloem with ongoing projects including maintaining a coral nursery and organising reef clean-up dives. Volunteer packages include diving, shared accommodation and all meals.

## ⌦ Sleeping

Saracen Bay is the most developed beach with over a dozen small 'resorts' lining the sand. Nearly all of Koh Rong Sanloem's resorts have 24-hour electricity. Wi-fi is still a rarity (and if available is sporadic at best). Most places offer healthily discounted rates for bungalows during June to October.

**Easy Tiger**  GUESTHOUSE $

(☑ 096 915 3370; www.easytigerbungalows.com; M'Pai Bay; dm/r/bungalow US$7.50/15/30) This friendly guesthouse in M'Pai Bay village has plenty of home-spun appeal, thanks to its helpful owners. There's simple dorms and small private rooms in the main building. Out back are sturdy basic bungalows with large verandahs for those seeking more privacy. However, it's the restaurant and communal feel that make this place a winner.

### Chill Inn
GUESTHOUSE $

(☑ 016 824211; www.chillinncambodia.com; M'Pai Bay; dm US$7.50) The hammock-strung bar out front is M'Pai Bay's laid-back night spot, while the super-simple dorm provides all the basic dossing needs. A cracking spot for those who favour kicked-back ambience over amenities.

### The Drift
GUESTHOUSE $

(☑ 015 865388; www.facebook.com/thedriftsam loem; M'Pai Bay; dm/r US$8/15) A new player on the M'Pai Bay scene, The Drift has spick-and-span dorms and a couple of private rooms in a cute wooden house on the sand. There's a good social vibe with home-cooked meals (US$3) often eaten communally.

### Lazy Beach
RESORT $$

(☑ 017 456536; www.lazybeachcambodia.com; bungalows US$60) Alone on the southwest coast of Koh Rong Samloem, the 16 bungalows at this idyllic getaway front one of the must stunning beaches you'll find anywhere. They have balconies and hammocks outside, and spiffy stone-floor bathrooms and duelling queen-size beds inside. The restaurant-common area is stocked with books and board games, making it a good fit for families.

### The Beach Resort
RESORT $$

(☑ 034-666 6106; www.thebeachresort.asia; Saracen Bay; dm US$7.50, bungalow with/without bathroom US$35/25, deluxe US$50-85; ☎) This lively resort caters for the full gamut of budgets with an open-air dorm, bijou seafront bungalows and deluxe stone-walled options. It's also the stop-off point for Sihanoukville's Party Boat, whose day-trippers fill up the bar area most afternoons, which – depending on your outlook – will either be a major plus or minus to staying here.

### Green Blue Resort
RESORT $$

(☑ 096 725 0054; www.greenblueresort.com; Saracen Bay; dm US$10, bungalow US$65-80) Green Blue has a delightfully homey feel with bungalows strung with pot plants and vines, some set back from the seafront amid a well-tended garden. A small basic dorm out back caters for budgeteers. Electricity only in the evening.

### ★ Cita Resort
RESORT $$$

(☑ 096 261 2418; www.citaresort.com; Saracen Bay; bungalow US$85-90) At the southern end of Saracen Bay, this intimate resort has just five beautifully conceived raised bungalows with upper-level bedrooms fronted by sea-view balconies, open-air bathrooms and shaded hammock-strung lounging area below. The fantastic restaurant here dishes up fresh pasta and other Italian specialities.

### Secret Paradise
RESORT $$$

(www.secretparadiseresort.asia; Saracen Bay; bungalow US$100) Beach living with serious style – Secret Paradise has huge glass-door bungalows, featuring cane furniture and snazzy bathrooms, all with seafront verandahs. Service is impeccable and the restaurant is strong on tasty Khmer cuisine.

## ✖ Eating & Drinking

There are no separate restaurants in Saracen Bay, but all the resorts have attached restaurants so there's quite a good selection of food on offer. Koh Rong Sanloem is more about relaxing than partying so there's not much

---

### DIVING IN CAMBODIA

Cambodia might not be as famous for diving as neighbouring Thailand, but heading below the surface here offers up some serious dive highlights. Though fish stock may indeed be lower than in other Asian dive destinations (a consequence of years of irresponsible fishing practices, now being reversed by marine conservation organisations), the waters surrounding the southern islands off Sihanoukville are famed for their biodiverse coral life and unique array of macro life, particularly seahorses and nudibranchs.

The best of Cambodia's diving is among the fringing reefs of Koh Rong Sanloem and Koh Koun, which are home to a mind-boggling collection of weird and wacky nudibranchs, starfish and seahorses. Commonly spotted fish include angelfish, damselfish and scorpionfish. Further afield, the islands of Koh Tang and Koh Prins offer a plethora of marine life from bamboo shark and bluespotted ribbontail ray to wrasse and batfish. Whale sharks have also been sighted by divers here.

Two of the most experienced dive operators in the area, who know the best dive sites for macro life, are Cambodian Diving Group (p207) and Coral Garden Dive Resort (p207).

happening after dark. The Beach Resort usually has a bit of a drinking scene.

### Fishing Hook
INTERNATIONAL $

(M'Pai Bay; mains US$2.50-5.50; ⊗6-10.30pm) Some of the finest food on Koh Rong Sanloem is served up at this place perched on M'Pai Bay pier. The menu waltzes from Khmer-influenced seafood (such as grilled fish in tamarind sauce) to more global offerings, while the cushion-strewn dining terrace over the water is the epitome of beach-casual ambience.

### Good Vibz
BAR

(www.good-vibz-camp.com; ⊗approx Dec-Apr) Veering off the walking trail from Saracen Bay to Sunset Beach, 436 steps lead up the hill to this secluded jungle-bar that throws weekly raves and daily events including movie nights with films projected on a large screen amid the jungle backdrop. For those who can't bear to leave there's also accommodation in hammocks (US$1) and tents (from US$3).

## ❶ Getting There & Away

Both **Speed Ferry Cambodia** (www.speedferry cambodia.com; one way/return US$13/26) and **TBC Speed Boat** (☑ 088 781 1711; www. tbckohrongspeedboat.com; one way/return US$12.50/$20) connect Saracen Bay with Sihanoukville. Speed Ferry Cambodia also stops at M'Pai Bay.

Speed Ferry Cambodia has departures from Saracen Bay Pier at 9.30am and 3.30pm, which continue to drop off/pick up passengers at M'Pai Bay (about 15 minutes later) and Koh Rong Island (US$5 to hop between the islands) before heading for Sihanoukville.

Speed Ferry Cambodia uses Orchid Resort, near Saracen Bay Pier, as its office. You should make sure to validate the ticket for your return journey here one day before travel to make sure you get a seat.

TBC Speed Boat departs Saracen Bay Pier for Sihanoukville at 10.30am, 1.30pm and 4pm.

Schedules change frequently depending on the season so always double check when you buy your ticket.

# Koh Sdach Archipelago ប្រជុំកោះស្ដេច

Just off Botum Sakor National Park's (p181) southwest tip, this is a modest archipelago of 12 small islands, most of them uninhabited. Basing yourself at one of the two islands with accommodation – Koh Sdach (King

Island) and Koh Totang – you can spend a day or two exploring the other islands, some of which have utterly isolated beaches and good snorkelling. Most island-hopping tours target Koh Ampil, which is a cluster of three tiny islands surrounding a spit of sand, and the long white beaches on either side of Koh Smach.

Koh Sdach has the only village of any size in the entire archipelago and is thoroughly off the tourist trail with the small local economy based entirely around fishing. The village pier is around 10 minutes by outboard (speedboat) from the point where the new four-lane highway that cuts through Botum Sakor National Park terminates on the mainland. Although this highway has made the archipelago infinitely easier to access, it's part of a huge tourism development that is permanently changing the southwest coast of Botum Sakor, once known for pristine beaches backed by virgin forest (an 18-hole golf course has been opened along the mainland coast).

Fortunately, the islands appear to be largely excluded from the development agenda, and existing resorts are far enough from the mainland that the commotion is out of earshot, if not completely out of eyeshot. Koh Sdach has 24-hour electricity.

## 🛏 Sleeping & Eating

### Mean Chey Guesthouse
GUESTHOUSE $

(☑ 011 983806; Koh Sdach; r US$7.50) Budget travellers will have to settle for this simple guesthouse with 15 powder-blue concrete cottages close to the main fishing village on the northwest side of Koh Sdach. The Yvonne restaurant on the premises has lovely views of the neighbouring islands and serves French and Khmer food.

### Nomads Land
RESORT $$$

(☑ 011 916171; http://nomadslandcambodia. com; Koh Totang; bungalows s/d incl meals from US$60/90; ⊗Nov-May) 🌿 It's hard to imagine a more relaxed place than Nomads. Owner Karim has made this the greenest resort in the islands with five funky bungalows powered by solar panels and rain water collected for drinking. It sits on a white beach on Koh Totang, an island speck, which is 15 minutes from the mainland's Poi Yopon village by the resort's boat.

## ❶ Getting There & Away

Getting to the Koh Sdach archipelago can be rather convoluted. The easiest, but most expensive, way is to hire private transport from Koh Kong (US$60), Sihanoukville (US$80) or Phnom Penh (US$90) and travel overland via the new Chinese highway to the village of Poi Yopon on the mainland opposite Koh Sdach.

Much cheaper is to take any public bus travelling down NH48 and get off at the turnoff for the Chinese highway, 6km west of Andoung Tuek. From here you can either get a local minibus (US$7.50, two hours, mornings only) or *moto* driver (US$15 to US$20 depending on your negotiating skills) to take you to Poi Yopon.

Hiring an outboard from Poi Yopon to Koh Sdach costs about US$10. Nomads Land (p209) has its own private boat, which can pick you up, and it can also can organise taxis to Poi Yopon.

A much more adventurous (or frustrating, depending on your outlook) option is to try to get on the local cargo ferry from Sihanoukville to Koh Sdach Island. This leaves Sihanoukville's Royal Pier in the main port area daily, or every other day (depending on various factors), between noon and 2pm (US$10, 4½ hours with a stop or two along the way) and makes the return leg from Koh Sdach at 8pm.

# KAMPOT PROVINCE

Kampot Province (ខេត្តកំពត) has emerged as one of Cambodia's most alluring destinations thanks to a hard-to-beat combination of easygoing towns and lush countryside riddled with honeycombed limestone caves.

The province is renowned for producing some of the world's finest pepper. Durian haters be warned: Kampot is also Cambodia's main producer of this odoriferous fruit.

## Kampot កំពត

📞 033 / POP 39,500

It's not hard to see why travellers become entranced by Kampot. This riverside town, with streets rimmed by dilapidated shophouse architecture, has a dreamy quality; as if someone pressed the snooze button and the entire town forgot to wake up.

Eclipsed as a port when Sihanoukville was founded in 1959, Kampot makes an excellent base for exploring Bokor National Park, Kep, and the superb cave-temples and verdant countryside of the surrounding area.

### ◎ Sights

Kampot is more about ambience than actual sights and the most enjoyable activity is strolling or cycling through the central old town district where lanes are lined with crumbling shophouses, many built in the mid-20th century by the town's then vibrant Chinese merchant population. The best streets, a couple of which have been well restored in recent years, are between the triangle delineated by the central Durian Roundabout, the post office and the old French bridge.

**Kampot Traditional
Music School** CULTURAL CENTRE
(www.kcdi-cambodia.com; St 724; ⊙2-5pm Mon-Tue & 5-7pm Fri) 🖉 FREE During visitor hours you are welcome to observe training sessions and/or performances at this school that trains children who are orphaned or have disabilities in traditional music and dance. Donations are very welcome.

**Kampot Provincial Museum** MUSEUM
(សារមន្ទីរខេត្តកំពត; River Rd; admission US$2; ⊙3-6pm Tue & Thu, 8-11am & 3-6pm Sat & Sun) This tiny new museum, inside the finely-preserved French colonial–era Old Governor's Mansion, traces the history of Kampot and the outlying area, drawing on the knowledge and experience of Jean-Michel Filippi, a cultural anthropologist and some-time resident of the area.

Well, we think it does anyway, as on our last visit we tried to access it twice during its supposed opening hours and found it firmly closed. If it is open during your Kampot visit, it's worthwhile stopping by.

**Kampot Prison** HISTORIC BUILDING
(ពន្ធនាគារ ខេត្តកំពត; St 736) You can view the beautiful, but hugely decrepit, French colonial–era old prison building from outside Kampot prison gate. The guards are used to tourists stopping by, but ask before you start taking photographs.

**Old French Bridge** BRIDGE
Destroyed during the Khmer Rouge period, Kampot's old French bridge was later repaired in a mishmash of styles. It's officially closed for safety reasons; locals simply climb over the barrier to walk across. Watch your step extremely carefully if you do decide to walk on it.

### 🏃 Activities & Courses

Kampot is fast creating a niche for itself as a base for adventure sports and activities. Climbing and water sports on the Kampong Bay River are the main attractions.

### Climbodia
ROCK CLIMBING

(📞 095 581951; www.climbodia.com; Phnom Kbal Romeas, off NH33; half-day US$35-40, full-day US$70) Cambodia's first outdoor rock-climbing outfit offers highly recommended half-day and full-day programs of climbing, abseiling and caving amid the limestone formations of Phnom Kbal Romeas, 5km south of Kampot. *Via ferratas* (cabled routes) have been established across some of the cliffs and the variety of programs cater for both complete novices and the more experienced.

### SUP Asia
WATER SPORTS

(📞 093 980550; www.supasia.org; Kompong Bay River east bank; 2½hr tour US$25; ☺ daily mid-Oct–Jul) SUP (stand-up paddleboarding) has come to Kampot in a big way with this company offering an alternative form of touring the river. Daily tours depart at 8.30am and 3.30pm, taking in the riverbank sights of the local area (with a SUP lesson beforehand). There's also a two-day (18km) trip that traverses the Kampong Bay River to the sea.

### Khmer Roots Cafe
COOKING COURSE

(📞 088 356 8016; http://khmerrootscafe.com; off NH33; cooking course incl return transport from Kampot US$20; ☺ 10am-4pm) More than just a cooking class, Khmer Roots Cafe is a slice of Cambodian rural life set amid owner Soklim's shady trees and organic vegetable gardens about one hour east of Kampot. Classes usually include preparing two dishes (including gathering the ingredients), lunch and the opportunity to explore the tranquil countryside afterwards.

### Seeing Hands Massage 5
MASSAGE

(River Rd; per hr US$5; ☺ 7am-11pm) Blind masseurs offer soothing bliss.

## 👉 Tours

Everybody and their grandmother wants to sell you a tour in Kampot. The main day trips are to Bokor Hill Station (US$12 to $15), and a countryside tour that usually includes Phnom Chouk Cave, the nearby salt fields, a pepper farm, Kep and Koh Tonsay (US$18 to $20).

Alternatively, you can hire a *remork* driver and cobble together your own tour of the caves, Kep and surrounding countryside. Depending on locations, a half-/full-day tour costs about US$15/25.

Sunset cruises and evening boat trips to watch fireflies are also popular. Be aware on the firefly tours that seeing fireflies isn't guaranteed due to their unpredictable nature.

### FESTIVAL TIME

Launched in 2015, the Kampot Writers & Readers Festival (www.kampot writersfestival.com) brings four days of literary discussions, poetry readings, art exhibitions, concerts and creative workshops to Kampot in November.

### Bart the Boatman
BOAT TOUR

(📞 092 174280; 2 people US$40) Known simply as Bart the Boatman, this Belgian expat runs original private boat tours along the small tributaries of the Kampong Bay River. His backwater tour is highly recommended by travellers.

### Captain Chim's
BOAT TOUR

(📞 012 321043; Captain Chim's Guesthouse, St 724; sunset boat trip per person US$5) Sunset cruises and firefly-watching trips on a traditional boat include a cold beer and are a bargain. Also on offer are fishing trips for US$11 including lunch, and bicycle hire (US$2 per day).

### Kampot Dreamtime Tours
BOAT TOUR

(📞 089 908417; www.kampotrivercruises.com; River Rd) Sunset river trips leave from the dock just across the road from Rikitikitavi (p213) at 4pm and cruise out to the river mouth in a boat formerly owned by King Norodom Sihanouk. Wine, cheese and a seafood barbecue are included.

### Sok Lim Tours
TOUR

(📞 012 796919; www.soklimtours.com; St 730; ☺ 8am-7pm) Kampot's longest-running outfit is well regarded and organises all the usual day tours and river cruises. For private countryside tours they have good English-speaking *remork* driver-guides who understand the process and history behind Kampot pepper. If there's no one in the actual office, they'll be in the neighbouring Jack's Place restaurant.

### Quad Cambodia Kampot
ADVENTURE TOUR

(📞 088 938 1242; www.quadcambodiakampot.wix. com/quadcambodiakampot; River Rd; sunset 1½hr tour 1 person US$23, 2 people US$33) A revved-up approach to local sightseeing in the Kampot countryside, sunset quad-biking tours depart at 4.15pm. There are also longer tours (from US$36 per person) that head further afield.

## 🛏 Sleeping

When it comes to accommodation, Kampot is a tale of two cities. In town most hotels and guesthouses are in, or near, the old

# Kampot

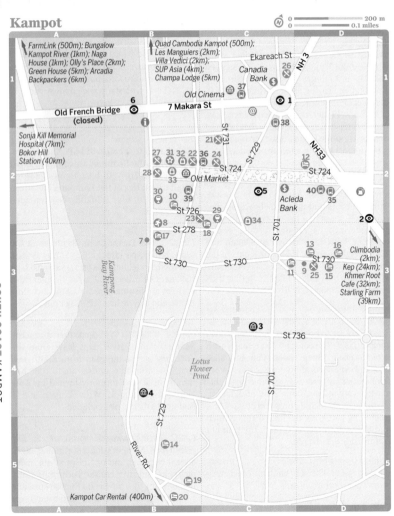

FarmLink (500m); Bungalow Kampot River (1km); Naga House (1km); Olly's Place (2km); Green House (5km); Arcadia Backpackers (6km)

Quad Cambodia Kampot (500m); Les Manguiers (2km); Villa Vedici (2km); SUP Asia (4km); Champa Lodge (5km)

Ekareach St

Canadia Bank

Old Cinema

Old French Bridge (closed)

7 Makara St

Sonja Kill Memorial Hospital (7km); Bokor Hill Station (40km)

St 731

St 729

NH33

St 724

St 724

Old Market

Acleda Bank

Kampong Bay River

St 726

St 278

St 730

St 730

St 701

Climbodia (2km); Kep (24km); Khmer Root Cafe (32km); Starling Farm (39km)

St 736

Lotus Flower Pond

St 701

St 729

River Rd

Kampot Car Rental (400m)

SOUTH COAST KAMPOT

---

town, a stone's throw from all the cafes and restaurants. Out of town, a series of places are strung out along the riverbank offering a complete chill-out (or complete party, depending on which one you pick) experience. If you fall for Kampot's charms, it might be worth sampling both areas.

## Central Kampot

**Magic Sponge**  GUESTHOUSE **$**
(☏017 946428; www.magicspongekampot.com; St 730; dm US$4, r with air-con US$10-15, without air-con US$15-20; ❄❖❄) This popular backpacker place has a rooftop dorm with impressive through breezes, personalised fans and reading lights. Good-value private rooms are exceptionally well cared for and bright. Downstairs is a movie lounge and a lively bar-restaurant with happy hours from noon to 8pm and well-regarded Indian food. There's even minigolf in the garden.

**Pepper Guesthouse**  GUESTHOUSE **$**
(☏017 822626; guesthousepepper@yahoo.com; St 730; dm US$3, r with fan US$10, bungalow US$25; ❄❖❄) We're big fans of this homely, locally run guesthouse in a slightly creaky mid-century villa. Fan-only rooms have bags of character with beautiful old wood floors

# Kampot

(room 101 is the best), while out in the front garden are two rather upmarket bungalows with rain showers and tasteful decor.

**Blue Buddha Hotel**    HOTEL **$**
(☏071 637 2924; www.bluebuddhahotel.com; St 730; d/tr/f US$22/27/38; ⊛❋🛜) Raising the bar for budget digs in Kampot, Blue Buddha has helpful owners and spacious, minimalist-style rooms with comfortable beds, cable TV, minibar and big modern bathrooms. Guests also benefit from a swag of discounts at businesses around town, and free bike hire.

**Captain Chim's Guesthouse**    GUESTHOUSE **$**
(☏012 321043; www.facebook.com/captain-chims-guest-house; St 724; dm US$3; r with/without air-con US$13/8; ❋🛜) This family-run guesthouse offers simple, spick-and-span rooms and a spacious dorm with its own balcony. Bathrooms only have cold water. Guests get free laundry and free bicycle hire.

**The Mad Monkey Hostel**    HOSTEL **$**
(☏033-666 8853; www.madmonkeyhostels.com/kampot; River Rd; dm US$5, d with/without air-con US$25/18; ⊛❋@🛜) Part of the Mad Monkey hostel empire, this place lures backpackers in with good-sized (fan-only)

dorms and a poolside bar area that's always home to a youthful party scene.

**Nyny Guesthouse**    HOTEL **$**
(☏077 901460; nynyhotel@yahoo.com; St 730; s/d US$6/8, with air-con US$13/15; ❋🛜) Bargain basement prices with solid facilities are on offer at this blandly modern hotel. Rooms are sparkling clean and come with showers that have dependable hot water.

★ **Rikitikitavi**    BOUTIQUE HOTEL **$$**
(☏012 235102; www.rikitikitavi-kampot.com; River Rd; r incl breakfast US$48-53, f US$58; ⊛❋🛜) One of Cambodia's best-run boutique hotels, Rikitikitavi's rooms are a lesson in subtle luxury, fusing Asian-inspired decor with modern creature comforts. Ceilings are graced with stunning beams, and palm panels and beautiful artwork adorn the walls. Plus you get swish contemporary bathrooms and mod-con amenities such as flat-screen TVs, DVD player, fridge and kettle. Service is sublime. Highly recommended.

**The Columns**    BOUTIQUE HOTEL **$$**
(☏092 128300; www.the-columns.com; St 728; r incl breakfast US$45-59, ste US$75; ❋🛜) Set in a row of thoughtfully restored shophouses

near the riverfront, this boutique hotel blends classic and modern with minimalist rooms featuring a touch of mid-century furniture, iPhone docking stations, flat-screen TVs and slick modern bathrooms. Downstairs is Green's, an inviting cafe with a lovely old tilework floor and a menu of healthy salads and shakes.

**Two Moons** HOTEL **$$**
(☑033-932857; www.twomoonshotel.com; River Rd; r US$35-50, ste US$70-85, r with shared bathroom US$15-20; ⊜❋☎☒) Bright, contemporary rooms in the main building opening on to a communal balcony, and there's some jazzy top floor 'penthouse' suites, perfect for families. The sprawling garden, with inviting pool area and good bar-restaurant, is home to a traditional wooden Khmer house with a couple of atmospheric budget rooms.

**Mea Culpa** GUESTHOUSE **$$**
(☑012 504769; www.meaculpakampot.com; St 729; r US$25-27; ❋☎) This modern villa has 11 rooms with plenty of homely appeal, while the location, south of the centre, guarantees a relaxed, peaceful vibe. The garden restaurant here spins the best pizza in town, straight from a wood-fired oven.

## On the River

Most of the out-of-town places aren't *that* far out of town – usually just a 10-minute *remork* ride from the centre. All of them are on the river and have over-water pavilions or docks to facilitate swimming.

**Bungalow Kampot River** BUNGALOW **$**
(☑033-666 6418; sokvireak25@gmail.com; Tuk Chhou Rd; bungalow US$6-10; ☎) For back-to-basics living and serious relaxation this Cambodian-owned family place comes up trumps. The river-terrace restaurant (meals from US$2) is the spot to contemplate sunset while accommodation is in rustic palm-thatch bungalows (think mattress on the floor, mosquito net and fan). Stilted bungalows have private bathrooms.

**Olly's Place** BUNGALOW **$**
(☑092 605837; www.ollysplacekampot.com; Tuk Chhou Rd; dm US$3, r US$6-8; ☎) This mellow, intimate retreat is run by French-speaking Belgian Olly. Thatched bungalows and basic rooms are ridiculously good value considering the relaxed vibe and plum location. Use of windsurfers and paddleboards is free.

**Naga House** BUNGALOW **$**
(☑012 289916; www.facebook.com/nagahouse kampot; Tuk Chhou Rd; bungalow US$7-12; ☎) This classic backpacker hang-out offers basic ground-level and stilted thatched bungalows (all with shared bathroom) amid lush foliage. There's an extremely social bar-restaurant on the riverfront that often rocks into the night and regularly hosts live music and DJ sets.

**Arcadia Backpackers** HOSTEL **$**
(☑077 219756; www.arcadiabackpackers.com; Tuk Chhou Rd; dm US$5-8, r with bathroom US$17-20, without bathroom US$10, bungalow US$25; ☎) Kampot's biggest backpacker party scene, Arcadia is about sunbathing on the river pontoon during the day and later, joining in the revelry at the bar-restaurant that regularly cranks into the wee hours. Those after some semblance of sleep would be wise not to opt for the US$5 dorm.

**★ Green House** BUNGALOW **$$**
(☑092 791958; www.greenhousekampot.com; Tuk Chhou Rd; bungalow with bathroom US$20-30, without bathroom US$12; ☎) This gorgeously conceived riverfront pad is all about tranquillity and has both palm-thatch bungalows (with shared facilities) and colourful wooden cottages with balconies; the best right on the riverbank (children under 12 not accepted). The historic teak-wood main building, which houses the restaurant (open from 7am to 8.45pm), was once home to the legendary Phnom Penh bar 'Snowy's' (aka 'Maxine's'), transported lock stock and barrel here in 2011.

**Champa Lodge** BUNGALOW **$$**
(☑092 525835; www.champalodge.com; Kompong Kreang; bungalow US$38-60; ☎) Set on a bend in the river amid traditional Cambodian countryside scenes, Champa is a rural hideaway with arty rooms set in traditional Khmer wooden houses, all with verandahs to sloth out on and admire the bucolic views. Kayak and bike hire is available if you can drag yourself away. The restaurant-bar includes a great selection of Belgian beers.

**Les Manguiers** RESORT **$$**
(☑092 330050; www.mangokampot.com; Kompong Bay River east bank; r with shared bathroom US$11-24, bungalow US$32-80; @☎) This rambling garden complex has swags of extras with free canoes and bikes, badminton, table tennis and a children's playground. You can jump into the river from one of four over-water gazebos. There's a variety of accom-

**LOCAL KNOWLEDGE**

## KAMPOT PEPPER

Before Cambodia's civil war, no Paris restaurant worth its salt would be without pepper from Kampot Province, but the country's pepper farms were all but destroyed by the Khmer Rouge, who believed in growing rice, not spice.

Today, thanks to a group of eco-entrepreneurs and foodies who are passionate about pepper, Kampot-grown peppercorns, delicate and aromatic but packing a powerful punch, are making a comeback.

Kampot pepper is grown on family farms that dot Phnom Voar and nearby valleys northwest of Kompong Trach, where the unique climate and farmers' fidelity to labour-intensive growing techniques produce particularly pungent peppercorns. In fact, Kampot pepper is so extraordinary that it's Cambodia's first-ever product to receive a 'geographical indication' (GI), just like French cheeses. Increased sales have made a huge difference for Kampot's pepper families, and especially for the girls who are able to marry now their parents can afford their dowries.

Peppercorns are picked from February to May. Black pepper is plucked from the trees when the corns are starting to turn yellow and turns black during sun-drying; red pepper is picked when the fruit is completely mature; and mild white pepper is soaked in water to remove the husks. September to February is the season for green pepper, whose sprigs have to be eaten almost immediately after harvesting – the crab market restaurants (p223) of Kep are one of the best places to experience its gentle freshness. A packet of pepper makes an excellent souvenir or gift: it's lightweight, unbreakable and, if stored properly – that is, *not* ground! – will stay fresh for years.

**FarmLink** (☑ 033 690 2354; www.farmlink-cambodia.com; ⊘ 7.30-11.30am & 1.30-4.30pm Mon-Fri) In Kampot you can purchase pouches of peerless pepper at the FarmLink boutique, one of the pioneers of GI pepper production. You can see pepper being dried in the garden out the front and visitors can see the pepper sorting room. It's just over the New Bridge; take the first right and look for it on the left.

**Sothy's Pepper Farm** (☑ 088 951 3505; www.mykampotpepper.asia; Phnom Voar, Kep district, off NH33; ⊘ 9am-5pm) By far the friendliest pepper farm to visit, Sothy's has a shop and offers short tours that explain the history and process behind the Kampot pepper industry. It's nearer to Kep than Kampot.

**Starling Farm** (www.starlingfarm.com; Kampot district, off NH33; ⊘ 7am-5pm) Has an on-site shop and restaurant. The farm doesn't run tours (or offer any information) but you can go have a look at the nearest pepper field by yourself. The scenery on the way out here from Kampot is the real highlight.

modation from large, bright simple rooms to stilted wooden bungalows, all with fan and cold water. Meals are served *table d'hôte* style.

**Villa Vedici**  RESORT **$$**
(☑ 089 290714; www.villavedici.com; Kompong Bay River east bank; r US$30-45, bungalows from US$55; ❄@ 🛜 ≋) A playground for kids and adults alike offering kitesurfing, a speedboat for water-skiing and wakeboarding, plus a PlayStation on a gargantuan flat-screen in the main building's airy living room. Rooms are functional rather than frilly, but guests tend to spend most of their time here lapping up the rays beside the lovely pool.

 **Eating**

For cheap eats, the bustling **night market** (NH3; ⊘ 4pm-midnight) is full of food stalls

where you can chow down on simple noodle and rice dishes, grilled meat and Khmer desserts such as sticky rice with coconut sauce.

Many of the guesthouses are worthy of a meal. Mea Culpa has wood-fired pizzas, Magic Sponge (p212) has good Indian food, or enjoy a meal on the water at one of the out-of-town riverside places – Green House is particularly good.

**Cafe Espresso**  CAFE **$**
(St 731; mains US$4-6; ⊘ 8.30am-4pm Tue-Fri, 9am-4.30pm Sat & Sun; 🛜 ☑) A blink-and-you'll-miss-it cafe; we advise you don't blink. The Aussie owners are real foodies and offer a global menu that traipses from vegetarian *quesadillas* to Brazilian-style pork sandwiches with some especially tempting breakfast options. But it is caffeine-cravers who will

be really buzzing, thanks to their regionally grown coffee blends, roasted daily in house.

### Epic Arts Café
CAFE $

(www.epicarts.org.uk; St 724; mains US$2-4; ☺7am-4pm; 🛜) 🍴 A great place for breakfast, homemade cakes, infused tea and light lunches, this mellow eatery is staffed by young people who are deaf or have a disability. Profits fund arts workshops for Cambodians with a disability and it's possible to learn some sign language at 3pm every Friday.

### Jack's Place
CAMBODIAN $

(St 730; mains US$2.50-6; ☺7am-10pm; 🛜🍴) A friendly, local family-run place, this relaxed open-air restaurant dishes up *yao hon* (Khmer hot-pots), *char kroeung* (vegetable and peanut stir-fry) and a whole host of Cambodian staples. The soups here are delicious and there's also sandwiches and burgers.

### Ellie's
CAFE $

(St 726; mains US$3-5; ☺8am-4pm Wed-Mon; 🛜🍴) Eggs Benedict, French toast, English muffins – Ellie's whips up some of the most scrumptious breakfasts in town for travellers pining for a taste of home. The cakes and original sandwich fillings, such as pumpkin, spinach and feta, make for a tasty lunch too.

### Captain Chim's
CAMBODIAN $

(St 724; mains US$1-3; ☺7am-10pm; 🛜) Some of Kampot's best budget bites are found here. Best known for breakfast, Khmer faves such as *loc lak* (salad featuring marinated, stir-fried beef) will fill you up at any time of day.

### ★ Rikitikitavi
INTERNATIONAL $$

(www.rikitikitavi-kampot.com; River Rd; mains US$5-8; ☺7am-10pm; 🛜🍴) Named after the mongoose in Rudyard Kipling's *The Jungle Book,* this riverfront terrace is all about the ambience. It's known for its Kampot pepper chicken, burritos, slow-cooked curry and salads. Happy hour from 5pm to 7pm brings 2-for-1 cheer on all cocktails. This is the best place in town to kick back and enjoy a sundowner.

### Veronica's Kitchen
INTERNATIONAL $$

(River Rd; mains US$4.75-6; ☺7.30am-10pm; 🛜) This easygoing and friendly open-air restaurant is run by a local family and has a considered menu of classic Khmer and European dishes that manages to please everyone. It's a top riverfront spot for a late-afternoon beer.

### Rusty Keyhole
INTERNATIONAL $$

(River Rd; small/large/extra-large ribs US$5/7.50/10; ☺8am-11pm Nov-May, 11am-11pm Jun-Oct; 🛜) This popular riverfront bar-restaurant turns out a global menu of comfort food and Khmer home cooking. Most people are here for their famous ribs; order in advance, but beware the enormous extra-large portions.

### Baraca
TAPAS $$

(St 726; tapas US$1.50-3, mixed plate for 2 people US$10; ☺5-10pm; 🛜🍴) A cosy, colourful place with a slight bohemian edge, Baraca serves inventive tapas with cherry-picked influences from Asia, the Mediterranean and the Middle East. A must for lovers of small-plate dining. Out the back their **guesthouse** (📋 011 290434; www.baraca.org; St 726; d US$12-16, f US$20; 🛜) has simple, airy rooms with high ceilings and original tilework floors.

## 🍷 Drinking & Entertainment

### KAMA
BAR

(Kampot Arts and Music Association; St 726; ☺6pm-midnight Wed-Sun; 🛜) Owned by Julien Poulson, a founding member of the acclaimed band, Cambodian Space Project, KAMA is part boho bar, part art space. It spins tunes from an eclectic vinyl collection, plays movies nightly and hosts creative events. Pop in for a beer, or their dish of the day, and check out what's happening while you're in town.

### Oh Neils
BAR

(River Rd; ☺5pm-late; 🛜) The liveliest of the little bars that dot the riverfront in Kampot, Oh Neils has walls plastered with rock 'n' roll memorabilia and a who's who soundtrack of classic tunes from down the decades.

### Ecran
CINEMA

(St 724; per movie 10,000r; ☺11am-9pm Wed-Mon) Ecran (French for screen) is a little movie-cafe offering big-screen films and a private room for movie watching. Cambodian classics such as *The Killing Fields* screen daily, plus cult classics and more. Handmade noodles and dumplings are available (US$2 to $2.50), plus drinks.

## 🔒 Shopping

### Tiny Kampot Pillows
HANDICRAFTS, CLOTHING

(www.tinykampotpillows.com; 2000 Roundabout; ☺10am-6pm) Textile shop selling, well, lots of tiny pillows in handwoven silk, plus plenty of other accessories from clothing to bags.

### Dorsu
CLOTHING

(www.dorsu.org; St 724; ☺10am-5.30pm) Ethical fashion from Kampot. The lovely range of high-quality wardrobe staples here are all designed and produced locally by a small team.

**Kepler's Kampot Books**    BOOKS
(St 724; ⊗8am-8pm) This is the place for secondhand books in Kampot.

## ❶ Information

The free and often hilarious *Kampot Survival Guide* (www.kampotsurvivalguide.com) takes a tongue-in-cheek look at local expat life. There's also the free *Coastal* guide to Kampot and Kep, with heaps of info on local businesses.

There's a strip of copy shops with internet access southwest of the Durian Roundabout on 7 Makara St. Wi-fi is free at most guesthouses, cafes and restaurants.

**Acleda Bank** (St 724; ⊗ 8am-3.30pm Mon-Fri, to 11.30am Sat, ATM 24hr)

**Canadia Bank** (Durian Roundabout; ⊗8am-3.30pm Mon-Fri, to 11.30am Sat, ATM 24hr)

**Sonja Kill Memorial Hospital** (🖉emergency 078 265782, outpatient clinic 077 666752; www.skmh.org; NH3, 7km west of Kampot) The best hospital in the area with state-of-the-art medical facilities and highly trained local and expatriate doctors.

**Tourist Information Centre** (🖉033-655 5541; lonelyguide@gmail.com; River Rd; ⊗7am-7pm) Led by the knowledgeable Mr Pov, Kampot's tourist office doles out free advice, sells tours and can arrange transport to area attractions such as caves, falls and Kompong Trach.

## ❶ Getting There & Away

Kampot, on NH3, is 148km southwest of Phnom Penh, 105km east of Sihanoukville and 25km northwest of Kep.

**Capitol Tours** (🖉092 665001; NH33) and **Phnom Penh Sorya** (NH33) sell tickets from offices opposite the Total petrol station near the Four Nagas Roundabout. Both have a 7am departure to Phnom Penh (US$5 to US$6, four hours). Capitol has another service at 1pm. Sorya's service goes via Kep (US$2, 45 minutes).

Most people opt to travel to Phnom Penh by faster, more comfortable, minivan services. **Giant Ibis** (🖉095 666809; www.giantibis. com; 7 Makara St) has minivans to Phnom Penh (US$9, 2½ hours) departing at 8.30am and 2.45pm. **Kampot Express** (🖉077 555123; www.kampotexpress.com; St 729 ) runs minivans to Phnom Penh (US$8, 2¾ hours) at 8am,1pm and 4.30pm. To Sihanoukville, **Kampot Tours & Travel** (🖉092 125556; St 710) (US$5, 8am and 3.30pm, two hours) and **Champa Mekong Travel** (🖉033-630 0036; St 724; US$5; 8am, 10.30am, 3.30pm; two hours) are the two main minivan companies. For Kep (US$3, 30 minutes), Kampot Tours & Travel have services at 9.30am and 2pm, while Champa minivans leave at 10.30am and 3pm. The morning service to Kep from both companies carries on to Ha Tien in Vietnam (US$8, 1½ hours).

All guesthouses can arrange tickets and pick-ups.

A *moto* to Kep should cost about US$6 (*remork* US$12).

## ❶ Getting Around

A *moto* ride in town costs around 2000r (*remork* US$1). To get to the riverside guesthouses on the edge of town it should cost between US$2 to US$4, depending on where they're located.

Bicycles (US$2 per day) and motorbikes (about US$5 per day) can be rented from many guesthouses around town.

**Kampot Car Rental** (🖉 088 5102702; www.facebook.com/kampotcarrental; River Rd; per day from US$20; ⊗7am-8pm) Self-drive car hire gives you the freedom to explore at a bargain price. Check the small print.

---

# Around Kampot

The limestone hills east of Kampot towards Kep are littered with caves. Phnom Chhnork, surrounded by blazingly green countryside, is a real gem and can easily be visited in an afternoon along with Phnom Sorsia.

**Phnom Chhnork**    CAVE
(ភ្នំឆ្នក; admission US$1; ⊗7am-6pm) Phnom Chhnork is a short walk through a quilt of rice paddies from Wat Ang Sdok, where a monk collects the entry fee and a gaggle of friendly local kids offer their services as guides.

From the bottom, a 203-step staircase leads up the hillside and down into a cavern as graceful as a Gothic cathedral. The view from up top, and the walk to and from the wat, is especially magical in the late afternoon.

Inside the cave you'll be greeted by a stalactite elephant, with a second elephant outlined on the flat cliff face to the right. Tiny chirping bats live up near two natural chimneys that soar towards the blue sky, partly blocked by foliage of an impossibly green hue.

Within the main chamber stands a remarkable 7th-century (Funan-era) brick temple, dedicated to Shiva. The temple's brickwork is in superb condition thanks to the protection afforded by the cave. Poke your head inside and check out the ancient stalactite that serves as a *linga*. A slippery passage, flooded in the rainy season, leads through the hill.

To get to Phnom Chhnork turn left off the NH33 about 5.5km east of Kampot. Look for a sign reading 'Phnom Chhngok Resort' across the road from a Cham mosque. From the turnoff it's 6km to the cave on a bumpy road. A return *moto* ride from Kampot costs about US$6 (*remork* US$10).

### Phnom Sorsia
CAVE

(ភ្នំសូសៀ, Phnom Sia; ⊘7am-6pm) FREE Phnom Sorsia is home to several natural caves. From the parking area, a stairway leads up the hillside to a gaudy modern **temple**. From there, steps lead left up to **Rung Damrey Saa** (White Elephant Cave). A slippery, sloping staircase where one false step will send you into the abyss leads down and then up and then out through a hole in the other side. Exit the cave and follow the right-hand path which leads back to the temple.

To see the **Bat Cave** take the steps leading to the right from the temple. Inside the cave, bats flutter and chirp overhead, flying out to the forest and back through a narrow natural chimney. Locals use bamboo poles to hunt the creatures by swatting them out of the air. The circuit ends near a hilltop stupa with impressive views.

The turnoff to Phnom Sorsia is on NH33, 13.5km southeast of Kampot and 1.3km northwest of the White Horse Roundabout near Kep. Look for a sign reading 'Phnom Sorsia Resort' – from there a dirt road leads about 1km northeast through the rice fields.

### Tek Chhou Rapids
RIVER

(ទឹកឈូ; admission US$1) Hugely popular with locals, these modest rapids are surrounded by food stalls and – a prerequisite for any proper Khmer day out – picnicking platforms. A *remork* here from Kampot costs around US$5.

Thanks to the hydroelectric dams upriver (part of the US$280 million project that flooded small parts of Bokor National Park), the term 'rapids' is something of a misnomer but this is still a top spot for riverside relaxation and a chance to take in the local scene.

# Bokor Hill Station
កស្ដានីយភ្នំបូកគោ

The once abandoned French retreat of Bokor Hill Station FREE, inside the 1581-sq-km **Bokor National Park** (ឧទ្យានជាតិបូកគោ, Preah Monivong National Park; admission motorbike/car 2000r/4000r) is famed for its refreshingly cool climate and creepy derelict buildings that had their heyday during the 1920s and 1930s. On cold, foggy days it can get pretty spooky up here as mists drop visibility to nothing and the wind keens through abandoned buildings.

It's appropriate, then, that the foggy showdown that ends the Matt Dillon crime thriller *City of Ghosts* (2002) was filmed here.

These days the hill station is becoming more famous for the ugly modern casino, which blights the summit, the Thansur Bokor Highland Resort. It's part of a development project that includes a golf course and numerous holiday villas on sale at speculative prices. This construction has sadly all but destroyed the pleasingly eerie atmosphere of bygone Bokor.

## History

In the early 1920s the French, ever eager to escape the lowland heat, established a hill station atop Phnom Bokor (1080m), known for its dramatic vistas of the coastal plain one vertical kilometre below.

The hill station was twice abandoned to the howling winds: first when Vietnamese and Khmer Issarak (Free Khmer) forces overran it in the late 1940s while fighting for independence from France, and again in 1972 when the Lon Nol regime left it to the Khmer Rouge forces that were steadily taking over the countryside. Because of its commanding position, the site was strategically important to all sides during the civil war and was one location the Vietnamese really had to fight for during their 1979 invasion. For several months, the Khmer Rouge held out in the Catholic church while the Vietnamese shot at them from the Bokor Palace, 500m away.

## ◎ Sights

### Bokor Palace
HISTORIC BUILDING

(ដំណាក់បូកគោ) FREE Opened in 1925, this once grand hotel was a chief playground for hobnobbing French officials. As you wander through the building, you'll need your imagination to envisage the lavish interiors that adorned the opulent ballroom and guestrooms as today the hotel is a vast, empty shell with just scraps of original floor tilework still hanging on.

### Catholic Church
CHURCH

FREE The squat belfry of the Romanesque-style Catholic church still holds aloft its cross, and fragments of glass brick cling to the corners of the nave windows; one side window holds the barest outline of a rusty crucifix. It's easy to imagine a small crowd of French colonials in formal dress assembled here for Sunday Mass. The subdividing walls inside were built by the Khmer Rouge. A bit up the hill, a sheer drop overlooks rainforest.

### Wat Sampov Pram                    BUDDHIST TEMPLE

(វត្តសំពៅប្រាំ) Lichen-caked Wat Sampov Pram (Five Boats Wat) offers tremendous views over the jungle to the coastline below, including Vietnam's Phu Quoc Island. Wild monkeys like to hang out around the wat.

### Popokvil Falls                          WATERFALL

(ទឹកធ្លាក់ពពកវិល) From the Thansur Bokor Highland Resort, the road heads north to two-tiered Popokvil Falls, which are at their most impressive from July to October.

## 🛈 Getting There & Away

To visit the hill station you can either go on one of the numerous day trips organised in Kampot or rent a motorbike and travel under your own steam. The road up here is brand-spanking new – built by the Thansur Bokor Highland Resort – so it's in excellent condition.

# Kep                              កែប

📱 036 / POP 35,000

Founded as a seaside retreat for the French elite in 1908 and a favoured haunt of Cambodian high-rollers during the 1960s, today tourists are being drawn back to Kep (Krong Kep, also spelled Kaeb). Some travellers find Kep a tad soulless because it lacks a centre. Others are oddly charmed by its torpid pace.

This dearth of a central hub (not to mention a complete absence of a long sandy shoreline) hasn't stopped Kep's proliferation of boutique resorts. Hotels here squarely target a cultured beach crowd, happier to go for a hike amid the butterly-filled trails of Kep National Park and hang out in their hammock with a glass of wine, than party.

Famed for its spectacular sunsets and splendid seafood, Kep also has a glut of luxurious villa ruins that hark back to its pre-war heyday. Kep's evacuation under Khmer Rouge rule, followed in the 1980s by systematic looting, mean today these decaying shells of modernist mansions, now entangled with forest, stand as relics from another age that met a sudden and violent end.

## ⊙ Sights

Scattered throughout Kep are the mildewed shells of handsome mid-20th-century villas that speak of happier, carefree times, and of the terrible years of Khmer Rouge rule and civil war. All built according to the precepts of the modernist style, with clean lines and little adornment, they keep the memory of Kep's short and sweet heyday alive. Today

many are covered in graffiti and shelter squatters (and, some say, ghosts). There are good examples along NH33A, heading north from the Northern Roundabout. Don't get your hopes up about buying one, as they were all snapped up for a song in the mid-1990s by well-connected speculators.

### ★ Kep National Park                          PARK

(ឧទ្យានជាតិកែប; admission 4000r) The interior of Kep peninsula is occupied by Kep National Park, where an 8km circuit, navigable by foot and mountain bike, winds through thick forest passing by wats and viewpoints. Quirky yellow signs point the way and show trailheads to off-shooting walking paths that lead into the park's interior. The 'Stairway to Heaven' trail is particularly worthwhile, leading up the hill to a pagoda, a nunnery and the Sunset Rock viewpoint.

The main park entrance is behind Veranda Natural Resort.

Fuel up or chill out after your hike at Led Zep Cafe (p224), which is on the trail 300m into the walk from the main entrance. The owner, Christian, was the driving force in creating, mapping and signposting the trails and continues to look after the park environment.

### Koh Tonsay (Rabbit Island)                 ISLAND

(កោះ ទន្សាយ) If you like a rustic beachcomber lifestyle, Koh Tonsay's 250m-long main beach is for you, but come now as the island is tagged for development. The beach is one of the nicest of any of the Kep-area islands, but don't expect sparkling white sand. This one has shorefront flotsam, chickens and wandering cows. Restaurant-shacks and rudimentary bungalows (from US$7 per night) rim the sand.

Boats to Rabbit Island (30 minutes) leave from Rabbit Island pier at 9am, returning to Kep at 4pm (US$10 return). Kep guesthouses can arrange boat tickets or you can head to the Koh Tonsay Boat Ticket Office at the pier. Private boats to Rabbit Island can be arranged at the pier office and cost about US$25 return.

Other Kep-area islands include Koh Pos (Snake Island; about 30 minutes beyond Rabbit Island), which has a deserted beach and fine snorkelling but no overnight accommodation. Getting out there costs about US$50 for an all-day trip by 10-person boat. There's also small, beachless Koh Svay (Mango Island), whose summit offers nice views.

The island's named because locals say it resembles a rabbit – an example of what too much local brew can do to your imagination.

SOUTH COAST KEP

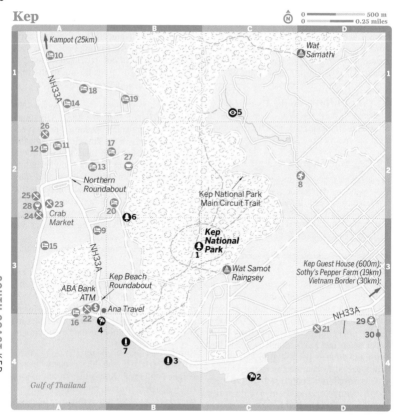

**Kep Butterfly Farm**  FARM

(កសិដ្ឋានមេអំបៅកែប; Jasmine Valley Trail, Kep National Park; donations accepted; ⊙9am-6pm) FREE This small and beautifully kept flower-filled garden is home to myriad butterflies. You can cycle or motorbike here or hike here from the Kep National Park trail by taking the off-shooting 'Connection Path' track.

## 🐾 Beaches

Most of Kep's beaches are too shallow and rocky to make for good swimming. It is possible to swim off the beach or the jetty at the Sailing Club, but the water is particularly shallow here.

**Kep Beach**  BEACH

This handkerchief-sized strip of sand is Kep's only proper beach. In the pre-war period, powder-white sand was trucked in from other beaches and this practice began again in 2013, ensuring the beach is in better shape

than it had been for years. It's still somewhat pebbly and can get packed on weekends. The eastern end of the shaded promenade along the beach is marked by Sela Cham P'dey, a statue depicting a nude fisher's wife waiting for her husband to return.

**Coconut Beach**  BEACH

This 'beach' has dining platforms and food shacks, but not really any sand as such. It begins a few hundred metres southeast of Kep Beach, just past the town's famous giant crab statue.

## 🏃 Activities

**Sailing Club**  WATER SPORTS

(☑078 333686; www.knaibangchatt.com/the-sailing-club; ⊙8am-5pm) Open to all, the club hires out sea kayaks (US$5 per hour), Hobie Cats (from US$15 per hour) and windsurfers (US$12 per hour). Decent mountain bikes are also available at US$10 per day.

# Kep

### Magic Tree
TREE CLIMBING

(☑ 099 896859; maxdiscoverycambodia.wordpress. com; US$8) Max Discovery Cambodia organise a range of events and team-building around Kep, and the Magic Tree is an alternative experience for families. Explore the interior of a huge old ficus tree in Kep National Park with safety ropes and instruction.

### Ranch de la Plantation
HORSE RIDING

(☑ 097 847 4960; www.kep-plantation.com; 1/2hr US$20/34; ⊙8am-6pm) Horse rides are available through the lower reaches of Kep National Park and into the countryside around town. Horses can be a little cantankerous so are more suited to experienced adult riders.

### Marine Conservation Cambodia
VOLUNTEERING

(www.marineconservationcambodia.org; Koh Seh) ⬦ Based on the island of Koh Seh (18km from Kep) Marine Conservation Cambodia works to preserve the marine environment around Kep and combat the destruction caused to sealife by illegal fishing. Volunteers can get hands-on practice, getting involved with patrols to spot illegal fishing, as well as learning about marine conservation and helping with research projects.

## ⌖ Tours

Kep makes a good base for visiting Sothy's Pepper Farm (p215), and several delightful cave temples, including Wat Kiri Sela (p224) near Kompong Trach, and Phnom Chhnork (p217) and Phnom Sorsia (p218) on the road to Kampot. The best way to see the sights is to hire one of the many English-speaking *re-mork* drivers in town (about US$20 per day) and tailor your own countryside tour.

## 🛏 Sleeping

Kep meanders along the shoreline for a good 5km, with resorts and guesthouses speckled along the length of the main road and snuggled along the dirt tracks that wander up the hills leading to Kep National Park.

### ★ Botanica Guesthouse
BUNGALOW **$**

(☑ 097 899 8614; www.kep-botanica.com; NH33A; r with fan/air-con US$19/29; ❄☏⊛) A little way from the action (if Kep can be said to have any action), Botanica offers exceptional value for money with attractive bungalows boasting contemporary bathrooms. There is a small swimming pool and guests can use free bicycles to hit the beach.

### Tree Top Bungalows
BUNGALOW **$**

(☑ 012 515191; www.keptreetop.com; bungalow with/without bathroom US$25/5, treehouse bungalow from US$10; @ ☏) Chilled out to the max, the bamboo 'treehouse' bungalows here are as quirky as it gets (each pair shares a bathroom). Back down on the ground are solid, roomy bungalows with private bathrooms, and Kep's cheapest rooms – shacks separated by flimsy partitions.

### Kimly Lodge
GUESTHOUSE **$**

(☏ 012 721200; www.kimlylodge.com; d US$25, bungalow from US$45; ❈ 🛜 🏊 ) Smart, good-value rooms with tiled floors, cosy decor and spotless bathrooms are a real budget find. Out the back large cottage-style bungalows have stone-walled bathrooms and little verandahs.

### Kep Guest House
HOSTEL **$**

(☏ 097 374 8080; www.kepguesthouse.com; NH33A; dm US$5-7, r US$9-17; ❈ 🛜 ) This modest hostel is Kep's nicest backpacker pad with bright, airy and clean rooms, and a dorm with double beds. There's great sea views from the rooftop restaurant. The US$17 room has air-con.

### Bacoma
BUNGALOW **$**

(☏ 088 411 2424; bacoma@live.com; NH33A; r US$10-36; 🛜 ) Cheap and cheerful rondavels (circular thatched dwellings) in the garden all have mosquito nets and fan, with a generous helping of sparkling clean shared bathrooms. There are also roomy bungalows and traditional Khmer houses with private bathroom.

### Le Coco De Mer
BUNGALOW **$**

(☏ 090 880413; www.lecocodemerbungalows.com; bungalow with fan/air-con incl breakfast US$25/35; ❈ 🛜 ) Set in a relaxed, peaceful garden, Le Coco De Mer is tucked just up the hill from the main road. Simple but sweet wooden bungalows (fan only), with hammocks strung from porch, are delightfully rustic, while spacious concrete cottages offer air-con to beat the Kep heat.

### ★ Saravoan Hotel
BOUTIQUE HOTEL

(☏ 036-639 3909; www.saravoanhotel-kep.com; d/tw/f US$45/50/55; ❹ ❈ 🛜 🏊 ) This new player on the scene has brought contemporary minimalist design to Kep. Spacious rooms with polished concrete floors, stone-wall detailing and floor-to-ceiling glass doors that open out onto balconies with the best sea view in town. The terrace pool area (again with sea views) is just the place to cool off after exploring Kep National Park.

### Tara Lodge
GUESTHOUSE **$$**

(☏ 097 623 6167; www.taralodge-kep.com; d incl breakfast US$50-60, f US$75; ❹ ❈ 🛜 ) The hugely friendly Tara Lodge gets a big tick from us for its comfortable, large rooms (with all the mod-cons) secreted within a verdant garden of palms and flowers, and set around a glistening pool. This is a secluded spot for some serious downtime. The upstairs terrace-restaurant has wonderful views.

### Le Flamboyant Resort
RESORT **$$**

(☏ 017 491010; www.flamboyant-hotel.com; NH33A; d incl breakfast from US$60; ❹ ❈ 🛜 🏊 ) Although less flamboyant than the name would suggest, this attractive, large garden property (complete with lawn-mowing horse) has a boutique resort feel. Cottage-style bungalows have blue accents and wood detailing, and open out onto dinky verandahs. There are two swimming pools, a small spa hut and a good restaurant on site.

### Sea View Bungalows
RESORT **$$**

(☏ 097 695 8582; www.seaviewbungalows.com; bungalows incl breakfast from US$40; ❈ 🛜 🏊 ) This family-friendly bungalow resort sprawls along the hillside amid a rambling mature garden with pool. It's far enough away to feel secluded, but still central enough to easily walk to Kep's crab market. Both spacious family suites and standard bungalows are comfortable and kept spick-and-span, though the decor is a bit dull.

### Veranda Natural Resort
RESORT **$$$**

(☏ 012 888619; www.veranda-resort.asia; Kep Hillside Rd; r incl breakfast from US$80; ❈ 🛜 🏊 ) The hillside bungalows here are built of wood, bamboo and stone, and are connected by a maze of stilted walkways, making it a memorable spot for a romantic getaway. Check out a few rooms because the size, shape and price vary wildly. The food is excellent and sunset views from the restaurant pavilion are stunning.

### Le Ponton Hotel
BOUTIQUE HOTEL **$$$**

(☏ 017 780061; www.lepontonhotel.com; bungalow incl breakfast from US$80; ❹ ❈ 🛜 🏊 ) This hotel radiates an effortless beach-holiday vibe with its colourful lounging areas and very attractive pool area. Bungalow-style rooms with little balconies are simple but chic, and are set within a wonderful tropical garden of blooming flowers and well-tended trees. It's strolling distance to both the crab market and Kep Beach.

### Knai Bang Chatt
BOUTIQUE HOTEL **$$$**

(☏ 078 888556; www.knaibangchatt.com; s/d incl breakfast from US$188/319; ❹ ❈ @ 🛜 🏊 ) Kep's first stab at a design hotel occupies a cluster of 1960s waterfront villas, with rooms that could have fallen out of the pages of a slick magazine. For this price though, we would have expected all the lovely glass to be cleaned to properly appreciate the sea views. It's on the seafront, with only a sliver of a beach.

#  Eating

Eating at the **crab market** – a row of wooden waterfront restaurants by a wet fish market – is a quintessential Kep experience. Fresh crabs fried with Kampot pepper are a taste sensation. Crabs are kept alive in pens tethered a few metres off the pebbly beach. You can dine at one of the restaurants or buy crab for around 35,000r a kilo and have your guesthouse prepare it. There are lots of great places to choose from at the crab market, so keep an eye on where the Khmer crowd are eating. Some of Kep's hotels offer fine dining. Knai Bang Chatt's seafront Strand dining pavilion and Veranda Natural Resort are a couple of the top tables, and have great views to boot.

### ★ Kimly                                     SEAFOOD $$
(☏ 036-904077; Crab Market; mains US$2.50-8; ⊗ 10am-10pm) Of the longest-running restaurant-shacks in the crab market, this is the one most recommended by locals. Kimly does crab every which way – 27 ways, to be exact – all for US$6 to US$7, or supersize it for an extra two bucks. The Kampot pepper crab is truly mouth-watering.

### La Baraka                          INTERNATIONAL $$
(Crab Market; mains US$6-10; ⊗ 11am-10pm; 🛜)
A breath of fresh air from the crab market's other identikit menus, La Baraka serves up a mix of European and Asian flavours with bags of seafood dishes such as swordfish carpaccio. For non-fish lovers there's also great pizza and pasta. Their terrace, over the waves, is sunset cocktail perfection.

### Breezes                                    FUSION $$
(NH33A; mains US$5-10; ⊗ noon-9.30pm; 🛜)
Sitting right on the shoreline, this inviting alfresco restaurant on the road out towards the Rabbit Island pier boasts sleek furnishings, excellent food and fine views of Rabbit Island. Dishes are Asian (not necessarily Khmer), Western and fusion.

### Brise de Kep                      INTERNATIONAL $$
(☏ 036-633 6339; Kep Beach; mains US$3-9; ⊗ 7am-10pm) Mixing up a selection of French and Asian dishes, this restaurant with sea views is strong on seafood specials, including tuna, barracuda and shellfish.

### ★ Sailing Club                             FUSION $$
(mains US$7-12.50; ⊗ 10am-10pm; 🛜) With a small beach, breezy wooden bar and a wooden

SOUTH COAST KEP

---

## GETTING TO VIETNAM: KEP TO HA TIEN

**Getting to the border** The Prek Chak–Xa Xia **border crossing** (⊗ 6am-5.30pm) has become a popular option for linking Kampot and Kep with Ha Tien, and then onwards to either the popular Vietnamese island of Phu Quoc, or to Ho Chi Minh City.

The easiest way to get to the Prek Chak border and on to Ha Tien, Vietnam, is to catch a minivan from Phnom Penh (US$16, five hours), Sihanoukville (US$16, four hours), Kampot (US$8, 1½ hours) or Kep (US$5, one hour) to the border. Virak Buntham (p84) plies this route from Phnom Penh. From Kampot and Kep, Kampot Tours & Travel (p217) are the most reliable service.

Note that even travellers who've bought a through ticket to Ho Chi Minh City or Phu Quoc usually have to change buses at the border.

A more flexible alternative from Phnom Penh or Kampot is to take any bus to Kompong Trach, then a *moto* (about US$3) for 15km, on a good road, to the border.

In Kep, guesthouses can arrange a direct *remork* (US$13, one hour) or taxi (US$20, 30 minutes). Rates and times are almost double from Kampot. Private vehicles take a new road that cuts south to the border 10km west of Kompong Trach.

**At the border** Vietnam grants 15-day visas on arrival for nationals of several European and Asian countries. Other nationalities, and anyone staying longer than 15 days, must purchase a visa in advance.

At Prek Chak, *motos* ask US$5 to take you to the Vietnamese border post 300m past the Cambodian one, and then all the way to Ha Tien (15 minutes, 7km). You'll save money walking across no-man's land and picking up a *moto* on the other side for US$2 to US$3.

**Moving on** Travellers bound for Phu Quoc should arrive in Ha Tien no later than 12.30pm to secure a ticket on the 1pm ferry (230,000d or about US$11, 1½ hours). Extreme early risers may be able to make it to Ha Tien in time to catch the 8am ferry. The scheduled buses from Cambodia to Ha Tien arrive before the 1pm boat departs.

jetty poking out into the sea, this is one of Cambodia's top sundowner spots. The Asian fusion food is excellent and you can get your crab fix here too. Try the Kep Special Fish (served in a Kampot pepper and coconut sauce) for a local taste sensation.

## 🍷 Drinking & Nightlife

**Toucan** BAR

(Crab Market; ⏰ 11am-midnight; 📶) The terrace here is the best spot for a drink (or five) once the sun goes down. There's usually a few punters propping up the bar until midnight or so, which counts as a late night for Kep.

**Led Zep Cafe** CAFE

(Kep National Park; ⏰ 9.30am-6pm) A lovely, secluded cafe on the Kep National Park trail. Enjoying a chilled lime juice on the wide terrace with knock-out views overlooking the coast is the perfect pick-me-up after a hike.

## ❶ Information

For all things Kep-related, www.visitkep.com is a useful online resource.

There's no bank in Kep but there is an **ABA Bank ATM** (⏰ 24 hr) at Kep Beach.

Nearly all hotels and many restaurants have free wi-fi.

## ❶ Getting There & Around

Kep is 25km from Kampot and 41km from the Prek Chak–Xa Xia border crossing to Vietnam.

Buses stop at Kep Beach in front of a line of travel agencies which all sell bus and minibus tickets. **Ana Travel** (📞 036-652 3999; Kep Beach; ⏰ 9am-6pm) has the best onward bus information. You can also purchase bus tickets from most guesthouses.

Phnom Penh Sorya (p84) and **Hua Lian** (Map p46; 📞 223025; Monireth Blvd & Olympic Stadium) buses head to Phnom Penh at 7.30am, 1pm and 2.30pm (US$5, four hours). A private taxi to Phnom Penh (2½ hours) costs US$40 to US$45.

Virak Buntham's (p199) Ha Tien–Sihanoukville bus rumbles through Kep at 7.30pm (US$7, three hours). However, it's more comfortable to take the minivan services to Sihanoukville (US$6 to US$7, 2½ hours) via Kampot (US$3, ½ hour) run by **Kampot Tours & Travel** (Map p190; 📞 in Kampot 092 125556; Ana Travel, Serendipity Beach Rd) and Champa Mekong Travel (p217) departing at 10.30am and 2.30pm.

A *remork* to Kampot costs about US$12; private taxis are US$20. *Remorks* hang out at Kep Beach roundabout. There are very few *moto* drivers in town.

Motorbike rental is US$5 to US$7 per day; ask your guesthouse or any travel agency.

# Around Kep

**Wat Kiri Sela** BUDDHIST TEMPLE

(វត្តគិរីសីលា; ⏰ 7am-6pm) This Buddhist temple sits at the foot of Phnom Kompong Trach, a dramatic karst formation riddled with more than 100 caverns and passageways. From the wat, an underground passage leads to a fishbowl-like formation, surrounded by vine-draped cliffs and open to the sky. Various stalactite-laden caves shelter reclining Buddhas and miniature Buddhist shrines.

The closest town is Kompong Trach. From here, take the dirt road opposite the Acleda Bank, on NH33 in the town centre, for 2km.

Kompong Trach is 28km northeast of Kep on NH33, making it an easy day trip from both Kep and Kampot.

At the wat, note that friendly local kids with torches (flashlights), keen to put their evening-school English to use, are eager to serve as guides. Make sure you tip them if you use them.

# TAKEO PROVINCE

Often referred to as 'the cradle of Cambodian civilisation', Takeo Province (ខេត្តតាកែវ) was part of what Chinese annals called 'water Chenla', no doubt a reference to the extensive annual floods that still blanket much of the area. Today this impoverished rural province is a backwater that sees few tourists. Those who do make it here get some of Cambodia's most ancient and fascinating temples virtually to themselves.

The temples of Tonlé Bati (p90) and Phnom Chisor (p91) lie in Takeo but are usually visited as day trips from Phnom Penh.

## Takeo តាកែវ

📞 032 / POP 40,000

There's not much happening at all in the languid, lakeside provincial capital of Takeo, but it makes a good base from which to take a motorboat ride to the pre-Angkorian temples of Angkor Borei (p227) and Phnom Da (p227) and experience river life.

The main attraction in town is eating freshwater lobster on the waterfront (rainy season only).

# Takeo

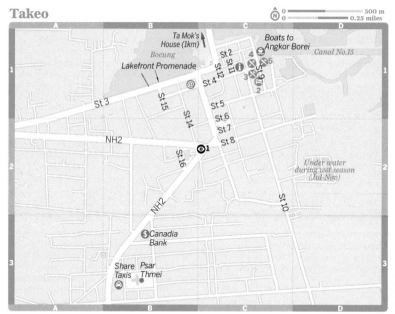

## ◉ Sights & Activities

Although it's nothing compared to Kampot, some attractive French-era shophouses, slowly slouching into genteel decay, line the streets around Psar Nat. The building housing Psar Nat itself is a concrete monstrosity built after the overthrow of the Khmer Rouge.

**Ta Mok's House**                    HISTORIC BUILDING
(ផ្ទះតាម៉ុក; ⊘7am-5pm) **FREE** A pleasant stroll via a 150m-long railings-free bridge takes you to the house of Takeo Province's most notorious native son, Ta Mok (aka 'The Butcher'), the Khmer Rouge commander of the Southwestern Zone, where he presided over horrific atrocities. Ta Mok's House is now occupied by a police training facility, but you can wander around the grounds. Ta Mok also had a residence near Anlong Veng.

## 🛌 Sleeping

Few people stay overnight in Takeo as it is day-tripping distance from Phnom Penh or a brief detour on a road trip south to Kep or Kampot.

**Meas Family Homestay**              HOMESTAY **$**
(☑011 925428; http://cambodianhomestay.com; Ang Tasaom District; adult/child incl all meals

US$17/13; @ 🛜) This popular and friendly family homestay has 11 rooms in a spacious compound located just off the road between Angk Tasaom and Takeo. The rates include some delicious home-cooked Khmer food and cooking classes are available. It's possible to volunteer to teach English at the local school.

**Daunkeo Guesthouse**                GUESTHOUSE **$**
(☑032-210303; www.daunkeo.com; St 9; s/d with fan US$6/8, with air-con US$13/15; ❄🛜) The smartest guesthouse in Takeo, Daunkeo is spread over three modern villas. Spotlessly clean and efficiently run, its air-con rooms include satellite TV and hot-water showers. Anoint yourself a VIP with a suite-like room for just US$25.

## GETTING TO VIETNAM: TAKEO TO CHAU DOC

**Getting to the border** The remote and seldom-used Phnom Den–Tinh Bien border crossing (☉7am-5pm) between Cambodia and Vietnam lies about 60km southeast of Takeo town in Cambodia and offers connections to Chau Doc. Most travellers prefer the Mekong crossing at Kaam Samnor or the newer Prek Chak crossing near Ha Tien to the south. Take a share taxi (10,000r), a chartered taxi (US$25) or a *moto* (US$10) from Takeo to the border (48km).

**At the border** Several European and Asian nationalities can get 15-day Vietnam visas on arrival; everyone else needs to arrange one in advance. Coming into Cambodia from Vietnam, note that e-visas are not accepted for entry here.

**Moving on** Travellers are at the mercy of Vietnamese *xe om* (*moto*) drivers and taxis for the 30km journey from the border to Chau Doc. Prepare for some tough negotiations. Expect to pay somewhere between US$5 and US$10 by bike, more like US$20 for a taxi.

## ✖ Eating

There are food stalls around **Independence Monument**. In the evening, this is the place to snack on Cambodian desserts or enjoy a *tukalok* (fruit shake).

**Stung Takeo**  CAMBODIAN $
(St 9; small/large mains US$3/5; ☉7am-9pm) Perched over the seasonal lake, this is easily Takeo's best restaurant for both food and ambience. The seafood-heavy menu is full of traditional local flavour, such as squid and Kampot pepper. This is also the place to come for remarkably good – and affordable – freshwater lobster. The season for these toothsome creatures is approximately August to November.

**Delikes**  INTERNATIONAL $
(St 10; mains US$2-5; ☉6am-8pm; 🛜) This small place serves excellent Asian breakfasts, tasty fresh spring rolls and salads, and a range of pizzas. Their green mango and dried shrimp salad makes for a light but flavourful lunch.

**Psar Nat**  MARKET $
(St 10; ☉6am-about 8pm) The food court here has a dozen stalls that are great for breakfast soup, *num kong* (delectably chewy Khmer doughnuts) and *num kroch* (fried dumplings filled with beans and palm sugar).

## ℹ Information

**Canadia Bank** (NH2; ☉8am-3.30pm Mon-Fri, to 11.30am Sat, ATM 24hr)
**Takeo Tourism** (✆032-931323; ☉7.30-11am & 2-5pm Mon-Fri, 7.30-11am Sat & Sun) May be able to arrange an English-speaking guide (US$15 to US$20) to the temples.

## ℹ Getting There & Around

Takeo is on NH2, 77km south of Phnom Penh, 40km north of Kirivong and 48km north of the Phnom Den-Tinh Bien border crossing to Vietnam.

No bus company currently serves Takeo. To Phnom Penh direct, take a shared taxi (US$5 per seat, US$25 for the whole taxi) from a *lot* (NH3) in front of **Psar Thmei** (Central Market, NH2). For a more roundabout journey, hop on a nine-seater *remork* (seat 2000r) from Psar Thmei, a *remork* (US$4) from Psar Thmei or the hospital or a *moto* (US$3) wherever you spot one, and head to Angk Tasaom; the chaotic transport junction 13km west of Takeo on NH3. Here you can flag down both northbound buses to Phnom Penh and southbound buses to Kampot and Kep.

Occasional share taxis (10,000r) and minivans (5000r) make the 45-minute trip down to Kirivong, or you can hire a *moto* for US$10. To get to the Phnom Den–Tinh Bien border crossing for Vietnam, go to Kirivong and switch to a *moto* (US$2) for the final 8km. A private taxi to Kirivong is US$20, plus US$5 more to the border.

# Angkor Borei & Phnom Da

Angkor Borei was known as Vyadhapura when it served as the capital of 'water Chenla' in the 8th century. It was also an important centre during the earlier Funan period (1st to 6th centuries), when Indian religion and culture were carried to the Mekong Delta by traders, artisans and priests from India, as the great maritime trade route between India and China passed by the Mekong Delta. The earliest datable Khmer inscription (AD 611) was discovered here and hints of this past greatness can be found in the 5.7km moated wall that still surrounds this impoverished riverine townlet.

The 45-minute open-air motorboat ride to reach here from Takeo, along Canal No 15, dug in the 1880s, is one of the best opportunities you'll have in Cambodia to see rural riverside living. Today Angkor Borei is home to a small archaeological museum displaying local Funan and Chenla era artefacts. In wet season, when the water levels are high enough, the boat then continues for 15 minutes to Phnom Da, with its temple featuring striking bas-reliefs and ancient hand-cut caves. When arriving by boat isn't possible, you can hop on a *moto* at Angkor Borei.

## ◉ Sights

**Angkor Borei**
**Archaeological Museum**　　　MUSEUM
(សារមន្ទីរបុរាណវិទ្យាអង្គរបុរី; ☑ 012 201638; admission US$1; ⊗ 8am-4.30pm) This modest archaeological museum occupies a Khmer-style building a bit east of Angkor Borei's road bridge. Featured inside are locally discovered Funan- and Chenla-era artefacts, including human bones, pottery, jewellery and stone carvings. The dark-red statues are copies of important works now in Phnom Penh's National Museum (p42) or Paris' Musée Guimet.

**Phnom Da**　　　TEMPLE
(ប្រាសាទភ្នំដា; admission US$2) The twin hills of Phnom Da are spectacularly isolated Mont-St-Michel-style by annual floods. One hill is topped by a temple whose foundations date from the 6th century, although the temple itself was rebuilt in the 11th century. Exceptionally, the temple entrance faces north; the other three sides have blind doors decorated with bas-relief *nagas*.

Five artificial caves pockmark the two hills, used for centuries as Hindu and Buddhist shrines and, during the Vietnam War, as hideouts by the Viet Cong.

Phnom Da's finest bas-relief carvings are not in situ, having been taken to museums in Angkor Borei, Phnom Penh and Paris.

Nearby, on the second hillock, is 8m-high Wat Asram Moha Russei, a restored Hindu sanctuary that probably dates from around AD 700.

## ❶ Getting There & Away

Hiring a boat from Takeo's dock costs around US$35 return for up to four people. The canal leading out to Angkor Borei is clearly delineated in the dry season but surrounded by flooded rice fields the rest of the year. In the rainy season the water can get rough in the afternoon, so it's a good idea to head out early.

Angkor Borei can also be reached year-round via a circuitous land route from the north.

When the water levels are too low you will have to travel by *moto* for the 10-minute ride from Angkor Borei to Phnom Da (US$5 return).

# Phnom Bayong
# & Around　　　ភ្នំបាយ័ងនិងកោរ

Affording breathtaking views of Vietnam's pancake-flat Mekong Delta, the cliff-ringed summit of Phnom Bayong (313m) is graced by a 7th-century Chenla temple built to celebrate a victory over Funan. The *linga* originally in the inner chamber is now in Paris' Musée Guimet, but a number of flora- and fauna-themed bas-relief panels can still be seen; for example, on the lintels of the three false doorways, and carved into the brickwork.

The sweltering climb up to the temple takes about 1½ hours (bring plenty of water), or you can hire a *moto* in Kirivong to take you up in less than 20 minutes (US$10). It's a treacherous path, which explains the high price.

Gentle Kirivong Waterfall (Chruos Phaok Waterfall) is reached by a 1.5km access road that begins about 1km south of Kirivong. Market stalls here sell the area's most famous products: topaz and quartz, either cut like gems or carved into tiny Buddhas and *nagas*. It's a popular destination for locals on a day out.

## ❶ Getting There & Away

Phnom Bayong is about 3km west of the northern edge of Kirivong; the turnoff is marked by a painted panel depicting the temple.

Kirivong is on NH2, 40km south of Takeo and 8km north of the Phnom Den–Tinh Bien border crossing. From Takeo, a *moto* to Kirivong costs about US$10 (US$15 return).

Infrequent minibuses and share taxis to Phnom Penh (via Takeo) leave from Kirivong's Ton Lop Market on NH2 in the centre of town.

To get to the Vietnam border, a *moto* (US$2) from Kirivong is the best bet. Coming *from* the border, you may have to ask the Cambodian border officials to call a *moto* or taxi to pick you up.

# Northwestern Cambodia

POP 4 MILLION / AREA 71,157 SQ KM

## Best Temples

➡ Prasat Preah Vihear (p262)

➡ Banteay Chhmar (p254)

➡ Sambor Prei Kuk (p267)

➡ Preah Khan (p263)

➡ Banteay Top (p254)

## Best Local Life

➡ Banteay Chhmar Homestay (p255)

➡ Phoum Kandal & Chong Kos Floating Villages (p229)

➡ Soksabike (p240)

➡ Isanborei (p268)

## Why Go?

Looking for temples without the tourist hordes? The remote temples of Northwest Cambodia are a world apart. While hilltop Prasat Preah Vihear is the big-hitter, the other temple complexes – wrapped by vines and half-swallowed by jungle – are all fabulous to explore.

In the region's heart is Tonlé Sap, one of the world's most fish-rich lakes and a birder's paradise. Boat trips from Kompong Chhnang and Krakor (near Pursat) to the rickety floating villages that cluster along this important waterway allow you to dip your toes in lake life.

When forays into the region's far-flung corners are complete, the Northwest has one more surprise up its sleeve. Laid-back Battambang, with its colonial architecture and burgeoning arts scene, is the main city here. There's a wealth of brilliant sights all within day-tripping distance from town – making it a worthy pit stop after all the hard travelling is done.

## When to Go
### Battambang

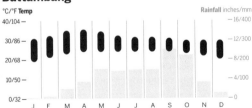

**Dec & Jan** Head to remote temples to explore while pleasant temperatures prevail.

**Aug & Sep** Rainy season is in full throttle in lush countryside studded with palms.

**Nov** Best for back-country exploration, with roads neither too muddy nor too dusty.

# KOMPONG CHHNANG PROVINCE

Kompong Chhnang Province (ខេត្តកំពង់ឆ្នាំង) is a relatively wealthy province, thanks to its proximity to the capital, its fishing and agricultural industries and abundant water resources.

## Kompong Chhnang កំពង់ឆ្នាំង

📋 026 / POP 45,000

While nothing much may be happening in the sleepy centre of Kompong Chhnang (Clay Pot Port), the bustling dock on the Tonlé Sap River is the jumping-off point for serene boat rides to two floating villages. Skimming through the watery streets in a tiny wooden paddle-boat as the late afternoon sun sends a shimmer over the river is a gorgeous way to end a day.

Outside of town you'll find a lush landscape of yellow-green rice fields. Here, in the tiny hamlets where cows slumber beside curvaceous hay bales, the area's distinctive pottery is crafted underneath stilted homes, providing another reason to linger.

## ⊙ Sights

Combining Ondong Rossey and Phnom Santuk for a *moto* (motorcycle taxi) or

## Kompong Chhnang

bicycle tour makes for a rewarding circuit. There are no road signs, so it's a good idea to go with a local.

★**Phoum Kandal &
Chong Kos Floating Villages**    VILLAGE

Much less visited than other floating villages, the Tonlé Sap River hamlets of Phoum Kandal (ភូមិកណ្ដាល) and Chong Kos (ចុងកោះ) are a colourful vision of brightly painted wooden houses, with tiny terraces strung with hammocks, all built on rickety DIY pontoons. To fully explore the villages, hire a wooden boat (with captain) at Kompong Chhnang dock (US$10 per hour, up to three people) to paddle you through these fully buoyant towns, complete with shops, satellite TV – check out the ingenious bamboo electricity poles! – and mobile vegetable vendors.

A one-hour boat ride will allow you to see one village; with 1½ or two hours, you have enough time to visit both. Bigger, motorised tourist boats are available for river tours for US$15 per hour, but these only circle the perimeter of the villages. Hiring a paddle-boat is a more tranquil option: you can glides within the maze of watery streets to glimpse how village life functions when everything floats.

Phoum Kandal (directly southeast of the boat dock) is an ethnic Vietnamese village, while Chong Kos (to the north) is Khmer.

**Ondong Rossey**    VILLAGE

(អណ្ដូងប្រស្សៀ) The quiet village of Ondong Rossey, where the area's famous red pottery is made under every house, is a delightful 7km ride west of town through serene rice fields dotted with sugar palms, many with bamboo ladders running up the trunk. The unpainted pots, decorated with etched or appliqué designs, are either turned with a foot-spun wheel (for small pieces) or banged into shape with a heavy wooden spatula (for large ones).

The golden-hued mud piled up in the yards is quarried at nearby **Phnom Krang Dai Meas** and pounded into fine clay before being shaped and fired; only at the last

**NORTHWESTERN CAMBODIA KOMPONG CHHNANG**

## Kompong Chhnang

# North-western Cambodia Highlights

**1** Chilling out amid the colonial-tinged charms of **Battambang** (p236), surrounded by verdant countryside and hilltop temples.

**2** Soaking up the stupendous vistas from atop **Prasat Preah Vihear's** (p262) dramatic mountain perch.

**3** Gliding on a paddle-boat through the watery thoroughfares of Phoum Kandal and Chong Kos floating villages, just outside **Kompong Chhnang** (p229).

**4** Exploring the vine-entwined brick temples of Southeast Asia's first temple city: the impressive pre-Angkorian ruins of **Sambor Prei Kuk** (p267).

**5** Admiring the intricate Avalokiteshvara bas-reliefs at the massive 12th-century complex of **Banteay Chhmar** (p254).

**6** Traversing the lonely road out to **Preah Khan** (p264) to stand in awe at its mighty, jungle-encroached *gopura* (entrance pavilion).

stage does it acquire a pinkish hue. Pieces can be purchased at the **Pottery Development Center**, although you'll get better deals buying directly from the pottery makers at their houses.

**Phnom Santuk** VIEWPOINT
(ភ្នំសន្ទុក) Phnom Santuk, a rocky hillock behind **Wat Santuk**, is a few kilometres southwest of Kompong Chhnang. The boulder-strewn summit affords fine views of the countryside, including Tonlé Sap, 20km to the north.

## 🛏 Sleeping & Eating

There are plenty of food stalls at the two markets, **Psar Leu** (⊙7am-6pm) and **Psar Krom** (⊙6am-6pm).

**Chanthea Borint Hotel** GUESTHOUSE **$**
(📞026-988622; cbrint@yahoo.com; Prison St; r with fan/air-con US$8/15; ❄❅🖥) Set in a shady garden, this 30-room family pad offers the most charming and friendly accommodation in town. The rooms are small but tidy and well cared for. The restaurant serves breakfast only.

**Sovann Phum Hotel** HOTEL **$**
(📞026-989333; sovannphumkpchotel@yahoo.com; NH5; r with fan/air-con from US$8/15; ❅@🖥) A step up from most Kompong Chhnang options in cleanliness and style, this is a popular spot for the NGO crowd. It has 30 good-sized rooms with modern bathrooms and plenty of light, plus a decent restaurant.

**Soksan Restaurant** CAMBODIAN **$**
(NH5; mains US$2-2.50; ⊙6am-8pm) It lacks English signage but there's an English menu at this restaurant next to Kompong Chhnang's taxi park. It specialises in fried everything, and soups – or be adventurous and order the porcupine fish with omelette.

**Phnom Mea Bakery** BAKERY **$**
(NH5; baked goods 2000-5000r; ⊙7am-5pm) This little place turns out freshly baked baguettes, sandwiches, pastries and tasty pizza. An excellent option for packed lunches.

## ℹ Information

*Remork-moto (tuk tuk)* driver **Channy** (📞077 357361; srinchanny@yahoo.com) is the one-stop shop for all things informative about Kompong Chhnang. He hangs out near the taxi park when he's not with customers.

**Acleda Bank** (NH5; ⊙8am-3.30pm Mon-Fri, to 11.30am Sat, ATM 24hr)

**Canadia Bank** (NH5; ⊙8am-3.30pm Mon-Fri, to 11.30am Sat, ATM 24hr)

## ℹ Getting There & Away

Kompong Chhnang is 91km north of Phnom Penh, 93km southeast of Pursat and 198km southeast of Battambang.

**BUS**

You can buy tickets for Rith Mony and several other companies at the **bus stand** (NH5) – a vendor-cart with bus company signage in front – found north of the taxi park. You can also flag down buses on the NH5 at the Acleda Bank corner.

Buses south to Phnom Penh (12,000r, two hours), and north to Pursat (12,000r, two hours) and Battambang (20,000r, 3½ hours) pull through town hourly throughout the day.

**TAXI**

The fastest way to get to Phnom Penh is by share taxi (20,000r, 1½ hours). They wait at the **taxi park** west of Psar Leu. Share taxis do not generally serve destinations to the northwest, such as Battambang.

## ℹ Getting Around

A several-hour *remork* tour taking in the pottery villages and Phnom Santuk costs around US$8. A *moto* should be about US$5. A *moto/remork* to the port is US$1/2 one way.

Chanthea Borint Hotel rents bicycles (US$2 for the day).

# PURSAT PROVINCE

Pursat Province (ខេត្តពោធិ៍សាត់), Cambodia's fourth-largest, stretches from the remote forests of Phnom Samkos, on the Thai border, eastwards to the fishing villages and marshes of Tonlé Sap lake. Famed for its oranges, it encompasses the northern reaches of the Cardamom Mountains, linked with the town of Pursat by disreputable roads.

## Pursat ពោធិ៍សាត់

📞052 / POP 38,000

You know you've hit Pursat when huge marble monument shops begin to rim the roads – if you're in the market for a life-size statue of a rearing horse, you're in the right place. This dusty provincial capital, known for its carvers, is no beauty but it makes a good base for a day trip to the floating village of Kompong Luong or an expedition into the wilds of the Central Cardamoms Protected Forest.

# Pursat

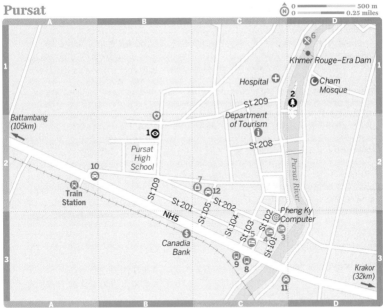

## ◉ Sights

**Koh Sampovmeas**  PARK

(កោះសំពៅមាស, Golden Ship Island) This bizarre island-park, built up in the shape of a ship, is Pursat's place to see and be seen towards sunset. Young locals drop by for aerobics (classes from 5pm) or a game of badminton, while power-walkers pound the circuit between the manicured lawns and Khmer-style pavilions.

**Bun Rany Hun Sen Development Centre**  ARTS CENTRE

(St 109; ⊙7-11am & 2-5pm Mon-Fri, 7-11am Sat) Teaches cloth and mat weaving, sewing, marble carving and other artisanal skills to young people, and sells the items they make from a large shop on premises. There are some real bargains here on beautiful *krama* (chequered scarves) and baskets. Travellers are welcome to visit classes.

## 🛏 Sleeping & Eating

**KM Hotel**  HOTEL $

(☑052-953168; www.kmhotel.com.kh; St 101; r US$20, deluxe US$45; 🕸🛜🌊) Bringing a whole new level of comfort to Pursat's hotel scene, this 146-roomed hotel is ridiculously good value, with mammoth rooms hosting flatscreen TVs and new beds that guarantee a contented sleep. The bathrooms, with old

## Pursat

### ◉ Sights

| | |
|---|---|
| 1 | Bun Rany Hun Sen Development Centre ........................B2 |
| 2 | Koh Sampovmeas ...............................D1 |

### 🛏 Sleeping

| | |
|---|---|
| 3 | KM Hotel ...............................................C3 |
| 4 | Phnom Pech Hotel.............................C3 |
| 5 | Thansour Thmey Hotel .......................C3 |

### ✕ Eating

| | |
|---|---|
| 6 | Magic Fish Restaurant .......................D1 |
| | Reak Smey Angkor Restaurant..................................(see 4) |

### 🛍 Shopping

| | |
|---|---|
| 7 | Psar Chaa..............................................C2 |

### ⓘ Transport

| | |
|---|---|
| 8 | Phnom Penh Sorya...............................C3 |
| 9 | Rith Mony...............................................C3 |
| 10 | Taxis to Battambang...........................A2 |
| 11 | Taxis to Phnom Penh ..........................C3 |
| 12 | Taxis to Pramoay................................C2 |

showers, are a let-down, but we're not complaining because look outside and you'll find not one but two huge swimming pools.

**Thansour Thmey Hotel**  HOTEL $

(☑012 962395; thansourthmey@gmail.com; St 102; r with fan/air-con US$7/15; 🕸🛜) Hello,

## THE KHMER ROUGE AIRPORT

The Khmer Rouge were not known as great builders, but in 1977 and 1978 slave labourers built an airfield using cement of such high quality that even today the 2440m runway and access roads look like they were paved just last week.

No one knows for sure but it seems that **Kompong Chhnang Airport** (KZC), never operational under the Khmer Rouge, was intended to serve as a base for launching air attacks against Vietnam. Chinese engineers oversaw the work of tens of thousands of Cambodians suspected of disloyalty to the Khmer Rouge. Anyone unable to work was killed, often with a blow to the head delivered with a bamboo rod. In early 1979, as Vietnamese forces approached, almost the entire workforce was executed. Estimates of the number of victims, buried nearby in mass graves, range from 10,000 to 50,000.

In the late 1990s, a plan to turn the airport into a cargo hub for air-courier companies came to nought. These days, local teenagers come out here to tool around on their motorbikes while cows graze between the taxiway and the runway. On sunny days the sun creates convincing mirages.

On an anonymous slope a few kilometres away, the Khmer Rouge dug a **cave** – said to be 3km deep – apparently for the purpose of storing weapons flown in from China. Now home to swirling bats, it can be explored with a torch (flashlight) – but lacking ventilation, it gets very hot and humid.

On a hillside near a cluster of bullet-pocked cement barracks, stripped of anything of value, is a massive cement water tank. Inside it's a remarkable echo chamber.

The airport is about 12km west of town. Take NH5 towards Battambang for 7km and then turn left onto a concrete road.

classic Khmer wood carvings. If you've always wanted to sleep in an intricately carved bed, now is your chance. Rooms are tidy and the restaurant, which serves Khmer and Chinese dishes (mains 10,000r to 16,000r), is one of the best in Pursat.

**Phnom Pech Hotel** HOTEL **$**
(052-951515; St 101; r with fan US$8, with aircon US$13-15; ) This long-running local has clean, though tired, rooms. The friendly manager is quite helpful with travel advice.

**Reak Smey Angkor Restaurant** CAMBODIAN **$**
(St 101; mains 4000-8000r; 7am-9pm) Hugely popular with Khmer tour groups, this family-run restaurant dishes up an extensive menu of local favourites, with plenty of noodle soups and fried-rice options. There's also a small menu of omelettes and Western breakfast plates.

**Magic Fish Restaurant** CAMBODIAN **$**
(St 101; mains 8000-15,000r; 10am-9pm) Just north of the Khmer Rouge–era dam, this riverside place has tasty Khmer dishes and great river views.

## 🛈 Information

Cheata at the Phnom Pech Hotel is relatively switched on if you need information on getting around the province, including to more remote bits such as the Cardamoms.

**Canadia Bank** (NH5; 8am-3.30pm Mon-Fri, to 11.30am Sat, ATM 24hr)

**Department of Tourism** (012 838854; 7-11am & 2-5pm Mon-Fri) Has a booklet on Pursat sightseeing and a map of the province and city.

## 🛈 Getting There & Around

Pursat is 105km southeast of Battambang and 185km northwest of Phnom Penh along NH5.

Buses pass through Pursat virtually all day long, shuttling southeast to Kompong Chhnang and Phnom Penh (20,000r, four hours) hourly; and north to Battambang (15,000r, 1½ hours), hourly from around 11am onwards. **Phnom Penh Sorya** (NH5) has direct trips to Kompong Cham (US$9, six hours, 11.30am) and Siem Reap (US$6, five hours, 7.30am) via Battambang.

Share taxis serve Phnom Penh (24,000r, three hours) from NH5 just east of the bridge. Share taxis to Battambang (16,000r, two hours) depart from NH5 on the western edge of town.

Pick-ups and share taxis to the remote Cardamoms outpost of Ou Som (40,000r, 3¼ hours) and the town of Pramoay (Veal Veng; 30,000r, 2½ hours) via Kravanh (one hour) and Rovieng (two hours) leave from next to the old market, Psar Chaa.

Phnom Pech Hotel rents out bicycles (US$3 a day) and motorbikes (US$10). *Moto/remork* drivers in town charge US$10/15 for a return trip to Kompong Luong.

# Kompong Luong     កំពង់ហ្លួង

POP 10,000

Kompong Luong has all the amenities you'd expect to find in an oversized fishing village, except that here everything floats on water. The result is a partly ethnic-Vietnamese Venice without the dry land. The cafes, shops, chicken coops, fish ponds, ice-making factory, petrol station and karaoke bars are kept from sinking by boat hulls, barrels or bunches of bamboo, as are the Vietnamese pagoda, the blue-roofed church and the colourful houses. In the dry season, when water levels drop and Tonlé Sap lake shrinks, the entire aquapolis is towed, boat by boat, a few kilometres north.

The population of this fascinating and picturesque village is partly Vietnamese, so (reflecting their ambiguous status in Cambodian society) you may find the welcome here slightly more subdued than in most rural Cambodian towns, at least from the adults. Khmer Rouge massacres of Vietnamese villagers living around Tonlé Sap were commonplace during the first half of the 1990s, and even as late as 1998 more than 20 Vietnamese were killed in a pogrom near Kompong Chhnang.

The way to explore Kompong Luong is, naturally, by boat. The official tourist rate to charter a four-passenger wooden motorboat (complete with life-jackets) at Kompong Luong boat landing is US$10 per hour for one to three passengers (US$13 for four to five, US$15 for six to seven).

Kompong Luong has three **homestays** (per person per night not incl boat ride US$4-6; ⊗) available with local families. This is an interesting way to discover what everyday life is really like on the water. Meals are available for US$2 and host families can provide boats for village exploring. You can book a homestay when you arrive at the boat landing.

## ❶ Getting There & Around

The jumping-off point to Kompong Luong is the town of Krakor, 32km east of Pursat. From Krakor to the boat landing, where tours begin, it's 1.5km to 6km, depending on the time of year.

# Northern Cardamom Mountains     ភ្នំក្រវ៉ាញ

As the Central Cardamoms Protected Forest (CCPF) and adjacent wildlife sanctuaries slowly open up to ecotourism, Pursat is emerging as the Cardamoms' northern gateway.

## ❶ Getting There & Away

Roads and bridges in the area have been upgraded to service a new hydrodam in Ou Som, and you can now get into the park at any time of the year. Areas in and near the CCPF are still being de-mined, so stay on roads and well-trodden trails.

From Psar Chaa in Pursat, share taxis and pick-ups serve Kravanh (one hour), Rovieng (two hours) and Pramoay (three hours) year-round. From Pramoay, the track south to Ou Som is in rougher shape. It's passable by *moto* year-round, but taxis can't handle it during the height of the wet season. The road south from Ou Som to Koh Kong is much better and can accommodate taxis year-round. In the dry season you can go from Pursat all the way to Koh Kong by share taxi.

You can also get to Pramoay via a dirt road (no public transport) from Samlaut in Pailin Province.

Phnom Aural Wildlife Sanctuary is best accessed from Kompong Speu, 45km west of Phnom Penh.

# Central Cardamoms Protected Forest (CCPF)     ព្រៃអភិរក្សភ្នំក្រវ៉ាញ

The CCPF's enforcement ranger teams get technical and financial support from Conservation International (www.conservation.org) and operate out of three stations in the north.

Rangers and military police based at Kravanh ranger station, deep in the Cardamoms jungle in the Tang Rang area south of Pursat, play an unending game of cat-and-mouse with loggers, poachers and encroachers.

The most valuable contraband at the front-line Rovieng ranger station is aromatic *mreah prew* (sassafras, or safrole) oil, extracted from the roots of the endangered *Cinnamomum parthenoxylon* tree. One tonne of wood produces just 30L of the oil, which has a delightful, sandalwood-like scent. Local people use it in traditional medicine, but it's safrole oil's use as the precursor in the production of the drug MDMA that has caused the most illegal logging of this tree species.

A few kilometres from Rovieng (and 53km southwest of Pursat) are the L'Bak Kamronh Rapids, which attract Khmers on holidays. About 25km west of Rovieng, in Pramoay Commune, the old-growth Chhrok Preal Forest can be visited with a guide.

To pre-arrange a guide, homestay or guesthouse near the Kravanh or Rovieng ranger stations, try contacting forestry official **Peau Somanak** (✆ 017 464663; smpeov@gmail.com) for advice.

## Phnom Samkos Wildlife Sanctuary ទីជម្រកសត្វព្រៃភ្នំសំកុស

Sandwiched between the CCPF and the Thai frontier, the Phnom Samkos Wildlife Sanctuary (3338 sq km) is well and truly out in the sticks. It is threatened by timber laundering and agricultural concessions.

Boasting Cambodia's second-highest peak, Phnom Samkos (1717m), the sanctuary's main town is Pramoay (Veal Veng), 125km west of Pursat. This remote little outpost has three **guesthouses** (r US$5). Local *moto* drivers can take visitors to nearby ethnic minority villages.

From Pramoay it takes about an hour to tackle the track south to Ou Som, next to the Atai dam, where there's a CCPF ranger station.

### 🏃 Activities

**O'Soam Tourism Centre**                    TOUR
(☎ 089 899895; www.osoamtour.wordpress.com) In the isolated settlement of Ou Som, villagers have long eked out a meagre living by poaching and logging. To create income-generating opportunities in the area that harness the local environment sustainably, the O'Soam Community Centre offers a range of ecotourism activities for those interested in experiencing a region of Cambodia that has long been under the radar for travellers.

Hiking and boat trips in the surrounding countryside, as well as trips to Phnom Samkos, can be organised. Local accommodation is provided by a couple of simple guesthouses and homestays (US$5 per person).

## Phnom Aural Wildlife Sanctuary ទីជម្រកសត្វព្រៃភ្នំឱរ៉ាល់

Sadly, Phnom Aural Wildlife Sanctuary (2538 sq km), just east of the CCPF, is rapidly being destroyed from the south and the east by corrupt land speculation and rampant illegal logging.

Hiking up Phnom Aural (1813m), Cambodia's highest peak, can be done in a day but most do it in two or three days, including transport to and from Phnom Penh. Guides (US$25 to US$30 per day) who know the way, and where to find water, can be hired through the village chief in Sra Ken, at the base of the mountain.

To get there, travel from Phnom Penh to the town of Kompong Speu (45km), where early-afternoon minibuses depart for Spean Dach (12,000r, 2½ hours), then hire a *moto* to Sra Ken (US$10, one hour). Overnight in Sra Ken, which has homestay accommodation (about US$4 to US$6), and head up the mountain the next morning. On the second day you can camp on the mountain or return to Sra Ken.

# BATTAMBANG PROVINCE

Battambang Province (ខេត្តបាត់ដំបង; Bat Dambong), is said by proud locals to produce Cambodia's finest rice, sweetest coconuts and tastiest oranges (don't bring this up in Pursat). It has a long border with Thailand and a short stretch of the Tonlé Sap shoreline.

Battambang has passed from Cambodia to Thailand and back again several times over the past few centuries. Thailand ruled the area from 1794 to 1907 and again during WWII (1941 to 1946), when the Thais cut a deal with the Japanese and the Vichy French.

# Battambang បាត់ដំបង
☎ 053 / POP 147,000

There's something about Battambang that visitors just love. Forget the fact that there's really not all that much to do in the city proper: the colonial architecture teetering into genteel disrepair, the riverside setting, the laid-back cafes – they all make up for it. It's the perfect blend of relatively urban modernity and small-town friendliness.

Outside the city's confines, meanwhile, timeless hilltop temples and bucolic villages await – not to mention the most scenic river trip in the country, which links Battambang with Siem Reap.

That Cambodia's best-known circus (the magnificent Phare Ponleu Selpak) is here is no coincidence: the city has an enduring tradition of producing many of Cambodia's best-loved singers, actors and artists.

### ◉ Sights

Much of Battambang's charm lies in its early 20th-century architecture; a mix of vernacular shophouses and French colonial construction that makes up the historic core of the city. Some of the finest colonial buildings are dotted along the waterfront (St 1), especially just south of Psar Nath (St 1), itself an architectural monument, albeit a modernist one.

Phnom Penh–based **KA Architecture Tours** (www.ka-tours.org) **FREE** has collaborat-

**LOCAL KNOWLEDGE**

## BATTAMBANG'S EMERGING ART SCENE

Before the Khmer Rouge era, Battambang had a long history as the nation's central hub for art and culture. Today a new generation of artists are building on this heritage and Battambang is regaining its reputation as Cambodia's capital of culture. A small clutch of galleries, shops and funky bars have set up around St 2½, creating an informal arts district right in the heart of town. Check out the local scene at these places:

**Sammaki Gallery** (St 2½; ⊙1-6pm Mon-Fri) 🖉 Battambang's original contemporary-art gallery, focused on the work of local young artists. Supported by the Cambodian Children's Trust.

**Sangker Art Space** (St 1½) A little art space and gallery that runs regular exhibitions by Battambang's artists.

**Lotus Bar & Gallery** (p244) At the heart of Battambang's artistic life, Lotus' upstairs gallery hosts exhibitions showcasing the town's diverse and eclectic artistic community. Owner Darren Swallow helped found the Sammaki Gallery.

**Choco l'art Café** (p243) This cafe-gallery often hosts exhibitions and other art projects.

**Make Maek Art Space** (66 St 2½) This gallery and workshop, run by respected local painter Mao Soviet, displays many of his works. It was closed last time we came through town but check out if it's reopened when you visit.

---

ed with Battambang Municipality to create two heritage walks in the historic centre of Battambang, available as a free download from its website. The walks concentrate both on the French period and on the modernist architecture of the '60s. This is a great way to spend half a day exploring the city.

**Battambang Museum** MUSEUM
(សារមន្ទីរខេត្តបាត់ដំបង; St 1; admission US$1; ⊙8-11am & 2-5.30pm) This small and rather dusty museum displays a trove of fine Angkorian lintels and statuary from all over Battambang Province, including pieces from Prasat Banan and Sneng. Signs are in Khmer, English and French.

A mammoth museum enlargement and modernisation project was in the planning stages when we were last in town and may be well under way by the time you visit.

**Governor's Residence** NOTABLE BUILDING
The two-storey Governor's Residence, with balconies and wooden shutters, is a handsome legacy of the early 1900s. The interior is closed but it's possible to stroll the grounds. It was designed by an Italian architect for the last Thai governor, who departed in 1907.

**Train Station** HISTORIC BUILDING
(St 102) Here at Battambang's disused train station, the time on the stopped clock is always 8.02. Just along the tracks to the south, you can explore a treasure trove of derelict French-era repair sheds, warehouses and rolling stock.

**Wats** BUDDHIST TEMPLE
Battambang's Buddhist temples survived the Khmer Rouge period relatively unscathed thanks to a local commander who ignored orders from on high. Some of the best are **Wat Phiphétaram** (St 4), **Wat Damrey Sar** (វត្តដំរីស, White Elephant Pagoda; St 127) and **Wat Kandal** (វត្តកណ្ដាល; Riverside Rd).

**Wat Kor Village** VILLAGE
(ភូមិវត្តកô) About 2km south of central Battambang, the village of Wat Kor is centred around a temple of the same name. It's a great place to wander, especially late in the afternoon when the opposite (east) bank of the Sangker River is back-lit in amber tones by the sinking sun. Picturesque bridges span the river, the spires of Wat Kor glow bright platinum and Khmer village life is on full display.

About 1.5km beyond Wat Kor, you'll encounter a cluster of Khmer heritage houses that the village is known for. Built of now-rare hardwoods almost a century ago and surrounded by orchard gardens, they have wide verandahs and exude the ambience of another era.

Two of the approximately 20 heritage houses in the Wat Kor area are open to visitors: **Bun Roerng House** (suggested donation US$1) and neighbouring **Khor Sang House** (suggested donation US$1). The owner of each will give you a short tour in French or English. They have floors worn lustrous by a century of bare feet and are decorated with old furniture and family photos.

# Battambang

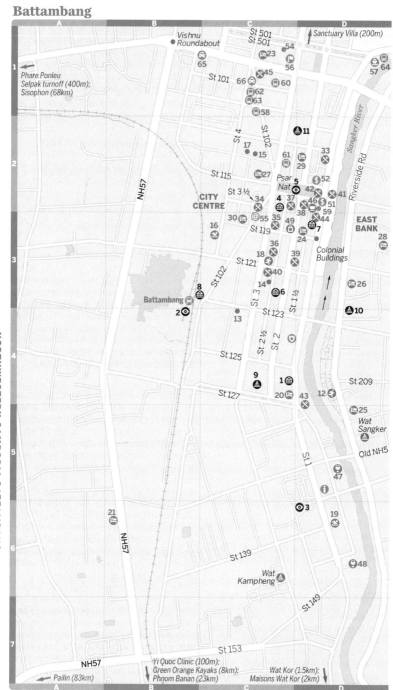

St 501
St 501

Vishnu
Roundabout

Sanctuary Villa (200m)

Phare Ponleu
Selpak turnoff (400m);
Sisophon (68km)

St 101

St 4

St 102

St 115

CITY
CENTRE

St 3½

Psar
Nat

EAST
BANK

St 119

St 102

St 121

Colonial
Buildings

St 3

Battambang

St 1½

St 123

St 2½

St 2

St 125

St 209

St 127

Wat
Sangker

Old NH5

St 1

Wat
Kampheng

St 139

St 149

NH57

St 153

NH57

Pailin (83km)

Yi Quoc Clinic (100m);
Green Orange Kayaks (8km);
Phnom Banan (23km)

Wat Kor (1.5km);
Maisons Wat Kor (2km)

Sangker River

Riverside Rd

NORTHWESTERN CAMBODIA BATTAMBANG

Bun Roerng House was built in 1920 by a local lawyer. During our last visit, the current owners were planning to turn the rear section of the house into homestay accommodation which, when finished, could be a unique option for architecture/history fans. Khor Sang House was built in 1907 by the French-speaking owner's grandfather, who served as a secretary to the province's last Thai governor. The rear section dates from 1890.

## 🏃 Activities

Non-guests can use the pool at **Delux Villa** (☑ 077 336373; www.deluxvilla.com; St 4; 🛜) for US$5.

### Green Orange Kayaks          KAYAKING
(☑ 017 736166; www.fedacambodia.org; Ksach Poy; half-day US$12) ✎ Kayaks can be rented from Green Orange Kayaks, part of FEDA, a local NGO that runs a community centre in the village of Ksach Poy, 8km south of Battambang. Half-day, self-guided kayaking trips begin at Ksach Poy's Green Orange Cafe. From there you paddle back to the city along the Sangker River. A guide (US$3) is optional. Booking ahead is highly recommended.

FEDA also run a guesthouse, the **Green Orange Village Bungalow** (☑ 012 207957; www.fedacambodia.org; Ksach Poy; tr per person US$5) ✎, in Ksach Poy. Ask for Ngarm.

### Aerobics Classes          HEALTH & FITNESS
(Riverside Rd; per person 1000r) Head to Battambang's East Bank to see the locals burning off the rice carbs doing aerobics from about 6am to 7am and 5pm to 7pm daily. Just five minutes of working out should be enough to teach you some numbers in Khmer.

### Seeing Hands Massage          MASSAGE
(☑ 078 337499; St 121; per hr US$6; ⊙ 7am-10pm) ✎ Trained blind masseurs offer soothing work-overs.

### Victory Club          SWIMMING
(St 1; pool access US$2; ⊙ 6am-8pm) Has a 25m pool.

### Khmer New Generation Organization          VOLUNTEERING
(☑ 092 790597; www.kngocambodia.org; Bospo village) ✎ Khmer New Generation Organization, a local NGO, is always looking for volunteer teachers to help out with its English-language teaching program. Commitments of one month or longer are preferred.

# Battambang

**Children's Action for
Development**                    VOLUNTEERING
(☑ 092 301697; www.cadcambodia.org) 🏃 Children's Action for Development, a nonprofit in Pheam Ek (13km from Battambang), provides free English instruction to local kids and welcomes short-term volunteer teachers.

## 👉 Tours

**Soksabike**                        CYCLING
(☑ 012 542019; www.soksabike.com; half-day US$23-27, full-day US$34-40; ⊙ departs 7.30am) 🏃 Based at Kinyei cafe (p244), Soksabike is

a social enterprise aiming to connect visitors with the Cambodian countryside and its people. Half-day/full-day trips cover 25km/40km and include stops at family-run industries such as rice-paper making and the *prahoc* (fermented fish paste) factory, and a visit to a local home. Tour prices depend on group size.

**Butterfly Bicycle Tours**            CYCLING
(☑ 089 297070; www.butterflytour.asia; St 309; half-day tour US$15-17; ⊙ departs 7.30am & 1.30pm) Begun by a group of local university students, Butterfly's bicycle tours are focused either on landscapes, sights or traditional life

in the local area. The traditional livelihoods tour gets rave reviews from visitors.

### Battambang Bike
CYCLING

(☑ 097 482 4104; www.thebattambangbike.com; St 2½; tours US$18) Leads a variety of bike tours, including a half-day city tour and a half-day cycle trip to Phnom Sampeau. They also run free Saturday fun-rides and rent both city and mountain bikes (US$2 to $5 per day).

## 🍴 Courses

### Coconut Lyly
COOKING COURSE

(☑ 016 399339; www.coconutlyly.com; St 111; per person US$10) Classes are run by Chef Lyly, a graduate from Siem Reap's Paul Dubrule Cooking School. Half-day classes (start times 9am and 3.30pm) include a visit to Psar Nath, preparing four typically Khmer dishes (recipe book included) and then eating your handiwork afterwards. The excellent restaurant here is open from 8am to 10pm.

### Nary Kitchen
COOKING COURSE

(☑ 012 763950; www.narykitchen.com; St 111; half-day course US$10) This popular cooking class includes a visit to the local market, three-course menu and a keepsake recipe book. Courses start at 9am and 3.30pm, lasting about three hours, plus time to eat. If you're more interested in eating than cooking, its restaurant is open from 8am to 10pm.

### Australian Centres for Development
LANGUAGE COURSE

(☑ 053-677 7772; www.acdcambodia.weebly.com; St 123; ✐) Offers well-regarded Khmer language classes, with one-to-one lessons available as well as regular weekly classes.

## 🛏 Sleeping

Most of Battambang's budget options are clustered close to Psar Nath, while midrange and luxury accommodation tends to be either on the east bank or out of the centre, and requires a short *remork* or *moto* ride to get to the tourist belt in the old quarter.

### City Centre

### ★ Angkor Comfort Hotel
HOTEL $

(☑ 077 306410; www.angkorcomforthotel.com; St 1; r with air-con US$15; ➲ ✵ ☎) The Angkor's huge rooms are sparkling clean and come with white linen on the bed, flatscreen TVs, enough power-points to charge up all your devices at once, and modern bathrooms with walk-in showers – these are midrange amenities on a backpacker budget.

### Royal Hotel
HOTEL $

(☑ 016 912034; www.royalhotelbattambang.com; St 115; r with air-con US$20-25; ✵ @ ☎) An old-timer on the Battambang scene, the Royal is deservedly popular. Some rooms may be faded but all are decently sized and come with fridge and TV. Staff here are some of the most clued-up in town.

### Senghout Hotel
HOTEL $

(☑ 012 530327; www.senghouthotel.com; St 2; r with fan US$10-15, with air-con US$15-35; ✵ ☎ ✵) Known for its on-the-ball staff who are quick to help with traveller queries, the Senghout has a variety of nicely decorated rooms. Some can be a bit poky, so check out a few before deciding. The rooftop pool is a key drawcard.

### Ganesha Family Guesthouse
GUESTHOUSE $

(☑ 092 135570; www.ganeshaguesthouse.com; St 1½; dm US$4.50, r US$11-14; ☎) The best of Battambang's cheapies, Ganesha has a light-filled dorm with double-wide beds, and small private rooms with bamboo furniture and tiled bathrooms (cold water only). Downstairs is an inviting cafe.

### Tomato Guesthouse
GUESTHOUSE $

(☑ 053-690 7374; www.facebook.com/tomato guesthouse; St 119; dm/d US$1.50/3; ☎) The cafe downstairs is always bustling and upstairs are tiny, en suite rooms – just don't try to swing a cat in them. Or else you can bed down in the spectacularly cheap dorm.

### Banan Hotel
HOTEL $

(☑ 053-953242; www.bananhotel.com; NH5; r incl breakfast US$20, deluxe US$25-40; ✵ @ ☎ ✵) With wood panelling in abundance, this hotel has immaculate rooms (more expensive ones come with balconies) and friendly service, plus there's an annexe with a rooftop pool.

### Sanctuary Villa
BOUTIQUE HOTEL $$

(☑ 097 216 7168; r incl breakfast US$60-90; ✵ @ ☎ ✵) This intimate poolside boutique in a lush garden has seven attractive villas furnished with traditional woods, tasteful silks and throw rugs – but the out-of-the-way location won't be for everybody. From the White Horse roundabout on NH5 go 500m north and take a right.

### Maisons Wat Kor
BOUTIQUE HOTEL $$$

(☑ 098 555377; www.maisonswatkor.com; Wat Kor village; s/d from US$81/94; ✵ ☎ ✵) About 2km south of central Battambang, Maisons Wat Kor is a secluded sanctuary of just eight rooms in traditional-style Khmer houses. Rooms are light-filled, spacious and come with

**DON'T MISS**

## AN EVENING UNDER THE BIG TOP

Battambang's signature attraction is the internationally acclaimed circus (*cirque nouveau*) of **Phare Ponleu Selpak** (ហ្វារពន្លឺសិល្បៈ; ☑ 053-952424; www.phareps.org; adult/student US$14/7), a multi-arts centre for disadvantaged children. Even though they also run shows in Siem Reap, it's worth timing your visit to Battambang to watch this amazing spectacle where it all began. Performances are at 7pm on Monday, Thursday and Saturday, with a Friday show added between November to February. Tickets are sold at the door from 6pm.

Phare, as it's known to locals, does a ton of stuff – contrary to popular belief it is not just a circus. It trains musicians, visual artists and performing artists as well. Many of the artists you'll bump into around town, such as Ke of Choco l'art Café fame (opposite), lived and studied at Phare. Guests are welcome to take a **guided tour** (US$5; ⊙ Mon-Fri 8-11am & 2-5pm) of the Phare complex during the day and observe circus, dance, music, drawing and graphic-arts classes. This is definitely $5 well spent.

To get here from the Vishnu Roundabout on NH5, head west for 900m and then turn right (north) and continue another 600m.

contemporary bathrooms. The saltwater swimming pool surrounded by lush foliage provides plenty of opportunity for chill-out time.

**Au Cabaret Vert**   BOUTIQUE HOTEL **$$$**
(☑ 053-656 2000; www.aucabaretvert.com; NH57; r incl breakfast US$85; ❋ ☎ ☀) Contemporary meets colonial at this resort on the western edge of town. Rooms are stylish and include flatscreen TV and rain shower. The swimming pool is a natural, self-cleaning pond.

## East Bank

★**Here Be Dragons**   HOSTEL **$**
(☑ 089 264895; www.herebedragonsbattambang.com; Riverside East; dm US$3, r US$8-10; ☎) A funky fun bar, leafy front garden for relaxing, and free beer on arrival make Here Be Dragons a top backpacker base. Six-bed dorms come with lock-boxes, while sunny private rooms are cheerfully decked out with brightly coloured bedding. The quiet location next to the riverside park on the East Bank is a bonus.

**La Villa**   BOUTIQUE HOTEL **$$**
(☑ 053-730151; www.lavilla-battambang.net; Riverside Rd; d incl breakfast from US$70; ❋ @ ☎ ☀) For a taste of colonial life, try this French-era villa renovated in vintage 1930s style, one of the most romantic boutique hotels in Cambodia. Gauzy mosquito nets drape over four-poster beds, original tile work graces the floors and art deco features decorate every corner, creating an old-world ambience that can't be beaten.

**Sangker Villa Hotel**   BOUTIQUE HOTEL **$$**
(☑ 097 764 0017; www.sangkervilla.com; off St 203; r incl breakfast US$45-55; ❋ ☎ ☀) Sangker Villa may lack the pizzazz of Battambang's fancier poolside boutiques, but beats them hands-down on price. Out the back, the poolside bar provides a tranquil retreat, while bright, simply decorated rooms come with contemporary bathrooms.

★**Bambu Hotel**   HOTEL **$$$**
(☑ 053-953900; www.bambuhotel.com; St 203; r incl breakfast from US$90; ❂ ❋ @ ☎ ☀) Bambu's spacious rooms are designed in a Franco-Khmer motif with gorgeous tiling, stone-inlaid bathrooms and exquisite furniture. The fusion restaurant is one of the best in town and the poolside bar invites lingering. Above all else though, it's Bambu's gracious staff that set it in a category above Battambang's other boutique offerings. Book ahead – it's extremely popular.

## ✖ Eating

For excellent Cambodian cuisine, also try cooking-school restaurants (p241) around town.

For street food, there are three night markets. The original **night market** (snacks & mains r2000-8000; ⊙ 4-9pm) is at the northeast corner of Psar Nath and dishes up barbecued chicken, fish and pork. The **new night market** (St 1; mains 4000-8000r; ⊙ 6pm-midnight) is across the road along the riverfront, and is more of a sit-down affair. There's another **riverside night market** (St 1; mains r4000-8000; ⊙ 3pm-midnight), across from the Battambang Museum.

## 🏂 City Centre

### ★ Lonely Tree Cafe
CAFE **$**

(www.thelonelytreecafe.com; St 121; mains US$4-5.50; ⊙10am-10pm; 📶) 🍴 Upstairs from the shop of the same name, this uber-cosy cafe serves Spanish tapas–style dishes and a few Khmer options under a soaring, bamboo-inlaid ceiling. Its mascot is an actual tree on the road to Siem Reap. Proceeds support cultural preservation and the disabled, among other causes.

### Coconut Water
INTERNATIONAL **$**

(St 119; mains US$2-3.50; ⊙8am-9pm; 🍴) 🍴 Eat in the snug 1st-floor cafe or amid the cushions on the shaded rooftop. There's great breakfast options and a small list of Khmer staples, or you can munch on a caramelised chicken or tofu burger. Profits support various community projects.

### Flavours of India
INDIAN **$**

(85 St 2½; mains US$3.50-5; ⊙9am-10.30pm; 📶🍴) The Battambang outpost of a popular Phnom Penh Indian restaurant, the inspiration for which came about when some curry-craving expats ordered takeaway all the way from the capital (290km to the southeast). Opt for the *thalis* (US$5 to US$7) for an excellent-value meal.

### Vegetarian Foods Restaurant
VEGETARIAN **$**

(St 102; mains 1500-3000r; ⊙6.30am-5pm; 🍴) This hole-in-the-wall eatery serves some of the most delicious vegetarian dishes in Cambodia, including rice soup, homemade soy milk and dumplings for just 1000r. Tremendous value.

### Fresh Eats Café
INTERNATIONAL **$**

(www.mpkhomeland.org; St 2½; mains US$2.50-4; ⊙9am-9pm; 📶) 🍴 Run by an NGO that helps disadvantaged youth, this place complements its Khmer specialities with build-your-own baguettes, great salads and pasta. There's a small handicrafts boutique on site.

### Lan Chov Khorko Miteanh
NOODLES **$**

(145 St 2; mains 4000-6000r; ⊙9am-9pm) More conveniently known as Chinese Noodle by resident foreigners, the Chinese chef here does bargain dumplings and serves fresh noodles a dozen or more ways, including with pork or duck soup.

### Choco l'art Café
CAFE **$**

(www.chocolartcafe.com; St 117; breakfasts & mains US$1.50-6; ⊙9am-midnight Wed-Mon; 📶) Run with gusto by local painter Ke and his French partner, Soline, this inviting gallery-cafe sees foreigners and locals alike gather to drink and eat Soline's wonderful bread, pastries and (for breakfast) crêpes. Live music gets going occasionally.

### ★ Jaan Bai
FUSION **$$**

(📞078 263144; jaanbai@cambodianchildrenstrust.org; cnr St 1½ & St 2; small plates US$3, mains US$4-10; ⊙11am-10.30pm Tue-Sun; 📶🍴) 🍴 Jaan Bai ('rice bowl' in Khmer) is Battambang's foodie treat, with a sleekly minimalist interior offset by beautiful French-Khmer tile work lining the wall. The menu likewise is successfully bold. Order a few of the small plates to savour their range of flavours, or go all-out with the tasting menu: seven plates plus wine for US$15 per person (minimum two people).

You're eating for a good cause. Jaan Bai trains and employs vulnerable youth through the Cambodia Children's Trust (www.cambodianchildrenstrust.org).

### Cafe Eden
CAFE **$$**

(www.cafeedencambodia.com; St 1; mains US$4-7; ⊙7.30am-9pm Wed-Mon; 📶) 🍴 This American-run social enterprise offers a relaxed space for a hearty breakfast or an afternoon coffee. The compact lunch-and-dinner menu is Asian-fusion style, with some great burgers on offer as well. They also do the best chips in town. At the back, their boutique sells a small range of clothing and crafts.

### The Kitchen
INTERNATIONAL **$$**

(St 1; mains US$5-7; ⊙10am-10pm; 📶) The Kitchen has an easygoing vibe, with colourful wall art and dangling kitchen implements used as decoration. The menu dishes up a bit of everything, wandering from Mexican (burritos and tacos) to pan-Asian with ease. There's some good bar-snack options, too.

## 🏂 East Bank

A lively restaurant scene is developing on the East Bank, especially along Old NH5.

### Bamboo Train Cafe
INTERNATIONAL **$**

(Old NH5; mains 8000-16,000r; ⊙7am-10pm) The affable owner ensures this place is always popular. The eclectic menu contains pizza, pasta, curries and a delicious tofu *amok*.

### Battambang BBQ & Buffet
BARBECUE **$**

(Old NH5; mains 10000-16000r; ⊙4-10pm) Offering an all-inclusive tabletop barbecue and serve-yourself buffet, this place is

NORTHWESTERN CAMBODIA BATTAMBANG

**DON'T MISS**

## ALL ABOARD THE BAMBOO TRAIN

Battambang's **Bamboo Train** (return ride for 2 or more passengers each US$5, for 1 passenger US$10; ⊙7am-dusk) is one of the world's unique rail journeys. From O Dambong, 3.7km east of Battambang's old French bridge (Wat Kor Bridge), the train bumps 7km southeast to O Sra Lav along warped, misaligned rails and vertiginous bridges left by the French. The journey takes 20 minutes each way, with a 20-minute stop at O Sra Lav in between.

Each bamboo train – known in Khmer as a *norry* (nori) – consists of a 3m-long wooden frame, covered lengthwise with slats made of ultralight bamboo, that rest on two barbell-like bogies, the aft one connected by fan belts to a 6HP gasoline engine. Pile on 10 or 15 people, or up to three tonnes of rice, crank it up and you can cruise along at about 15km/h.

The genius of the system is that it offers a brilliant solution to the most ineluctable problem faced on any single-track line: what to do when two trains going in opposite directions meet. In the case of bamboo trains, the answer is simple: one car is quickly disassembled and set on the ground beside the tracks so that the other can pass. The rule is that the car with the fewer passengers has to cede priority.

With the advent of good roads, the bamboo train would have become defunct if it hadn't been for its reinvention as a tourist attraction. Yes, it is super-touristy – complete with some very determined children touting bracelets when you disembark at O Sra Lav – but there's no denying that whizzing along the click-clacking rails is a huge amount of fun.

There is talk of upgrading the railway and ending the operation of the bamboo train in the near future, but there are plans to relocate it within the province.

unbelievably popular with local Khmers and domestic tourists. Exceptional value.

★**La Villa**  INTERNATIONAL $$
(☑053-730151; Riverside Rd; mains US$5-15; ⊙11am-3pm & 6-9pm; 🛜) Battambang's most atmospheric dinner option dishes up delectable Khmer, Vietnamese, French and Italian dishes, plus wines from around the world. Specialities include a tender fish fillet in lemon sauce. Sit inside under the glass atrium or bask in the colonial glow of the courtyard outside.

### 🍷 Drinking & Nightlife

★**Kinyei**  CAFE
(www.kinyei.org; 1 St 1½; coffee US$1.25-2.50, snacks US$1-2.50; ⊙7am-7pm; 🛜) 📶 Want to know where we go for our morning coffee in Battambang? National barista champs have been crowned here. All your espressos, flat whites and cappuccinos are on offer and there's a small menu of breakfast options and light bites.

**Lotus Bar & Gallery**  CAFE
(St 2½; ⊙11am-late; 🛜) In a beautifully renovated shophouse, the street-level bar is a fine place to mingle with all sorts of characters. Upstairs is a gallery, while downstairs you might get film, musical performances or a themed party on any given night. The menu

(mains US$4 to US$8) meanders from Middle East–inspired mezze platters to pizza, with some Khmer specialities thrown in.

**Here Be Dragons**  BAR
(Riverside Rd; ⊙11am-late; 🛜) Before there was the popular hostel, there was the popular bar Dragons. They haven't forgotten their roots. The bar frequently rumbles 'til late with a mix of backpackers and expats. There's a Wednesday pub quiz.

**Riverside Balcony Bar**  BAR
(cnr St 1 & St 149; ⊙4-11pm Tue-Sun; 🛜) Set in a gorgeous wooden house high above the riverfront, Australian-run Riverside is Battambang's original bar and a mellow place for a sundowner. The small menu mixes pub grub and Khmer classics (mains US$3.50 to US$7.50).

**River**  BAR
(St 1; ⊙6am-11pm) Locals flock here during the evening for the riverfront breezes and for the football and movies this place blasts out on its outdoor screen.

### 🛍 Shopping

**Lonely Tree Shop**  TEXTILES
(St 121; ⊙10am-10pm) 📶 Fine silk bags, chunky jewellery, fashionable shirts and skirts. Definitely not your run-of-the-mill charity gift shop.

### Jewel in the Lotus
VINTAGE

(St 2½; ⊙ 11am-10pm) A wonderful trinket shop selling all kinds of ephemera and kitsch, plus old photos and prints by local artists. Worth stopping in even if you're not buying.

### Bric-a-Brac
HOMEWARES

(☑ 077 531562; www.bric-a-brac.asia; 112 St 2; ⊙ 11am-8pm) This swish place sells handmade *passementrie* (trimmings) items, textiles, antiques and accessories. Upstairs is a bijou hotel of just three arty, designed rooms.

### Rachana Handicrafts
TEXTILES

(⊙ 7.30am-5.30pm) 🖉 A tiny, NGO-run sewing workshop on the outskirts of town that trains disadvantaged women and sells purses, stuffed toys, *kramas* and cotton and silk accessories.

## ℹ Information

For information on what's happening in town, look out for copies of the free *Battambang Buzz* magazine at restaurants, bars and hotels.

The city map available at the tourist office details scenic routes to the bamboo train and other attractions outside of town.

Free wi-fi access is the norm at hotels and most cafes and restaurants.

**ANZ Royal Bank** (St 1; ⊙ 8.30am-4pm Mon-Fri, ATM 24hr)

**Canadia Bank** (Psar Thom; ⊙ 7.30am-3.30pm Mon-Fri, to 11.30am Sat, ATM 24hr)

**Handa Medical Centre** (☑ 095 520654; NH5; ⊙ clinic 9am-3.30pm, emergency 24hr) Has two ambulances and usually a European doctor or two in residence.

**Institut Français** (French Institute; www. institutfrancais-cambodge.com; St 501; ⊙ 8am-noon & 2-6pm Mon-Fri) Valiantly trying to keep French culture alive in the age of the Anglophones, the French Institute has an upstairs *médiathèque* with books and DVDs available for free browsing.

**Tourist Information Office** (☑ 012 534177; www.battambang-town.gov.kh; St 1; ⊙ 8-11am & 2-5pm Mon-Fri) Moderately useful office with a great map of Battambang.

**Yi Quoc Clinic** (☑ 053-953163, 012 530171; off NH57; ⊙ 24hr) The best clinic in town.

## ℹ Getting There & Away

Battambang is 290km northwest of Phnom Penh along NH5 and 80km northeast of Pailin along NH57 (formerly NH10).

### BOAT

The riverboat to Siem Reap (US$20, daily 7am) squeezes through narrow waterways and passes by protected wetlands, taking from five hours in the wet season to nine or more hours in the height of the dry season. Cambodia's most memorable boat trip, it's operated on alternate days by **Angkor Express** (☑ 012 601287) and **Chann Na** (☑ 012 354344).

In the dry season, passengers are driven to a navigable section of the river. The best seats are away from the noisy motor. It may be possible to alight at the Prek Toal Bird Sanctuary and then be picked up there the next day for US$5 extra. Be aware that these boats, while scenic, are not always popular with local communities along the way, as the wake has caused small boats to capsize and fishing nets are regularly snagged. Many travellers also complain of overcrowding and safety issues – there are rarely enough life jackets to go around.

### BUS

Like Phnom Penh, Battambang does not have a central bus station. Most companies are clustered in the centre just south of the intersection of NH5 and St 4.

To Phnom Penh, Capitol Tour and Phnom Penh Sorya have the most day buses. For a quicker journey, opt for the more expensive express minivan services run by Golden Bayon Express (US$10, 4½ hours, 7am and 8.30am) or Mekong Express (US$12, 4½ hours, 7.30am, 8.45am, 9.30am, 1pm, 2.30pm and 5pm). Unless you don't mind arriving at an ungodly hour in the morning, the sleeper bus options offered to Phnom Penh by various companies are not worth it.

Mekong Express and Golden Bayan also run express minivans to Siem Reap.

Buses to Bangkok involve a change at the border – usually to a minibus on the Thai side.

If you're pinching pennies, Capitol Tour generally has the lowest prices, followed by Phnom Penh Sorya.

**Capitol Tour** (☑ 053-953040; St 102)
**Golden Bayon Express** (☑ 070 968966; St 101)
**Mekong Express** (☑ 088 576 7668; St 3)
**Phnom Penh Sorya** (☑ 053-953904; St 4)
**Ponleu Angkor Khmer** (☑ 053-952366; St 4)
**Rith Mony** (☑ 011 575572; St 1)

### TAXI

At the **taxi station** (NH5), share taxis to Phnom Penh (40,000r, 4½ hours) and Pursat (16,000, two hours) leave from the southeast corner. Taxis to Poipet (20,000r, 1¾ hours), Sisophon (20,000r, 1¼ hours) and Siem Reap (26,000r, three hours) leave from north of the market out on NH5.

Share taxis to Pailin (20,000r, 1¼ hours) and the Psar Pruhm–Ban Pakard border leave from the corner of St 101 and St 4. Hiring a private taxi (US$35 to US$40) gives you the option of stopping off at Phnom Sampeau and Sneng on the way.

## BUSES FROM BATTAMBANG

| DESTINATION | DURATION (HR) | COST (US$) | COMPANIES | FREQUENCY |
|---|---|---|---|---|
| Bangkok | 9 | 15-16 | Mekong Express, PP Sorya | 10.30am, 11.30am, noon |
| Kompong Cham | 7½ | 7.50-10 | PP Sorya, Rith Mony | 9.30am |
| Pailin | 1½ | 3-4 | Ponleu Angkor, Rith Mony | 1pm, 3pm |
| Phnom Penh | 5-6 | 5-12 | all companies | regularly until 2.30pm |
| Poipet | 2¼ | 4-4.50 | Capitol, PP Sorya, Rith Mony | 7.45am, 1pm |
| Siem Reap | 3-4 | 4.50-5 | Capitol, Golden Bayon Express, Mekong Express, PP Sorya | 7.45am, 8am, 9.45am, 1pm, 2pm |

## ❶ Getting Around

English- and French-speaking *remork* drivers are commonplace in Battambang, and all are eager to whisk you around on day trips. A half-day trip out of town to a single sight like Phnom Sampeau might cost US$12, while a full day trip taking in three sights – Phnom Sampeau, Phnom Banan and the bamboo train, for instance – costs US$16 to US$20, depending on your haggling skills. A *moto* costs about half that.

A *moto* ride in town costs around 2000r, while a *remork* ride starts from US$1.

**Gecko Moto** (☑ 089 924260; St 3; ⊙ 8am-7pm) and Royal Hotel rent out motorbikes for US$7 to US$8 per day. Bicycles can be rented at the Royal Hotel, Soksabike, Battambang Bike and several other guesthouses for about US$2 per day.

## Around Battambang

The countryside around Battambang is littered with old temples and other worthwhile sights. Admission to Phnom Sampeau, Phnom Banan and Wat Ek Phnom costs US$3 for a combined ticket. If you purchase the ticket at one site, it's valid all day long at the other two. For details on sites not mentioned below, check out the guidebook *Around Battambang* (US$10) by Ray Zepp, which has details on temples, wats and excursions in the Battambang and Pailin areas. Proceeds go to monks and nuns working to raise HIV/AIDS awareness and to help AIDS orphans.

## Phnom Sampeau · ភ្នំសំពៅ

At the summit of this fabled limestone outcrop, 12km southwest of Battambang along NH57 (towards Pailin), a complex of **temples** (admission US$3 combined ticket) affords gorgeous views.

As you descend from the summit's golden stupa, dating from 1964, turn left under the gate decorated with a bas-relief of Eiy Sei (an elderly Buddha). A deep canyon, its vertical sides cloaked in greenery, descends 144 steps through a natural arch to a 'lost world' of stalactites, creeping vines and bats; two Angkorian warriors stand guard.

Near the westernmost of the two antennas at the summit, two government artillery pieces, one with markings in Russian, the other in German, are still deployed. Near the base of the western antenna, jockey for position with other tourists on the sunset lookout pavilion. Looking west you'll spy **Phnom Krapeu** (Crocodile Mountain), a one-time Khmer Rouge stronghold.

About halfway up to the summit, a road leads under a gate and 250m up to the **Killing Caves of Phnom Sampeau**, now a place of pilgrimage. A staircase, flanked by greenery, leads into a cavern where a golden reclining Buddha lies peacefully next to a glass-walled memorial filled with bones and skulls – the remains of some of the people bludgeoned to death by Khmer Rouge cadres and then thrown through the skylight above. Next to the base of the stairway is the old memorial, a rusty cage made of chicken wire and cyclone fencing and partly filled with human bones.

Back down at the hill base, people gather every evening to witness a natural spectacle. At dusk (around 5.30pm) a thick column of bats pours out of a massive cave high up on the north side of the cliff face. The mesmerising display lasts a good 30 minutes as millions of bats head out in a looping line to their feeding grounds near Tonlé Sap.

Access up to Phnom Sampeau is via a cement road or – if you're in need of a workout – a steep staircase. The road is too steep for *remorks*. English-speaking *moto* drivers hang out near the base of the hill, at a line of restaurants around the ticket office, and can whisk you up the hill for US$4 return.

## Phnom Banan ប្រាសាទភ្នំបាណន់

The temple of Prasat Banan can easily be combined with a visit to Phnom Sampeau for a good half-day trip by *moto* or *remork*.

### ◎ Sights

**Prasat Banan** TEMPLE
(admission US$3 combined ticket) It's a 358-stone-step climb up Phnom Banan to reach Prasat Banan, but the incredible views across surrounding countryside from the top are worth it. Udayadityavarman II, son of Suryavarman I, built Prasat Banan in the 11th century; some locals claim the five-tower layout here was the inspiration for Angkor Wat, although this seems optimistic. There are impressive carved lintels above the doorways to each of the towers and bas-reliefs on the upper parts of the central tower.

From the temple, a narrow stone staircase leads south down the hill to three caves, which can be visited with a local guide. Prasat Banan is 23km south of Battambang.

**Prasat Phnom Banon Winery** WINERY
(កន្លែងផលិតស្រាទំពាំងបាយជូរ ភ្នំបាណន់; Bot Sala Village; wine tasting US$2; ◎6am-6pm)

Midway between Battambang and Phnom Banan, in an area known for its production of chilli peppers (harvested from October to January), Cambodia's only winery grows shiraz and cabernet sauvignon grapes to make reds, and tropics-resistant Black Queen and Black Opal grapes to make rosés. Both taste completely unlike anything you've ever encountered in a bottle with the word 'wine' on the label.

Officially recognised by Cambodia's Ministry of Industry, Mines & Energy, Banon belongs to that exclusive club of wineries whose vintages improve significantly with the addition of ice cubes. Also made here is Banon brandy, which has a heavenly bouquet and a taste that has been compared to turpentine. Sampling takes place in an attractive garden pavilion.

The winery is 10km south of Battambang and 8km north of Phnom Banan.

## Kamping Poy កំពីងពួយ

Also known as the Killing Dam, Kamping Poy was one of the many grandiose Khmer Rouge projects intended to re-create the sophisticated irrigation networks that helped

**WORTH A TRIP**

### TEMPLES & VILLAGE LIFE ON THE ROAD TO WAT EK PHNOM

The rural lanes that squiggle out from Battambang are brimming with paddy field panoramas and tiny villages where traditional crafts and produce are made. The roads leading to Wat Ek Phnom are particularly rewarding to explore and make for a great half-day circuit, soaking up a mix of historic sights and village life. Some highlights:

**Pheam Ek Village** About 5km north of Battambang is the village of Pheam Ek, whose speciality industry is making rice paper for spring rolls. All along the road, in family workshops, you'll see rice paste being steamed and then placed on a bamboo frame for drying in the sun. Wat Ek Phnom is 5.5km further on.

**Wat Ek Phnom** (វត្តឯកភ្នំ; admission US$3 combined ticket) Hidden behind a colourful modern pagoda and a gargantuan Buddha statue is this atmospheric, partly collapsed 11th-century temple. Wat Ek Phnom measures 52m by 49m and is surrounded by the remains of a laterite wall and an ancient *baray* (reservoir). A lintel showing the Churning of the Ocean of Milk can be seen above the east entrance to the central temple, whose upper flanks hold some fine bas-reliefs.

**Prahoc Factory** After leaving Wat Ek Phnom, turn southwest towards Battambang; just before the bridge across the Sangker River, is a local factory which produces Cambodian *prahoc* (fermented fish paste). The bamboo trays of fish drying in the sun along the roadside are hugely photogenic.

**Wat Somrong Knong** Just over the bridge, on the eastern side of the Sangker River, is Wat Somrong Knong. The gorgeous 18th-century pagoda here was used as a prison during the Khmer Rouge era; the area behind the wat was used as a killing field, where it's believed around 10,000 people were executed. A memorial has been erected at the site. From here, take the road southwest for 6km to arrive back in Battambang.

Cambodia wax mighty under the kings of Angkor. As many as 10,000 Cambodians are thought to have perished during its construction, worked to death under the shadow of executions, malnutrition and disease.

There's little to see but people come to picnic, and hire row boats (10,000r for two hours) out on the water.

These days, thanks to the dam, the Kamping Poy area is one of the few parts of Cambodia to produce two rice crops a year.

Kamping Poy is 27km west of Battambang (go via NH5 and follow the irrigation canal). It's easy to combine a visit here with a stop at Phnom Sampeau.

## Sneng ស្នែង

This town, located on NH57 20km southwest of Battambang towards Pailin, is home to two small yet interesting temples. **Prasat Yeay Ten** (ប្រាសាទយាយទែន; NH57), dedicated to Shiva, dates from the end of the 10th century and, although in a ruinous state, has above its doorways three delicately carved lintels that somehow survived the ravages of time and war; the eastern one depicts the Churning of the Ocean of Milk. The temple is situated on the east side of the highway, so close to the road that it resembles an ancient Angkorian tollbooth.

Behind Prasat Yeay Ten is a contemporary wat; tucked away at the back of the wat compound are three **brick sanctuaries** (off NH57) that have some beautifully preserved carvings around the entrances.

# PAILIN PROVINCE

Pailin (ខេត្តប៉ៃលិន) is best known for its gem mines (now pretty much exhausted), a surfeit of land mines and for being a refuge for Khmer Rouge pensioners.

During the civil war, the Pailin area's gem and timber resources – sold on international markets with help from Thai army generals – served as the economic crutch that kept the Khmer Rouge war machine hobbling along. In the mid-1990s, it was a staging area for regular dry-season offensives that overran government positions as far east as Phnom Sampeau.

In 1996 the Khmer Rouge supremo in these parts, Ieng Sary – or Brother Number Three during the Democratic Kampuchea regime – defected to the government side with 3000 heavily armed troops. His reward

> ### ⓘ LAND MINE ALERT!
>
> Pailin and nearby parts of Battambang Province (especially the districts of Samlot and Rotanak Mondol) are some of the most heavily land-mined places in the world. De-mining sites are commonplace, sometimes quite close to the highway. Numerous amputees bear sad tribute to the horror of land mines. Stay *on* the beaten track in these parts. Public roads are OK, but farm roads are risky, and venturing into Pailin's beautiful forests on foot is definitely *not* a good idea.

was amnesty and free rein in Krong Pailin, a mini-province carved out of Battambang Province to serve as a Khmer Rouge fiefdom. Only in 2007 were Ieng and his wife arrested for war crimes and crimes against humanity. He died in March 2013, well before the completion of the trial. Ieng's son, Ieng Vuth, currently serves as deputy governor of Pailin.

# Pailin ប៉ៃលិន

🖉 055 / POP 35,000

The remote Wild West town of Pailin has little to recommend it except a particularly colourful hilltop temple. That said, the forested Cardamom foothills surrounding the city are beautiful. Just don't wander into them by yourself – or you may literally be walking into a minefield.

## ◉ Sights & Activities

**Wat Phnom Yat** BUDDHIST TEMPLE
(វត្តភ្នំយ៉ាត; off NH57) From NH57, stairs lead through a garish gate up to Wat Phnom Yat, a psychedelic temple centred on an ancient po (sacred fig) tree. A 27m Buddha looms over the top of the staircase, while a path leads up to the colourful temple and the large golden stupas at the top of the hill.

Along the path a life-sized cement tableau shows naked sinners and their punishments: being heaved into a cauldron (the impious), de-tongued (liars) and forced to climb a spiny tree (adulterers). Medieval European triptychs don't portray a hell that is nearly so scary – a highly pertinent message given who lives around here. The sunrises and sunsets at the top are usually nice enough to take your mind off the fire and brimstone.

# Pailin

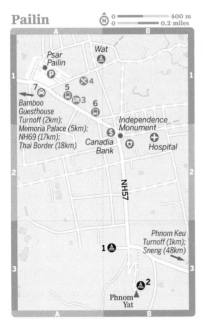

## Wat Khaong Kang
BUDDHIST TEMPLE

(វត្តកោងកាង) At the base of Phnom Yat hill, an impressive gate from 1968 leads to Wat Khaong Kang, an important centre for Buddhist teaching before the Khmer Rouge madness. The exterior wall is decorated with an especially long bas-relief of the Churning of the Ocean of Milk. The last time we pulled through town it couldn't be viewed due to vital restoration work, but that should be finished by the time you visit.

## Phnom Keu Waterfall
WATERFALL

(ទឹកធ្លាក់ភ្នំគយ, Blue Mountain Waterfall; motorbike/car 3000/10000r) There are numerous waterfalls dropping out of the Cardamoms south of Pailin. The most accessible one, which has water year-round, is Phnom Keu. To get there turn right off NH57 1.5km east of Wat Phnom Yat, then proceed 5km on a rough road (which gets dodgy in the rainy season). From the entrance, cross the small river via the dirt road and walk about 3km to the falls.

The area's other waterfalls are more difficult to access due to being at their most impressive during the rainy season, when the roads are often impassable – and getting to the more remote falls is risky because of the lingering presence of land mines.

## 🛏 Sleeping & Eating

### Bamboo Guesthouse
GUESTHOUSE **$**

(☑ 012 405818; r US$15-35; ✸ 🗢) Bamboo is an oasis of calm on Pailin's northwestern outskirts, with 27 comfortable bungalows. The restaurant serves excellent Khmer and Thai food (mains US$4 to US$8) in outdoor pavilions. From the market head west on NH57 for 2km, turn right and proceed 800m.

### Pailin Ruby Guesthouse
GUESTHOUSE **$**

(☑ 016 477933; NH57; s with fan US$6-8, d with fan US$8-11, s with air-con US$11, d with air-con US$13-16; ✸ 🗢) A good-value place in the centre, with 48 clean, spacious rooms. It's worth paying for the air-con options as they have natural light.

### Memoria Palace
RESORT **$$**

(☑ 015 430014; www.memoriapalace.com; hut US$45, bungalow US$55-105; ✸ 🗢 ✸) Located 5km west of Pailin, this resort has humongous bungalows with boutique touches and great views, and a 20m-long hilltop swimming pool. There's also three fan-only, palm-thatch huts. The restaurant (mains US$5 to US$10) is Pailin's best; breakfast is included. To get here go straight where the highway bends sharply to the right 500m beyond the turnoff to Bamboo Guesthouse.

### Leang Sreng Restaurant
CAMBODIAN **$**

(meals US$1-3; ◎ 6am-11pm) This informal place serves up steaming bowls of *pho*-style Vietnamese beef noodle soup. Just look for the sign decorated with a laughing cow.

## ℹ Information

English-speaking manager Theara of the Memoria Palace hotel is about the only useful source of information in Pailin. He can put together tours that take in gem mines, farms and waterfalls, among others.

**NORTHWESTERN CAMBODIA PAILIN**

## GETTING TO THAILAND: PAILIN TO CHANTHABURI

**Getting to the border** The laid-back Psar Pruhm–Ban Pakard **border crossing** (⊘7am-8pm) is 102km southwest of Battambang and 18km northwest of Pailin via good sealed roads.

First get to Pailin from Battambang. In Pailin, patient travellers might get a share taxi (6000r) to the border. If nothing is going, take a *moto* (US$5) or private taxi (US$10), or catch the buses coming through at about 1.30pm.

**At the border** Immigration officials usually quote US$35 for Cambodian tourist visas here. Formalities are extremely straightfoward and quick on both sides. Ignore all offers from touts on the Thai side of the border to help with visas.

**Moving on** On the Thai side, you can avoid being overcharged for transport to Chanthaburi (150B by minibus, one hour) by hopping on a *moto* (50B) to the nearby *sŏrngtăaou* (pick-up truck) station. From Chanthaburi's bus station there are buses to Bangkok.

On the Cambodian side, *motos* and taxis whisk you to Pailin from a stop about 150m east of the border post, near the Victoria Casino entrance. If you cross early enough, the 7.30am public buses from the border straight to Phnom Penh via Battambang are an option. A private taxi from the border to Battambang costs US$40.

**Canadia Bank** (NH57; ⊘8am-3.30pm Mon-Fri, to 11.30am Sat, ATM 24hr)

### ❶ Getting There & Away

NH57 (sometimes still called Highway 10) from Battambang to Pailin is now in excellent shape, making for a straightforward journey by bus, car or motorbike.

**Rith Mony** (☑092 290 909) and Punleu Angkor Khmer each have morning buses that originate in Psar Pruhm at the Thai border around 7.30am, pick up passengers in Pailin around 8am, and continue to Phnom Penh (38,000r, eight hours) via Battambang (15,000r, 1½ hours).

Share taxis to Battambang (20,000r, one hour) leave from the taxi stand opposite Psar Pailin on NH57.

A rough track goes from Treng District, about 25km east of Pailin, southward through the Cardamom Mountains to Koh Kong via Samlaut and Pramoay. NH59, a sealed highway, originates about 6km west of Pailin and runs north to Poipet along the Thai border.

## Samlaut          សំឡូត

The northernmost tip of the Cardamom Mountains – home to elephants, gibbons, pangolins, hornbills and many other endangered creatures – covers the southern half of Pailin Province (pretty much everything south of NH57). Known as the **Samlaut Multiple Use Area** (600 sq km), this expanse of forested mountains is contiguous with two Thai parks (Namtok Klong Kaew National Park and Khlong Kreua Wai Wild-

life Sanctuary), with which it is joined as a transboundary **Peace Park**. Countless land mines make the area too dangerous for trekking, however.

Samlaut is administered and patrolled with help from the Maddox Jolie-Pitt Foundation (www.mjpasia.org), named after the Cambodian-born adopted son of its founder and president, the American actress Angelina Jolie.

## BANTEAY MEANCHEY PROVINCE

Sandwiched between the casinos of Poipet, Cambodia's most important border crossing with Thailand, and the glories of Angkor, agricultural Banteay Meanchey Province (ខេត្តបន្ទាយមានជ័យ) often gets overlooked by travellers rushing on to Siem Reap or Battambang. If you're not in a hurry though, the fabulous jungle-temple ruins of Banteay Chhmar are well worth a stopover.

## Poipet          ប៉ោយប៉ែត
☑054 / POP 89,500

Long the armpit of Cambodia, notorious for its squalor, scams and sleaze, Poipet (pronounced 'poi-*peh*' in Khmer) has recently splurged on a facelift and no longer looks like the post-apocalyptic place it once was. Thanks mainly to the patronage of neighbouring Thais, whose own country bans gambling, its casino resorts – with names like Tropicana and Grand Diamond City – are turning the town into Cambodia's little Las Vegas. However, beyond the border zone it's still a chaotic, rubbish-strewn strip mall sprinkled with dodgy massage parlours. The Khmers' gentle side is little in evidence, but don't worry, the rest of the country does not carry on like this. The faster you get used to making quick conversions between Cambodian riel, US dollars and Thai baht, all of which are in use here, the easier it'll be. A good rule of thumb is 4000r = US$1 = 30B.

Poipet extends southeast from the border (the filthy O Chrou stream) for a few kilometres along NH5. Useful landmarks are Acleda Bank, 500m east of the border, and Canadia Bank another 500m further on.

## 🛏 Sleeping & Eating

Hotels in the baht-only casino zone advertise rooms for 1000B to 2000B – good value given the facilities. Cheap hotels and guesthouses, some of them brothels, are strung out along NH5 and around the bus station. As a general rule, however, don't plan on sticking around unless you are an inveterate gambler.

The cheapest eats are around the market and along NH5 near Acleda Bank. The casino zone's night market, a block north of NH5, has clean, well-lit restaurants and pubs. The all-you-can-eat Thai buffets (250B) offered by most hotels in the casino zone are a great deal.

**City Poipet Hotel**                        HOTEL $
(☎ 054-967576; citypoipethotel@gmail.com; d with fan/air-con from US$8/15; ❀ 🛜 ) By far the nicest crash pad in Poipet, it has a whiff of style, plus decent wi-fi. It's behind Acleda Bank.

**Destiny Cafe**                              CAFE $
(NH5; dishes US$2-3.50; ⊙ 7am-7pm; 🛜 ) ✎ A fine place to hang out if you have some time to kill, with tasty Khmer and Western eats, good coffee and friendly staff. They support an array of community projects in the local area so you're eating for a good cause. It's a five-minute walk beyond Canadia Bank.

---

### GETTING TO THAILAND: POIPET TO ARANYA PRATHET

**Getting to the border** The original land Poipet–Aranya Prathet **border crossing** (⊙ 7am-8pm) between Cambodia and Thailand is by far the busiest and the one most people take when travelling between Bangkok and Siem Reap. It has earned itself a bad reputation over the years, with scams galore to help tourists part with their money, especially those coming in from Thailand.

Frequent buses and share taxis run from Siem Reap and Battambang to Poipet. Don't get off the bus until you reach the big roundabout adjacent to the border post. Buying a ticket all the way to Bangkok (usually involving a change of buses at the border) can expedite things and save you the hassle of finding onward transport on the Thai side. The most convenient option is to take the 8am through-bus to Mo Chit bus station in Bangkok, run by Nattakan in Siem Reap. This costs an inflated US$28, but it's the only bus service that allows you to continue to Bangkok on the same bus you board in Siem Reap.

**At the border** Be prepared to wait in sweltering immigration lines on both sides – waits of two or more hours are not uncommon, especially in the high season. Show up early in the morning to avoid the crowds. You can pay a special 'VIP fee' (aka a bribe) of 200B on either side to skip the lines. There is no departure tax to leave Cambodia despite what Cambodian border officials might tell you. Entering Thailand, most nationalities are issued 15-day visa waivers free of charge.

Coming in from Thailand, under no circumstances should you deal with any 'Cambodian' immigration officials who might approach you on the Thai side – this a pure scam. Entering Cambodia, the official tourist visa fee is US$30 but it's common to be charged $35. If you don't mind waiting around, you can usually get the official rate if you politely hold firm. Procuring an e-visa (US$37) before travel won't save you any money but will save your stress levels.

**Moving on** Minibuses wait just over the border on the Thai side to whisk you to Bangkok (B300, four hours, every 30 minutes). Or make your way 7km to Aranya Prathet by *tuk tuk* (80B) or *sŏrngtăaou* (15B), from where there are regular buses to Bangkok's Mo Chit station between 4am and 6pm (223B, five to six hours). Make sure your *tuk tuk* driver takes you to the main bus station in Aranya Prathet for your 80B, not to the smaller station about 1km from the border (a common scam). The 1.55pm train is another option to Bangkok.

## ❶ LAND MINE ALERT!

Banteay Meanchey and Oddar Meanchey (p255) are among the most heavily land-mined provinces in Cambodia. Do *not*, under any circumstances, stray from previously trodden paths. If you've got your own wheels, travel only on roads or trails regularly used by locals.

## ❶ Information

Don't change money at the places suggested by touts, no matter how official they look. In fact, there's no need to change money at all, as baht work just fine here.

**ANZ Bank** (NH5; ⊘ 8am-3.30pm Mon-Fri, to 11.30am Sat, ATM 24hr) Located 1.2km east of the border roundabout.

**Canadia Bank** (NH5; ⊘ 8am-3.30pm Mon-Fri, to 11.30am Sat, ATM 24hr) About 1km east of the border roundabout.

## ❶ Getting There & Away

It's worth mastering the transport tricks of this scam-ridden border to save both hassle and money.

Poipet has two bus stations: the **Poipet Tourist Passenger International Terminal**, situated 9km east of town in the middle of nowhere, and the **main bus station**, which is at the main market, one block north of Canadia Bank off NH5. Unless you don't mind overpaying, avoid the international tourist terminal. Unfortunately this is easier said than done, as upon exiting immigration you'll be herded towards a 'free' tourist shuttle to this terminal, where onward buses depart to Phnom Penh (US$15, eight hours, 406km), Siem Reap (US$9, 2½ hours, 153km) and Battambang (US$10, 2½ hours, 116km). Share/private taxis to Siem Reap from the international terminal cost an inflated US$12/48.

Rather than give these scam artists your business, stay solo and walk or take a *moto* (2000r) for 1km along NH5 to the bus company offices near Canadia Bank, or to the main bus station nearby. You'll get 'real' bus fares here that are about half of what you pay at the international tourist terminal.

Unfortunately, the vast majority of buses depart in the morning (before 10.30am). If you can't get a bus, just take a share taxi – these also depart from the NH5 around Canadia Bank – onward to Siem Reap (seat/whole taxi US$5/35), Battambang (seat/whole taxi US$4.25/30) or Phnom Penh (seat/whole taxi US$8/42). Don't take the taxis that hang out near the roundabout by the border – these charge tourists at least double.

The many bus companies here include Capitol Tour, Phnom Penh Sorya, Kampuchea Angkor Express and Rith Mony. Several companies offer trips to Bangkok (US$10) until about 1pm.

All roads leading out of Poipet are sealed and in fine condition.

## ❶ Getting Around

*Moto* drivers wait at the big roundabout to whisk you around the town proper – pay 2000r for a short ride.

# Sisophon ស៊ីសុផុន

📋 054 / POP 61,600

Sisophon (also confusingly known as Svay, Svay Sisophon, Srei Sophon and Banteay Meanchey) is strategically situated at north-west Cambodia's great crossroads, the intersection of NH5 and NH6. This dusty transit hub doesn't have much going for it, but it's the nearest town to use as a base for exploring the Angkorian temples of Banteay Chhmar.

Those looking for a rural base for their temple visit will find it more rewarding to support the community homestay project operating in the village of Banteay Chhmar itself.

## ◉ Sights

**École d'Art et de Culture Khmers** ARTS CENTRE
(School of Khmer Art & Culture; www.krousar-thmey.org; ⊘ 7-11am & 2-5pm Mon-Fri, 7-11am Sat) 🖉 Housed in a traditional Khmer-style building, this school teaches underprivileged children traditional music, *apsara* dancing, painting, sculpture and shadow puppetry. You can observe classes but read the clearly posted ground rules first (note: no photos).

## 🛏 Sleeping & Eating

There's a line of grilled-meat stands along St 2 that are great for a cheap, filling meal. The one directly opposite the Pyramid Hotel is particularly friendly.

**Nasa Hotel** HOTEL $
(📞 011 777702; NH6; r US$15-20; ❄ ✴ 🛜) This apricot-coloured concrete box stands out like a sore thumb on the main road. Inside you'll find well-cared-for rooms that unfortunately lack natural light but come with satellite TV, hot water and fridge. It's the best deal in town.

## Sisophon

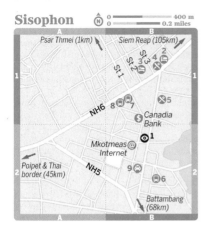

**Pyramid Hotel**     HOTEL **$**
(📱054-668 8881; www.pyramid-hotel.com; St 2; r with air-con from US$15; 🌀 📶) A solid bet, the Pyramid has 44 small but spick-and-span rooms in a quiet but central location just off the main highway. They also have a good restaurant on site.

**Mirror Restaurant**     CAMBODIAN **$**
(mains US$2-7) This modern diner offers traditional Cambodian *phnom pleung* ('hill of fire', or DIY barbecue) for 30,000r, plus sizzling barbecue chicken.

**Kim Heng Restaurant**     ASIAN **$**
(NH6; mains 9000-10,000r; ⊙8am-9pm) Nothing fancy, just a small menu of Asian staples –

### GETTING TO THAILAND: SISOPHON TO SURIN

**Getting to the border** The O Smach–Chong Chom **border crossing** connects Cambodia's Oddar Meanchey Province and Thailand's Surin Province, but it is very remote. Share taxis link Siem Reap and Sisophon with Samraong via NH68. From Samraong, take a *moto* (US$5) or a charter taxi (US$15) for the smooth drive to O Smach (30 minutes, 40km) and its frontier casino zone. The crossing itself is easy. Note that if you're entering Cambodia, e-visas cannot be used at this border.

**Moving on** On the Thai side, walk to the nearby bus stop, where regular buses depart to Surin throughout the day (60B, 1½ hours, 70km).

including fried sour cabbage and sweet-and-sour pork – all served with mountains of rice.

### ℹ️ Information

**Canadia Bank** (⊙8am-3.30pm Mon-Fri, to 11.30am Sat, ATM 24hr)

**Mkotmeas Internet** (per hr 2000r; ⊙7am-8pm)

### ℹ️ Getting There & Away

Sisophon is 45km east of Poipet, 105km west of Siem Reap and 68km northwest of Battambang.

Most long haul buses call in at the **bus station** in the centre of town. Capitol Tour, Rith Mony and Phnom Penh Sorya each have four or five buses per day south to Battambang (7000r, 1½ hours) and Phnom Penh (US$7, eight hours). Capital Tour and Sorya also have a couple of buses to Poipet. A few morning buses from Poipet come through en route to Siem Reap (two hours).

**Mekong Express** (NH56) has a central office with express minivan services to Siem Reap (US$5, two hours) at 9.45am and 3.45pm; and four to Phnom Penh (US$14, six hours) between 7.30am and 4pm. **Mean Chey Express** (📱054-665 1999; dara_muong@yahoo.com; NH6) also runs comfortable minivans to Phnom Penh (US$9, 6½ hours).

From the **taxi park**, near the bus station, share taxis serve Poipet (15,000r, 40 minutes), Siem Reap (14,000r, two hours), Battambang (10,000r, 1¼ hours) and Phnom Penh (US$10, six hours); a private taxi to Siem Reap costs about US$30. There are also share taxis to Samraong via Kralanh for the O Smach border crossing (25,000r, three hours).

Share taxis to other northbound destinations, including Banteay Chhmar (p255), depart from **Psar Thmei** (St 1).

# Banteay Chhmar បន្ទាយឆ្មារ

Beautiful, peaceful and covered in astonishingly intricate bas-reliefs, Banteay Chhmar is one of the most impressive remote temple complexes beyond the Angkor area; it was constructed by Cambodia's most prolific builder, Jayavarman VII (r 1181–1219), on the site of a 9th-century temple. The Global Heritage Fund (www.globalheritagefund.org) is assisting with conservation efforts here, and it is now a top candidate for Unesco World Heritage Site status. Next to the ruins, Banteay Chhmar village is part of a worthwhile Community-Based Tourism (CBT) scheme offering homestays, activities and guides for temple tours to assist with community development in the area. If you're looking for an opportunity to delve into Cambodian rural life and spend some quality time amid a temple complex far away from the crowds, this is is a great opportunity. All activities can be booked through the CBT Office.

## ◉ Sights

★ **Banteay Chhmar**  BUDDHIST TEMPLE
(admission US$5; ⊙8am-6pm) Now atmospherically encroached by forest, Banteay Chhmar housed one of the largest and most impressive Buddhist monasteries of the Angkorian period and was originally enclosed by a 9km-long wall. It is one of the the few temples to feature the Bayon-style four-faced Avalokiteshvaras with their mysterious and iconic smiles. The temple is also renowned for its 2000 sq metres of intricate carvings that depict war victories, scenes from daily life and a spectacular bas-relief of multi-armed Avalokiteshvaras.

The sequence of eight multi-armed Avalokiteshvaras, on the exterior of the southern section of the temple's western ramparts, is unique to Banteay Chhmar. Unfortunately several of these were dismantled and trucked into Thailand in a brazen act of looting in 1998; only two figures – one with 22 arms, the other with 32 – remain in situ, but the dazzling, intricate artistry involved in creating these carvings is still easily evoked. The segments of the looted bas-reliefs that were intercepted by the Thais are now on display in Phnom Penh's National Museum (p42).

On the temple's east side, a huge bas-relief on a partly toppled wall dramatically depicts naval warfare between the Khmers (on the left) and the Chams (on the right), with the dead (some being devoured by crocodiles) at the bottom. Further south (to the left) are scenes of land warfare with infantry and elephants. There are more martial bas-reliefs along the exterior of the temple's south walls.

The once-grand entry gallery is now a jumble of fallen sandstone blocks, though elsewhere a few intersecting galleries have withstood the ravages of time, as have some almost-hidden 12th-century inscriptions. Sadly, all the *apsaras* (nymphs) have been decapitated by looters.

**Banteay Top**  BUDDHIST TEMPLE
(បន្ទាយទ័ព) FREE Banteay Top (Fortress of the Army) may be small, but its impressively tall, damaged towers are highly photogenic. Constructed around the same time as Banteay Chhmar, it may be a tribute to the army of Jayavarman VII, which confirmed Khmer dominance over the region by comprehensively defeating the Chams.

To get here from Banteay Chhmar, head towards Sisophon along NH56 for 7km, take the left-hand turn through the red ornamental gate and head east down the track for 5km.

**Prasat Ta Prohm**  BUDDHIST TEMPLE
(ប្រាសាទតាព្រហ្ម) FREE Prasat Ta Prohm is the easiest of Banteay Chhmar's nine satellite temples to visit. This small ruined temple is topped by a well-preserved example of a Bayan-style four-faced Avalokiteshvaras. To get here, exit Banteay Chhmar by its south gate, cross the main road (NH56) and take the dirt track just to your right. After about 100 metres a walking trail veers off to the left and ends at the temple.

**Banteay Chhmar
Satellite Temples**  BUDDHIST TEMPLE
FREE Along with Prasat Ta Prohm, there are nine fascinating satellite temples in the vicinity of Banteay Chhmar, all in a ruinous state and some accessible only if you chop through the jungle. These include Prasat Samnang Tasok, Prasat Mebon, Prasat Prom Muk Buon, Prasat Yeay Choun, Prasat Pranang Ta Sok and Prasat Chiem Trey. To explore these lesser-seen temples, hire a guide from the CBT Office.

## 🏃 Activities

If you've got some time up your sleeve, spending a day or two in the area to soak up local village life is well worth while. The CBT Office rents out bicycles (US$1.50 per day) for exploring and can arrange village tours, as well as *kuyon* (tractor) transport (US$10 per group) or a *moto* (US$5) to Banteay Top.

## 🛏 Sleeping & Eating

**CBT Homestay Program** HOMESTAY $
(☑ 097 516 5533, 012 435660; www.visitbanteay chhmar.org; r US$7) 🍴 Thanks to the homestay project run by the CBT Office, it's possible to stay in Banteay Chhmar and three nearby hamlets. Rooms are inside private homes and come with mosquito nets, fans that run when there's electricity (6pm to 10pm) and downstairs bathrooms. Part of the income goes into a community development fund.

**Banteay Chhmar Restaurant** CAMBODIAN $
(NH56; mains US$1.50-4) Near the temple's eastern entrance, this rustic restaurant is the only place to dine without pre-ordering. It serves really tasty Khmer food.

## 🛍 Shopping

**Soieries du Mékong** HANDICRAFTS
(Mekong Silk Mill; www.soieriesdumekong.com; NH56; ⏰ 7.30am-noon & 1.30-5pm Mon-Fri) It is possible to see silk being woven and to purchase top-quality silk products destined for the French market at Soieries du Mékong, 150m south of where NH56 from Sisophon meets the *baray* (the reservoir surrounding the temple). It's affiliated with the French NGO Enfants du Mékong (www.enfants dumekong.com).

## ⓘ Orientation

The main road through town runs west-to-east south of the *baray*, and then takes a 90-degree turn north just after it. The market and taxi park are at the turn; a few hundred metres north is the temple's main (eastern) entrance.

## ⓘ Information

**Community-Based Tourism Office** (CBT Office; ☑ 097 516 5533, 012 435660; www.visitbanteaychhmar.org; NH56) Besides arranging homestays and guides, this pioneering office also arranges activities that allow travellers a small insight into village life (such as ox-cart rides and traditional music shows) and can arrange trips to outlying temples by local transport. The office is opposite and a bit south of the Banteay Chhmar main (eastern) entrance.

## ⓘ Getting There & Away

Banteay Chhmar is 61km north of Sisophon and about 50km southwest of Samraong along NH56.

The last 10km of this road was a mess when we visited as it was being upgraded, but should be better by the time you read this. The temple can also be visited on a long day trip from Siem Reap.

From Sisophon's Psar Thmei (1km north of NH6), most northbound share taxis go only as far as Thmor Puok, although a few continue on to Banteay Chhmar (15,000r, one hour) and Samraong. A *moto* from Sisophon to Banteay Chhmar will cost US$15 to US$20 return, and a taxi US$50 to US$60 return.

# ODDAR MEANCHEY PROVINCE

Far-flung and dirt-poor, Oddar Meanchey Province (ខេត្តឧត្តរមានជ័យ) produces very little apart from opportunities for aid organisations. Khmer Rouge sites around Anlong Veng attract those curious about Cambodia's brutal modern history, while two remote international border crossings with Thailand (Choam–Chong Sa Ngam and O Smach–Chong Chom) are becoming more popular as roads improve.

## Anlong Veng អន្លង់វែង

For almost a decade this was the ultimate Khmer Rouge stronghold, home to Pol Pot, Nuon Chea, Khieu Samphan and Ta Mok, among the most notorious leaders of Democratic Kampuchea. Anlong Veng fell to government forces in April 1998 and about the same time Pol Pot died mysteriously nearby. Soon after, Prime Minister Hun Sen ordered that NH67 be bulldozed through the jungle to ensure that the population didn't have second thoughts about ending the war.

Today Anlong Veng is a poor, dusty town with little going for it except the nearby Choam–Chong Sa Ngam border crossing, which connects with a pretty isolated part of Thailand. For those with an interest in contemporary Cambodian history though, the area's Khmer Rouge sites are an important part of the picture. In this area, most of the residents, and virtually the entire political leadership and upper class, are ex-Khmer Rouge or their descendents.

The town's focal point is the Dove of Peace Roundabout at the junction of NH67 and the new highway east to Preah Vihear. The monument is a gift from Hun Sen. About 600m north of the monument, the NH67 crosses a bridge and continues 16km to the Thai border.

## LAND MINES: CAMBODIA'S UNDERGROUND WAR

Cambodia is a country scarred by years of conflict – and some of the deepest scars lie just inches beneath the surface. The legacy of land mines here is one of the worst anywhere in the world, with an estimated four to six million still planted around the countryside. Although the conflict ended more than a decade ago, Cambodia's civil war is still claiming new victims: civilians who have stepped on a mine or been injured by unexploded ordnance (UXO), also known as explosive remnants of war (ERW).

The first massive use of mines came in the mid-1980s, when Vietnamese forces (using forced local labour) constructed a 700km-long minefield along the entire Cambodian–Thai border. After the Vietnamese withdrawal, more mines were laid by the Cambodian government to prevent towns, villages, military positions, bridges, border crossings and supply routes from being overrun, and by Khmer Rouge forces to protect areas they still held. Even more government mines were laid in the mid-1990s in offensives against Khmer Rouge positions around Anlong Veng and Pailin.

Today Cambodia has one of the highest number of amputees per capita of any country: more than 40,000 Cambodians have lost limbs due to mines and other military explosives. Despite extensive mine risk education (MRE) campaigns, an average of about 15 Cambodians are injured or killed every month. This is a vast improvement on the mid-1990s, when the monthly figure was more like 300, but it's still wartime carnage in a country officially at peace.

To complicate matters, areas that seem safe in the dry season can become dangerous in the wet, as the earth softens. It's not uncommon for Cambodian farmers to settle on land during the dry season only to have their lives shattered a few months later when a family member has a leg blown off.

Several groups are working furiously to clear the country of mines – one reason the mine-casualty rate has dropped (other reasons include increased awareness and improved roads). When travelling in more remote parts of the northwest you're likely to see de-mining teams run by the Cambodian Mine Action Authority (www.cmaa.gov.kh), the HALO Trust (www.halotrust.org), and the Mines Advisory Group (www.maginternational.org) in action.

Some sage advice about mines:

➡ In remote areas, never leave well-trodden paths.

➡ Never touch anything that looks remotely like a mine or munitions.

➡ If you find yourself accidentally in a mined area, retrace your steps only if you can clearly see your footprints. If not, stay where you are and call for help – as advisory groups put it, 'better to spend a day stuck in a minefield than a lifetime as an amputee'.

➡ If someone is injured in a minefield, do *not* rush in to assist even if they are crying out for help – find someone who knows how to safely enter a mined area.

➡ Do not leave the roadside in remote areas, even for the call of nature. Your limbs are more important than your modesty.

In 1997 more than 100 countries signed a treaty banning the production, stockpiling, sale and use of land mines under any circumstances. However, the world's major producers refused to sign, including China, Russia and the USA. Cambodia was a signatory to the treaty, but mine clearance in Cambodia is, tragically, too often a step-by-step process. For the majority of Cambodians, the underground war goes on.

For more on the scourge of land mines, visit the Cambodia Landmine Museum (p124) near Siem Reap.

## ◉ Sights

The main sights in Anlong Veng are locations once associated with Ta Mok (Uncle Mok, aka Brother Number Five). To his former supporters, many of whom still live in Anlong Veng, he was harsh but fair, a benevolent builder of orphanages and schools, and a leader who kept order, in stark contrast to the anarchic atmosphere that prevailed once government forces took over. But to most Cambodians, Pol Pot's military enforcer – responsible for thousands of deaths in successive purges during the terrible years of

Democratic Kampuchea – was best known as 'the Butcher'. Arrested in 1999, he died in July 2006 in a Phnom Penh hospital, awaiting trial for genocide and crimes against humanity.

### Ta Mok's House
HISTORIC SITE

(ផ្ទះតាម៉ុក; suggested donation for caretaker US$1) On a peaceful lakeside site, Ta Mok's House is a spartan structure with a bunker in the basement, five childish wall murals downstairs (one of Angkor Wat, four of Prasat Preah Vihear) and three more murals upstairs, including an idyllic wildlife scene. About the only furnishings that weren't looted are the floor tiles.

To get here, head north from the bridge on NH67 for 600m, turn right (signposted for the house) and continue 200m past the so-called Tourism Information hut.

### Ta Mok's Lake
LAKE

(បឹង តាម៉ុក) Swampy Ta Mok's Lake was created on Brother Number Five's orders, but the water killed all the trees; their skeletons are a fitting monument to the devastation he and his movement left behind. In the middle of the lake, due east from Ta Mok's House, is a small brick structure – an outhouse, and all that remains of Pol Pot's residence in Anlong Veng.

### Ta Mok's Grave
MONUMENT

(ផ្នូរតាម៉ុក; admission US$2) From the turnoff to Ta Mok's house, driving a further 7km north takes you to Tumnup Leu village, where a signposted right turn brings you 200m to a fork. Take the left fork and proceed another 200m to Ta Mok's Angkorian-style mausoleum, built by a rich grandson in 2009. The cement tomb bears no name or inscription. Locals come here to light incense and, in a bizarre local tradition, hope his spirit grants them a winning lottery number.

The mausoleum is on the grounds of a modest pagoda; take a hard right (south) as you enter the grounds to find the grave.

## 🛏 Sleeping

### Bot Uddom Guesthouse
GUESTHOUSE $

(☑ 011 500507; r with air-con from US$15; ❄ 🗑) Some of the large, spotless rooms here come with massive hardwood beds. The annexe looks out on Ta Mok's Lake (well, swamp). It's a few hundred metres east of the Dove of Peace roundabout on the road to Preah Vihear.

### Monorom Guesthouse
HOTEL $

(☑ 065-690 0468; NH67; r with fan/air-con US$6/15; ❄ ❄ 🗑) The air-con rooms here are nondescript, but it's central, clean and everything works. Fan-only rooms are a bit dreary. It's 200m north of the main roundabout. No English spoken.

## 🍴 Eating

North of the roundabout are a few restaurants, while south of the roundabout blazing braziers barbecue chicken, fish and eggs on skewers at the lively **night market**.

### Monorom Restaurant
CAMBODIAN $

(NH67; mains 8000-16,000r; ⊗ 8am-10pm) Attached to the hotel of the same name, Monorom dishes up a small but decently tasty selection of typical fried vegetable and meat dishes and breakfast noodle soups. It's pretty much the only place in town with an English menu.

### Mab Phkay Pich
CAMBODIAN, THAI $

(NH67; mains 16,000-20,000r; ⊗ 6am-10pm) This popular place serves tasty Khmer and Thai food in private pavilions. Situated 500m north of town and a few buildings south of the turnoff to Ta Mok's house.

## ⓘ Information

**Acleda Bank** (⊗ 7.30am-2pm Mon-Fri, to noon Sat, ATM 24hr)

**Votha Internet Service** (NH67; per hr 3000r; ⊗ 7am-9pm) Doubles as the Rith Mony bus terminal.

## ⓘ Getting There & Around

Anlong Veng is 124km north of Siem Reap along nicely sealed NH67, and about 76km west of Sra Em, the turnoff for Prasat Preah Vihear.

The bus depots are on NH67, just north of the roundabout, while share taxis gather on NH67 just southwest of the roundabout.

Share taxis to Siem Reap (20,000r, 1½ hours) and Sra Em (20,000r, two hours) are most frequent in the morning. A private taxi to Sra Em costs US$30.

**Rith Mony** (NH67), **Ponleu Angkor Khmer** (NH67) and **Liang US Express** (☑ 092 905026; NH67) have early-morning bus services to Phnom Penh (US$10, seven hours) via Siem Reap (US$5, two hours) at 7.30am and 8.30am.

A *moto* circuit to the Thai border and back, via Ta Mok's house and grave, costs about US$8. To explore the sights along the Dangrek Mountain track as well, expect to pay around US$20 for a three-to-four-hour circuit.

NORTHWESTERN CAMBODIA DANGREK MOUNTAINS

## GETTING TO THAILAND: ANLONG VENG TO PHUSING

**Getting to the border** The remote Choam–Chong Sa Ngam **border crossing** connects Anlong Veng in Oddar Meanchey province with Thailand's Si Saket Province. A *moto* from Anlong Veng to the border crossing, 16km away, costs US$3 or US$4 (more like US$5 in the reverse direction). This road is sealed and in good condition. The crossing is right next to the smugglers' market.

**At the border** Formalities are straightforward, but note that if you are coming in from Thailand, e-visas are not accepted here. Cambodian visas on arrival are usually charged at US$35.

**Moving on** Once in Thailand, it should be possible to find a *sŏrngtăaou* to Phusing and from there a bus to Khu Khan or Si Saket. Another option is the casino buses, which leave hourly to/from Khu Khan (30 minutes) and Phusing.

Local *moto* driver **Vong Bun Lim** (☑ 088 909 1802) knows the routes to most of the sights around Anlong Veng and in the Dangrek Mountains; he speaks decent English.

# Dangrek Mountains ភ្នំដងរែក

For years the world wondered where Pol Pot and his cronies were hiding out: the answer was right here in the densely forested Dangrek Mountains, close enough to Thailand that they could flee across the border if government forces drew nigh. North of Anlong Veng, hidden within these hill slopes near the Thai frontier, are a number of key Khmer Rouge sites.

About 2km before the border the road splits to avoid a house-sized boulder. A group of **statues** (NH67) hewn entirely from the boulder by the Khmer Rouge can be seen and have now been preserved as a shrine. The statues depict a woman carrying bundles of bamboo sticks on her head and two uniformed Khmer Rouge soldiers (the latter were decapitated by government forces).

Just after you arrive in the bustling border village, look for a sign for the **cremation site of Pol Pot** (admission US$2) on the east side of NH67 (it's 50m south of and opposite the Sangam Casino entrance). Pol Pot's ashes lie under a rusted corrugated iron roof surrounded by rows of partly buried glass bottles. The Khmer Rouge leader was hastily burned here in 1998 on a pile of rubbish and old tyres – a fittingly inglorious end, some say, given the suffering he inflicted on millions of Cambodians.

Bizarre as it may sound, Pol Pot is remembered with affection by some locals, and people sometimes stop by to light incense. According to neighbours, every last bone fragment has been snatched from the ashes by visitors in search of good-luck charms. Pol Pot's spirit, like that of his deputy Ta Mok, is said to give out winning lottery numbers.

The Choam–Chong Sa Ngam border crossing is a few hundred metres north of here, near a ramshackle smugglers' market. From behind the smugglers' market, a dirt road with potholes the size of parachutes – navigable only by 4WD vehicles and motorbikes (and not navigable at all in the depth of the wet season) – heads east, parallel to the Dangrek escarpment. Domestic tourists head along this road to get to **Peuy Ta Mok** (ពើយតាម៉ុក; Ta Mok's Cliff) to enjoy spectacular views of Cambodia's northern plains.

About 4km east along the dirt track after Peuy Ta Mok (when the trail forks at the water-lily lake, take the left-hand track) you'll arrive at **Pol Pot's house**. Surrounded by a cinderblock wall, the jungle hideout was comprehensively looted, though you can still see a low brick building whose courtyard hides an underground bunker. This narrow part of the track is navigable only by motorbike. Much more difficult to get to is **Khieu Samphan's house**, buried in the jungle on the bank of a stream about 5km east of Pol Pot's house.

# PREAH VIHEAR PROVINCE

Vast, remote and hardly touched by tourism, Preah Vihear Province (ខេត្តព្រះវិហារ) is home to three of Cambodia's most impressive Angkorian legacies. Stunningly perched on a promontory high in the Dangrek Mountains, Prasat Preah Vihear became Cambodia's second Unesco World Heritage Site in 2008, sparking an armed stand-off with Thailand. Further south are the lonely, jungle-engulfed temples of Preah Khan – imbued with a secret-world atmosphere due to the sheer isolation. More easily accessible is

10th-century capital Koh Ker (p169), which is a straightforward toll-road drive away from Siem Reap (via Beng Mealea).

Preah Vihear Province is genuine 'outback' Cambodia and remains desperately poor – in part because many areas were under Khmer Rouge control until 1998, and in part because until recently its transport infrastructure was in a catastrophic state. The needs of the Cambodian army in its confrontation with Thailand have expedited dramatic road upgrades in the province, making travel more straightforward, although public transport is still in short supply on some routes.

# Preah Vihear City

🗹 064 / POP 25,000

Preah Vihear City, still commonly known by its old name, Tbeng Meanchey (គុបដៃមានជ័យ), is a sleepy provincial capital where dogs lounging in the middle of the street are only occasionally jolted awake

by passing vehicles. There's very little to see or do here, but the town is useful as a base for journeys to Prasat Preah Vihear, Preah Khan and Koh Ker. Note that a closer base for Prasat Preah Vihear is Sra Em, only 27km south of the temple.

With the smooth highway, running 130km east to Thala Boravit and the new bridge over the Mekong to Stung Treng, Preah Vihear City and the province's remote temples are also a good stop-off for travellers heading east, between the temples of Angkor and Stung Treng, Ratanakiri and Champasak Province in southern Laos.

## 🛏 Sleeping

**Home Vattanak Guesthouse**  HOTEL **$**
(🗹064-636 3000; St A14; r from US$15; ⊖✳@🛜) The 27 well-maintained rooms at this sparkling-clean hotel include wonderful beds, decent bathrooms and luxuries such as flatscreen TVs. Its central but quiet location, tucked down a quiet side street, is an extra bonus.

**Lyhout Guesthouse**  HOTEL **$**
(🗹012 737116; www.lyhoutguesthouse.blogspot. com; Koh Ker St; r US$15-35; ✳🛜) Smart rooms here have wooden desks and white bedspreads adorned with handsome bedrunners. Upgrade yourself to VIP status for an ornate Khmer-carving headboard on the bed, and a fridge and kettle in your room.

**Heng Heng Guesthouse**  HOTEL **$**
(🗹012 900992; Mlou Prey St; r with fan/air-con from US$7/12; ✳🛜) Rooms at this peach concrete monstrosity are a bit time-worn but nonetheless a good deal. Grab a room up on

NORTHWESTERN CAMBODIA PREAH VIHEAR CITY

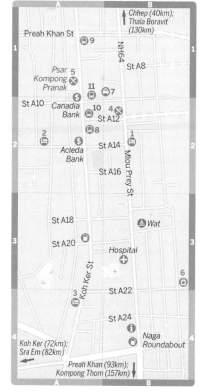

Preah Vihear City · 0 — 100 m / 0 — 0.05 miles

## Preah Vihear City

### 🛌 Sleeping

### 🍴 Eating

### 🛍 Shopping

### 🚌 Transport

the top floor for its sweeping public balcony (alas, with no furniture).

##  Eating

There are several small restaurants dishing up cheap-and-cheerful noodle soups and other Cambodian staples along Koh Ker St.

**Phnom Tbaeng Restaurant**     CAMBODIAN **$**
(Mlou Prey St; mains 12,000-20,000r; ⊙5am-9pm) This open-air restaurant is one of the few places in town with an English menu. Dishes include prawn soup, *tom yam,* noodle soups and steamed fish – as well as more adventurous options such as fried eel and pig's intestines.

**Psar Kompong Pranak**     MARKET **$**
(Koh Ker St; mains 2000-4000r) The northern side of Psar Kompong Pranak is home to plenty of food stalls hawking Khmer-style baguettes, grilled chicken and simple rice and noodle dishes.

## Shopping

**Weaves of Cambodia**     HANDICRAFTS
(☑092 346415; www.weavescambodia.com; ⊙7am-11am & 1-5pm Mon-Fri, 7am-11am Sat) Originally established by the Vietnam Veterans of America Foundation, Weaves of Cambodia, known locally as Chum Ka Mo, is a silk-weaving centre that provides work and rehabilitation for land-mine and polio victims, widows and orphans. Hand-loomed silk scarves (US$30 to US$40) and sarongs (US$70) cost half of what you'll pay in Phnom Penh.

It is now part of the silk empire of Vientiane-based American textile designer Carol Cassidy.

## ℹ Information

**Canadia Bank** (⊙8am-3.30pm Mon-Fri, to 11.30am Sat, ATM 24hr)
**Tourist Office** (☑097 997 9698, 088 885 9366; Mlou Prey St; ⊙7.30-11am & 2-5pm Mon-Fri) With-it, English-speaking Mr Thin is the man in charge here. He and his colleague Heng, an expert on temples, can guide you to Preah Khan and a few lesser-known temples in the province.

## ℹ Getting There & Around

Preah Vihear City is 157km north of Kompong Thom, 82km south of Sra Em, 72km east of Koh Ker and 185km northeast of Siem Reap. These roads are now all in good shape.

**GST Transport** (Koh Ker St), **Liang US Express** (Koh Ker St) and **Thong Ly** (St A10) have 7am buses to Phnom Penh (US$5, seven hours). **Phnom Penh Sorya's** (☑092 273713; Koh Ker St) service to the capital leaves at 7.30am (US$5). All buses travel via Kompong Thom (15,000r, two hours). For Siem Reap, transfer in Kompong Thom.

Share taxis leave from the **bus and taxi station** (St A10) and go to Kompong Thom (25,000r, 1½ hours), Siem Reap (40,000r, three hours, morning only), Sra Em (20,000r, one hour, morning only), Stung Treng (24,000r, two hours) and Choam Ksant (15,000r, one hour). Share taxis to Stung Treng travel via the new bridge across the Mekong from Thala Boravit.

**Asia Van Transfer** (☑012 505673, 063-963855; www.asiavantransfer.com) operates a private minivan between Siem Reap and Stung Treng that passes through Preah Vihear City. Going to Stung Treng (1¾ hours) it leaves at 11.15am; to Siem Reap (2¾ hours) it leaves at 4.15pm.

Private taxis can be hired at the taxi station to Siem Reap (US$70), Prasat Preah Vihear (one way/return US$45/70) and Preah Khan (US$60 return).

# Prasat Preah Vihear    ប្រាសាទព្រះវិហារ

Cambodia's most dramatically situated Angkorian monument, 800m-long Prasat Preah Vihear is perched on an escarpment in the Dangrek Mountains (625m); with breath-

---

## ℹ LAND MINE ALERT!

Until as recently as 1998, land mines were used by the Khmer Rouge to defend Prasat Preah Vihear against government forces. During the past decade, organisations made headway in clearing the site of these enemies within. However, the advent of a border conflict with Thailand led to this area being heavily militarised once again. Both sides denied laying new land mines during the armed stand-off between 2008 and 2011, but rumours persist, as several Thai and Cambodian soldiers were killed by mines in the vicinity of the temple. So do *not*, under any circumstances, stray from marked paths around Prasat Preah Vihear.

The rest of the province is heavily land-mined, too, especially around Choam Ksant. Those with their own transport should travel only on roads or trails regularly used by locals.

taking views of lowland Cambodia, 550m below, stretching as far as the eye can see.

For generations, Prasat Preah Vihear (called Khao Phra Wiharn by the Thais) has been a source of tension between Cambodia and Thailand. This area was ruled by Thailand for several centuries, but returned to Cambodia during the French protectorate, under the treaty of 1907. In 1959 the Thai military seized the temple from Cambodia; then–Prime Minister Sihanouk took the dispute to the International Court of Justice in the Hague, gaining worldwide recognition of Cambodian sovereignty in a 1962 ruling.

The next time Prasat Preah Vihear made international news was in 1979, when the Thai military pushed more than 40,000 Cambodian refugees across the border in one of the worst cases of forced repatriation in UN history. The area was mined and many – perhaps several hundred – refugees died from injuries, starvation and disease before the occupying Vietnamese army could cut a safe passage and escort them on the long walk south to Kompong Thom.

Prasat Preah Vihear hit the headlines again in May 1998 when the Khmer Rouge regrouped here after the fall of Anlong Veng and staged a last stand that soon turned into a final surrender. The temple was heavily land-mined during these final battles and de-mining was ongoing up until the outbreak of the conflict with Thailand. Re-mining seems to be the greater threat right now, with both sides accusing the other of using land mines.

In July 2008 Prasat Preah Vihear was declared Cambodia's second Unesco World Heritage Site. The Thai government, which claims 4.6 sq km of territory right around the temple (some Thai nationalists even claim the temple itself), initially supported the bid, but the temple soon became a pawn in Thailand's chaotic domestic politics. Within a week, Thai troops crossed into Cambodian territory, sparking an armed confrontation that has taken the lives of several dozen soldiers and some civilians on both sides. The Cambodian market at the bottom of the Monumental Stairway, which used to be home to some guesthouses, burned down during an exchange of fire in April 2009. In 2011 exchanges heated up once more and long-range shells were fired into civilian territory by both sides.

In July 2011 the International Court of Justice ruled that both sides should withdraw troops from the area to establish a demilitarised zone. Then in November 2013,

the ICJ confirmed its 1959 ruling that the temple belongs to Cambodia, although it declined to define the official borderline, leaving sovereignty of some lands around the temple open to dispute. The border dispute has died down in recent years, but tensions could reignite any time, especially if the Yellow Shirts regain control in Thailand.

During our most recent visit, there was still a large military presence in and around the temple – ostensibly for security, though it might make some visitors uncomfortable, and money or cigarettes are occasionally requested by soldiers. Always check the latest security situation when in Siem Reap or

## Prasat Preah Vihear

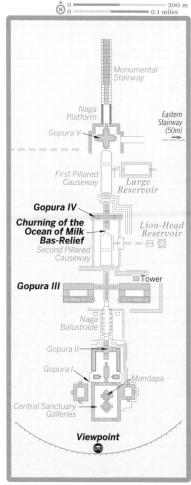

## ❶ ACCESSING PRASAT PREAH VIHEAR

➡ Driving in from Sra Em, your first stop is the **information centre** (Kor Muy; ⊘7am-4.30pm) in the village of Kor Muy (23km north from Sra Em). This is where you pay for entry, secure an English-speaking guide if you want one (US$15), and arrange transport via *moto* (US$5 return) or 4WD (US$25 return, maximum six passengers) up the 6.5km temple access road.

➡ Bring your passport with you when visiting Prasat Preah Vihear. You'll be asked for your passport number when buying your ticket.

➡ The first 5km of the access road are gradual enough, but the final 1.5km is extremely steep; nervous passengers might consider walking this last bit, especially if it's wet. Private vehicles are allowed up this road, but you'll need a motorbike or 4WD. Parking at the top costs 2000/5000r for a motorbike/car.

➡ Another option is to walk up the Eastern Staircase – look for signs to the 'Ancient Staircase' on the road from Sra Em before you get to the information centre in Kor Muy.

➡ It used to be possible to get to Prasat Preah Vihear from Thailand, where paved roads from Kantharalak led almost up to the Monumental Stairway. However, due to the long stand-off between Thailand and Cambodia, access from the Thai side has been forbidden since mid-2008. That could of course change, so check the situation on the ground.

Phnom Penh before making the long overland journey here.

## ❂ Sights

★ **Prasat Preah Vihear**        BUDDHIST TEMPLE
(admission US$10; ⊘7.30am-4.30pm) An important place of pilgrimage during the Angkorian period, Prasat Preah Vihear was built by a succession of seven Khmer monarchs, beginning with Yasovarman I (r 889–910) and ending with Suryavarman II (r 1112–1152). Like other temple-mountains from this period, it was designed to represent Mt Meru and dedicated to the Hindu deity Shiva.

The temple is laid out along a north–south processional axis with five cruciform *gopura* (pavilions), decorated with exquisite carvings, separated by esplanades up to 275m long.

From the parking area, walk up the hill to toppled and crumbling Gopura V at the north end of the temple complex. From here, the grey-sandstone Monumental Stairway leads down to the Thai border. Back when the temple was open from the Thai side, this stairway was how most tourists entered the temple complex. Thailand claims this part of the temple is theirs. That Gopura V appears on both the 50,000r and 2000r banknotes is an emphatic statement that Cambodia disagrees.

East of Gopura V you'll see a set of stairs dropping into the abyss. This is the 1800m Eastern Stairway. Used for centuries by pilgrims climbing up from Cambodia's northern plains, it was recently de-mined, rebuilt as a 2242-step wooden staircase and reopened.

Walking south up the slope from Gopura V, the next pavilion you get to is Gopura IV. On the pediment above the southern door, look for an early rendition of the Churning of the Ocean of Milk, a theme later depicted awesomely at Angkor Wat.

In Gopura I the galleries, with their inward-looking windows, are in a remarkably good state of repair, but the Central Sanctuary is just a pile of rubble. Outside, the cliff affords a stupendous viewpoint to Cambodia's northern plains, with the holy mountain of Phnom Kulen (487m) looming in the distance. This is a fantastic spot for a picnic.

The best guidebook to Prasat Preah Vihear's architecture and carvings is *Preah Vihear* by Vittorio Roveda (published 2010). These days it may be hard to find in Cambodia, as it was published in Thailand and the text is in English and Thai.

## ▬ Sleeping

All accommodation in the area is in Sra Em, the bustling junction town 30km south of the temple.

**Sok San Guesthouse**        GUESTHOUSE $
(☑097 715 3839; s/d with fan US$8/10, with air-con from US$13/15; ❋☏) Sok San has a variety of dimly lit rooms and a restaurant with decent Thai and Cambodian food. Cheaper rooms are small and windowless. Air-con ones come with mismatched furniture and windows (which look out onto the corridor). It's 1km west of Sra Em centre.

**Preah Vihear**
**Boutique Hotel**  BOUTIQUE HOTEL $$$
(☑ 088 346 0501; www.preahvihearhotel.com; Ok-
nha Franna St; d incl breakfast US$35-90; ❋ ☎ ☲ )
A slick boutique in the unlikeliest of plac-
es, the PVBH is looking to coax higher-end
temple goers from Siem Reap to stay a
night. With lush bedding and a shimmering
20m pool to cool off in outside, it has a pret-
ty good case. It's about 1km out of town on
the road to Prasat Preah Vihear.

 **Eating**

A string of simple BBQ shacks and basic
restaurants cluster around Sra Em's main
roundabout.

**Pkay Broek Restaurant**  CAMBODIAN $
(mains US$2.50-6; ⊙ 6am-10pm) Located 3km
west of the centre on the road to Anlong
Veng, Pkay Prek Restaurant is famous for its
grill-it-yourself *phnom pleung* ('hill of fire',
translated as 'Korean Fire Beef' on its menu).

ⓘ **Information**

There is no bank or ATM in Sra Em. Be sure to
bring enough cash with you.

ⓘ **Getting There & Away**

Sra Em is 80km from Anlong Veng and 200km
from Siem Reap. The roads up here in this
northernmost part of Cambodia have improved
dramatically in recent years.

With a private car you can get to Prasat Preah
Vihear in about 2½ hours from Siem Reap. The
day trip usually takes in Koh Ker and/or Beng
Mealea and/or Banteay Srei en route and costs
US$100 to US$150.

It makes much more sense to break up the long
trip with a night in Sra Em, which is 23km from
Kor Muy, where the temple information office
is, and 30km from the temple proper. From Sra
Em's central roundabout, take a *moto* to Kor Muy
(US$10 to US$15 return), where another *moto*
will take you up to the temple (US$5 return).
There is no public transport to Kor Muy.

From the roundabout, share taxis go to Siem
Reap (US$10, 2½ hours), Phnom Penh (US$15,
eight hours), Preah Vihear City (US$5, one
hour) and Anlong Veng (US$5, one hour). Trips
to all destinations besides Siem Reap are in the
morning only.

**Liang US Express** has a morning bus from Sra
Em to Phnom Penh (US$10, 10 hours) via Preah
Vihear City and Kompong Thom, while **Rith Mony**
(☑ 097 865 6018) has a morning bus to Phnom
Penh (US$10, 10 hours) via Siem Reap (20,000r,
3½ hours).

# Veal Krous Vulture Feeding Station
ស្ថានីយ៍ដាក់ចំណីក្តាត វាលគ្រួស

In order to save three critically endangered
species – the white-rumped, slender-billed
and red-headed vultures – the Wildlife Con-
servation Society (www.wcs.org) set up a
'vulture restaurant' in the village of Dong-
phlet, northeast of Chhep on the edge of
the Preah Vihear Protected Forest. A cow
carcass is put out in a field, and visitors
waiting in a nearby bird hide watch as these
incredibly rare vultures move in to devour
the carrion.

Visits are offered by Siem Reap–based
**Sam Veasna Center** (SVC; ☑ 063-963710;
www.samveasna.org).

Trips here involve an overnight at a WCS
forest camp. Access to the site is year-round,
but try to give SVC at least a week's notice to
assure your spot.

# Preah Khan

For tantalising lost-world ambience,
the **Preah Khan Temple Enclosure**
(ប្រាសាទព្រះខាន់; admission 10,000r) can't be
beaten. Covering almost 5 sq km, this temple
complex (not to be confused with the temple
of the same name at Angkor) is the largest
temple enclosure constructed during the
Angkorian period – quite a feat when you
consider the competition.

Preah Khan's history is shrouded in mys-
tery, but it was long an important religious
site, and some structures here date back
to the 9th century. Both Suryavarman II,
builder of Angkor Wat, and Jayavarman
VII lived here at various times during their
lives, suggesting Preah Khan was some-
thing of a second city in the Angkorian em-
pire. Originally dedicated to Hindu deities,
Preah Khan was reconsecrated to Mahaya-
na Buddhist worship during a monumental
reconstruction in the late 12th and early
13th centuries.

Wrapped by vines and trees, and thanks
to its back-of-beyond location, the site is
astonishingly peaceful and you'll very like-
ly be the only visitor. One entry fee gains
you admission to all of the temples in the
enclosure.

Locals say there are no land mines in
the vicinity of Preah Khan, but stick to the
marked paths just to be on the safe side.

## TMATBOEY: ON THE TRAIL OF THE GIANT IBIS

Cambodia's remote northern plains, the largest remaining block of deciduous diptero-carp forest, seasonal wetlands and grasslands in Southeast Asia, have been described as Southeast Asia's answer to Africa's savannahs. Covering much of northwestern Preah Vihear Province, they are one of the last places on earth where you can see Cambodia's national bird, the critically endangered giant ibis.

Other rare species that can be spotted here include the woolly-necked stork, white-rumped falcon, green peafowl, Alexandrine parakeet, grey-headed fish eagle and no fewer than 16 species of woodpecker, as well as owls and raptors. Birds are easiest to see from January to April.

In a last-ditch effort to ensure the survival of the giant ibis, protect the only confirmed breeding sites of the white-shouldered ibis and save the habitat of other globally endangered species, including the sarus crane and the greater adjutant, the Wildlife Conservation Society (www.wcs.org) set up a pioneering community-ecotourism project here.

Situated in the isolated village of Tmatboey inside the **Kulen Promtep Wildlife Sanctuary (តំបន់អភិរក្សសត្វលែនព្រហ្មទេព**; www.samveasna.org), the initiative provides local villagers with education, income and a concrete incentive to do everything possible to protect the ibis. All visitors make a conservation donation to the village conservation fund to help with maintenance and improvements to the project.

Tmatbouey village lies about 5km off the smooth new highway that links Preah Vihear City and Sra Em. The turnoff is 46km southeast of Sra Em and 39km northwest of Preah Vihear. The village is accessible year-round. To arrange a four-day, three-night visit contact the Siem Reap–based Sam Veasna Center (SVC; p263). Visitors sleep in wooden bungalows with bathrooms and solar hot water.

For those wanting to explore an even more remote corner of Cambodia, the Kulen Promtep Wildlife Sanctuary's newest birding site is based out of the tiny outpost village of Prey Veng – about 60km from Tmatboey (as the giant ibis flies). Here the WCS and SVC aim to replicate the success of Tmatboey to ensure conservation of this habitat. More than 150 bird species have been spotted here, including the giant ibis, greater adjutant and white-winged duck.

As well as birding, Prey Veng offers great opportunities for hiking through the open dry forest to a hilltop Angkorian temple. Prey Veng's community-managed guesthouses provide simple accommodation.

Trips to both Tmatboey and Prey Veng can include visits to Beng Mealea, Koh Ker and Prasat Preah Vihear en route and are often combined with visits to Veal Krous Vulture Feeding Station. Contact SVC for tour pricing details.

## ⦿ Sights

**Prasat Damrei**　　　　　　BUDDHIST TEMPLE
(ប្រាសាទដំរី; Elephant Temple) Prasat Damrei lies at the eastern end of a 3km-long *baray* (reservoir) and is the first temple on the Preah Khan access road. On the summit of this small pyramid temple, two of the original exquisitely carved elephants can still be seen; two others are at Phnom Penh's National Museum (p42) and the Musée Guimet in Paris.

**Prasat Preah Stung**　　　　BUDDHIST TEMPLE
(ប្រាសាទព្រះស្ទឹង) At the western end of Preah Khan's *baray* stands Prasat Preah Stung (known to locals as Prasat Muk Buon or Temple of the Four Faces). It's particularly memorable because its central tower

(held up by bamboo scaffolding) is adorned with four enigmatic, Bayon-style faces of Avalokiteshvara.

**★Preah Khan**　　　　　　BUDDHIST TEMPLE
(ប្រាសាទព្រះខាន់) From Prasat Preah Stung, the Preah Khan Temple Enclosure access road leads 400m southwest to the magnificently well-preserved eastern **gopu-ra** (entrance pavilion) of Preah Khan itself, which is surrounded by a (now dry) moat similar to the one around Angkor Thom. Once through the grand gateway, a trail meanders past a **dharmasala** (pilgrim's rest house) and through another crumbling pavilion to the **central temple area** of half-toppled *prangs* (temple towers), entangled with trees and overgrown by forest.

As recently as the mid-1990s, the central structure was thought to be in reasonable shape, but at some point in the second half of the decade, looters arrived seeking buried statues under each *prang*. Assaulted with pneumatic drills and mechanical diggers, the ancient temple never stood a chance – many of the towers simply collapsed in on themselves, leaving the mess we see today. Once again a temple that had survived so much couldn't stand the onslaught of the 20th century and its all-consuming appetite.

Among the carvings found at Preah Khan was the bust of Jayavarman, now in Phnom Penh's National Museum (p42) and widely copied as a souvenir for tourists. The body of the statue was discovered in the 1990s by locals who alerted authorities, making it possible for a joyous reunion of head and body in 2000.

Most locals refer to this temple as Prasat Bakan; scholars officially refer to it as Bakan Svay Rolay, combining the local name for the temple and the district name. Khmers in Siem Reap often refer to it as Preah Khan-Kompong Svay.

### Prasat Preah Thkol
BUDDHIST TEMPLE

(ប្រាសាទព្រះថ្កុល) In the centre of Preah Khan's *baray* is Prasat Preah Thkol (known by locals as Mebon), an island temple similar in style to the Western Mebon at Angkor.

### ❶ Getting There & Away

Traditionally, Preah Khan has been the toughest of Preah Vihear Province's remote temples to reach, but upgraded provincial highways and a new dirt road to the temple itself have improved things dramatically. You can now visit Preah Khan year-round, although it's still easiest in the dry season.

There's no public transport, so you'll need to drive yourself or hire a *moto* or a taxi in Preah Vihear City or Kompong Thom, or in Siem Reap for an extra-long day trip.

To get there turn west off smooth NH62 in Svay Pak, about 64km south of Preah Vihear City and 93km north of Kompong Thom. From here an all-season dirt road (substantially pitted with potholes) via Sangkom Thmei commune takes you to Ta Seng, about 56km from the highway and just 4km from the temple. These last 4km are in good shape.

Coming from Siem Reap there are other options for hard-core trail bikers. The most straightforward route is to take NH6 to Stoeng and then head north. You can also take NH6 to Kompong Kdei, head north to Khvau and then ride east on a difficult stretch of NH66 (see below).

An amazing alternative is to approach from Beng Mealea along the ancient Angkor road (Cambodia's own Route 66 – NH66). You'll cross about 10 splendid Angkorian naga bridges, including the remarkable 77m-long Spean Ta Ong, 7km west of Khvau. The road from Beng Mealea to Khvau is now in fine condition. However, it deteriorates rapidly after Khvau. The 23km from Khvau to Ta Seng are impassable in the rainy season.

Only experienced bikers should attempt these alternative routes on rental motorbikes, as conditions range from difficult to extremely tough from every side – and you could end up lost in the middle of nowhere.

# KOMPONG THOM PROVINCE

For those not wanting to rush between Phnom Penh and Siem Reap, Kompong Thom Province (ខេត្តកំពង់ធំ) makes for a rewarding stopover thanks to several intriguing sights spread across the countryside surrounding provincial capital Kompong Thom.

## Kompong Thom
កំពង់ធំ

📞 062 / POP 68,000

This friendly, bustling commercial town rims the NH6 with the lazy curves of the Sen River winding through the centre. The town may be sparse on attractions but it's a prime launching pad for exploring nearby sights. Both the serene, tree-entwined temples of Sambor Prei Kuk and the colourful wats of Phnom Santuk are easy half-day trips, while good accommodation and eating options make Kompong Thom an excellent base from which to head out on a long day trip to Preah Khan.

### ❍ Sights & Activities

Stung Sen St, east of the NH6, is lined by plenty of creaky, pastel-washed wooden houses and makes for a lovely stroll in the late afternoon.

Sambor Village Hotel offers a variety of river cruises, including a sunset cruise and a longer journey to the boat pagodas of Trey Leak village.

### Kompong Thom Museum
MUSEUM

(NH6; ⊙ 9am-4pm) **FREE** This seriously bijou museum (it's one room) actually packs a pretty good punch with statuary and stelae from local sites, including a fine selection of beautiful pieces from Sambor Prei Kuk

# Kompong Thom

Kompong Thom Museum (2km);
Sambor Prei Kuk (30km);
Siem Reap (150km)

St 105
Wat Kompuong
NH 6
St 103
St 101
St 102
Stung Sen
2 1
Stung Sen St
7
Psar Kompong Thom
9
Run Amok (100m);
Sambor Village Hotel (200m)
8
4
Prachea Thepatay St (Democracy St)
Canadia Bank
St 1
St 3
3
St 5
St 6
6
St 7
St 8
Elephant & Tigers Statue
5
St 10
Kakaoh (13km); Santuk Silk Farm (15km);
Phnom Santuk Turnoff (15km)

## ⊨ Sleeping

**Arunras Hotel**  HOTEL $
(☏062-961294; NH6; s/d with fan US$5/8, d with air-con US$15; ❋❸) Dominating Kompong Thom's accommodation scene, this corner establishment has 58 good-value rooms with Chinese-style decoration and on-the-ball staff. The popular restaurant downstairs dishes up tasty Khmer fare. It operates the slightly cheaper, 53-room **Arunras Guesthouse** (☏012 865935; NH6; s/d with fan US$6/8, with air-con US$10/13; ❋❸) next door. Extra bonus for the lazy traveller: buses through town stop literally right outside the door.

**Vimean Sovann Guesthouse**  HOTEL $
(☏078 220333; St 7; s/d with fan US$6/7, with air-con US$12/14; ❋❸) It may not look like much from the outside, but hiding inside are the smartest budget rooms in town, all with fresh paint, new bathroom fixtures and cute wall art. Opt for the spacious double rooms (with two beds), which come with private balcony.

**Ponleu Thmey Guesthouse**  HOTEL $
(☏012 910896; NH6; s/d with fan US$3/6, with air-con US$13/14; ❋❸) Popular with NGO workers, Ponleu Thmey has simple but super-clean fan rooms for the budget-conscious, along with smart air-con options that come with flatscreen TV.

⭐**Sambor Village Hotel**  BOUTIQUE HOTEL $$
(☏062-961391; www.samborvillage.asia; Prachea Thepatay St; s/d US$50/55; ❋@❸❋) This French-owned place brings boutique to Kompong Thom. Spacious, bungalow-style rooms with four-poster beds and chic bathrooms are set amid a tranquil verdant garden with

(it's well worth poking your head in on your way back from the site itself).

**French Governor's Residence**  HISTORIC BUILDING
(Stung Sen St) About 500m west of Kompong Thom bridge is the dilapidated old French governor's residence (no entry), chiefly interesting as being next to three old mahogany trees that hold an extraordinary sight: hundreds of large bats (in Khmer, chreoun), with 40cm wingspans. They spend their days suspended upside-down like winged fruit, fanning themselves with their wings to keep cool. Head here around dusk (from about 5.30pm or 6pm) to see them fly off in search of food.

**Im Sokhom Travel Agency**  TOUR
(☏012 691527; St 3) Runs guided tours, including cycling trips to Sambor Prei Kuk, and can arrange transport by *moto* to Sambor Prei Kuk (US$10) or Phnom Santuk and Santuk Silk Farm (US$8).

## THE IRON KUY OF CAMBODIA

The Kuy are an ethnic minority found in northern Cambodia, Southern Laos and North-eastern Thailand. In Cambodia, the Kuy have long been renowned as smelters and smiths. It is thought that the Kuy may have produced iron – used for weaponry, tools and construction supports – since the Angkorian period.

The Kuy stopped smelting iron around 1950, but high-quality smithing continues to be practised in some communities. When travelling along NH62 between Kompong Thom and Preah Vihear City, it is possible to stop at Rumchek, about 2km south of the iron mines of Phnom Dek. Kuy smith Mr Ma Thean lives in Rumchek and can produce a traditional Kuy jungle knife in just one hour. The experience includes a chance to work the bellows and is a good way to support a dying art.

an inviting pool under the shade of a mango tree. The upstairs terrace restaurant has international cuisine and impressive hardwood flooring. Free use of mountain bikes. Located riverside, about 700m east of NH6.

## ✖ Eating

**Prum Bayon Restaurant**                CAMBODIAN $
(Prachea Thepatay St; mains incl rice 6000-10,000r; ⊙5am-9pm) Lacking English signs but with an English menu, this immensely popular feeding station is where locals come for flavourful Khmer cooking.

**Psar Kompong Thom**                CAMBODIAN $
(NH6; mains 2000-4000r; ⊙4pm-2am) Sit on a plastic chair at a neon-lit table outside Kompong Thom's main market and dig into chicken rice soup, chicken curry noodles and Khmer-style baguettes.

★**Kompong**
**Thom Restaurant**                CAMBODIAN $$
(NH6; mains US$3-8; ⊙6.30am-9pm; 🛜🍴) With delightful bow-tied waiters and a pocket-sized terrace overlooking the river, this restaurant is easily Kompong Thom's best. Unique concoctions featuring water buffalo and stir-fried eel feature on the menu of Khmer classics, which come in generous portions.

**Run Amok**                INTERNATIONAL $$
(Prachea Thepatay St; mains US$2.50-8.75; ⊙3-9pm Mon-Sat; 🛜) If you're in the mood for comfort food, this bamboo-walled place is a real gem. The big menu of pizzas and burgers is a winner, as is their fantastic selection of ice cream.

## ❶ Information

**Canadia Bank** (NH6; ⊙8am-3.30pm Mon-Fri, 8-11.30am Sat, ATM 24hr)

**Tourist Information Office** (Stung Sen St; ⊙8am-11am & 2-5pm Mon-Fri) Hands out a pamphlet on Kompong Thom sights.

## ❶ Getting There & Around

Kompong Thom is 165km north of Phnom Penh, 147km southeast of Siem Reap and 157km south of Preah Vihear City.

Dozens of buses travelling between Phnom Penh (US$5, four hours) and Siem Reap (US$5, two hours) pass through Kompong Thom. They drop off passengers right in front of the Arunras Hotel (which is also where you flag down a bus when you're leaving town).

Share taxis are the fastest way to Phnom Penh (US$5) and Siem Reap (US$5). Heading north to Preah Vihear City, share taxis (US$5) depart in the morning only. Most taxi services depart from the **taxi park**, one block east of the **Tela Station** on NH6; Phnom Penh taxis depart from the Tela Station.

**Im Sokhom Travel Agency** (p266) rents bicycles (US$1 a day) and motorbikes (US$5 a day).

# Around Kompong Thom

## Sambor Prei Kuk                សំបូរ៍ព្រៃគុក

Cambodia's most impressive group of pre-Angkorian monuments, **Sambor Prei Kuk** (www.samborpreikuk.com; admission US$3) encompasses more than 100 mainly brick temples huddled through the forest, among them some of the oldest structures in the country. Originally called Isanapura, it served as the capital of Upper Chenla during the reign of the early 7th-century King Isanavarman and continued to serve as an important learning centre during the Angkorian era.

The main temple area consists of three complexes, each enclosed by the remains of two concentric walls. Their basic layout – a central tower surrounded by shrines, ponds and gates – may have served as an inspiration for the architects of Angkor five centuries later. Many of the original statues are now in the National Museum (p42) in Phnom Penh.

In the early 1970s, Sambor Prei Kuk was bombed by US aircraft in support of the Lon Nol government's doomed fight against the Khmer Rouge. Some of the craters, ominously close to the temples, can still be seen. The area's last land mines were cleared in 2008.

Sambor Prei Kuk today has a serene and soothing atmosphere, with the sandy trails between temples looping through shady forest, making for a pleasant stroll. It's well worth hiring a guide from the local community to show you around (half/full day US$6/10). Guides hang out at the parking area, next to the main ruins complex.

By the ticket office near the bridge, about 500m before the parking area, is a giant handicrafts market with *kramas*, baskets and other products made by local villagers.

## ◎ Sights

**Prasat Sambor**　　　　　TEMPLE
(ប្រាសាទសំបូរ) The principal temple group, Prasat Sambor (7th and 10th centuries) is dedicated to Gambhireshvara, one of Shiva's many incarnations (the other groups are dedicated to Shiva himself). Several of Prasat Sambor's towers retain brick carvings in fairly good condition, and there is a series of large *yoni* (female fertility symbols) around the central tower.

**Prasat Yeai Poeun**　　　　　TEMPLE
(ប្រាសាទយាយព័ន្ធ, Prasat Yeay Peau) Prasat Yeai Poeun is arguably the most atmospher-ic ensemble, as it feels lost in the forest. The eastern gateway is being both held up and torn asunder by an ancient tree, the bricks interwoven with the tree's extensive, probing roots. A truly massive tree shades the western gate.

**Prasat Tao**　　　　　TEMPLE
(ប្រាសាទតោ, Lion Temple) The largest of the Sambor Prei Kuk complexes, Prasat Tao boasts excellent examples of Chenla carving in the form of two large, elaborately coiffed stone lions. It also has a fine, rectangular pond, Srah Neang Pov.

## 🛏 Sleeping & Eating

You'll find plenty of restaurants (mains US$2 to US$4) serving local fare around the new handicrafts market near the temple entrance.

**Isanborei**　　　　HOMESTAY $
(☑ 017 936112; www.samborpreikuk.com; dm/d US$4/6) 🍃 This organisation works hard to encourage visitors to Sambor Prei Kuk to stay another day. Besides running a community-based homestay program, Isanborei offers cooking courses, rents bicycles (US$2 per day) and organises ox-cart rides. It also operates a stable of *remorks* to whisk you safely to/from Kompong Thom (US$15 one way).

## ℹ Getting There & Away

To get here from Kompong Thom, follow NH6 north for 5km before continuing straight on NH62 towards Preah Vihear (the paved road to Siem Reap veers left). After 11km turn right at the laterite sign and continue for 14km on a brand-new sealed road to the temple entrance.

From Kompong Thom, a return trip *moto* ride out here (under an hour) should cost US$10, and a *remork* about US$13.

---

## Phnom Santuk　　　　ភ្នំសន្ទុក

Its forest surrounded summit adorned with a gleeful medley of Buddha images and pagodas, Phnom Santuk (admission US$2) is the most important holy mountain (207m) in this region and a hugely popular site of Buddhist pilgrimage.

Reached by slogging your way up 809 stairs, with the upper staircase home to troops of lounging monkeys – or you can wimp out and take the paved 2.5km road – Santuk's extraordinary ensemble of colourful wats and stupas are a kaleidoscope mish-mash of old and new Buddhist statuary and monuments.

### OFF THE BEATEN TRACK

## IN SEARCH OF THE BENGAL FLORICAN

The northeastern shores of the Tonlé Sap are home to scores of bird species, including the critically endangered Bengal florican. Vaguely resembling a pheasant, the Bengal florican is one of the 'big six' critically endangered birds (along with two Ibis species and three vulture species) that twitchers flock to Cambodia to see.

Straddling the borders of Siem Reap and Kompong Thom provinces, the Stung Chikreng Bengal Florican Conservation Area (BFCA) is the best place in the world to spot this rare bird. The Siem Reap–based Sam Veasna Center (p263) runs birding trips to the BFCA out of Siem Reap.

Near the main white-walled pagoda is pyramid-shaped Prasat Tuch, which features an intricately carved sandstone exterior. Just beneath the southern side of the summit there are a number of reclining Buddhas; several are modern incarnations cast in cement, while others were carved into the living rock in centuries past.

Phnom Santuk has an active wat and the local monks are always interested in receiving foreign tourists. Boulders located just below the summit afford panoramic views south towards Tonlé Sap.

For travellers spending the night in Kompong Thom, Phnom Santuk is a good place from which to catch a magnificent sunset over the rice fields, although this means descending in the dark (bring a torch/flashlight).

## 🛈 Getting There & Away

The turnoff to Phnom Santuk is about 15km south of Kompong Thom. The entrance is well marked on the east side of the NH6 at about the 149km marker. From the highway it's about 2km to the base of the temple stairs. From Kompong Thom, a return trip by *moto* costs about US$8, and a *remork* about US$10.

## Kakaoh                    កកោះ

The village of Kakaoh straddles the NH6 about 13km south of Kompong Thom and 2km north of the Phnom Santuk entrance. It is famous for its stonemasons, who fashion giant Buddha statues, decorative lions and other traditional Khmer figures with hand tools and a practised eye. It's fascinating to watch the figures, which range in height from 15cm to over 5m, slowly emerge from slabs of stone. Statues range wildly in price – from US$20 for a statuette to US$3500 (not including excess baggage charges) for a 2.5m-high Buddha carved from a single

block of the highest-quality stone. They are often donated to wats by wealthy Khmers.

## Santuk Silk Farm          កសិដ្ឋានស្ូត្រ សន្ទក

The **Santuk Silk Farm** (☑ 012 906604; www. santuksilks.com; ⊙ 7am-11am & 1-5pm Mon-Fri, 7am-11am Sat) FREE is one of the few places in Cambodia where you can see the entire process of silk production, starting with the seven-week life-cycle of the silkworm. The farm employs 18 locals, mostly women, as artisan weavers; you can watch them weave scarves (US$20 to US$45) and other items. The entrance is 200m north of the Phnom Santuk entrance, on the opposite (west) side of NH6.

Silkworms are delicate creatures that feed only on mulberry leaves and have to be protected from predators such as geckos, ants and mosquitoes. Although most of the raw silk used here comes from China and Vietnam, the local worms produce 'Khmer golden silk', so-called because of its lush golden hue.

The farm is run by Budd Gibbons, an American Vietnam War veteran who's lived in Cambodia since 1996, and his Cambodian wife. If possible, call ahead before your visit so they can put the scarves out. Groups of five or more can pre-order an excellent home-cooked meal.

## Prasat Kuha Nokor ប្រាសាទគុហានគរ

This 11th-century Buddhist temple, constructed during the reign of Suryavarman I, is in extremely good condition thanks to a lengthy renovation before the civil war. It is on the grounds of a modern wat and is an easy-enough stop for those with their own transport. The temple is signposted from NH6 about 70km southeast of Kompong Thom and 22km north of Skuon; it's 2km from the main road. From NH6, you can get a *moto* to the temple.

# Eastern Cambodia

POP 6.25 MILLION / AREA 68,472 SQ KM

## Best Wildlife Experiences

➡ Gibbons (p286)

➡ Doucs (p301)

➡ Dolphin-spotting around Kratie (p279)

➡ Birdwatching in Seima Protected Forest (p301)

➡ Elephant Valley Project (p298)

## Best Places to Stay

➡ Tree Top Ecolodge (p289)

➡ Terres Rouges Lodge (p289)

➡ Koh Trong Community Homestay I (p281)

➡ Mayura Hill Hotel & Resort (p299)

➡ Nature Lodge (p297)

## Why Go?

Home to diverse landscapes and peoples, the 'Wild East' shatters the illusion that Cambodia is all paddy fields and sugar palms. There are plenty of those in the lowland provinces, but in the northeast they yield to the mountains of Mondulkiri and Ratanakiri Provinces, where ecotourism is playing a major role in the effort to save dwindling forests from the twin ravages of illegal logging and land concessions.

Rare forest elephants and vocal primates are found in the northeast, and endangered freshwater Irrawaddy dolphins can be seen year-round near Kratie and Stung Treng. Thundering waterfalls, crater lakes and meandering rivers characterise the landscape, and trekking, biking, kayaking, ziplining and elephant experiences are all taking off. The rolling hills and lush forests also provide a home to many ethnic minority groups, known collectively as Khmer Leu (Upper Khmer) or *chunchiet* (ethnic minorities).

## When to Go
### Kratie

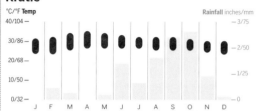

| | |
|---|---|
| °C/°F **Temp** | Rainfall inches/mm |

**Sep & Oct** Mondulkiri is particularly beautiful as blooming wildflowers colour the landscape.

**Mar & Apr** Low water levels make for great dolphin-watching and kayaking.

**May & Jun** The Ratanakiri and Mondulkiri highlands offer escape from the heat of the lowlands.

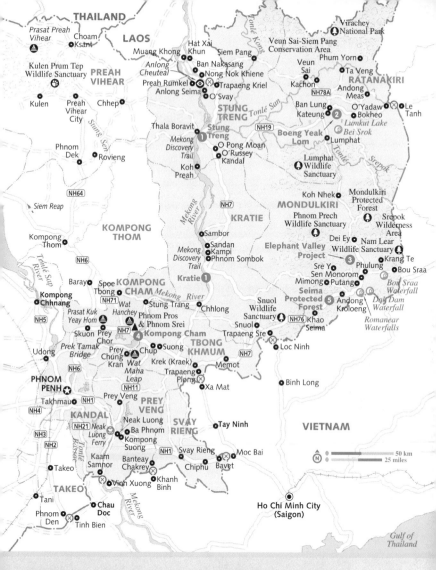

# Eastern Cambodia Highlights

① Kayaking with rare freshwater Mekong Irrawaddy dolphins near **Kratie** (p279) or **Stung Treng** (p284).

② Diving into the crystal-clear waters of the crater lake of **Boeng Yeak Lom** (p286) in Ratanakiri.

③ Walking with elephants in their element at the **Elephant Valley Project** (p298).

④ Soaking up the charms of relaxing **Kompong Cham** (p272), gateway to historic temples, lush countryside and friendly locals.

⑤ Spotting black-shanked doucs and gibbons in Mondulkiri's **Seima Protected Forest** (p301).

# KOMPONG CHAM PROVINCE

Kompong Cham Province (ខេត្តកំពង់ចាម) draws a steady trickle of visitors thanks to its role as a gateway to the northeast. Attractions include several pre-Angkorian and Angkorian temples, as well as some atmospheric riverbank rides for cyclists and motorbikers. The provincial capital offers an accessible slice of the real Cambodia: a land of picturesque villages, pretty wats and fishing communities.

Kompong Cham used to be the most heavily populated province in Cambodia, but was divided in two in a spat of post-election gerrymandering that saw the birth of Tbong Khmum Province.

---

## Kompong Cham　　កំពង់ចាម

✔ 042 / POP 73,000

Kompong Cham is a peaceful provincial capital spread along the banks of the Mekong. It was an important trading post during the French period, the legacy of which is evident as you wander through the streets of crumbling yet classic buildings.

Long considered Cambodia's third city after Phnom Penh and Battambang, Kompong Cham has lately been somewhat left in the dust by the fast-growing tourist towns of Siem Reap and Sihanoukville. However, Kompong Cham remains a travel hub and acts as the stepping stone to eastern Cambodia. The big bridge south of the centre, Spean Kizuna, was the first to span the Mekong's width in Cambodia.

### ◉ Sights & Activities

There's still a fair-sized population of Cham Muslims in the area (hence the name 'Kompong Cham'). One Cham village is on the east bank of the Mekong north of the French lighthouse; its big, silver-domed mosque is clearly visible from the right bank. Another one is south of the bridge just beyond Wat Day Doh, which is worth a wander en route.

Aerobics takes place on the riverfront near the bridge at dusk if you want to get down with the locals.

**Wat Nokor Bachey**　　　BUDDHIST TEMPLE

(វត្តនគរបាជ័យ; admission US$2) The original fusion temple, Wat Nokor is a modern Theravada Buddhist pagoda squeezed into the walls of an 12th-century Mahayana Buddhist shrine of sandstone and laterite. It's a kitschy kind of place; many of the older building's archways have been incorporated into the new building as shrines for worship. On weekdays there are only a few monks in

## Kompong Cham

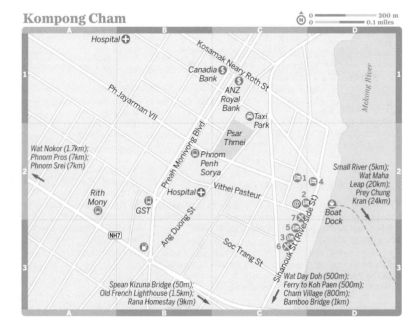

### KRAMA CHAMELEON

The colourful chequered scarf known as the *krama* is almost universally worn by rural Khmers and is still quite popular in the cities. The scarves are made from cotton or silk, and the most famous silk *kramas* come from Kompong Cham and Takeo provinces.

*Kramas* have a multitude of uses. They are primarily used to protect Cambodians from the sun, the dust and the wind, and it is for this reason many tourists end up investing in one during a visit. However, they are also slung around the waist as mini-sarongs, used as towels for drying the body, knotted at the neck as decorations, tied across the shoulders as baby carriers, placed upon chairs or beds as pillow covers, used to tow broken-down motorbikes and stuffed inside motorbike tyres in the advent of remote punctures – the list goes on.

the complex and it's peaceful to wander among the alcoves and their hidden shrines.

The entry price includes admission to Phnom Pros and Phnom Srei, both just outside town. To get here, head towards Phnom Penh and take the left fork at the large roundabout, 2.5km west of the bridge. The temple is down a pretty dirt road.

#### Koh Paen                                          ISLAND

(កោះប៉ែន) For a relaxing bicycle ride, it's hard to beat Koh Paen, a rural island in the Mekong River, connected to the southern reaches of Kompong Cham town by an elaborate **bamboo bridge** (toll 500-1000r) in the dry season or a local **ferry** (with/without bicycle 1500/1000r) in the wet season. The bamboo bridge is an attraction in itself, built entirely by hand each year and looking from afar like it is made of matchsticks. The island offers a slice of rural local life, with fruit and vegetable farms and traditional wooden houses. During the dry season, several sandbars appear around the island. Bicycles can be hired from some local guesthouses.

#### Old French Lighthouse              HISTORIC BUILDING

(ប៉មបាវាំងចាស់) Looming over the Mekong River opposite town is an old French lighthouse. For years it was an abandoned shell, but it's been renovated – and features an

incredibly steep and precarious staircase (more like a series of ladders). Don't attempt the climb if you're scared of heights. There are great views across the Mekong from the summit, especially at sunset.

### 🛏 Sleeping

Most visitors prefer to stay on the riverfront for a view over the Mekong, but keep in mind that there is an early-morning soundtrack, including boat horns and the muezzin's call from the Cham mosque across the river.

#### ★ Moon River Guesthouse         GUESTHOUSE $

(☎016 788973; moonrivermekong@gmail.com; Sihanouk St; r with fan US$7-11, with air-con US$13-19; ❄ 🗺) One of the newer riverfront guesthouses, Moon River is a great all-rounder with smart, spacious rooms, including some triples. Downstairs is a popular restaurant-bar that serves hearty breakfasts and draws a crowd by night.

#### Daly Hotel                                      HOTEL $

(☎042-666 6631; www.dalyhotel.net; d/tw US$18/20, VIP US$40; ❄ 🗺) A swish hotel one block from the river, the Daly is the best of the many Khmer-style high-rise hotels in town. Rooms are large and bright with wall-mounted flatscreen TVs, spick-and-span bathrooms and luscious linen.

#### Mekong Sunrise                          GUESTHOUSE $

(☎011 449720; bong_thol@yahoo.com; Sihanouk St; dm US$3, r with fan US$5-7, with air-con US$12; ❄ 🗺) A backpacker crash pad over a popular riverfront bar-restaurant, Mekong Sunrise has spacious upper-floor rooms with access to a sprawling rooftop. Furnishings are sparse, but it's cheap enough and there's a pool table.

#### Monorom 2 VIP Hotel                      HOTEL $

(☎092 777102; www.monoromviphotel.com; Sihanouk St; r US$15-50; ❄ @ 🗺) The smartest option on the riverfront; rooms include heavy wood furnishings and inviting bathtubs. The lavish suites have private balconies grandstanding the Mekong and large bathrooms loaded with toiletries. The cheapest rooms are, however, windowless.

**OBT Homestay**  HOMESTAY **$**
(☏017 319194; p_sophal@yahoo.com; volunteer/tourist incl 2 meals US$5/10) The Organization for Basic Training accepts volunteers to teach English to local kids, but ordinary travellers looking to spend a few days going local in a Khmer village are also welcome. Tours by ox-cart, horse or boat along the Mekong are available. It's in Chiro village, on the east bank of the Mekong about 5km north of the French lighthouse.

**Mekong Hotel**  HOTEL **$**
(☏042-941536; Sihanouk St; r with fan/air-con US$8/16, VIP US$27; ❄☎) This old-timer is still popular thanks to a prime riverfront location and big, bright, relatively well-maintained rooms. The hangar-like hallways are wide enough for an ultimate frisbee tournament.

**Rana Homestay**  HOMESTAY **$$**
(☏012 686240; http://rana-ruralhomestay-cambodia.webs.com; per person US$25) Located in the countryside beyond Kompong Cham, this homestay offers an insight into electricity-free life in rural Cambodia. The price includes all meals and tours of the local area. There's a two-night minimum stay, a two-person minimum and advance booking is required.

## ✖ Eating

**★Smile Restaurant**  CAMBODIAN **$**
(www.bdsa-cambodia.org; Sihanouk St; mains US$3-5; ⊙6.30am-9pm; ☎) 🍴 Run by the Buddhism and Society Development Association, this handsome nonprofit restaurant is a huge hit with the NGO crowd for its big breakfasts and authentic Khmer cuisine, such as *char k'dau* (stir-fry with lemongrass, hot basil and peanuts) and black-pepper squid. Western dishes are on the menu as well, and it sells BSDA-made *kramas* and trinkets.

**Lazy Mekong Daze**  INTERNATIONAL **$**
(Sihanouk St; mains US$3-5.50; ⊙7.30am-last customer; ☎) One of the go-to places to gather after-dark thanks to a mellow atmosphere, a pool table and a big screen for sports and movies. The menu includes a range of Khmer, Thai and Western food, plus the best wood-fired pizzas in town, chilli con carne and tempting ice creams.

**Destiny Coffee House**  CAFE **$**
(12 Vithei Pasteur St; mains US$3-5; ⊙7am-5.30pm Mon-Sat; ☎🍴) This stylish cafe has relaxing sofas and a contemporary look. The international menu includes delicious hummus with dips, lip-smacking homemade cakes, breakfast burritos, salads and wraps.

**Mekong Crossing**  INTERNATIONAL **$**
(Sihanouk St; mains US$2-5; ⊙6am-10pm; ☎) Occupying a prime corner on the riverfront, this old favourite has recently had a successful facelift and serves an enticing mix of Khmer curries and Western favourites, such as big burgers and tasty sandwiches. Doubles as a popular bar by night.

## ℹ Information

**ANZ Royal Bank** (Preah Monivong Blvd; ⊙8.30am-4pm Mon-Fri, ATM 24hr) ATM charges US$5 for withdrawals.

**Canadia Bank** (Preah Monivong Blvd; ⊙8am-3.30pm Mon-Fri, 8-11.30am Sat, ATM 24hr) Free ATM withdrawals for some cards, plus free cash advances on credit cards.

**Lazy Mekong Daze** (above) Hands out a decent map that highlights the major sights in and around Kompong Cham.

### BUSES FROM KOMPONG CHAM

| DESTINATION | PRICE | DURATION (HR) | FREQUENCY |
| --- | --- | --- | --- |
| Ban Lung | 32,000r | 7 | 10am |
| Kratie via Chhlong | 20,000r | 2 | 9.30am |
| Kratie via Snuol | 21,000r | 4 | 10.30am, 2pm |
| Pakse, Laos | US$22 | 12 | 10am |
| Phnom Penh | 20,000r | 3 | hourly till 3.45pm |
| Sen Monorom | 28,000r | 5 | 11.45am |
| Siem Reap | 24,000r | 5 | 7.30am, 9.30am, noon |
| Stung Treng via Chhlong | 30,000r | 5 | 10.30am |

## GETTING TO VIETNAM: KOMPONG CHAM TO TAY NINH

**Getting to the border** The Trapeang Phlong–Xa Mat **border crossing** (⊙7am-5pm) has become increasingly popular for those travelling between northeast Cambodia and Ho Chi Minh City. From Kompong Cham take anything heading east on NH7 towards Snuol, and get off at the roundabout in Krek (Kraek), on NH7, 55km east-southeast of Kompong Cham. From there, it's 13km south by *moto* (US$3) along NH72 to snoozy Trapeang Phlong, marked by a candy-striped road barrier and a few tin shacks.

**At the border** This border is a breeze: just have your Vietnamese visa ready.

**Moving on** On the Vietnamese side, motorbikes and taxis go to Tay Ninh, 45km to the south – but be prepared to negotiate a bit harder than in Cambodia.

**Mekong Internet** (Vithei Pasteur; per hr 1500r; ⊙6.30am-10pm) Among a cluster of internet cafes on Vithei Pasteur St.

### ⓘ Getting There & Away

Phnom Penh is 120km southwest. If you are heading north to Kratie or beyond, arrange transport via the sealed road to Chhlong rather than taking a huge detour east to Snuol on NH7.

**Phnom Penh Sorya** (www.phnompenhsorya. com; Preah Monivong Blvd) is the most reliable bus company operating out of Kompong Cham. **GST** (☑012 734052; Preah Monivong Blvd) has morning buses to Battambang, Kratie and Siem Reap. **Rith Mony** (NH7) adds buses to Ban Lung, Battambang and Siem Reap.

Share taxis (15,000r) and overcrowded local minibuses (10,000r) also do the dash to Phnom Penh from the **taxi park** near the New Market (Psar Thmei). The trip takes two hours or more depending on traffic in the capital. Morning share taxis and minibuses to Kratie (US$5, two hours) depart when full from the **Caltex station** at the main roundabout, and there are morning minibuses from the taxi park also.

There are no longer any passenger boats to other towns running on the Mekong from here.

### ⓘ Getting Around

Kompong Cham has a surplus of *moto* and *remork-moto (tuk tuk)* drivers who speak great English and can guide you around the sites. If you sip a drink overlooking the Mekong, one of them will find you before too long. **Mr Vannat** (☑012 995890; vannat_kompongcham@yahoo. com) is the veteran of the group and has a 4WD for hire (he also speaks French), but all of these guys are pretty good. Figure on US$10 to US$15 per day for a *moto* and US$15 to US$20 for a *remork* (slightly more if including Wat Maha Leap in your plans). Return-trip *remork* journeys to Wat Hanchey or Phnom Pros and Phnom Srei are a negotiable US$10.

Most guesthouses and restaurants on the riverfront rent motorbikes (US$3 to US$5 per day) and bicycles (US$1 per day), including Lazy Mekong Daze (opposite).

## Around Kompong Cham

### Phnom Pros & Phnom Srei ភ្នំប្រុសភ្នំស្រី

'Man Hill' and 'Woman Hill' are the subjects of local legends with many variations, one of which describes a child taken away at infancy only to return a powerful man who falls in love with his own mother. Disbelieving her protestations, he demands her hand in marriage. Desperate to avoid this disaster, the mother cunningly devises a deal: a competition between her team of women and his team of men to build the highest hill by dawn. If the women win, she won't have to marry him. As they toil into the night, the women build a huge fire, with flames reaching high into the sky. The men, mistaking this for sunrise, lay down their tools – and the impending marriage is foiled. Locals love to relay this tale, each adding their own details as the story unfolds. Admission to the hills is US$2 and includes entry to Wat Nokor Bachey (p272).

**Phnom Srei** has fine views of the countryside during the wet season and a very strokeable statue of Nandin (a sacred bull that was Shiva's mount). **Phnom Pros** is a good place for a cold drink among the inquisitive monkeys that populate the shady trees. The area between the two hills was once a killing field; a small, gilded brick stupa on the right as you walk from Man Hill to Woman Hill houses a pile of skulls.

The hills are about 7km out of town on the road to Phnom Penh. Opposite the entrance to Phnom Pros lies **Cheung Kok** village, home to a local ecotourism initiative, run by the NGO Amica (www.amica-cambodge.org), aimed at introducing visitors to rural life in Kompong Cham.

## SHOULD YOU RIDE AN ELEPHANT?

According to legend, more than one million elephants were used in the construction of Angkor Wat; in reality the numbers were closer to 6000, but elephants have long played an important role in Cambodian history. They were the tractors and tanks that gave the god-kings of Angkor the means to project their power across the region. Originally these elephants were trapped in the wild by the kingdom's indigenous communities.

This illustrious history was cut short by conflict, as domestic elephants were marked as a 'legitimate war target' – they were either killed or their owners fled to neighbouring countries. Contemporary Cambodia has very few captive elephants left – just 79 at the last count – and their numbers are dwindling due to overwork and old age, with most employed in the tourism industry. The biggest hope for the survival of their species lies with Cambodia's healthy wild population, which stands at more than 500 and is protected by Cambodia's remaining forests, as captive elephants are no longer being bred.

The modern-day relationship between elephants and tourism is a complex one. There are now more elephants working to carry tourists around than to haul timber or rice, so their care is dependent on the dollars tourism generates, and once captured they cannot return to the wild. However, the elephant is a highly intelligent animal and animal-welfare groups advocate that riding elephants is actually detrimental to their health. If you do decide to ride an elephant, take a closer look at the animal and its work environment:

➡ Are the elephant's ribs visible? If so, this elephant is too thin to work and should be fed and rested.

➡ Are there open wounds or abscesses on the elephant? Injured elephants should not be working.

➡ The elephant should have a shaded area to rest, with clean water and food available.

➡ There should be enough slack in the chain so that it can move around – they need enough space so they don't have to defecate near where they eat.

➡ The seat placed on the elephant should be made of light bamboo (not heavy wood), and there should be thick layers of padding between the seat and the skin.

➡ There should be rubber hoses to line the binding ropes, or they will abrade the skin.

➡ Elephants should work for only four hours a day, carrying no more than two adults at once.

➡ The elephant carer should not have to use the bullhook or whip the elephant with every command.

If there is a clear problem with the elephant don't be afraid to refuse to ride it. Politely explain your concerns.

For those who want to learn more about these noble creatures, Mondulkiri offers the animal-friendly option of walking with elephants (p298) instead of riding atop them – an excellent insight into their natural behaviour. For more on issues with elephant welfare and tourism, check out www.earasia.org.

*Compiled with assistance from Jack Highwood, Founder, Elephant Valley Project*

---

Villagers teach visitors about harvesting rice, sugar palm and other crops. There is also a small shop in the village selling local handicraft products.

## Wat Maha Leap      វត្តមហាលាភ

Sacred Wat Maha Leap is one of the last remaining wooden pagodas left in the country. More than a century old, it was only spared devastation by the Khmer Rouge because they converted it into a hospital. Many of the Khmers who were put to work in the surrounding fields perished here; 500 bodies were thrown into graves on site, which are now camouflaged by a tranquil garden.

The pagoda itself is beautiful. The wide black columns supporting the structure are complete tree trunks, resplendent in gilded patterns. The Khmer Rouge painted over the designs to match their austere philosophies, but monks later stripped it back to its original glory. Sadly, the roof collapsed in 2012 and repairs were still under way at the time of writing.

The journey to Wat Maha Leap is best done by boat from Kompong Cham. Follow the Mekong downstream for a short distance before peeling off on a sublime tributary known as Small River, which affords awesome glimpses of rural Cambodian life. A guided trip on a 40HP outboard (US$50 return trip, including stops in nearby weaving villages) gets there in less than an hour each way. Outboards can be found at the boat dock.

Small River is navigable only from July to December; at other times, travel overland. It's pretty difficult to find on your own without some knowledge of Khmer, as there are lots of small turns along the way, so hire a *moto* (US$10 per return trip including a stop in Prey Chung Kran, one hour each way). It's 20km by river and almost twice that by road.

## Prey Chung Kran          ប្រែចម្រាន

Kompong Cham is famous for high-quality silk. The tiny village of Prey Chung Kran is set on the banks of the river and nearly every household has a weaving loom. Under the cool shade provided by their stilted homes, weavers work deftly to produce *kramas* that are fashionable and traditional. The most interesting thing to watch is the dyeing process, as the typical diamond-and-dot tessellations are formed at this stage. Prey Chung Kran is about 4km from Wat Maha Leap. There are additional weavers all along the road between Wat Maha Leap and Prey Chung Kran.

## Wat Hanchey          វត្តហ្មានជ័យ

Wat Hanchey is a hilltop pagoda that was an important centre of worship during the Chenla period when, as today, it offered some of the best Mekong views in Cambodia. During the time of the Chenla empire, this may have been an important transit stop on journeys between the ancient cities of Thala Boravit (near Stung Treng to the north) and Angkor Borei (near Takeo to the south).

Sitting in front of a large, contemporary wat is a remarkable brick sanctuary dating from the 8th century. The well-preserved inscriptions on the doorway are in ancient Sanskrit. A hole in the roof lets in a lone shaft of light. The foundations of several other 8th-century structures, some of them destroyed by American bombs, are scattered around the compound, along with a clutch of bizarre fruit and animal statues.

The trip out here takes about 30 minutes from Kompong Cham on a motorbike. Cy-

cling here through the pretty riverbank villages is a good way to pass half a day.

## Rubber Plantations          ចំការកៅស៊ូ

Kompong Cham was the heartland of the Cambodian rubber industry; rubber plantations still stretch across the province. Many of them are back in business and some of the largest plantations can be visited. Using an extended scraping instrument, workers graze the trunks until the sap appears, which they let drip into the open coconut shells on the ground. At Chup Rubber Plantation, about 15km east of Kompong Cham, you can observe harvesting in action and wander at will around the **factory** (រោងចក្រ; admission US$1) where workers process the rubber.

# KRATIE PROVINCE

Pretty Kratie Province (ខេត្តក្រចេះ) spans the Mekong, from which much of Kratie's population makes its living. Beyond the river, it's a remote and wild land that sees few outsiders. Many visitors are drawn to the rare freshwater Irrawaddy dolphins found in Kampi, about 15km north of the provincial capital. The town of Kratie is a little charmer and makes a good base from which to explore the surrounding countryside.

## Kratie          ក្រចេះ

☑ 072 / POP 44,000

A supremely mellow riverside town, Kratie (pronounced kra-*cheh*) has an expansive riverfront and some of the best Mekong sunsets in Cambodia. It is the most popular place in the country to see Irrawaddy dolphins (p279), which live in the Mekong River in ever-diminishing numbers. There is a rich legacy of French-era architecture, as it was spared the wartime bombing that destroyed so many other provincial centres.

As a travel hub Kratie is the natural place to break the journey when travelling overland between Phnom Penh and Champasak in southern Laos.

### ⊙ Sights & Activities

The main draw here is the chance to spot the elusive Irrawaddy dolphin. Riding a bike around Koh Trong (p281) or along the banks of the Mekong River is always rewarding.

Kratie

## Kratie

**⊕ Activities, Courses & Tours**
1 Sorya Kayaking Adventures ............... A1

**⊙ Sleeping**
2 Le Bungalow ......................................... A1
3 Silver Dolphin Guesthouse ................B4
4 U-Hong II Guesthouse .........................A3

**⊗ Eating**
5 Jasmine Boat Restaurant ...................A3
6 Le Bungalow ........................................A2
7 Red Sun Falling ...................................A2
8 Tokae Restaurant ................................B3

### 👉 Tours

**CRDTours** TOUR
(☑ 099 834353; www.crdtours.org; St 3; ⊗ 8am-noon & 2-5.30pm) ✒ Run by the Cambodian Rural Development Team, this company focuses on sustainable tours along the Mekong Discovery Trail (p283). Homestays, volunteer opportunities and various excursions are available on the Mekong island of **Koh Pdao**, 20km north of Kampi. The typical price is US$38 to US$60 per day, including all meals and tours. Tours and homestays on **Koh Preah** (near Stung Treng) and **Koh Trong** are also possible. Mountain bike tours from Kratie to Koh Pdao are another option.

CRDT can also organise boat trips from Stung Treng to Kratie, sleeping in remote river villages along the way (US$130 to US$300 per person, depending on numbers).

**Cambodian Pride Tours** TOUR
(☑ 088 836 4758; www.cambodianpridetours.com) Local tours operated by experienced, Kratie-born guide Sithy, who is keen to promote real-life experiences in his community, such as visiting family members and learning about farming methods.

### 🛏 Sleeping

For something even more relaxed than Kratie, consider staying directly on the island of Koh Trong (p281), where homestays and two midrange guesthouses await.

**Silver Dolphin Guesthouse** HOSTEL $
(☑ 012 999810; silver.dolphinbooking@yahoo.com; 48 Rue Preah Suramarit; dm US$4, r US$4-14; ✳@🛜) This backpacker hostel is a great deal. The dorm is spacious, with a soaring ceiling, and even the cheapest doubles have a TV, bathroom and some furniture. There is a popular upstairs bar-restaurant with a

**Wat Roka Kandal** BUDDHIST TEMPLE
(វត្តរកាកណ្ដាល; admission 2000r) About 2km south of Kratie on the road to Chhlong is this beautiful little temple dating from the 19th century, one of the oldest in the region. To see the beautifully restored interior, ask around for someone with the key. Even if you can't get in, the shaded grounds, adjacent to some lovely traditional wooden houses, are worth a wander.

**Sorya Kayaking Adventures** KAYAKING
(☑ 090 241148; www.soryakayaking.com; Rue Preah Suramarit) Sorya has a fleet of eight kayaks and runs half-day and multiday trips (with homestay accommodation) on the Mekong north of Kratie, or on the Te River to the south. This is a great way to get close to the dolphins. Other highlights include a small flooded forest north of Kampi, Vietnamese floating villages, and a sunset trip around Koh Trong. There's a small cafe on site and it sells handicrafts woven by disadvantaged widows.

riverfront balcony. Owner Pech speaks great English and French.

**Le Tonlé Tourism Training Center** GUESTHOUSE $
(☎ 072-210505; www.letonle.org; St 3; r US$10-20; ❄ 🛜) 🖉 Following on from the success of its long-running Le Tonlé project (p282) in Stung Treng, CRDT has opened a slightly smarter operation in Kratie. The expanded property has nine attractively rustic rooms in a beautiful wooden house and delicious food prepared by at-risk program trainees. Some rooms have bathrooms, some rooms share.

**U-Hong II Guesthouse** GUESTHOUSE $
(☎ 085 885168; 119 St 10; r US$4-13; ❄ @ 🛜) A lively little shoes-off guesthouse between the market and the riverfront. There are eight rooms here, plus 11 more in a nearby annex, some with air-con. There is a buzzing bar-restaurant that boasts the most extensive cocktail list in town.

**Balcony Guesthouse** GUESTHOUSE $
(☎ 016 604036; www.balconyguesthouse.net; Rue Preah Suramarit; r US$5-20; ❄ @ 🛜) This long-running backpacker place was moving north up the riverfront at the time of writing. Expect more of the same formula, with tasteful rooms and a popular little bar by night.

**Mekong Dolphin Hotel** HOTEL $$
(☎ 072-666 6666; www.mekongdolphinhotel.com; Rue Preah Sumamarit; r US$20-50; ❄ 🛜) Looming large on the riverfront, this hotel is the smartest in town, offering slick river-view rooms for US$35 and suites for your inner VIP at US$50. Room amenities include a safe and hairdryer; the hotel even has a small gym and sauna (if Kratie isn't hot enough for you already).

**River Dophin Hotel** HOTEL $$
(☎ 072-210570; www.riverdolphinhotel.com; r US$35-55; ❄ @ 🛜 🏊) Stranded somewhat inland from the riverfront action, it is none-theless a deservedly popular place thanks to a high level of comfort and service (for Kratie) and one of the town's only swimming pools. Add US$5 for breakfast. Non-guests can use the pool for US$3 per day.

**Le Bungalow** BOUTIQUE HOTEL $$
(☎ 012 660902; www.rajabori-kratie.com; Rue Preah Suramarit; r without/with bathroom US$31/65; ❄ @ 🛜) Akin to a boutique homestay, here you'll find three rooms in a traditional wooden house decorated with Sino-Khmer furnishings from the colonial period. Two rooms are spacious and have modern bathrooms, while the third is more suited to children travelling with their parents and has an outside bathroom.

## ✖ Eating

When in Kratie, keep an eye out for two specialities sold on the riverfront and elsewhere: *krolan* (sticky rice, beans and coconut milk steamed inside a bamboo tube) and *nehm* (tangy raw, spiced river fish wrapped in banana leaves). The south end of the *psar* (market) turns into a carnival of barbecue stands

---

### DOLPHIN-WATCHING AROUND KRATIE

The freshwater Irrawaddy dolphin (*trey pisaut* in Khmer) is an endangered species throughout Asia, with shrinking numbers inhabiting stretches of the Mekong in Cambodia and Laos, and isolated pockets in Bangladesh and Myanmar. The dark-blue to grey cetaceans grow to 2.75m long and are recognisable by their bulging foreheads and small dorsal fins. They can live in fresh or salt water, although they are seldom seen in the sea.

Before the civil war, locals say, Cambodia was home to as many as 1000 dolphins. However, during the Pol Pot regime many were hunted for their oils, and their numbers continue to plummet even as drastic protection measures have been put in place, including a ban on fishing and commercial motorised boat traffic on much of the Mekong between Kratie and Stung Treng. The dolphins continue to die at an alarming rate, and experts now estimate that there are fewer than 85 Irrawaddy dolphins left in the Mekong between Kratie and the Lao border.

The best place to see them is at Kampi, about 15km north of Kratie, on the road to Sambor. A *moto/remork* should be around US$7/10 return, depending on how long the driver has to wait. Motorboats shuttle visitors out to the middle of the river to view the dolphins at close quarters. It costs US$9 per person for one to two persons and US$7 per person for groups of three to four. Encourage the boat driver to use the engine as little as possible once near the dolphins, as the noise is sure to disturb them. It is also possible to see them near the Lao border in Stung Treng province (p281).

hawking meat-on-a-stick by night. Noteworthy restaurants can also be found at Balcony Guesthouse and the more upmarket Le Bungalow (Rue Preah Suramarit; mains US$4-16).

**Red Sun Falling** INTERNATIONAL $
(Rue Preah Suramarit; mains US$2-4; ☉7am-9pm; ☎) One of the liveliest spots in town, the long-running Red Sun has a relaxed cafe ambience, a supreme riverfront location, used books for sale and a good selection of Asian and Western meals.

**Tokae Restaurant** CAMBODIAN $
(St 10; mains US$2-4; ☉6am-11pm; ☎) Look out for Cambodia's largest *tokae* (gecko) on the wall and you've found this excellent little eatery. The menu offers a good mix of cheap Cambodian food like curries and *amok* (a baked fish dish), plus equally affordable Western breakfasts and comfort food.

**Jasmine Boat Restaurant** INTERNATIONAL $$
(Rue Preah Sumarmarit; meals US$1.50-22; ☎) Occupying a prime spot above the Mekong River, this is the only place on the river in town. The boat-shaped restaurant has a mixed menu of affordable Khmer specials and pricey international meat dishes, but it's a great spot to drink a coffee or a beer any time of day.

## ⓘ Information

All of the recommended guesthouses are pretty switched on to travellers' needs. U-Hong II and Silver Dolphin guesthouses have public internet access.

---

### GETTING TO VIETNAM: KRATIE TO BINH LONG

**Getting to the border** The Trapeang Sre–Loc Ninh border crossing (☉7am-5pm) is useful for those trying to get straight to Vietnam from Kratie or points north. First get to the bustling junction town of Snuol by bus, share taxi or minibus from Sen Monorom, Kratie or Kompong Cham. In Snuol catch a *moto* (US$5) for the 18km trip southeastward along smooth NH74.

**At the border** As always you'll need a prearranged visa to enter Vietnam, and US$30 for a visa-on-arrival to enter Cambodia.

**Moving on** On the Vietnamese side, the nearest town is Binh Long, 40km to the south. Motorbikes wait at the border.

---

**Canadia Bank** (Rue Preah Suramarit; ☉8.30am-3.30pm Mon-Fri, ATM 24hr) ATM offering cash withdrawals, plus currency exchange.

## ⓘ Getting There & Away

Kratie is 250km northeast of Phnom Penh (via the Chhlong road) and 141km south of Stung Treng.

**Phnom Penh Sorya** (☏081 908005) operates three buses per day to Phnom Penh (US$8, eight hours) along the slow route (via Snuol); Sorya's bus from Laos comes through at roughly 3.30pm and goes to Phnom Penh via the much-shorter Chhlong route (US$8, six hours). Sorya buses to Siem Reap involve a change in Suong.

Going the other way, Sorya's bus from Phnom Penh to Pakse, Laos (US$16, eight hours) via Stung Treng collects passengers in Kratie at about 11.30am. Sorya also has a 1pm bus to Ban Lung (US$8, five hours) and a 3pm bus to Stung Treng (US$5, three hours). **Rith Mony** (☏012 818737) also has a bus to Ban Lung (US$8, 11.30am).

Express vans, which pick you up from your guesthouse, are a faster way to Phnom Penh (US$7, four hours, about six per day), and usually offer transfers onward to Sihanoukville. There's also an express van to Siem Reap (US$13, six hours, 7.30am). Share taxis (US$10) head to Phnom Penh between 6am and 8am, with possible additional departures after lunch.

For Sen Monorom, take a local minibus from the **taxi park** (30,000r, four hours, two or three early-morning departures) or head to Snuol and change. Local minibuses also serve Ban Lung, with most departures between 11am and 2pm.

## ⓘ Getting Around

Most guesthouses can arrange bicycle (from US$1) and motorbike (from US$5) hire. An English-speaking *motodup* will set you back US$10 to US$15 per day, and a *remork* about US$20 to US$25, depending on the destinations.

---

# Around Kratie

## Phnom Sombok វត្តភ្នំហាន់ដំរយ

Phnom Sombok is a small hill with an active wat, located on the road from Kratie to Kampi. The hill offers the best views across the Mekong on this stretch of the river and a visit here can easily be combined with a trip to see the dolphins for an extra couple of dollars.

---

## Sambor សំបូរ

Sambor was the site of a thriving pre-Angkorian city during the time of Sambor

## KOH TRONG, AN ISLAND IN THE MEKONG

Lying across the water from Kratie is the island of Koh Trong (កោះត្រង), a 6km-long sandbar in the middle of the river. Cross here by boat and enjoy a slice of rural island life. Attractions include an old stupa and small floating village, as well as the chance to encounter one of the rare Mekong mud turtles that inhabit the western shore.

There are two homestays on the island. Best is **Koh Trong Community Homestay I** (mattress per person US$4, r US$8), set in an old wooden house, offering two proper bedrooms and fancy-pants bathrooms (that is, thrones not squats). It is located about 2km north of the ferry dock near Rajabori Villas. Ride your bike, take a *moto* (US$1) or ride an ox-cart. **Rajabori Villas** (012 770150; www.rajabori-kratie.com; r incl breakfast US$60-200;) is a boutique lodge with a swimming pool and bungalows that provide the best accommodation in the Kratie region. It's located at the northern tip of the island; a private boat from Kratie costs US$4/5 per day/night. Practically next door is the slightly more rustic **Arun Mekong** (017 663014; www.arunmekong.wordpress.com; r US$22-27, bungalows US$33), with a nice mix of tastefully furnished rooms and bungalows. Electricity runs only from 6pm to 11pm here.

Catch the little **ferry** (with/without bicycle 2000r/1000r) from the port in Kratie. Bicycle rental is available on the island near the ferry landing for US$1, or do the loop around the island on a *moto* (US$2.50) steered by a female *motodup*, a rarity for Cambodia.

Prei Kuk and the Chenla empire. Not a stone remains in the modern town of Sambor, which is locally famous for having the largest wat in Cambodia, complete with 108 columns. Known locally as **Wat Sorsor Moi Roi** (Hundred Columns Temple), it was constructed on the site of a 19th-century wooden temple, a few pillars of which are still located at the back of the compound.

The **Mekong Turtle Conservation Centre** (012 712071; www.mekongturtle.com; adult/child US$4/2; 8.30am-4.30pm) is located within the temple grounds. Established by Conservation International (www.conservation.org), it is home to several species of turtle, including the rare Cantor's giant softshell, which was only rediscovered along this stretch of the Mekong in 2007. One of the largest freshwater turtles, it can grow to nearly 2m in length. Hatchlings are nurtured here for 10 months before being released in the wild. Tourists can participate in the release on select weeks, usually in September and May/June. Check the website for the exact dates.

To get to Sambor, follow the Kampi road north to Sandan, before veering left along a reasonable 10km stretch of road. It's about 35km in total.

## Chhlong

ឈ្លង

Chhlong is a somnolent riverside town 31km south of Kratie. The main attraction is the old governor's residence, a gorgeous, yellow-and-white French colonial mansion near the river.

Once a top-end boutique hotel, it is now shuttered up and falling into disrepair. Architecture buffs might also drop in at the House of a Hundred Pillars (1884), about 500m north of Le Relais. According to the house's owner, the Khmer Rouge removed many of the pillars – so today only 56 remain. A few more decrepit French colonial buildings line the river.

Chhlong is worth a wander if you are driving through with your own transport, but probably not worth a special trip from Kratie. Keen cyclists might like to follow the old river road between Kratie and Chhlong, as it passes through some traditional Cham minority villages along the way.

# STUNG TRENG PROVINCE

Stung Treng Province (ខេត្តស្ទឹងត្រែង) is a transit point between the popular destinations of Ratanakiri Province and Kratie Province. A new bridge over the Mekong in Stung Treng is part of the new highway running west to Preah Vihear City, cutting about four hours off the journey from Champasak (Southern Laos) to Siem Reap, a key route on the Southeast Asia backpacker trail. Unfortunately for Stung Treng, it makes it even easier to pass through on the way to somewhere else.

Loaded with largely untapped tourist potential, Stung Treng could benefit hugely from the increased traffic if people stuck around. The main attractions are up near the

Lao border, where you can kayak out to a pod of Irrawaddy dolphins then continue downstream along a pretty stretch of the Mekong dotted with flooded forest. Further north, thundering rapids cascade over the border from Laos, a spectacular sight that's a continuation of the huge Khone Falls. Further east, hard-core travellers can access Virachey National Park from remote Siem Pang.

# Stung Treng     ស្ទឹងត្រែង

📞 074 / POP 35,000

Located on the Tonlé San near its confluence with the Mekong, Stung Treng is a quiet town with limited appeal, but sees a lot of transit traffic heading north to Laos, south to Kratie, east to Ratanakiri and west to Siem Reap. Some locals call the Tonlé San the 'Tonlé Kong', as it merges with the Tonlé Kong (known as the Sekong in Laos) 10km east of town. Just north of the town centre, a major bridge across the San leads north to Laos.

## ◉ Sights & Activities

Dolphin-watching and kayaking trips near the Lao border can be done as day trips out of Stung Treng.

**Thala Boravit**                              TEMPLE

(ថាឡាបុរវត្ត) This crumbling temple is across the new Mekong bridge from Stung Treng. It is hardly worth the effort for the casual visitor, but temple fiends may feel the urge to tick it off. Thala Boravit was an important Chenla-period trading town on the river route connecting the ancient city of Champasak and the sacred temple of Wat Phu with the ancient cities of Sambor Prei

Kuk (Isanapura) and Angkor Borei. For all its past glories, there is very little to see today.

**Mekong Blue**                                 SILK

(មេគង្គប្លូ; 📞 012 622096; www.mekongblue.com; ⏰ 7.30-11.30am & 2-5pm Mon-Sat) 🚩 Part of the Stung Treng Women's Development Centre, Mekong Blue is a silk-weaving centre on the outskirts of Stung Treng. Mekong Blue specialises in exquisite silk products for sale and export. At this centre it is possible to observe the dyers and weavers, most of whom come from vulnerable or impoverished backgrounds. The centre is located about 4km east of the centre on the riverside road that continues under the bridge. There is a small showroom on site with a selection of silk on sale, plus a cafe. However, it only serves cold drinks unless you book a meal in advance.

## 🛏 Sleeping

**Le Tonlé Tourism
Training Centre**                          GUESTHOUSE $

(📞 074-973 638; www.letonle.org; s US$6-10, d US$8-12; 🛜) Located in a shady spot on the riverfront about 500m west of the port, this small guesthouse doubles as a training centre for underprivileged locals getting started in the tourism industry. The four rooms are simple but tastefully furnished, and share an immaculate bathroom and a comfy balcony, where delicious meals can be ordered in advance.

**Riverside Guesthouse**                   GUESTHOUSE $

(📞 012 257257; kimtysou@gmail.com; r US$5-8; @) Overlooking the riverfront area, the Riverside has long been a popular travellers' hub. Rooms are basic, but then so are the prices. It's a good spot for travel information and there's a popular bar-restaurant downstairs.

**Mekong Bird Lodge**                      BUNGALOW $

(📞 012 796699; www.mekongbirdeco-lodge.com; s/d/tw US$13/15/18) This self-styled ecolodge sits on a bluff overlooking a peaceful Mekong

## Stung Treng

Tonlé San

Rany Neh Internet (350m);
Tourist Information
Centre (2km);
Tonlé San Bridge (2.5km);
Mekong Blue (3.7km)

Le Tonlé Tourism
Training Centre
(500m)

Xplore-
Asia

Psar    Canadia
Bank

Hospital ✚

Phnom Penh
Sorya

Mekong Bridge
(6km)

## Stung Treng

## THE MEKONG DISCOVERY TRAIL

It's well worth spending a couple of days exploring the various bike rides and activities on offer along the **Mekong Discovery Trail** (www.mekongdiscoverytrail.com), an initiative to open up stretches of the Mekong River around Stung Treng and Kratie to community-based tourism. Once managed by the government with foreign development assistance, the project is now being kept alive by private tour companies, such as Xplore-Asia (p283) in Stung Treng and CRDTours (p278) in Kratie.

It deserves support, as it intends to provide fishing communities an alternative income in order to protect the Irrawaddy dolphin and other rare species on this stretch of river.

There's a great booklet with routes and maps outlining excursions around Kratie and Stung Treng, but you'll be hard-pressed to secure your own copy; ask tour operators if you can photograph theirs. The routes can be tackled by bicycle or motorbike. They range in length from a few hours to several days, with optional overnights in village homestays. Routes criss-cross the Mekong frequently by ferry and traverse several Mekong islands, including Koh Trong (p281).

eddy north of town. It has a lush tropical garden, but remains exceedingly rustic. Sturdy wood bungalows are spacious and have balconies with sunset views, but lack furniture (beyond beds). Request a mosquito net. To get here, turn left at the sign 4km north of the Tonlé San bridge and continue 1.5km.

**Golden River Hotel**      HOTEL **$$**
(☑ 074-690 0029; www.goldenriverhotel.com; r US$15-35; ❄ @ ☎) Still the best all-rounder in town, the Golden River has 50 well-appointed rooms complete with hot-water bathrooms, fridges and TVs. Rooms at the front with a view cost a few dollars more.

## ✗ Eating

On the riverside promenade west of the ferry dock, a handful of street-side vendors peddle cold beer and noodle soup until late in the evening.

**Ponika's Palace**      INTERNATIONAL **$**
(mains US$2-5; ❄ 6am-10pm) Need a break from *laab* (a spicy salad with chicken, pork or fish) after Laos? Burgers, pizza and English breakfast grace the menu, along with Indian food and wonderful Khmer curries. Affable owner Ponika speaks English and cold beer is available to slake a thirst.

**Dara Canteen**      INTERNATIONAL **$**
(mains US$2-5; ❄ 7am-9pm) This is a good refuge for French travellers thanks to the French-speaking owner, and sells wholesome baguettes and a good-value US$5 filet mignon.

## ❶ Information

**Canadia Bank** (❄ 8.30am-3.30pm Mon-Fri, ATM 24hr) Has an international ATM.

**Rany Neh Internet** (per hr 4000r; ❄ 7am-8pm) Internet access.

**Riverside Guesthouse** (☑ 012 257257; kim tysou@gmail.com) Specialises in getting people to/from Laos, Siem Reap or just about anywhere else. Also runs boat tours to the Lao border, with a trip to see the resident dolphin pod (US$100/120 for two/four people). English-speaking guides offer motorbike tours around the province.

**Tourist Information Centre** (☑ 074-210001; ❄ 8-11am & 2-5pm) Inconveniently located near the Tonlé San bridge; it's rare to find it open.

**Xplore-Asia** (☑ 011 433836, 074-973456; www. xplore-cambodia.com) Doles out brochures, booklets and advice, and tailors one- to several-day cycling-and-kayak combo tours along the Mekong Discovery Trail (above), including kayaking with the dolphins. Rents out kayaks (US$10 per day), motorbikes (US$10 per day) and sturdy Trek mountain bikes (US$5 per day).

## ❶ Getting There & Away

NH7 north to the Lao border is in reasonable shape these days, but the same cannot be said for the stretch south to Kratie.

Express minibuses with guesthouse pick-ups as early as 4am are the quickest way to Phnom Penh (US$10 to US$13, eight hours). Book through Riverside Guesthouse.

**Phnom Penh Sorya** (☑ 092 181805) has a 6.30am bus to Phnom Penh (US$10, nine hours) via Kratie (US$5, three hours) and Kompong Cham (US$8, six hours). Sorya's bus from Laos to Phnom Penh comes through Stung Treng around 11.30am. Additionally, local minibuses to Kratie depart regularly until 2pm from the market area.

There is a comfortable tourist van to Ban Lung (US$6, two hours, 8am), with additional morning trips in cramped local minibuses from the market (US$5, three hours).

## GETTING TO LAOS: STUNG TRENG TO DON DET

**Getting to the border** The remote Trapeang Kriel–Nong Nok Khiene border crossing (☉6am-6pm), 60km north of Stung Treng, is a popular crossing point on the Indochina overland circuit. For many years, there was a separate river crossing here, but that's no longer open. Phnom Penh Sorya, in partnership with Pakse-based Lao operator Sengchalean, has buses from Phnom Penh straight through to Pakse's 2km Bus Station (US$27, 12 to 14 hours). This bus leaves Phnom Penh at 6.45am, with pick-ups with possible in Kompong Cham (around 9.30am), Kratie (around 11.30am) or Stung Treng (around 3pm). Trips in the other direction depart Pakse at 7.30am. Services to Laos from Siem Reap are also possible, with a bus change in Soung. The only other option to the border is a private taxi (around US$35 to US$40) or *moto* (around US$15) from Stung Treng.

**At the border** Both Lao and Cambodian visas are available on arrival. Entering Laos, it costs US$35 to US$42 for a visa, depending on nationality, plus a US$2 fee (dubbed either an 'overtime' or a 'processing' fee, depending on when you cross) upon both entry and exit.

Entering Cambodia, they jack up the price of a visa to US$25 from the normal US$20. The extra US$5 is called 'tea money', as the border guards have been stationed at such a remote crossing. In addition, the Cambodians charge US$1 for a cursory medical inspection upon arrival in the country, and levy a US$2 processing fee upon exit. These fees might be waived if you protest, but don't protest for too long or your bus may leave without you. The bus companies want their cut too, so they charge an extra US$1 to US$2 to handle your paperwork with the border guards. To avoid this fee, insist on doing your own paperwork and go through immigration alone.

**Moving on** Aside from the Sorya bus, there's virtually zero traffic on either side of the border. If you're dropped at the border, expect to pay 150,000/50,000 kip (US$12/4) for a taxi/*sǎhm-lór* heading north to Ban Nakasang (for Don Det).

The new highway west from Thala Boravit to Preah Vihear via Chhep is in great shape. **Asia Van Transfer** (✍ in Siem Reap 063-963853; www.asiavantransfer.com) has an express minibus to Siem Reap at 2pm daily (US$23, five hours), with a stop in Preah Vihear City (US$12, three hours).

Riverside Guesthouse rents out motorbikes (from US$5) while Riverside and Ponika's Place have bicycles for hire (US$1 to US$2).

## Around Stung Treng

In addition to the homestay program at Preah Rumkel, there are worthwhile community-based tourism initiatives, including homestays, in O'Russey Kandal, about 28km south of Stung Treng, and in Koh Preah, about 15km south of Stung Treng. Both programs have a slew of tours and activities on offer and there are volunteer opportunities as well.

Contact Mlup Baitong (ម្លុប់បៃតង; ✍012 899471; www.mlup-baitong.org) in Stung Treng for information on O'Russey Kandal, and CRDT (p278) in Kratie for information on Koh Preah. Xplore-Asia (p283) can also help organise homestay-based itineraries.

### Preah Rumkel ព្រះរំកិល

This small village is emerging as hotbed of ecotourism thanks to its proximity to the Anlong Cheuteal Irrawaddy dolphin pool near the Lao border. With wetlands recognised by the Ramsar List of Wetlands of International Importance (www.ramsar. org), dozens of islands, a rich array of bird life and various rapids and waterfalls cascading down from Laos, this is one of the Mekong River's wildest and most beautiful stretches.

The half-dozen frolicking dolphins in the Anlong Chuteal pool (known as Boong Pa Gooang in Laos) can easily be sighted from shore in Preah Rumkel, where there is an excellent community-based homestay (✍011 899891; mlup@online.com.kh; per person US$3, plus per meal US$3) program if you want to stay another day. There's a US$2 per person charge to see the dolphins.

Excursions out of Preah Rumkel include a hike up a nearby mountain and a boat/hiking trip to view the rampaging Mekong rapids cascading down from Laos. The rapids are an awesome display of nature's force, especially in the wet season.

Hire a longtailed boat in O'Svay or, closer to the Laos border, Anglong Morakot, to explore the area and view the dolphins at Anlong Cheuteal. Boats cost a negotiable US$25 return trip to Preah Rumkel and the dolphin pool. Add US$10 if you want to continue upstream to the rapids. Anlong Morakot is only 4km from the border so travellers coming in from Laos could get there in about 10 minutes on the back of a *moto* (about US$2). Be sure to arrange onward transport to Stung Treng – either at the border or in advance through Xplore-Asia (p283) or Riverside Guesthouse (p282) in Stung Treng. These companies can also prearrange your *moto* and boat ride from the border to Preah Rumkel. A taxi to Stung Treng from this area costs about US$45.

Better yet, through Xplore-Asia (p283) you can kayak with the dolphins and then paddle downstream to O'Svay, or through bird-rich flooded forests all the way to Stung Treng. A full-day kayak excursion south of O'Svay costs US$65 per person; add US$20 per person to include the boat trip upstream to the dolphin pool and the Mekong rapids.

## Siem Pang     សៀមប៉ាង

📃 074 / POP 5000

A relatively prosperous town that stretches for about 6km along the Tonlé Kong, Siem Pang is a good place to observe rural life or just relax by the riverside in a remote outpost.

Siem Pang acts as the western gateway to Virachey National Park (p293) and is renowned for its rich wildlife. Rare giant ibis and white-shouldered ibis roost around here. You can arrange a park permit (preferably well in advance) and find a guide through Theany Guesthouse.

**BirdLife International** (📞 097 974 5966, in Phnom Penh 023-993631; www.birdlife.org) runs a 'vulture restaurant' (feeding station) that attracts all three species of critically endangered vultures found in Cambodia. It's set up for research rather than tourism, but if you time your visit for the twice-monthly 'feed', which involves killing a water buffalo or cow and leaving it in a field near an observation hideout, you may get a chance to spot the vultures. Or you can up the ante with US$300 to organise a private feed.

A ferry takes passengers (1000r) and motorbikes (2500r) across the river, where the scenic trail to Veun Sai (p291) in Ratanakiri starts. **Theany Guesthouse** (📞 077 257773;

r US$7.50-10) offers one-way motorbike rentals for this ride (US$70, including the cost of returning the motorbike to Siem Pang), along with simple rooms in a traditional wooden house. The upstairs rooms are cheaper but there is decent breeze through the verandah.

Regular morning and occasional afternoon vans make the trip from Stung Treng to Siem Pang (US$5, 2½ hours). From Stung Treng, drive 50km north on NH7, turn right, and proceed another 52km on an unsealed road. There are no longer any public boats along the Tonlé Kong to/from Stung Treng.

# RATANAKIRI PROVINCE

Popular Ratana kiri Province (ខេត្តរតនគិរី) is making a name for itself as a diverse region of outstanding natural beauty that provides a remote home for a mosaic of minority peoples. The Jarai, Tompuon, Brau, Kavet and Kreung are the Khmer Leu (Upper Khmer) people, with their own languages, traditions and customs. There is also a large Lao population throughout the province and multiple languages can be heard in villages such as Veun Sai.

Adrenaline-pumping activities are abundant. Swim in clear volcanic lakes, shower under waterfalls or trek in the vast Virachey National Park – it's all here. Tourism is taking off even as the lowland elite plunder the place at an alarming pace. Ratanakiri is the frontline in the battle for land, and the slash-and-burn minorities are losing out thanks to their tradition of collective ownership. The forest is disappearing at an alarming rate, being replaced by rubber plantations and cashew-nut farms. Hopefully someone will wake up and smell the coffee – there's plenty of that as well – before it's too late.

Gem mining is big business in Ratanakiri, which is hardly surprising given that the name means 'hill of the precious stones'. There is good-quality zircon mined in several parts of the province, as well as other semiprecious stones. Just don't get suckered into a dream deal, as gem scams here are as old as the hills themselves.

Roads in Ratanakiri are not as impressive as the sights. In the dry season, prepare to do battle with the dust of 'red-earth Ratanakiri', which will leave you with orange skin and ginger hair. The roads look like a papaya shake during the wet season. The ideal time

## THE REAL GIBBON EXPERIENCE

The Mekong region is awash in tours that have 'gibbon' in their name, but don't guarantee gibbons. Here in Ratanakiri you get to observe gibbons in their natural habitat.

**Veun Sai Gibbon Ecotours** (☏ 097 752 9960; veunsaicbet@gmail.com) was established as a community-based ecotourism project (CBET) by Conservation International (CI; www.conservation.org); the project is located within the Veun Sai-Siem Pang Conservation Area (VSSPCA), just outside the border of Virachey National Park north of Veun Sai. You stay at least one night in the jungle sleeping in hammocks or in a community-based homestay, rising before dawn to spend time with semi-habituated northern buff-cheeked gibbons. This species was discovered only in 2010 and the population in Veun Sai is believed to be one of the largest at about 500 individuals. Hearing their haunting dawn call echo through the jungle and seeing them swing through the canopy is memorable. These tours also offer the opportunity to experience dense jungle, open savannah, rivers and waterfalls, and to visit Kavet and Lao villages.

CI has an exclusive arrangement with the village near the gibbon site to run these tours. The gibbon-viewing season runs from 1 November to mid-June (it's too wet at other times) and the visits are limited to six people at a time. The tours cost US$100 to US$200 per person for a one-night/two-day tour, depending on group size and which tour company you choose. The fee includes entrance to the VSSPCA, guide, homestays and camps, and all meals. Most companies in Ban Lung can arrange these trips on behalf of CI. For more details on the gibbon-spotting experience, contact the CBET. CBET payments are used as a substitute for destructive forest use, so this is a very worthwhile way to contribute something positive to wildlife conservation and community development.

to explore is November, after the rains have stopped and before the dust begins to swirl.

# Ban Lung បានលុង

☏ 075 / POP 40,000

Affectionately known as *dey krahorm* ('red earth') after its rust-coloured affliction, Ban Lung provides a popular base for a range of Ratanakiri romps.

The town itself is busy and lacks the backwater charm of Sen Monorom in Mondulkiri, but with attractions such as Boeng Yeak Lom just a short hop away, there is little room for complaint. Many of the minorities from the surrounding villages come to Ban Lung to buy and sell at the market.

## ⊙ Sights & Activities

There are no real sights in the centre of town. The big draw is Boeng Yeak Lom, while multiday treks around Ban Lung are picking up steam. Elephant rides are offered near Ka Tieng Waterfall, but are not recommended due to the well-being of the animals (p276). Save your elephant experience for walking with the herd (p298) in Mondulkiri.

**Boeng Yeak Lom**                                    LAKE
(បឹងយក្សឡោម; admission US$1) At the heart of the protected area of Yeak Lom is a beaut-

iful, emerald-hued crater lake set amid the vivid greens of the towering jungle. It is one of the most peaceful locations Cambodia has to offer and the water is extremely clear. Several wooden piers are dotted around the perimeter, making it perfect for swimming. A small Cultural & Environmental Centre has a modest display on ethnic minorities in the province and hires out life jackets for children.

The lake is believed to have been formed 700,000 years ago and some believe it must have been formed by a meteor strike as the circle is so perfect. The indigenous minority people in the area have long considered Yeak Lom a sacred place and their legends talk of mysterious creatures that inhabit the waters, but don't let that put you off swimming.

The local Tompuon minority has a 25-year lease to manage the lake through to 2021, and proceeds from the entry fee go towards improving life in the nearby villages. However, developers – backed by local politicians – have long been clamoring for the sacred lands around the lake. One can only hope they are kept at bay and that Boeng Yeak Lom is preserved in all of its pristine glory, an all-too-rare occurrence in Cambodia.

To get to Boeng Yeak Lom from Ban Lung's central roundabout head east towards Vietnam for 3km, turn right at the prominent minorities statue and proceed 2km or so. *Motos* charge US$4 to US$5 return (more if you make them wait), while *remorks* have been known to charge up to US$10 return. It takes about an hour to reach the lake on foot from Ban Lung.

**Waterfalls**                                          WATERFALL
(per waterfall 2000r) Tucked amid the sprawling cashew and rubber plantations just west of Ban Lung are three waterfalls worth visiting: **Chaa Ong**, **Ka Tieng** and **Kinchaan**. All are within a 20-minute *moto* ride of town, and visits to all three are usually included in tour companies' half- and full-day excursions. The turnoffs to all three waterfalls are 200m west of the new bus station, just beyond a Lina petrol station. There's signage but it's barely visible.

The tallest and most spectacular of the three is 25m-high Chaa Ong – it's set in a jungle gorge and you can clamber behind the waterfall or venture underneath for a power

## Ban Lung

### Activities, Courses & Tours

### Sleeping

### Eating

shower. However, it dries up from about January to May. Ka Tieng is the most enjoyable, as it drops over a rock shelf, allowing you to clamber all the way behind. There are some vines on the far side that are strong enough to swing on for some Tarzan action. Kinchaan Waterfall is impressively set against jungle foliage and offers some swimming holes.

The Chaa Ong turnoff is on the right (north) side of NH19; the waterfall is 5.5km from the highway along a dirt road. The turnoff to Ka Tieng and Kinchaan is on the left side of NH19; proceed 5.5km to a fork in the road. Go left 200m to Kinchaan, or right 2.5km to Ka Tieng.

You can access all three falls year-round, but think twice about driving yourself on a motorbike in the rainy season, as the red-clay access roads are extremely slippery when wet and you're almost guaranteed to wipe out. *Motos* (return US$6 for one waterfall, or US$10 for all three) and *remorks* (US$10/20 for one/three waterfalls) can get you here safely.

## ☞ Tours

Overnight treks with nights spent camping or staying in minority villages north of Veun Sai or Ta Veng are popular. Day tours usually take in some combination of waterfalls, Boeng Yeak Lom, elephant rides, minority villages, gem mines and jungle walks. Figure on US$45 to $50 per day per person for a couple (less for bigger groups).

Keep in mind that trekking in Virachey National Park is the exclusive domain of Vi-

rachey National Park Eco-Tourism Information Center (p290). Private tour operators also offer multiday treks, but these only go as far as the park's buffer zone. There's little forest left standing outside the park boundary, so be careful that you're not being taken for a loop – literally – around and around in the same small patch of forest. Despite being shut out from the park, private operators can still design creative treks that take in minority villages and scenic spots around the province.

Some of the accommodation in town – Backpacker Pad (Backpacker Banlung Tours), Tree Top Ecolodge (Smiling Tours), Terres Rouges (which can provide French-speaking guides) and Yaklom Hill Lodge – are good at arranging tours, plus there are also several dedicated tour companies.

### Highland Tours                                     TOUR
(☏ 097 658 3841; highland.tour@yahoo.com) Kimi and Horng are husband-and-wife graduates of the Le Tonlé Tourism Training Centre (p282) in Stung Treng who have moved to the highlands to run a range of tours, including fun day trips and a multiday tour from I Tub village (northwest of Veun Sai) to Siem Pang by bike, then on to Stung Treng by boat. Horng is the only female guide in Ratanakiri.

### Khieng                                             TOUR
(☏ 097 923 0923; khamphaykhieng@yahoo.com) Bespectacled Khieng is an indigenous Tompuon guide who runs unique one- to two-night trips in fairly well-preserved jungle around Lumphat, with overnight stays in

---

### RESPONSIBLE TREKKING AROUND RATANAKIRI

Overnight treks in the forests of Ratanakiri are very popular these days. Diehard trampers spend up to eight days sleeping in replica US Army hammocks and checking out some of the country's last virgin forest in and around Virachey National Park.

Where possible, we recommend using indigenous guides for organised treks and other excursions around Ban Lung. They speak the local dialects and can secure permission to visit cemeteries that are off-limits to Khmer guides. Unfortunately, with a few notable exceptions (see above), the level of English among indigenous guides tends to be only fair. If you need a more fluent English guide, we suggest hiring both an English-speaking Khmer guide and a minority guide, if it's within your budget.

A loose association of Tompuon guides is based at Boeng Yeak Lom – they can take you on an exclusive tour of several Tompuon villages around Boeng Yeak Lom. (They have neither a phone number nor an email so you'll just have to show up.) You can observe weavers and basket-makers in action, learn about animist traditions and eat a traditional indigenous meal of bamboo-steamed fish, fresh vegetables, 'minority' rice and rice wine.

Among private tour companies, only Yaklom Hill Lodge (opposite) employs a full-time indigenous (Tompuon) guide, but you'll need to request him. Virachey National Park also employs some indigenous guides and uses minority porters, while the tour companies we list can all hire indigenous guides on request.

minority villages. His tours are cheap and he seems genuinely interested in seeing money go to Tompuon communities and guides, so tip him well. He also has an impressive hand-drawn map of Ratanakiri province. Khieng can often be found around Boeng Yeak Lom.

**DutchCo Trekking Cambodia** TOUR
(☑097 679 2714; www.trekkingcambodia.com) One of the most experienced trekking operators in the province, run by – wait for it – a friendly Dutchman. Runs four- to five-day treks north of Veun Sai through Kavet villages and community forests, and one- to two-day trips around Kalai (south of Veun Sai), among many other tours.

**Parrot Tours** TOUR
(☑012 764714; www.jungletrek.blogspot.com) Sitha Nan is a national-park-trained guide with expert local knowledge. Parrot runs a range of overnight treks in the forests north of Itub, home to throngs of gibbons.

# 🛏 Sleeping

There are a host of bog-standard high-rise hotels near the market, but none worth writing home about.

⭐**Tree Top Ecolodge** BUNGALOWS $
(☑012 490333; www.treetop-ecolodge.com; d US$7, cottage with cold/hot water US$12/15; 🛜) This is one of the best places to stay in Cambodia's 'wild east', with oodles of atmosphere. 'Mr T's' place boasts rough-hewn walkways leading to huge bungalows with mosquito nets, thatched roofs and hammock-strewn verandahs with verdant valley vistas. Like the bungalows, the restaurant is fashioned from hardwood and dangles over a lush ravine. Up-to-date travel advice is plentiful, especially for those Laos bound.

**Banlung Balcony** GUESTHOUSE $
(☑097 809 7036; www.balconyguesthouse.net; Boeng Kansaign; d US$4-7; @🛜) This is one of Ban Lung's best deals at the budget end of the market. The rooms are basic but have high ceilings and wooden floors, and there's a huge public balcony. The restaurant-bar has decent food and a snooker table (which is a lot harder to master than a standard pool table).

**Backpacker Pad** HOSTEL $
(☑088 944 1616; banlungbackpackerpad@yahoo.com; dm US$2, d without/with bathroom US$4/5; 🛜) Popular Backpacker Pad is the cheapest deal in town, with small rooms or communal dorms at rock-bottom prices. The cosy

common area out front is a good place to meet other travellers. Owner Sophat is a great source of info and runs an eponymous tour company.

**Flashpacker Pad** HOTEL $
(☑093 785259; flashpackerpad@gmail.com; Boeng Kansaign; r with fan/air-con from US$7/9; ✱🛜) Quite literally a flashpacker pad run by Backpacker Pad. The rooms have a touch of class, with flatscreens and indigenous-made runners on white bedspreads. Go for a room with a view for misty mornings on the lake. Also a good source of tour and transport information. Great value.

**Lakeside Chheng Lok Hotel** HOTEL $
(☑012 957422; lakeside.chhenglokhotel@gmail.com; Boeng Kansaign; r with fan/air-con from US$5/15; ✱@🛜✱) The ever-expanding Lakeside has tacked on a swimming pool, a vast new wing and a sister hotel in recent years. There's a lot of choice here, from large but generic air-con rooms to bare-bones fan-cooled rooms.

**Thy Ath Lodge** HOTEL $
(☑017 386396; thy.ath.lodge@gmail.com; Boeng Kansaign; r US$15-25) This lakeside lodge is run by a friendly family who make their guests feel very at home. Rooms are spacious and airy; options include suite-like cottages out front – an absolute steal for US$25.

**Yaklom Hill Lodge** LODGE $
(☑011 725881; www.yaklom.com; s/d/tr US$10/15/20) 🖉 Ratanakiri's only true ecolodge, staffed by Tompuon, is set amid lush forest near Boeung Yeak Lom, 5km east of Ban Lung's central roundabout. It will appeal to those who like nature. The all-wood bungalows are atmospheric but starting to show their age, and can get damp. A generator enables hot showers and light from 6pm to 9pm. Hiking trails lead to the lake and beyond. Breakfast is included in the low season.

**Ratanak Sombath Hotel** HOTEL $$
(☑075-655 5556; ratanaksombathhotel@gmail.com; US$15-35; ✱) One of a new breed of high-rise hotels popping up around town, this is exceedingly good value, offering spacious rooms with all the trimmings, such as a minibar and safety-deposit box. There's even a swimming pool, which draws a local crowd at weekends.

⭐**Terres Rouges Lodge** BOUTIQUE HOTEL $$
(☑075-974051; www.ratanakiri-lodge.com; Boeng Kansaign; s/d incl breakfast US$46/52, ste

US$86-92; ❉ @ 🛜 ⛱ ) Even as competition hots up, Terres Rouges remains one of the most atmospheric places to stay in provincial Cambodia. The fan-cooled standard rooms are done up in classy colonial style, with beautiful Cambodian furniture, tribal artefacts and a long common verandah. Suites consist of spacious Balinese-style bungalows with open-plan bathrooms, set in the gorgeous garden.

If you're travelling with kids or looking for a little more comfort in Ban Lung, this option is a no-brainer.

**Ratanak Resort**      BOUTIQUE HOTEL **$$**
( 📞 092 244114; www.ratanakresort.com; r US$39-100; ⛱ ) Located a few kilometres out of town on a bluff near Yeak Lom Lake, Ratanak is a stylish, all-wooden resort with accommodation in upmarket bungalows. Rooms include four-poster beds with billowing drapes and useful extras for the dapper adventurer, such as a bathrobe and hair dryer. The small infinity pool here is open to non-guests for US$5.

## ✕ Eating & Drinking

Among the guesthouses, Terres Rouge has the most sophisticated menu, while Treetop and Banlung Balcony are also reliable. To get down with the locals, head to the lakefront near Coconut Shake Restaurant around sunset, plop down on a mat, and order cheap beer and snacks from waterfront shacks.

Night owls don't have much to divert them. Banlung Balcony has a great bar occasionally brimming with backpackers, as does Backpacker Pad.

**★ Green Carrot**      INTERNATIONAL **$**
(US$2-6; ⏱ 7am-10pm; 🛜 ) A great little hole-in-the-wall restaurant that turns out surprisingly sophisticated food, including healthy salads, sandwiches and wraps, plus a good range of Khmer favourites. It even does a decent burger and some very affordable pizzas. Happy hour has two-for-one on cocktails from 6pm to 8pm.

**Cafe Alee**      INTERNATIONAL **$**
(mains US$1.50-5.50; ⏱ 7am-last customer; 🛜 ) Cafe Alee has one of the more interesting menus in town, including a generous smattering of vegetarian options, a hearty lasagne and the full gamut of Khmer food (minus the MSG that sometimes shows up in local restaurants). It also serves hearty breakfasts for trekkers.

**Sal's Restaurant & Bar**      INTERNATIONAL **$**
(mains US$1.75-5; ⏱ 5-10pm) This welcoming restaurant-bar, popular with Ban Lung's small expat community, is the place to come for comfort food from home, including Indian curries, spicy Mexican and great burgers. All dishes are freshly prepared, so order ahead if you don't want a long wait.

**Taman**      CAMBODIAN **$**
(dishes 6000-12,000r; ⏱ 6am-8pm; 🛜 ) Locals flock to this place for wholesome Cambodian and Chinese breakfasts, including steaming bowls of noodle soup – guaranteed to give an energy boost ahead of a trek in the forest. It's a block east of the market.

**Everest**      INDIAN **$**
(mains US$3-4; ⏱ 7am-11pm; 🛜 ) It's Ban Lung, not Brick Lane, but the extensive range of Indian flavours on offer here is a welcome relief from the over-familiar Ratanakiri menu of Cambodian dishes, burgers and pasta.

**Coconut Shake Restaurant**      CAMBODIAN **$**
(Boeng Kansaign; mains 6000-16,000r; ⏱ 7am-9pm) The best coconut shakes in the northeast cost just 4000r at this little place overlooking the lake. It has fried noodles and other Khmer fare if you're feeling peckish.

**Rith Any Banh Chav**      CAMBODIAN **$**
(dishes US$1; ⏱ 2-7pm) The owner here specialises in *banh chav* – a dish of meat, baby shrimps, sprouts, vegies and spices wrapped inside a thin egg pancake that's wrapped inside a lettuce leaf, and dipped in a zesty sweet-chilli sauce.

**Pteas Bay Khmer**      INTERNATIONAL **$$**
(Boeng Kansaign; US$4-15) This wooden restaurant has an imposing setting above the shores of Boeng Kansaign, making it a good stop by day or night. The menu includes some classic Cambodian dishes, homemade pasta and some select cuts of meat.

## ℹ Information

Visitors will find guesthouses or tour companies to be most useful in the quest for local knowledge.

**Canadia Bank** ( ⏱ 8.30am-3.30pm Mon-Fri, ATM 24hr) Full-service bank with an international ATM.

**Srey Mom Internet** (per hr 4000r; ⏱ 6.30am-10pm) Fan-cooled internet access.

**Virachey National Park Eco-Tourism Information Centre** ( 📞 075-974013, 097 896 4995; virachey@camintel.com; ⏱ 8am-noon & 2-5pm)

---

### GETTING TO VIETNAM: BAN LUNG TO PLEIKU

**Getting to the border** Opened to tourists in 2008, the O'Yadaw–Le Thanh **border crossing** (⊙7am-5pm) is 70km east of Ban Lung along smooth NH19. From Ban Lung, guesthouses advertise a 6.30am van to Pleiku in Vietnam (from US$8, three hours), involving a change of vehicles at the border. These pick you up at your guesthouse for a surcharge, which is easier than trying to arrange a ticket independently. Alternatively, take a local minibus to O'Yadaw from Ban Lung's new bus station, and continue 25km to the border by *moto*.

**At the border** Formalities are straightforward and lines nonexistent – just make sure you have a Vietnamese visa if required, as visas are not issued at the border.

**Moving on** Once on the Vietnamese side of the frontier, the road is nicely paved and *motos* wait to take you to Duc Co (20km), where there are buses to Pleiku, Quy Nhon and Hoi An.

---

The place to organise trekking in Virachey National Park.

## ⓘ Getting There & Away

Ban Lung is 510km northeast of Phnom Penh and 129km east of O Poang Moan, the junction town 19km south of Stung Treng. Highway NH19 between Ban Lung and O Pong Moan is flat, empty and fully sealed, but leave early as very little public transport departs Ban Lung in the afternoon.

There is a vast bus station on the western outskirts of town, 2.5km west of Ban Lung's main roundabout, but guesthouses and tour companies can arrange pick-ups in town, which is much more convenient.

**Phnom Penh Sorya** (☏077 880062; www.ppsoryatransport.com), Rith Mony and Thong Ly operate early-morning buses to Phnom Penh (US$9 to US$10, 11 hours) via Kratie and Kompong Cham, but these are slow compared with express minivans. Long-distance bus services to Siem Reap or Pakse are also promoted, but in reality this is a hassle, as you will be forced to change buses, often with significant wait times, in Kompong Cham or Stung Treng respectively.

Speedy express-van services pick you up at your guesthouse and head to Phnom Penh (US$15, eight hours, 6am and 1pm) and Stung Treng (US$7, two hours, around 8am). Organise these through your guesthouse. Call Backpacker Pad or Tree Top Ecolodge to arrange an express van pick-up if coming from Phnom Penh.

There is also a daily minivan south to Sen Monorom (US$8, two hours, 8am) in Mondulkiri. Various local slow minibuses also depart in the morning to Phnom Penh (50,000r, 10 hours), Stung Treng (20,000r, three hours) and O'Yadaw (12,000r, 1½ hours), and throughout the day to Lumphat (10,000r, one hour) and Kratie (25,000r, four hours). From O'Yadaw you can cross the border into Vietnam.

Pick-up trucks head to more remote Ratanakiri villages from the **taxi park** next to the market. Share taxis out of Ban Lung are rare.

Ratanakiri's airport has been closed to commercial flights for years.

## ⓘ Getting Around

Bicycles (US$1 to US$3), motorbikes (US$5 to US$7), cars (from US$30) and 4WDs (from US$50) are available for hire from most guesthouses in town.

**Cheng Heng** (☏088 851 6104; ⊙6am-8pm) has some 250cc trail bikes for rent (US$25) in addition to a stable of well-maintained smaller motorbikes (US$6 to US$8).

*Motodups* hang out around the market and some double as guides. Figure on US$15 to US$20 per day for a good English-speaking driver-guide. A *moto* to Yeak Lom costs about US$4 to US$5 return; to Veun Sai is US$15 return; and to any waterfall is about US$6 or so return.

*Remorks* have finally made it to Ban Lung, but there are only a handful in town and they are expensive by Cambodian standards – about double what a *moto* costs.

---

# Around Ban Lung

## Veun Sai                                   វិនៃសៃ

⚑075 / POP 3000

Located on the banks of Tonlé San, Veun Sai is a cluster of Chinese, Lao and *chunchiet* (ethnic minority) villages. Originally, the town was located on the north bank of the river and known as Virachey, but these days the main settlement is on the south bank. From the south side, cross the river on a small **ferry** (500/3000r without/with a motorbike) and walk west for a couple of kilometres, passing through the Khmer village, a Lao community and a small *chunchiet* area, before finally emerging in a wealthy Chinese village complete with large wooden houses and inhabitants who still speak

Chinese. Note how neat and tidy it is compared with the surrounding communities.

The Veun Sai area is known for Tompuon cemeteries, but most of them are closed to outsiders these days. The bans are at least partially the result of tourists flaunting behavioral protocols.

At the time of writing, the closest cemetery to Veun Sai open to visitors was an ethnic Kachah cemetery in Kaoh Paek, a 45-minute boat ride upriver from Veun Sai. Expect to pay around US$40 for the boat trip from Veun Sai, or about half that from Kachon, 10km upriver (east) of Veun Sai. Tour companies in Ban Lung charge US$50 for an excursion here.

Veun Sai is 39km northwest of Ban Lung on an unsealed but smooth all-weather road. It is easy enough to get here under your own steam on a motorbike or with a vehicle. English-speaking guides ask US$15 or so return to take you out here on a *moto*.

Skilled motorbike and mountain-bike riders can ride from Veun Sai to Siem Pang (65km) in Stung Treng via Itub (a few hours' walk south of the gibbon zone) along a scenic trail that begins on the north side of the river.

## Ta Veng ⟨តាវែង⟩

Ta Veng is an insignificant village on the southern bank of Tonlé San, but it acts as one of the main gateways to Virachey National Park and the base for many treks run by private operators in the park's buffer zone. It was in the Ta Veng district that Pol Pot, Ieng Sary and other leaders of the Khmer Rouge established their guerrilla base in the 1960s. Locals say nothing today remains of the remote base, although, in a dismal sign of decline, they point out that Ta Veng had electricity before the war.

Ta Veng is about 57km north of Ban Lung on a roller-coaster road through the mountains that affords some of the province's better views. The road passes through several minority villages, where it is possible to break the journey. There are some very steep climbs in sections, and for this reason it wouldn't be much fun in the rain. Travel by motorbike or charter a vehicle. It is possible to hire small boats in Ta Veng for river jaunts (US$15 to US$20 in the local area or US$80 to US$90 for the five-hour trip to Veun Sai).

---

### TREAD LIGHTLY IN THE HILLS

Tourism can bring many benefits to highland communities; however, there are also negatives, such as increased litter and pollutants, domination of the tourism business by lowland Khmers at the expense of highland minorities, and the tendency of tourists to disregard local customs and taboos. One way to offset the negatives is to hire indigenous guides. Not only does this ensure that your tourist dollars go directly to indigenous communities, but it will also enrich your own visit. Indigenous guides can greatly improve your access to the residents of highland communities, who are animists and speak Khmer only as a second language. They also understand taboos and traditions that might be lost on Khmer guides. Their intimate knowledge of the forests is another major asset.

More tips on visiting indigenous communities responsibly:

#### Interaction

➡ Be polite and respectful, especially with elderly people.

➡ Dress modestly.

➡ Taste traditional wine if you are offered it, especially during a ceremony. Refusal will cause offence.

➡ Honour signs discouraging outsiders from entering a village; for instance, during a spiritual ceremony. A good local guide will be able to detect these signs.

➡ Learn something about the community's culture and language and demonstrate something good about yours.

#### Gifts

➡ Individual gifts create jealousy and expectations. Instead, consider making donations to the local school, medical centre or community fund.

## Lumkut Lake & Bokheo
បឹងលំកុដ និងបរកែវ

Lumkut is a large crater lake hemmed in by dense forest on all sides, similar to the more illustrious and accessible Boeng Yeak Lom. To get to the lake turn south off the highway to O'Yadaw about 33km east of Ban Lung. The lake is 15km south along a rough road. Access is difficult in the rainy season, so most visitors opt for the convenience of Yeak Lom.

On the way to the lake you can stop off in Bokheo, the current hot spot for gem mining, 29km east of Ban Lung. Locals dig a large pit in the ground and then tunnel horizontally in their search for amethyst and zircon. The mines tend to move around so ask around where to find them.

## Virachey National Park
ឧទ្យានជាតិវីរជ័យ

One of the largest protected areas in Cambodia, stretching for 3325 sq km east to Vietnam, north to Laos and west to Stung Treng Province, is **Virachey National Park** (admission US$5). The park has never been fully explored and is home to a number of rare mammals, including elephants, clouded leopards, tigers and sun bears, although your chances of seeing any of these creatures are extremely slim. However, you'll probably hear endangered gibbons and might spot great hornbills, giant ibis, Germain's peacock-pheasants and other rare birds. So important is the park to the Mekong region that it was designated an Asean Heritage Park in 2003. However, the bad news is that it is seriously under threat from developers, and Cambodian authorities have already leased more remote regions of the park to Vietnamese rubber plantation developers.

Virachey has one of the most organised ecotourism programs in Cambodia, focusing on small-scale culture, nature and adventure trekking. The program aims to involve and benefit local minority communities. All treks into the park must be arranged through the Virachey National Park Eco-Tourism Information Centre (p290) in Ban Lung. The park offers two- to eight-day treks led by English-speaking rangers. Private operators offer tours in the park buffer zone but are forbidden from taking tourists into the park proper. However, private tour companies can be useful in setting things

➡ If you do give individual gifts, keep them modest (such as pens, pencils and notebooks).

➡ Do not give children sweets or money.

➡ Do not give clothes, as communities are self-sufficient.

### Shopping

➡ Haggle politely and always pay the agreed (and fair) price.

➡ Do not ask to buy a villager's personal household items, tools, or the jewellery or clothes they are wearing.

➡ Do not buy village treasures, such as altar pieces or totems.

### Photographs

➡ Do not photograph altars.

➡ Do not use a flash.

➡ Do not photograph without asking permission first, and this includes children. Some hill tribes believe the camera will capture their spirit.

➡ Do not show up for 15 minutes and expect to be granted permission to take photos. Invest some time in getting to know the villagers first.

### Travel

➡ Make a point of travelling in small, less disruptive groups.

➡ Try to spend some real time in minority villages – at least several hours if not an overnight. If you don't have a few hours to invest, don't go.

---

### RESPECT THE DEAD

The *chunchiet* (ethnic minorities) of Ratanakiri bury their dead amid the jungle, carving effigies of the deceased to stand guard over the graves. When a lengthy period of mourning is complete, villagers hold a celebration and add two carved wooden likenesses of elephant tusks to the structures. Newer tombs of wealthy individuals have been cast in concrete and show some modern touches, such as sun-shades and mobile phones.

There are many cemeteries scattered throughout the forests of Ratanakiri, but most of them are strictly off-limits to visitors. Cemeteries are sacred sights for the *chunchiet* – enter them only with permission from the village chief and preferably in the company of a local. If you are lucky enough to be allowed into a cemetery, touch nothing, act respectfully and ask permission before taking photos.

Unfortunately, there have been many reports of tourists ignoring clearly marked signs (in English) urging outsiders to abstain from entering *chunchiet* cemeteries. Worse, un-scrupulous art collectors and amateur anthropologists from Europe have been buying up the old effigies from poor villagers.

---

up in advance with park staff, who are not always responsive.

The signature trek is an eight-day, seven-night Phnom Veal Thom Wilderness Trek (one/two people US$400/350). It starts from Ta Veng with an overnight homestay in a Brau village. The trek then goes deep into the heart of the Phnom Veal Thom grasslands, an area rich in wildlife such as sambar deer, gibbons, langurs, wild pigs, bears and hornbills. Trekkers return via a different route and pass through areas of evergreen forest. The price includes transport by *moto* to the trail head, park admission, food, guides, porters, hammocks and boat transport. Prices drop the larger the group. There are also one- and two-night treks available in the park.

---

## Lumphat លំផាត់

POP 2000

The former provincial capital of Lumphat, on the banks of Tonlé Srepok, is a shadow of its former self thanks to sustained US bombing raids in the early 1970s. The Tonlé Srepok is believed to be the river depicted in the seminal antiwar film *Apocalypse Now*, in which Martin Sheen's Captain Benjamin Willard goes upriver into Cambodia in search of renegade Colonel Kurtz, played by Marlon Brando.

Bei Srok (ប៊ីស្រុក; Tuk Chrouu Bram-pul; admission 2000r) is a popular waterfall with seven gentle tiers. It's about 20km east of Lumphat. You can also get here on a rough road that leads south-southwest from Boeng Yeak Lom. Many Ban Lung tour companies offer Bei Srok as a day tour combined with some abandoned gem mines nearby and

bomb-crater spotting around Lumphat. Access is difficult to impossible in the rainy season.

To get to Lumphat from Ban Lung, take the road to Stung Treng for 10km before heading south. The 35km journey takes about 45 minutes. Pick-ups to the taxi park in Ban Lung leave early in the morning from Lumphat and return in the afternoon on most days.

# MONDULKIRI PROVINCE

A world apart from lowland Cambodia, Mondulkiri Province (ខេត្តមណ្ឌលគិរី) is the original Wild East of the country. Climatically and culturally it's also another world, which comes as a relief after the heat of the plains. This region is home to the hardy Bunong people and their noble elephants, and it's possible here to visit traditional villages and learn about elephants in their element at the Elephant Valley Project (p298).

The landscape is a seductive mix of pine clumps, grassy hills and windswept valleys that fade beguilingly into forests of jade green and hidden waterfalls. Wild animals, such as bears, leopards and especially elephants, are more numerous here than elsewhere, although sightings are usually limited to birds, monkeys and the occasional wild pig.

Mondulkiri means 'Meeting of the Hills', an apt sobriquet for a land of rolling hills. In the dry season it's a little like Wales with sunshine; in the wet season, like Tasmania with more rain. At an average elevation of 800m, it can get quite chilly at night, so bring something warm.

Mondulkiri is the most sparsely populated province in the country, with just four people per square kilometre. Almost half the inhabitants come from the Bunong minority group, with other minorities making up much of the rest of the population. Hunting remains the profession of choice for many minorities.

Conservationists have grand plans for the province, creating wildlife sanctuaries and initiating sustainable tourism activities, but are facing off against speculators and industrialists queuing up for natural resources.

# Sen Monorom    សែនមនោរម្យ

📞 073 / POP 10,000

The provincial capital of Mondulkiri, Sen Monorom is really an overgrown village, a charming community set in the spot where the legendary hills meet. In the centre of town are two lakes, leading some dreamers to call it 'the Switzerland of Cambodia'.

The area around Sen Monorom is peppered with minority villages and picturesque waterfalls, making it the ideal place to spend some time. Many of the Bunong people from nearby villages come here to trade: the distinctive baskets they carry on their backs make them easy to distinguish from the immigrant lowlanders. Set at 800m, when the winds blow Sen Monorom is notably cooler than the rest of Cambodia, so bring warm clothing.

## ◉ Sights & Activities

Not much happens in Sen Monorom itself, but there are a few worthwhile sights within a short motorbike ride or a long walk from town. Headline activities include the nearby Elephant Valley Project (p298) and the new Mayura Zipline (p300) at Bou Sraa Waterfall.

**Monorom Falls**    WATERFALL
(ទឹកធ្លាក់មនោរម្យ) FREE A 10m drop into a popular swimming hole, Monorom Falls is lovely if you can beat the crowds. From the west side of the airstrip, head northwest for 2.3km, turn left and proceed 1.5km. There's no legible sign at the turnoff.

**Wat Phnom Doh Kromom**    BUDDHIST TEMPLE
(វត្តភ្នំដោះក្រមុំ) Looming over the northeast corner of the airstrip, Wat Phnom Doh Kromom has Mondulkiri's best sunset vista – a wooden platform lets you take in the views. Continue another 5km north beyond to the wat for **Samot Cheur** (Ocean of Trees), another viewpoint overlooking an emerald forest to the east.

## ☞ Tours

As in Ratanakiri, multiday forest treks are immensely popular. We recommend securing indigenous Bunong guides for these trips: they know the forests intimately and can break the ice with the locals in any Bunong villages you visit.

Drop in to the **Mondulkiri Resource and Documentation Centre** (MRDC; 📞 097 408 7806; www.mondulkiri-centre.org; Hefalump Cafe), located above the Hefalump Cafe, for information on the **WEHH** (📞 097 273 9566; http://bunongtourism.wordpress.com; from US$55) tour program, which offers an intimate look at Bunong culture in the Dak Dam community. Operated in partnership with NGO Nomad RSI, itineraries include life on a Bunong farm, the handicrafts of the Bunong and a

---

### COMMUNITY HOMESTAYS IN MONDULKIRI

WWF (p297) has recently helped two villages in Mondulkiri's Phnom Prich Wildlife Sanctuary launch projects geared to giving tourists a glimpse into traditional Bunong lifestyles. One is located in Dei Ey, about 55km north of Sen Monorom; the other is in Sre Y, about 30km northwest of Sen Monorom. Contact Nimith at WWF for details on both projects, which can also be booked through the Hefalump Cafe (p300) in Sen Monorom.

Dei Ey offers homestays, traditional meals, walking with elephants owned by the local Bunong, and trekking. Cultural activies such as resin-collecting and honey-making are also on the docket. Prices for a two-day trip start at US$135 for one person and go down substantially with each additional person. Included are transport, meals, guides and accommodation in the Dei Ey Community Lodge. Sre Y has a similar program, involving walking with elephants, followed by a trek to a waterfall, then returning to Sen Monorom on mountain bikes.

Portions of the proceeds from these initiatives go into a community fund designed to improve local livelihoods and protect the forest.

# Sen Monorom

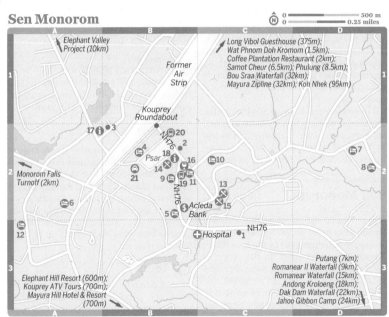

## Sen Monorom

trek into old-growth Bunong forest. Prices start from US$55 per person, subject to the size of the group.

Other guesthouse-based tour operators, such as Nature Lodge and Green House, usually employ Bunong people as porters on longer excursions, but you should request this service.

Many guesthouses in town run the full gamut of treks and tours around Sen Mono-

rom. Figure on about US$50 per person per day for overnight trips, including all meals, transfer to the trail head by *moto,* and an English-speaking guide. Per-person prices drop for larger groups.

**Adventure Rider Asia**     BIKE TOURS
(☑ 078 250350; www.adventureriderasia.com; NH76; tours per day from US$75) Reini tailors trail-bike tours on the rugged back roads of

Mondulkiri and well beyond for multiday trips. Tours include a high-quality bike and full riding gear. Lessons are available for bikers who want to learn to ride a dirt bike.

**Green House** TOUR
(☑017 905659; www.greenhouse-tour.blogspot. com; NH76) 🌱 Owner Sam Nang is a good source of information about Mondulkiri. Green House operates the **Elephant Community Program**, which offers affordable elephant encounters for US$35 per person, plus some longer overnight tours. As well as treks, Green House also offers full-day mountain-bike tours (from US$20), plus Trek and Giant mountain bikes (US$8 per day) and motorbikes (US$7) for hire.

**Kouprey ATV Tours** ADVENTURE TOUR
(☑088 888 8629; Mayura Hill Resort; tours US$29) Quad biking has come to the hills of Mondulkiri – and it's a whole lot of fun. Organised by Mayura Hill Resort, the trip takes in some of Sen Monorom's main sights, including the Monorom Falls, Samot Cheur ('Ocean of Trees') and the Wat Phnom Doh Kromom viewpoint. It's great value and a fun way to get a bit of ATV experience under your belt in a low-traffic environment.

**Mondulkiri Sanctuary** ECOTOUR
(☑011 494449; www.mondulkirisanctuary.org) 🌱 Established by LEAF (Local Environmental Awareness Foundation), this is a small wildlife corridor near the Otai River. Day visits run for US$45 per person (8- to 14-year-olds half-price; under 8s free) and overnight trips with camping out in the forest can be arranged. Group numbers are limited to 12 people per day. Volunteers are also welcome. Unlike Elephant Valley Project (p298), tours are also run at weekends.

**Mondulkiri Trail** TOUR
(☑088 593 5588; www.mondulkiritourguide.com; tours per person from US$50) Operated by experienced motorbike driver Monyhong, who can take you deep into the bush – either on a day trip out of Sen Monorom or on overnights to Kratie, Ratanakiri or beyond.

**Sam Veasna Center** WILDLIFE TOURS
(☑012 520828; www.samveasna.org; Hefalump Cafe, Sen Monorom) 🌱 Works with the international NGO Wildlife Conservation Society (WCS; www.wcscambodia.org) in promoting wildlife and birdwatching tours in the Seima Protected Forest, west of town. By the time you read this, a Sam Veasna staffer

should be embedded in the Hefalump Cafe for information on primate tracking and bird-spotting in Seima.

**WWF** ECOTOUR
(☑073-690 0096; www.panda.org) 🌱 Involved in a host of ecotourism initiatives around Mondulkiri and runs its own set of tours north of Sen Monorom in the Phnom Prich Wildlife Sanctuary and Mondulkiri Protected Forest.

## 🛏 Sleeping

Hot water is a nice bonus in chilly Mondulkiri, but it usually costs a little more. Places without hot-water showers can usually provide flasks of boiling water for bathing. There is rarely need for air-conditioning in this neck of the woods. The Elephant Valley Project (p298) offers an alternative lodging experience in the jungle

★**Nature Lodge** GUESTHOUSE $
(☑012 230272; www.naturelodgecambodia.com; r US$10-30; 🐕) Sprawling across a windswept hilltop near town are 30 solid wood bungalows with private porches, hot showers and mosquito nets. Among them are incredible Swiss Family Robinson–style chalets with sunken beds and ante-rooms. The magnificent restaurant has comfy nooks, a pool table and an enviable bar where guests chill out and swap travel tales.

Trek-fuelling burgers and pasta are the speciality, plus plenty of vegetarian options. An array of tours are neatly outlined on the menu, including the affiliated Mondulkiri Sanctuary elephant experience.

**Indigenous Peoples Lodge** BUNGALOW $
(☑012 317368; indigenouspeopleslodge@gmail. com; r US$7-20; @🐕) Run by a Bunong family, this is a great place to stay with a whole range of accommodation set in minority houses, including a traditional thatched Bunong house with an upgrade or two. The cheapest rooms involve a share bathroom, but are good value. Perks include free internet and free drop-offs in town.

**Phanyro Guesthouse** GUESTHOUSE $
(☑017 770867; r US$8-12; 🐕) This is a favourite with visiting volunteers and NGOs, offering a clutch of tasteful cottages perched on a ridge overlooking the river valley. The rooms fail to exploit the views, but are well looked after and have hot water.

**Tree Lodge** BUNGALOWS $

(🕿 097 723 4177; www.treelodgecambodia.com; r US$5-15; 🛜) Basic A-frame huts made from native materials extend in perfect linear formation down a hill at the back; there are also some smarter new bungalows. Hang out at the restaurant, where hammocks and tasty Khmer food await. The young family in charge are very welcoming and can help with tour arrangements.

**Happy Elephant** GUESTHOUSE $

(🕿 097 616 4011; www.mondulkiri-elephant.com; dm US$2, r US$5-8; 🛜🐾) French-Khmer couple Vivi and Mot are your hosts with the most at this backpacker pad, which features sturdy cold-water bungalows on a hill behind the Phat Gecko bar-restaurant. They also offer tours and treks for those without a game plan.

## WALKING WITH ELEPHANTS

For an original elephant experience, visit the **Elephant Valley Project** (EVP; 🖉 099 696041; www.elephantvalleyproject.org; ⊘ Mon-Fri). The project entices local mahouts to bring their overworked or injured elephants to this 1600-hectare sanctuary. It's very popular, so make sure you book well ahead. You can visit for a whole (US$85) or half day (US$55). It does not take overnight visitors on Friday and Saturday nights and is not open to day visitors on Saturday and Sunday.

A Briton with a contagious passion for elephants, project founder Jack Highwood is on a mission to improve the lot of Mondulkiri's working elephants – the EVP is a place where 'elephants get to be elephants again'. While Bunong tradition calls for giving elephants a certain amount of down time, Highwood says that economic incentives to overwork elephants prove too great for the impoverished mahouts of Mondulkiri. In addition to toting tourists around on their backs, elephants are hired to haul around anything and everything, including illegally cut timber. 'In Mondulkiri, the elephant is basically seen as a cheap tractor', he says.

Most tour companies in Mondulkiri stress that their tours employ only humanely treated elephants. Highwood commends this, but says it's the exception rather than the rule. 'Mondulkiri's remaining 48 elephants are often in a highly stressed state because there are just not enough to go around', he says. 'They are generally too old to work and made to do things they aren't meant to be doing.'

Enter the EVP. Mahouts who bring their elephants here are paid a competitive working wage to retire their elephants full-time to the forest and ecotourism. Mahouts continue to work with their elephants, feeding and caring for them and making sure they are as content as possible. The elephants, for their part, can spend their days blasting through the forest in search of food and hanging out by the river spraying mud on one another.

Visitors are not allowed to ride the elephants here. Instead, you simply walk through the forest with them and observe them in their element. In the process you learn a lot about not only elephant behaviour but also Bunong culture and forest ecology. Other project components include funding forestry protection for wild elephants, health care and other support for Bunong communities in the project area in exchange for use of the forest – and, most importantly, health and veterinary care for all the elephants in Mondulkiri, not just those resident in the valley. The Wildlife Conservation Society lauds the EVP for helping to protect the eastern reaches of the Seima Protected Forest.

The overnight options include a stay in exquisite bungalows tucked into the jungle on a ridge overlooking the valley. A two-day package in dorm-style accommodation costs US$125, while private bungalows cost US$145. Longer stays of three days in the dorm/ bungalow (US$235/265) and five days (US$405/455) are also available. Prices include full board.

Access to the site is tightly controlled, so don't show up unannounced as there are free-range elephants wandering around. It's popular so book well in advance before your arrival in Mondulkiri. The maximum number of day-trippers allowed per day is 12.

If you are in Mondulkiri at the weekend, you may want to consider an alternative elephant experience, such as visiting a community-owned elephant in the villages of Putang or Phulung and watching the elephants forage in the forest, as promoted by the Green House (p297) and its Elephant Community Program.

### Sovannkiri Guesthouse
HOSTEL $

(☑ 097 474 4528; dm US$3; r US$5-8) Run by a Tasmanian-Khmer couple, this guesthouse was on the move at the time of writing – so will be bigger and better by the time you read this. It offers clean, affordable rooms and the big dorm beds can sleep two. The popular restaurant has great Western food in town, reliable Khmer food and an attached bar.

### Avocado Guesthouse
GUESTHOUSE $

(☑ 011 803884; avocado-guest-house@gmail.com; r US$10-25; ☎) A smart new guesthouse near the market, the rooms here are some of best equipped in town for this sort of money. Rooms are US$5 cheaper if you forsake the air-con, a wise move in the cooler months of November to February. There's a small cafe downstairs.

### Long Vibol Guesthouse
GUESTHOUSE $

(☑ 012 589958; www.longvibol.com; r US$8-25; ☎) An attractive wooden resort set amid a lush garden just outside the centre. The 20 rooms are smallish but well-appointed. Tour guide legend Vibol retired from trekking and is the mayor of Sen Monorom. His old tours are still available with new guides.

### Green House Guesthouse
GUESTHOUSE $

(Boran Sortha Guesthouse; ☑ 017 905 659; r US$5-20; ❄☎) Partnered with the tour company of the same name, here you'll find a wide range of rooms from singles with cold water right through to a two-bedroom family suite with air-con. It's also confusingly known as the Boran Southa Guesthouse.

### Pech Kiri Motel
HOTEL $

(☑ 012 932102; pichkiri@gmail.com; r US$8-30; ❄☎) Once upon a time, this was the only game in town, and it's still going strong under the lively direction of Madame Deu. Cheap rooms are near the front, while more opulent new hotel rooms are at the back.

### Elephant Hill Resort
HOTEL $$

(☑ 016 510520; www.elephanthillresort.com; r US$60-80) Perhaps inspired by their neighbours at Mayura Hill, the rooms here are set in spacious villas that double as suites. Each villa includes a lounge, a bedroom and an indulgent *two* bathrooms. It's a good option for families looking for a comfortable mid-range option.

### ★ Mayura Hill Hotel & Resort
HOTEL $$$

(☑ 077 980980; www.mayurahillresort.com; r incl breakfast US$100-125, ste incl breakfast US$150; ❄☎✉) Setting a new standard for lodgings in Mondulkiri, Mayura Hill is a lovely place to stay for those with the budget. The 14 villa rooms are tastefully appointed with woods and silks and the family villa includes a bunk for the children. Facilities include a swimming pool and a five-a-side football pitch! The restaurant is most sophisticated in town.

## 🍴 Eating & Drinking

Most of the guesthouses here have restaurants, the most noteworthy of which are Nature Lodge, Sovannkiri Guesthouse and Mayura Hill.

### Hefalump Cafe
CAFE $

(cakes US$1-3; ⊙7am-6pm Mon-Fri, 9am-4pm Sun; ☎) 🌿 A collaboration of various NGOs and conservation groups in town, this cafe doubles as a training centre for Bunong people in hospitality. Local coffee or Lavazza, a range of teas, and some delicious homemade cakes make this a great spot to plan your adventures over a cuppa.

### Coffee Plantation Resort
CAMBODIAN $

(www.chormkacafe.com; mains US$2.50-7; ⊙7am-9pm; ☎) As the name suggests, it's set on the grounds of an extensive coffee plantation, but offers some excellent local flavours, as well as the homegrown coffee. The *banh chaeuv* savoury pancakes are a wholesome meal for just US$2.50; there's also delicious honey-roasted chicken.

### Khmer Kitchen
CAMBODIAN $

(mains US$2-4; ⊙6am-10pm; ☎) This unassuming street-side eatery whips up some of the most flavoursome Khmer food in the hills. The *kari saik trey* (fish coconut curry) and other curries are particularly noteworthy, plus they also offer a smattering of international dishes.

### Green House Restaurant & Bar
INTERNATIONAL $

(mains US$1.50-3.50; ⊙7am-11pm; ☎) As well as internet access and tour information on the menu, Green House is a popular place for inexpensive Khmer and Western dishes. It also doubles as bar by night with cheap beer and cheeky cocktails set to a soundtrack of ambient reggae beats.

### Cafe Phka
BAKERY

(dishes US$1.50-5) Taught the art of baking by some Swedish residents in Sen Monorom, this is the source of the delicious cakes that turn up in the Hefalump Cafe each day. Try

> **DON'T MISS**
>
> ## MAYURA ZIPLINE AT BOU SRAA FALLS
>
> The new **Mayura Zipline** (☑ 088 888 8629; Bou Sraa Falls; US$69) is an adrenaline rush in the extreme, as the longest 300m-line passes right over the top of Bou Sraa Falls. The zipline course starts on the far bank of the river; there are a total of six lines to navigate, plus a suspension bridge. The first four zips are warm-ups for the high-speed flight over the waterfall; the course finishes with a short tandem line for couples or new friends.
>
> It's a shorter, faster course than Flight of the Gibbon Angkor (p98), which is reflected in the pricing. It takes around one hour or so to navigate for smaller groups. While it doesn't have gibbons, it does have a bird's eye view of Bou Sraa – which is spectacular. Contact guesthouses and hotels for advance bookings or just show up at the new information centre at the falls. Discounts are sometimes available on the price.

carrot cake or banana and cinnamon cake, or go healthy with a sandwich or salad first. It has a nice garden setting by a small stream.

**Mondulkiri Pizza**                          PIZZA $
(☑ 097 522 2219; small/large pizza US$5/10; ⊘ 10am-10pm) The big electric oven here churns out the best pizzas in the hills. Staff can also deliver to your door if you're feeling lazy after a long trek.

**Chilli on the Rocks**                          BAR
Sleepy Sen Monorom has a real bar at long last. Run by a friendly Swedish couple, there is cheap beer, strong cocktails and a menu of international bites, including a tasty tapas platter to go with the drinks. Closing hours are flexible, depending on the crowd.

## ℹ Information

The leading guesthouses in town are also good sources of tourist information.
**Acleda Bank** (NH76; ⊘ 8.30am-3.30pm, ATM 24hr) Changes major currencies and has a Visa-only ATM.
**Hefalump Cafe** (⊘ 7am-6pm Mon-Fri, 9am-4pm Sun) This NGO-run cafe doubles as a 'drop-in centre' for Bunong people and is the best source of information on sustainable tourism in Mondulkiri Province, including the Elephant Valley Project, the Seima Protected Forest and responsible tours to Bunong communities.

## ℹ Getting There & Away

The stretch of NH76 connecting Sen Monorom to Snuol and Phnom Penh (370km) is in fantastic shape and passes through large tracts of protected forest. Hardcore dirt bikers may still prefer the old French road, known as the 'King's Highway', that heads east from Kao Seima, which runs roughly parallel to NH76 and pops out near Andong Kroloeng, about 25km from Sen Monorom.

**Phnom Penh Sorya** (☑ 097 723 4177; www.ppsoryatransport.com) runs a 7.30am bus to Phnom Penh (35,000r, eight hours). Kim Seng Express runs comfortable minivans (US$11) that do the trip in five hours, with six departures each day between 7am and 2pm. Virak-Buntham also operates a minibus to Phnom Penh (US$12), with departures at 7.15am and 1.30pm.

Vehicles to Phnom Penh no longer go via Kompong Cham, but take a new shortcut across Prey Veng Province. Any advertised trip to Siem Reap usually involves a change of vehicle in Soung.

Local minibuses (departing from the taxi park) are the way to Kratie (30,000r, four hours). Count on at least one early-morning departure and two or three departures around 12.30pm. Reserve the morning van in advance.

There are now minibuses plying the new road to Ban Lung in Ratanakiri; they cost US$8 and take about two hours.

## ℹ Getting Around

English-speaking *moto* drivers cost about US$15 to US$20 per day. Sample return trip *moto* prices for destinations around Sen Monorom are US$12 to Bou Sraa, US$10 to Dak Dam Waterfall, US$5 to Samot Cheur and US$3 for Monorom Falls.

Most guesthouses rent out motorbikes for US$6 to US$8 and a few have bicycles for US$2. Adventure Rider Asia (p296) has well-maintained 250cc dirt bikes for US$30 a day. Pick-up trucks and 4WDs can be chartered for the day; they cost about US$50 around Sen Monorom in the dry season, and more again in the wet season.

# Around Sen Monorom

## Bou Sraa Waterfall      ទឹកជ្រោះប៊ូស្រា

Plunging into the dense Cambodian jungle below, **Bou Sraa Waterfall** (admission 5000r) is one of the country's most impressive falls. Famous throughout the country, this double-drop waterfall has an upper tier of some 10m and a spectacular lower tier with a thundering 25m drop. Getting here is a 33km, one-hour journey east of Sen Monorom on a mostly sealed road.

To get to the bottom of the lower falls, cross the bridge over the river and follow a path to a precipitous staircase that continues to the bottom; it takes about 15 minutes to get down. The snack stalls and sellers lining the path to the bottom of the main falls are to relocate to a purpose-built dining and market area under the management of the Mayura Zipline team, including attractive wooden picnic pavilions for dining and a more sophisticated range of dishes than is currently on offer.

## Other Waterfalls

Other popular waterfalls in Mondulkiri include **Romanear Waterfall** (ទឹកធ្លាក់រមនា), 18km southeast of Sen Monorom, and **Dak Dam Waterfall** (ទឹកជ្រោះដាក់ដាំ), 25km southeast of Sen Monorom. Both are very difficult to find without assistance, so it's best to take a *moto* driver or local guide. Romanear is a low, wide waterfall with some convenient swimming holes. Dak Dam is similar to the Monorom Falls, albeit with

a greater volume of water. The waterfall is several kilometres beyond the Bunong village of Dak Dam and locals are able to lead the way if you can make yourself understood.

There is also a second Romanear Waterfall, known rather originally as **Romanear II** (ទឹកធ្លាក់រមនាពីរ), which is near the main road between Sen Monorom and Snuol. It's a small waterfall with a pretty jungle setting.

## Bunong Villages

Several Bunong villages around Sen Monorom make for popular excursions, although the frequently visited villages that appear on tourist maps have assimilated into modern society. In general, the further out you go, the less exposed the village. Trips to Bunong villages can often be combined with waterfalls or elephant treks. Each guesthouse has a preferred village to send travellers to, which is a great way to spread the wealth.

# Seima Protected Forest

កំបន់ការពារវ័ព្រឈើកែវសីមា

The 3000-sq-km Seima Protected Forest may host the country's greatest treasure trove of

---

### MONKEY BUSINESS IN MONDULKIRI

A recent Wildlife Conservation Society study estimated populations of 20,600 black-shanked doucs and more than 1000 yellow-cheeked crested gibbons in Seima Protected Forest, the world's largest known populations of both species. Thanks to an new project supported by the Sam Veasna Center (SVC) in the Bunong village of Andong Kraloeng, Jahoo Gibbon Camp is offering treks into the wild to spot these primates, thus providing local villagers with an incentive to conserve the endangered primates and their habitat by earning a sustainable income.

Treks wind their way through mixed evergreen forest and waterfalls and offer an excellent chance of spotting other species such as doucs and macaques, while viewing the tracks of more elusive species such as bear, gaur (wild cattle) and elephant. There is also an enormous diversity of birdlife, including the spectacular giant hornbill. Registered guides accompany visitors together with local Bunong guides to identify the trails.

A conservation contribution is included in the cost of the trip, which supports community development projects; an additional contribution is paid by each visitor and by SVC if doucs and/or gibbons are spotted, providing a direct incentive for the village to protect these rare wildlife species. This is a new project and price of tours are dependent on transport and group size: sample prices are around $80 per person for a one-day tour, or US$150 for an overnight tour at a rustic tented camp known as the Jahoo Gibbon Camp, including guides and food.

For information and booking contact the Sam Veasna Center (p297) in Sen Monorom. The Jahoo Gibbon Camp lies within the protected forest near the highway, just 25km southwest of there. Access is relatively easy in the dry season, but a bit harder in the wet season.

## MONDULKIRI PROTECTED FOREST: THE AFRICAN EXPERIENCE IN CAMBODIA

Before the civil war, the grasslands of northern Mondulkiri were home to huge herds of gaur, banteng and wild buffalo. Visitors who witnessed their annual migrations compared the experience to Africa's Serengeti and its annual wildebeest migrations. Sadly, like Uganda and other African countries, thousands of animals were killed (and are still killed) for bush meat. WWF (p297) has been working hard to return this area to its former glory through conservation initiatives in the Mondulkiri Protected Forest, one of the largest protected areas in Cambodia, which provides a home to leopards, bears, langurs, gibbons, wild cows and rare bird life (tigers have not been spotted since 2007). During our most recent visit, we saw several herds of banteng, a rare type of wild cow.

Ecotourism is part of the mix, but several initiatives have been scrapped due to the remoteness of the location. Another problem is that many of the cats, bears and other exotic prowlers that patrol the area are more elusive than banteng. Check with the WWF to find out the latest on tours into this area.

mammalian wildlife. Besides unprecedented numbers of black-shanked doucs and yellow-cheeked crested gibbons, an estimated 150 wild elephants – accounting for more than half of the total population in Cambodia – roam the park, along with bears and seven species of cat. The bird life is also impressive, and the jungle, which is lusher and denser than the dry forest in eastern Mondulkiri, has been relatively well preserved.

The Wildlife Conservation Society (WCS; www.wcscambodia.com) supports the government's Forestry Administration to manage the forest, and there is a range of ecotourism enterprises in development, including douc and gibbon-spotting in Andong Kroloeng. WCS' partner and birdwatching specialist **Sam Veasna Center** (☑ 012 520828; www.samveasna.org) runs birdwatching trips in Seima, not far from Kao Seima, with highly trained guides for around US$100 per person per day; there's always a flat US$30 per person conservation fee. Guests usually opt to sleep in Sen Monorom.

For the latest developments on tours in the park contact the Hefalump Cafe (p300) in Sen Monorom.

The road to Sen Monorom passes right through Seima Protected Forest, so keep an eye out for monkeys if driving through.

# Koh Nhek                    កោះញែក
☑ 073 / POP 6000

The final frontier as far as Mondulkiri goes, this village in the far north of the province is a strategic place on the overland route between Sen Monorom and Ratanakiri Province. This is traditionally where the road from Sen Monorom ended and the cattle track to Lumphat (in Ratanankiri) began. Now it's a rest stop on the new Mondulkiri–Ratanakiri highway, with several guesthouses and restaurants.

As well as making it easier for travellers to get from Mondulkiri to Ban Lung, the new road should provide a little economic boost to Koh Nhek; a new branch of Acleda Bank (with no ATM) here is a sign of changing times.

The best accommodation here is the **Phnom Kroal Guesthouse** (☑ 015 779799; penyon@gmail.com; bungalows US$15), on the road north to Ratanakiri. Rooms are set in spacious bungalows with tasteful furnishings and a large bathroom, making the price an absolute giveaway. **Sovankiri Guesthouse** (☑ 099 367000; r US$10-13) is another central option with some bungalows out the back.

**Ly Sochea Restaurant** (mains 6000-15,000r) is opposite Acleda Bank and offers some tasty Khmer fare. There is no menu as such, but the owners will invite you into the kitchen to point at their well-organised ingredients.

# Understand Cambodia

# Cambodia Today

**The political landscape shifted dramatically in the 2013 election, with major opposition gains adding up to some interesting times for Cambodia. The economy continues to grow at a dramatic pace, albeit from what was 'Year Zero' just a few decades ago, but many observers are beginning to question at what cost to the delicate environment.**

## Best on Film

**The Killing Fields** (1984) This definitive film on the Khmer Rouge period in Cambodia tells the story of American journalist Sydney Schanberg and Cambodian photographer Dith Pran during and after the war.

**Apocalypse Now** (1979) In Francis Ford Coppola's masterpiece, a renegade colonel, played by Marlon Brando, goes AWOL in Cambodia. Martin Sheen plays a young soldier sent to bring him back, and the ensuing encounter makes for a powerful indictment of war.

**The Last Reel** (2014) This award-winning homegrown Cambodian film explores the impact of Cambodia's dark past on the next generation.

## Best in Print

**Hun Sen's Cambodia** (Sebastian Strangio) A no-holds-barred look at contemporary Cambodia and the rule of Prime Minister Hun Sen.

**The Gate** (François Bizot) Bizot was kidnapped by the Khmer Rouge, and later held by them in the French embassy.

**Voices from S-21** (David Chandler) A study of the Khmer Rouge's interrogation and torture centre.

**Cambodia's Curse** (Joel Brinkley) A Pulitzer Prize–winning journalist pulls no punches in his criticism of the government and donors alike.

## Politics

The Cambodian People's Party (CPP) has dominated the politics of Cambodia since 1979 when it was installed in power by the Vietnamese. Party and state are intertwined and the CPP leadership has been making plans for the future with dynastic alliances between its offspring.

However, this control was shaken in the last election when the united opposition was able to make significant gains. Long-standing opposition leader Sam Rainsy joined with Human Rights Party leader Kem Sokha to launch the Cambodia National Rescue Party (CNRP). While official results from the National Election Commission (NEC) confirmed a CPP victory, official opposition counts suggested the CNRP may have actually won the popular vote by a slight majority. As a result the CNRP boycotted the National Assembly and refused to take its seats.

Following months of demonstrations and political wranglings, the opposition ended its boycott. Since that time, both sides have agreed to support a 'culture of dialogue', which means promoting conversation over criticism. However, heated topics remain, including the shared border with Vietnam and land reform. When it comes to land issues, it is ironic that the former communist, Hun Sen, is backing the elite tycoons, and the ex-banker, Sam Rainsy, is backing the masses with a land-redistribution scheme. Such is Cambodia, an enigmatic land of confusion and contradictions.

Huge geopolitical forces are at play in the region with China's push into the South China Sea. Cambodia finds itself caught in the middle of a simmering conflict between its two closest allies, China and Vietnam, and cannot please both; it has already alienated some of its

Asean partners by appearing to kowtow to China. How long can Cambodia walk the geopolitical tightrope without falling off?

## Economy

Badly traumatised by decades of conflict, Cambodia's economy was long a gecko amid the neighbouring dragons. This has slowly started to change, as the economy has been liberalised and investors are circling to take advantage of the new opportunities.

The government, long shunned by international big business, is keen to benefit from these newfound opportunities. China has come to the table to play for big stakes, and is now annually pledging as much as all the other international donors put together, with no burdensome strings attached.

Aid was long the mainstay of the Cambodian economy, and NGOs have done a lot to force important sociopolitical issues onto the agenda. However, Cambodia remains one of Asia's poorest countries and income is desperately low for many families. The official minimum wage is only US$140 per month and there have recently been regular demonstrations and strikes for higher wages in the garment sector.

## Land Concessions Versus Environment

Cambodia's pristine environment may be a big draw for adventurous ecotourists, but much of it is currently under threat. Ancient forests are being razed to make way for plantations, rivers are being sized up for major hydroelectric power plants and the South Coast is being explored by leading oil companies. Places like the Cardamom Mountains are in the front line, and it remains to be seen whether the environmentalists or the economists will win the debate.

Several hydroelectric power plants have been built by the Chinese in the Cardamom Mountains in recent years and a controversial scheme to develop a plant in the remote Areng Valley is still on the table. This is an area of original forest and a habitat for rare species like the Siamese crocodile and the dragonfish. All this adds up to an ever-stronger economy, but it's unlikely to encourage the ecotourism that is just starting to take off.

## Media

The governing CPP controls most of the national television stations, radio stations and newspapers. Opposition demonstrations or antigovernment activities are rarely reported via official channels. However, social media is plugging the gap and a new generation of young Cambodians are avid Facebook and YouTube users. With opposition support officially hovering around the 50% mark, some of the official media may need to change its tune to remain in touch with the popular mood.

POPULATION: **16 MILLION**

LIFE EXPECTANCY: **65 YRS**

INFANT MORTALITY: **45 PER 1000 BIRTHS**

GDP: **US$16.71 BILLION (2014)**

ADULT LITERACY RATE: **78%**

### if Cambodia were 100 people

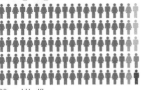

90 would be Khmer
5 would be of Vietnamese origin
3 would be Cham
1 would be of Chinese origin
1 would be an ethnic minority

### origin of visitors (%)

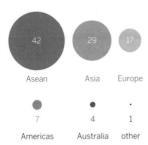

42 Asean
29 Asia
17 Europe
7 Americas
4 Australia
1 other

### population per sq km

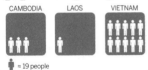

CAMBODIA    LAOS    VIETNAM

≈ 19 people

# History

'The good, the bad and the ugly' is a simple way to sum up Cambodian history. Things were good in the early years, culminating in the vast Angkor empire, unrivalled in the region during four centuries of dominance. Then the bad set in, from the 13th century, as ascendant neighbours steadily chipped away at Cambodian territory. In the 20th century it turned downright ugly, as a brutal civil war culminated in the genocidal rule of the Khmer Rouge (1975–79), from which Cambodia is still recovering.

## The Origin of the Khmers

Like many legends, the one about the origin of Cambodia is historically opaque, but it does say something about the cultural forces that brought Cambodia into existence, in particular its relationship with its great subcontinental neighbour, India. Cambodia's religious, royal and written traditions stemmed from India and began to coalesce as a cultural entity in their own right between the 1st and 5th centuries AD.

Very little is known about prehistoric Cambodia. Much of the southeast was a vast, shallow gulf that was progressively silted up by the mouths of the Mekong, leaving pancake-flat, mineral-rich land ideal for farming. Evidence of cave-dwellers has been found in the northwest of Cambodia, and carbon dating on ceramic pots found in the area shows that they were made around 4200 BC. Examinations of bones dating back to around 1500 BC suggest that the people living in Cambodia at that time resembled the Cambodians of today. Early Chinese records report that the Cambodians were 'ugly' and 'dark' and went about naked. A healthy dose of scepticism may be required, however, when reading the reports of imperial China concerning its 'barbarian' neighbours.

## The Early Cambodian Kingdoms

Cambodian might didn't begin and end with Angkor. There were a number of powerful kingdoms present in this area before the 9th century.

From the 1st century AD, the Indianisation of Cambodia occurred through trading settlements that sprang up on the coastline of what is now southern Vietnam, but was then inhabited by the Khmers. These

Cambodia's Funan-period trading port of Oc-Eo, now located in Vietnam's Mekong Delta, was a major commercial crossroads between Asia and Europe, and archaeologists there have unearthed Roman coins and Persian pottery.

| TIMELINE | 4200 BC | AD 100 | 245 |
|---|---|---|---|
| | Cave-dwellers capable of making pots inhabit caves around Laang Spean; archaeological evidence suggests their vessels were similar to those still made in Cambodia today. | The religions, language and sculpture styles of India start to take root in Cambodia with the arrival of Indian traders and holy men. | The Chinese Wei emperor sends a mission to the countries of the Mekong region and is told that a barbarous but rich country called Funan exists in the Delta region. |

settlements were important ports of call for boats following the trading route from the Bay of Bengal to the southern provinces of China. The largest of these nascent kingdoms was known as Funan by the Chinese, and may have existed across an area between modern Phnom Penh and the archaeological site of Oc-Eo in Kien Giang Province in southern Vietnam. Funan would have been a contemporary of Champasak in southern Laos (then known as Kuruksetra) and other lesser fiefdoms in the region.

Funan is a Chinese name and may be a transliteration of the ancient Khmer word *bnam* (mountain). Although very little is known about Funan, much has been made of its importance as an early Southeast Asian centre of power.

It is most likely that between the 1st and 8th centuries Cambodia was a collection of small states, each with its own elites who strategically intermarried and often went to war with one another. Funan was no doubt one of these states, and as a major sea port would have been pivotal in the transmission of Indian culture into the interior of Cambodia.

The little that historians do know about Funan has mostly been gleaned from Chinese sources. These report that Funan-period Cambodia (1st century to 6th century AD) embraced the worship of the Hindu deities Shiva and Vishnu and, at the same time, Buddhism. The *linga* (phallic totem) appears to have been the focus of ritual and an emblem of kingly might, a feature that was to evolve further in the Angkorian cult of the god-king. The people practised primitive irrigation, which enabled successful cultivation of rice, and traded raw commodities such as spices and precious stones with China and India.

From the 6th century, Cambodia's population gradually concentrated along the Mekong and Tonlé Sap Rivers, where the majority of people remain today. The move may have been related to the development of wet-rice agriculture. Between the 6th and 8th centuries, Cambodia was a collection of competing kingdoms, ruled by autocratic kings who legitimised their rule through hierarchical caste concepts borrowed from India.

India wasn't the only power to have a major cultural impact on Cambodia. The island of Java was also influential, colonising part of 'water Chenla' in the 8th century.

Cambodia's turbulent past is uncovered in a series of articles, oral histories and photos on an excellent website called Beauty and Darkness: Cambodia in Modern History. Find it at www.mekong.net/cambodia.

HISTORY THE EARLY CAMBODIAN KINGDOMS

## THE LEGEND OF KAUNDINYA & THE NAGA PRINCESS

Cambodia came into being, so the legend says, through the union of a princess and a foreigner. The foreigner was an Indian Brahman named Kaundinya and the princess was the daughter of a *naga* (mythical serpent-being) king who ruled over a watery land. One day, as Kaundinya sailed by, the princess paddled out in a boat to greet him. Kaundinya shot an arrow from his magic bow into her boat, causing the fearful princess to agree to marriage. In need of a dowry, her father drank up the waters of his land and presented them to Kaundinya to rule over. The new kingdom was named Kambuja.

| 600 | 802 | 889 | 924 |
|---|---|---|---|
| The first inscriptions are committed to stone in Cambodia in ancient Khmer, offering historians the only contemporary accounts of the pre-Angkorian period other than from Chinese sources. | Jayavarman II proclaims independence from Java in a ceremony to anoint himself a *devaraja* (god-king) on the holy mountain of Phnom Kulen, marking the birth of the Khmer Empire of Angkor. | Yasovarman I moves the capital from the ancient city of Hariharalaya (Roluos today) to the Angkor area, 16km to the northwest, and marks the location with three temple mountains. | Usurper king Jayavarman IV transfers the capital to Koh Ker and begins a mammoth building spree, but the lack of water sees the capital move back to Angkor just 20 years later. |

This era is generally referred to as the Chenla period. Like Funan, this is a Chinese term and there is little to support the idea that Chenla was a unified kingdom that held sway over all of Cambodia. Indeed, the Chinese themselves referred to 'water Chenla' and 'land Chenla'. Water Chenla was located around Angkor Borei and the temple mount of Phnom Da, near the present-day provincial capital of Takeo, and land Chenla in the upper reaches of the Mekong River and east of Tonlé Sap, around Sambor Prei Kuk, an essential stop on a chronological jaunt through Cambodia's history.

## The Rise of the Angkorian Empire

Gradually the Cambodian region was becoming more cohesive. Before long the fractured kingdoms of Cambodia would merge to become a sprawling Asian empire.

A popular place of pilgrimage for Khmers today, the sacred mountain of Phnom Kulen, northeast of Angkor, is home to an inscription that tells of Jayavarman II (r 802–50) proclaiming himself a 'universal monarch', or *devaraja* (god-king) in 802. It is believed that he may have resided in the Buddhist Shailendras' court in Java as a young man and was inspired by the great Javanese temples of Borobudur and Prambanan near present-day Yogyakarta. Upon his return to Cambodia, he instigated an uprising against Javanese control over the southern lands of Cambodia. Jayavarman II then set out to bring the country under his control through alliances and conquests, becoming the first monarch to rule most of what we call Cambodia today.

### JAYAVARMAN VII

A devout follower of Mahayana Buddhism, Jayavarman VII (r 1181–1219) built the city of Angkor Thom and many other massive monuments. Indeed, many of the temples visited around Angkor today were constructed during Jayavarman VII's reign. However, Jayavarman VII is a figure of many contradictions. The bas-reliefs of the Bayon depict him presiding over battles of terrible ferocity, while statues of the king depict a meditative, otherworldly aspect. His program of temple construction and other public works was carried out in great haste, no doubt bringing enormous hardship to the labourers who provided the muscle, and thus accelerating the decline of the empire. He was partly driven by a desire to legitimise his rule, as there may have been other contenders closer to the royal bloodline, and partly by the need to introduce a new religion to a population predominantly Hindu in faith. However, in many ways he was also Cambodia's first progressive leader, proclaiming the population equal, abolishing castes and embarking on a program of school, hospital and road building.

| 1002 | 1112 | 1152 | 1177 |
|---|---|---|---|
| Suryavarman I comes to power and expands the extent of the kingdom by annexing the Buddhist kingdom of Louvo (known as Lopburi in modern-day Thailand). He also increases trade links with the outside world. | Suryavarman II commences the construction of Angkor Wat, the mother of all temples, dedicated to Vishnu and designed as his funerary temple. | Suryavarman II is killed in a disastrous campaign against the Dai Viet (Vietnamese), provoking this rising northern neighbour and sparking centuries of conflict between the two countries. | The Chams launch a surprise attack on Angkor by sailing up the Tonlé Sap. They defeat the powerful Khmers and occupy the capital for four years. |

Jayavarman II was the first of a long succession of kings who presided over the rise and fall of the greatest empire mainland Southeast Asia has ever seen, one that was to bequeath the stunning legacy of Angkor. The key to the meteoric rise of Angkor was a mastery of water and an elaborate hydraulic system that allowed the ancient Khmers to tame the elements. The first records of the massive irrigation works that supported the population of Angkor date to the reign of Indravarman I (r 877–89), who built the *baray* (reservoir) of Indratataka. His rule also marks the flourishing of Angkorian art, with the building of temples in the Roluos area, notably Bakong.

By the turn of the 11th century, the kingdom of Angkor was losing control of its territories. Suryavarman I (r 1002–49), a usurper, moved into the power vacuum and, like Jayavarman II two centuries before, re-unified the kingdom through war and alliances, stretching the frontiers of the empire. A pattern was beginning to emerge, which was repeated throughout the Angkorian period: dislocation and turmoil, followed by reunification and further expansion under a powerful king. Architecturally, the most productive periods occurred after times of turmoil, indicating that newly incumbent monarchs felt the need to celebrate, even legitimise, their rule with massive building projects.

By 1066 Angkor was again being riven by conflict, becoming the focus of rival bids for power. It was not until the accession of Suryavarman II (r 1112–52) that the kingdom was again unified. Suryavarman II embarked on another phase of expansion, waging costly wars in Vietnam and the region of central Vietnam known as Champa. He is immortalised as the king who, in his devotion to the Hindu deity Vishnu, commissioned the majestic temple of Angkor Wat. For an insight into events in this epoch, see the bas-reliefs on the southwest corridor of Angkor Wat, which depict Suryavarman II's reign.

Suryavarman II had brought Champa to heel and reduced it to vassal status, but the Chams struck back in 1177 with a naval expedition up the Mekong and into Tonlé Sap Lake. They took the city of Angkor by surprise and put King Dharanindravarman II to death. The following year a cousin of Suryavarman II rallied the Khmer troops and defeated the Chams in yet another naval battle. The new leader was crowned Jayavarman VII in 1181.

## Decline & Fall of Angkor

Angkor was the epicentre of an incredible empire that held sway over much of the Mekong region, but like all empires, the sun was to eventually set.

A number of scholars have argued that decline was already on the horizon at the time Angkor Wat was built, when the Angkorian empire was at the height of its remarkable productivity. There are indications

The commercial metropolis that is now Ho Chi Minh City (Saigon) in Vietnam was, in 1600, a small Cambodian village called Prey Nokor.

| 1181 | 1219 | 1253 | 1296 |
|---|---|---|---|
| The Chams are vanquished as Jayavarman VII, the greatest king of Angkor and builder of Angkor Thom, takes the throne, changing the state religion to Mahayana Buddhism. | Jayavarman VII dies aged in his 90s, and the empire of Angkor slowly declines due to a choking irrigation network, religious conflict and the rise of powerful neighbours. | The Mongols of Kublai Khan sack the Thai kingdom of Nanchao in Yunnan, sparking an exodus southwards, which brings Thais into direct conflict with the weakening Khmer empire. | Chinese emissary Chou Ta Kuan spends one year living at Angkor and writes *The Customs of Cambodia*, the only contemporary account of life in the great Khmer capital. |

One of the definitive guides to Angkor is *A Guide to the Angkor Monuments* by Maurice Glaize, first published in the 1940s and now out of print. Download it free at www.theangkor guide.com.

that the irrigation network was overworked and slowly starting to silt up due to the massive deforestation that had taken place in the heavily populated areas to the north and east of Angkor. This was exacerbated by prolonged periods of drought in the 14th century, which was more recently discovered through the advanced analysis of dendrochronology, or the study of tree rings, in the Angkor area.

Massive construction projects such as Angkor Wat and Angkor Thom no doubt put an enormous strain on the royal coffers and on the thousands of slaves and common people who subsidised them in hard labour and taxes. Following the reign of Jayavarman VII, temple construction effectively ground to a halt, largely because his public works had quarried local sandstone into oblivion and left the population exhausted.

Another challenge for the later kings was religious conflict and internecine rivalries. The state religion changed back and forth several times during the twilight years of the empire, and kings spent more time engaged in iconoclasm, defacing the temples of their predecessors, than building monuments to their own achievements. From time to time this boiled over into civil war.

Angkor was also losing control over the peripheries of its empire. At the same time, the Thais were ascendant, having migrated south from Yunnan, China, to escape Kublai Khan and his Mongol hordes. The Thais, first from Sukothai, later Ayuthaya, grew in strength and made repeated incursions into Angkor before finally sacking the city in 1431 and making off with thousands of intellectuals, artisans and dancers from the royal court. During this period, perhaps drawn by the opportunities for sea trade with China and fearful of the increasingly bellicose Thais, the Khmer elite began to migrate to the Phnom Penh area. The capital shifted several times over the centuries but eventually settled in present-day Phnom Penh.

From 1500 until the arrival of the French in 1863, Cambodia was ruled by a series of weak kings beset by dynastic rivalries. In the face of such intrigue, they sought the protection – granted, of course, at a price – of either Thailand or Vietnam. In the 17th century, the Nguyen lords of southern Vietnam came to the rescue of the Cambodian king in return for settlement rights in the Mekong Delta region. The Khmers still refer to this region as Kampuchea Krom (Lower Cambodia), even though it is well and truly populated by the Vietnamese today.

In the west, the Thais controlled the provinces of Battambang and Siem Reap from 1794 and held influence over the Cambodian royal family. Indeed, one king was crowned in Bangkok and placed on the throne at Udong with the help of the Thai army. That Cambodia survived through the 18th century as a distinct entity is due to the preoccupations of its neighbours: while the Thais were expending their energy and resources fighting the Burmese, the Vietnamese were wholly absorbed by internal

Chinese emissary Chou Ta Kuan lived in Angkor for a year in 1296, and his observations have been republished as *The Customs of Cambodia* (2000), a fascinating insight into life during the height of the empire.

| 1353 | 1431 | 1516 | 1594 |
|---|---|---|---|
| Lao prince Chao Fa Ngum ends his Angkor exile and is sponsored by his Khmer father-in-law on an expedition to conquer the new Thai kingdoms, declaring himself leader of Lan Xang (Land of a Million Elephants). | The Thais sack Angkor definitively, carting off most of the royal court to Ayuthaya, including nobles, priests, dancers and artisans. | King Ang Chan I ascends the throne, defeats the Thais in a battle that gives modern-day Siem Reap its name and 'rediscovers' the great walled city of Angkor Thom on a hunting expedition. | The temporary Cambodian capital of Lovek falls when, legend says, the Siamese fire a cannon of silver coins into its bamboo defences. Soldiers cut down the bamboo to retrieve the silver, leaving the city exposed. |

strife. The pattern continued for more than two centuries, the carcass of Cambodia pulled back and forth between two powerful tigers.

# The French in Cambodia

The era of yo-yo-ing between Thai and Vietnamese masters came to a close in 1863, when French gunboats intimidated King Norodom I (r 1860–1904) into signing a treaty of protectorate. Ironically, it really was a protectorate, as Cambodia was in danger of going the way of Champa and vanishing from the map. French control of Cambodia developed as a sideshow to its interests in Vietnam, uncannily similar to the American experience a century later, and initially involved little direct interference in Cambodia's affairs. The French presence also helped keep Norodom on the throne despite the ambitions of his rebellious half-brothers.

By the 1870s, French officials in Cambodia began pressing for greater control over internal affairs. In 1884 Norodom was forced into signing a treaty that turned his country into a virtual colony, sparking a two-year rebellion that constituted the only major uprising in Cambodia before WWII. The rebellion only ended when the king was persuaded to call upon the rebel fighters to lay down their weapons in exchange for a return to the status quo.

During the following decades, senior Cambodian officials opened the door to direct French control over the day-to-day administration of the country, as they saw certain advantages in acquiescing to French power. The French maintained Norodom's court in splendour unseen since the heyday of Angkor, helping to enhance the symbolic position of the monarchy. In 1907 the French were able to pressure Thailand into returning the northwest provinces of Battambang, Siem Reap and Preah Vihear in return for concessions of Lao territory to the Thais. This meant Angkor came under Cambodian control for the first time in more than a century.

The French did very little to encourage education in Cambodia, and by the end of WWII, after 70 years of colonial rule, there were no universities and only one high school in the whole country.

## THE NAME GAME

Cambodia has changed its name so many times over the last few decades that there are understandable grounds for confusion. To the Cambodians, their country is Kampuchea. The name is derived from the word 'Kambuja', meaning 'those born of Kambu', the mythical founder of the country. It dates back as far as the 10th century. The Portuguese 'Camboxa' and the French 'Cambodge', from which the English name 'Cambodia' is derived, are adaptations of 'Kambuja'.

It was the Khmer Rouge that insisted the outside world use the name Kampuchea. Changing the country's official English name back to Cambodia was intended as a symbolic move to distance the present government in Phnom Penh from the bitter connotations of the name Kampuchea, which Westerners associate with the Khmer Rouge regime.

| 1772 | 1834 | 1863 | 1884 |
|---|---|---|---|
| Cambodia is caught between the powerful Vietnamese and Siamese, and the latter burn Phnom Penh to the ground, another chapter in the story of inflamed tensions that persist to this day. | The Vietnamese take control of much of Cambodia during the reign of Emperor Minh Mang and begin a slow revolution to 'teach the barbarians their customs'. | The French force King Norodom I into signing a treaty of protectorate, which prevents Cambodia being wiped off the map and thus begins 90 years of French rule. | Rebellion against French rule in Cambodia erupts in response to a treaty giving French administrators wide-ranging powers. The treaty is signed under the watch of French gunboats in the Mekong River. |

During the US bombing campaign, more bombs were dropped on Cambodia than were used by all sides during WWII.

King Norodom I was succeeded by King Sisowath (r 1904–27), who was succeeded by King Monivong (r 1927–41). Upon King Monivong's death, the French governor-general of Japanese-occupied Indochina, Admiral Jean Decoux, placed 19-year-old Prince Norodom Sihanouk on the Cambodian throne. The French authorities assumed young Sihanouk would be pliable, but this proved to be a major miscalculation.

During WWII, Japanese forces occupied much of Asia, and Cambodia was no exception. However, with many in France collaborating with the occupying Germans, the Japanese were happy to let their new Vichy France allies control affairs in Cambodia. The price was conceding to Thailand (a Japanese ally of sorts) much of Battambang and Siem Reap Provinces once again, areas that weren't returned until 1947. However, after the fall of Paris in 1944 and with French policy in disarray, the Japanese were forced to take direct control of the territory by early 1945.

After WWII the French returned, making Cambodia an autonomous state within the French Union, but retaining de facto control. The immediate postwar years were marked by strife among the country's various political factions, a situation made more unstable by the Franco-Vietminh War then raging in Vietnam and Laos, which spilled over into Cambodia. The Vietnamese, as they were also to do 20 years later in the war against Lon Nol and the Americans, trained and fought with bands of Khmer Issarak (Free Khmer) against the French authorities.

## The Sihanouk Years

The postindependence period was one of peace and prosperity. It was Cambodia's golden era, a time of creativity and optimism. Phnom Penh grew in size and stature, the temples of Angkor were the leading tourist destination in Southeast Asia and Sihanouk played host to a succession of influential leaders from across the globe. However, dark clouds were circling, as the American war in Vietnam became a black hole, sucking in neighbouring countries.

For more on the incredible life and times of Norodom Sihanouk, read the biography *Prince of Light, Prince of Darkness* (1994) by Milton Osborne.

In late 1952 King Sihanouk dissolved the fledgling parliament, declared martial law and embarked on his 'royal crusade', a travelling campaign to drum up international support for his country's independence. Independence was proclaimed on 9 November 1953 and recognised by the Geneva Conference of May 1954, which ended French control of Indochina. In 1955 Sihanouk abdicated, afraid of being marginalised amid the pomp of royal ceremony. The 'royal crusader' became 'citizen Sihanouk'. He vowed never again to return to the throne. Meanwhile his father became king. It was a masterstroke that offered Sihanouk both royal authority and supreme political power. His newly established party, Sangkum Reastr Niyum (People's Socialist Community), won every

| 1907 | 1941 | 1942 | 1947 |
|---|---|---|---|
| French authorities successfully negotiate the return of the northwest provinces of Siem Reap, Battambang and Preah Vihear, which have been under Thai control since 1794. | A young King Sihanouk ascends the throne aged just 19 years old, beginning an incredible political career that will span about 70 years. | Japanese forces occupy Cambodia, leaving the administration in the hands of Vichy France officials, but fanning the flames of independence as the war draws to a close. | The provinces of Battambang, Siem Reap and Sisophon, seized by the Thais during the Japanese occupation, are returned to Cambodia. |

seat in parliament in the September 1955 elections and Sihanouk was to dominate Cambodian politics for the next 15 years.

Though he feared the Vietnamese communists, Sihanouk considered South Vietnam and Thailand – both allies of the mistrusted USA – the greatest threats to Cambodia's security, even its survival. In an attempt to fend off these many dangers, he declared Cambodia neutral and refused to accept further US aid, which had accounted for a substantial chunk of the country's military budget. He also nationalised many industries, including the rice trade, which angered many

## SIHANOUK: THE LAST OF THE GOD-KINGS

Norodom Sihanouk was a towering presence in the topsy-turvy world of Cambodian politics. A larger-than-life character of many enthusiasms and shifting political positions, amatory exploits dominated his early life. Later he became the prince who stage-managed the close of French colonialism, led Cambodia during its golden years, was imprisoned by the Khmer Rouge and, from privileged exile, finally returned triumphant as king. He was many things to many people, but whatever else he was, he proved himself a survivor.

Sihanouk, born in 1922, was not an obvious contender for the throne, as he was from the Norodom branch of the royal family. He was crowned in 1941, at just 19, with his education incomplete. In 1955 Sihanouk abdicated and turned his attention to politics, his party winning every seat in parliament that year. By the mid-1960s Sihanouk had been calling the shots in Cambodia for a decade.

The conventional wisdom was that 'Sihanouk is Cambodia', his leadership the key to national success. However, as the country was inexorably drawn into the American war in Vietnam and government troops battled with a leftist insurgency in the countryside, Sihanouk was increasingly seen as a liability.

On 18 March 1970, the National Assembly voted to remove Sihanouk from office. He went into exile in Beijing and joined the communists. Following the Khmer Rouge victory on 17 April 1975, Sihanouk returned to Cambodia as head of the new state of Democratic Kampuchea. He resigned after less than a year and was confined to the Royal Palace as a prisoner of the Khmer Rouge. He remained there until early 1979 when, on the eve of the Vietnamese invasion, he was flown back to Beijing.

Sihanouk never quite gave up wanting to be everything for Cambodia: international statesman, general, president, film director and man of the people. On 24 September 1993, after 38 years in politics, he settled once more for the role of king. On 7 October 2004 he once again abdicated, and his son King Sihamoni ascended the throne. However, Sihanouk's place in history is assured, the last in a long line of Angkor's god-kings.

Norodom Sihanouk passed away on 15 October 2012 in Beijing and his body was flown back to Cambodia a few days later. More than a million Cambodians lined the streets from the airport to the Royal Palace and his body was laid in state for 100 days before an elaborate state funeral.

| 1953 | 1955 | 1962 | 1963 |
|---|---|---|---|
| Sihanouk's royal crusade for independence succeeds and Cambodia goes it alone without the French on 9 November, ushering in a new era of optimism. | King Sihanouk abdicates the throne to enter a career in politics; he founds the Sangkum Reastr Niyum (People's Socialist Community) party and wins the election with ease. | The International Court rules in favour of Cambodia in the long-running dispute over the dramatic mountain temple of Preah Vihear, perched on the Dangkrek Mountains on the border with Thailand. | Pol Pot and Ieng Sary flee from Phnom Penh to the jungles of Ratanakiri. With training from the Vietnamese, they launch a guerrilla war against Sihanouk's government. |

Chinese-Cambodians. In 1965 Sihanouk, convinced that the USA had been plotting against him and his family, broke diplomatic relations with Washington and veered towards the North Vietnamese and China. In addition, he agreed to let the communists use Cambodian territory in their battle against South Vietnam and the USA. Sihanouk was taking sides, a dangerous position in a volatile region.

These moves and his socialist economic policies alienated conservative elements in Cambodian society, including the army brass and the urban elite. At the same time, left-wing Cambodians, many of them educated abroad, deeply resented his domestic policies, which stifled political debate. Compounding Sihanouk's problems was the fact that all classes were fed up with the pervasive corruption in government ranks, some of it uncomfortably close to the royal family. Although most peasants revered Sihanouk as a semidivine figure, in 1967 a rural-based rebellion broke out in Samlot, Battambang, leading him to conclude that the greatest threat to his regime came from the left. Bowing to pressure from the army, he implemented a policy of harsh repression against left-wingers.

By 1969 the conflict between the army and leftist rebels had become more serious, as the Vietnamese sought sanctuary deeper in Cambodia. Sihanouk's political position had also decidedly deteriorated – due in no small part to his obsession with film-making, which was leading him to neglect affairs of state. In March 1970, while Sihanouk was on a trip to France, General Lon Nol and Prince Sisowath Sirik Matak, Sihanouk's cousin, deposed him as chief of state, apparently with tacit US consent. Sihanouk took up residence in Beijing, where he set up a government-in-exile in alliance with an indigenous Cambodian revolutionary movement that Sihanouk had nicknamed the Khmer Rouge. This was a definitive moment in contemporary Cambodian history, as the Khmer Rouge exploited its partnership with Sihanouk to draw new recruits into its small organisation. Talk to many former Khmer Rouge fighters and they'll say that they 'went to the hills' (a euphemism for joining the Khmer Rouge) to fight for their king and knew nothing of Mao or Marxism.

Lon Nol's military press attaché was known for his colourful, even imaginative media briefings that painted a rosy picture of the increasingly desperate situation on the ground. With a name like Major Am Rong, few could take him seriously.

## Descent into Civil War

The lines were drawn for a bloody era of civil war. Sihanouk was condemned to death in absentia, a harsh move on the part of the new government that effectively ruled out any hint of compromise for the next five years. Lon Nol gave communist Vietnamese forces an ultimatum to withdraw their units within one week, which amounted to a declaration of war, as the Vietnamese did not want to return to the homeland to face the Americans.

On 30 April 1970, US and South Vietnamese forces invaded Cambodia in an effort to flush out thousands of Viet Cong and North Vietnamese

| 1964 | 1969 | 1970 | 1971 |
| --- | --- | --- | --- |
| After the US-sponsored coup against President Diem in South Vietnam, Sihanouk veers to the left, breaking diplomatic ties with the USA and nationalising the rice trade, antagonising the ethnic Chinese business community. | US President Nixon authorises the secret bombing of Cambodia, which starts with the carpet bombing of border zones, but spreads to the whole country, continuing until 1973 and killing up to 250,000 Cambodians. | Sihanouk throws in his lot with the Khmer Rouge after being overthrown by Prince Sirik Matak and military commander Lon Nol, and is sentenced to death in absentia, marking the start of a five-year civil war. | Lon Nol, leader of the Khmer Republic, launches the disastrous Chenla offensive against Vietnamese communists and their Khmer Rouge allies in Cambodia. He suffers a stroke, but struggles on as leader until 1975. |

troops who were using Cambodian bases in their war to overthrow the South Vietnamese government. As a result of the invasion, the Vietnamese communists withdrew deeper into Cambodia, further destabilising the Lon Nol government. Cambodia's tiny army never stood a chance and within the space of a few months, Vietnamese forces and their Khmer Rouge allies overran almost half the country. The ultimate humiliation came in July 1970 when the Vietnamese occupied the temples of Angkor.

In 1969 the USA launched Operation Menu, the secret bombing of suspected communist base camps in Cambodia. For the next four years, until bombing was halted by the US Congress in August 1973, huge areas of the eastern half of the country were carpet-bombed by US B-52s, killing what is believed to be many thousands of civilians and turning hundreds of thousands more into refugees. Undoubtedly, the bombing campaign helped the Khmer Rouge in their recruitment drive, as more and more peasants were losing family members to the aerial assaults. While the final, heaviest bombing in the first half of 1973 may have saved Phnom Penh from a premature fall, its ferocity also helped to harden the attitude of many Khmer Rouge cadres and may have contributed to the later brutality that characterised their rule.

Savage fighting engulfed the country, bringing misery to millions of Cambodians; many fled rural areas for the relative safety of Phnom Penh and provincial capitals. Between 1970 and 1975, several hundred thousand people died in the fighting. During these years, the Khmer Rouge came to play a dominant role in trying to overthrow the Lon Nol regime, strengthened by the support of the Vietnamese, although the Khmer Rouge leadership would vehemently deny this from 1975 onwards.

The leadership of the Khmer Rouge, including Paris-educated Pol Pot and Ieng Sary, had fled into the countryside in the 1960s to escape the summary justice then being meted out to suspected leftists by Sihanouk's security forces. They consolidated control over the movement and began to move against opponents before they took Phnom Penh. Many of the Vietnamese-trained Cambodian communists who had been based in Hanoi since the 1954 Geneva Accords returned down the Ho Chi Minh Trail to join their 'allies' in the Khmer Rouge in 1973. Many were dead by 1975, executed on the orders of the anti-Vietnamese Pol Pot faction. Likewise, many moderate Sihanouk supporters who had joined the Khmer Rouge as a show of loyalty to their fallen leader rather than a show of ideology to the radicals were victims of purges before the regime took power. This set a precedent for internal purges and mass executions that were to eventually bring the downfall of the Khmer Rouge.

It didn't take long for the Lon Nol government to become very unpopular as a result of unprecedented greed and corruption in its ranks. As the USA bankrolled the war, government and military personnel found

*To the End of Hell: One Woman's Struggle to Survive Cambodia's Khmer Rouge* is the incredible memoir of Denise Affonço, one of the only foreigners to live through the Khmer Rouge revolution, due to her marriage to a senior intellectual in the movement.

HISTORY DESCENT INTO CIVIL WAR

| 1973 | 1975 | 1977 | 1979 |
|---|---|---|---|
| Sihanouk and his wife, Monique, travel down the Ho Chi Minh Trail to visit Khmer Rouge allies at the holy mountain of Phnom Kulen near Angkor, a propaganda victory for Pol Pot. | The Khmer Rouge march into Phnom Penh on 17 April and turn the clocks back to Year Zero, evacuating the capital and turning the whole nation into a prison without walls. | The Pol Pot faction of the Khmer Rouge launches its bloodiest purge against the Eastern Zone of the country, sparking a civil war along the banks of the Mekong and drawing the Vietnamese into the battle. | Vietnamese forces liberate Cambodia from Khmer Rouge rule on 7 January 1979, just two weeks after launching the invasion, and install a friendly regime in Phnom Penh. |

The Documentation Center of Cambodia is an organisation established to document the crimes of the Khmer Rouge as a record for future generations. Its excellent website has a wealth of information about Cambodia's darkest hour. Take your time to visit www.dccam.org.

lucrative means to make a fortune, such as inventing 'phantom soldiers' and pocketing their pay, or selling weapons to the enemy. Lon Nol was widely perceived as an ineffectual leader, obsessed by superstition, fortune tellers and mystical crusades. This perception increased with his stroke in March 1971 and for the next four years his grip on reality seemed to weaken as his brother Lon Non's power grew.

Despite massive US military and economic aid, Lon Nol never succeeded in gaining the initiative against the Khmer Rouge. Large parts of the countryside fell to the rebels and many provincial capitals were cut off from Phnom Penh. Lon Nol fled the country in early April 1975, leaving Sirik Matak, who refused evacuation to the end, in charge. 'I cannot alas leave in such a cowardly fashion... I have committed only one mistake, that of believing in you, the Americans' were the words Sirik Matak poignantly penned to US ambassador John Gunther Dean. On 17 April 1975 – two weeks before the fall of Saigon (now Ho Chi Minh City) – Phnom Penh surrendered to the Khmer Rouge.

## The Khmer Rouge Revolution

Upon taking Phnom Penh, the Khmer Rouge implemented one of the most radical and brutal restructurings of a society ever attempted; its goal was a pure revolution, untainted by those that had gone before, to transform Cambodia into a peasant-dominated agrarian cooperative. Within days of the Khmer Rouge coming to power, the entire population of Phnom Penh and provincial towns, including the sick, elderly and infirm, was forced to march into the countryside and work as slaves for 12 to 15 hours a day. Disobedience of any sort often brought immediate execution. The advent of Khmer Rouge rule was proclaimed Year Zero. Currency was abolished and postal services ground to a halt. The country cut itself off from the outside world.

In the eyes of Pol Pot, the Khmer Rouge was not a unified movement but a series of factions that needed to be cleansed. This process had already begun with attacks on Vietnamese-trained Khmer Rouge and Sihanouk's supporters, but Pol Pot's initial fury upon seizing power was directed against the former regime. All of the senior government and military figures who had been associated with Lon Nol were executed within days of the takeover. Then the centre shifted its attention to the outer regions, which had been separated into geographic zones. The loyalist Southwestern Zone forces, under the control of one-legged general Ta Mok, were sent into region after region to 'purify' the population, a process that saw thousands perish.

The cleansing reached grotesque heights in the final and bloodiest purge against the powerful and independent Eastern Zone. Generally considered more moderate than other Khmer Rouge factions, the East-

| 1980 | 1982 | 1984 | 1985 |
|---|---|---|---|
| Cambodia is gripped by a terrible famine, as the dislocation of the previous few years means that no rice has been planted or harvested, and worldwide 'Save Kampuchea' appeals are launched. | Sihanouk is pressured to join the Khmer Rouge as head of the Coalition Government of Democratic Kampuchea (CGDK), a new military front against the Vietnamese-backed government in Phnom Penh. | The Vietnamese embark on a major offensive in the west of Cambodia and the Khmer Rouge and its allies are forced to retreat to refugee camps and bases inside Thailand. | There is a changing of the guard at the top and Hun Sen becomes Prime Minister of Cambodia, a title he still holds today with the Cambodian People's Party (CPP). |

ern Zone was ideologically, as well as geographically, closer to Vietnam. The Pol Pot faction consolidated the rest of the country before moving against the east from 1977 onwards. Hundreds of leaders were executed before open rebellion broke out, sparking a civil war in the east. Many Eastern Zone leaders fled to Vietnam, forming the nucleus of the government installed by the Vietnamese in January 1979. The people were defenceless and distrusted – 'Cambodian bodies with Vietnamese minds' or 'duck's arses with chicken's heads' – and were deported to the northwest with new, blue *kramas* (scarves). Had it not been for the Vietnamese invasion, all would have perished, as the blue *krama* was a secret party sign indicating an eastern enemy of the revolution.

It is still not known exactly how many Cambodians died at the hands of the Khmer Rouge during the three years, eight months and 20 days of its rule. The Vietnamese claimed three million deaths, while foreign experts long considered the number closer to one million. Yale University researchers undertaking ongoing investigations estimated that the figure was close to two million.

Hundreds of thousands of people were executed by the Khmer Rouge leadership, while hundreds of thousands more died of famine and disease. Meals consisted of little more than watery rice porridge twice a day, but were meant to sustain men, women and children through a back-breaking day in the fields. Disease stalked the work camps, malaria and dysentery striking down whole families; death was a relief for many from the horrors of life. Some zones were better than others, some leaders fairer than others, but life for the majority was one of unending misery and suffering in this 'prison without walls'.

As the centre eliminated more and more moderates, Angkar (the organisation) became the only family people needed and those who did not agree were sought out and crushed. The Khmer Rouge detached the Cambodian people from all they held dear: their families, their food, their fields and their faith. Even the peasants who had supported the revolution could no longer blindly follow such insanity. Nobody cared for the Khmer Rouge by 1978, but nobody had an ounce of strength to do anything about it...except the Vietnamese.

## Enter the Vietnamese

Relations between Cambodia and Vietnam have historically been tense, as the Vietnamese have slowly but steadily expanded southwards, encroaching on Cambodian territory. Despite the fact the two communist parties had fought together as brothers in arms, old tensions soon came to the fore.

From 1976 to 1978, the Khmer Rouge instigated a series of border clashes with Vietnam, and claimed the Mekong Delta, once part of

Journalist Henry Kamm spent many years filing reports from Cambodia in the 1970s and '90s, and his book *Cambodia: Report from a Stricken Land* is a fascinating insight into recent events.

| 1989 | 1991 | 1993 | 1994 |
|---|---|---|---|
| As the effects of President Gorbachev's *perestroika* (restructuring) begin to impact on communist allies, Vietnam feels the pinch and announces the withdrawal of its forces from Cambodia. | The Paris Peace Accords are signed, in which all parties, including the Khmer Rouge, agree to participate in free and fair elections supervised by the UN. | The pro-Sihanouk royalist party Funcinpec, under the leadership of Prince Ranariddh, wins the popular vote, but the communist CPP threatens secession in the east to muscle its way into government. | The Khmer Rouge targets foreign tourists in Cambodia, kidnapping and killing groups travelling by taxi and train to the South Coast, reinforcing Cambodia's overseas image as a dangerous country. |

the Khmer empire. Incursions into Vietnamese border provinces left hundreds of Vietnamese civilians dead. On 25 December 1978 Vietnam launched a full-scale invasion of Cambodia, toppling the Pol Pot government two weeks later. As Vietnamese tanks neared Phnom Penh, the Khmer Rouge fled westward with as many civilians as it could seize, taking refuge in the jungles and mountains along the Thai border.

The Vietnamese installed a new government led by several former Khmer Rouge officers, including current Prime Minister Hun Sen, who had defected to Vietnam in 1977. The Khmer Rouge's patrons, the Chinese communists, launched a massive reprisal raid across Vietnam's northernmost border in early 1979 in an attempt to buy their allies time. It failed and after 17 days the Chinese withdrew, their fingers badly burnt by their Vietnamese enemies. The Vietnamese then staged a show trial in Cambodia in which Pol Pot and Ieng Sary were condemned to death in absentia for their genocidal acts.

A traumatised population took to the road in search of surviving family members. Millions had been uprooted and had to walk hundreds of kilometres across the country. Rice stocks were decimated, the harvest left to wither and little rice planted, sowing the seeds for a widespread famine in 1979 and 1980.

As the conflict in Cambodia raged, Sihanouk agreed in 1982, under pressure from China, to head a military and political front opposed to the Phnom Penh government. The Sihanouk-led resistance coalition brought together – on paper, at least – Funcinpec (the French acronym for the National United Front for an Independent, Neutral, Peaceful and Cooperative Cambodia), which comprised a royalist group loyal to Sihanouk; the Khmer People's National Liberation Front, a noncommunist grouping under former prime minister Son Sann; and the Khmer Rouge, officially known as the Party of Democratic Kampuchea and by far the most powerful of the three. The crimes of the Khmer Rouge were swept aside to ensure a compromise that suited the realpolitik of the day.

For much of the 1980s Cambodia remained closed to the Western world, save for the presence of some humanitarian aid groups. Government policy was effectively under the control of the Vietnamese, so Cambodia found itself very much in the Eastern-bloc camp. The economy was in tatters for most of this period, as Cambodia, like Vietnam, suffered from the effects of a US-sponsored embargo.

In 1984 the Vietnamese overran all the major rebel camps inside Cambodia, forcing the Khmer Rouge and its allies to retreat into Thailand. From this time the Khmer Rouge and its allies engaged in guerrilla warfare aimed at demoralising its opponents. Tactics used by the Khmer Rouge included shelling government-controlled garrison towns, planting

> For the full flavour of Cambodian history, from humble beginnings in the prehistoric period through the glories of Angkor and right up to the present day, grab a copy of *The History of Cambodia* (1994), by David Chandler.

> During much of the 1980s, the second-largest concentration of Cambodians outside Phnom Penh was in the Khao-I-Dang refugee camp on the Thai border.

| 1995 | 1996 | 1997 | 1998 |
| --- | --- | --- | --- |
| Prince Norodom Sirivudh is arrested and exiled for allegedly plotting to kill Prime Minister Hun Sen, removing another potential rival from the scene. | British de-miner Christopher Howes, working in Cambodia with the Mines Advisory Group (MAG), is kidnapped by the Khmer Rouge and later killed, together with his interpreter Houn Hourth. | Second Prime Minister Hun Sen overthrows First Prime Minister Norodom Ranariddh in a military coup, referred to as 'the events of 1997' in Cambodia. | Pol Pot passes away on 15 April as Anlong Veng falls to government forces, and many observers ponder whether the timing is coincidental. |

## THE POLITICS OF DISASTER RELIEF

The Cambodian famine became a new front in the Cold War, as Washington and Moscow jostled for influence from afar. As hundreds of thousands of Cambodians fled to Thailand, a massive international famine relief effort, sponsored by the UN, was launched. The international community wanted to deliver aid across a land bridge at Poipet, while the new Vietnamese-backed Phnom Penh government wanted all supplies to come through the capital via Kompong Som (Sihanoukville) or the Mekong River. Both sides had their reasons – the new government did not want aid to fall into the hands of its Khmer Rouge enemies, while the international community didn't believe the new government had the infrastructure to distribute the aid – and both fears were right.

Some agencies distributed aid the slow way through Phnom Penh, and others set up camps in Thailand. The camps became a magnet for half of Cambodia, as many Khmers still feared the return of the Khmer Rouge or were seeking a new life overseas. The Thai military convinced the international community to distribute all aid through their channels and used this as a cloak to rebuild the shattered Khmer Rouge forces as an effective resistance against the Vietnamese. Thailand demanded that, as a condition for allowing international food aid for Cambodia to pass through its territory, food had to be supplied to the Khmer Rouge forces encamped in the Thai border region as well. Along with weaponry supplied by China, this international assistance was essential in enabling the Khmer Rouge to rebuild its military strength and fight on for another two decades.

thousands of mines in rural areas, attacking road transport, blowing up bridges, kidnapping village chiefs and targeting civilians. The Khmer Rouge also forced thousands of men, women and children living in the refugee camps it controlled to work as porters, ferrying ammunition and other supplies into Cambodia across heavily mined sections of the border.

The Vietnamese, for their part, laid the world's longest minefield, known as K-5 and stretching from the Gulf of Thailand to the Lao border, in an attempt to seal out the guerrillas. They also sent Cambodians into the forests to cut down trees on remote sections of road to prevent ambushes. Thousands died of disease and from injuries sustained from land mines. The Khmer Rouge was no longer in power, but for many the 1980s were almost as tough as the 1970s – one long struggle to survive.

Only a handful of foreigners were allowed to visit Cambodia during the Khmer Rouge period of Democratic Kampuchea. US journalist Elizabeth Becker was one who travelled there in late 1978; her book *When the War Was Over* (1986) tells her story.

## The UN Comes to Town

The arrival of Mikhail Gorbachev in the Kremlin saw the Cold War draw to a close. It was the furthest-flung Soviet allies who were cut adrift first, leaving Vietnam internationally isolated and economically crippled. In September 1989 Vietnam announced the withdrawal of all its troops from Cambodia. With the Vietnamese gone, the opposition coalition,

| 1999 | 2000 | 2002 | 2003 |
|---|---|---|---|
| Cambodia finally joins Asean after a two-year delay, taking its place among the family of Southeast Asian nations, which welcome the country back onto the world stage. | The Cambodian Freedom Fighters (CFF) launch an 'assault' on Phnom Penh. Backed by Cambodian-American dissidents, the attackers are lightly armed, poorly trained and politically inexperienced. | Cambodia holds its first ever local elections at commune level, a tentative step towards dismantling the old communist system of control and bringing grass-roots democracy to the country. | The CPP wins the election, but political infighting prevents the formation of the new government for almost a year until the old coalition with Funcinpec is revived. |

still dominated by the Khmer Rouge, launched a series of offensives, forcing the now-vulnerable government to the negotiating table.

Diplomatic efforts to end the civil war began to bear fruit in September 1990, when a peace plan was accepted by both the Phnom Penh government and the three factions of the resistance coalition. According to the plan, the Supreme National Council (SNC), a coalition of all factions, would be formed under the presidency of Sihanouk. Meanwhile the UN Transitional Authority in Cambodia (Untac) would supervise the administration of the country for two years, with the goal of free and fair elections.

Untac undoubtedly achieved some successes, but for all of these it was the failures that were to cost Cambodia dearly in the 'democratic' era. Untac was successful in pushing through many international human-rights covenants; it opened the door to a significant number of non-governmental organisations (NGOs); and, most importantly, on 25 May 1993, elections were held with an 89.6% turnout. However, the results were far from decisive. Funcinpec, led by Prince Norodom Ranariddh, took 58 seats in the National Assembly, while the Cambodian People's Party (CPP), which represented the previous communist government, took 51 seats. The CPP had lost the election, but senior leaders threatened a secession of the eastern provinces of the country. As a result, Cambodia ended up with two prime ministers: Norodom Ranariddh as first prime minister, and Hun Sen as second prime minister.

Even today, Untac is heralded as one of the UN's success stories. Another perspective is that it was an ill-conceived and poorly executed peace because so many of the powers involved in brokering the deal had their own agendas to advance. To many Cambodians who had survived the 1970s, it was unthinkable that the Khmer Rouge would be allowed to play a part in the electoral process after presiding over a genocide.

The UN's disarmament program took weapons away from rural militias who for so long provided the backbone of the government's provincial defence network against the Khmer Rouge and this left communities throughout the country vulnerable to attack. Meanwhile the Khmer Rouge used the veil of legitimacy conferred upon it by the peace process to re-establish a guerrilla network throughout Cambodia. By 1994, when it was finally outlawed by the government, the Khmer Rouge was arguably a greater threat to the stability of Cambodia than at any time since 1979.

Untac's main goals had been to 'restore and maintain peace' and 'promote national reconciliation', and in the short term it achieved neither. It did oversee free and fair elections, but these were later annulled by the actions of Cambodia's politicians. Little was done during the UN period to try to dismantle the communist apparatus of state set up by

During the 1960s, Cambodia was an oasis of peace while wars raged in neighbouring Vietnam and Laos. By 1970 that had all changed. For the full story, read *Sideshow: Kissinger, Nixon and the Destruction of Cambodia,* by William Shawcross (1979).

| 2004 | 2005 | 2006 | 2007 |
|---|---|---|---|
| In a move that catches observers by surprise, King Sihanouk abdicates the throne and is succeeded by his son King Sihamoni, a popular choice as Sihamoni has steered clear of politics. | Cambodia joins the WTO, opening its markets to free trade, but many commentators feel it could be counterproductive, as the economy is so small and there is no more protection for domestic producers. | Lawsuits and counter lawsuits see political leaders moving from conflict to courtroom in the new Cambodia. The revolving doors stop with opposition leader Sam Rainsy back in the country and Prince Ranariddh out. | Royalist party Funcinpec continues to implode in the face of conflict, intrigue and defections, with democrats joining Sam Rainsy, loyalists joining the new Norodom Ranariddh Party and others joining the CPP. |

the CPP, a well-oiled machine that continues to ensure that former communists control the civil service, judiciary, army and police today.

## The Slow Birth of Peace

When the Vietnamese toppled the Pol Pot government in 1979, the Khmer Rouge disappeared into the jungle. The guerrillas eventually boycotted the 1993 elections and later rejected peace talks aimed at establishing a ceasefire. In 1994 the Khmer Rouge resorted to a new tactic of targeting tourists, with horrendous results for a number of foreigners in Cambodia. During 1994 three people were taken from a taxi on the road to Sihanoukville and subsequently shot. A few months later another three foreigners were seized from a train bound for Sihanoukville and in the ransom drama that followed they were executed as the army closed in.

The government changed course during the mid-1990s, opting for more carrot and less stick in a bid to end the war. The breakthrough came in 1996 when Ieng Sary, Brother No 3 in the Khmer Rouge hierarchy and foreign minister during its rule, was denounced by Pol Pot for corruption. He subsequently led a mass defection of fighters and their dependants from the Pailin area, and this effectively sealed the fate of the remaining Khmer Rouge. Pailin, rich in gems and timber, had long been the economic crutch that kept the Khmer Rouge hobbling along. The severing of this income, coupled with the fact that government forces now had only one front on which to concentrate their resources, suggested the days of civil war were numbered.

By 1997 cracks were appearing in the coalition and the fledgling democracy once again found itself under siege. But it was the Khmer Rouge that again grabbed the headlines. Pol Pot ordered the execution of Son Sen, defence minister during the Khmer Rouge regime, and many of his family members. This provoked a putsch within the Khmer Rouge leadership, and the one-legged hardliner general Ta Mok seized control, putting Pol Pot on 'trial'. Rumours flew about Phnom Penh that Pol Pot would be brought there to face international justice, but events dramatically shifted back to the capital.

A lengthy courting period ensued in which both Funcinpec and the CPP attempted to win the trust of the remaining Khmer Rouge hardliners in northern Cambodia. Ranariddh was close to forging a deal with the jungle fighters and was keen to get it sewn up before Cambodia's accession to Asean, as nothing would provide a better entry fanfare than the ending of Cambodia's long civil war. He was outflanked and subsequently outgunned by Second Prime Minister Hun Sen. On 5 July 1997, fighting again erupted on the streets of Phnom Penh as troops loyal to the CPP clashed with those loyal to Funcinpec. The heaviest exchanges were around the airport and key government buildings, but before long

| 2008 | 2009 | 2010 | 2011 |
|---|---|---|---|
| Elections are held and the CPP increases its share of the vote to 58%, while the opposition vote is split across several parties. | Comrade Duch, aka Kaing Guek Eav, commandant of the notorious S-21 prison, goes on trial for crimes committed during the Khmer Rouge regime. | As the annual Bon Om Tuk (Water Festival) draws to a close on 22 November, more than 350 people die as revellers swarm across a narrow bridge in huge numbers. | The simmering border conflict over the ancient temple of Preah Vihear spills over into actual fighting between Cambodia and Thailand. A ceasefire is negotiated by Asean chair Indonesia. |

the dust had settled and the CPP once again controlled Cambodia. Euphemistically known as 'the events of 1997' in Cambodia, much of the international community condemned the violence as a coup.

As 1998 began, the CPP announced an all-out offensive against its enemies in the north. By April it was closing in on the Khmer Rouge strongholds of Anlong Veng and Preah Vihear, and amid this heavy fighting Pol Pot evaded justice by dying a natural death on 15 April in the captivity of his former Khmer Rouge comrades. The fall of Anlong Veng in April was followed by the fall of Preah Vihear in May, and the surviving big three, Ta Mok, Khieu Samphan and Nuon Chea, were forced to flee into the jungle near the Thai border with their remaining troops.

The 1998 election result reinforced the reality that the CPP was now the dominant force in the Cambodian political system and on 25 December Hun Sen received the Christmas present he had been waiting for: Khieu Samphan and Nuon Chea were defecting to the government side. The international community began to pile on the pressure for the establishment of some sort of war-crimes tribunal to try the remaining Khmer Rouge leadership. After lengthy negotiations, agreement was finally reached on the composition of a court to try the surviving leaders of the Khmer Rouge. The CPP was suspicious of a UN-administered trial as the UN had sided with the Khmer Rouge–dominated coalition against the government in Phnom Penh, and the ruling party wanted a major say in who was to be tried and for what. The UN for its part doubted that the judiciary in Cambodia was sophisticated or impartial enough to fairly oversee such a major trial. A compromise solution – a mixed tribunal of three international and four Cambodian judges requiring a super majority of two plus three for a verdict – was eventually agreed upon. For more on recent events in Cambodia, see p304.

## Moving Towards Democracy?

Western powers, including the USA and UK, ensured the Khmer Rouge retained its seat at the UN general assembly in New York until 1991, a scenario that saw those responsible for the genocide representing their victims on the international stage.

In 2002 Cambodia's first-ever local elections were held to select village- and commune-level representatives, an important step in bringing grassroots democracy to the country. Despite national elections since 1993, the CPP continued to monopolise political power at local and regional levels and only with commune elections would this grip be loosened. The national elections of July 2003 saw a shift in the balance of power, as the CPP consolidated its grip on Cambodia and the Sam Rainsy Party overhauled Funcinpec as the second party. This trend continued into the 2008 election when the CPP's majority grew. However, the 2013 election saw a massive reversal in the trend as the opposition managed to stay united through the election campaign. The return of Cambodia National Rescue Party (CNRP) leader Sam Rainsy from self-imposed exile saw his party come close to victory over the CPP.

| 2012 〉 | 2013 〉 | 2014 〉 | 2015 〉 |
|---|---|---|---|
| Cambodia assumes the chair of Asean and hosts the Asia-Pacific Economic Cooperation (APEC) summit. US President Obama flies into Phnom Penh, but doesn't meet with Prime Minister Hun Sen. | In Cambodia's fifth postwar election the united opposition Cambodia National Rescue Party (CNRP) wins 55 seats in the National Assembly. CNRP cites voting irregularities but the CPP ignores calls for an investigation. | The opposition CNRP finally enters the National Assembly, one year on from the divisive election. | The governing CPP and the opposition CNRP agree on a 'culture of dialogue' to avoid unnecessary tension, but the issue of the Cambodia-Vietnam border flares up. |

# Pol Pot & the Khmer Rouge Trials

**The Khmer Rouge controlled Cambodia for three years, eight months and 20 days, a period etched into the consciousness of the Khmer people. The Vietnamese ousted the Khmer Rouge on 7 January 1979, but Cambodia's civil war rumbled on for another two decades before drawing to a close in 1999. Finally, more than 20 years after the collapse of the Khmer Rouge regime, serious discussions began about a trial to bring those responsible for the deaths of about two million Cambodians to justice. These trials commenced in 2006 and continue to this day.**

## The Khmer Rouge Tribunal

### Case 001

Case 001, the trial of Kaing Guek Eav, aka Comrade Duch, began in 2009. Duch was seen as a key figure as he provided the link between the regime and its crimes in his role as head of S-21 prison. Duch was sentenced to 35 years imprisonment in 2010, but this was reduced to just 19 years in lieu of time already served and his cooperation with the investigating team. For many Cambodians this was a slap in the face, as Duch had already admitted overall responsibility for the deaths of about 17,000 people. Convert this into simple numbers and it equates to about 10 hours of prison time per victim. However, an appeal verdict announced on 3 February 2012 extended the sentence to life imprisonment.

To learn more about the origins of the Khmer Rouge and the Democratic Kampuchea regime, read *How Pol Pot Came to Power* (1985) and *The Pol Pot Regime* (1996), both written by Yale University academic Ben Kiernan.

### Case 002

Case 002 began in November 2011, involving the most senior surviving leaders of the Democratic Kampuchea (DK) era: Brother Number Two Nuon Chea (age 84), Brother Number Three and former foreign minister of Democratic Kampuchea Ieng Sary (age 83) and former DK head of state Khieu Samphan (age 79). Justice may prove elusive, however, due to the slow progress of court proceedings and the advancing age of the defendants. Ieng Sary died on 14 March 2013 and his wife and former DK Minister of Social Affairs Ieng Thirith (age 78) was ruled unfit to stand trial due to the onset of dementia. Both Nuon Chea and Khieu Samphan received life sentences for crimes against humanity in August 2014, but are currently facing additional charges of genocide.

### Case 003

Case 003 against head of the DK navy, Meas Muth, and head of the DK air force, Sou Met, is politically charged and threatened to derail the entire tribunal during 2011. Investigations into this case stalled back in 2009 under intense pressure from the Cambodian government, which wanted to draw a line under proceedings with the completion of Case 002. Prime Minister Hun Sen made several public statements objecting to the continuation of Case 003 and the subsequent impasse has led to criticism from many quarters, including Human Rights Watch. Many independent observers have called for the replacement of at least two

Pol Pot travelled up the Ho Chi Minh trail to visit Beijing in 1966, at the height of the Cultural Revolution there. He was obviously inspired by what he saw, as the Khmer Rouge went even further than the Red Guards in severing links with the past.

Cambodian judges for their lack of political impartiality, and German judge Siegfried Blunk resigned under pressure for failing to conduct full investigations into Case 003. It remains to be seen who will prevail in this battle of wills, but to many observers the entire credibility of the trial continues to remain under threat. Neither Meas Muth nor Sou Met have yet been arrested despite their whereabouts being well known.

## Cost

More than US$200 million has been spent to date, against a backdrop of allegations of corruption and mismanagement on the Cambodian side. Some Cambodians feel the trial will send an important political message about accountability that may resonate with some of the Cambodian leadership today. However, others argue that the trial is a major waste of money, given the overwhelming evidence against surviving senior leaders, and that a truth and reconciliation commission may have provided more compelling answers for Cambodians who want to understand what motivated the average Khmer Rouge cadre.

# Pol Pot & His Comrades

## Pol Pot: Brother Number One

Pol Pot is a name that sends shivers down the spines of Cambodians and foreigners alike. It is Pol Pot who is most associated with the bloody madness of the regime he led between 1975 and 1979, and his policies heaped misery, suffering and death on millions of Cambodians.

Pol Pot was born Saloth Sar in a small village near Kompong Thom in 1925. As a young man he won a scholarship to study in Paris, where he came into contact with the Cercle Marxiste and communist thought, which he later transformed into a politics of extreme Maoism.

In 1963 Sihanouk's repressive policies sent Saloth Sar and his comrades fleeing to the jungles of Ratanakiri. It was from this moment that Saloth Sar began to call himself Pol Pot. Once the Khmer Rouge was allied with Sihanouk, following his overthrow by Lon Nol in 1970 and subsequent exile in Beijing, its support soared and the faces of the leadership became familiar. However, Pol Pot remained a shadowy figure, leaving public duties to Khieu Samphan and Ieng Sary.

When the Khmer Rouge marched into Phnom Penh on 17 April 1975, few people could have anticipated the hell that was to follow. Pol Pot and his clique were the architects of one of the most radical and brutal revolutions in the history of humankind. It was Year Zero and Cambodia was on a self-destructive course to sever all ties with the past.

After being ousted by the Vietnamese, Pol Pot was not to emerge as the public face of the revolution until the end of 1976, after he returned from a trip to see his mentors in Beijing. He granted almost no interviews to foreign media and was seen only on propaganda movies produced by government TV. Such was his aura and reputation that, by the last year of the regime, a cult of personality was developing around him.

The Khmer Rouge period is politically sensitive in Cambodia, due in part to the connections the current leadership has with the communist movement – so much so that the history of the genocide was not taught in high schools until 2009.

Pol Pot spent much of the 1980s living in Thailand and was able to rebuild his shattered forces and once again threaten Cambodia. His enigmatic persona increased as the international media speculated on his real fate. His demise was reported so often that when he finally passed away on 15 April 1998, many Cambodians refused to believe it until they had seen his body on TV or in newspapers. Even then, many were sceptical and rumours continue to circulate about exactly how he met his end. Officially he was said to have died from a heart attack, but a full autopsy was not carried out before his body was cremated on a pyre of burning tyres.

For more on the life and times of Pol Pot, pick up one of the excellent biographies written about him: *Brother Number One* by David Chandler or *Pol Pot: The History of a Nightmare* by Phillip Short.

### Nuon Chea: Brother Number Two

Long considered one of the main ideologues and architects of the Khmer Rouge revolution, Nuon Chea studied law at Bangkok's Thammasat University before joining the Thai Communist Party. He was appointed Deputy Secretary of the Communist Party of Kampuchea upon its secretive founding in 1960 and remained Pol Pot's second in command throughout the regime's rule, with overall responsibility for internal security. He was sentenced to life imprisonment in 2014 and awaits further trial at the ECCC for additional charges of genocide as part of Case 002.

### Ieng Sary: Brother Number Three

One of Pol Pot's closest confidants, Ieng Sary fled to the jungles of Ratanakiri in 1963, where he and Pol Pot both underwent intensive guerrilla training in the company of North Vietnamese communist forces. Ieng Sary was one of the public faces of the Khmer Rouge and became foreign minister of Democratic Kampuchea. Until his death, he maintained that he was not involved in the planning or execution of the genocide. However, he did invite many intellectuals, diplomats and exiles to return to Cambodia from 1975, the majority of whom were subsequently tortured and executed in S-21 prison. He helped hasten the demise of the Khmer Rouge as a guerrilla force with his defection to the government side in 1996 and was given an amnesty for his earlier crimes.

### Khieu Samphan: Brother Number Nine

Khieu Samphan studied economics in Paris and some of his theories on self-reliance were credited with inspiring Khmer Rouge economic policies. During the Sihanouk years of the 1960s, Khieu Samphan spent several years working with the Sangkum government and putting his more moderate theories to the test. During a crackdown on leftists in 1967, he fled to the jungle to join Pol Pot and Ieng Sary. During the DK period, he was made head of state from 1976 to 1979. Along with Nuon Chea, he was sentenced to life imprisonment in 2014 and awaits further trial for genocide charges as part of Case 002.

### Comrade Duch: Commandant of S-21

Born Kaing Guek Eav in Kompong Thom in 1942, Duch initially worked as a teacher before joining the Khmer Rouge in 1967. Based in the Cardamom Mountains during the civil war of 1970–75, he was given responsibility for security and political prisons in his region, where he refined his interrogation techniques. Following the Khmer Rouge takeover, he was moved to S-21 prison and was responsible for the interrogation and execution of thousands of prisoners. He fled Phnom Penh as Vietnamese forces surrounded the city, and his whereabouts were unknown until he was discovered living in Battambang Province by British photojournalist Nic Dunlop. The first to stand trial and be sentenced in Case 001, Comrade Duch cooperated through the judicial process. He was sentenced to life imprisonment in early 2012.

## The Future

It remains to be seen whether the wheels of justice will turn fast enough to deliver a verdict on the remaining Khmer Rouge leaders on trial. However, that justice has already been served in the case of Comrade Duch (and at least partially for Brothers Two and Nine) has provided a measure of closure for some victims. Keep up to date with the latest developments in the trial by visiting the official website of the Cambodian Tribunal Monitor (www.cambodiatribunal.org).

The 2010 film *Enemies of the People* follows Cambodian journalist and genocide survivor Thet Sambath as he wins the confidence of Brother Number Two in the Khmer Rouge, Nuon Chea, eventually coaxing him to give new testimony on his role in the genocidal regime.

Khieu Samphan tries to exonerate himself in his 2004 publication, *Cambodia's Recent History and the Reasons Behind the Decisions I Made.*

Pick up a copy of *When Clouds Fell From the Sky* (2015) by Robert Carmichael, a book that tells the story of a Cambodian diplomat's disappearance on his return to Cambodia in 1977 and his family's search for justice more than 30 years later.

POL POT & THE KHMER ROUGE TRIALS THE FUTURE

# People & Culture

**A tumultuous history, an incredible heritage of architecture, sculpture and dance, a modern arts scene, and a fascinating mosaic of people and faiths all coalesce to form Cambodia's rich national character.**

## The National Psyche

Since the glory days of the Angkorian empire, the Cambodian people have been on the losing side of many a battle – their country all too often a minnow amid the circling sharks – and popular attitudes have been shaped by this history. At first glance, Cambodia appears to be a nation of shiny, happy people, but look deeper and it is a country of evident contradictions. Light and dark, rich and poor, love and hate, life and death – all are visible on a journey through the kingdom. Most telling of all is the evidence of the nation's glorious past set against the more recent tragedy of its present.

Angkor is everywhere: on the flag, the national beer, cigarettes, hotels and guesthouses – anything and everything. It's a symbol of nationhood and fierce pride – no matter how ugly things got in the bad old days, the Cambodians built Angkor Wat and it doesn't get bigger than that.

Contrast this with the abyss into which the nation was sucked during the years of the Khmer Rouge. Pol Pot is a dirty word in Cambodia due to the death and suffering he inflicted on the country.

As for Cambodian attitudes towards their regional neighbours, these are complex. Thais aren't always popular, as some Cambodians feel they fail to acknowledge their cultural debt to Cambodia and generally look down on their less affluent neighbour. Cambodian attitudes towards the Vietnamese are more ambivalent. There is a certain level of mistrust, as many feel the Vietnamese aspire to colonise their country. (Many Khmers still call the lost Mekong Delta 'Kampuchea Krom', meaning 'Lower Cambodia'.) However, this mistrust is balanced with a grudging respect for the Vietnamese role in Cambodia's 'liberation' from the Khmer Rouge in

Jayavarman VII (r 1181–1219) was a Mahayana Buddhist who directed his faith towards improving the lot of his people, with the construction of hospitals, universities, roads and shelters.

### THE POPULATION OF CAMBODIA

Cambodia's second postwar population census was carried out in 2008 and put the country's population at about 13.5 million. The current population is estimated at around 16 million and, with a rapid growth rate of about 2% per year, it's predicted to reach 20 million by 2025.

Phnom Penh is the largest city, with a population of nearly two million. Other major population centres include the boom towns of Siem Reap, Sihanoukville, Battambang and Poipet.

The much-discussed imbalance of men to women due to years of conflict is not as serious as it was in 1980, but it's still significant: there are about 95 males to every 100 females, up from 86.1 to 100 in 1980. There is, however, a marked imbalance in age groups: more than 40% of the population is under the age of 16.

## CAMBODIAN GREETINGS

Cambodians traditionally greet each other with the *sompiah,* which involves pressing the hands together in prayer and bowing, similar to the *wai* in Thailand. The higher the hands and the lower the bow, the more respect is conveyed – important to remember when meeting officials or the elderly. In recent times this custom has been partly replaced by the handshake but, although men tend to shake hands with each other, women usually use the traditional greeting with both men and women. It is considered acceptable (or perhaps excusable) for foreigners to shake hands with Cambodians of both sexes.

1979. But when liberation became occupation in the 1980s, the relationship soured once more.

## The Cambodian Way of Life

For many older Cambodians, life is centred on family, faith and food, an existence that has stayed the same for centuries. Family is more than the traditional nuclear family; it's the extended family of third cousins and obscure aunts – as long as there is a bloodline, there is a bond. Families stick together, solve problems collectively, listen to the wisdom of the elders and pool resources. The extended family comes together during times of trouble and times of joy, celebrating festivals and successes, and mourning deaths and disappointments. Whether the Cambodian house is big or small, there will be a lot of people living inside.

For the majority of the population still living in the countryside, these constants carry on as they always have: several generations sharing the same roof, the same rice and the same religion. But during the dark decades of the 1970s and 1980s, this routine was ripped apart by war and ideology, as the peasants were dragged into a bloody civil war and later forced into slavery. The Khmer Rouge organisation Angkar took over as the moral and social beacon in the lives of the people. Families were forced apart, children turned against parents, brothers against sisters. The bond of trust was broken and is only slowly being rebuilt today.

For the younger generation, brought up in a postconflict, postcommunist period of relative freedom, it's a different story – arguably thanks to their steady diet of MTV and steamy soaps. Cambodia is experiencing its very own '60s swing, as the younger generation stands ready for a different lifestyle from the one their parents had to swallow. This creates plenty of friction in the cities, as rebellious teens dress as they like, date whoever they wish and hit the town until all hours. More recently this generational conflict spilled over into politics as the Facebook generation helped deliver a shock result that saw the governing Cambodian People's Party (CPP) majority slashed in half.

Cambodia is set for major demographic shifts in the next couple of decades. Currently just 20% of the population lives in urban areas, which contrasts starkly with the country's more developed neighbours, such as Malaysia and Thailand. Increasing numbers of young people are likely to migrate to the cities in search of opportunity, forever changing the face of contemporary Cambodian society. However, for now at least, Cambodian society remains much more traditional than that of Thailand and Vietnam, and visitors need to keep this in mind.

## Multiculturalism

According to official statistics, more than 90% of the people who live in Cambodia are ethnic Khmers, making the country the most ethnically homogeneous in Southeast Asia. However, unofficially, the figure is probably smaller due to a large influx of Chinese and Vietnamese in

The Cambodian and Lao people share a close bond, as Fa Ngum, the founder of the original Lao kingdom of Lan Xang (Land of a Million Elephants), was sponsored by his Khmer father-in-law.

Lowland Khmers are being encouraged to migrate to Cambodia's northeast where there is plenty of available land. But this is home to the country's minority peoples, who have no indigenous concepts of property rights or land ownership, so this may see their culture marginalised in coming years.

## KHMER KROM

The Khmer Krom people of southern Vietnam are ethnic Khmers separated from Cambodia by historical deals and Vietnamese encroachment on what was once Cambodian territory. Nobody is sure just how many of them there are and estimates vary from one million to seven million, depending on who is doing the counting.

The history of Vietnamese expansion into Khmer territory has long been a staple of Khmer textbooks. King Chey Chetha II of Cambodia, in keeping with the wishes of his Vietnamese queen, first allowed Vietnamese to settle in the Cambodian town of Prey Nokor in 1623. It was obviously the thin end of the wedge, as Prey Nokor is now better known as Ho Chi Minh City (Saigon).

The Vietnamese government has pursued a policy of forced assimilation since independence, which has involved ethnic Khmers taking Vietnamese names and studying in Vietnamese. According to the Khmer Kampuchea Federation (KKF), the Khmer Krom continue to suffer persecution, including lack of access to health services, religious discrimination and outright racism. Several monks have been defrocked for nonviolent protests in recent years and the Cambodian government has even assisted in deporting some agitators, according to Human Rights Watch.

Many Khmer Krom would like to see Cambodia act as a mediator in the quest for greater autonomy and ethnic representation in Vietnam, but the Cambodian government takes a softly, softly approach towards its more powerful neighbour, perhaps borne of the historic ties between the two political dynasties.

For more about the ongoing struggles of the Khmer Krom, visit www.khmerkrom.org.

the past century. Other ethnic minorities include Cham, Lao and the indigenous peoples of the rural highlands.

### Ethnic Khmers

The Khmers have inhabited Cambodia since the beginning of recorded regional history (around the 2nd century), many centuries before Thais and Vietnamese migrated to the region. Over the centuries, the Khmers have mixed with other groups residing in Cambodia, including Javanese and Malays (8th century), Thais (10th to 15th centuries), Vietnamese (from the early 17th century) and Chinese (since the 18th century).

### Ethnic Vietnamese

The Vietnamese are one of the largest non-Khmer ethnic groups in Cambodia. According to government figures, Cambodia is host to around 100,000 Vietnamese, though unofficial observers claim the real figure may be somewhere between half a million and one million. The Vietnamese play a big part in the fishing and construction industries in Cambodia. There is still some distrust between the Cambodians and the Vietnamese, though, even of the Vietnamese who have been living in Cambodia for generations.

### Ethnic Chinese

Friends of Khmer Culture (www.khmerculture.net) is dedicated to supporting Khmer arts and cultural organisations, and Meta House, an exhibition space in Phnom Penh, promotes Khmer arts and culture.

The government claims there are around 50,000 ethnic Chinese in Cambodia, but informed observers estimate half a million to one million in urban areas. Many Chinese Cambodians have lived in Cambodia for generations and have adopted the Khmer culture, language and identity. Until 1975, the ethnic Chinese controlled the economic life of Cambodia and in recent years they have re-emerged as a powerful economic force, mainly due to increased investment by overseas Chinese.

### Ethnic Cham

Cambodia's Cham Muslims (known locally as the Khmer Islam) officially number around 200,000. Unofficial counts put the figure higher at around 500,000. The Cham live in villages on the banks of the Mekong and Tonlé Sap rivers, mostly in the provinces of Kompong Cham, Kompong Speu and Kompong Chhnang. They suffered vicious persecution between 1975 and 1979, when a large part of their community was targeted. Many Cham mosques that were destroyed under the Khmer Rouge have since been rebuilt.

### Ethno-Linguistic Minorities

Cambodia's diverse Khmer Leu (Upper Khmer) or *chunchiet* (ethnic minorities), who live in the country's mountainous regions, probably number around 100,000.

The majority of these groups live in the northeast of Cambodia, in the provinces of Ratanakiri, Mondulkiri, Stung Treng and Kratie. The largest group is the Tompuon (many other spellings are also used), who number nearly 20,000. Other groups include the Bunong, Kreung, Kavet, Brau and Jarai.

The hill tribes of Cambodia have long been isolated from mainstream Khmer society, and there is little in the way of mutual understanding. They practise shifting cultivation, rarely staying in one place for long. Finding a new location for a village requires a village elder to mediate with the spirit world. Very few of the minorities retain the sort of colourful traditional costumes found in Thailand, Laos and Vietnam.

# Religion

### Buddhism

Buddhism arrived in Cambodia with Hinduism but only became the official religion from the 13th and 14th centuries. Most Cambodians today practise Theravada Buddhism. Between 1975 and 1979 many of Cambodia's Buddhist monks were murdered by the Khmer Rouge and nearly all of the country's wats (more than 3000) were damaged or destroyed. In the late 1980s, Buddhism once again became the state religion and today young monks are a common sight throughout the country. Many wats have been rebuilt or rehabilitated and money-raising drives for this work can be seen on roadsides across the country.

The ultimate goal of Theravada Buddhism is nirvana – 'extinction' of all desire and suffering to reach the final stage of reincarnation. By feeding monks, giving donations to temples and performing regular worship at the local wat, Buddhists hope to improve their lot, acquiring enough merit to reduce their number of rebirths.

Every Buddhist male is expected to become a monk for a short period in his life, optimally between the time he finishes school and starts a career or marries. Men or boys under 20 years of age may enter the *sangha* (monastic order) as novices. Nowadays men may spend as little as 15 days to accrue merit as monks.

### Hinduism

Hinduism flourished alongside Buddhism from the 1st century AD until the 14th century. During the pre-Angkorian period, Hinduism was represented by the worship of Harihara (Shiva and Vishnu embodied in a single deity). During the time of Angkor, Shiva was the deity most in favour with the royal family, although in the 12th century he was superseded by Vishnu. Today some elements of Hinduism are still incorporated into important ceremonies involving birth, marriage and death.

### Animism

Both Hinduism and Buddhism were gradually absorbed from beyond the borders of Cambodia, fusing with the animist beliefs already present among the Khmers before Indianisation. Local beliefs didn't disappear

PEOPLE & CULTURE RELIGION

Look out for Chinese and Vietnamese cemeteries dotting the rice fields of provinces to the south and east of Phnom Penh. Khmers do not bury their dead, but practise cremation, and the ashes may be interred in a stupa in the grounds of a wat.

There are 25 female parliamentarians out of 123 seated in the National Assembly in Cambodia, making up 20% of MPs.

Among Cambodia's 25 provinces, Kandal has the densest population, with more than 300 people per sq km. Mondulkiri has the sparsest population, with just four people per sq km.

The purest form of animism is practised among the minority people known as Khmer Leu. Some have converted to Buddhism, but the majority continue to worship spirits of the earth and skies and their forefathers.

but were incorporated into the new religions to form something uniquely Cambodian. The concept of Neak Ta has its foundations in animist beliefs regarding sacred soil and the sacred spirit around us. Neak Ta can be viewed as a mother-earth concept, an energy force uniting a community with its earth and water. It can be represented in many forms, from stone or wood to termite hills – anything that symbolises both a link between the people and the fertility of their land. The sometimes phallic representation of Neak Ta helps explain the popularity of Hinduism and the worship of the *lingam* (phallic symbol).

### Islam

Cambodia's Muslims are descendants of Chams, who migrated from what is now central Vietnam after the final defeat of the kingdom of Champa by the Vietnamese in 1471. Like Buddhists in Cambodia, the Cham Muslims call the faithful to prayer by banging a drum, rather than with the call of the muezzin.

### Christianity

Christianity has made limited headway into Cambodia compared with neighbouring Vietnam. There were a number of churches in Cambodia before the war, but many of these were systematically destroyed by the Khmer Rouge, including Notre Dame Cathedral in Phnom Penh. Christianity made a comeback of sorts throughout the refugee camps on the Thai border in the 1980s, as a number of food-for-faith-type charities set up shop dispensing religion with every meal. Many Cambodians changed their public faith for survival, before converting back to Buddhism on their departure from the camps, earning the moniker 'rice Christians'.

The famous Hindu epic the *Ramayana* is known as the *Reamker* in Cambodia. Reyum Publishing issued a beautifully illustrated book, *The Reamker* (1999), telling the story.

## The Arts

The Khmer Rouge's assault on the arts was a terrible blow to Cambodian culture. Indeed, for a number of years the consensus among Khmers was that their culture had been irrevocably lost. The Khmer Rouge not only did away with living bearers of Khmer culture but also destroyed cultural artefacts, statues, musical instruments, books and anything else that served as a reminder of a past it was trying to efface. The temples of Angkor were spared as a symbol of Khmer glory and empire, but little else survived. Despite this, Cambodia is witnessing a resurgence of traditional arts and a growing interest in experimentation in modern arts and cross-cultural fusion.

### Architecture

Khmer architecture reached its peak during the Angkorian era (9th to 14th centuries). Some of the finest examples of architecture from this period are Angkor Wat and the structures of Angkor Thom.

Today most rural Cambodian houses are built on high wood pilings (if the family can afford it) and have thatched roofs, walls made of palm mats and floors of woven bamboo strips resting on bamboo joists. The shady space underneath is used for storage and for people to relax at midday. Wealthier families have houses with wooden walls and tiled roofs, but the basic design remains the same.

To learn more about New Khmer Architecture, pick up a copy of *Building Cambodia: New Khmer Architecture 1953–1970* by Helen Grant Ross and Darryl Collins.

The French left their mark in Cambodia in the form of some handsome villas and government buildings built in neoclassical style, pillars and all. Some of the best architectural examples are in Phnom Penh, but most of the provincial capitals have at least one or two examples of architecture from the colonial period. Battambang and Kampot are two of the best-preserved colonial-era towns, with handsome rows of shophouses and the classic governors' residences.

During the 1950s and 1960s, Cambodia's so-called golden era, a group of young Khmer architects shaped the capital of Cambodia in their own image, experimenting with what is now called New Khmer Architecture. Vann Molyvann was the most famous proponent of this school of architecture, designing a number of prominent Phnom Penh landmarks such as the Olympic Stadium, the Chatomuk Theatre and Independence Monument. The beach resort of Kep was remodelled at this time, as the emergent Cambodian middle class flocked to the beach, and there are some fantastic if dilapidated examples of New Khmer Architecture around the small town. Boutique hotels Knai Bang Chatt and Villa Romonea in Kep are both restored examples from this period.

To discover examples of New Khmer Architecture, visit the website of Khmer Architecture Tours (www.ka-tours.org) or sign up for one of its walking tours of Phnom Penh or Battambang. The website includes downloadable printouts for DIY tours of each city.

The first major international feature film to be shot in Cambodia was *Lord Jim* (1964), starring Peter O'Toole.

PEOPLE & CULTURE THE ARTS

## Cinema

Back in the 1960s, the Cambodian film industry was booming. Between 1960 and 1975, more than 300 films were made, some of which were exported all around Asia, including numerous films by then head-of-state Norodom Sihanouk. However, the advent of Khmer Rouge rule saw the film industry disappear overnight and it didn't recover for more than a quarter of a century.

The film industry in Cambodia was given a new lease of life in 2000 with the release of *Pos Keng Kong* (The Giant Snake). A remake of a 1960s Cambodian classic, it tells the story of a powerful young girl born from a rural relationship between a woman and a snake king. It's an interesting love story, albeit with dodgy special effects, and achieved massive box-office success around the region.

The success of *Pos Keng Kong* heralded a mini revival in the Cambodian film industry and local directors now turn out several films a year. However, many of these are amateurish horror films of dubious artistic value.

At least one overseas Cambodian director has enjoyed major success in recent years: Rithy Panh's *People of the Rice Fields* was nominated for the Palme d'Or at the Cannes Film Festival in 1995. The film touches only fleetingly on the Khmer Rouge, depicting the lives of a family living an arduous existence in the rice fields. His other films include *One Night after the War* (1997), the story of a young Khmer kickboxer falling for a bar girl in Phnom Penh; and the award-winning *S-21: The Khmer Rouge*

Rithy Panh's 1996 film *Bophana* tells the true story of Hout Bophana, a beautiful young woman, and Ly Sitha, a regional Khmer Rouge leader, who fall in love and are executed for their 'crime'.

### SIHANOUK & THE SILVER SCREEN

Between 1965 and 1969 Sihanouk (former king and head of state of Cambodia) wrote, directed and produced nine feature films, a figure that would put the average workaholic Hollywood director to shame. Sihanouk took the business of making films very seriously, and family and officials were called upon to play their part: the minister of foreign affairs acted as the male lead in Sihanouk's first feature, *Apsara* (1965), and his daughter Princess Bopha Devi, the female lead. When, in the same movie, a show of military hardware was required, the air force was brought into action.

Sihanouk often took on the leading role himself. Notable performances saw him as a spirit of the forest and as a victorious general. Perhaps it was no surprise, given the king's apparent addiction to the world of celluloid dreams, that Cambodia should challenge Cannes with its Phnom Penh International Film Festival. The festival was held twice, in 1968 and 1969. Also perhaps unsurprisingly, Sihanouk won the grand prize on both occasions. He continued to make movies in later life and made around 30 films during his remarkable career.

Rithy Panh's *The Missing Picture* (2013) became the first Cambodian film to be shortlisted for Best Foreign Language Film at the 2014 Oscars.

*Killing Machine* (2003), a powerful documentary in which survivors from Tuol Sleng are brought back to confront their guards.

The definitive film about Cambodia is *The Killing Fields* (1985), which tells the story of American journalist Sydney Schanberg and his Cambodian assistant Dith Pran. Most of the footage was actually shot in Thailand, as it was filmed in 1984 when Cambodia was effectively closed to the West.

Quite a number of international films have been shot in Cambodia in recent years, including *Tomb Raider* (2001), *City of Ghosts* (2002) and *Two Brothers* (2004), all worth seeking out for their beautiful Cambodian backdrops. Australian independent feature film *Wish You Were Here,* partly shot in Cambodia in 2011, opened the Sundance Festival in 2012.

For more on Cambodian films and cinema, pick up a copy of *Kon: The Cinema of Cambodia* (2010), published by the Department of Media and Communication at the Royal University of Cambodia. Also look out for the Cambodia International Film Festival (www.cambodia-iff.com), held in Phnom Penh every December.

## TOP 10 TIPS TO EARN THE RESPECT OF THE LOCALS

Take your time to learn a little about the local culture in Cambodia. Not only will you avoid inadvertently causing offence, but it will also ingratiate you with your hosts. Here are a few top tips:

**Dress code** Respect local dress standards, particularly at religious sites. Covering the upper arms and upper legs is appropriate, although some monks will be too polite to enforce this. Always remove shoes before entering a temple, as well as hats. Nude sunbathing is considered totally inappropriate, even on beaches.

**Make a contribution** Since most temples are maintained through donations, remember to make a contribution when visiting a temple. When visiting a Khmer home, a small token of gratitude in the form of a gift is always appreciated.

**Meet and greet** Learn the Cambodian greeting, the *sompiah,* and use it when introducing yourself to new friends. When beckoning someone over, always wave towards yourself with the palm down, as palm up with fingers raised can be suggestive, and even offensive.

**A woman's touch** Monks are not supposed to touch or be touched by women. If a woman wishes to pass something to a monk, the object should be placed within reach of the monk or on his 'receiving cloth'.

**Keep your cool** No matter how high your blood pressure rises, do not raise your voice or show signs of aggression. This will lead to a 'loss of face' and cause embarrassment to the locals, ensuring the situation gets worse rather than better.

**Business cards** Exchanging business cards is an important part of even the smallest transaction or business contact in Cambodia. Get some printed before you arrive and hand them out like confetti. Always present them with two hands.

**Deadly chopsticks** Leaving a pair of chopsticks sitting vertically in a rice bowl looks very much like the incense sticks that are burned for the dead.

**Mean feet** Cambodians like to keep a clean house and it's usual to remove shoes when entering somebody's home. It's rude to point the bottom of your feet towards other people. Never, ever point your feet towards anything sacred, such as an image of Buddha.

**Hats off** As a form of respect to the elderly or other esteemed people, such as monks, take off your hat and bow your head politely when addressing them. Never pat or touch an adult on the head.

**Toothpicks** While digging out those stubborn morsels from between your teeth, it's polite to use one hand to perform the extraction and the other hand to cover your mouth.

## Dance

More than any of the other traditional arts, Cambodia's royal ballet is a tangible link with the glory of Angkor. Its traditions stretch long into the past, when the dance of the *apsara* (heavenly nymph) was performed for the divine king. Early in his reign, King Sihanouk released the traditional harem of royal *apsara* that came with the crown.

Dance fared particularly badly during the Pol Pot years. Very few dancers and teachers survived. In 1981, with a handful of teachers, the University of Fine Arts was reopened and the training of dance students resumed.

Much of Cambodian royal dance resembles that of India and Thailand (the same stylised hand movements, the same sequined, lamé costumes and the same opulent stupa-like headwear), as the Thais incorporated techniques from the Khmers after sacking Angkor in the 15th century. Although royal dance was traditionally an all-female affair (with the exception of the role of the monkey), more male dancers are now featured. Known as *robam preah reachtrop* in Khmer, the most popular classical dances are the Apsara dance and the Wishing dance.

Folk dance is another popular element of dance performances that are regularly staged for visitors in Phnom Penh and Siem Reap. Folk dances draw on rural lifestyle and cultural traditions for their inspiration. One of the most popular folk dances is *robam kom arek,* involving bamboo poles and some nimble footwork. Also popular are fishing and harvest-themed dances that include plenty of flirtatious interaction between male and female performers.

Other celebrated dances are only performed at certain festivals or at certain times of the year. The *trot* is very popular at Khmer New Year to ward off evil spirits from the home or business. A dancer in a deer costume runs through the property pursued by a hunter and is eventually slain.

Chinese New Year (*Tet* to the Vietnamese in Cambodia) sees elaborate lion dances performed all over Phnom Penh and other major cities in Cambodia.

Contemporary dances include the popular *rom vong* or circle dance, which is likely to have originated in neighbouring Laos. Dancers move around in a circle taking three steps forward and two steps back. Hip hop and break-dancing is fast gaining popularity among urban youngsters and is regularly performed at outdoor events.

## Music

The bas-reliefs on some of the monuments in the Angkor region depict musicians and *apsara* holding instruments similar to the traditional Khmer instruments of today, demonstrating that Cambodia has a long musical tradition all of its own.

Customarily, music was an accompaniment to a ritual or performance that had religious significance. Musicologists have identified six types of Cambodian musical ensemble, each used in different settings. The most traditional of these is the *arek ka,* an ensemble that performs at weddings. The instruments of the *arek ka* include a *tro khmae* (three-stringed fiddle), a *khsae muoy* (single-stringed bowed instrument) and *skor areak* (drums), among others. *Ahpea pipea* is another type of wedding music that accompanies the witnessing of the marriage and *pin peat* is the music that is heard at ballet performances and shadow-puppet displays.

Much of Cambodia's golden-era music from the pre-war period was lost during the Pol Pot years. The Khmer Rouge targeted singers, and the great Sinn Sisamouth, Ros Sereysothea and Pen Ron, Cambodia's

Amrita Performing Arts (www.amrita performingarts. org) has worked on a number of ground-breaking dance and theatre projects in Cambodia, including collaborations with French and Japanese performers.

One of the greatest '70s legends to seek out is Yos Olarang, the Jimi Hendrix of Cambodia, with his screaming vocals and wah-wah pedals. His most famous song, 'Jis Cyclo', is an absolute classic.

PEOPLE & CULTURE THE ARTS

most famous songwriters and performers, all disappeared in the early days of the regime.

After the war, many Khmers settled in the USA, where a lively Khmer pop industry developed. Influenced by US music and later exported back to Cambodia, it has been enormously popular.

A new generation of overseas Khmers growing up with influences from the West is producing its own sound. Cambodians are now returning to the homeland raised on a diet of rap in the US or France, and lots of artists are breaking through, such as the KlapYaHandz collective started by Sok 'Cream' Visal.

There's also a burgeoning pop industry, many of whose stars perform at outdoor concerts in Phnom Penh. It's easy to join in the fun by visiting one of the innumerable karaoke bars around the country. Preap Sovath is the Robbie Williams of Cambodia and, if you flick through the Cambodian channels for more than five minutes, the chances are he will be performing. Meas Soksophea is the most popular female singer, the Adele of Cambodia with a big voice, but it's an ever-changing industry and new stars are always waiting in the wings.

Dengue Fever is the ultimate fusion band, rapidly gaining a name for itself beyond the USA and Cambodia. Cambodian singer Chhom Nimol fronts five American prog rockers who dabble in psychedelic sounds. Another fusion band fast gaining a name for itself is the Cambodian Space Project, comprising a mix of Cambodians and expats. They regularly play in Phnom Penh and are well worth catching if you're in town at the same time.

One form of music unique to Cambodia is *chapaye,* a sort of Cambodian blues sung to the accompaniment of a two-stringed wooden instrument similar in sound to a bass guitar played without an amplifier. There are few old masters, such as Kong Nay (the Ray Charles of Cambodia), left alive, but *chapaye* is still often shown on late-night Cambodian TV before transmission ends. Kong Nay has toured internationally in countries such as Australia and the USA, and has even appeared with Peter Gabriel at the WOMAD music festival in the UK.

For more on Cambodian music, pick up a copy of *Dontrey: The Music of Cambodia* (2011), published by the Department of Media and Communication at the Royal University of Cambodia. There is also an excellent rockumentary feature called *Don't Think I've Forgotten,* which is about Cambodia's lost rock-and-roll era; watch it at www.dtifcambodia.com.

## Sculpture

The Khmer empire of the Angkor period produced some of the most exquisite carved sculptures found anywhere on earth. Even in the pre-Angkorian era, the periods generally referred to as Funan and Chenla, the people of Cambodia were producing masterfully sensuous sculpture that was more than just a copy of the Indian forms on which it was modelled. Some scholars maintain that the Cambodian forms are unrivalled, even in India itself.

The earliest surviving Cambodian sculpture dates from the 6th century AD. Most of it depicts Vishnu with four or eight arms. A large eight-armed Vishnu from this period is displayed at the National Museum in Phnom Penh.

Also on display at the National Museum is a statue of Harihara from the end of the 7th century, a divinity who combines aspects of both Vishnu and Shiva but looks more than a little Egyptian with his pencil moustache and long, thin nose – a reminder that Indian sculpture drew from the Greeks, who in turn were influenced by the Pharaohs.

Innovations of the early Angkorian era include freestanding sculpture that dispenses with the stone aureole that in earlier works sup-

## SPORT IN CAMBODIA

The national sport of Cambodia is *pradal serey* (Cambodian kickboxing). It's similar to kickboxing in Thailand (don't make the mistake of calling it Thai boxing over here, though) and there are regular weekend bouts on CTN and TV5. It's also possible to go to the TV arenas and watch the fights live.

Football is another national obsession, although the Cambodian team is a real minnow, even by Asian standards. Many Cambodians follow the Premier League in England religiously and regularly bet on games.

The French game of *pétanque*, also called *boules,* is also very popular here and the Cambodian team has won several medals in regional games.

ported the multiple arms of Hindu deities. The faces assume an air of tranquillity, and the overall effect is less animated.

The Banteay Srei style of the late 10th century is commonly regarded as a high point in the evolution of Southeast Asian art. The National Museum has a splendid piece from this period: a sandstone statue of Shiva holding Uma, his wife, on his knee. Sadly, Uma's head was stolen some time during Cambodia's turbulent years. The Baphuon style of the 11th century was inspired to a certain extent by the sculpture of Banteay Srei, producing some of the finest works to have survived today.

The statuary of the Angkor Wat period is felt to be conservative and stilted, lacking the grace of earlier work. The genius of this period manifests itself more clearly in the immense architecture and incredible bas-reliefs of Angkor Wat itself.

The final high point in Angkorian sculpture is the Bayon period from the end of the 12th century to the beginning of the 13th century. In the National Museum, look for the superb representation of Jayavarman VII, an image that projects both great power and sublime tranquillity.

As the state religion swung back and forth between Mahayana Buddhism and Hinduism during the turbulent 13th and 14th centuries, Buddha images and bodhisattvas were carved only to be hacked out by militant Hindus on their return to power. By the 15th century stone was generally replaced by polychromatic wood as the material of choice for Buddha statues. A beautiful gallery of post-16th-century Buddhas from around Angkor is on display at the National Museum.

Cambodian sculptors are rediscovering their skills now that there is a ready market among visitors for reproduction stone carvings of famous statues and busts from the time of Angkor.

# Food & Drink

**It's no secret that the dining tables of Thailand and Vietnam are home to some of the finest food in the world, so it should come as no surprise to discover that Cambodian cuisine is also rather special. Unlike the culinary colossi that are its neighbours, Cambodia is not that well known in international food circles, but all that looks set to change. Just as Angkor has put Cambodia on the tourist map, so too *amok* (baked fish with lemongrass-based *kreung* paste, coconut and chilli in banana leaf) could put the country on the culinary map.**

As well as eating the notorious tarantulas of Skuon, Cambodians also like to eat crickets, beetles, larvae and ants. Some scientists have suggested insect farms as a way to solve food problems of the future. This time, Cambodia might be ahead of the curve.

Cambodia has a great variety of national dishes, some similar to the cuisine of neighbouring Thailand and Laos, others closer to Chinese and Vietnamese cooking, but all come with a unique Cambodian twist.

Freshwater fish forms a huge part of the Cambodian diet thanks to the natural phenomenon that is the Tonlé Sap lake. The fish come in every shape and size, from the giant Mekong catfish to teeny-tiny whitebait, which are great beer snacks when deep-fried. The French left their mark, too, with baguettes becoming the national bread and Cambodian cooks showing a healthy reverence for tender meats.

Cambodia is a crossroads in Asia, the meeting point of the great civilisations of India and China, and, just as its culture has drawn on both, so too has its cuisine. You're bound to find something that takes your fancy, whether your tastes run to spring rolls or curry. Add to this a world of dips and sauces to complement the cooking and a culinary journey through Cambodia becomes as rich a feast as any in Asia.

## Staples & Specialities

No matter what part of the world you come from, if you travel much in Cambodia, you are going to encounter food that is unusual, strange, maybe even immoral, or just plain weird. The fiercely omnivorous Cambodians find nothing strange in eating insects, algae, offal or fish bladders. They will dine on a duck foetus, brew up some brains or snack on some spiders. They will peel live frogs to grill on a barbecue or down wine infused with snake to increase their virility.

To the Khmers there is nothing 'strange' about anything that will sustain the body. To them a food is either wholesome or it isn't; it's nutritious or it isn't; it tastes good or it doesn't. And that's all they worry about. They'll try anything once, even a burger.

### Rice, Fish & Soup

Cambodia's abundant waterways provide the fish that is fermented into *prahoc* (fermented fish paste), which forms the backbone of Khmer cuisine. Built around this are the flavours that give the cuisine

## COOKING COURSES

If you are really taken with Cambodian cuisine, it's possible to learn some tricks of the trade by signing up for a cooking course. This is a great way to introduce your Cambodian experience to your friends – no one wants to sit through the slide show of photos, but offer them a mouth-watering meal and they will all come running. There are courses available in Phnom Penh, Siem Reap, Battambang and Sihanoukville, and more are popping up all the time.

its kick: the secret roots, the welcome herbs and the aromatic tubers. Together they give the salads, snacks, soups and stews a special aroma and taste that smacks of Cambodia.

Rice from Cambodia's lush fields is the principal staple, enshrined in the Khmer word for 'eating' or 'to eat', *nyam bai* – literally 'eat rice'. Many a Cambodian, particularly drivers, will run out of steam if they run out of rice. It doesn't matter that the same carbohydrates are available in other foods, it is rice and rice alone that counts. Battambang Province is Cambodia's rice bowl and produces the country's finest yield.

For the taste of Cambodia in a bowl, try the local *kyteow,* a rice-noodle soup that will keep you going all day. This full, balanced meal will cost you just 5000r in markets and about US$2 in local restaurants. Don't like noodles? Then try the *bobor* (rice porridge), a national institution, for breakfast, lunch and dinner, and best sampled with some fresh fish and a splash of ginger.

A Cambodian meal almost always includes a *samlor* (traditional soup), which will appear at the same time as the other courses. *Samlor machou bunlay* (hot and sour fish soup with pineapple and spices) is popular.

Much of the fish eaten in Cambodia is freshwater, from the Tonlé Sap or the Mekong River. *Trey ahng* (grilled fish) is a Cambodian speciality (*ahng* means 'grilled' and can be applied to many dishes). Traditionally, the fish is eaten as pieces wrapped in lettuce or spinach leaves and then dipped into *teuk trey,* a fish sauce that is a close relative to Vietnam's *nuoc mam,* but with the addition of ground peanuts.

## Salads

Cambodian salad dishes are popular and delicious, although they're quite different from the Western idea of a cold salad. *Phlea sait kow* is a beef and vegetable salad flavoured with coriander, mint and lemongrass. These three herbs find their way into many Cambodian dishes.

## Desserts & Fruit

Desserts can be sampled cheaply at night markets around the country. One sweet snack to look out for is the ice-cream sandwich. Popular with the kids, it involves putting a slab of homemade ice cream into a piece of sponge or bread.

Cambodia is blessed with many tropical fruits and sampling these is an integral part of a visit to the country. All the common fruits can be found in abundance, including *chek* (banana), *menoa* (pineapple) and *duong* (coconut). Among the larger fruit, *khnau* (jackfruit) is very common, often weighing more than 20kg. The *tourain* (durian) usually needs no introduction, as you can smell it from a mile off; the exterior is green with sharp spikes, while inside is a milky, soft interior regarded by the Chinese as an aphrodisiac.

The fruits most popular with visitors include the *mongkut* (mangosteen) and *sao mao* (rambutan). The small mangosteen has a purple skin that contains white segments with a divine flavour, while the rambutan has an interior like a lychee and an exterior covered in soft red and green spikes.

Best of all, although common throughout the world, is the *svay* (mango). The Cambodian mango season is from March to May. Other varieties of mango are available year round, but it's the hot-season ones that are a taste sensation.

# Drinks

Cambodia has a lively local drinking culture, and the heat and humidity will ensure that you hunt out anything on offer to quench your thirst. Coffee, tea, beer, wine, soft drinks, fresh fruit juices and some of the

*Teuk trey* (fish sauce), one of the most popular condiments in Cambodian cooking, cannot be taken on international flights, in line with regulations on carrying strong-smelling or corrosive substances.

FOOD & DRINK DRINKS

Some Cambodian nightclubs allow guests to rent premium bottles of spirits, like Johnnie Walker Blue Label, to display on the table – a way of maintaining face despite the fact it's actually Johnnie Walker Red Label in the glass.

The local brew for country folk is sugar-palm wine, distilled daily direct from the trees and fairly potent after it has settled. Sold in bamboo containers off the back of bicycles, it's tasty and cheap, although only suitable for those with a cast-iron stomach.

more exotic 'fire waters' are all widely available. Tea is the national drink, but these days it is just as likely to be beer in the glass.

## Beer

It's never a challenge to find a beer in Cambodia and even the most remote village usually has a stall selling a few cans. Angkor is the national beer, produced in vast quantities in a big brewery down in Sihanoukville. It costs around US$2 to US$3 for a 660ml bottle in most restaurants and bars. Draught Angkor is available for around US$0.50 to US$1.50 in the main tourist centres. Other popular local brands include Cambodia Beer, aiming to topple Angkor as the beer of choice, and provincial favourite Crown Lager.

A beer brand from neighbouring Laos, Beerlao, is very drinkable and is also one of the cheapest ales available. Tiger Beer is produced locally and is a popular draught in the capital. Some Khmer restaurants have a bevy of 'beer girls', each promoting a particular beer brand. They are always friendly and will leave you alone if you prefer not to drink.

A word of caution for beer seekers in Cambodia: while the country is awash with good brews, there's a shortage of refrigeration in the countryside. Go native and learn how to say, '*Som teuk koh*' (Ice, please).

## Wine & Spirits

Local wine in Cambodia generally means rice wine; it is popular with the minority peoples of the northeast. Some rice wines are fermented for months and are super strong, while other brews are fresher and taste more like a demented cocktail. Either way, if you are invited to join a session in a minority village, it's rude to decline. Other local wines include light sugar-palm wine and ginger wine.

In Phnom Penh and Siem Reap, foreign wines and spirits are sold in supermarkets at bargain prices, given how far they have to travel. Wines from Europe and Australia start at about US$5, while the famous names of the spirit world cost between US$5 and US$15.

Friends is one of the best-known restaurants in Phnom Penh, turning out a fine array of tapas, shakes and specials to help street children in the capital. Its cookbook The Best of Friends is a visual feast showcasing its best recipes.

## Tea & Coffee

Chinese-style *tai* (tea) is a bit of a national institution, and in most Khmer and Chinese restaurants a pot will automatically appear for no extra charge as soon as you sit down. *Kaa fey* (coffee) is sold in most restaurants. It is either black or *café au lait,* served with dollops of condensed milk.

## Water & Soft Drinks

Drinking tap water *must* be avoided, especially in the provinces, as it is rarely purified and may lead to stomach complications. Locally produced mineral water starts at 1000r per bottle at shops and stalls.

Although tap water should be avoided, it is generally OK to have ice in your drinks. Throughout Cambodia, *teuk koh* (ice) is produced with treated water at local ice factories, a legacy of the French.

### BOTTOMS UP

When Cambodians propose a toast, they usually stipulate what percentage must be downed. If they are feeling generous, it might be just *ha-sip pea-roi* (50%), but more often than not it is *moi roi pea-roi* (100%). This is why they love ice in their beer, so they can pace themselves over the course of the night. Many a *barang* (foreigner) has ended up face down on the table at a Cambodian wedding when trying to outdrink the Khmers without the aid of ice.

All the well-known soft drinks are available in Cambodia. Bottled drinks are about 1000r, while canned drinks cost about 2000r, and more again in restaurants or bars.

*Teuk kalohk* are popular throughout Cambodia. They are a little like fruit smoothies and are a great way to wash down a meal.

# Dining Out

Whatever your tastes, some eatery in Cambodia is sure to help out, be it the humble peddler, a market stall, a local diner or a slick restaurant.

It's easy to sample inexpensive Khmer cuisine throughout the country, mostly at local markets and cheap restaurants. For more refined Khmer dining, the best restaurants are in Phnom Penh and Siem Reap, where there is also the choice of excellent Thai, Vietnamese, Chinese, Indian, French and Mediterranean cooking. Chinese and Vietnamese food is available in towns across the country due to the large urban populations of both of these ethnic groups.

There are few Western fast-food chains in Phnom Penh as yet, with the exception of KFC and Burger King, but there are a few local copycats. The most successful have been Lucky Burger and BB World, with lots of branches in the capital.

There are often no set hours for places to eat but, as a general rule of thumb, street stalls are open from very early in the morning until early evening, although some stalls specialise in the night shift. Most restaurants are open all day, while some of the fancier places are only open for lunch (usually 11am to 2.30pm) and dinner (usually 5pm to 10pm).

## Dining Out with Kids

Both Phnom Penh and Siem Reap have child-friendly eateries, although most restaurants in Cambodia are pretty friendly towards children. Some international restaurants have a children's menu available. High chairs are generally only found at international restaurants and fast-food outlets. Baby-changing facilities are almost nonexistent in Cambodian restaurants. Check out the relevant destination chapters for child-friendly recommendations.

## Street Snacks

Street food is an important part of everyday Cambodian life. Like many Southeast Asians, Cambodians are inveterate snackers. They can be found at impromptu stalls at any time of the day or night, delving into a range of unidentified frying objects. Drop into the markets for an even greater range of dishes and the chance of a comfortable seat. It's a cheap, cheerful and cool way to get up close and personal with Khmer cuisine.

Here's a list of five top street snacks to look out for in Cambodia:

**Banh chev** Rice pancake stuffed with yummy herbs, bean sprouts and a meat or fish staple.

**Bobor** Rice porridge, like congee in China, popular with dried fish and egg or zip it up with chilli and black pepper.

**Chek chien** Deep-fried bananas; these are a popular street snack at any time of day.

**Loat** Small white noodles that almost look like bean sprouts; they taste delicious fried up with beef.

**Nam ben choc** Thin rice noodles served with a red chicken curry or a fish-based broth.

# In the Cambodian Kitchen

Enter the Cambodian kitchen and you will learn that fine food comes from simplicity. Essentials consist of a strong flame, clean water, basic cutting utensils, a mortar and pestle, and a well-blackened pot or two.

---

**We Dare You**

**Crickets** Anyone for cricket?

**Duck foetus** Unborn duck, feathers and all.

**Durian** Nasally obnoxious spiky fruit, banned on flights.

**Prahoc** Fermented fish paste, almost a biological weapon.

**Spiders** Just like it sounds: deep-fried tarantulas.

FOOD & DRINK DINING OUT

Before it became a member of the World Trade Organization (WTO), copyright protection was almost unknown in Cambodia. During that period there were a host of copycat fast-food restaurants, including Khmer Fried Chicken, Pizza Hot and Burger Queen, all now sadly defunct.

One of the most popular street snacks in Cambodia is the unborn duck foetus. The white duck eggs contain a little duckling, feathers and all. Don't order *kaun pong tier* if you want to avoid this.

Cambodians eat three meals a day. Breakfast is either *kyteow* or *bobor*. Baguettes are available at any time of day or night, and go down well with a cup of coffee.

Lunch starts early, around 11am. Traditionally, lunch is taken with the family, but in towns and cities many workers now eat at local restaurants or markets.

Dinner is the time for family bonding. Dishes are arranged around the central rice bowl and diners each have a small eating bowl. The procedure is uncomplicated: spoon some rice into your bowl, and lay 'something else' on top of it.

When ordering multiple courses from a restaurant menu, don't worry – don't even think – about the proper succession of courses. All dishes are placed in the centre of the table as soon as they are ready. Diners then help themselves to whatever appeals to them, regardless of who ordered what.

### Table Etiquette

Sit at the table with your bowl on a small plate, chopsticks or fork and spoon at the ready. Some Cambodians prefer chopsticks and some prefer fork and spoon, but both are usually available. Each place setting will include a small bowl, usually located at the top right-hand side for the dipping sauces.

When serving yourself from the central bowls, use the communal serving spoon so as not to dip your chopsticks or spoon into the food. To begin eating, just pick up your bowl with your left hand, bring it close to your mouth and spoon in the food.

Some dos and don'ts:

➡ Do wait for your host to sit first.

➡ Don't turn down food placed in your bowl by your host.

➡ Do learn to use chopsticks.

➡ Don't leave chopsticks in a V-shape in the bowl, a symbol of death.

➡ Do tip about 5% to 10% in restaurants, as wages are low.

➡ Don't tip if there is already a service charge on the bill.

➡ Do drink every time someone offers a toast.

➡ Don't pass out face down on the table if the toasting goes on all night.

## Vegetarians & Vegans

For the scoop on countryside cooking in Cambodia, pick up *From Spiders to Waterlilies* (2009), a cookbook produced by Romdeng restaurant in Phnom Penh.

Few Cambodians understand the concept of strict vegetarianism and many will say something is vegetarian to please the customer when in fact it is not. If you are not a strict vegetarian and can deal with fish sauces and the like, you should have few problems ordering meals, and those who eat fish can sample Khmer cooking at its best. In the major tourist centres, many of the international restaurants feature vegetarian meals, although these are not budget options.

In Khmer and Chinese restaurants, stir-fried vegetable dishes are readily available, as are vegetarian fried-rice dishes, but it is unlikely these 'vegetarian' dishes have been cooked in separate woks from other fish- and meat-based dishes. Indian restaurants in the popular tourist centres can cook up genuine vegetarian food, as they usually understand the vegetarian principle better than the *prahoc*-loving Khmers.

# Environment

**Cambodia's landscape ranges from the highs of the Cardamom Mountains to the lows of the Tonlé Sap basin, and includes some critically endangered species clinging on in the protected areas and national parks. However, these species and their habitat are under threat from illegal logging, agricultural plantations and hydroelectric dams for electricity. Cambodia faces a challenge to balance the economy and its need for electricity against the desire to develop sustainable ecotourism.**

## The Land

Cambodia's borders as we know them today are the result of a classic historical squeeze. As the Vietnamese moved south into the Mekong Delta and the Thais pushed west towards Angkor, Cambodia's territory, which in Angkorian times stretched from southern Burma to Saigon and north into Laos, began to shrink. Only the arrival of the French prevented Cambodia from going the way of the Chams, who became a people without a state. In that sense, French colonialism created a protectorate that actually protected.

Cambodia's highest mountain, at 1813m, is Phnom Aural in Pursat Province.

Modern-day Cambodia covers 181,035 sq km, making it a little more than half the size of Vietnam or about the same size as England and Wales combined. To the west and northwest it borders Thailand, to

### TONLÉ SAP: HEARTBEAT OF CAMBODIA

Tonlé Sap, the largest freshwater lake in Southeast Asia, is an incredible natural phenomenon that provides fish and irrigation waters for half the population of Cambodia. It is also home to 90,000 people, many of them ethnic Vietnamese, who live in 170 floating villages.

Linking the lake with the Mekong at Phnom Penh is a 100km-long channel known as the Tonlé Sap River. From June to early October, wet-season rains rapidly raise the level of the Mekong, backing up the Tonlé Sap River and causing it to flow northwestward into the Tonlé Sap lake. During this period, the lake surface increases in size by a factor of four or five, from 2500–3000 sq km up to 10,000–16,000 sq km, and its depth increases from an average of about 2m to more than 10m. An unbelievable 20% of the Mekong's wet-season flow is absorbed by the Tonlé Sap. In October, as the water level of the Mekong begins to fall, the Tonlé Sap River reverses direction, draining the waters of the lake back into the Mekong.

This extraordinary process makes Tonlé Sap an ideal habitat for birds, snakes and turtles, as well as one of the world's richest sources of freshwater fish: the flooded forests make for fertile spawning grounds, while the dry season creates ideal conditions for fishing. Experts believe that fish migrations from the lake help to restock fisheries as far north as China.

This unique ecosystem was declared a Unesco Biosphere Reserve in 2001, but this may not be enough to protect it from the twin threats of upstream dams and rampant deforestation. Dams are already in operation on the Chinese section of the Mekong, known locally as the Lancang, and the massive new Xayaboury Dam in Laos is now under construction, the first major dam on the Middle or Lower Mekong.

You can learn more about Tonlé Sap and its unique ecosystem at the Gecko Centre (p127) near Siem Reap.

The Tonlé Sap provides a huge percentage of Cambodians' protein intake, 70% of which comes from fish. The volume of water in the Tonlé Sap can expand by up to a factor of 70 during the wet season.

the northeast Laos, to the east Vietnam, and to the south is the Gulf of Thailand.

Cambodia's two dominant geographical features are the mighty Mekong River and a vast lake, the Tonlé Sap. At Phnom Penh the Mekong splits into three channels: the Tonlé Sap River, which flows into, and out of, the Tonlé Sap lake; the Upper River (usually called simply the Mekong or, in Vietnamese, Tien Giang); and the Lower River (the Tonlé Bassac, or Hau Giang in Vietnamese). The rich sediment deposited during the Mekong's annual wet-season flooding has made central Cambodia incredibly fertile. This low-lying alluvial plain is where the vast majority of Cambodians live – fishing and farming in harmony with the rhythms of the monsoon.

In Cambodia's southwest quadrant, much of the landmass is covered by mountains: the Cardamom Mountains (Chuor Phnom Kravanh), covering parts of the provinces of Koh Kong, Battambang, Pursat and Krong Pailin, which are now opening up to ecotourism; and, southeast of there, the Elephant Mountains (Chuor Phnom Damrei), situated in the provinces of Kompong Speu, Koh Kong and Kampot.

Cambodia's 435km coastline is a big draw for visitors on the lookout for isolated tropical beaches. There are islands aplenty off the coast of Sihanoukville, Kep and Koh Kong.

Along Cambodia's northern border with Thailand, the plains collide with a striking sandstone escarpment more than 300km long that towers up to 550m above the lowlands: the Dangkrek Mountains (Chuor Phnom Dangkrek). One of the best places to get a sense of this area is Prasat Preah Vihear (p260).

Researchers estimate that about 50 to 100 wild elephants live in Mondulkiri Province. A similar number live in the Cardamom Mountains.

In the northeastern corner of the country, the plains give way to the Eastern Highlands, a remote region of densely forested mountains that extends east into Vietnam's Central Highlands and north into Laos. The wild provinces of Ratanakiri and Mondulkiri provide a home for many minority (hill-tribe) peoples and are taking off as an ecotourism hot spot.

## Wildlife

Cambodia's forest ecosystems were in excellent shape until the 1990s and, compared with its neighbours, its habitats are still relatively healthy. The years of war took their toll on some species, but others thrived in the remote jungles of the southwest and northeast. Ironically, peace brought increased threats as loggers felled huge areas of primary forest and the illicit trade in wildlife targeted endangered species. Due to years of inaccessibility, scientists have only relatively recently managed to research and catalogue the country's plant and animal life.

### Animals

Snake bites are responsible for more amputations in Cambodia than land mines these days. Many villagers go to their local medicine man for treatment and end up with an infection or gangrene; some even die.

Cambodia is home to an estimated 212 species of mammal, including tigers, elephants, bears, leopards and wild oxen. Some of the biggest characters, however, are the smaller creatures, including the binturong (nicknamed the bear cat), the pileated gibbon (the world's largest populations live in the Cardamoms and the Seima Protected Forest in Mondulkiri) and the slow loris, which hangs out in trees all day. The country also has a great variety of butterflies.

Most of Cambodia's fauna is extremely hard to spot in the wild. The easiest way to see a healthy selection is to visit the Phnom Tamao Wildlife Rescue Centre (p90) near Phnom Penh, which provides a home for rescued animals and includes all the major species.

A whopping 720 bird species find Cambodia a congenial home, thanks in large part to its year-round water resources. Relatively common birds include ducks, rails, cranes, herons, egrets, cormorants, pelicans, storks and parakeets, with migratory shorebirds, such as waders,

## TIGERS UNDER THREAT

In the mid-1990s, somewhere between 100 and 200 Cambodian tigers were being killed every year, their carcasses bringing huge sums around Asia (especially China) because of their supposed aphrodisiacal powers. By 1998 annual incidents of tiger poaching had dropped to 85 and in 2005 just two tigers were killed. Sadly, it's more likely that these estimates reflect a crash in tiger numbers rather than increased community awareness or more effective law enforcement.

Experts fear there may be fewer than 50 of the big cats left in the wild in Cambodia. Numbers are so low that, despite repeated efforts, camera traps set by researchers in recent years have failed to photograph a single tiger, though footprints and other signs of the felines' presence have been recorded. As far as anyone can tell, the surviving tigers live in very low densities in very remote areas, making it difficult for both poachers and scientists to find them, and hard for environmentalists to protect them.

At present, tigers are known to inhabit two areas: the central part of the Cardamom Mountains and Mondulkiri Province. In addition, they are thought to be present in small numbers in Ratanakiri and Preah Vihear.

For insights, stories and links about tigers in Cambodia and what's being done to protect them, visit the website of the Cat Action Treasury at www.felidae.org.

**ENVIRONMENT** WILDLIFE

plovers and terns, around the South Coast estuaries. Serious twitchers should consider a visit to Prek Toal Bird Sanctuary (p126); Ang Trapeng Thmor Reserve (p127), home to the extremely rare sarus crane, depicted on the bas-reliefs at Angkor; or the Tmatboey Ibis Project (p264), where the critically endangered giant ibis, Cambodia's national bird, can be seen. For details on birdwatching in Cambodia, check out the Siem Reap–based Sam Veasna Center (p126).

Cambodia is home to about 240 species of reptile, including nine species of snake whose venom can be fatal, such as members of the cobra and viper families.

### Endangered Species

Unfortunately, it is getting mighty close to checkout time for a number of species in Cambodia. The kouprey (wild ox), declared Cambodia's national animal by King Sihanouk back in the 1960s, and the Wroughton's free-tailed bat, previously thought to exist in only one part of India but discovered in Preah Vihear Province in 2000, are on the 'Globally Threatened: Critical' list, the last stop before extinction.

Other animals under serious threat in Cambodia include the Asian elephant, tiger, banteng, gaur, Asian golden cat, black gibbon, clouded leopard, fishing cat, marbled cat, sun bear, pangolin, giant ibis and Siamese crocodile.

Cambodia has some of the last remaining freshwater Irrawaddy dolphins (*trey pisaut* in Khmer), instantly identifiable thanks to their bulging forehead and short beak. Viewing them at Kampi, near Kratie, is a popular activity.

In terms of fish biodiversity, the Mekong is second only to the Amazon, but dam projects threaten migratory species. The Mekong giant catfish, which can weigh up to 300kg, is critically endangered due to habitat loss and overfishing.

The following environmental groups – staffed in Cambodia mainly by Khmers – are playing leading roles in protecting Cambodia's wildlife:

**Conservation International** (www.conservation.org)
**Fauna & Flora International** (www.fauna-flora.org)
**Maddox Jolie-Pitt Foundation** (www.mjpasia.org)

The *khting vor* (spiral-horned ox), so rare that no one had ever seen a live specimen, was considered critically endangered until DNA analysis of its distinctive horns showed that the creature had never existed – the 'horns' belonged to ordinary cattle and buffalo!

For a close encounter with tigers at the temples of Angkor, watch Jean-Jacques Annaud's 2004 film *Two Brothers*, the story of two orphaned tiger cubs during the colonial period.

In September 2005, three enforcement rangers working with NGO Fauna & Flora International to prevent illegal hunting and logging in the Cardamom Mountains were murdered in separate incidents, apparently by poachers. Then, in 2012, popular environmental activist Chhut Vuthy, founder of the Natural Resource Protection Group, was shot dead in Koh Kong Province.

**Wildlife Alliance** (WildAid; www.wildlifealliance.org)
**Wildlife Conservation Society** (www.wcs.org)
**WWF** (www.worldwildlife.org)

## Plants

No one knows how many plant species are present in Cambodia because no comprehensive survey has ever been conducted, but it's estimated that the country is home to 15,000 species, at least a third of them endemic.

In the southwest, rainforests grow to heights of 50m or more on the rainy southern slopes of the mountains, with montane (pine) forests in cooler climes above 800m and mangrove forests fringing the coast. In the northern mountains there are broadleaved evergreen forests, with trees soaring 30m above a thick undergrowth of vines, bamboos, palms and assorted woody and herbaceous ground plants. The northern plains support dry dipterocarp forests, while around the Tonlé Sap there are flooded (seasonally inundated) forests. The Eastern Highlands are covered with deciduous forests and grassland. Forested upland areas support many varieties of orchid.

The sugar palm, often seen towering over rice fields, provides fronds to make roofs and walls for houses, and fruit that's used to produce medicine, wine and vinegar. Sugar palms grow taller over the years, but their barkless trunks don't get any thicker, hence they retain shrapnel marks from every battle that has ever raged around them.

# National Parks

In the late 1960s Cambodia had six national parks, together covering 22,000 sq km (around 12% of the country). The long civil war effectively destroyed this system and it wasn't reintroduced until 1993, when a royal decree designated 23 areas as national parks, wildlife sanctuaries, protected landscapes and multiple-use areas. Several more protected forests were added to the list in the last decade, bringing the area of protected land in Cambodia to over 43,000 sq km, or around 25% of the country.

Cambodia became the first Southeast Asian country to establish a national park when it created a protected area in 1925 to preserve the forests around the temples of Angkor.

This is fantastic news in principle, but in practice the authorities don't always protect these areas in any way other than drawing a line on a map. The government has enough trouble finding funds to pay the rangers who patrol the most popular parks, let alone to recruit staff for the remote sanctuaries, though in recent years a number of international NGOs have been helping to train and fund teams of enforcement rangers.

## CAMBODIA'S MOST IMPORTANT NATIONAL PARKS

| PARK | SIZE | FEATURES | ACTIVITIES | BEST TIME TO VISIT |
|---|---|---|---|---|
| Bokor | 1581 sq km | hotel-casino, ghost town, views, waterfalls | trekking, cycling, wildlife watching | Nov–May |
| Kirirom | 350 sq km | waterfalls, vistas, pine forests | hiking, wildlife watching | Nov–Jun |
| Ream | 150 sq km | beaches, islands, mangroves, dolphins, monkeys | boating, swimming, hiking, wildlife watching | Nov–May |
| Southern Cardamoms Protected Forest | 1443 sq km | rivers, waterfalls, jungle, elephants | hiking, cycling, wildlife watching | Nov–Jun |
| Virachey | 3325 sq km | unexplored jungle, waterfalls | trekking, adventure, wildlife watching | Nov–Apr |

The Mondulkiri Protected Forest, at 4294 sq km, is now the largest protected area in Cambodia and is contiguous with Yok Don National Park in Vietnam. The Central Cardamoms Protected Forest, at 4013 sq km, borders the Phnom Samkos Wildlife Sanctuary to the west and the Phnom Aural Wildlife Sanctuary to the east, creating almost 10,000 sq km of designated protected land. The noncontiguous Southern Cardamoms Protected Forest (1443 sq km) is along the Koh Kong Conservation Corridor, whose ecotourism potential is as vast as its jungles are impenetrable.

## Environmental Issues

### Logging

The greatest threat to Cambodia's globally important ecosystems is logging for charcoal and timber and to clear land for cash-crop plantations. During the Vietnamese occupation, troops stripped away swaths of forest to prevent Khmer Rouge ambushes along highways. The devastation increased in the 1990s, when the shift to a capitalist market economy led to an asset-stripping bonanza by well-connected businessmen.

International demand for timber is huge and, as neighbouring countries such as Thailand and Vietnam began to enforce much tougher logging regulations, foreign logging companies flocked to Cambodia. At the height of the country's logging epidemic in the late 1990s, just under 70,000 sq km of the country's land area, or about 35% of its total surface area, had been allocated as concessions, amounting to almost all of Cambodia's forest land except national parks and protected areas. However, even in these supposed havens, illegal logging continued. According to environmental watchdog Global Witness (www.global witness.org), the Royal Cambodian Armed Forces (RCAF) is the driving force behind much of the recent logging in remote border regions.

In the short term, deforestation is contributing to worsening floods along the Mekong, but the long-term implications of logging are hard to assess. Without trees to cloak the hills, rains will inevitably carry away large amounts of topsoil during future monsoons and in time this will have a serious effect on Tonlé Sap.

From 2002 things improved for a time. Under pressure from donors and international institutions, all logging contracts were effectively frozen, pending further negotiations with the government. However, small-scale illegal logging continued, including cutting for charcoal production and slash-and-burn for settlement.

The latest threat to Cambodia's forests comes from 'economic concessions' granted to establish plantations of cash crops such as rubber, mango, cashew and jackfruit, or agro-forestry groves of acacia and eucalyptus to supply wood chips for the paper industry. The government argues these plantations are necessary for economic development and counts them as reforestation, but in reality the damage to the delicate ecosystem is irreparable and on a massive scale.

### Pollution & Sanitation

Phnom Penh's air isn't anywhere near as bad as Bangkok's, but as vehicles multiply it's getting worse. In provincial towns and villages, the smoke from garbage fires can ruin your dinner or lead to breathing difficulties and dry coughs.

Detritus of all sorts, especially plastic bags and bottles, can be seen in distressing quantities on beaches, around waterfalls, along roads and carpeting towns, villages and hamlets.

Cambodia has extremely primitive sanitation systems in urban areas, and nonexistent sanitary facilities in rural areas, with only a

Despite responsibility for nearly 20% of the Mekong River's waters, China is not a member of the Mekong River Commission (MRC). However, it began discussing its extensive dam developments with downstream MRC members in 2007.

According to Global Forest Watch (GFW; www.global forestwatch. org), Cambodia's deforestation has accelerated at a faster rate than any other country on earth since 2001. Cambodia lost a total of 2379 sq km of tree cover in 2010, at the peak of the problem. Since then, the numbers have declined, though the country still recorded a loss of 1780 sq km in 2014.

346

**DOING YOUR BIT**

Every visitor to Cambodia can make at least a small contribution to the country's ecological sustainability.

➡ Dispose of your rubbish responsibly.

➡ Drink fresh coconuts, in their natural packaging, rather than soft drinks in throwaway cans and bottles.

➡ Choose trekking guides who respect both the ecosystem and the people who live in it.

➡ Avoid eating wild meat, such as bat, deer and shark fin.

➡ Don't touch live coral when snorkelling or diving, and don't buy coral souvenirs.

➡ If you see wild animals being killed, traded or eaten, take down details of what and where, and contact the **Wildlife Alliance** (☑012 500094; wildlifealliance@online.com. kh), an NGO that helps manage the government's Wildlife Rapid Rescue Team. Rescued animals are either released or taken to the Phnom Tamao Wildlife Rescue Centre (p88).

tiny percentage of the population having access to proper facilities. These conditions breed and spread disease: epidemics of diarrhoea are not uncommon and it is the number-one killer of young children in Cambodia.

In the mid-1960s Cambodia was reckoned to have around 90% of its original forest cover intact. Estimates today vary, but 25% is common.

## Damming the Mekong

The Mekong rises in Tibet and flows for 4800km before continuing through southern Vietnam into the South China Sea. This includes almost 500km in Cambodia, where it can be up to 5km wide. With energy needs spiralling upwards throughout the region, it is very tempting for developing countries like Cambodia and its upstream neighbours to build hydroelectric dams on the Mekong and its tributaries.

Environmentalists fear that damming the mainstream Mekong may be nothing short of catastrophic for the flow patterns of the river, the migratory patterns of fish, the survival of the freshwater Irrawaddy dolphin and the very life of the Tonlé Sap. Plans currently under consideration include the Sambor Dam, a massive 3300MW project 35km north of Kratie. Preparatory work recently began for the Don Sahong (Siphandone) Dam just north of the Cambodia–Laos border.

Also of concern is the potential impact of dams on the annual monsoon flooding of the Mekong, which deposits nutrient-rich silt across vast tracts of land used for agriculture. A drop of just 1m in wet-season water levels on the Tonlé Sap would result in the flood area decreasing by around 2000 sq km, with potentially disastrous consequences for Cambodia's farmers.

Overseeing development plans for the river is the Mekong River Commission (MRC; www.mrcmekong.org). Formed by the United Nations Development Programme and involving Cambodia, Thailand, Laos and Vietnam, it is ostensibly committed to sustainable development.

Banned in Cambodia, the damning 2007 report *Cambodia's Family Trees*, by the UK-based environmental watchdog Global Witness (www. globalwitness. org), exposes Cambodia's most powerful illegal-logging syndicates.

## Sand Extraction

Sand dredging in the estuaries of Koh Kong Province, including inside the protected Peam Krasaop Wildlife Sanctuary, threatens delicate mangrove ecosystems and the sea life that depends on them. Much of the sand is destined for Singapore. For details, see Global Witness' 2009 report *Country for Sale* (www.globalwitness.org/reports/country-sale). Sand extraction from the Mekong River is also having an impact on local communities, as many riverbank collapses have been reported in recent years.

# Survival Guide

# Directory A–Z

## Accommodation

Accommodation in Cambodia has improved immensely during the past decade and everything is available, from the classic budget crash pad to the plush palace. Most hotels quote in US dollars, but some places in the provinces quote in riel, while those near the Thai border quote in baht.

### Hotels & Guesthouses

In Phnom Penh, Siem Reap and the South Coast, which see a steady flow of tourist traffic, hotels improve significantly once you start spending more than US$15 a night. If you spend between US$20 and US$50 you can arrange something very comfortable with the possible lure of a swimming pool. There has also been an explosion of boutique hotels in Phnom Penh, Siem Reap, Sihanoukville, Kep and Battambang and these are atmospheric and charming places to stay in the US$50 to US$100 range. Most smaller provincial cities also offer air-conditioned comfort in the US$10 to US$20 range.

There is now a host of international-standard hotels in Siem Reap, several in Phnom Penh and a couple on the coast in Sihanoukville and Kep. Most quote hefty walk-in rates and whack 10% tax and 10% service on as well. Book online for a lower rate, including taxes and service.

There are substantially discounted low-season (April through September) rates available at major hotels in Phnom Penh, Siem Reap and Sihanoukville. Discounts of 50% are common, as are specials such as 'stay three, pay two'. Check hotel websites for details on any promos or offers.

While many of the swish new hotels have lifts, older hotels often don't and the cheapest rooms are at the top of several flights of stairs.

Budget guesthouses used to be restricted to Phnom Penh, Siem Reap and Sihanoukville, but as tourism takes off in the provinces, they are turning up in most of the other provincial capitals. Costs hover around US$5 to US$10

## BOOK YOUR STAY ONLINE

For more accommodation reviews by Lonely Planet authors, check out http://lonelyplanet.com/hotels/. You'll find independent reviews, as well as recommendations on the best places to stay. Best of all, you can book online.

for a bed, usually with fan, bathroom and satellite TV.

Some guesthouses in Cambodia do not have hot water, but most places have at least a few more expensive rooms where it is available.

### Hostels

There has been a surge in backpacker hostels in recent years, particularly in popular destinations like Phnom Penh, Siem Reap and Sihanoukville. Lively and well run, the dorms are not always the best value and are often the same price as a private room in a locally owned guesthouse. However, most hostels also offer private rooms and some have bonus draws like a swimming pool.

### Homestays

Homestays are popping up in the provinces and offer a good way to meet the local people and learn about the Cambodian lifestyle.

There are several organised homestays around the country in provinces like Kompong Cham and Kompong Thom, as well as lots of informal homestays in out-of-the-way places such as Preah Vihear. The Mekong Discovery Trail includes several homestays between Kratie and the Lao border. There are also several homestays in Banteay Srei District near Siem Reap, which is a convenient option for those only planning to visit Angkor.

## Children

Children can live it up in Cambodia, as they are always the centre of attention and almost everybody wants to play with them. This is great news when it comes to babes in arms and little toddlers, as everyone wants to entertain them for a time or babysit while you tuck into a plate of noodles. For the full picture on surviving and thriving on the road, check out Lonely Planet's *Travel with Children*, which contains useful advice on how to cope on the road. There is also a rundown on health precautions for kids and advice on travel during pregnancy.

## Customs Regulations

If Cambodia has customs allowances, it is tight-lipped about them. You are entitled to bring into the country a 'reasonable amount' of duty-free items. Travellers arriving by air might bear in mind that alcohol and cigarettes are on sale at prices well below duty-free rates on the streets of Phnom Penh – a branded box of 200 cigarettes costs just US$13 and international spirits start as low as US$7 a litre.

Like any other country, Cambodia does not allow travellers to import any weapons, explosives or narcotics – some might say

that there are more than enough of these things in the country already.

It is also illegal to take ancient stone sculptures from the Angkor period out of the country.

## Discount Cards

Senior travellers and students are not eligible for discounts in Cambodia.

## Embassies & Consulates

Many countries now have embassies in Phnom Penh, though some travellers will find that their nearest embassy is in Bangkok. It's important to realise what an embassy can and can't do to help if you get into trouble. Generally speaking, it won't be much help if the trouble is your own fault. Visitors are bound by the laws of the country they are in. The embassy won't be sympathetic if you end up in jail after committing a crime, even if such actions are legal in your own country.

In genuine emergencies assistance may be available, but only if all other channels have been exhausted. If you have all your money and documents stolen, the embassy can assist with getting a new passport, but a loan for onward travel is out of the question.

**Australian Embassy** (Map p46; ☑023-213470; 16 National Assembly St, Phnom Penh)

**Chinese Embassy** (Map p46; ☑023-720920; 256 Mao Tse Toung Blvd, Phnom Penh)

**French Embassy** (Map p38; ☑023-430020; 1 Monivong Blvd, Phnom Penh)

**German Embassy** (Map p46; ☑023-216381; 76-78 St 214, Phnom Penh)

**Indian Embassy** (Map p38; ☑023-210912; 5 St 466, Phnom Penh)

**Indonesian Embassy** (Map p38; ☑023-216148; 1 St 466, Phnom Penh)

**Japanese Embassy** (Map p38; ☑023-217161; 194 Norodom Blvd, Phnom Penh)

**Lao Embassy** (Map p58;☑023-982632; 15-17 Mao Tse Toung Blvd, Phnom Penh)

## Electricity

230V/50Hz

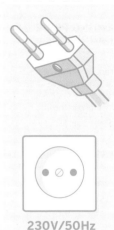

230V/50Hz

**Malaysian Embassy** (☎023-216177; 220 Norodom Blvd, Phnom Penh)

**Myanmar Embassy** (Map p46; ☎023-223761; 181 Norodom Blvd, Phnom Penh)

**Philippine Embassy** (Map p58; ☎023-222303; 15 St 422, Phnom Penh)

**Singaporean Embassy** (Map p46; ☎023-221875; 92 Norodom Blvd, Phnom Penh)

**Thai Embassy** (Map p38; ☎023-726306; 196 Norodom Blvd, Phnom Penh)

**UK Embassy** (Map p38; ☎023-427124; 27-29 St 75, Phnom Penh)

**US Embassy** (Map p52; ☎023-728000; 1 St 96, Phnom Penh)

**Vietnamese Embassy** (Map p58; ☎023-726274; 436 Monivong Blvd, Phnom Penh) Also has consulates in Battambang (Map p238; ☎053-952894; St 3; ⏱830-5.30pm Mon-Fri), issuing visas in a day; and Sihanoukville (Map p185; ☎034-934039; 310 Ekareach St; ⏱8am-noon & 2-4pm Mon-Sat), also with speedy visa processing.

## Food

See p336 for the low-down on food in Cambodia.

### EATING PRICE RANGES

The following price ranges refer to a standard main course. Unless otherwise stated, tax is included in the price.

**$** less than US$5

**$$** US$5-15

**$$$** more than US$15

## Insurance

Health insurance is essential. Make sure your policy covers emergency evacuation: limited medical facilities mean that you may have to be airlifted to Bangkok in the event of serious injury or illness.

Worldwide travel insurance is available at www.lonely planet.com/travel-insurance. You can buy, extend and claim online anytime – even if you're already on the road.

## Internet Access

Internet access is widespread, but there are not as many internet shops as there used to be now that wi-fi is more prevalent. Charges range from 1500r to US$2 per hour. Many hotels, guesthouses, restaurants and cafes now offer free wi-fi, even in the most out-of-the-way provincial capitals.

## Language Courses

The only language courses available in Cambodia at present are in Khmer and are aimed at expat residents of Phnom Penh rather than travellers. Try the Institute of Foreign Languages at the **Royal University of Phnom Penh** (Map p38; ☎012 866826; www.rupp.edu.kh; Russian Blvd). Also check out the noticeboards at popular guesthouses, restaurants and bars, where one-hour lessons are often advertised by private tutors. There are also regular listings under the classifieds in the *Phnom Penh Post* and the *Cambodia Daily*.

## Legal Matters

Marijuana is not legal in Cambodia and the police are beginning to take a harder line on it. There have been several busts (and a few setups, too) of foreigner-owned bars and restaurants where ganja was smoked – the days of free bowls in guesthouses are definitely history. Marijuana is traditionally used in some Khmer dishes, so it will continue to be around for a long time, but if you are a smoker, be discreet.

This advice applies equally to other narcotic substances, which are also illegal. And think twice about buying any pills from a 'friendly' street dealer, as they may turn out to be tranquillisers and you'll wake up as a robbery victim.

Travellers should note that they can be prosecuted under the law of their home country regarding age of consent, even when abroad.

## LGBT Travellers

While Cambodian culture is tolerant of homosexuality, the gay and lesbian scene here is certainly nothing like that in Thailand. Former King Norodom Sihanouk was a keen supporter of equal rights for same-sex partners and this seems to have encouraged a more open attitude among younger Cambodians. Both Phnom Penh and Siem Reap have a few gay-friendly bars, but it's a low-key scene compared with some parts of Asia.

With the vast number of same-sex travel partners – gay or otherwise – checking into hotels across Cambodia, there is little consideration over how travelling foreigners are related. However, it is prudent not to flaunt your sexuality. As with heterosexual couples, passionate public displays of affection are considered a basic no-no.

Recommended websites when planning a trip:

**Cambodia Gay** (www.cambodia-gay.com) Promoting the GLBT community in Cambodia.

**Siem Reap Gay Guide** (www.thesiemreapgayguide.com) Also produces a free printed guide.

**Sticky Rice** (www.stickyrice.ws) Gay travel guide covering Cambodia and Asia.

**Utopia** (www.utopia-asia.com) Gay travel information and contacts, including some local gay terminology.

## DANGEROUS DRUGS 101

Watch out for *yaba*, the 'crazy' drug from Thailand, known rather ominously in Cambodia as *yama* (the Hindu god of death). Known as ice or crystal meth elsewhere, it's not just any old diet pill from the pharmacist but homemade methamphetamines produced in labs in Cambodia and the region beyond. The pills are often laced with toxic substances, such as mercury, lithium or whatever else the maker can find. *Yama* is a dirty drug and more addictive than users would like to admit, provoking powerful hallucinations, sleep deprivation and psychosis. Steer clear of the stuff unless you plan on an indefinite extension to your trip.

Also be very careful about buying 'cocaine' in Cambodia. Most of what is sold as coke, particularly in Phnom Penh, is actually pure heroin and far stronger than what may be found elsewhere.

# Maps

The best all-rounder for Cambodia is the Gecko *Cambodia Road Map*. At 1:750,000 scale, it has lots of detail and accurate place names. Other popular foldout maps include Nelles *Cambodia, Laos and Vietnam Map* at 1:1,500,000, although the detail is limited, and the Periplus *Cambodia Travel Map* at 1:1,000,000, with city maps of Phnom Penh and Siem Reap.

Lots of free maps, subsidised by advertising, are available in Phnom Penh and Siem Reap at leading hotels, guesthouses, restaurants and bars.

# Money

Cambodia's currency is the riel, abbreviated in our listings to a lower-case 'r' written after the sum. Cambodia's second currency (some would say its first) is the US dollar, which is accepted everywhere and by everyone, though change may arrive in riel. Dollar bills with a small tear are unlikely to be accepted by Cambodians, so it's worth scrutinising the change you are given to make sure you don't have bad bills. In the west of the country,

the Thai baht (B) is also commonplace. If three currencies seems a little excessive, perhaps it's because the Cambodians are making up for lost time: during the Pol Pot era, the country had *no* currency. The Khmer Rouge abolished money and blew up the National Bank building in Phnom Penh.

The Cambodian riel comes in notes of the following denominations: 100r, 200r, 500r, 1000r, 2000r, 5000r, 10,000r, 20,000r, 50,000r and 100,000r.

Businesses may quote prices in US dollars or riel, but in the west it is sometimes baht. While this may seem inconsistent, this is the way it's done in Cambodia, and the sooner you get used to thinking comparatively in riel, dollars or baht, the easier your travels will be.

## ATMs

There are credit-card-compatible ATMs (Visa, MasterCard, JCB, Cirrus) in most major cities. There are also ATMs at the Cham Yeam, Poipet and Bavet borders if arriving by land from Thailand or Vietnam. Machines dispense US dollars or riel. Large withdrawals of up to US$2000 are possible, providing your account can

handle it. Stay alert when using ATMs late at night.

ANZ Royal Bank has the most extensive network, including ATMs at petrol stations, and popular hotels, restaurants and shops, closely followed by Canadia Bank. Acleda Bank has the widest network of branches in the country, including all provincial capitals, making remote travel that much easier to plan. Most ATM withdrawals incur a charge of US$3 to US$5, but ABA Bank offers free withdrawals.

## Bargaining

It is important to haggle over purchases made in local markets in Cambodia, otherwise the stallholder may 'shave your head' (local vernacular for 'rip you off'). Bargaining is the rule in markets, when arranging share taxis and pick-ups, and in some guesthouses. The Khmers are not ruthless hagglers, so a persuasive smile and a little friendly quibbling is usually enough to get a fair price. Try to remember that the aim is not to get the lowest possible price, but a price that is acceptable to both you and the seller. Remember that in many cases a few hundred riel is more important to a Cambodian with a family to support than to a traveller on an extended vacation.

## Cash

The US dollar remains king in Cambodia. Armed with enough cash, you won't need to visit a bank at all because it is possible to change small amounts of dollars for riel at hotels, restaurants and markets. It is always handy to have about US$10 worth of riel kicking around, as it is good for *motos*, *remork-motos* (tuk tuks) and markets. Pay for something cheap in US dollars and the change comes in riel.

The only other currency that can be useful is Thai baht, mainly in the west of the country. Prices in towns such as Koh Kong, Poipet and

## TIPPING TIPS

In many Cambodian restaurants, change will be returned in some sort of bill holder. If you leave the change there it will often be taken by the restaurant proprietor. If you want to make sure the tip goes to the staff who have served you, leave the tip on the table or give it to the individuals directly. In some places, there may be a communal tip box that is shared by staff.

Sisophon are often quoted in baht, and even in Battambang it is common.

In the interests of making life as simple as possible when travelling overland, organise a supply of US dollars before arriving in Cambodia. Cash in other major currencies can be changed at banks or markets in Phnom Penh or Siem Reap. However, most banks tend to offer a poor rate for any non-dollar transaction so it can be better to use moneychangers, which are found in and around every major market.

Western Union and Money-Gram are both represented in Cambodia for fast, if more expensive, money transfers. Western Union is represented by Acleda Bank, and Money-Gram by Canadia Bank.

### Credit Cards

Top-end hotels, airline offices and upmarket boutiques and restaurants generally accept most major credit cards (Visa, MasterCard, JCB and sometimes American Express), but many pass the charges straight on to the customer, meaning an extra 2% to 3% on your bill.

Cash advances on credit cards are available in Phnom Penh, Siem Reap, Sihanoukville, Kampot, Bat-

tambang, Kompong Cham and other major towns. Most banks advertise a minimum charge of US$5, but Canadia Bank offers this service for free.

Several travel agents and hotels in Phnom Penh and Siem Reap can arrange cash advances for about 5% commission; this can be particularly useful if you get caught short at the weekend.

### Tipping

Tipping is not traditionally expected here, but in a country as poor as Cambodia, tips can go a long way. Salaries remain extremely low and service is often friendly and attentive. Many of the upmarket hotels levy a 10% service charge, but this doesn't always make it to the staff. If you stay a couple of nights in the same hotel, try to remember to tip the staff who clean your room. Consider tipping drivers and guides, as the time they spend on the road means time away from home and family.

It is considered proper to make a small donation at the end of a visit to a wat, especially if a monk has shown you around; most wats have contribution boxes for this purpose.

### Travellers Cheques

Most branches of Acleda Bank change travellers cheques to cash, bringing financial freedom to far-flung provinces like Ratanakiri and Mondulkiri. It is best to have cheques in US dollars; expect

to pay about 2% commission to change them.

## Opening Hours

Most Cambodians get up very early and it's not unusual to see people out and about exercising at 5.30am if you are heading home – ahem, sorry, getting up – at that time.

**Banks** Hours vary slightly according to the bank, but most keep core hours of 8am to 3.30pm Monday to Friday, plus Saturday morning.

**Bars** Many are open all day, but some open only for the night shift, especially if they don't serve food.

**Government offices** Open from Monday to Friday and on Saturday mornings. They theoretically begin the working day at 7.30am, break for a siesta from 11.30am to 2pm, and end the day at 5pm. Attractions such as museums are normally open seven days a week.

**Local markets** These operate seven days a week and usually open and close with the sun, running from 6.30am to 5.30pm. They close for a few days during the major holidays of Chaul Chnam Khmer (Khmer New Year), P'chum Ben (Festival of the Dead) and Chaul Chnam Chen (Chinese New Year).

**Restaurants** Local restaurants generally open from about 6.30am until 9pm and may stay open throughout that time. International restaurants stay open a little later and sometimes close between sittings.

## SHOPPING

High-quality handmade crafts, including silk clothing and accessories, stone and wood carvings, and silver, are widely available, especially in Siem Reap, Phnom Penh and towns with particular handicraft specialities. Hill tribes in Mondulkiri and Ratanakiri produce hand-woven cotton in small quantities. In our coverage of Phnom Penh and Siem Reap, we focus on shops and organisations that contribute to reviving traditional crafts and supporting people who are disadvantaged or disabled.

**Shops** Tend to open from about 8am until 6pm, although shops in malls are usually open until about 8pm, as are supermarkets. There are 24-hour minimarts in most big cities.

## Photography

Many internet cafes in Cambodia will burn CDs or DVDs from digital images using card readers or USB connections. The price is about US$2.50 if you need a DVD or US$1.50 for a CD. Digital memory sticks are widely available in Cambodia and are pretty cheap. Digital cameras are a real bargain thanks to low tax and duty, so consider picking up a new model in Phnom Penh, rather than Bangkok or Saigon.

Make sure you have the necessary charger, plugs and transformer for Cambodia. Take care with some of the electrical wiring in guesthouses around the country, as it can be pretty amateurish.

### Photographing People

The usual rules apply. Be polite about photographing people, don't push cameras into their faces, and show respect for monks and people at prayer. In general, the Khmers are remarkably courteous people and if you ask nicely, they'll agree to have their photograph taken. The same goes for filming, although in rural areas you will often find children desperate to get in front of the lens and astonished at seeing themselves played back on an LCD screen. Some people will expect money in return for their photo being snapped; be sure to establish this before clicking away.

## Post

The postal service is hit and miss from Cambodia; send anything valuable by courier or from another country.

### FESTIVAL WARNING

In the run-up to major festivals such as P'chum Ben or Chaul Chnam Khmer, there is a palpable increase in the number of robberies, particularly in Phnom Penh. Cambodians need money to buy gifts for relatives or to pay off debts, and for some individuals theft is the quickest way to get this money. Be more vigilant at night at these times and don't take valuables out with you unnecessarily.

Ensure postcards and letters are franked before they vanish from your sight.

Letters and parcels sent further afield than Asia can take up to two or three weeks to reach their destination. Use a courier to speed things up; **EMS** (☏023-723511; www.ems.com.kh; Main Post Office, St 13, Phnom Penh) has branches at every major post office in the country. DHL and Fed Ex are present in major cities like Phnom Penh, Siem Reap and Sihanoukville.

## Public Holidays

Banks, ministries and embassies close down during public holidays and festivals, so plan ahead if visiting Cambodia during these times. Cambodians also roll over holidays if they fall on a weekend and take a day or two extra during major festivals. Add to this the fact that they take a holiday for international days here and there, and it soon becomes apparent that Cambodia has more public holidays than any other nation on earth!

**International New Year's Day** 1 January

**Victory over the Genocide** 7 January

**International Women's Day** 8 March

**International Workers' Day** 1 May

**International Children's Day** 8 May

**King's Birthday** 13-15 May

**King Mother's Birthday** 18 June

**Constitution Day** 24 September

**Commemoration Day** 15 October

**Independence Day** 9 November

**International Human Rights Day** 10 December

## Safe Travel

Cambodia is a pretty safe country for travellers these days, but remember the golden rule: *stick to marked paths in remote areas* (because of land mines).

The *Cambodia Daily* (www.cambodiadaily.com) and the *Phnom Penh Post* (www.phnompenhpost.com) are both good sources for breaking news. Check their websites before you hit the road.

### Crime & Violence

Given the number of guns in Cambodia, there is less armed theft than one might expect. Still, hold-ups and motorcycle theft are a potential danger in Phnom Penh and Sihanoukville. There is no need to be paranoid, just cautious. Walking or riding alone late at night is not ideal, particularly in rural areas.

There have been incidents of bag snatching in Phnom Penh in the last few years and the motorbike thieves don't let go, dragging passengers off *motos* (motorcycle taxis) and endangering lives.

Should anyone be unlucky enough to be robbed, it is important to note that getting help from the police, such as a police report, is going to cost you. The going rate depends on the size of the claim, but anywhere from US$5 to US$50 is a common charge.

Violence against foreigners is extremely rare, but it pays to take care in crowded bars or nightclubs in Phnom Penh. If you get into a stand-off with rich young Khmers in a bar or club, swallow your pride and back down. Many carry guns and have an entourage of bodyguards. Sihanoukville also has a reputation for occasional violent incidents, usually between rival groups of foreign business owners.

## Mines, Mortars & Bombs

*Never* touch any rockets, artillery shells, mortars, mines, bombs or other war material you may come across. The most heavily mined part of the country is along the Thai border area, but mines are a problem in much of Cambodia. In short: *do not stray from well-marked paths under any circumstances*. If you are planning any walks, even in safer areas such as the remote northeast, it is imperative you take a guide as there may still be unexploded ordnance (UXO) from the American bombing campaign of the early 1970s.

## Scams

Most scams are fairly harmless, involving a bit of commission here and there for taxi or *moto* drivers, particularly in Siem Reap.

There have been one or two reports of police set-ups in Phnom Penh, involving planted drugs. This seems to be very rare, but if you fall victim to the ploy, it may be best to pay them off before more police get involved at the local station, as the price will only rise when there are more mouths to feed.

There is quite a lot of fake medication floating about the region. Safeguard yourself by only buying prescription drugs from reliable pharmacies or clinics.

Beware the Filipino blackjack scam: don't get involved in any gambling with seemingly friendly Filipinos unless you want to part with plenty of cash.

Beggars in places such as Phnom Penh and Siem Reap may ask for milk powder for an infant in arms. Some foreigners succumb to the urge to help, but the beggars usually request the most expensive milk formula available and return it to the shop to split the proceeds after the handover.

## GOVERNMENT TRAVEL ADVICE

Travel advisories on government-run websites update nationals on the latest security situation in any given country.

**Australian Department of Foreign Affairs** (www.smartraveller.gov.au)

**Canadian Government** (www.voyage.gc.ca)

**German Foreign Office** (www.auswaertiges-amt.de)

**Japanese Ministry of Foreign Affairs** (www.anzen.mofa.go.jp)

**Netherlands Government** (www.minbuza.nl)

**New Zealand Ministry of Foreign Affairs** (www.safetravel.govt.nz)

**UK Foreign Office** (www.gov.uk/foreign-travel-advice)

**US Department of State** (www.travel.state.gov)

## Telephone

Cambodia's landline system was totally devastated by the long civil war, leaving the country with a poor communications infrastructure. The advent of mobile phones has allowed Cambodia to catch up with its regional neighbours by jumping headlong into the technology revolution. Mobile phones are everywhere in Cambodia, but landline access in major towns is also improving, connecting more of the country to the outside world than ever before. In this guide, landline area codes appear under the name of each city, but in many areas service is spotty.

With the explosion of wi-fi in towns and cities, it is usually possible to use FaceTime, Skype or Viber at any guesthouse, hotel, cafe or restaurant. Some guesthouses and hotels also have terminals in the lobby for the free use of guests.

For telephone listings of businesses and government offices, check out www.yp.com.kh.

### Mobile Phones

Mobile phones, whose numbers start with ☑01, 06, 07, 08 or 09, are hugely popular with both individuals and commercial enterprises.

When travelling with a mobile phone on international roaming, just select a network upon arrival, dial away and await a hefty phone bill once you return home. Note to self: Cambodian roaming charges are extraordinarily high.

Those who plan on spending longer in Cambodia should arrange a SIM card for one of the local service providers. Foreigners need to present a valid passport to get a local SIM card, but they are available free on arrival at Phnom Penh and Siem Reap international airports.

Most mobile companies now offer cheap internet-based phone calls accessed through a gateway number. Look up the cheap prefix and calls will be just US10¢ or less per minute.

## Time

Cambodia (like Laos, Vietnam and Thailand) is seven hours ahead of Greenwich Mean Time or Universal Time Coordinated (GMT/UTC). When it is midday in Cambodia, it is 10pm the previous evening in San Francisco, 1am in New York, 5am in London, 6am in Paris and 3pm in Sydney.

## Toilets

Cambodian toilets are mostly of the sit-down variety. The occasional squat toilet turns up here and there, particularly in the most budget of budget guesthouses in the provinces or out the back of provincial restaurants.

The issue of toilets and what to do with used toilet paper is a cause for concern. Generally, if there's a wastepaper basket next to the toilet, that is where the toilet paper goes, as many sewerage systems cannot handle toilet paper. Toilet paper is seldom provided in the toilets at bus stations or in other public buildings, so keep a stash with you at all times.

Many Western toilets also have a hose spray in the bathroom, aptly named the 'bum gun' by some. Think of this as a flexible bidet, used for cleaning and ablutions as well as hosing down the loo.

Public toilets are rare, the only ones in the country being along Phnom Penh's riverfront and some beautiful wooden structures dotted about the temples of Angkor. The charge is usually 500r for a public toilet, although they are free at Angkor. Most local restaurants have some sort of toilet.

Should you find nature calling in remote border areas, don't let modesty drive you into the bushes: *there*

*may be land mines not far from the road or track.* Stay on the roadside and do the deed, or grin and bear it until the next town.

## Tourist Information

Cambodia has only a handful of tourist offices, and those encountered by the independent traveller in Phnom Penh and Siem Reap are generally of limited help. However, in the provinces it is a different story, as the staff are sometimes happy to see visitors, if the office happens to be open. These offices generally have little in the way of brochures or handouts though. Generally speaking, fellow travellers, guesthouses, hotels and free local magazines are more useful than tourist offices.

Cambodia has no official tourist offices abroad and it is unlikely that Cambodian embassies will be of much assistance in planning a trip, besides issuing visas, which are available on arrival anyway.

## Travellers with Disabilities

Broken pavements, potholed roads and stairs as steep as ladders at Angkor ensure that for most people with mobility impairments, Cambodia is not going to be an easy country in which to travel. Few buildings have been designed with the disabled in mind, although new projects, such as the international airports at Phnom Penh and Siem Reap, and top-end hotels, include ramps for wheelchair access. Transport in the provinces is usually very overcrowded, but taxi hire from point to point is an affordable option.

On the positive side, the Cambodian people are usually very helpful towards all foreigners, and local labour is cheap if you need someone to accompany you at all

times. Most guesthouses and small hotels have ground-floor rooms that are reasonably easy to access.

The biggest headache also happens to be the main attraction – the temples of Angkor. Causeways are uneven, obstacles common and staircases daunting, even for able-bodied people. It is likely to be some years before things improve, although some ramping is now being introduced at major temples.

Wheelchair travellers will need to undertake a lot of research before visiting Cambodia. There is a growing network of information sources that can put you in touch with others who have wheeled through Cambodia before. Try contacting the following:

**Disability Rights UK** (http://disabilityrightsuk.org)

**Mobility International USA** (www.miusa.org)

**Society for Accessible Travel & Hospitality** (SATH; www.sath.org)

## Visas

Most visitors to Cambodia require a one-month tourist visa (US$30). Most nationalities receive this on arrival at Phnom Penh and Siem Reap airports, and at land borders, but citizens of Afghanistan, Algeria, Bangladesh, Iran, Iraq, Nigeria, Pakistan, Saudi Arabia, Sri Lanka and Sudan need to make advance arrangements. Passport holders from Asean member countries do not require a visa to visit Cambodia. One passport-sized photo is required and you'll be 'fined' US$2 if you don't have one. It is also possible to arrange a visa through Cambodian embassies overseas or an online e-visa (US$30, plus a US$5 processing fee) through the Ministry of Foreign Affairs (www.mfaic.gov.kh).

Those seeking work in Cambodia should opt for the business visa (US$35) as it is easily extended for long periods, including multiple entries and exits. A tourist visa can be extended only once and only for one month, and does not allow for re-entry.

Travellers are sometimes overcharged when crossing at land borders with Thailand, as immigration officials demand payment in baht and round up the figure considerably. Overcharging is also an issue at the Laos border, but not usually at Vietnam borders. Arranging a visa in advance can help avoid overcharging.

Overstaying a visa currently costs US$5 a day.

For visitors continuing to Vietnam, one-month single-entry visas cost US$55 and take two days in Phnom Penh, or just one day via the Vietnamese consulate in Sihanoukville. Most visitors to Laos can obtain a visa on arrival (US$30 to US$42) and most visitors heading to Thailand do not need a visa.

## Visa Extensions

Visa extensions are issued by the large immigration office located directly across the road from Phnom Penh International Airport.

Extensions are easy to arrange, taking just a couple of days. It costs US$45 for one month (for both tourist and business visas), US$75 for three months, US$155 for six months and US$285 for one year (the last three prices relate to business visas only). It's pretty straightforward to extend business visas ad infinitum. Travel agencies and some motorbike-rental shops in Phnom Penh can help with arrangements, sometimes at a discounted price.

## Volunteering

There are fewer opportunities for volunteering than one might imagine in a country as impoverished as Cambodia. This is partly due to the sheer number of professional development workers based here, and development is a pretty lucrative industry these days.

Cambodia hosts a huge number of NGOs, some of which do require volunteers from time to time. The best way to find out who is represented in the country is to drop in on the **Cooperation Committee for Cambodia**

### THE PERILS OF ORPHANAGE TOURISM

In recent years, visiting orphanages in the developing world – Cambodia in particular – has become a popular activity, but is it always good for the children and the country in the longer run? Tough question. 'Orphan tourism' and all the connotations that come with it are a disturbing development that is bringing unscrupulous elements into the world of caring for Cambodian children. There have already been reports of new orphanages opening up with a business model to bring in a certain number of visitors per month. In other cases, the children are not orphans at all, but are 'borrowed' from the local school for a fee.

In a report released in 2009, Save the Children stated that most children living in orphanages throughout the developing world have at least one parent still alive. More than eight million children worldwide are living in institutions, with most sent there by their families because of poverty rather than the death of a parent. Many are in danger of abuse and neglect from carers, as well as exploitation and international trafficking, with children aged under three most at risk.

The Save the Children report states: 'One of the biggest myths is that children in orphanages are there because they have no parents. This is not the case. Most are there because their parents simply can't afford to feed, clothe and educate them.' From 2005 to 2010, the number of orphanages in Cambodia almost doubled from 153 to 269. Of the 12,000 Cambodian children in institutions, only about 28% are genuine orphans without both parents.

Many orphanages in Cambodia are doing a good job in tough circumstances. Some are world class, enjoy funding and support from wealthy benefactors, and don't need visitors; others are desperate places that need all the help they can get. However, if a place is promoting orphan tourism, then proceed with caution, as the adults may not always have the best interests of the children at heart. Child-welfare experts also recommend that any volunteering concerning children should involve a minimum three-month commitment – having strangers drop in and out of their lives on short visits can be detrimental to a child's emotional well-being and development.

Friends International and Unicef joined forces in 2011 to launch the 'Think Before Visiting' campaign. Learn more at www.thinkchildsafe.org/thinkbeforevisiting before you inadvertently contribute to the problem.

(CCC; ☎023-214152; www.ccc-cambodia.org; 9-11 St 476) in Phnom Penh. This organisation has a handy list of all NGOs, both Cambodian and international, and is extremely helpful.

There are a couple of professional Siem Reap–based organisations helping to place volunteers. **ConCERT** (Map p96; ☎063-963511; www.concertcambodia.org; 560 Phum Stoueng Thmey; ☺9am-5pm Mon-Fri) has a 'responsible volunteering' section on its website that offers some sound advice on preparing for a stint as a volunteer. **Globalteer** (☎063-761802; www.globalteer.org) coordinates the Cambodia Kids Project and offers volunteer placements with various projects, but this does involve a weekly charge.

The other avenue is professional volunteering through an organisation back home that offers one- or two-year placements in Cambodia. One of the largest organisations is Voluntary Service Overseas (www.vso.org.uk) in the UK, but other countries also have their own organisations, including Australian Volunteers International (www.australianvolunteers.com) and New Zealand's Volunteer Service Abroad (www.vsa.org.nz). The UN also operates its own volunteer program; details are available at www.unv.org. Other general volunteer sites with links all over the place include www.voluntourism.org and www.goabroad.com/volunteer-abroad.

## Women Travellers

Women will generally find Cambodia a hassle-free place to travel, although some of the guys in the guesthouse industry will try their luck from time to time. Foreign women are unlikely to be targeted by local men, and will probably find Khmer men to be courteous and polite. At the same time it pays to be careful. As is the case in many places, walking or riding a bike alone late at night is risky, and if you're planning a trip off the beaten track it would be best to find a travel companion.

Khmer women dress fairly conservatively. It's best to follow suit, particularly when visiting wats. In general, long-sleeved shirts and long trousers or skirts are preferred. It is also worth having trousers for heading out at night on *motos,* as short skirts aren't very practical.

Tampons and sanitary napkins are widely available in the major cities and provincial capitals, but if you are heading into very remote areas for a few days, it is worth having your own supply.

## Work

Jobs are available throughout Cambodia, but apart from teaching English or helping out in guesthouses, bars or restaurants, most are for professionals and are arranged in advance. There is a lot of teaching work available for English-language speakers; salary is directly linked to experience. Anyone with an English-language teaching certificate can earn considerably more than those with no qualifications.

For information about work opportunities with NGOs, call into Phnom Penh's **Cooperation Committee for Cambodia** (CCC; ☎023-214152; www.ccc-cambodia.org; 9-11 St 476), which has a noticeboard for positions vacant. If you are thinking of applying for work with NGOs, you should bring copies of your education certificates and work references. However, most of the jobs available are likely to be on a voluntary basis, as most recruiting for specialised positions is done in home countries or through international organisations.

Other places to look for work include the classifieds sections of the *Phnom Penh Post* and the *Cambodia Daily,* and on noticeboards at guesthouses and restaurants in Phnom Penh.

# Transport

## GETTING THERE & AWAY

### Entering the Country

Cambodia has two international gateways for arrival by air – Phnom Penh and Siem Reap – and a healthy selection of land borders with neighbouring Thailand, Vietnam and Laos. Formalities at Cambodia's international airports are traditionally smoother than at land borders, as the volume of traffic is greater. Crossing at land borders is relatively easy, but immigration officers may try to wangle some extra cash, either for the visa or via some other scam. Anyone without a photo for their visa form will be charged about US$2 at the airport, and around 100B at land borders with Thailand.

Arrival by air is popular for those on a short holiday, as travelling overland to or from Cambodia puts a dent in the time in-country. Travellers on longer trips usually enter and exit by land, as road and river transport is very reasonably priced in Cambodia.

### Passport

Not only is a passport essential, but it also needs to be valid for at least six months or Cambodian immigration will not issue a visa.

It's also important to make sure that there is plenty of space left in the passport, as a Cambodian visa alone takes up one page.

Losing a passport is not the end of the world, but it is a serious inconvenience. To expedite the issuing of a new passport, keep a photocopy of your passport photo page.

## Air

### Airports & Airlines

**Phnom Penh International Airport** (សិប្បកម្មសាខាងព្រះ ពទូរប ព្រះ:ឈរវង្ស; PNH; ☎023-890890; www.cambodia-airports.com) Gateway to the Cambodian capital.

**Siem Reap International Airport** (Map p130; ☎063-761261; www.cambodia-airports.com) Serves visitors to the temples of Angkor. Both airports have a good range of services, including restaurants, bars, shops and ATMs.

**Sihanoukville International Airport** (☎012-333524; www.cambodia-airports.com) Currently only offers domestic links with Phnom Penh and Siem Reap.

Flights to Cambodia are expanding, but most connect only as far as regional capitals. However, budget airlines have taken off in recent years and are steadily driving down prices.

If you are heading to Cambodia for a short holiday and want a minimum of fuss, Thai Airways offers the eas-

iest connections from major cities in Europe, the USA and Australia. Singapore Airlines' regional wing, Silk Air, and budget airline Jetstar offer at least one flight per day connecting Cambodia to Singapore. Other regional centres with flights to Cambodia are Ho Chi Minh City (Saigon), Hanoi, Vientiane, Luang Prabang, Pakse, Kuala Lumpur, Seoul, Taipei, Hong Kong, Guangzhou and Shanghai. Further afield, there is also a route to Doha in the Middle East.

Domestic airlines in Cambodia tend to open up and close down regularly. Given the choice, enter the country on an international carrier rather than a local outfit.

Some airlines offer open-jaw tickets into Phnom Penh and out of Siem Reap, which can save some time and money. Tickets are available directly from the airlines or through travel agencies in Phnom Penh and Siem Reap.

**Air Asia** (www.airasia.com) Daily budget flights connecting Phnom Penh and Siem Reap to Kuala Lumpur and Bangkok.

**Asiana Airlines** (www.asiana.co.kr) Regular connections between Phnom Penh and Seoul.

**Bangkok Airways** (www.bangkokair.com) Daily connections from Phnom Penh and Siem Reap to Bangkok.

**Cambodia Angkor Air** (www.cambodiaangkorair.com) Daily connections from Phnom Penh and Siem Reap to Bangkok,

## CLIMATE CHANGE & TRAVEL

Every form of transport that relies on carbon-based fuel generates $CO_2$, the main cause of human-induced climate change. Modern travel is dependent on aeroplanes, which might use less fuel per kilometre per person than most cars but travel much greater distances. The altitude at which aircraft emit gases (including $CO_2$) and particles also contributes to their climate change impact. Many websites offer 'carbon calculators' that allow people to estimate the carbon emissions generated by their journey and, for those who wish to do so, to offset the impact of the greenhouse gases emitted with contributions to portfolios of climate-friendly initiatives throughout the world. Lonely Planet offsets the carbon footprint of all staff and author travel.

Ho Chi Minh City (Saigon) and Guangzhou; also from Phnom Penh to Vientiane and Hanoi.

**Cebu Pacific** (www.cebupacific air.com) Budget flights between Siem Reap and Manila three times a week.

**China Eastern Airlines** (www. ce-air.com) Regular flights from Phnom Penh to Shanghai.

**China Southern Airlines** (www. cs-air.com) Daily flights from Phnom Penh to Guangzhou.

**Dragon Air** (www.dragonair.com) Daily flights between Phnom Penh and Hong Kong.

**Eva Air** (www.evaair.com) Daily flights between Phnom Penh and Taipei.

**Jetstar** (www.jetstar.com) Daily budget flights from both Phnom Penh and Siem Reap to Singapore.

**Korean Air** (www.koreanair. com) Regular flights connecting Phnom Penh and Siem Reap with Seoul and Incheon.

**Lao Airlines** (www.laoairlines. com) Regular flights from Phnom Penh to Vientiane and from Siem Reap to Pakse and Luang Prabang.

**Malaysia Airlines** (www. malaysiaairlines.com) Daily connections from Phnom Penh and Siem Reap to Kuala Lumpur.

**Qatar Airways** (www.qatarair ways.com) Regular flights from Phnom Penh to Ho Chi Minh City and Doha.

**Silk Air** (www.silkair.com) Daily flights linking Phnom Penh and Siem Reap with Singapore, plus some flights between Siem Reap and Danang.

**Thai Airways** (www.thaiair.com) Daily flights connecting Phnom Penh and Bangkok.

**Vietnam Airlines** (www.viet namair.com.vn) Daily flights linking both Phnom Penh and Siem Reap with both Hanoi and Ho Chi Minh City, as well as Phnom Penh with Vientiane, and Siem Reap with Luang Prabang, Danang and Phu Quoc.

## Land

### Border Crossings

Cambodia shares one border crossing with Laos, five crossings with Thailand and seven with Vietnam. Cambodian visas are now available at all the land crossings with Laos, Thailand and Vietnam. Neighbouring visas are available on arrival in Laos and Thailand but are only available to limited nationalities on arrival in Vietnam, so check your passport status before heading to the border. Most borders are open during the core hours of 7am to 5pm. However, some of the most popular crossings are open later in the evening and other more remote crossings close for lunch.

There are few legal money-changing facilities at some of the more remote border crossings, so be sure to have some small-denomination US dollars handy.

Tourist visas are available at all crossings for US$30, but Cambodian immigration officers at the land border crossings, especially with Thailand, have a reputation

for petty extortion. Travellers are occasionally asked for a small 'immigration fee' of some kind or some sort of bogus health certificate costing US$1. More serious scams include overcharging for visas by demanding payment in Thai baht and forcing tourists to change US dollars into riel at a poor rate. Hold your breath, stand your ground, and don't let this experience flavour your impression of Cambodians overall.

Before making a long-distance trip, be aware of border closing times, visa regulations and any transport scams. Border details change regularly, so ask around or check the Lonely Planet Thorn Tree (lonely planet.com/thorntree).

#### LAOS

Cambodia and Laos share a remote frontier that includes some of the wildest areas of both countries. There is only one border crossing open to foreigners.

#### THAILAND

Cambodia and Thailand share an 805km border and there are now five legal international border crossings, and many more options for locals.

#### VIETNAM

Cambodia and Vietnam share a long frontier with a bevy of border crossings. Foreigners are currently permitted to cross at seven places. Cambodian visas are

# Border Crossings

0 — 50 km
0 — 25 miles

THAILAND

LAOS

Chong Jom
Smach
Samraong  Choam  Anlong  Sra Em
Veng
Chong Sa-Ngam  Prasat Preah Vihear
Muang Khong
Nong Nok Khiene
Le Thanh
Trapeang Kriel
Ban Lung  Yadaw
Aranya Prathet
Poipet  Sisophon
Siem Reap
Tbeng Meanchey
Battambang
Ban Pakard
Psar Pruhm
Pailin
Pursat
Kompong Luong
Krakor
Kompong Chhnang
Romeas
Kompong Thom
Kratie
Sen Monorom
Skuon
Kompong Cham
Snuol  Trapeang Sre
Loc Ninh
Udong
Khlong Yai
Hat Lek
Cham Yeam  Koh Kong City
Kompong Speu
PHNOM PENH
Trapeang Prey Phlong
Veng
Svay Rieng
Xa Mat
Tay Ninh
VIETNAM
Banteay Chakrey
Kaam Samnor
Bavet  Moc Bai
Takeo
Phnom Den
Khanh Binh
Vinh Xuong
HO CHI MINH CITY (SAIGON)
Sihanoukville  Kampot
Kep  Prek Chak
Xa Xia  Ha Tien
Tinh Bien
Chau Doc

now available at all crossings, but two-week Vietnamese visas are only available on arrival for a handful of nationalities.

## Car & Motorcycle

Car drivers and motorcycle riders will need registration papers, insurance documents and an International Driving Licence (although not officially recognised) to bring vehicles into Cambodia. It is complicated to bring in a car but relatively straightforward to bring in a motorcycle, as long as you have a *carnet de passage* (vehicle passport). This acts as a temporary import-duty waiver and should save a lot of hassles when dealing with Cambodian customs.

# Tours

In the early days of tourism in Cambodia, organised tours were a near necessity. The situation has changed dramatically and it is now much easier to organise your own trip. Budget and midrange travellers in particular can go it alone, as arrangements are cheap and easy on the ground. If you are on a tight schedule, it can pay to book a domestic flight in advance if you're planning to link the temples of Angkor and Siem Reap with Cambodia's capital, Phnom Penh. Once at Angkor, guides and all forms of transport under the sun are plentiful.

Flights and tours can be booked online at lonely planet.com/bookings.

Shop around before booking a tour, as there is lots of competition and some companies offer more interesting itineraries than others. The following are reliable companies based in Cambodia.

**About Asia** (063-760190; www.aboutasiatravel.com) Small bespoke travel company specialising in Siem Reap. Profits help build schools in Cambodia.

**Hanuman** (023-218396; www.hanuman.travel) Long-running, locally owned, locally operated company with innovative tours like Temple Safari. Big supporter of responsible tourism initiatives.

**Journeys Within** (☎063-964748; www.journeys-within.com) A boutique tourism company based in Siem Reap that offers various cross-border trips in addition to appealing tours within Cambodia. Operates a charitable arm helping schools and communities.

**Sam Veasna Center** (☎063-963710; www.samveasna.org) ✈ Day trips that combine birdwatching with visits to outlying temples.

There are also motorbike touring companies recommended later in this section (p363), as well as specialist travel companies in Siem Reap (p102) offering Angkor experiences and more.

# GETTING AROUND

## Air

### Airlines in Cambodia

Domestic flights offer a quick way to travel around the country. The problem is that the airlines themselves seem to come and go pretty quickly as well. There are currently three domestic airlines in Cambodia, operating flights between Phnom Penh and Siem Reap and Siem Reap and Sihanoukville. There are around seven flights a day between Phnom Penh and Siem Reap and it is usually possible to get on a flight at short notice. Book ahead in peak season. There are currently about three flights per day between Siem Reap and Sihanoukville in peak season.

**Bassaka Air** (☎023-217613; www.bassakaair.com) Offers at least one flight daily between Phnom Penh and Siem Reap and Siem Reap and Siem Reap.

**Cambodia Angkor Air** (☎023-212564; www.cambodiaangkorair.com) The national carrier offers four flights a day between Phnom Penh and Siem Reap and up to two flights a day between Siem Reap and Sihanoukville.

Prices are higher than the competition.

**Cambodia Bayon Airlines** (☎023-231555; www.bayonairlines.com) Has at least one flight daily between Phnom Penh and Siem Reap and Siem Reap and Sihanoukville.

### Helicopter

There are two private helicopter companies offering scenic flights over the temples of Angkor and charter flights for high-flyers.

**Helicopters Cambodia** (Map p96; ☎012 814500; www.helicopterscambodia.com) Has offices in Phnom Penh and Siem Reap and is affiliated with Helicopters New Zealand.

**Helistar** (Map p96; ☎088 888 0016; www.helistarcambodia.com) A reliable helicopter company with offices in both Phnom Penh and Siem Reap.

## Bicycle

Cambodia is a great country for experienced cyclists to explore. A mountain bike is the recommended set of wheels thanks to the notorious state of the roads. Most roads have a flat unpaved trail along the side, which is useful for cyclists.

Much of Cambodia is pancake flat or only moderately hilly. Safety, however, is a considerable concern on the newer surfaced roads, as local traffic travels at high speed. Bicycles can be transported around the country in the back of pick-ups or on the roof of minibuses.

Guesthouses and hotels in Cambodia rent out bicycles for around US$2 per day, or US$7 to US$15 for an imported brand such as Giant or Trek.

Top bikes, safety equipment and authentic spare parts are now readily available in Phnom Penh at very reasonable prices.

**PEPY Ride** (☎023-222804; www.pepyride.org) A bicycle and volunteer tour company offering adventures throughout Cambodia. PEPY promotes 'adventurous living, responsible giving' and uses proceeds to help build schools in rural Cambodia and fund education programs.

For more on cycling in Cambodia, see the Outdoor Adventures chapter (p28).

## Boat

Cambodia's 1900km of navigable waterways are not as important as they once were for the average tourist, given major road improvements. North of Phnom Penh, the Mekong is easily navigable as far as Kratie, but there are no longer regular passenger services on these routes, as buses have taken all the business. There are scenic boat services between Siem Reap and Battambang, and the Tonlé Sap lake is also navigable year-round, although only by smaller boats between March and July.

Traditionally the most popular boat services with foreigners are those that run between Phnom Penh and Siem Reap. The express services do the trip in as little as five hours, but it's not the most interesting boat journey in Cambodia, as the Tonlé Sap lake is like a vast sea, offering little scenery. It's more popular (and much cheaper) to take a bus on the paved road instead.

The small boat between Siem Reap and Battambang is more rewarding, as the river scenery is truly memorable, but it can take as long as a whole day with delays.

## Bus

The range of road transport is extensive. On sealed roads, the large air-conditioned buses are the best choice. Elsewhere in the country, a shared taxi or minibus is the way to go.

Bus services have come on in leaps and bounds in the last few years and the situation is getting even

## POPULAR LAND CROSSINGS

### Laos

For Laos, the Trapeang Kriel–Nong Nok Khiene crossing connects Stung Treng in Cambodia with Don Det in Laos.

### Thailand

| BORDER CROSSING | CAMBODIAN TOWN | CONNECTING TOWN |
| --- | --- | --- |
| Cham Yeam–Hat Lek | Koh Kong City | Trat |
| Choam–Chong Sa-Ngam | Anlong Veng | Phusing |
| O Smach–Chong Jom | Samraong | Surin |
| Poipet–Aranya Prathet | Siem Reap | Bangkok |
| Psar Pruhm–Ban Pakard | Pailin | Chanthaburi |

### Vietnam

| BORDER CROSSING | CAMBODIAN TOWN | CONNECTING TOWN |
| --- | --- | --- |
| Bavet–Moc Bai | Phnom Penh | Ho Chi Minh City |
| Kaam Samnor–Vinh Xuong | Phnom Penh | Chau Doc |
| O Yadaw–Le Thanh | Ban Lung | Pleiku, Quy Nhon, Hoi An |
| Phnom Den–Tinh Bien | Takeo | Chau Doc |
| Prek Chak–Xa Xia | Kep, Kampot | Ha Tien, Phu Quoc |
| Trapeang Phlong–Xa Mat | Kompong Cham | Tay Ninh, Ho Chi Minh City |
| Trapeang Sre–Loc Ninh | Kratie, Kompong Cham | Binh Long |

better as more roads are upgraded. Bus travel is arguably the safest way to get around the country these days. The services used most regularly by foreigners are those from Phnom Penh to Siem Reap, Battambang, Sihanoukville, Kompong Cham and Kratie, and the tourist buses from Siem Reap to Poipet.

'Express minibuses' now connect Phnom Penh and major cities around the country and these can be faster than the bigger buses. These minibuses are usually modern Ford Transits or Toyota HiAces and operate a one seat/one passenger policy. Older minibuses serve most provincial routes but are not widely used by Western visitors. They are very cheap but often uncomfortably overcrowded and sometimes driven by maniacs. Only really consider them if there is no alternative.

## Car & Motorcycle

Car and motorcycle rental are comparatively cheap in Cambodia and many visitors rent a car or bike for greater flexibility to visit out-of-the-way places and to stop when they choose. Almost all car rental in Cambodia includes a driver, which is good news given the abysmal state of many roads, the lack of road signs and the disregard for road rules displayed by some drivers.

### Driving Licences

A standard driving licence is not much use in Cambodia. In theory, to drive a car you need an International Driving Licence, usually issued through your automobile association back home, but Cambodia is not currently a recognised country. It is very unlikely that a driving licence will be of any use to most travellers, save for those

coming to live and work in Cambodia.

When it comes to renting motorcycles, it's a case of no licence required. If you can drive the bike out of the shop, you can drive it anywhere, or so the logic goes.

### Fuel & Spare Parts

Fuel is relatively expensive in Cambodia compared with other staples, at around 4000r to 5000r (US$1 to US$1.25) a litre. Fuel is readily available throughout the country, but prices generally rise in rural areas. Even the most isolated communities usually have someone selling petrol out of Fanta or Johnnie Walker bottles. Some sellers mix this fuel with kerosene to make a quick profit – use it sparingly, in emergencies only.

When it comes to spare parts, Cambodia is flooded with Chinese, Japanese and Korean motorcycles, so it's easy to get parts for Hondas,

Yamahas or Suzukis, but finding a part for a BMW or Harley is another matter. The same goes for cars – spares for Japanese cars are easy to come by, but if you are driving something obscure, bring substantial spares.

## Hire

### CAR

Car hire is generally only available with a driver and is most useful for sightseeing around Phnom Penh and Angkor. Some tourists with a healthy budget also arrange cars or 4WDs with drivers for touring the provinces. Hiring a car with a driver is about US$30 to US$35 for a day in and around Cambodia's towns. Heading into the provinces it rises to US$50 or more, plus petrol, depending on the destination. Hiring 4WDs will cost around US$60 to US$120 a day, depending on the model and the distance travelled. Driving yourself is just about possible, but this is inadvisable due to chaotic road conditions and personal liability in the case of an accident.

### MOTORCYCLE

It is possible to explore Cambodia by motorbike, but only experienced off-road bikers should take to these roads with a dirt bike. Novice riders should stick to riding smaller semi-automatic mopeds. Anyone planning a longer ride should try out the bike around Phnom Penh for a day or so first to make sure it is in good health.

Cambodia has some of the best roads (read worst roads) in the world for dirt biking, particularly in the provinces of Preah Vihear, Mondulkiri, Ratanakiri and the Cardamom Mountains. There are several specialised dirt-bike touring companies in Cambodia.

Drive with due care and attention, as medical facilities and ambulances are less than adequate beyond

Phnom Penh, Siem Reap and Battambang. If you have never ridden a motorcycle before, Cambodia is not the ideal place to start, but once out of the city it does get easier. If you're jumping in at the deep end, make sure you are under the supervision of someone who knows how to ride.

Motorcycles are available for hire in Phnom Penh and other provincial capitals. In Siem Reap (and at times in Sihanoukville), motorcycle rental is forbidden. It is usually possible to rent a 100cc motorcycle for between US$5 and US$10 per day; costs are around US$10 to US$25 for a 250cc dirt bike.

**Cambodia Expeditions** (www.cambodiaexpeditions. com) This team has been running motorbike tours and rallies in Cambodia since 1998. Very professional with some great routes in the north of the country.

**Dancing Roads** (www. dancingroads.com) Offers motorbike tours around the capital and gentle tours further afield to the South Coast. Based in Phnom Penh, the driver-guides are fun and friendly.

**Hidden Cambodia** (www. hiddencambodia.com) A Siem Reap–based company specialising in motorcycle trips throughout the country, including the remote temples of northern Cambodia and beyond.

**Red Raid Cambodia** (www. motorcycletourscambodia.com) More expensive but experienced French-run outfit offering trips throughout Cambodia, including the Cardamoms.

For more on dirt biking in Cambodia, see the Outdoor Adventures chapter (p28).

## Insurance

If you are travelling in a tourist vehicle with a driver, then the car is usually insured. When it comes to motorcycles, many rental bikes are not insured and you will have to sign a contract agreeing to a valuation for the bike if it is stolen. Make sure you have a strong lock and always leave the bike in guarded parking where available.

Do not even consider hiring a motorcycle if you are daft enough to be travelling in Cambodia without medical insurance. The cost of treating serious injuries, especially if you require an evacuation, is bankrupting for budget travellers.

## Road Conditions & Hazards

Whether travelling or living in Cambodia, it is easy to lull yourself into a false sense of security and assume that down every rural road is yet another friendly village. However, even with the demise of the Khmer Rouge, odd incidents of banditry and robbery do occur in rural

### ROAD SAFETY

Many more people are now killed and injured each month in traffic accidents than by land mines. While this is partly down to land mine awareness efforts and ongoing clearance programs, it is also due to a huge increase in the number of vehicles on the roads and drivers travelling at dangerous speeds. Be extremely vigilant when travelling under your own steam and take care crossing the roads on the high-speed national highways. It's best not to travel on the roads at night due to a higher prevalence of accidents at this time. This especially applies to bikers, as several foreigners are killed each year in motorbike accidents.

areas. There have also been some nasty bike-jackings in Sihanoukville. When travelling in your own vehicle, and particularly by motorcycle in rural areas, make certain you check the latest security information in communities along the way.

Be particularly careful about children on the road – you'll sometimes find kids hanging out in the middle of a major highway. Livestock on the road is also a menace; hit a cow and you'll both be pizza.

Other general security suggestions for those travelling by motorcycle:

➡ Try to get hold of a good-quality helmet for long journeys or high-speed riding.

➡ Carry a basic repair kit, including some tyre levers, a puncture-repair kit and a pump.

➡ Always carry a rope for towing on longer journeys in case you break down.

➡ In remote areas always carry several litres of water, as you never know when you will run out.

➡ Travel in small groups, not alone, and stay close together.

➡ Don't be cheap with the petrol, as running out of fuel in a rural area could jeopardise your health, especially if water runs out too.

➡ Do not smoke marijuana or drink alcohol and drive.

➡ Keep your eyes firmly fixed on the road; Cambodian potholes eat people for fun.

### Road Rules

If there are road rules in Cambodia it is doubtful that anyone is following them. Size matters and the biggest vehicle wins by default. The best advice if you drive a car or ride a motorcycle in Cambodia is to take nothing for granted.

In Cambodia traffic drives on the right. There are some traffic lights at junctions in Phnom Penh, Siem Reap and Sihanoukville, but where there are no lights, most traffic turns left into the oncoming traffic, edging along the wrong side of the road until a gap becomes apparent. For the uninitiated it looks like a disaster waiting to happen, but Cambodians are quite used to the system. Foreigners should stop at crossings and develop a habit of constant vigilance. Never assume that other drivers will stop at red lights; these are considered optional by most Cambodians, especially at night.

Phnom Penh is the one place where, amid all the chaos, traffic police take issue with Westerners breaking even the most trivial road rules. Make sure you don't turn left at a 'no left turn' sign or travel with your headlights on during the day (although, strangely, it doesn't seem to be illegal for Cambodians to travel without headlights at night). Laws requiring that bikes have mirrors and that drivers (not passengers, even children) wear helmets, are being enforced around the country by traffic police eager to levy fines. Foreigners are popular targets.

## Local Transport

### Bus

There are currently almost no local bus networks in Cambodia. Phnom Penh now has a few local bus routes that are proving popular with local students, but are not yet widely used by visitors.

### Cyclo

As in Vietnam and Laos, the cyclo (pedicab) is a cheap way to get around urban areas. In Phnom Penh cyclo drivers can either be flagged down on main roads or found waiting around markets and major hotels. It is necessary

to bargain the fare if taking a cyclo from outside an expensive hotel or popular restaurant or bar. Fares range from US$1 to US$3. There are few cyclos in the provinces, and in Phnom Penh the cyclo has almost been driven to extinction by the moto.

### Moto

Motos, also known as motodups (meaning moto driver), are small motorcycle taxis. They are a quick way of making short hops around towns and cities. Prices range from 2000r to US$1.50 or more, depending on the distance and town; expect to pay more at night. In the past it was rare for prices to be agreed in advance, but with the increase in visitor numbers, a lot of drivers have got into the habit of overcharging. It's probably best to negotiate up front, particularly in the major tourist centres, outside fancy hotels or at night.

### Outboards

Outboards (pronounced 'outboor') are the equivalent of Venice's vaporetto, a sort of local river-bus or taxi. Found all over the country, they are small fibreglass boats with 15HP or 40HP engines, and can carry up to six people for local or longer trips. They rarely run to schedules, but locals wait patiently for them to fill up or you can charter the whole boat and take off. Another variation are the

### THE MOTO BURN

Be careful not to put your leg near the exhaust pipe of a moto (motorcycle taxi) after long journeys; many travellers have received nasty burns, which can take a long time to heal in the sticky weather, and often require antibiotics to recover.

international longtail rocket boats that connect small villages on the upper stretches of the Mekong. Rocket is the definitive word and their safety is questionable.

## Remork-Moto

The *remork-moto (tuk tuk)* is a large trailer hitched to a motorcycle and pretty much operates as a low-tech local bus with oh-so-natural air-conditioning. They are used throughout rural Cambodia to transport people and goods, and are often seen on the edge of towns ready to ferry farmers back to the countryside.

Most popular tourist destinations, including Phnom Penh, Siem Reap and the South Coast, have their very own tourist versions of the *remork,* with a canopied trailer hitched to the back of the motorbike for two people in comfort or as many as you can pile on at night. Often referred to as *tuk tuks* by foreigners travelling in Cambodia, they're a great way to explore temples, as you get the breeze of the bike but some protection from the elements.

## Rotei Ses

*Rotei* means 'cart' or 'carriage' and *ses* is 'horse', but the term is used for any cart pulled by an animal. Cambodia's original 4WD, ox carts, usually pulled by water buffalo or cows, are a common form of transport in remote parts of the country, as only they can get through thick mud in the height of the wet season. Some local community-tourism initiatives now include cart rides.

## REMORK VERSUS TUK TUK

So just what are those motorbikes with the cute little carriages pulled behind? *Remork-motos? Remorks? Tuk tuks?* The debate rumbles on. Officially, Cambodians call them *remork-motos,* which is often shortened to *remork.* In Thailand, the high-octane three-wheeled taxis in Bangkok are known as *tuk tuks,* and this moniker has hopped across the border into common usage in Cambodia. However, some Cambodians take offence at the use of the name *tuk tuk,* so for the time being we are opting for *remork.* Remorkable.

## Taxi

Taxi hire in towns and cities is getting easier, but there are still very few metered taxis, with just a handful of operators in Phnom Penh. Guesthouses, hotels and travel agents can arrange cars for sightseeing in and around towns.

## Share Taxis

In these days of improving roads, share taxis are losing ground to 'express minibuses'. When using share taxis, it is an advantage to travel in numbers, as you can buy spare seats to make the journey more comfortable. Double the price for the front seat and quadruple it for the entire back row. It is important to remember that there aren't necessarily fixed prices on every route, so you have to negotiate. For major destinations they can be hired individually, or you can pay for a seat and wait for other passengers to turn up. Guesthouses are also very helpful when it comes to arranging share taxis – at a price, of course.

## Train

Cambodia's rail system is, like the old road network, one of the most notorious in Asia. There are currently no passenger services, but this may change as the railway continues to be rehabilitated by a private company. Eventually, the Cambodian network will be plugged into the Trans-Asian Railway, which will link Singapore and China, but connecting Phnom Penh with Ho Chi Minh City via a Mekong bridge will take a few years yet.

The rail network consists of about 645km of single-track metre-gauge lines. The 385km northwestern line, built before WWII, links Phnom Penh with Pursat and Battambang. The 254km southwestern line, which was completed in 1969, connects Phnom Penh with Takeo, Kampot and Sihanoukville. The prettiest sections of the network are between Takeo and Kampot and from there to Sihanoukville.

# Health

General health is more of a concern in Cambodia than most other parts of Southeast Asia, due to a lack of effective medical-treatment facilities, a prevalence of tropical diseases and poor sanitation. Once you venture into rural areas you are very much on your own, although most towns have a reasonable clinic these days.

If you feel particularly unwell, try to see a doctor rather than visit a hospital; hospitals in rural areas are pretty primitive and diagnosis can be hit and miss. If you fall seriously ill in Cambodia you should head to Phnom Penh or Siem Reap, as these are the only places in the country with decent emergency treatment. Pharmacies in the larger towns are remarkably well stocked and you don't need a prescription to get your hands on anything from antibiotics to antimalarials. Prices are also very reasonable, but do check the expiry date, as some medicine may have been on the shelves for quite a long time.

While the potential dangers can seem quite frightening, in reality few travellers experience anything more than an upset stomach. Don't let these warnings make you paranoid.

## BEFORE YOU GO

### Insurance

Do not visit Cambodia without medical insurance. Hospitals are extremely basic in the provinces and even in Phnom Penh the facilities are generally not up to international standards. Anyone who has a serious injury or illness while in Cambodia may require emergency evacuation to Bangkok. With an insurance policy costing no more than the equivalent of a bottle of beer a day, this evacuation is free. Without an insurance policy, it will cost between US$10,000 and US$20,000. Don't gamble with your health in Cambodia or you may end up another statistic.

### Vaccinations

Plan ahead for getting your vaccinations; some of them require more than one injection over a period of time, while others should not be given together.

Record all vaccinations on an International Certificate of Vaccination, available from your doctor. It is a good idea to carry this as proof of your vaccinations when travelling in Cambodia.

### Medical Checklist

Following is a list of items to consider including in your medical kit – consult your pharmacist for brands available in your country.

☐ aspirin or paracetamol – for pain or fever

☐ antihistamine – for allergies, or to ease the itch from insect bites or stings

☐ cold and flu tablets, throat lozenges and nasal decongestant

☐ multivitamins – especially for long trips, when dietary vitamin intake may be inadequate

☐ loperamide or diphenoxylate – 'blockers' for diarrhoea

☐ rehydration mixture – to prevent dehydration, which may occur during bouts of diarrhoea

### EVERYDAY HEALTH

Normal body temperature is up to 37°C (98.6°F); more than 2°C (4°F) higher indicates a high fever. The normal adult pulse rate is 60 to 100 beats per minute (children 80 to 100, babies 100 to 140). As a general rule, the pulse increases about 20 beats per minute for each 1°C (2°F) rise in fever.

## RECOMMENDED VACCINATIONS

Recommended vaccinations for a trip to Cambodia are listed here, but it is imperative that you discuss your needs with your doctor.

**Diphtheria and tetanus** Vaccinations for these two diseases are usually combined.

**Hepatitis A** This vaccine provides long-term immunity after an initial injection and a booster at six to 12 months. The hepatitis A vaccine is also available in a combined form with the hepatitis B vaccine – three injections over a six-month period are required.

**Hepatitis B** Vaccination involves three injections, with a booster at 12 months.

**Polio** A booster every 10 years maintains immunity.

**Tuberculosis** Vaccination against TB (BCG vaccine) is recommended for children and young adults who will be living in Cambodia for three months or more.

**Typhoid** Vaccination against typhoid may be required if you are travelling for more than a couple of weeks in Cambodia.

☐ insect repellent, sunscreen, lip balm and eye drops

☐ calamine lotion or aloe vera – to ease irritation from sunburn

☐ antifungal cream or powder – for fungal skin infections and thrush

☐ antiseptic (such as povidone-iodine) – for cuts and grazes

☐ bandages, plasters and other wound dressings

☐ water-purification tablets or iodine

☐ sterile kit (sealed medical kit containing syringes and needles) – highly recommended, as Cambodia has potential medical-hygiene issues

# IN CAMBODIA

## Availability & Cost of Health Care

Self-diagnosis and treatment of health problems can be risky: always seek professional medical help.

Antibiotics should ideally be administered only under medical supervision. Take only the recommended dose at the prescribed intervals and use the whole course, even if the illness seems to be cured earlier. Stop immediately if there are any serious reactions.

The best clinics and hospitals in Cambodia are found in Phnom Penh and Siem Reap. A consultation usually costs in the region of US$20 to US$50, plus medicine. Elsewhere, facilities are more basic, although a private clinic is usually preferable to a government hospital. For serious injuries, seek treatment in Bangkok.

## Infectious Diseases

### Dengue

This viral disease is transmitted by mosquitoes. There is only a small risk to travellers, except during epidemics, which usually occur during and just after the wet season.

Unlike the malaria mosquito, the *Aedes aegypti* mosquito, which transmits the dengue virus, is most active during the day and is found mainly in urban areas.

Signs and symptoms of dengue fever include a sudden onset of high fever, headache, joint and muscle pains (hence its old name, 'breakbone fever'), plus nausea and vomiting. A rash of small red spots appears three to four days after the onset of fever.

Seek medical attention if you think you may be infected. A blood test can diagnose infection, but there is no specific treatment for the disease. Aspirin should be avoided, as it increases the risk of haemorrhaging, but plenty of rest is advised.

There is no vaccine against dengue fever. The best prevention is to avoid mosquito bites at all times.

### Fungal Infections

Fungal infections occur more commonly in hot weather and are usually on the scalp, between the toes (athlete's foot) or fingers, in the groin and on the body (ringworm). Ringworm, a fungal infection, not a worm, is contracted from infected animals or other people. Moisture encourages these infections.

To prevent fungal infections wear loose, comfortable clothes, avoid artificial fibres, wash frequently and dry yourself carefully.

### Hepatitis

Hepatitis is a general term for inflammation of the liver. Several different viruses cause hepatitis, and they differ in the way that they are transmitted. The symptoms are similar in all forms of the illness, and include fever, chills, headache, fatigue, feelings of weakness, and aches and pains, followed by loss of appetite, nausea, vomiting, abdominal pain, dark urine, light-coloured faeces, jaundiced (yellow) skin and yellowing of the whites of the eyes.

Hepatitis A and E are both transmitted by ingesting contaminated food or water. Seek medical advice, but there is not much you can do apart from resting, drinking lots of fluids, eating lightly and avoiding fatty foods.

There are almost 300 million chronic carriers of hepatitis B in the world. It is spread through contact with infected blood, blood products or body fluids; for example, through sexual contact, unsterilized needles, blood transfusions or contact with blood via small breaks in the skin. Hepatitis C and D are spread in the same way as hepatitis B and can also lead to long-term complications.

## HIV/AIDS

Infection with the human immunodeficiency virus (HIV) may lead to acquired immune deficiency syndrome (AIDS), which is a fatal disease. Any exposure to blood, blood products or body fluids may put the individual at risk.

The disease is often transmitted through sexual contact or dirty needles, so vaccinations, acupuncture, tattooing and body piercing can be potentially as dangerous as intravenous drug use.

## Intestinal Worms

These parasites are most common in rural Cambodia. The various worms have different ways of infecting people. Some may be ingested in food such as undercooked meat (eg tapeworms) and some enter through your skin (eg hookworms). Consider having a stool test when you return home to check for worms and to determine the appropriate treatment.

## Malaria

This serious and potentially fatal disease is spread by mosquitoes. If you are travelling in endemic areas it is extremely important to avoid mosquito bites and to take tablets to prevent the disease developing if you become infected. There is no malaria in Phnom Penh, Siem Reap and most other major urban areas in Cambodia, so visitors on short trips to the most popular places do not need to take medication. Malaria self-test kits are widely available in Cambodia, but are not that reliable.

Symptoms of malaria include fever, chills and sweating, headache, aching joints, diarrhoea and stomach pains, usually preceded by a vague feeling of ill health. Seek medical help immediately if malaria is suspected, as, without treatment, the disease can rapidly become more serious or even fatal.

## Sexually Transmitted Infections (STIs)

Gonorrhoea, herpes and syphilis are among these infections. Sores, blisters or a rash around the genitals and discharges or pain when urinating are common symptoms. With some STIs, such as wart virus or chlamydia, symptoms may be less marked or not observed at all, especially in women. Reliable condoms are widely available throughout urban areas of Cambodia.

## Typhoid

Typhoid fever is a dangerous gut infection caused by contaminated water and food. Medical help must be sought.

In its initial stages sufferers may feel they have a bad cold or flu on the way, as early symptoms are a headache, body aches and a fever that rises a little each day until it is around 40°C (104°F) or higher. There may also be vomiting, abdominal pain, diarrhoea or constipation.

In the second week, the high fever continues and a few pink spots may appear on the body; trembling, delirium, weakness, weight loss and dehydration may occur.

## Traveller's Diarrhoea

Simple things like a change of water, food or climate can all cause a mild bout of diarrhoea, but a few rushed toilet trips with no other symptoms are not indicative of a major problem. Almost everyone gets a mild bout of the runs on a longer visit to Cambodia.

Dehydration is the main danger with diarrhoea, particularly in children or the elderly as it can occur quite quickly. Under all circumstances *fluid replacement* is the most important thing to remember. Stick to a bland diet as you recover. Commercially available oral rehydration salts are very useful; add them to boiled or bottled water.

Gut-paralysing drugs such as Lomotil or Imodium can be used to bring relief from the symptoms of diarrhoea, although they do not actually cure the problem. Only use these drugs if you do not have access to toilets and *must* travel.

# Environmental Hazards

## Food

There is an adage that says, 'If you can cook it, boil it or peel it you can eat it...otherwise forget it'. This is slightly extreme, but many travellers have found it is better to be safe than sorry. Vegetables and fruit should be washed with purified water or peeled where possible. Beware of ice cream that is sold in the street (or anywhere), as it might have melted and refrozen. Shellfish such as mussels, oysters and clams should be avoided, as should undercooked meat, particularly in the form of mince.

## Heat Exhaustion

Dehydration and salt deficiency can cause heat exhaustion. Take time to acclimatise to high temperatures, drink sufficient liquids and do not do anything too physically demanding.

Salt deficiency is characterised by fatigue, lethargy, headaches, giddiness and

## CONTACT LENSES

People wearing contact lenses should be aware that Cambodia is an extremely dusty country and this can cause much irritation when travelling. It is generally bearable in cars, but when travelling by motorcycle or pick-up, it is most definitely not. Pack a pair of glasses.

muscle cramps; salt tablets may help, but adding extra salt to your food is better.

Heatstroke can occur if the body's heat-regulating mechanism breaks down, causing the body temperature to rise to dangerous levels. Long, continuous periods of exposure to high temperatures and insufficient fluids can leave you vulnerable to heatstroke.

### Insect Bites & Stings

Bedbugs live in various places, but particularly in dirty mattresses and bedding, and are evidenced by spots of blood on bedclothes or on the wall. Bedbugs leave itchy bites in neat rows. Calamine lotion or Stingose spray may help.

All lice cause itching and discomfort. They make themselves at home in your hair (head lice), your clothing (body lice) or in your pubic hair (crabs). You catch lice through direct contact with infected people or by sharing combs, clothing and the like. Powder or shampoo treatment will kill the lice, and infected clothing should be washed in very hot, soapy water and left to dry in the sun.

Leeches may be present in damp rainforest conditions; they attach themselves to your skin to suck your blood. Trekkers often get them on their legs or in their boots. Salt or a lighted cigarette end will make them fall off.

Sandflies inhabit beaches (usually the more remote ones) across southeast Asia. They have a nasty bite that is extremely itchy and can easily become infected. Use an antihistamine to quell the itching, and, if you have to itch, use the palm of your hand and not your nails or infection may follow.

### Prickly Heat

Prickly heat is an itchy rash caused by excessive perspiration trapped under the skin. It usually strikes people who have just arrived in a hot climate. Keeping cool, bathing often, drying the skin, using a mild talcum or prickly heat powder, or finding air-conditioning may help.

### Snakes

To minimise the chances of being bitten by a snake, always wear boots, socks and long trousers when walking through undergrowth where snakes may be present.

### Water

The number-one rule is *be careful of water and ice*, although both are usually factory produced, a legacy of the French. If you don't know for certain that the water is safe, assume the worst. Reputable brands of bottled water or soft drinks are usually fine, but you can't safely drink tap water. Only use water from containers with a serrated seal. Tea and coffee are generally fine, as they're made with boiled water.

# Traditional Medicine

Traditional medicine or *thnam boran* is very popular in rural Cambodia. There are *kru Khmer* (traditional medicine men) in most districts of the country and some locals trust them more than modern doctors and hospitals. Working with tree bark, roots, herbs and plants, they boil up brews to supposedly cure all ills. However, when it comes to serious conditions like snake bites, their treatments can be counterproductive.

# Language

The Khmer language is spoken by approximately nine million people in Cambodia, and is understood by many in neighbouring countries. Although Khmer as spoken in Phnom Penh is generally intelligible to Khmers nationwide, there are several distinct dialects in other parts of the country. Most notably, inhabitants of Takeo Province tend to modify or slur hard consonant/ vowel combinations, especially those with 'r'. For example, *bram* (five) becomes *pe-am*, *sraa* (alcohol) becomes *se-aa*, and *baraang* (French for foreigner) becomes *be-ang*. In Siem Reap there's a Lao-sounding lilt to the local speech – some vowels are modified, eg *poan* (thousand) becomes *peuan*, and *kh'sia* (pipe) becomes *kh'seua*.

Though English is fast becoming Cambodia's second language, the Khmer population still clings to the Francophone pronunciation of the Roman alphabet and most foreign words. This is helpful to remember when spelling Western words and names aloud – 'ay-bee-see' becomes 'ah-bey-sey' and so on.

The pronunciation guides in this chapter are designed for basic communication rather than linguistic perfection. Read them as if they were English, and you shouldn't have problems being understood. Some consonant combinations are separated with an apostrophe for ease of pronunciation, eg 'j-r' in j'rook (pig) and 'ch-ng' in ch'ngain

## WANT MORE?

For in-depth language information and handy phrases, check out Lonely Planet's *Southeast Asia Phrasebook*. You'll find it at **shop.lonelyplanet.com**, or you can buy Lonely Planet's iPhone phrasebooks at the Apple App Store.

(delicious). Also note that k is pronounced as the 'g' in 'go'; kh as the 'k' in 'kind'; p as the final 'p' in 'puppy'; ph as the 'p' in 'pond'; r as in 'rum' (hard and rolling); t as the 't' in 'stand'; and th as the 't' in 'two'.

Vowels and vowel combinations with an h at the end are pronounced with a puff of air at the end. Vowels are pronounced as follows:

a and ah shorter and harder than aa
aa as the 'a' in 'father'
ae as the 'a' in 'cat'
ai as in 'aisle'
am as the 'um' in 'glum'
av like a nasal ao (without the 'v')
aw as the 'aw' in 'jaw'
awh as the 'aw' in 'jaw' (short and hard)
ay as ai (slightly nasal)
e as in 'they'
eh as the 'a' in 'date' (short and hard)
eu like 'oo' (with flat lips)
euh as eu (short and hard)
euv like a nasal eu (without the 'v')
ey as in 'prey'
i as in 'kit'
ia as the 'ee' in 'beer' (without the 'r')
ih as the 'ee' in 'teeth' (short and hard)
ii as the 'ee' in 'feet'
o as the 'ow' in 'cow'
œ as 'er' in 'her' (more open)
oh as the 'o' in 'hose' (short and hard)
ohm as the 'ome' in 'home'
ow as in 'glow'
u as the 'u' in 'flute' (short and hard)
ua as the 'ou' in 'tour'
uah as ua (short and hard)
uh as the 'u' in 'but'
uu as the 'oo' in 'zoo'

# BASICS

The Khmer language reflects the social standing of the speaker and the subject through personal pronouns and 'politeness words'. These range from the simple *baat* for men and *jaa* for women, placed at the end of a sentence and meaning 'yes' or 'I agree', to the very formal and archaic *Reachasahp* or 'royal language', a separate vocabulary reserved for addressing the king and very high officials. Many of the pronouns are determined on the basis of the subject's age and gender in relation to the speaker.

Foreigners are not expected to know all of these forms. The easiest and most general personal pronoun is *niak* (you), which may be used in most situations, for either gender. Men of your age or older can be called *lowk* (Mister). Women of your age or older can be called *bawng srei* (older sister) or, for more formal situations, *lowk srei* (Madam). *Bawng* is an informal, neutral pronoun for men or women who are (or appear to be) older than you. For the third person (he/she/they), male or female, singular or plural, the respectful form is *koat* and the common form is *ke*.

| Hello. | ជម្រាបសួរ | johm riab sua |
|---|---|---|
| Goodbye. | លាសិនហើយ | lia suhn hao-y |
| Excuse me./ Sorry. | សូមទោស | sohm toh |
| Please. | សូម | sohm |
| Thank you. | អរគុណ | aw kohn |
| You're welcome. | អត់អីទេ/ សូមអញ្ជើញ | awt ei te/ sohm onh-jernh |
| Yes. | បាទ/ចាស | baat/jaa (m/f) |
| No. | ទេ | te |

### How are you?
អ្នកសុខសប្បាយទេ? niak sohk sabaay te

### I'm fine.
ខ្ញុំសុខសប្បាយ kh'nyohm sohk sabaay

### What's your name?
អ្នកឈ្មោះអ្វី? niak ch'muah ei

### My name is ...
ខ្ញុំឈ្មោះ... kh'nyohm ch'muah ...

### Does anyone speak English?
ទីនេះមានអ្នកចេះ tii nih mian niak jeh
ភាសាអង់គ្លេសទេ? phiasaa awngle te

### I don't understand.
ខ្ញុំមិនយល់ទេ/ kh'nyohm muhn yuhl te/
ខ្ញុំស្តាប់មិនបាន kh'nyohm s'dap muhn baan te

# ACCOMMODATION

### Where's a hotel?
អ្នកតើលនៅឯណា? ohtail neuv ai naa

| I'd like a room ... | ខ្ញុំសុំបន្ទប់... | kh'nyohm sohm bantohp ... |
|---|---|---|
| for one person | សម្រាប់ មួយនាក់ | samruhp muy niak |
| for two people | សម្រាប់ ពីរនាក់ | samruhp pii niak |
| with a bathroom | ដែលមាន បន្ទប់ទឹក | dail mian bantohp tuhk |
| with a fan | ដែលមាន កង្ហារ | dail mian kawnghahl |
| with a window | ដែលមាន បង្អួច | dail mian bawng uoch |

### How much is it per day?
តម្លៃមួយថ្ងៃ damlay muy th'ngay
ប៉ុន្មាន? ponmaan

# DIRECTIONS

### Where is a/the ...?
...នៅឯណា? ... neuv ai naa

### How can I get to ...?
ផ្លូវណាទៅ...? phleuv naa teuv ...

### Go straight ahead.
ទៅត្រង់ teuv trawng

### Turn left.
បត់ឆ្វេង bawt ch'weng

### Turn right.
បត់ស្តាំ bawt s'dam

### at the corner
នៅកាច់ជ្រុង neuv kait j'rohng

### behind
នៅខាងក្រោយ neuv khaang krao-y

### in front of
នៅខាងមុខ neuv khaang mohk

### next to
នៅជាប់ neuv joab

### opposite
នៅទល់មុខ neuv tohl mohk

# EATING & DRINKING

**Where's a ...?** ...នៅឯណា? ... neuv ai naa

**food stall** កន្លែងលក់ kuhnlaing loak
អ្មប m'howp

**market** ផ្សារ psar

**restaurant** ភោជនីយដ្ឋាន resturawn

**Do you have a menu in English?**
មានម៉ឺនុយជា mien menui jea
ភាសាអង់គ្លេសទេ? piasaa awnglay te

**What's the speciality here?**
ទីនេះមានម្ហូប tii nih mien m'howp
អ៊ីពិសេសទេ? ei piseh te

**I'm vegetarian.**
ខ្ញុំតមសាច់ kh'nyohm tawm sait

**I'm allergic to (peanuts).**
កុំដាក់ (សណ្ដែកដី) kohm dak (sandaik dei)

**Not too spicy, please.**
សូមកុំធ្វើហឹរពេក sohm kohm twœ huhl pek

**This is delicious.**
អានេះឆ្ងាញ់ណាស់ nih ch'ngain nah

**The bill, please.**
សូមគិតលុយ sohm kuht lui

## Fruit & Vegetables

| | | |
|---|---|---|
| **apple** | ផ្លែប៉ោម | phla i powm |
| **banana** | ចេក | chek |
| **coconut** | ដូង | duong |
| **custard apple** | ទៀប | tiep |
| **dragonfruit** | ផ្លែស្រកានាគ | phlai srakaa neak |
| **durian** | ធុរេន | tourain |
| **grapes** | ទំពាំងបាយជូរ | tompeang baai juu |
| **guava** | ត្របែក | trawbaik |
| **jackfruit** | ខ្នុរ | khnau |
| **lemon** | ក្រូចឆ្មារ | krow-it ch'maa |
| **longan** | លៀន | mien |
| **lychee** | ផ្លែគូលែន | phlai kuulain |
| **mandarin** | ក្រូចខ្ទិច | krow-it khwait |
| **mango** | ស្វាយ | svay |
| **mangosteen** | មង្ឃុត | mongkut |

| | | |
|---|---|---|
| **orange** | ក្រូចពោធិ៍សាត់ | kroch pow saat |
| **papaya** | ល្ហុង | l'howng |
| **pineapple** | ម្នាស់ | menoa |
| **pomelo** | ក្រូចថ្លុង | kroch th'lohng |
| **rambutan** | សាវម៉ាវ | sao mao |
| **starfruit** | ស្ពឺ | speu |
| **vegetables** | បន្លែ | buhn lai |
| **watermelon** | ឪឡឹក | euv luhk |

## Meat & Fish

| | | |
|---|---|---|
| **beef** | សាច់គោ | sach kow |
| **chicken** | សាច់មាន់ | sach moan |
| **crab** | ក្ដាម | k'daam |
| **eel** | អន្ទង់ | ahntohng |
| **fish** | ត្រី | trey |
| **frog** | កង្កែប | kawng kaip |
| **lobster** | បង្គង | bawng kawng |
| **pork** | សាច់ជ្រូក | sach j'ruuk |
| **shrimp** | បង្គា | bawngkia |
| **snail** | ខ្យង | kh'jawng |
| **squid** | ម៉ឹក | meuk |

## Other

| | | |
|---|---|---|
| **bread** | នំប៉័ង | nohm paang |
| **butter** | ប៊ឺរ | bœ |
| **chilli** | ម្ទេស | m'teh |
| **curry** | ការី | karii |
| **fish sauce** | ទឹកត្រី | teuk trey |
| **fried** | បៀន/ឆា | jien/chaa |
| **garlic** | ខ្ទឹមស | kh'tuhm saw |
| **ginger** | ខ្ញី | kh'nyei |
| **grilled** | អាំង | ahng |
| **ice** | ទឹកកក | teuk koh |
| **lemongrass** | ស្លឹកគ្រៃ | sluhk krey |
| **noodles (egg/rice)** | មី/គុយទាវ | mii/kyteow |
| **pepper** | ម្រេច | m'rait |

| rice | បាយ | bai |
| salt | អំបិល | uhmbuhl |
| soup | ស៊ុប | sup |
| soy sauce | ទឹកស៊ីអ៊ីវ | teuk sii iw |
| spring rolls (fresh/fried) | ណែម/ឆាយ៉ាវ | naim/chaa yaw |
| steamed | ចំហុយ | jamhoi |
| sugar | ស្ករ | skaw |

## Drinks

| beer | ប៊ីយ៉ែរ | bii-yœ |
| coffee | កាហ្វេ | kaa fey |
| lemon juice | ទឹកក្រូចឆ្មា | teuk kroch ch'maa |
| orange juice | ទឹកក្រូចពោធិ៍សាត់ | teuk kroch pow sat |
| tea | តែ | tai |
| water | ទឹក | teuk |

# EMERGENCIES

**Help!**
ជួយខ្ញុំផង! juay kh'nyohm phawng

**Call the police!**
ជួយហៅប៉ូលិសមក! juay hav police mok

**Call a doctor!**
ជួយហៅ juay hav
គ្រូពេទ្យមក! kruu paet mok

**I've been robbed.**
ខ្ញុំត្រូវចោរប្លន់ kh'nyohm treuv jao plawn

**I'm ill.**
ខ្ញុំឈឺ kh'nyohm cheu

**I'm allergic to (antibiotics).**
ខ្ញុំមិនត្រូវជាតុ kh'nyohm muhn treuv thiat
(អង់ទីប៊ីយ៉ូទិក) (awntiibiowtik)

**Where are the toilets?**
បង្គន់នៅឯណា? bawngkohn neuv ai naa

# SHOPPING & SERVICES

**I want to see the ...**
ខ្ញុំចង់ទៅមើល... kh'nyohm jawng teuv mœl ...

**What time does it open?**
វាបើកម៉ោងប៉ុន្មាន? wia baok maong pohnmaan

**What time does it close?**
វាបិទម៉ោងប៉ុន្មាន? wia buht maong pohnmaan

**I'm looking for the ...**
ខ្ញុំរក... kh'nyohm rohk ...

| bank | ធនាគារ | th'niakia |
| post office | ប្រៃសណីយ៍ | praisuhnii |
| public telephone | ទូរស័ព្ទសាធារណៈ | turasahp saathiaranah |
| temple | វត្ត | wawt |

**How much is it?**
នេះថ្លៃប៉ុន្មាន? nih th'lay pohnmaan

**That's too much.**
ថ្លៃពេក th'lay pek

**No more than ...**
មិនលើសពី... muhn lœh pii ...

**What's your best price?**
អ្នកដាច់ប៉ុន្មាន? niak dach pohnmaan

**I want to change US dollars.**
ខ្ញុំចង់ដូរ kh'nyohm jawng dow
ដុល្លារអាមេរិក dolaa amerik

**What is the exchange rate for US dollars?**
មួយដុល្លារ muy dolaa
ដូរបានប៉ុន្មាន? dow baan pohnmaan

# TIME & DATES

**What time is it?**
ឥឡូវនេះម៉ោងប៉ុន្មាន? eileuv nih maong pohnmaan

| in the morning | ពេលព្រឹក | pel pruhk |
| in the afternoon | ពេលរសៀល | pel r'sial |
| in the evening | ពេលល្ងាច | pel l'ngiach |
| at night | ពេលយប់ | pel yohp |
| yesterday | ម្សិលមិញ | m'suhl mein |
| today | ថ្ងៃនេះ | th'ngay nih |
| tomorrow | ថ្ងៃស្អែក | th'ngay s'aik |

| Monday | ថ្ងៃចន្ទ | th'ngay jahn |
| Tuesday | ថ្ងៃអង្គារ | th'ngay ahngkia |
| Wednesday | ថ្ងៃពុធ | th'ngay poht |
| Thursday | ថ្ងៃព្រហស្បតិ៍ | th'ngay prohoah |
| Friday | ថ្ងៃសុក្រ | th'ngay sohk |
| Saturday | ថ្ងៃសៅរ៍ | th'ngay sav |
| Sunday | ថ្ងៃអាទិត្យ | th'ngay aatuht |

# TRANSPORT

| Where's the ...? | ...នៅឯណា? | ... neuv ai naa |
|---|---|---|
| **airport** | វាលយន្ត | wial yohn |
| | ហោះ | hawh |
| **bus stop** | ចំណត | jamnawt |
| | ឡានឈ្នួល | laan ch'nual |
| **train station** | ស្ថានីយ | s'thaanii |
| | ថេភ្លើង | roht ploeng |

| When does the ... leave? | ...ចេញម៉ោង ប៉ុន្មាន? | ... jeinh maong pohnmaan |
|---|---|---|
| **boat** | ទូក | duk |
| **bus** | ឡានឈ្នួល | laan ch'nual |
| **train** | ថេភ្លើង | roht ploeng |
| **plane** | យន្តហោះ | yohn hawh |

### What time does the last bus leave?

| ឡានឈ្នួលចុងក្រោយ ចេញទៅម៉ោងប៉ុន្មាន? | laan ch'nual johng krao-y jein teuv maong pohnmaan |
|---|---|

### I want to get off (here).

| ខ្ញុំចង់ចុះ(ទីនេះ) | kh'nyohm jawng joh (tii nih) |
|---|---|

### How much is it to ...?

| ទៅ...ថ្លៃប៉ុន្មាន? | teuv ... th'lay pohnmaan |
|---|---|

### Please take me to (this address).

| សូមជូនខ្ញុំទៅ (អាសយដ្ឋាននេះ) | sohm juun kh' nyohm teuv (aasayathaan nih) |
|---|---|

### Here is fine, thank you.

| ឈប់នៅទីនេះក៏បាន | chohp neuv tii nih kaw baan |
|---|---|

## Numbers

Khmers count in increments of five – after reaching the number five (*bram*), the cycle begins again with the addition of one, ie 'five-one' (*bram muy*), 'five-two' (*bram pii*) and so on to 10, which begins a new cycle. For example, 18 has three parts: 10, five and three.

There's also a colloquial form of counting that reverses the word order for numbers between 10 and 20 and separates the two words with *duhn: pii duhn dawp* for 12, *bei duhn dawp* for 13 and so on. This form is often used in markets, so listen keenly.

| 1 | មួយ | muy |
|---|---|---|
| 2 | ពីរ | pii |
| 3 | បី | bei |
| 4 | បួន | buan |
| 5 | ប្រាំ | bram |
| 6 | ប្រាំមួយ | bram muy |
| 7 | ប្រាំពីរ | bram pii |
| 8 | ប្រាំបី | bram bei |
| 9 | ប្រាំបួន | bram buan |
| 10 | ដប់ | dawp |
| 11 | ដប់មួយ | dawp muy |
| 12 | ដប់ពីរ | dawp pii |
| 16 | ដប់ប្រាំមួយ | dawp bram muy |
| 20 | ម្ភៃ | m'phei |
| 21 | ម្ភៃមួយ | m'phei muy |
| 30 | សាមសិប | saamsuhp |
| 40 | សែសិប | saisuhp |
| 100 | មួយរយ | muy roy |
| 1000 | មួយពាន់ | muy poan |
| 1,000,000 | មួយលាន | muy lian |
| **1st** | ទីមួយ | tii muy |
| **2nd** | ទីពីរ | tii pii |
| **3rd** | ទីបី | tii bei |
| **4th** | ទីបួន | tii buan |
| **10th** | ទីដប់ | tii dawp |

# GLOSSARY

**apsara** – heavenly nymph or angelic dancer, often represented in Khmer sculpture

**Asean** – Association of Southeast Asian Nations

**Avalokiteshvara** – Bodhisattva of Compassion and the inspiration for Jayavarman VII's Angkor Thom

**baray** – reservoir

**boeng** – lake

**Chenla** – pre-Angkorian period, 6th to 8th centuries

**chunchiet** – ethnic minorities

**CNRP** – Cambodia National Rescue Party

**CPP** – Cambodian People's Party

**cyclo** – pedicab; bicycle rickshaw

**devaraja** – cult of the god-king, established by Jayavarman II, in which the monarch has universal power

**devadas** – goddesses

**EFEO** – École Française d'Extrême Orient

**essai** – wise man or traditional medicine man

**Funan** – pre-Angkorian period, 1st to 5th centuries

**Funcinpec** – National United Front for an Independent, Neutral, Peaceful and Cooperative Cambodia; royalist political party

**garuda** – mythical half-man, half-bird creature

**gopura** – entrance pavilion in traditional Hindu architecture

**Hun Sen** – Cambodia's prime minister (1985–present)

**Jayavarman II** – the king (r 802–50) who established the cult of the god-king, kicking off a period of amazing architectural productivity that resulted in the extraordinary temples of Angkor

**Jayavarman VII** – the king (r 1181–1219) who drove the Chams out of Cambodia before embarking on an ambitious construction program, including the walled city of Angkor Thom

**Kampuchea** – the name Cambodians use for their country; to non-Khmers, it is associated with the bloody rule of the Khmer Rouge, which insisted that the outside world adopt for Cambodia the name Democratic Kampuchea from 1975 to 1979

**Khmer** – a person of Cambodian descent; the language of Cambodia

**Khmer Krom** – ethnic Khmers living in Vietnam

**Khmer Rouge** – a revolutionary organisation that seized power in 1975 and implemented a brutal social restructuring, resulting in the suffering and death of millions of Cambodians during its four-year rule

**krama** – scarf

**linga** – phallic symbols

**Mahayana** – literally, 'Great Vehicle'; a school of Buddhism (also known as the Northern School) that built upon and extended the early Buddhist teachings; see also Theravada

**moto** – small motorcycle with driver; a common form of transport in Cambodia

**Mt Meru** – the mythical dwelling of the Hindu god Shiva

**naga** – mythical serpent, often multiheaded; a symbol used extensively in Angkorian architecture

**nandi** – sacred ox, vehicle of Shiva

**NGO** – nongovernmental organisation

**NH** – national highway

**Norodom Ranariddh, Prince** – son of King Sihanouk and former leader of Funcinpec

**Norodom Sihanouk, King** – former king, head of state, film director and a towering figure in modern-day Cambodia

**Pali** – ancient Indian language that, along with Sanskrit, is the root of modern Khmer

**phnom** – mountain or hill

**Pol Pot** – the former leader of the Khmer Rouge; responsible for the suffering and deaths of millions of Cambodians; previously known as Saloth Sar

**prasat** – stone or brick hall with religious or royal significance

**preah** – sacred

**psar** – market

**Ramayana** – an epic Sanskrit poem composed around 300 BC featuring the mythical Ramachandra, the incarnation of the god Vishnu

**remork-moto** – trailer pulled by a motorcycle; often shortened to *remork*

**rom vong** – Cambodian circle dancing

**Sangkum Reastr Niyum** – People's Socialist Community; a national movement, led by King Sihanouk, that ruled the country during the 1950s and 1960s

**Sanskrit** – ancient Hindu language that, along with Pali, is the root of modern Khmer language

**stung** – river

**Suryavarman II** – the king (r 1112–52) responsible for building Angkor Wat and for expanding and unifying the Khmer empire

**Theravada** – a school of Buddhism (also known as the Southern School or Hinayana) found in Myanmar (Burma), Thailand, Laos and Cambodia; this school confined itself to the early Buddhist teachings; see also Mahayana

**tonlé** – large river

**UNDP** – UN Development Programme

**Unesco** – UN Educational Scientific and Cultural Organization

**Untac** – UN Transitional Authority in Cambodia

**vihara** – temple sanctuary

**WHO** – World Health Organization

**Year Zero** – 1975; the year the Khmer Rouge seized power

**yoni** – female fertility symbol

# Behind the Scenes

## SEND US YOUR FEEDBACK

We love to hear from travellers – your comments keep us on our toes and help make our books better. Our well-travelled team reads every word on what you loved or loathed about this book. Although we cannot reply individually to postal submissions, we always guarantee that your feedback goes straight to the appropriate authors, in time for the next edition. Each person who sends us information is thanked in the next edition – the most useful submissions are rewarded with a selection of digital PDF chapters.

Visit **lonelyplanet.com/contact** to submit your updates and suggestions or to ask for help. Our award-winning website also features inspirational travel stories, news and discussions.

Note: We may edit, reproduce and incorporate your comments in Lonely Planet products such as guidebooks, websites and digital products, so let us know if you don't want your comments reproduced or your name acknowledged. For a copy of our privacy policy visit lonelyplanet.com/privacy.

## OUR READERS

**Many thanks to the travellers who used the last edition and wrote to us with helpful hints, useful advice and interesting anecdotes:**

**A** Andrea Rudan, Andrew Pitman, Anna Januszewska, Annemiek Lauwerijssen **B** Ben Nye, Bill Weir **C** Christopher Moyle **E** Emma Leslie **F** Francesco Licciardi **G** Georgiena Ryan **H** Heather Delany **J** James & Kassie Bowen, John Voegeli, Jose Stolk, Julia Dorman-Tejada **K** Karen Barnett, Katia Parolini **L** Laura Mattina **M** Marcel Ponti, Marcelo de Moura, Marjolaine & Hanael Sfez, Martijn Wiegman **P** Paul Gruncell **R** Rebecca Tilbrook, Rochelle Roberts **S** Sal Bolton, Salvatore Travia, Sandra Seiger, Sara Derr, Signe Fribo, Simon Joseph, Sophie Carr, Stefaan Ooms, Steve Scena **T** Tim Bushell **W** Werner Bruyninx **Z** Zita Hooke

## WRITER THANKS

### Nick Ray

A huge and heartfelt thanks to the people of Cambodia, whose warmth and humour, stoicism and spirit make it a happy yet humbling place to be. Biggest thanks are reserved for my lovely wife, Kulikar Sotho, and our children, Julian and Belle, as without their support and encouragement the adventures would not be possible. Thanks also to Mum and Dad for giving me a taste for travel from a young age.

Thanks to fellow travellers and residents, friends and contacts in Cambodia who have helped shaped my knowledge and experience in this country. There is no room to thank everyone, but you all know who you are, as we meet for anything from beers to ecotourism conferences regularly enough.

Thanks also to my co-author Jess Lee for going the distance to ensure this is a worthy new edition. Finally, thanks to the Lonely Planet team who have worked on this title. The author may be the public face, but a huge amount of work goes into making this a better book behind the scenes and I thank everyone for their hard work.

### Jessica Lee

On the road, huge thanks to fellow author Nick, Ritthy, Martin, dive supremos Simon and Tom, Mr Jack, and 'other Jess' and Raph, and kudos to Leap, Arun, Heng and Lim for being some of the most brilliant motodups I've ever had the luck to come across. Back home, a big thanks to the best house sitter in the world, Shannon Wang. Most of all, thank you to the people of Cambodia who always make a journey here a joy.

# ACKNOWLEDGMENTS

Climate map data adapted from Peel MC, Finlayson BL & McMahon TA (2007) 'Updated World Map of the Köppen-Geiger Climate Classification', *Hydrology and Earth System Sciences*, 11, 1633–44.

Cover photograph: *Apsara* dancer, Angkor Wat; Matteo Colombo, Getty Images ©

Illustrations pp134-5: Michael Weldon.

## THIS BOOK

This 10th edition of *Cambodia* was researched and written by Nick Ray and Jessica Lee. Nick also wrote the previous two editions with Greg Bloom. This guidebook was produced by the following:

**Destination Editor** Laura Crawford

**Product Editors** Katie O'Connell, Amanda Williamson

**Senior Cartographers** David Kemp, Diana von Holdt

**Book Designer** Wibowo Rusli

**Assisting Editors** Michelle Bennett, Peter Cruttenden, Ali Lemer, Lauren O'Connell

**Cover Researcher** Naomi Parker

**Language Content** Branislava Vladisavljevic

**Thanks to** Kate Chapman, Andi Jones, Mao Monkolransey, Karyn Noble, Kirsten Rawlings, Luna Soo, Angela Tinson

# Index

INDEX C–H

# Map Legend

## Sights

- Beach
- Bird Sanctuary
- Buddhist
- Castle/Palace
- Christian
- Confucian
- Hindu
- Islamic
- Jain
- Jewish
- Monument
- Museum/Gallery/Historic Building
- Ruin
- Shinto
- Sikh
- Taoist
- Winery/Vineyard
- Zoo/Wildlife Sanctuary
- Other Sight

## Activities, Courses & Tours

- Bodysurfing
- Diving
- Canoeing/Kayaking
- Course/Tour
- Sento Hot Baths/Onsen
- Skiing
- Snorkelling
- Surfing
- Swimming/Pool
- Walking
- Windsurfing
- Other Activity

## Sleeping

- Sleeping
- Camping

## Eating

- Eating

## Drinking & Nightlife

- Drinking & Nightlife
- Cafe

## Entertainment

- Entertainment

## Shopping

- Shopping

## Information

- Bank
- Embassy/Consulate
- Hospital/Medical
- Internet
- Police
- Post Office
- Telephone
- Toilet
- Tourist Information
- Other Information

## Geographic

- Beach
- Gate
- Hut/Shelter
- Lighthouse
- Lookout
- Mountain/Volcano
- Oasis
- Park
- Pass
- Picnic Area
- Waterfall

## Population

- Capital (National)
- Capital (State/Province)
- City/Large Town
- Town/Village

## Transport

- Airport
- Border crossing
- Bus
- Cable car/Funicular
- Cycling
- Ferry
- Metro/MRT/MTR station
- Monorail
- Parking
- Petrol station
- Skytrain/Subway station
- Taxi
- Train station/Railway
- Tram
- Underground station
- Other Transport

*Note: Not all symbols displayed above appear on the maps in this book*

## Routes

- Tollway
- Freeway
- Primary
- Secondary
- Tertiary
- Lane
- Unsealed road
- Road under construction
- Plaza/Mall
- Steps
- Tunnel
- Pedestrian overpass
- Walking Tour
- Walking Tour detour
- Path/Walking Trail

## Boundaries

- International
- State/Province
- Disputed
- Regional/Suburb
- Marine Park
- Cliff
- Wall

## Hydrography

- River, Creek
- Intermittent River
- Canal
- Water
- Dry/Salt/Intermittent Lake
- Reef

## Areas

- Airport/Runway
- Beach/Desert
- Cemetery (Christian)
- Cemetery (Other)
- Glacier
- Mudflat
- Park/Forest
- Sight (Building)
- Sportsground
- Swamp/Mangrove

# OUR STORY

A beat-up old car, a few dollars in the pocket and a sense of adventure. In 1972 that's all Tony and Maureen Wheeler needed for the trip of a lifetime – across Europe and Asia overland to Australia. It took several months, and at the end – broke but inspired – they sat at their kitchen table writing and stapling together their first travel guide, *Across Asia on the Cheap*. Within a week they'd sold 1500 copies. Lonely Planet was born.

Today, Lonely Planet has offices in Franklin, London, Melbourne, Oakland, Beijing and Delhi, with more than 600 staff and writers. We share Tony's belief that 'a great guidebook should do three things: inform, educate and amuse'.

# OUR WRITERS

### Nick Ray

Coordinating writer, Phnom Penh, Siem Reap, Temples of Angkor, Eastern Cambodia. A Londoner of sorts, Nick comes from Watford, the sort of town that makes you want to travel. He lives in Phnom Penh with his wife, Kulikar, and children, Julian and Belle. He has written for countless guidebooks on the Mekong region, including Lonely Planet's *Vietnam, Cambodia, Laos & Northern Thailand* and *Myanmar* books, as well as *Southeast Asia on a Shoestring*. When not writing, he is often out exploring the remote parts of Cambodia as a location scout and manager for the world of television and film, including everything from *Tomb Raider* to *Top Gear*. Motorbikes are a part-time passion and he has travelled through most of Indochina on two wheels.

Read more about Nick at:
http://auth.lonelyplanet.com/profiles/nickjray

### Jessica Lee

South Coast, Northwestern Cambodia. Jess first journeyed to Cambodia in the late '90s and fell for its vine-wrapped temples and palm-studded rice-field vistas. She's criss-crossed the country several times since then and this welcome return to the nation saw her exploring remote temples in some of Cambodia's most far-flung corners and checking out the fast-changing scenes upon the sand of the South Coast's islands. Jess is also an author on Lonely Planet's *Turkey*, *Egypt* and *Vietnam* titles. She blogs about travel at www.roadessays.wordpress.com.

Read more about Jessica at:
http://auth.lonelyplanet.com/profiles/jessicalee1

**Published by Lonely Planet Publications Pty Ltd**
ABN 36 005 607 983
10th edition – August 2016
ISBN 978 1 74321 874 7
© Lonely Planet 2016   Photographs © as indicated 2016
10 9 8 7 6 5 4 3 2 1
Printed in China